ETHNIC CHICAGO

Ethnic Chicago

A Multicultural Portrait

Fourth Edition

Edited by

Melvin G. Holli and Peter d'A. Jones

WILLIAM B. EERDMANS PUBLISHING COMPANY
GRAND RAPIDS, MICHIGAN

Copyright © 1977, 1981, 1984, 1995 by Wm. B. Eerdmans Publishing Co.
255 Jefferson Ave. S.E., Grand Rapids, Michigan 49503

First edition 1977
Fourth edition 1995

Printed in the United States of America

06 05 04 03 02 01   8 7 6 5 4 3

Library of Congress Cataloging-in-Publication Data

Ethnic Chicago : a multicultural portrait / edited by
Melvin G. Holli and Peter d'A. Jones.—4th ed.
        p.   cm.
Includes bibliographical references and index.
ISBN 0-8028-0753-8 (paper)
1. Minorities—Illinois—Chicago.
2. Chicago (Ill.)—Ethnic relations.
I. Holli, Melvin G.   II. Jones, Peter d'Alroy.
F548.9.A1E85   1995
305.8′009773′11—dc20   95-3130
                                                CIP

Contents

ETHNIC INSTITUTIONS

For
Flight Sergeant Brian A. Jones
who never got to America
and
Sylvia Erickson Holli
whose family know something of
the immigrant epic

Introduction: Ethnic Life in Chicago

History offers very few clear, simple moral battles. Ethnic history is no exception. The complex history of the medley of ethnic groups that live in Chicago is played against the backdrop of United States ethnic history as a whole. This kaleidoscopic story cannot be understood without an even wider stage set of world ethnic history.

In the very recent past, the national revolutions of 1989-1992 in Eastern Europe and the former Soviet Union remind us how fragile the political world is. Most nations are constructed of imperfect confederations, ethnic groups tied together out of habit, convenience, and economic necessity. When some nations fall apart, ancient ethnic hostilities come out into the open air. Even in the United States, where the national tradition is the "Melting Pot," the fortunes of ethnicity rise and fall with each trend of political life. For instance, the issues in the debate on multiculturalism in America (and "political correctness") fill the screen in the early 1990s.

The editors of this book on ethnic Chicago had to contend with the "ethnic revival" of the 1970s and early 1980s, which spread doubts about the "myth" of the Melting Pot and put firmly in place the rival "myth" of Cultural Pluralism. Though out of fashion for a time, the Melting Pot still remains. The French-Indian *metis* (described by Jacqueline Peterson) were lost without a trace; ethnic cultures of the Italians, the Irish, and the Germans were in the process of being melted; but the sturdier cultures of the Poles, Jews, Ukrainians, Greeks, and Mexicans (although within a "Hispanic" form) still endure. Even when they meet or integrate into a national civilization, ethnic cultures leave a lasting impression: witness the evolving impact of Chicago's Germans on the city's industry and technology, which defies time, and on high culture, exemplified by Chicago's symphony orchestra. The Irish have shaped the character of Chicago's urban politics and the Catholic Church for what appears to be a long time. That is what the Melting Pot was all about: it never prescribed total

1

destruction of newcomer cultures (as some commentators mistakenly believed).[1]

Israel Zangwill, who did more to popularize the Melting Pot metaphor than anyone, with his 1908 melodrama of that name, turned to music for the source of another metaphor. The young Russian-Jewish hero of his play, David Quixano, yearned to write the "great American symphony." As an amalgamationist (albeit temporarily — he joined up with the Zionists later), Zangwill meant this to imply that the instruments of the orchestra blend together as one musical voice. It is interesting and ironic that Zangwill's major intellectual opponent, Horace Kallen, champion of "cultural pluralism" and ethnic separatism, also turned to music for his metaphor, speaking of a possible "orchestration of mankind." In his orchestration, presumably each musical instrument would maintain the integrity of its separate sound and identity.

One image, two opposing lessons: assimilation or fragmentation, melting pot or cultural pluralism. But Americans cannot seek aid in metaphors, however fitting or clever they may be. The *behavior* of some Americans betrays their inner thoughts: ethnicity is changing in the United States. European immigration is much smaller than it used to be, relative to the numbers of people living here; some whites are removed by generations from their immigrant ancestors, to at least the fourth generation (the United States is the country of birth for themselves, both of their parents, and all four of their grandparents).[2] And an increasing part of the white population is now of mixed ethnic ancestry. These 13.3 million "unhyphenated Americans" who answered *American* on the 1980 census form, despite the ongoing "ethnic revival" that was all the rage politically, chose to be "American" first and foremost.

Meanwhile, we have the multicultural debate with us. The dean of American liberal historians, A. M. Schlesinger Jr., in *The Disuniting of America: Reflections on a Multicultural Society* (New York: Norton, 1992) talks about the "cult of ethnicity." Is the American Dream really a power structure covering subjugated cultures? No, says Schlesinger, for the West has created democratic remedies as well as diseases in its time: the movement to end slavery (and the obscenities of racism, polygamy, clitoridectomy, wife-burning, foot-binding and the like), the movement for women's rights, to end torture and to advance human rights, to promote free speech, free journalism, free thought, and so forth. The "multiculturalists" must take account of these achievements and not look with disdain at the American experiment and the benefits of the melting pot. The valuable ideal of ethnic diversity should not be a hindrance to political unity.

1. Philip Gleason, "Confusion Compounded: The Melting Pot in the 1960s and 1970s," *Ethnicity* 6 (March 1979): 10-20. Andrew Greeley's intellectually provocative *Why Can't They Be Like Us?* (Philadelphia: E. P. Dutton, 1971) was an important stimulus for academic ethnic research.
2. R. D. Alpha and M. B. Chamlim, *American Sociological Review* 48 (1988): 240-47; S. Lieberson and Mary C. Waters, *From Many Strands: Ethnic and Racial Groups in Contemporary America* (New York: Russell Sage Fdn., 1988).

We have sought, as editors, to avoid those simplistic, too easily grasped polarized scenarios such as "black" versus "white," "WASP" versus "ethnic," "host" society versus "immigrant," in favor of a more realistic approach. The inner complexity of each immigrant group was also a fact of ethnic life. "Ethnic democracy" in a multicultural, ideologically egalitarian society such as ours emerges only with painful slowness over the years, as group after group jockeys for position. Ethnic history is not a mere local argument, a battle for "freedom" and against "prejudice." We seek an ethnic history for its own sake, a richly detailed and informing portrait, warts and all, of varying ethnic communities, their values, social structures, inner dynamics, and everyday lifestyles. The mainstream American culture, which had been forged long before the newcomers of the mass migrations arrived (those of the 1880s, '90s and 1900s) was a product of English, Scotch-Irish, Irish, Welsh, Dutch, Swedes, American Indians, blacks, Germans, and so many people that it belies the title "Anglo-Saxon." The mainstream culture even then was not the Anglo-Saxon, Puritan culture, but an already *melted* culture. The later immigrants found that they would fit into "America," with all its faults, and there were many.

Ethnic history in Chicago goes on, as it must. The latest news concerns the Asian Americans. The fastest growing minority in the United States, doubling over the last decade (to 7.3 million), Asians comprise in the American nation at large: Chinese, Japanese, Asian Indians, Filipinos, Koreans, Vietnamese, Laotians, Thais, Cambodians, Hmong, Pakistanis, and Indonesians. Many are highly skilled and college educated and possess a hard-work ethic that theorist Max Weber associated with Protestant northern Europeans. Although many work as entrepreneurs or at middle-level (or even high-level) white-collar positions, they complain about a "glass ceiling" that keeps them in lower-level management. They dislike being stereotyped as passive and unaggressive, and they resent having their allegedly poor English-language skills pointed out (according to a 1992 report of the U.S. Civil Rights Commission on "Civil Rights Issues Facing Asian Americans in the 1990s"). In contrast to the historic pattern of turn-of-the-century immigrants, most Asians do not gather in ethnic inner-city ghettos, except to conduct business. Instead they settle in the suburbs. Three-fifths of them live outside of Chicago proper, in DuPage County, northwest Cook County, and the northern suburbs. They enjoy the highest median family incomes of any newcomer group.

The Founding Fathers were genuinely confused about America's ethnic future, but they agreed to admit all and sundry. They had no way of realizing in what great numbers the immigrants would come to these shores, or how this would transform America. They would have been astonished at the arrival of the Asian Americans! We Americans fluctuate between separatism and "Americanization," between "desegregation" and "Black Power," between antidiscrimination laws and fears of "affirmative discrimination." The cauldron of American values bubbles on.

Israel Zangwill defended his metaphor of the melting pot in this way in 1914 (when the shadow of the First World War was looming over Europe):

The process of American amalgamation is not assimilation or simple surrender to the dominant type, as is popularly supposed, but an all-round give-and-take by which the final type may be enriched or impoverished.[3]

*   *   *

Essays from previous editions of *Ethnic Chicago* that appear in Section I, "Ethnic Groups," have been revised, updated, and in several cases completely rewritten to take into account new developments within their ethnic groups. New essays include Anita Olson's demographic study of Chicago's Swedes, James Grossman's definitive essay on the migration and settlement of African Americans in Chicago, Dominic Candeloro's scholarly treatment of Chicago's Italians, and Melvin Holli's revisionist essay on German Chicago. Also new is the multi-authored Latino chapter covering three major heritage groups: Mexican, Puerto Rican, and Cuban. And finally, in this section are three new chapters on Asian Americans: Susan Lee Moy on the Chinese, Padma Rangaswamy on Asian Indians, and Joseph Ahne on the Koreans, a path-breaking essay on Chicago's new entrepreneurial immigrants. All three chapters complement an intellectually provocative and updated chapter by Mosako Osako on Japanese Chicago.

Section II, "Ethnic Institutions," is not to be found in any of the earlier editions (1977, 1981, 1984) and adds a dimension to our study of ethnicity. Focusing on six key ethnic institutions (saloons, sports, crime, churches, neighborhoods, and cemeteries), this section illuminates the institutional elements that have received very little attention from previous scholars of ethnicity. For instance, differences between the "parochials" and the "universals" among ethnic saloons; crime as a "queer ladder" of upward mobility for some ethnics but not for others; ethnic church building styles; a revisionist examination of the myth of the stable neighborhood; and the final resting place of ethnicity, the cemetery.

These original essays are the product of long years of careful and thorough research by seasoned scholars and respected authorities of their various ethnic groups and group institutions. Evocative, frequently revisionist, and consistently informative, these selections capture in Chicago, America's heartland city, a microsocial view of the national ethnic processes of adjustment, survival, identity, and even melting into the American melting pot.

---

3. Quoted in "The Melting Pot and Afterward," in R. J. Meister, ed., *Race and Ethnicity in Modern America* (Lexington, Massachusetts, 1974); on the question of identity see the late Arthur Mann's thoughtful *The One and the Many: Reflections on the American Identity* (Chicago, 1979); for a theoretical restatement of the complexity of assimilation see Ewa Morawska, "The Sociology and Historiography of Immigration," in *Immigration Reconsidered: History, Sociology and Politics* (New York: Oxford University Press, 1990), 218f.

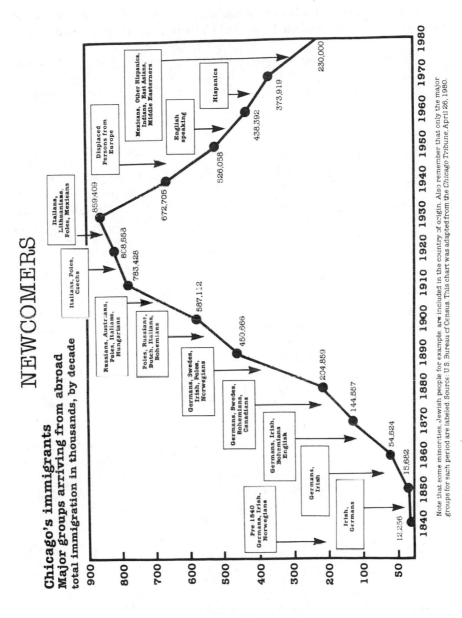

NEWCOMERS

Chicago's immigrants
Major groups arriving from abroad
total immigration in thousands, by decade

Italians, Lithuanians, Poles, Mexicans

Italians, Poles, Czechs

Russians, Austrians, Poles, Italians, Hungarians

Poles, Russians, Dutch, Italians, Bohemians

Germans, Swedes, Irish, Poles, Norwegians

Germans, Swedes, Bohemians, Canadians

Germans, Irish, Bohemians, English

Germans, Irish

Irish, Germans

Pre-1840 Germans, Irish, Norwegians

Displaced Persons from Europe

Mexicans, Other Hispanics, Indians, East Asians, Middle Easterners

English speaking

Hispanics

859,409
808,553
783,428
587,112
450,666
204,859
144,557
54,624
15,682
12,256
672,705
526,058
438,392
373,919
230,000

1840 1850 1860 1870 1880 1890 1900 1910 1920 1930 1940 1950 1960 1970 1980

900 800 700 600 500 400 300 200 100 50

Note that some minorities, Jewish people for example are included in the country of origin. Also remember that only the major groups for each period are labeled. Source: U.S. Bureau of Census. This chart was adapted from the *Chicago Tribune*, April 26, 1980.

Ethnic Groups

The opening chapter, Jacqueline Peterson's study of the French-Indian founding fathers of Chicago, is a fluent, evocative portrait of eighteenth- and early nineteenth-century frontier people. She skillfully describes the microsocial history of the founding families, their homes, occupations, systems of social status, concerns, and lifestyles. This patient study provides us with a unique picture of an early frontier settlement under the profit-seeking aegis of the American Fur Company. Many sorts of folk were tolerated and accepted in those days: Indians, French, Anglos, *metis*, and other mixed-bloods. For a few brief frontier years, the society was casually multiracial, occupying what Richard White has called the "middle ground."[4] Then this mixed culture vanished under the impact of an invasion of Americanizing Yankees. The newcomers, with their built-in, inner-directed sense of linear "progress," their capacity for deferred gratification, and their readiness, as Peterson puts it, to "cheat the present," swept everything before them. The clash of values proved too much for a premodern folk: some of the refugees trekked westward to the Indian reservations; others fled to remote trapping outposts to insulate themselves from change. And yet some were absorbed and "melted" into the majority culture.

Michael F. Funchion deals succinctly with the formative years of Irish culture in Chicago, and with the important suggestion that the classic "ghetto hypothesis" does not apply to the Irish. The "famine" Irish had come with a love of Ireland, a hatred for England, and their Catholic religion as their main resources. Beginning as humble canal diggers and laborers, these sons of the Emerald Isle soon came to dominate the "Irish trinity" of American urban life: the priesthood, the police, and politics.

Every Catholic bishop in Chicago from 1847 to 1916, with one exception, was Irish. The police force in Chicago was disproportionately Irish by the 1890s. And most Chicago mayors since 1933 have been of Irish Catholic heritage. Ironically, some of the Irish successes in American life may be attributed to Anglo oppression: the English had Anglicized the Irish to a point where they could become the leaders of the newcoming fresh immigrants. With the language of "perfidious Albion" and a goodly store of native wit, the Irish went on to conquer the American city, introducing and leading their often less fortunate coreligionists from Europe toward the American mainstream. The Irish had yet another advantage that Funchion wryly points out: they could get in touch with their roots much more easily than could most other third-generation Americans because they spoke the language of their ancestors, and for that the English were responsible.

In Melvin G. Holli's persuasive account, the rapid "melting" of Germans

---

4. Richard White, *The Middle Ground: Indians, Empires, and Republics in the Great Lakes Region, 1650-1815* (Cambridge: Cambridge University Press, 1991).

in Chicago, through the impact of two world wars (as Holli says of the Germans, they were the nation's first ethnic war *victims*), must not obscure their unique cultural, social, labor, and artisan benefits to the city of Chicago from the earliest days: "Public expression of German ethnicity today is nowhere proportionate to the number of German Americans in the nation's population." As Holli's revisionist study shows, *Deutschtum's* fall from its most favored nation status was brought about in part by the bellicose propaganda of German leaders in Germany and unfortunately in the German-American population. Yet Chicago's Germans were vitally important to an industrializing city and gave to its high culture, in both music and theater, an enduring legacy.

Chicago's Swedes, though fewer in number than the Germans, were drawn to residential areas and occupations similar to those of German immigrants. They settled in localities that had a heavily northern and western European flavor, and their own presence contributed to it. Primarily Lutheran and middle class in ethos and outlook, though poor and often just off the boat, Swedes would be among the first of the nineteenth-century immigrants to Chicago to begin moving toward the less densely populated areas of the city and to the suburbs, as Anita R. Olson shows in her chapter.

Irving Cutler, the geographer of Chicago, is also renowned for his lectures and knowledge of Chicago's Jewish population. With authority and marvelous visual evidence, Cutler chronicles the progress of Jews from shtetl to suburb. The mapping and photo documentation add a special dimension to his text. Cutler intertwines into his narrative biographical examples of ghetto successes: Benny Goodman, Paul Muni, Arthur Goldberg, and Julius Rosenwald. Jews worked hard, and within a generation they were at the upper reaches of occupational and income achievement. Jewish socialism, once a heady and feisty idea in the ghetto, was a vanishing phenomenon by the 1950s, a victim of the high individual achievements of the group. Jews created their own worldly utopias, not through Karl Marx, but through education, occupation, and high income. Yet it was not all work, as Cutler shows in his sketches of a colorful street life, an active theater, and even a Chicago version of a "borscht belt" resort that grew and flourished. "From Shtetl to Suburb" is an important dimension of that Jewish urban epic in the twentieth century.

The enigma of Polish Chicago — now that the Polish homeland is free of Soviet domination and entering the free-market economy — seems to reflect an age-old American ethnic problem: how to be "American" and still be "Polish." Edward R. Kantowicz, an expert on American Catholicism and on Polish America, in his insightful and original study of the survival of Chicago's large Polish community, has selected one of the most in-group peoples to be found anywhere. In Europe, Poles survived as Poles over many decades when there was politically no Polish nation. They brought to America with them this deep, tenacious attitude toward national identity and did not lose it in the streets of Chicago or Milwaukee. Thus Kantowicz's theme is "Survival through Solidarity."

Yet there is a price to be paid for a group's single-mindedly internalizing its energies. There is no doubt that the Poles of Chicago achieved a greater sense of wholeness than most ethnic groups; but, as Kantowicz indicates, the cost was a diminished influence in the wider non-Polish community. Building from within, Polish Americans created a solid "Polonia," a nation within a nation, on the basis of their churches, their superb building and loan associations, their parochial schools, and their fraternal associations. Even the major division within the group, between the nationalists and religionists, was milder than splits within comparable groups, such as Lithuanians and Bohemians. (Here, as throughout his chapter, Kantowicz makes cross-ethnic comparisons, noting, for example that Italians, unlike Poles, were content to use the American public school system). The price that first- and second-generation Poles paid for their commitment to separate treatment within the Catholic Church and their insistence on Polish priests and parishes, for example, was low general influence in the higher levels of the Church, which lacked Polish leaders. The same was true in the secular realm of the city, and for that matter in state and national politics. There are lessons here for other ethnic groups as well.

Dominic Candeloro's sensitive and urbane discussion of Chicago's Italians extends from the pre-1880 period to the more enlightened attitude of the 1990s, when things "Italian" were encouraged instead of discouraged by American society. Many of Chicago's Italians were immigrants from the impoverished south of Italy, the *Mezzogiorno*. They were peasant Catholic families who hated government and authority, schools, and voluntary associations (outside the family); but they obtained work in Chicago's various industries, railway yards, city construction projects, and the smaller businesses of shoemaking, fruit and vegetable peddling, barbering and the needle trades. In politics they remained underrepresented and had to cope with the legacy of Al Capone, the substrata of the underworld of the 1920s, and Prohibition. The second generation of Chicago's Italians (roughly between 1920 and 1940) were mostly born in Chicago and became middle-class Americans. Their search for respect from the rest of American society has culminated in the tolerant climate of today, far from the poverty, crime, and political ignorance of the ethnic past. Italian family life was a blessing: it brought the *contadini* (small peasant farmers) to America seeking *pan e lavoro* (bread and work), and they found what they wanted. They were no longer "birds of passage," but settlers and Americans.

Andrew T. Kopan presents the story of Greek American survival through education, an ethnic odyssey that challenges much of the conventional wisdom about ethnics and puts in print for a larger audience the extraordinary entrepreneurial talents of this ethnic group. Chicago's Hellene immigrants were no "Golden Greeks" with great means; they were humble rural folk who came to America with neither education nor urban skills. Yet such was the drive to succeed expressed by these enterprising folk that by 1920 some 10,000 were self-employed, mostly in small businesses in Chicago.

A second important theme underscored by Kopan is that Chicago's Greeks appeared to have reversed the natural process of language deterioration in the second generation. Because of a poor homeland school system, Chicago's first-generation Greeks had a relatively high illiteracy rate (27 percent); yet the second generation, through after-school programs and church schools, often developed a more fluent command of the Greek language than their parents had. The Greeks in our time stand near the very top rungs of American education, occupation, and income ladder. Yet these signal successes, as Kopan points out, did not allow the Greeks to be swallowed up by the vastness of America: they retained important components of their ethnicity, such as the Greek language.

Chicago's Ukrainians are a people with their own special and often poignant cultural resonances, and yet they are a very poorly understood group. Filling in this lacuna in the historical record, Myron B. Kuropas, a former White House Ethnic Adviser to President Gerald Ford, examines the Ukrainian identity crisis and the political struggle here for an independent overseas homeland. (At last, since 1992, with the dissolution of the former Soviet Union, Ukraine is formally "free.") Following a time-tested pattern that Poles, Bohemians, and others had employed during World War I, Ukrainians tried to use the United States as a base for launching an independent state of Ukraine in the Soviet Union. But the pendulum of history no longer swung to the tune of self-determination as it had in Woodrow Wilson's time, and utilizing European political models led to disappointment. In addition, the Ukrainian nationalist movement in the United States was unfairly tainted and smeared, linked by its detractors to the Nazi movement that arose in Germany in the 1930s. Even so, Ukrainians triumphed over these adversities and realized one of their primary goals: the assertion both in the United States and abroad of a clear title to being a distinctive ethno-cultural people with a strong sense of future nationhood. In this effort the Chicago and American host played a vital role: as Kuropas puts it, "For many a Ukrainian emigré, the United States was not an ethnic melting pot but rather a school for his ethno-national development."

The historic aspirations of American blacks (or African Americans) have been to integrate, assimilate, and enter into the American cultural mainstream. Though the back-to-Africa movement of the 1920s and the black power and black Muslim movements of the 1960s seem to contradict that goal, those movements involved but a small fraction of blacks and have less historic force or trajectory behind them than the 150-year quest to enter into the mainstream. In politics, blacks wanted to be part of the system; in housing they wished to integrate. The fact that the barriers of race often impeded such advances does not invalidate their intent. The long-term historic black direction, then, has not been toward cultural pluralism or black separatism; it has rather been in the opposite direction — toward integration and assimilation, toward the figurative if not the literal melting pot.

In contrast to the separatism of the Polish community, most black Americans in Chicago, during the years before the Great Migration of World War I and the 1920s, would have chosen as much local and national political influence and integration as they could have won — if circumstances and white-dominated politics had permitted. In his cogent essay on the Great Migration to Chicago, James Grossman depicts the economic *pull* of Chicago and the North welcoming the migrating blacks, against the *push* of the racist society in Dixie and the South, which rejected black Southerners and militated against their staying where they were. The aphorism "Causes are not the same as motivations" is at the heart of Grossman's article, which is a true *social* history of this episode of black history. Some blacks "made it" in Chicago and seized their destinies against all odds of white society. Chicago offered paved streets, running water, electric lights, sewers, police and fire services. Yet there was a constant battle between the black "Old Settlers" and the black "Newcomers" from the rural, impoverished South. Throughout the very worst years of trial and violence, the abiding faith in America that so many blacks maintained was troubled but was hardly ever in doubt.

Meanwhile, a black middle class was growing in Chicago, as perceived by journalists, scholars, and casual observers. Social pathology was not the whole scene of African-American Chicago. William Braden, the news reporter, gives a positive portrait of the values and lifestyle of middle-class blacks in Chatham, a locality of the Windy City, in his article, "Chatham: An African-American Success Story." The "community of excellence," as black residents called Chatham, was one of many growing revelations of the black *middle-class* presence in the city.

The melting pot has laid claim to a sizable segment of the nation's ethnic population, and it will undoubtedly claim even more as American history advances. In their essay on the Latino population of Chicago today, Jorge Casuso and Eduardo Camacho claim that by the year 2000 one-quarter of all ethnics in Chicago will be Hispanic. In 1990 there were 352,000 Mexicans, 120,000 Puerto Ricans, and 10,000 Cubans in Chicago. Though *Hispanic* (or *Latino*) is an umbrella term comprising twenty separate nations and many more races and ethnic groups, only the above three groups are included in the chapter. They differ from other ethnic groups in America in religion, family patterns, the way they treat the elderly and children, and above all in the trait of *machismo*. Yet vast socio-economic and political differences exist among these Hispanics. Mexicans and Puerto Ricans are young, poor, and uneducated, and they have differences between themselves. The Mexican population of Chicago is the largest Hispanic group and still booming, presenting a challenge to Chicago's schools with its rapidly growing numbers. The poorest Hispanic group is the Puerto Ricans. They are not immigrants — they are citizens — but after three decades in Chicago they have made little social progress out of the *barrio* life. Cubans are middle-class political refugees, and they have the highest income levels of the Hispanic group. Although still culturally part of the land they left, they have entered the American economic mainstream.

The latest of the ethnic groups that have found themselves in Chicago are the Asian Americans. The first Chinese in America were from peasant families hailing from Kwangtung Province in the south of China, and they immigrated to California. By 1880 or so, the Chinese had founded a "Chinatown" in Chicago; the Chinese population of Chicago grew in the 1920s and '30s in the laundry and restaurant businesses. With the welcome repeal of Chinese exclusion in 1943 and the family reunification program, the Chinese population grew even larger and extended into the suburbs after the 1950s. The first 100 years of the Chinese in Chicago is the subject of an essay by Susan Lee Moy.

The communist takeover of mainland China in 1949 caused a leap in Chicago's Chinese population to about 6,000 in the 1950s; and in the 1970s, the Nixon era, the change in United States and Chinese relations brought new migrants from mainland China as well as from Hong Kong, Taiwan, and Southeast Asia. The 1980 United States Census counted about 28,000 Chinese in Chicago; and more were to come, especially from mainland China, in the 1980s and 1990s. The traditional image of Chinatown diminished. Class divisions among Chinese people were increased as Cantonese folk, who had been here for ages, clashed with Mandarin, the higher-social-order newcomers who had more education. Finally, the fall of Saigon in 1975 brought many Chinese "capitalists" and businessmen to Chicago.

The Japanese people of Chicago, by contrast, are on the way to assimilation. Like German Americans, Japanese Americans had the misfortune of having an ancestral homeland that waged war against the United States. Japanese American culture became a war victim, as Masako Osako relates, when World War II caught the Japanese Americans in the unenviable position of being on the wrong side as enemy aliens. In a chapter that makes some comparisons to Chinese Americans, Osako examines how the pains of the relocation camp experience set the *Nisei* on the road to assimilation: the Japanese redirected their own culture through the vale of hardship and tears in the camps, not toward rejection of America but toward absorption. Many Japanese were released during the war and dispersed throughout the nation to small colonies that provided few marriage partners or cultural facilities. But having survived this trial, the *Nisei* soon emerged as the "model ethnics," a phrase many dislike. Japanese Americans seemingly assuaged the pains of rejection by vaulting up the education, occupation, and income scales with astonishing speed. The social engine behind this progress, according to Osako, is a strong family structure and an emphasis on hard work, discipline, and achievement. The *Nisei* case offers little support for the argument that discrimination depresses occupational success. In his provocative summary, Osako suggests that Japanese Americans may be the first racial minority to integrate and assimilate biologically into the dominant white stock of America.

Padma Rangaswamy portrays the later Asian immigrants to Chicago, the Indians, as a "model minority" in their thirty years of growth inside ethnic Chicago. For a start, the Asian Indian community was dominated by a highly educated professional elite of doctors, engineers, scientists, and college professors for whom America (and "the West") held glamour and mystique. Only the newest-arrived Asians are the traditional Indian "poor"; but both groups share the rich and diverse cultural heritage of India. The Asian Indians were scattered all over the suburban map of the Chicago area, not in "ghetto" zones. They maintained togetherness in ways other than by living in close proximity: by meeting regularly at social and professional functions, and through a wide variety of temples and churches — Hindu especially, but also Muslim, Sikh, Jain, Zoroastrian, and Christian. Despite being scattered, a large concentration of Indians could be found in the 1970s and '80s on Chicago's North Side, with its proliferation of Indian shops and restaurants on Devon Avenue.

The last essay in this section is Joseph Ahne's chapter on the Koreans, whom he calls the "new entrepreneurial immigrants." Koreans have been in Chicago since the end of World War I, the successors of those Korean sugar plantation workers who first landed in Hawaii in 1903. They established their churches and student clubs, general stores, and restaurants in the Chicago area, but until the Korean War era they were "marginal" immigrants and few in number. In the post-Korean War years, a generation of students, many of them transients, came to dominate the leadership of the Chicago Korean community. But since 1968 there has been a surge of Korean immigrants, who come with middle-class educations or aspirations. Many of these are still first-generation Korean Americans.

Ahne describes the episode of the Koreans who went first to Germany as coal miners (with college degrees!) and nurses, and then came to Chicago, in fascinating detail. Chicago Koreans have been active in the retail market, always self-employed as "entrepreneurs," and to some extent in medicine, nursing, real estate, and academic life. Korean shopkeepers moved into black districts of Chicago, often replacing Jews, and have come into conflict over racial and social issues. Korean Americans recapture for us the pain and the promise of the hard-working first-generation entrepreneur. They are different from the older first-generation European immigrants of eighty to a hundred years ago because of their middle-class training and their passion for middle-class status. Like the Cubans, Chicago's Koreans are entering the economic mainstream — as measured by their high median income levels — even though many are still strongly tied to their homeland culture. Koreans have felt the real frustrations of the melting pot, up close.[5]

5. For a lucid explanation of the problems that "middleman minorities" face in other poor, third-world societies and inner-city neighborhoods, see Thomas Sowell, "Middleman Minorities," *American Enterprise*, May-June, 1993, pp. 30-41.

Ethnic Institutions

Ethnic *space* is something about which Perry Duis, the noted social historian, concerns himself in his researches into the nooks and crannies of Chicago history. The saloon is a prime institution of ethnic life. Duis takes the reader on a "pub crawl" into Scandinavian taverns (Swedish, Danish, and Norwegian) and Italian, Polish and Bohemian, German, Irish and black saloons, and creates for us a morphology of ethnic saloon types. In this polyglot world he discovers both parochial and universal kinds of saloons, the latter typified by the German and Irish. The universal type would shape the saloon style for Chicago.

Urban sports were strongly influenced by ethnicity, and the American *quid pro quo* was that ethnicity was strongly influenced by urban sports. Most of the "new" immigrants (post–1870) and the internal migrants from the American South had little or no sporting tradition to transfer to America, except the Germans and their Turnvereins and the Czechs and their Sokols. In other cases, long-forgotten sports such as Irish hurling and Gaelic football were revived for political reasons by independence supporters in the 1870s and 1880s in Ireland and were adopted by some Irish-American groups as a source of ethnic pride and solidarity. Yet they never rivalled the Irish-American affinity for American sports such as boxing, baseball, and basketball. The "yankee" sport of baseball was also adopted by African Americans who, facing discrimination, formed their own teams and leagues. Overall, sports played an important role as a "step toward assimilation," notes historian Steve Riess.

In Chicago there is a great interest in ethnic crime, which is the subject of Mark Haller's pertinent chapter. The criminal life appealed to some of the "poor working stiffs" in Chicago, who were mainly Italian, Irish, Jewish, and black in the 1920s. The underworld included policy gambling (betting on numbers), sports bookmaking, prostitution and the crime of the red light areas, alcohol bootlegging, labor racketeering, and general services in illegal goods. The pursuit of crime afforded a means of upward (and sometimes downward) mobility. Other means of upward mobility were available (sports, entertainment and nightlife, taxi dance halls, local machine politics, Chicago's labor unions), but in some cases these were also tainted with criminal activities. As Haller points out, to the eyes of the social underdog, "the whole world was a racket." Even so, the Germans and the Scandinavians were not a part of this organized underworld, nor were the overwhelming majority of those who comprised "ethnic Chicago."

A masterly sweep through the ethnic churches in Chicago is provided by Edward Kantowicz, who has already given us the penetrating chapter on Chicago's Poles. The Catholic church was self-organized into "ethnic leagues" in the 1910s and 1920s: the major league was Irish and Polish; the minor league was Slovak, Lithuanian, Bohemian, and Italian. "The twin spires of church steeple and factory smokestack dominated the ethnic neighborhoods of Chicago," declares Kantowicz, and the churches of each nationality "jostled one another" as they proclaimed, "Here we are!" The golden age of church architecture was initiated when many Chicago parishes began building on a large scale. But ethnicity "tended to fragment the Protestant, Catholic, and Jewish religions." In Chicago, Cardinal G. W. Mundelein "tried to pursue a policy of Americanization" — of ecumenicism. "The people of the United States must be American or something else. They cannot serve two masters," said Mundelein in 1916. His staff did not welcome Mexicans and Puerto Ricans as openly as it had welcomed previous immigrants from Europe. The Chicago bishops, preoccupied with suburban growth, had no intention of building new parishes in the city after World War II. Instead, "many formerly European ethnic churches have become thriving Mexican, Puerto Rican, or Filipino parishes simply by the weight of numbers," Kantowicz observes.

We turn to Dominic Pacyga, an urban historian who has amassed a repertoire of Chicago resources for his essay on Chicago's ethnic neighborhoods. Pacyga displays a skillful facility in handling an enormous volume of complex sources. As a revisionist, he points to the reality of neighborhood change rather than to the myth of neighborhood stability. Pacyga's essay gives the reader a sense of what it is really like in the ethnic neighborhoods of Chicago.

We conclude our section on "ethnic institutions" with a chapter by Helen Sclair on Chicago's ethnic cemeteries since the early nineteenth century. An expert almost without rival, Sclair has unearthed a wealth of information about what she calls "underground rites." Among the burial grounds covered in her pioneering essay are Native American, Irish, English, Scotch, Dutch, Jewish, German Protestant and Catholic, Luxembourg, Polish, Bohemian, Scandinavian, Italian, Lithuanian, Ukrainian, Serbian, Chinese, Japanese, and African American. Sclair closes her tour of these "memorial parks" with a cogent observation: the "convergence toward a broadly conceived 'Americanized' burial style appears to be in the making." The melting pot appears to have its triumph in the end.[6]

---

6. For a thoughtful appraisal of the problems implicit in an exaggerated pluralism, see John Higham, *Send These to Me: Jews and Other Immigrants in Urban America* (New York: Atheneum, 1975), pp. 197f.

ETHNIC GROUPS

CHAPTER 1

The Founding Fathers: The Absorption of French-Indian Chicago, 1816-1837

JACQUELINE PETERSON

*If we write histories of the way in which heterogeneous people arrived
on a frontier, come to form themselves into a community . . . we shall
be writing something complementary to histories of disintegration. We
shall be writing the history of becoming whole.*

Robert Redfield, The Little Community

I

*Have you built your ship of death, O have you?
O build your ship of death, for you will need it.
    And die the death, the long and painful death
    that lies between the old self and the new.*

D. H. Lawrence, "The Ship of Death"

Riding from the east toward Chicago, a visitor today can see, even in bright
midday, the hulking steel mills of Gary burning miles off in the distance. Orange
and black clouds hang heavy in the sky as if to warn of some terrible pestilence.
Travelers grimly lock themselves in airtight spaces away from the stench of
sulphur, and hurry by.

Rising with the Chicago Skyway bridge, the traveler wonders what kind of
unheavenly vision William B. Ogden, early nineteenth-century industrialist and

---

This chapter derives from research initially begun under the supervision of the late
Professor Gilbert Osofsky at the University of Illinois at Chicago Circle. It owes much
to his inspiration and is written in his honor.

railroad maker, could have had. A century after him, the corroded assemblage of steel girders, rail tracks, foundries, breweries, and shipping cranes fans out below the bridge like a giant black erector set devastated in a fiery holocaust. Humans do not easily belong here. Beyond the curve of the bridge is Wolf Lake. The vision is startling, for there in the midst of angry waste and decay — and Wolf Lake itself is an industrial sewage dump — is a scene that has eluded time: the grassy marshes, frozen in winter, which swell and flood the lowlands in spring; the shallow lakes and ponds broken only by narrow glacial or man-made ridges; the stunted scrub oak, poplar, and pines; the reed-covered banks lying low in the water so that a canoe need only be pushed up a foot or two to rest on the shore. It is all there, except for the stillness and the wild rice of the marshes.[1]

This neglected landscape is what Chicago must have looked like as late as 1833. It was an inhospitable spot. Its sloughs defied the cart and buggy: "No Bottom" signs marked much of what was later to become a bastion of straight-laced skyscrapers; ladies "calling" in long silk dresses were often seen wading barefoot in the knee-deep mud. Only canoes or hollowed-out skows made their way with ease across the wet grasslands or wound a path through the wild rice blanketing the Chicago River's branches and streams.[2]

The desolation of the unbroken prairie stretching to the south as far as the eye could reach — as far as Springfield — inspired dread and, only occasionally, admiration. The interminable vista reduced people to miniature stature. The gnawing loneliness did not come from a lack of human company; it came rather from the land, a terrain that took nothing in halfway measure.[3]

Old settlers, army scouts, fur trappers, and the Indians before them waited

---

1. Earliest descriptions of the Chicago portage, with its frozen marshes and floods, are those of Marquette, Joliet, and LaSalle, 1674-1682. See A. T. Andreas, *History of Chicago, From the Earliest Period to the Present Time* (Chicago, 1884), I, 44-45. Later descriptions can be found in Henry Rowe Schoolcraft, "A Journey up the Illinois River in 1821," in Milo M. Quaife, ed., *Pictures of Illinois One Hundred Years Ago* (Chicago, 1918), pp. 120-121; Gurdon Hubbard, "Recollections of First Year," Gurdon Hubbard Papers, Chicago Historical Society; Charles Cleaver, *Early Chicago Reminiscences* (Chicago, 1882), pp. 28, 30, 46; Edwin O. Gale, *Early Chicago and Vicinity* (Chicago, 1902), p. 105; Colbee C. Benton, in Paul Angle, ed., *Prairie State: Impressions of Illinois* (Chicago, 1968), p. 114; Bessie Louise Pierce, *A History of Chicago, 1673-1848* (New York, 1937), pp. 6-12.

2. Cleaver, pp. 28-29; Andreas, p. 192; "Remarks of Hon. George Bates," *Michigan Historical Collections*, 40 vols. (Lansing, 1877-1929), II, 180-181.

3. William H. Keating was one of the more outspoken critics of Chicago as a site for future settlement. See his *Narrative of an Expedition to the Source of St. Peter's River, Lake Winnepeek, Lake of the Woods, etc. Performed in the Year 1823 . . .* (London, 1825), I, 162-163, 165-166. For more favorable comments, see James Herrington to Jacob Herrington, Chicago, January 27, 1831, in Alphabetical File: James Herrington, Chicago Historical Society; "Recollections of First Year," p. 20; Charles Butler Journal, Friday, August 2, 1833, in Letter File: Charles Butler, Chicago Historical Society; Benton, *A Visitor to Chicago in Indian Days*, Paul M. Angle and James R. Getz, eds. (Chicago, 1957), p. 76; Andreas, p. 129. Charlotte Erickson's "The British Immigration in the Old Northwest, 1815-1860," in David M. Ellis, ed., *The Frontier in American Development* (Ithaca, N.Y., 1969), is an interesting study of the British exception to the American farmer's aversion to prairie living during this period.

in the silent heat of summer for the brown prairie grasses to burst into flame in the momentary blaze of fusion of sun and horizon. They listened on white winter nights to the thunder of a nor'easter lashing and breaking the frozen piles on the shore and sending the ice-clogged waters of the Chicago River scurrying backward to ravage its tributary banks. Wolves howled at the shore, and weeks without sun or moon made the inhabitants as blind men whose only guide was the sound of the wind.[4]

It would later occur to easterners that a way to shut out the lonesome vastness was to reshape the landscape. These town builders, less innovative than in need of psychological fortification, laid the imprint of a grid for city streets and in so doing cut through hill, stream, and forest, drained scores of marshes, raised buildings a full story above lake level, and absorbed a population of more than 4,000 within four short years of incorporation (1833-37), whose members filled the more subtle fortresses of judicial, political, religious, and social organization.[5] The master planners had conceived a blueprint for the systematic production of civilization. But it was unnatural; it could have been anywhere.

Its place name was *Checagou,* and that, at least, we owe to its earliest inhabitants. Archaeological diggings at the end of the nineteenth century indicated that prior to the European invasion there were at least twenty-one major Indian villages in Chicago's environs, all located on waterways: the Chicago River and its branches, the Des Plaines, the DuPage, the Calumet, and the lakeshore. In early historic times, the rolling Illinois and Wabash country was held by bands of the Miami and Illinois tribal confederations. The Miami maintained permanent summer residence at Chicago, where native women planted, harvested, and stored maize, squash, and beans. Miami hunters tracked the southern Illinois plains in search of buffalo. In spring and summer whole bands gathered to construct fresh mat-covered houses, to kindle a new fire for the coming year, to attend clan feasts, and to open and bless the sacred medicine bundles. By winter the Miami and the Illinois split into family hunting units to farm the waterways for muskrat and beaver.[6]

The Miami tribe was one of nine major Great Lakes Indian groups that

---

4. Gale, pp. 105-106; Cleaver, p. 28; Andreas, p. 207. Wolves were numerous on Chicago's north side as late as 1834.

5. See Cleaver, p. 30, for description of street drainage and building raising. Population estimates for the years 1833-1837 vary somewhat: Andreas claimed that the town grew from 200 in 1833 to 4,000 in 1837 (p. 142); a visitor's estimate in 1833 was 350, as cited in Angle, p. 64. Pierce (p. 14) lists 3,989 whites and 77 blacks in 1837.

6. See the Augustus Dilg Collection and the Albert Scharf Papers, Chicago Historical Society. See also Andreas, Ch. 1, and Louis Deliette, "Memoir Concerning the Illinois Country," Theodore C. Pease and Raymond C. Werner, eds., *Collections of the Illinois State Historical Library,* XXIII, French Series 1 (1934) (a copy signed "DeGannes" is in the Edward Everett Ayer Collection, Newberry Library, Chicago); Hiram Beckwith, *The Illinois and Indiana Indians* (Chicago, 1884), pp. 99-117; Raymond E. Hauser, "An Ethnohistory of the Illinois Indian Tribe, 1673-1832" (Ph.D. diss., Northern Illinois University, 1973).

Jean Baptiste Point du
Sable, a French-speaking
Negro from Santo
Domingo, who according
to tradition founded the
city of Chicago. From
Intercollegian *Wonder Book*
(Chicago, 1927).

developed, between 1600 and 1760, a distinctive tribal identity and culture. They
numbered only 4,000 on the eve of the great white migration, a scant percentage
of the approximately 100,000 natives who occupied the region. Living far to the
north on the upper shores of Lake Michigan and Lake Superior, the numerically
dominant Ojibway (25,000-30,000), adventurers and nomadic hunters, were to
become the prototypes for the white fur traders. To the south, along the western
shore of Lake Michigan, camped the seminomadic Fox, Sauks, Winnebago, and
the Menomini wild rice gatherers. Along the eastern shore lived the farming-
hunting Potawatomi and the highly structured urban communities of the
Huron and Ottawa farmers. At the bottom bowl of the lake were the Miami
and the Illinois tribes.[7]

The wide range of Indian cultural variation that developed in the years
1600-1760 is indicative of a stabilizing geographic and ecological order, al-

7. For geographic movement and settlement patterns of the Great Lakes tribes, see George
Quimby, *Indians in the Upper Great Lakes Region, 11,000 B.C. to A.D. 1800* (Chicago, 1960) and
James E. Fitting and Charles Cleland, "Late Prehistoric Settlement Patterns in the Upper Great
Lakes," *Ethnohistory,* XVI (1969), 289-302. For cultural variations, see W. Vernon Kinietz, *The
Indians of the Western Great Lakes, 1615-1760* (Occasional Contributions from the Museum of
Anthropology of the University of Michigan, No. 10, 1940; reprinted by University of Michigan
Press, 1965).

though a reverse effect was already in motion by the end of that period.[8] Tribes with a relatively static population, a value system ranking leisure above energy expenditure, and a subsistence economy had little need to wander further out beyond the boundaries marking economic survival, except in years of famine or natural catastrophe. The tribal world, a primarily "spiritual" entity, overlay — in fact, was identical with — the geographic area necessary for subsistence. The tribal worldview was centripetal and cyclical — inward-turning and bent to the symbiotic balance of nature's resources.

Each Great Lakes tribe claimed in seeming perpetuity its own loosely defined territorial domain. No one was foolish enough to think that he might, individually, hold title over the land; but tribes and kin hunting units did, through years of tradition, "own" the lands they occupied. Their boundaries were by and large respected. Warfare was a manifestation of tribal honor or of personal revenge, not of geographical or territorial conquest. There was no reason to obtain more territory.

The arrival of the European fur trade, particularly in its Anglo-Saxon phase, had a profound effect on the Indian conception of time and spatial integrity. All the land, even regions of which the Great Lakes tribes had neither heard nor seen, was said to "belong" to Frenchmen and Englishmen. The natives must have thought them vain, these God-like white men who set their linear-progressive stamp on times and places as yet unknown and who vied with one another for the "protection" of their "primitive" wards. Europeans had no respect for the cyclical stores of nature; nor did they respect the spiritual knowledge of the "savage." They scoffed at the notion that nature's vicissitudes were personally directed — for good or for evil — toward humans. Natural phenomena were to be understood and then controlled.

Perhaps — although current research signals otherwise — the native momentarily accepted the "superior" notion that a land which had seemed only comfortably to support a population ratio of one per square mile was suddenly limitless in its abundance. Indeed, for the Indian hunter the land was not without limits, and the diminishing herds of elk, caribou, and deer led the natives, already increasingly dependent on European material culture, away from the maize fields into the vast stretches of forest and finally onto the trails of the white fur-trader. These trails, long used by Indian messengers, heavy with wampum and running to announce war, death, birth, or high council, had never been avenues of ingress. They crossed boundaries never surveyed, but which ensured the integrity of distinct tribal cultures. With the coming of the fur trade, the ancient roads became highways of destruction.[9]

8. Quimby, p. 110.
9. *Ibid.*, pp. 109-115. The 1600-1760 estimated population density of the Great Lakes tribes of one per square mile assumes that Great Lakes peoples were subsistence farmers as well as hunters during this period. A growing literature concerns the impact of the fur trade upon Indian society:

Competition for hunting grounds and trade routes had by 1800 despoiled most of the diversity and autonomy of the Great Lakes tribes. Early nineteenth-century residents of and visitors to Chicago regarded their Indian neighbors as little more than stray dogs — vermin-infested scavengers. These were, of course, insensitive observers; but a direct result of the fur traffic had indeed been the emergence between 1760 and 1800 of a pan-Indian culture in the Lakes region, one that mimicked the peripatetic, band-oriented Chippewa social structure and depended heavily on imported trade goods. The art of pottery making was lost around 1780. Maize cultivation, once an activity central to the unity of village life, was now carried on primarily for white consumption. Ironically, years of famine brought on by the depletion in game reserves found Chicago-area Potawatomi buying back at grossly inflated prices corn meal that they had earlier cultivated.[10]

The rapid transition to a fur-trading culture by all of the Great Lakes tribes was propelled by a mistaken supposition that a white-Indian alliance might prove reciprocally enriching. Unfortunately, the disintegration of stable and coexisting tribal structures was the necessary price of the formation of a new social order. Tribal disintegration, even in its earliest stages, had devastating consequences. The tearing of a social fabric woven by oral tradition left the individual native defenseless in the face of a more sophisticated technology. Indian magic lost face to the gun.

The importation of European goods and foodstuffs destroyed the meaningful division of labor between the sexes. Potters, weavers, basketmakers, stoneworkers, and planters lost their occupations and status rank. Time, once the gentle discipline behind seasons, duties, and things spiritual, became an albatross. Intricate patterns of consanguineous and affineal recognition and avoidance were destroyed by intermarriage with whites, who refused to "avoid" certain relatives, tantamount to incest. Acceptance of "half-blood" chiefs confused, fragmented, and ultimately defused the potency of clan identification. Above all, the never-ending search for peltry broke up villages and kin groupings and clouded recognition of tribal boundaries. The result was prolonged intertribal war.[11]

---

see, most recently, Calvin Martin, "The European Impact on the Culture of a Northeastern Algonquian Tribe: An Ecological Interpretation," *William and Mary Quarterly*, XXXI, Ser. 1 (1974), 3-26.

10. Quimby, pp. 147-151. See also Quimby, *Indian Culture and European Trade Goods* (Madison, Wis., 1966); Harold Hickerson, *The Chippewa and Their Neighbors: A Study in Ethnohistory* (New York, 1970); Felix M. Keesing, "The Menomini Indians of Wisconsin," *Memoirs of the American Philosophical Society*, X (1939); and Arthur J. Ray, *Indians in the Fur Trade: Their Role as Trappers, Hunters, and Middlemen in the Lands Southwest of Hudson Bay 1660-1870* (Toronto, 1974).

11. Quimby, *Indians in the Upper Great Lakes*, pp. 151 and *passim*. That traditional authority was threatened is indicated by the tribal attempt to integrate British and American fathers into the patrilineal clan structure. Britishers were made members of a new clan, "the Lion," and Americans, "the Eagle."

Ancient runners' trails from the north, south, and east crossed at Chicago. With the establishment of fur-trading centers at St. Louis, Green Bay, Detroit, Fort Wayne, and Sandusky, the Miami and Illinois saw their hunting grounds invaded from three sides. From the north and west came the Sauk, Fox, and Kickapoo, and from the east marauding Iroquois bands. By the time Fort Dearborn was first built in 1803, the Miami had largely been driven toward the Wabash Valley.[12]

The Potawatomi were already bending under white influence. Earlier habitation near Detroit and Green Bay had exposed their members to intimate contact with French and British traders. Considerable intermarriage had occurred: dark-skinned daughters of mixed marriages were often trained and educated in French-Canadian homes, while sons were encouraged to enter the trade with their fathers. Signs of a metal age were everywhere: elaborate silver breastplates, crosses, earbobs, and crescent-shaped gorgets; iron spear- and arrowheads; copper cooking utensils; copper studs ornamenting the avenging end of tribal war clubs; and finely crafted tomahawks and hatchets.[13]

The influence of educated mixed-bloods within the tribe increased out of all proportion to their actual numbers. By 1833, on the eve of Potawatomi removal, a fair number of mixed-blood leaders had assumed, by American appointment, "chiefly" status. Such "chiefs" and their followers eventually came into the villages to live side by side with British and French traders, sharing food, equipment, and advice. They built one- or two-room log and bark huts, and they took on the trappings of European civilization in language, dress, and material wealth. Their social movement between white and Indian lifestyles seems to have been fluid, and their services were at least temporarily needed — as buffers between antagonistic cultures.[14] The majority of Potawatomi, meanwhile, still camped in band villages along streams and rivers. Their mat-covered, dome-shaped wigwams did not impinge on the landscape but followed its curves and hollows, forming a loose circle on high, level ground. They retained the language of their ancestors, the traditional religious beliefs, the tribal authority, and the social structure. However, their lives, like those of their mixed-blood leaders, had been irreparably altered: they had become part of a larger community.[15]

12. Andreas, pp. 34-45; James A. Clifton, *The Prairie People: Continuity and Change in Potawatomi Indian Culture, 1665-1965* (Lawrence, Kan., 1977); Erminie Wheeler-Voegelin and David B. Stone, *Indians of Illinois and Northwestern Indiana* (New York, 1974).

13. Quimby, pp. 147-151; John Kinzie Papers and Accounts, Chicago Historical Society; the Chicago Historical Society's collection of material artifacts, particularly the Fort Dearborn display; Arthur Woodward, *The Denominators of the Fur Trade* (Pasadena, Cal., 1970), pp. 22-23, and *passim.*

14. Madore Beaubien Papers, Beaubien Family Papers (including information on Chief Alexander Robinson) and Billy Caldwell Papers, Chicago Historical Society. See also Jacqueline Peterson, "Ethnogenesis: Métis Development and Influence in the Great Lakes Region, 1690-1836" (Ph.D. diss., University of Illinois, Chicago Circle, 1977).

15. Juliette Kinzie, *Wau-bun, The Early Days in the Northwest* (Chicago, 1932), pp. 193-194; Beaubien Family Papers, Chicago Historical Society.

Ancient runners' trails and waterways met at Fort Dearborn (Chicago).
Courtesy of the Illinois State Historical Library.

No member of the fur-trade world — either white or native — escaped the anguish dealt by the extinction of "the occupation" and the transition to a highly organized and stratified society launched by the Yankee invasion of the Old Northwest. Most white traders were neither prosperous nor urban in outlook. Rather, they blended into the pan-Indian culture developing in the Great Lakes region, learning Ojibway, the *lingua franca* of the trade, as their Indian counterparts learned a French *patois*. They adopted many of the customs and habits of the tribes with whom they wintered. They too were the victims of lavishly financed entrepreneurial ventures emanating from New York and Montreal, which culminated in a regionwide monopoly between 1811 and 1834 that was led by John Jacob Astor's American Fur Company.[16] When Astor's profits

16. John Kinzie Papers and Accounts, Chicago Historical Society; "Recollections of First Year," Gurdon S. Hubbard Papers; American Fur Company Papers, Letter Books, Chicago Historical Society; John Jacob Astor to Ramsay Crooks, New York, Mar. 17, 1817, in *Collections of the State Historical Society of Wisconsin* (Madison, 1854-1931), XIX, 451. See also Gordon Charles Davidson, *The Northwest Company* (New York, 1918); David Lavender, *The Fist in the Wilderness* (Garden

dipped sharply between 1828 and 1834, he merely sold his Great Lakes holdings and moved the trade beyond the Mississippi. His white and Indian employees — clerks, traders, *voyageurs,* and *engagés* — were left behind to stagger into the new world rising from the east.

Traditionally, the lower Great Lakes fur trade has been divided into pre-Astor entrepreneurial and post-Astor monopoly phases. That division implies that, prior to the formation of the American Fur Company, access to the trade was open to anyone with gumption, and that profitable competition was carried on by small French-Canadian, British, and mixed-blood traders throughout the region. However, this does not appear to have been the case. Few people of little means realized profits from the fur trade; most lived barely above the subsistence level and were perpetually in debt to supply agencies at Detroit, Montreal, or Michilimackinac. In collusion with British investors, Astor's Southwest Fur Company held a virtual monopoly over the Chicago region prior to the War of 1812, which forced his British partners to sell their American interests. A reorganized "American" Fur Company (AFC) was the result.

What actual competition existed prior to the AFC consisted of eastern capitalists who supplied local middlemen traders through their personal agents at Detroit and Michilimackinac. Such high-level competition survived throughout the Astor regime. The Detroit houses of Conant & Mack and William Brewster financed the ventures of two of the most successful traders in the Chicago area between 1820 and 1828.[17] The local traders themselves were never able to compete successfully. They lacked both capital and the respect of their employers. Despite a wealth of field experience, such men were regularly refused promotion to the inner executive chambers of the great trading houses. Most seriously, prices of pelts and trade goods were fixed in the East and abroad.[18]

The Chicago of 1816-1834 was thus a community of such middlemen traders and their employees — clerks, *voyageurs,* and *engagés* of French, British, American, Indian, and mixed extraction. They existed for the most part under the aegis of the AFC. Their work, social aspirations, and group solidarity revolved around the profit-and-loss ledger kept by Astor's chief assistants at Michilimackinac, Ramsay Crooks and Robert Stuart, and the annual trek to the

City, N.Y., 1964); John D. Haeger, "The American Fur Company and the Chicago of 1812-1835," *Journal of the Illinois State Historical Society* (Summer 1968), 117-139.

17. Account Books, American Fur Company Papers, Chicago Historical Society. Details of the estates of the American Fur Company's competition at Chicago, William Wallace and John Crafts, are given in Ernest B. East's "Contributions to Chicago History from Peoria County Records," Part I, *Journal of the Illinois State Historical Society* (Mar.-Dec. 1938), 197-207. See especially Robert Stuart to John Crafts, Aug. 20, 1824; Mar. 2, 1825; Aug. 26, 1824, American Fur Company Papers, Chicago Historical Society.

18. John Kinzie Papers and Accounts, Chicago Historical Society; Robert Stuart to Astor, Sep. 12, 1825, American Fur Company Papers, Chicago Historical Society.

"great house" on that island. Thus, in the following discussion of early Chicago lifeways, one must not forget the hidden specter of a ruling class looking sternly down Lake Michigan from its storehouse at Mackinac. Entrance to this ruling class was closed to local men. The exclusion of Chicago residents between 1816 and 1834 meant that they were already accustomed to taking orders from outsiders when the eastern speculators arrived. It also meant that the natural instinct of men to acquire status, dignity, and personal gain would exercise itself in other spheres. This was as true for the Potawatomi as for the British, French-Canadian, and "métis" employees of the trade.

The multiracial settlement of the early 1800s at Chicago was no utopian paradise. Exchanges between Indian and white culture had produced an ordering of financial and social status, though perhaps less sophisticated than that of the eastern newcomers. Slander, theft, moral outrage, extravagant competition, hints of petty squabbling, and even murder marked the social lives of the old settlers. But those lives were also marked by the security of clan; a tenuous kind of racial harmony; an easy, enveloping spirit that gathered in the entire village; and a peaceful, irreverent disdain for "progress."

II

The earth keeps some vibration going
There in your heart, and that is you.
And if the people find you can fiddle,
Why fiddle you must, for all your life.

— Edgar Lee Masters, "Fiddler Jones"

Chicago, on the eve of the Fort Dearborn garrison's second coming in 1816, lay fallow, as it had lain for centuries, awaiting the imperceptible retreat of Lake Michigan's glacial waters to dry out its sandy bottom. Riders on horseback, skirting the sand dunes of the lower bowl of the lake, must have been struck, as they took the northward curve, with the notion that they were treading on ground already claimed. Such men were not geologists, but when they saw the blue mist veiling the high hill in the distance, they named it Blue Island. This mound and its less auspicious neighbor, Stony Island, were by some chance of nature built of sturdier bedrock than the surrounding terrain. The mounds had been spared the leveling scrape of the last glacier. And when American soldiers arrived in 1816, the triple arms of the Chicago River still embraced much of the land for six months of the year.[19]

19. Quimby, pp. 1-20. In 1800, most of the land at Chicago was free of water at least half of the year. The lake continues to recede.

The lifeways of Chicago's early nineteenth-century inhabitants were of necessity waterways. A liquid boundary arc stretched from Wilmette *(Ouillmette)* at the northern lakeshore, down the north branch of the Chicago River to Wolf Point, following the river's south branch to what became 35th Street, and then cutting across to the southern lakeshore. Within this arc were scattered at least fifteen families whose lives were interdependent — united by blood, occupational survival, common values, and the river. As if by instinct, residents set their log and bark cabins and barns on the high bank and let their lives lean to the current. Such houses rarely had more than one or two rooms and fewer windows, but their inhabitants chose, without need of plat, the level ground, and placed their doors toward the river road and the yellow sundown prairie.

The human landscape was as careless as the meandering river, but was not without design. A respect for space and the needs of field and stable kept households apart; but there was another meaning to the sprawl. Long before a greedy state legislature — anticipating an Illinois-Michigan Canal — put Chicago on the map, and lots, streets, and ward boundaries were platted, the settlement had its geographic divisions. In addition to the Yankee garrison ensconced on the south bank of the main river branch, four other kin groups or clans had claimed their "turf": the British (Mc)Kinzies and their southern relatives Clybourne and Hall on the north side; the French-Indian Ouillmette, Beaubien, and LaFramboise families on the far north, west, and south sides.

So dispersed was the settlement that it was impossible for the eye to encompass it in a single sweeping glance from the fort's blockhouse, which occupied the highest ground. To an outsider accustomed to the comforting spectacle of shelters huddled together, Chicago seemed hardly to exist at all. United States Army Engineer William H. Keating recorded "but a few huts, inhabited by a miserable race of men, scarcely equal to the Indians from whom they are descended . . . [whose] log or bark houses are low, filthy and disgusting." Yet the town probably had a stable population of more than 150 outside the garrison prior to 1831. By its own enduring admission, it was a community.[20]

The view to the south of the fort covered a wide grassy plain that stretched for several miles beyond the garrison's orchards and corn fields at the foot of the stockade. A half mile down the lakeshore lay several scattered shanties used by the fort and the American Fur Company and a commodious, though jerry-built house occupied by Jean Baptiste Beaubien, AFC agent, and his mixed-blood family. To the west the plain was interrupted by a thin stand of trees lining the south branch of the river. Hidden among the timber was an establishment called Hardscrabble.[21]

The name Hardscrabble, perhaps derived from limestone outcroppings

20. Cleaver, pp. 15-16; Juliette Kinzie, pp. 205-211; Keating, pp. 165-166.

21. Juliette Kinzie, pp. 209-211; Benton in Paul Angle, *Prairie State,* pp. 112-114; Surgeon John Cooper's description in James Grant Wilson Papers, Chicago Historical Society; Captain John Whistler, 1808, Fort Dearborn Paper, Chicago Historical Society.

in the vicinity, is suggestive of a single farm but actually included at least ten cabins, a major house and post, and sleeping quarters for *voyageurs* spread out along the river bank. Title to this establishment, as to almost every other dwelling in the community, was obscure. Located at the entrance to Mud Lake, the spring portage route to the Des Plaines, Illinois, and Mississippi rivers, Hardscrabble rivaled Beaubien's cabin at the lakefront as a trading location. While Beaubien, as well as AFC agents before him, had the advantage of intercepting the first shipments of trade goods from Detroit and Michilimackinac in late summer, the traders at Hardscrabble were the first to see the *bâteaux* returning heavy with pelts in the spring.

Although Hardscrabble was most consistently occupied by the LaFramboise clan and other mixed-blood traders like Alexander Robinson, it became from time to time the seat of serious competition with the AFC. Prior to being bought out by Astor in 1824, John Crafts, representing Conant & Mack of Detroit, conducted his business there. Afterward, when Crafts had taken over the lakefront store for the AFC, William H. Wallace of Detroit traded at Hardscrabble until his death in 1827. Antoine Ouillmette, whose home and trading store hugged the lakeshore ten miles north of the principal settlement, also had a connection with the place. Wallace was paying him rent in 1827.[22]

"Improvements" at Chicago lacked the value easterners would later assign to them. Lots and houses were swapped for as little as a cord of wood and a pair of moccasins, or changed hands as the casual winnings off a fast pony or a shrewd card game. Residents almost never registered their property at the early Wayne and Crawford county seats. Their rudely fashioned cabins did not weather the winds or the damp, and the thatched or bark-shingled roofs inevitably invited fire. Like the portable wigwams of their Indian neighbors, such houses had little material worth. But, that is not to say that the early residents did not value permanence and stability; rather, their sense of community was not embodied in a tidy row of whitewashed domiciles legally bound and named.[23]

The "Kinzie mansion" was an exception. Although the Kinzie title is still unrecovered, presumably the house on the north bank opposite the fort was the same property that Jean Baptiste Point du Sable registered and sold in 1800 to Jean Lalime, post interpreter and Kinzie's rival. Lalime resided in the house

22. Robert Stuart to John Kinzie, Oct. 22, 1825, American Fur Company Papers, Chicago Historical Society; Juliette Kinzie, p. 215; testimony of Mary Galloway, wife of Archibald Clybourne, in Andreas, *History of Chicago*, p. 103; Ernest B. East, "The Inhabitants of Chicago, 1825-1831," *Journal of the Illinois State Historical Society* (1944), 155.

23. Keating, in Angle, p. 84; Marshall Smelser, "Material Customs in the Territory of Illinois," *Journal of the Illinois State Historical Society* (Apr. 1936), 17; Andreas, p. 134; Beaubien Family Papers, Chicago Historical Society; "Beaubiens of Chicago," MS in Frank Gordon Beaubien Papers, Chicago Historical Society.

prior to 1804, when the vituperative redbeard Kinzie arrived and immediately took firm possession.[24]

By 1831 the family had abandoned the mansion to a tenant postmaster. Perched on a sandhill, it had seen fifty years of storm and drift and seemed impatient to slide into the river. In its heyday, the house had been an impressive example of the French *habitant* architecture of the Mississippi Valley, the *poteaux en terre*. It had five rooms — a spacious salon with a small room off each corner — and a wide piazza running the length of the river side. Behind it were stables, a bakehouse, huts for employees, and, characteristically, a garden and orchard fenced by a palisade. Although presumably similar to other dwellings in the vicinity, the Kinzie mansion was certainly the largest — and the only house with a palisade.[25]

Smaller homes of similar construction were indiscriminately lumped with "log cabins" by early travelers. However, the typical American "log cabin" of Swedish-Finnish origin was formed of logs set horizontally, with a fireplace at one end of the building. Cabins of this style were not unknown at Chicago, but prior to 1820 they were vastly outnumbered by houses of a primitive French-Canadian design, the *pieux en terre*, whose origins probably owe something to the Huron longhouse.[26] Typically, the French-Canadian dwelling was constructed of roughhewn logs set vertically into a trench and chinked with grass and mud mortar. The thatched or shingled roof was peaked high to facilitate runoff; the fireplace sat astride the roof's center. Ordinarily, the logs were covered with bark slabs, but when the timber was clean-shaven and whitewashed, the structure took on the appearance of stone or frame. It is not surprising that Mark Beaubien's "pretentious" two-story, blue-shuttered tavern, the Sauganash, was mistaken for a New England frame house. There is no

24. Information concerning Jean Baptiste Point du Sable is elusive. For a brief sketch, see Lyman Draper interview with Robert Forsyth in Lyman S. Draper Manuscripts, S, XXII (1868), 104, Wisconsin Historical Society, Madison, Wisconsin. See also Milo M. Quaife, *Checagou* (Chicago, 1933), p. 90; Pierce, *A History of Chicago*, p. 13; William C. Smith to James May, Fort Dearborn, Dec. 9, 1803, William C. Smith Papers, Chicago Historical Society; "Beaubiens of Chicago," Frank Gordon Beaubien Papers, Chicago Historical Society. The Wayne County records at Detroit, Michigan, show the sale of du Sable's house to Lalime, as well as several Indian grants of land to Kinzie at Detroit. Pierre Menard claimed to have purchased a tract of land on the north bank of the Chicago River from an "Indian" named Bonhomme and later sold it to the Kinzies for $50. No houses are mentioned in these transactions.

25. Juliette Kinzie, p. 210. There is a drawing in the Augustus Dilg Collection, Chicago Historical Society, of the old Kinzie house which fairly matches Mrs. Kinzie's description. See also John Wentworth, *Early Chicago* (Chicago, 1876), p. 23, and Elizabeth Therese Baird, "Reminiscence of Early Days on Mackinac Island," *Collections of the State Historical Society of Wisconsin*, XIV, 25. For a description of the "poteaux en terre" of the lower Illinois country, see John Reynolds, *The Pioneer History of Illinois* (Belleville, Ill., 1852), pp. 30-31.

26. Smelser, pp. 18-19; John McDermott, ed., *The French in the Mississippi Valley* (Urbana, Ill., 1965), pp. 26-40. For a description of "half-breed" housing, see John H. Fonda in *Collections of the State Historical Society of Wisconsin*, V, 232; Peterson, *op. cit.*, Ch. 5.

Typical métis home, *poteaux en terre,* showing the bark-covered upright log structure
and French picket fence.   Courtesy of The Newberry Library.

evidence, however, that the *I* frame, with its central hall, preceded the Yankee influx of 1833.[27]

Fanning out beyond the "mansion," the numerous members of the Kinzie clan populated the wooded sloughs along the north bank and east of the north branch of the Chicago River. The north side was barely habitable: a dense growth of trees, knee-deep in water, choked out the sunlight, and the bogs were unfit for cultivation. When William B. Ogden's brother-in-law purchased the better part of the "Kinzie Addition" on speculation in the early 1830s, he was forced to initiate an extensive drainage program to render it fit for settlement. Yet from the very beginning this gloomy marsh spelled status, as did the Kinzie name.[28]

27. Jane F. Babson, "The Architecture of Early Illinois Forts," *Journal of the Illinois State Historical Society* (Spring 1968), 9-40; Fred Kniffer, "Folk Housing: Key to Diffusion," *Annals of the Association of American Geographers* (Dec. 1965); interview by Milo M. Quaife of Emily (Beaubien) LeBeau, Aug. 3, 1911, in Emily LeBeau Papers, Chicago Historical Society.

28. "The water lay 6 inches to 9 inches deep the year round," according to Cleaver, p. 30. See also "William B. Ogden," *Fergus Historical Series,* No. 17 (Chicago, 1882), 45; Benton in Angle, p. 114; Quaife, *Checagou,* p. 78.

John Kinzie — "Father of Chicago." Courtesy of Chicago Historical Society.

Viewed variously as the "father of Chicago" and as a common horse thief, Kinzie in fantasy obscures Kinzie in fact. A British subject and native of the Grosse Pointe district of Detroit, John Kinzie entered the fur trade early, after developing a fair skill as a silversmith. Ruthlessly ambitious, he soon wormed his way into the Detroit circle of merchant agents and found a patron for his Sandusky, Maumee, and St. Joseph trading "adventures." He apparently realized the potential value of territory in advance of the line of settlement. In 1795, he, his half-brother Thomas Forsyth, and other Detroit entrepreneurs almost succeeded in a conspiracy to grab title to Indian lands in Michigan and Indiana before General Anthony Wayne could finalize the Treaty of Greenville.[29]

Between 1804 and 1812, Kinzie at Chicago and Forsyth at Peoria together carved out a small empire in northern Illinois. Kinzie was unquestionably the most powerful man at Chicago during this period, outranking even the garrison officers, who were humbled monthly by Kinzie currency advanced to cover their overdue military pay. Most of the French-Indian inhabitants — the Mirandeaus, Ouillmettes, LaFramboises, and Robinsons — worked for Kinzie and Forsyth during these years, although it might well be a mistake to label them simply *voyageurs* or *engagés*. At least one mixed-blood, Captain Billy Caldwell, son of an Irish officer and a Mohawk mother, served as clerk, a position of some

29. John Kinzie Papers and Accounts, Chicago Historical Society; F. Clever Bald, *Detroit's First American Decade, 1796-1805* (Ann Arbor, 1948), p. 12. See also Eleanor Lytle Kinzie Gordon, *John Kinzie, the Father of Chicago: A Sketch* (1910). This inflated family history suggests that Kinzie lived in New York City and ran off to Quebec to learn a silversmith's trade, a plausible though unsubstantiated story.

responsibility.[30] But whatever the aspirations of local residents, guile, intimidation, and the soporific effects of British rum were devices Kinzie used to ensure that renegade trappers thought twice before embarking for Detroit to strike a separate bargain for their beaver pelts. Kinzie's recorded malevolence is limited to the murder of Jean Lalime in 1812, but hints of other threats abound.[31]

Despite Kinzie's local influence, he never escaped the pecuniary grasp of the Detroit merchants. Caught in the vast financial octopus that spread its tentacles to Montreal, London, and as far as Peking, Kinzie owed his livelihood to George McDougall, supply agent at Detroit, who in turn made his commission off trade goods sold by Forsyth and Richardson in Montreal. After he was imprisoned following the Fort Dearborn Massacre in 1812 because of his British sympathies, Kinzie's credit collapsed, and he was forced to sell all his real property. His debt to George McDougall alone was a hefty $22,000.[32]

When the second Fort Dearborn garrison returned to rebuild the post in 1816, an aging Kinzie followed. The wrath of the Potawatomi had been aimed at the Americans; thus the "Kinzie mansion," Hardscrabble, J. B. Beaubien's house on the southern lakeshore, and other assorted cabins stood unchanged. Even the scattered remains of the massacred whites, left to rot on the beach, had settled comfortably into temporary sandy graves. The bleached bones seemed ominous, and the garrison hastily shoved them into wooden coffins and dropped them into higher ground. But for John Kinzie it was a homecoming.

Time had been a visitor. The Kinzie family reclaimed its place on the north bank, but John never recovered his former status. The fort, more self-assured after the recent United States victory, had little need for a quarrelsome old trader whose past allegiances were suspect. Still, from a Yankee perspective, a Britisher was more comely than a Frenchman; before his death in 1828, Kinzie did manage to wangle brief appointments as interpreter and subagent (the latter a gratuity extended by his Indian agent son-in-law).[33]

The American Fur Company took him more seriously. An established trader, well known among the Potawatomi and mixed-blood *voyageurs,* Kinzie was viewed by Ramsay Crooks at Michilimackinac as the new company's key to the consolidation of the Illinois country. Yet, Kinzie failed to meet Crooks's expectations: although he was reinforced by a second AFC trader, J. B. Beaubien,

30. John Kinzie Papers and Accounts; Quaife, p. 95; Pierce, p. 21; Lyman S. Draper Manuscripts, S, XXII (1868), 102, Wisconsin Historical Society, Madison, Wisconsin; Clifton, "Captain Billy Caldwell."

31. Surgeon John Cooper of the first garrison at Fort Dearborn said that Kinzie was a man of "ungovernable temper" who had bitter quarrels with people. Cooper also charged Kinzie with Lalime's murder. See the James Grant Wilson Papers, Chicago Historical Society. See also *Hyde Park-Kenwood Voices,* III, No. 8 (1960), in John Kinzie Papers; Matthew Irwin to William Eustis, Chicago, July 3, 1812, in Lewis Cass Papers, II, Clements Library, Ann Arbor, Michigan.

32. Bald, p. 76; John Kinzie Papers and Accounts.

33. John Kinzie Papers and Accounts; Andreas, pp. 90-91; Lewis Cass to John Calhoun, Jan. 9, 1819, Lewis Cass Papers, Burton Historical Collection, Detroit Public Library.

Kinzie's efforts to overwhelm the competition at Chicago were in vain. In desperation, Astor bought out his competitor's agent, John Crafts, and turned control of the Chicago trade over to him. After Crafts's death in 1825, Kinzie again assumed control, with Beaubien retaining one-third share. The Creole Beaubien, who had an Indian wife, received short shrift at the hands of Ramsay Crooks and Robert Stuart at the big house: he was treated as a perpetual "second" man, even though his lines of connection with the mixed-blood trappers ran deeper than Kinzie's. When Kinzie died, Astor, plagued by a diminishing return, sold his Illinois interests to Gurdon Hubbard, the American Fur Company agent on the Wabash.[34]

The Chicago settlement in Kinzie's day was dependent to a man on the fur trade. The social hierarchy, therefore, tended to coincide with rank in the occupation, at least in the eyes of the Detroit and Michilimackinac suppliers. The Kinzie family stood at the top of the social pyramid, closely followed by the Beaubiens, and then the mixed-blood families of LaFramboise, Ouillmette, Mirandeau, Billy Caldwell, and Alexander Robinson. The Indian *engagés* and hunters occupied the base — or so the Kinzies would have said. Whether their version of the community structure was accurate, however, was largely unimportant. The subtle mechanisms that draw human beings together are for the most part unspoken; the sum of individual visions that converge to form a collective consciousness is never large enough to explain the whole. The view from the bottom of the social pyramid would no doubt have been considerably different. The Beaubiens and LaFramboises were well-loved by the Potawatomi; and Billy Caldwell and Alexander Robinson carried political weight within the local bands.[35]

With the ebb of "the occupation," the struggle for power and position began anew. The Kinzies would quite naturally choose to align with the fort: the Yankee garrison was the self-styled "bringer of civilization," and the Kinzies had always felt culturally superior to their French Creole and Indian neighbors. They had paid the bad debts of their Indian employees and sheltered numerous children of the Ouillmette and Mirandeau lines, who, while serving as maids and stable boys, were given the opportunity to observe Anglo-Saxon manners and virtues. Still, a turn to the fort was a sharp shift in allegiance: the garrison had always seemed alien, an intrusion on the measured rhythm of the Chicago community.[36]

34. John Kinzie Papers and Accounts; Robert Stuart to Astor, Sept. 12, 1825, American Fur Company Papers; Robert Stuart to J. B. Beaubien, Sept. 11, 1825, American Fur Company Papers; Gurdon Hubbard, Jan. 2, 1828, Gurdon S. Hubbard Papers.

35. Conway, p. 405 and *passim;* Charles J. Kappler, ed., *Indian Affairs. Law and Treaties* (Washington, D.C., 1904), II, 402-404; James R. Clifton, "Captain Billy Caldwell: The Reconstruction of an Abused Identity," paper read at the American Historical Association meetings, Dec. 1976, Washington, D.C.

36. Eleanor L. K. Gordon, *John Kinzie, Father of Chicago,* p. 28; John Kinzie Papers and

At some imperceptible point around 1820, however, the fort merged with the community to become for a brief period its ruling class. Why the inhabitants of Chicago allowed this to happen is unknown. It may have been the unconscious drift of a people who had lost their moorings. Direction had always floated down from Detroit or Mackinac, and when — simultaneously — Ramsay Crooks began to pack his bags and the fur boats came home empty, residents panicked. The paternal symbolism of the fort became, at that point, too obvious to resist. Union with the fort took two forms. For most of Chicago's inhabitants it was a simple matter of making the best use of the fort's presence. A garrison at the northern mouth of a new state would mean the influx of people (though in numbers more vast than the enterprising Beaubiens ever imagined). Overnight, a number of trading cabins were hastily converted to taverns, hostelries, and food-supply stores.[37]

The Kinzies beat a more direct path. Treating the garrison like a territorial clan, they marched through the front gate and brought home as relatives the highest ranking officials. Kinzie's elder son, John Harris, married Connecticut-born Juliette Magill, niece of the government Indian agent, Alexander Wolcott; his daughters Ellen Marion and Maria Indiana married Alexander Wolcott and Captain (later General) David Hunter, respectively; and his younger son, Robert Allen, married Gwinthlean Whistler, daughter of the commandant of the fort. As added insurance, both John Harris and Robert Allen became Army officers. These were calculated moves to retain status, and they succeeded. The family's prestige had been on the wane between 1816 and 1828, but in the eyes of the first Yankee arrivals in 1832-33, Kinzie was once again the foremost name in Chicago.[38]

Juliette Magill Kinzie was aware of that fact when, on a gray winter night in 1831, she first stood with her new husband on the threshold of Elijah Wentworth's trading store and sometime inn at Wolf Point and looked down the main branch of the river flowing eastward toward Lake Michigan. To her right she could make out the silhouette of the two bastions of Fort Dearborn nestled in the elbow of the river's sharp bend to the south; to her left, directly across the river from the fort, was the old Kinzie home hidden somewhere in the darkness among the sand hills. It was Juliette's initial visit, but she already knew her place.[39]

Accounts; Ramsay Crooks to John Kinzie, Oct. 29, 1819 and Aug. 11, 1819, and Robert Stuart to Kinzie, 1826-1827, in American Fur Company Papers.

37. Between 1829 and 1830 alone, prominent Chicagoans Archibald Clybourne, Samuel Miller, Archibald Caldwell, Mark Beaubien, Alexander Robinson, and Russell Heacock were licensed to keep tavern. See Ernest East, "Contributions to Chicago History from Peoria County Records," Part II, *Journal of the Illinois State Historical Society* (1938), 328-329; "Beaubiens of Chicago," Frank Gordon Beaubien Papers, Chicago Historical Society.

38. Kinzie Family Papers; Gale, p. 125.

39. Juliette Kinzie, p. 209.

A few hours earlier, on the last leg of a three-day journey on horseback, she and her husband, John Harris Kinzie, and their company of French-Canadian employees and guides had stumbled up the frozen bank of the Des Plaines River to warm themselves in front of Bernardus Laughton's fireplace. Mrs. Kinzie was shocked to find a stove and carpet in the middle of the Illinois wilderness. However, her hostess, Mrs. Laughton, was not comforted by such accoutrements of civilization. Like so many women — and men — set adrift on the prairie, she waited nervously, with her arms tightly folded, for the westward advance of her "Eastern family" to catch up.[40]

Mrs. Kinzie had more romantic illusions, born in part of her husband's success as an Indian agent at Fort Winnebago and his unusual apprenticeship to Robert Stuart at Michilimackinac, and in part by her own sense of *noblesse oblige*. Although she had never been to Chicago, she understood her rank in the social order. With the old trader Kinzie gone, she and John Harris Kinzie were the acknowledged leaders of the clan. In view of their Anglo-Saxon ancestry, they presumably were the leaders of the community as well.[41]

A different Kinzie kin group had begun to trickle into the north side as early as 1816: this was a bastard southern line fathered during the American Revolution by the elder John Kinzie; the mother was a young white woman who had been an Indian captive. Juliette Kinzie and other family historians chose to ignore it. However, its importance for early town development was great indeed, and its numbers, even if unacknowledged, served to reinforce the hegemony of the Kinzie name. The anxious adoption of Yankee values by John Kinzie's legitimate second crop of children must be given a fair share of the credit for the testy snubbing, feuding, and in-house squabbling that marked the relations of the two branches between 1816 and 1833. Unofficial marriages and separations were common enough in unorganized territory, and children of different mothers were usually united without stigma or anguish. When threatened by outside competition or family death, the two sets of Kinzie children could act as a unit, but the alliance was tenuous and easily broken.

In the late 1770s, John Kinzie and a trading companion, Alexander Clark, had either ransomed or been "given" two Giles County, Virginia girls whom Tecumseh's Shawnees had captured in a raid. Margaret and Elizabeth Mackenzie set up housekeeping with John Kinzie and Alexander Clark near Sandusky, and over the next decade John Kinzie had three children: James, William, and Elizabeth. Clark fathered a son, whom he named John Kinzie Clark for his friend.[42]

---

40. *Ibid.*, p. 205.

41. See Keating in Angle, *Prairie State*, pp. 84-86. Mrs. Kinzie's *Wau-bun*, while an important historical document, is unfortunately skewed to favor the family's social aspirations.

42. Juliette Kinzie Papers, Chicago Historical Society; Eleanor L. K. Gordon, pp. 6-7. Trader Clark's first name is listed variously as John and Alexander. Mrs. Kinzie omitted this branch of the Kinzie family in her *Wau-Bun*.

Family historian Juliette
Kinzie, an easterner with
a sense of *noblesse oblige*.
Courtesy of Chicago
Historical Society.

After the Revolution, the Mackenzie girls' father, hearing of his daughters' residence at Detroit, rode north to fetch them and their children. For whatever cause — a brutish John Kinzie, a distaste for the northern frontier, or the fear of reprisal due their British husbands — Elizabeth and Margaret fled to Virginia with their children and in short order married Jonas Clybourne and Benjamin Hall, respectively, also of Giles County.[43] As early as 1816, however, a renegade James Kinzie had sought out his natural father and was trading in Chicago. Kinzie apparently took his son in and treated him kindly. His wife Eleanor undoubtedly harbored reservations: as the eldest Kinzie, James threatened the succession rights of her sons, John Harris and his younger brother, Robert Allen. Ironically, in terms of native habits and inclinations, James was the obvious inheritor of John Kinzie's prairie domain. While Kinzie's daughters were acquiring polish at schools in Detroit and the East, and John and Robert were clerking for the AFC, James and his father worked the trade, chased wolves, raced horses, and got roaring drunk together. Had the rowdy old man lived until 1833, he might well have been a source

43. Gordon, *loc. cit.*; Andreas, pp. 101-102.

of embarrassment to his own "refined" children. As it turned out, John Kinzie became a legend; James became the embarrassment.[44]

The southern contingent of the Kinzie clan kept arriving. Word from James of fertile land and a burgeoning Illinois population brought his sister Elizabeth and his mother's and aunt's new families, the Halls and Clybournes. Others who came included John Kinzie Clark (thenceforth known as "Indian Clark"); the Caldwells, relatives of the Halls; and the Virginia-bred Miller brothers, one of whom married Elizabeth Kinzie. By 1829 they were at least twenty strong, too large a population to ignore.[45]

The southerners introduced a diversity of occupations unknown in early Chicago, breaking down the monolithic clutch of the fur trade several years before the easterners brought their crockery and sewing needles. The first attempts were at tavern-keeping, but by 1829 the southern members of the Kinzie clan were also engaged in butchering, tanning, intensive farming, ferrying, and blacksmithing. In addition, it seems clear that the Halls and Clybournes operated a still, Kentucky whiskey having replaced British rum as the liquid staple after 1812. The entire group built their log cabins on the east side of the north branch, running from the forks up to Rolling Meadows, and they settled in, in an uneasy harmony with their northside relatives and neighbors.[46]

The territorial space in which all families met — both occupationally and socially — was Wolf Point, a sort of "free zone." Located on the western, prairie side of the juncture between the two river branches, the Point was about midway between Hardscrabble and Clybourne's cattle yard at Rolling Meadows. A natural intersection, it served for nearly twenty years as the hub of village life — the scene of frolicking, trade, religion, education, and politics.

The Potawatomi were camping there after 1816, and they did not bother to move when stores and cabins were erected. By 1820, the LaFramboise brothers, mixed-blood "chiefs" Alexander Robinson and Billy Caldwell, and James Kinzie were operating out of trading huts at the Point. Shortly thereafter, James Kinzie built the Wolf Tavern and the Green Tree Tavern, which sported a false second-story front and a gallery, because Kinzie said he "wanted a white man's house." By 1828 the itinerant Methodist preachers Jesse Walker and William See were exhorting audiences weekly in a meetinghouse that was also used irregularly as a school for Chicago's French-Indian children.[47]

---

44. Andreas, p. 100; John Kinzie Papers; Robert Stuart to John Crafts, Mar. 2, 1825, American Fur Company Papers.

45. Andreas, pp. 100-102; Wentworth, *Early Chicago*, Supplemental Notes, pp. 34-35.

46. East, "Contributions," Part II, 329-331, 336-339; East, "The Inhabitants of Chicago, 1825-1831," *passim.*

47. The canal section, platted and sold in 1831, held the only lots on the market when the Eastern speculators began to arrive in 1833. Its location, the central loop, gave it a speculative advantage over areas further away from the new harbor. The Kinzie family did not pre-empt the Point, and it went to southerners who did not have a flair for exciting the Eastern interest. See Andreas, pp. 111, 130-132; also Gale, p. 54.

The territorial space in which all families met, Wolf Point was a sort of "free zone," the hub of village life for twenty years. Courtesy of The Newberry Library.

That same year Mark Beaubien, younger brother of Jean Baptiste Beaubien, was running a tavern that was later expanded into the famed "Sauganash," named for Billy Caldwell, on the bank opposite the Point to the south. Archibald Clybourne and Sam Miller also managed a tavern on the riverbank to the north. A few years later, David Hall and Robert Kinzie erected their own trading stores at the Point; and Miller and Hall's tannery operated to the north of Miller's tavern. By 1832 the Point was a bustling paradise of exotica. Races and accents mingled freely, as if the mere place had momentarily destroyed the compartments in people's minds and the territorial divisions of the town.[48] Next to survival, "frolicking" was the major preoccupation of the town. No one expected to make a fast buck; that heady prospect had not yet presented itself. Instead, winter and summer, residents spent a part of their day and uncounted evenings at the Point, swapping tales, playing at cards, racing on foot or horseback, trading, dancing, and flying high on corn "likker," rum, and French brandy. Social class and clan affiliation had no bearing here: it was physical prowess, a witty tongue, or a graceful step that brought people into community.

Full-blooded Indian employees of the Kinzies, who were barred from the dinner table, could hold the whole village captive by the gymnastic fluidity of the Discovery Dance at Wolf Point. The French-Indian Beaubien and LaFramboise girls, who had the gayest feet on earth, found admiring partners among the Virginia farmers, who were just as willing as they to dance until dawn. Whiskey was the official solvent. Everyone — even the women — drank, often from the

48. Mark Beaubien Papers, Chicago Historical Society; Andreas, pp. 106, 288-289.

Mark Beaubien "kept tavern like hell."
Courtesy of Chicago Historical Society: Charles D. Mosher, photographer.

same bottle. It probably was not only the "dissipated" Indians who camped out on the prairie; Virginia boys, too, hitched their ponies and rolled in the long grass to sleep off a night's hilarity. No wonder easterners and ministers were shocked to find a people so ignorant of the healthful, refreshing qualities of water. Liquor was a "problem" all over the state — over the whole region, for that matter.[49]

Perhaps whiskey was seen as a device to break down the barriers between strangers who seemed to have little in common. Or its fantasy-producing properties may have lent a rosier cast to otherwise gray and frightened lives, going nowhere but into the grave. Outwardly, liquor was called a tonic, a body-builder, and a daily necessity for many frontiersmen. That Mark Beaubien's tavern, the Sauganash, was the focal point of the community, therefore, should not seem odd. Its opening in 1826 coincided with several important changes. A declining fur trade threatened the occupational security of many of Chicago's earliest residents, and the population was suddenly growing: the Clybournes, Halls,

49. For the *habitant* dancing tradition, see John Reynolds, *The Pioneer History of Illinois,* pp. 52-53. Cleaver, *Early Chicago Reminiscences,* pp. 5-12; John H. Kinzie Papers; "John Dean Caton Recollections," *Reception to the Settlers of Chicago Prior to 1840, by the Calumet Club of Chicago, Tuesday evening, May 27, 1879* (Chicago, 1879), 36-37. For a discussion of the liquor problem, see Marshall Smelser, pp. 11-13; Thomas Forsyth to General William Clark, Peoria, Apr. 9, 1824, Thomas Forsyth Papers, Folder 2, Missouri Historical Society, St. Louis, Missouri.

Galloways, Scotts, Sees, more Mirandeaus, and John K. Clark had already arrived; and the full-grown children of the first families — the Kinzies and Beaubiens — were returning from school and looking for mates.

There was more to the convergence at Beaubien's place than social need. There were, after all, other taverns: Barney Laughton's on the "Aux Plaines," for example, was a favorite resort of the younger Kinzies. And since hospitality was a primary avenue to status, there was always a drinking circle at John Kinzie's, at Hardscrabble, and at J. B. Beaubien's house at the lakeshore. But Mark Beaubien, at a pivotal juncture in Chicago's history, offered more: entertainment and a defiant middle finger to the world.[50]

Beaubien joked that he "kept tavern like hell," and he evidently did. From 1826 until 1835, several years after the Yankee flood, when Mark tried a new venture, the Beaubien house was bursting its seams nightly. The Sauganash boarded and lodged upwards of twenty or thirty travelers and single townsmen at a time; by 1834 meals and blankets were being served in shifts. No one complained. After his bustling, round wife, the former Monique Nadeau, had cleared the table, Mark commenced the show. He played the fiddle like a madman, and full-blooded Potawatomi, French Creoles, Yankees, and Virginians could not keep from dancing.[51]

Dancing was a principal amusement among French *habitants,* and it became, next to drinking, the most significant community-binding ritual at Chicago. Everyone came and everyone danced. Besides the graceful French-Canadian cotillions, residents learned southern reels, the athletic War and Discovery dances, and the sedate social dances of the Potawatomi. There was hardly a man in Chicago in 1832 who did not know how to paint his body, decorate his hair with eagle feathers, and leap in frenzied exultation, terrorizing effete easterners. When town dances were formalized and limited by invitation in the 1830s, they were called *wabanos* or Grand Wa-ba-nos, a reference to an Indian medicine society noted for its all-night revelries. The name retained the native flavor. But something had changed: the Potawatomi and most of the mixed-bloods were noticeably absent from the guest lists.[52]

Mark Beaubien liked everyone, and the feeling was mutual. Among the Yankee reminiscences of Chicago's early years, the stories about Mark are the

50. Juliette Kinzie, p. 205; Beaubien Family Papers.

51. "John Wentworth's Recollections," Calumet Club, pp. 42, 48; Cleaver, p. 13. Beaubien's tavern was only 16 by 24 feet, yet in 1833-34, forty people were being boarded in shifts. No one knows how many people actually slept there in a given evening.

52. "John Wentworth's Recollections," Calumet Club, pp. 49, 71. In the winter of 1835-36, prominent Easterners and the Kinzies built the Lake House on the North Side. Gale said, "They ain't going to call it no tavern," and Cleaver said there was a joke circulating that no one worth less than $10,000 would be allowed to stay there. Weekly dancing parties were held there by invitation only. At least some of the French Creoles were being included: there is an 1843 dance ticket in the Beaubien Family Papers requesting the company of the "misses Beaubien." See also "Beaubiens of Chicago," Frank Gordon Beaubien Papers; Gale, p. 118.

most poignant — filled with memories of handsome Creole charm, mirth, and abundant kindness to Indians and Yankees alike. His first loves were fiddle playing, horse racing at the Point (or later across a rickety bridge erected in front of the Sauganash in 1831, which he was supposed to be "tending" as toll collector), and propagation. The most prolific man in town, he fathered twenty-three children, many of them named after early settlers he esteemed. He gave away to friends valuable lots he had purchased when the first Michigan-Illinois Canal lands were platted and sold. The only land he apparently possessed when Chicago was incorporated as a city in 1837 was a sixty-four-acre tract at the mouth of the Calumet River, which the Indians had given to "their good friend Mark Beaubien" in the 1833 cession.[53]

The Sauganash was more than a watering hole and ballroom; it also saw its share of the meetings of the Chicago Debating Society (J. B. Beaubien presiding in 1831) and of local politics, seen in the chartering of the town. Chicago's incorporation in 1837 was largely a response to outside interest in the Canal and the downstate need for a local county seat. The village had certainly been large enough to incorporate earlier, but it had evidently not occurred to residents to legalize their community status. However, the early settlers were not unmindful of politics and government: when the area was still part of Peoria County between 1825 and 1831, Chicago men, particularly the Virginians, had avidly sought political office.[54]

Prior to 1827, when the Chicago precinct was organized, all offices were appointive. The commissioners at Peoria gave preference to the men of rank in Chicago, but they also appointed men who appeared eager for position. Old John Kinzie and Jean Baptiste Beaubien were made justices of the peace in 1825 (Alexander Wolcott replaced the deceased Kinzie in 1828), and the southern newcomers Archibald Clybourne and John K. Clark received the nod for constable in 1825 and 1827. Local notables also recommended Billy Caldwell's appointment as justice of the peace, and he was installed on April 18, 1826.[55] Until 1828, J. B. Beaubien, John Kinzie, and Alexander Wolcott, the Indian agent, presided as election judges. James Kinzie later replaced his deceased father in that office. The job of election clerk was in fact that of messenger (the trip to and from Peoria with the voting returns paid $16.00), and that office went to

---

53. On the Beaubien farm at Grosse Pointe, see Bald, p. 35. Beaubien was early Chicago's most colorful character, according to most easterners' recollections. He is mentioned in nearly every old settler's reminiscences, especially in Gale, Cleaver, the John Wentworth Papers, Chicago Historical Society, and "Sketch of Hon. J. Young Scammon," *Chicago Magazine,* Mar. 1857, reprinted in *Fergus Historical Series,* No. 5 (Chicago, 1876). See "Beaubiens of Chicago," Frank Gordon Beaubien Papers and Beaubien Family Papers, for particulars, and Andreas (p. 107) for a physical description: "His favorite dress on 'great occasions' was a swallow-tail coat with brass buttons. . . . He was in his glory at a horse-race."

54. Andreas, pp. 85, 174; East, "Contributions," Part I, pp. 191-197.

55. East, "Contributions," Part I, pp. 191-197; Wentworth, *Early Chicago,* p. 41.

Dancing was a principal amusement among French *habitants;* next to drinking, it
was the most important community-binding ritual in Chicago.
Courtesy of the Illinois State Historical Library.

John K. Clark in 1825; Alexander Robinson and Henley Clybourne for the two
years following; and the Reverend Jesse Walker in 1832.[56]

A surprisingly large turnout participated in nine elections between 1825
and 1831. Thirty-five men registered in the first general election in 1896; thirty-
three in 1828; and thirty-two in 1830. Nearly all of the available Kinzies
(Canadian and southern) participated, as did most of the French Creole and
mixed-blood men of the south and west sides. No political preference emerged
during these three elections. The most obvious comment that can be made of
the returns is that the village voted with the fort.[57]

Beginning in 1828, however, local elections were of a different species.
Chicagoans took a provincial view of politics, and when the candidates were
familiar, a high-spirited campaign ensued. The election in 1830 to replace
Wolcott as justice of the peace, for instance, drew fifty-six voters. The southerners clamored for office. In 1828, Henley Clybourne was elected constable,
along with David Hunter; together they represented the Kinzie clan and the
fort. Archibald Clybourne tried unsuccessfully in 1828 and 1830 to win election
as justice of the peace; and in 1832 he ran as an Independent for Congress,

56. *Ibid.*
57. See Jean Baptiste Beaubien Papers for original voting lists; "Beaubiens of Chicago," Frank
Gordon Beaubien Papers; Andreas, pp. 600-602.

losing to the Democratic candidate from Jacksonville. But in 1828 he did manage to win appointment, along with Samuel Miller, as trustee for the school section land sale and as treasurer of the First Court of Cook County Commissioners. James Kinzie was elected first sheriff of Cook County in 1831, but in 1832 he was beaten by Stephen Forbes, a Yankee schoolteacher.[58]

Despite the small trickle of Yankees into Chicago up to 1832, Forbes's election was the first clear indication that Chicago's old settlers were about to lose the control they had exerted over their own political destinies. The experiment in political and occupational independence had been too brief to test whether Chicagoans could flourish apace with the rest of the state, under their own leadership. Their confusion and fear of autonomy was still manifest in 1833: when given the opportunity to elect a president of the town trustees, they chose Thomas J. V. Owen, the government Indian agent. A month later, as United States commissioner, Owen concluded a land cession treaty between the united Potawatomi, Ottawa, and Chippewa nations and the government that in effect disfranchised half of Chicago's residents. J. B. Beaubien's mixed-blood son Madore was a member of Owen's Board of Town Trustees in 1833, and John H. Kinzie was elected president in 1834. Thereafter, not one old settler held a position of importance in town or city government. Early residents simply could not compete with the horde of Yankees who descended on the prairie village between 1832 and 1836.[59]

The problem was not one of wits. Early Chicago settlers placed a surprisingly high value on education. Despite the historical impression that Yankees brought to a spiritually and educationally impoverished hinterland a fully developed cultural matrix, the cornerstone of which was the school, Chicago residents were already remarkably well educated, though somewhat less than godly. Perhaps because Chicago was in many ways an extension of urban Detroit (Kinzie and the Beaubien brothers were raised in the same Grosse Pointe district), many of the early settlers were more enlightened than their rural counterparts downstate. However, the southern branch of the Kinzie clan certainly lacked literary and scientific polish. No poets, orators, or physicians rose from their ranks. The most prominent Virginian was the lay Methodist exhorter William See, who flapped his long blacksmith arms like a scarecrow when he preached and ended his delivery with something between a curtsy and a bow. See organized the first church meeting at the Point, but he always became so entangled in the web of his own scattered thoughts that he failed to bring many sinners to Christ.[60]

Bereft of formal religion until 1833, the Catholic French Creoles and

58. Andreas, p. 602; East, "The Inhabitants of Chicago," *passim*.

59. Regarding the first Board of Trustees, see Andreas, pp. 174-175; *Chicago Democrat* (Dec. 10, 1833).

60. John Kinzie Papers, Madore Beaubien Papers, and Beaubien Family Papers; for a vivid description of Rev. See, see Juliette Kinzie, p. 216.

mixed-bloods and the Episcopal Kinzies turned to the secular world. They packed their sons and daughters off to Detroit boarding and finishing schools or to Isaac McCoy's Indian mission school at Niles, Michigan. The Kinzie family connection was presumably with Mrs. Pattinson's establishment at Detroit, since John Kinzie, desperately in debt in 1815, had sold his Grosse Pointe farm to Mrs. Pattinson's husband. Kinzie's legal sons both attended school in Detroit, and his daughters went on to college in Middletown, Connecticut.[61] Some of the LaFramboise children studied in Detroit, as did the daughters of the Beaubien brothers. Madore and Charles Henry Beaubien, Jean Baptiste's sons by his first marriage to an Ottawa woman, after a stint at McCoy's Indian school, were sent to Hamilton College and Princeton, respectively. Captain Billy Caldwell, son of a British army officer, was highly literate, an eloquent speaker, and received a Catholic education at Detroit.[62]

Periodically, the early settlers tried to induce private tutors to come to Chicago. Most of these attempts were ill-fated. Family tutoring was a common means of working one's way west or locating a husband, and most teachers did not last the year. Female teachers, paid by the town as late as 1837, still had to be recruited semiannually. The Kinzies and Beaubiens turned to family members: for example, John Harris Kinzie first studied under his father's half brother, Robert Forsyth, and when Charles Henry Beaubien returned from Princeton, he ran a school at home for the Beaubien-LaFramboise children.[63]

The first Yankee schoolteacher arrived unsolicited in 1830. A native of Vermont, Stephen Forbes was received with a mixture of apprehension and curiosity by those who had met his sister, the priggish Mrs. Laughton. Yet there was dire need for his services: the Beaubien and LaFramboise roosts were bursting. Forbes taught in the Beaubien house for a year and then quit to become sheriff. Perhaps he disliked his clientele; the pupils were overwhelmingly of mixed blood. The southerners did not send their offspring to Forbes' school; in fact, there is no indication that children on the north branch received any education at all until the town school districts were formed in 1837.[64]

In 1832, Thomas Watkins taught in the meeting-house at the Point. His pupils, again, were largely French-Indian, although a growing number of Yankee families sent their children there. Watkins apparently also agreed to take full-blooded Indian children into the school. Billy Caldwell, convinced that literacy

61. For a description of private schools in Detroit, see Bald, pp. 88-91; Beaubien Family Papers.

62. "The Beaubiens of Chicago," Frank Gordon Beaubien Papers; Madore Beaubien and Billy Caldwell Papers; Clifton, "Captain Billy Caldwell."

63. John Kinzie Papers; Madore Beaubien, 1881 and 1882 letters, Madore Beaubien Papers; Andreas, pp. 204-209.

64. Andreas, p. 205; Mary Ann Hubbard, *Family Memories* (printed for private circulation, 1912), p. 68.

was a key to native survival, offered to pay the tuition of any Potawatomi child who would wear European clothing. None accepted this offer.[65]

The year 1833 was pivotal in the annals of Chicago religion and education, as it was in almost every other sphere. The return of the Fort Dearborn garrison during the Black Hawk War of 1832 brought an eastern Presbyterian minister, the Reverend Jeremiah Porter, and a schoolmarm from Michilimackinac with dreams of a female academy. Chicago's ungodliness scandalized Porter, but he quickly formed a church group around a coterie of eastern arrivals of 1831-32 and members of the garrison. Porter's group was not so much pious or devout as it was conscious of a need for formality. Porter shared the meetinghouse at the Point with the Methodists for a brief time, but the congregation pushed for a separate church building. Porter's first communion was embellished with the use of Major Wilcox's silver service. The new six-hundred-dollar church opened its doors six months later. Unfortunately, women filled out the congregation while their men caused "a wanton abuse of the holy day by . . . sin[ning] against clear light and abus[ing] divine compassion and love." On that communion Sunday, enterprising Yankee males were busy unloading two vessels in the new harbor.[66]

The Methodists still operated at the Point, reinforced in 1831 and 1833 by the Reverends Stephen Beggs and Jesse Walker, both southerners. By 1834 a revivalistic spirit produced a host of new members, primarily of southern origin, who erected a church on the north side. At the time, it seemed a logical place to build, since most of the Kinzie-Clybourne-Hall clan had settled on the north branch. However, it was not long before the Methodists felt "outclassed" by the wealthy Yankees settling in Ogden's improved "Kinzie's Addition." The congregation bodily moved its church across the river in 1836 to the area just west of the fort, Chicago's new "free zone."[67]

Although Baptists, Catholics, and Episcopalians each established a church in 1833, religion exerted little control over the everyday social and moral lives of most residents. An exception was the devout collection of Episcopalian Methodists who met at the home of Mark Noble on Thursday evenings for prayer and discussion. The group organized the first Sunday School in 1832, which was interdenominational in character.[68] Noble's enthusiastic followers represented in their piety and temperance the only persons in town — with the possible exception of some of Porter's "highfalutin" Presbyterians — who resisted the understandably attractive urge to accommodate themselves to the casual transcultural lifestyle around them. They did not join Beaubien's Debating Society; nor did they frequent the favorite haunts of early residents, the

65. Andreas, p. 205; letter from John Watkins in Calumet Club, pp. 73-74.
66. Andreas, pp. 299-301; Rev. Jeremiah Porter, *Early Chicago's Religious History* (Chicago, 1881), pp. 54-58.
67. Andreas, pp. 288-289; Gale, p. 60.
68. Andreas, p. 289; Porter, pp. 56-57.

Sauganash Tavern — favorite haunt of Chicago pioneers.
Courtesy of Chicago Historical Society.

Sauganash and Laughton's Tavern. Instead, they performed charitable acts, nourished the school system and church attendance, and, though books were scarce, promoted an interest in literature. Mark Noble carried his entire library to the Sunday School wrapped in his pocket handkerchief, and his own timber built the Methodists' northside chapel. Arthur Bronson, east coast financier and cohort of William B. Ogden, was so impressed with Noble's endeavors that he shipped one hundred free books to the school.[69]

Eighteen thirty-three was a time of ambivalence and guarded optimism. The population had doubled since 1831. There was talk of a canal, of pre-emption, of a land cession, and of the official incorporation of Chicago as a county seat — with all the legal and social trappings. But no one was sure any of this would come about. Lots in the emerging central business district on the south side, formed by the sale of the township's school section, were still going for as little as $200 and were traded away with nonchalance. The Yankee influx had been gradual, so gradual that one easterner's assimilation into the lifeways of the older settlers was accomplished before his next potential ally against the reigning social order arrived.[70]

The Yankee influence was felt in institutional ways: churches and classical academies; ordinances for fire, garbage disposal, vagrant cattle, shooting, and

69. Gale, p. 60; Andreas, p. 289.
70. Andreas, pp. 174, 111-124; Beaubien Family Papers.

horse-racing; and lawyers predominating among the arrivals of 1833. But the more subtle matrix of social habits and relations had not been significantly altered. Hospitality (rather than privacy and exclusivity), essential to the native, French Creole, and southern prestige systems, was still an unspoken requirement. Personal antagonisms that might generate complex patterns of avoidance in private life were inappropriate when the community gathered to act out its wholeness. There were no "private" parties. One's home, more than just a compartment for the family and one's prejudices, displayed the extent of one's generosity. A spacious house, able to fit the whole crowd under its rafters, was a distinct social attribute.[71]

The first Yankees did not build spacious homes; in fact, most rented back rooms or boarded at the Sauganash or at one of James Kinzie's taverns. In a way, they became adopted relatives who danced, drank, and caroused until dawn, and sometimes through the following day with the rest. Eastern visitors were startled to see dark-skinned maidens with beaded leggings under their black stroud dresses jigging with army officers, and genteel ladies twirling on the arms of southern hayseeds. All under the merry auspices of Mark Beaubien and his fiddle.[72]

Wolf-hunting, horse-racing, card-sharking, and shooting matches were still in vogue, although mostly removed beyond the town limits. Army officers and later "pillars of the city" met weekly — on Wednesday morning — at the Sauganash for a bracer, before heading out over the wolf-bedeviled prairie with Hamilton-educated Madore Beaubien, in brilliant headdress, whooping at the forefront. Rev. Jeremiah Porter noticed, to his chagrin, that there were as many Yankees as French-Canadians gambling at cards on the Sabbath (a reputable Sunday pastime for French *habitants*). French *carioles* raced across the ice in winter, and those who lacked a sleigh built their own rude version from timber cut on the north side. Ice-skating by moonlight was a favorite community activity, concluded, as usual, by a rowdy warming at the Sauganash.[73]

Chicago residents did not need holidays to celebrate. However, New Year's Eve warranted something spectacular, particularly for the French-Canadians. In the early years, the *Guignolée* and the *Reveillon* enlivened New Year's festivities all over the territory. Around 1833, Madore Beaubien and the "boys" fitted up the garrison's sizable skow with runners and made the rounds of village houses, adding sleigh party revelers at each stop. By the end of the evening the excite-

71. Andreas, pp. 132-133; *Chicago Democrat,* Nov. 26, 1833; Wentworth, *Early Chicago,* pp. 39-40.

72. John Wentworth to Lydia Wentworth, Nov. 10, 1836, John Wentworth Papers, Chicago Historical Society; Madore Beaubien Papers; Harriet Martineau, in *Reminiscences of Early Chicago* (Chicago, 1912), p. 30; Cleaver, p. 27.

73. Charles Fenno Hoffman, in *Reminiscences of Early Chicago,* pp. 21-22; Beaubien Family Papers; Porter, p. 78; Cleaver, pp. 5, 12. According to Cleaver, large hunts of over 100 men were still being held in 1834. He describes improvised sleighs built by setting crockery crates filled with

ment was so out of hand that the group completely broke up a local tavern. The next morning, the "boys" paid $800 in damages without blinking an eye.[74]

There was something frenetic about the village scene. An unhoped-for material prosperity was in the wind, and residents rocked nervously on their heels — waiting. But there was also the scent of death. Black Hawk was defeated. His people, pushed into the turbulent Mississippi, had fallen like straw before the American scythe. Stragglers on the shore were dying of starvation or at the hands of the Sioux. What were white folks to do? What was anyone to do, in 1833, but wait?[75]

III. Epilogue

. . . If lost to honor and to pride
Thou wilt become the white man's bride
Then go within the strong armed wall
Partake the pomp of brilliant hall
And wreath above thy maiden brow
The sparkling gems to which they bow.

— "The Muse of the Forest,"
written for *The Chicago Democrat,* February 18, 1834

Chicago's future was secured by the tail end of the summer of 1833. The town received its corporate seal, elected its first set of trustees, and let it be known that the school section was to be auctioned off in order to raise funds for civic improvements, notably a courthouse. Settlers were notified of their pre-emption rights, and there was a dash — at least by some — to register their homesteads. The united Potawatomi, Chippewa, and Ottawa nation ceded all its land east of the Mississippi in exchange for 5,000,000 acres of promised soil west of the Missouri.*[76]

---

hay on two young saplings shaved at the end to create runners. See Reynolds, p. 229, for the French Creole habit of cardplaying on Sunday.

74. Cleaver, p. 12. For descriptions of the *Guignolée* and other French customs transplanted in the Illinois country, see Natalia Maree Belting, *Kaskaskia Under the French Regime,* Illinois Studies in the Social Sciences, XXIX, No. 3 (Urbana, 1948); J. M. Carriere, *Life and Customs in the French Villages of the Old Illinois Country* (Report of the Canadian Historical Association, 1939).

75. See Andreas, pp. 267-271, for a treatment of Chicago's role in the Black Hawk War; interview with Madore Beaubien, *Chicago Times,* May 16, 1882, in "Beaubiens of Chicago," p. 39, Frank Gordon Beaubien Papers.

*A surprising number of French-Indians and non-Indian husbands went west with the Potawatomi. Over half of the registered voters between 1828 and 1830 were, or were thought to be, in Indian country during the 1850s.

76. Andreas, pp. 122-128, 174-175; Kappler, ed., pp. 402-403; Charles Royce, *Indian Land Cessions in the United States,* 18th Annual Report of the Bureau of American Ethnology (Wash-

The year 1833 began with a sigh of relief. The Indian war was over, and the cholera that left a hundred army graves on the south bank had spent its malignancy in the winter freeze. General Scott's remaining troops were on their way east to spread the news about a lush green wilderness in Wisconsin and northern Illinois. Food, rationed during the Black Hawk scare, was once more in adequate supply. People got back to the normal business of running their small industries and drinking it up at Beaubien's.[77]

But it was not quite the same. The Yankee stream continued, increasing its breadth and current. The newcomers were primarily young men, single and ambitious, whose main goal in life was not to amass great wealth (although many would change their minds when given the opportunity), but to find a place that suited them and their talents, a place with which to grow. Chicago was not the first stop for many, nor the last for a few. The majority probably agreed, however, that Chicago was an advantageous place in which to settle during the 1830s. All occupational classes were arriving. Whereas the 1831-32 migration had seen a lopsided preponderance of merchants and a few professionals, 1833 witnessed a flock of lawyers and tradesmen who anticipated a growing urban center.[78]

In small numbers the New Englanders seemed to have been assimilated. Yet one by one they added cement to a structurally different worldview. Linear progress, historians would later call it: the belief that the future was only attainable by cheating the present, by conserving time, currency, energy, and emotion, and by walking a straight line. The Indians did not think people's lives should be bottled up like so much stale spring water. Nor did the French or the southerners (or Old John Kinzie when he lived). The Indians thought rather that the circle was the more natural version of things. The sun was round, the year was round, and if a hill was round, what sense did it make to cut a straight line through it?

Nineteenth-century Yankees, obsessed with their rightness, could not wean the native and his French sympathizer away from such notions. The simultaneous disappearance of the French, the Canadian *métis*, and the Indian from Illinois indicates a similarity in worldview and survival technique not generally granted significance. The lack of Yankee initiative among *habitants* of the Mississippi valley may be traced to more than an enslaving land system. The New Englanders had more success with the Kinzies and their southern

ington, 1899), pp. 750-751; Anselm J. Gerwing, "The Chicago Indian Treaty of 1833," *Journal of the Illinois State Historical Society* (1964); Wentworth, *Early Chicago,* pp. 39-40.

77. Andreas, pp. 120-121; "Biography of Thomas Church," *Fergus Historical Series,* No. 5 (Chicago, 1876), p. 42.

78. Andreas, pp. 131-133. See Daniel Elazar, *Cities of the Prairie* (New York, 1970), pp. 153-180, for Illinois migration streams; "List of Settlers of Chicago Who Came Between January, 1831, and December, 1836," in Rufus Blanchard, *Discovery and Conquest of the Northwest, With the History of Chicago* (Wheaton, 1879), pp. 424-433.

kinsmen, though the latter had difficulty adjusting to Yankee aloofness and smug moralism as the years passed.[79]

The transition seemed relatively simple in 1833. Many of the town elders were dead: Francis LaFramboise, John Kinzie, Benjamin Hall, and Alexander Wolcott. Young men remained but, like their Yankee counterparts, most were under thirty-five, and a fair share of those were under twenty-five. Before the horde of speculators arrived briefly in 1833 for the sale of the school section, and came to stay during the Illinois-Michigan Canal sales of 1835, Chicago was a town of "boys."

There was something innocent, almost naive, about the young men's optimism. Robert Allen Kinzie, John Kinzie's youngest son, pre-empted 160 acres on the north bank, but rejected an opportunity to register land at the Point because the family would never use all they had acquired. Early in 1833, while on an eastern buying trip for his trading store, the same young man was flabbergasted when he was offered $20,000 — by a shrewder judge of land values than he, Mr. Arthur Bronson — for his tract of swamp. In 1835, Bronson sold the acreage to his silent partner, Samuel Butler, for $100,000. In late summer of the same year, William B. Ogden, newly arrived to dispose of his brother-in-law's property, sold one-third of the property for the same amount. Ogden was not impressed at the time. But Robert Allen Kinzie was: his family might have been millionaires had they known.[80]

Mark Beaubien, only thirty-three and one of the "boys" himself, continued to pack travelers into the Sauganash, putting up curtains as sleeping partitions. When they laid out the town in 1831, his tavern sat in the middle of the street. "Didn't expect no town," he said, and the ease with which he continued to give away his lots suggests that he didn't care if it came.[81] Madore Beaubien took a Yankee partner, John Boyer, and married his daughter. The store foundered, but Madore had a high time selling fancy vests, hats, and laces to his Indian friends while the venture lasted. Like his uncle Mark, he sold his lots too early to share in any of the wealth. And he lost his Yankee wife. The second time around, Madore married a Potawatomi woman.[82]

The southerners expanded their cattle raising, butchering, and tanning operation at Rolling Meadows and cashed in on the eastern demand for beef. The newly dredged harbor, begun in 1833, turned meatpacking into Chicago's most profitable business in the 1830s, with the exception of platting and selling "paper towns." Archibald Clybourne, the man probably least admired by the old settlers, was easily the most successful in the later city. This negative rela-

79. See Madore Beaubien Papers. Mark Beaubien spoke of the affinity of French Creoles for the Potawatomi and Potawatomi culture on his deathbed, in "Beaubiens of Chicago," Frank Gordon Beaubien Papers.

80. Andreas, pp. 130-131; Kinzie Family Papers; "William B. Ogden," *Fergus Historical Series*, No. 17 (Chicago, 1882); "John Dean Caton Recollections," Calumet Club, p. 35; John Wentworth to Lydia Wentworth, Nov. 10, 1836, John Wentworth Papers.

81. Beaubien Family Papers; "Beaubiens of Chicago," Frank Gordon Beaubien Papers.

82. Beaubien Family Papers; store inventory, Madore Beaubien Papers.

tionship held true for John H. Kinzie as well, who retained his former prestige as leader of the north side's first family until his death, even though he proved a financial lightweight.[83]

Chicago's French-Indian families and Kinzie's employees appeared to resent his growing air of condescension. Even in the early years, when Kinzie was Indian agent at Fort Winnebago, the habitually sly, joking French-Canadian *engagés* referred to him as "Quinze Nez." Creole *voyageurs* made an art of the French-English double entendre: they called the Judge of Probate, for example, "le juge trop bête." Always sniffing for a way up, Kinzie did not fool his employees. Worse yet was Kinzie's romance-stricken wife, who reveled in her husband's noble attention to the poor "savage."[84]

The route an old settler had to take to rise in the increasingly eastern social milieu, and the amount of selling out that had to occur, is best illustrated by Kinzie's use of his wife's illusions. During the 1830s easterners in Chicago took a fancy to the finer aspects of Indian culture. Yankees were not particularly interested in seeing the display firsthand, but they welcomed Kinzie's tales of the wilderness, his rendition of sacred Potawatomi legend, his war paint, and his mock stag dance. Incredibly, he was so brash as to take an Indian show (in which he was the principal star) to the 1834-35 state legislature at Jacksonville for the purpose of "delighting" the delegates into passing a bill funding the proposed canal which was to cross land more or less taken from the Indians only a year earlier. Madore Beaubien must have burned down to his toes.[85]

The unmarried Yankee men lived together at the several boarding houses in a manner akin to rival fraternities. They gave in for the most part to the wilder ways of the young early settlers. John Wentworth, one of the "boys" for a time, and later mayor, claimed that he had never seen so much smoking and drinking. He found that the early churches also resembled fraternities, and he urged all of his friends to attend the Baptist services, where the best crowd gathered. The more contemplative Yankees, not so much averse to as timid about the drinking and shouting, were seated nightly in one or the other dry goods store playing checkers. Such games provided a political forum for the numerous young lawyers in town, who immediately swept novice officerholders like James Kinzie, Madore Beaubien, and Samuel Miller off their feet and out the governmental door.[86]

Aside from politics, there was still a healthy rapport among the young men in 1833. The Yankees relished a horse race as much as the early residents,

---

83. Andreas, p. 103.

84. Juliette Kinzie, pp. 227-229.

85. John Harris Kinzie Papers, 1833-1837, Chicago Historical Society; Harriet Martineau, *Reminiscences of Early Chicago*, p. 32; Martineau, "Strange Early Days," *Annals of Chicago*, IX (Chicago, 1876).

86. Cleaver, pp. 13, 24; Gale, p. 122; John Wentworth to Lydia Wentworth, Nov. 10, 1836, in John Wentworth Papers.

Mark Beaubien: "Didn't expect no town" — Chicago, 1840.
Courtesy of the Illinois State Historical Library.

and Mark Beaubien's daughters, as well as the dapper gentleman himself, drew the Yankees in as if magnetized. The old territorial divisions of the town were in a state of confusion, and new lines of class and race demarcation had not yet been drawn. Nearly all the Yankees lived on the near south side, the "free zone" which had replaced the Point as the central community meeting place. The boarding houses provided a kind of protective limbo, around which the bewildering array of conflicting values clashed but did not affect the people's lives. They were in the eye of the storm, and Mark Beaubien was Peter Pan. The "boys" were never going to grow up.[87]

The town found its adulthood abruptly and painfully. In early September 1833, the newly elected president of the town board, Robert C. V. Owen, called a grand council of the chiefs and headmen of the united Indian nations to discuss treaty arrangements for their removal west of the Mississippi. Owen, acting in his capacity as United States government commissioner, opened the proceedings by explaining to the assembly that he had heard that they wished to sell their

87. Cleaver, p. 27.

lands. This was a blatant untruth. But the Indians unfortunately had no precedent for supposing that they would be allowed to keep their territory, even if they chose to. They deliberated.[88]

The 5,000 men, women, and children took their time, however, spending nearly three weeks at Chicago. They camped along the lakeshore and at the Point and enlarged their already mammoth debts to the local white traders, Robert Allen Kinzie among them. The bulk of the traffic was in liquor — alcohol enough to put them all in a drunken stupor for a week. Tipsy families wept together beside their tents, and in the sober morning there was still the wailing.[89]

On September 26 the treaty was concluded. Under a spacious open shed, specially constructed on the north side of the river for the occasion, the officers and spectators gathered. The chiefs did not arrive until the sun was red in the sky, and again they delayed while two old chiefs, wobbling with whiskey, made incoherent rebuttals. Then they signed. The commissioners sat with the sundown blaze in their faces, appearing, ironically, as brothers of the men they were herding away. Facing east, the Indians huddled in darkness.[90]

88. Andreas, pp. 122-125.

89. *Ibid.*, p. 123; Charles Latrobe, *A Rambler in North America* (London, 1836), pp. 201, 207, 210-211.

90. Andreas, p. 124; Latrobe, pp. 213-214. For the influence of mixed-bloods in Potawatomi

The spectacle rocked the inner heart of the town. Yankees were horrified at so pagan and slovenly a group; sympathy gave way to disgust. "Half-breeds" who had been raised as part of the community shunned their previous friends. By order of the court in 1834, Justice of the Peace Beaubien publicly posted a "no trespassing" sign at Hardscrabble. White traders, new and old, hustled the sales while they could and then went home to estimate the amount of indebtedness the tribe had accumulated. The treaty allotted $150,000 to settle past liens, but the final settlement was $175,000. Undoubtedly many traders inflated the sum due; it seems that every white man in Chicago got a slice. The American Fur Company received an outrageous $20,000. The various members of the Kinzie family, including some of the Forsyths, received the next largest payment.[91]

In addition to the land west of the Missouri and the allotment to collectors, the treaty provided for cash payment in lieu of reservations, which was requested by innumerable "mixed-bloods" who wished to remain in Chicago. However, only three applicants' reservations were granted; the rest were given a pittance, ranging downward from $1800. A hungry Kinzie family again received a sizable grant, far exceeding the sums distributed among the French-Indians. The fourth and fifth clauses of the treaty provided for a twenty-year annual payment of $14,000, and $100,000 in goods to be distributed after ratification.[92] Goods worth $65,000 were presented to the nation on October 4. In preparation, the traders had ordered vast stores of whiskey (one trader alone asked for fifteen barrels). Fortunately, a prevailing south wind hindered ship passage up the river, and the traders were forced to content themselves with selling the supply on hand, as well as overpriced trinkets, blankets, knives, and so forth.[93]

It was a black Sunday. Worshipers did the only thing respectable people knew how to do: they hid within their churches from the drunken shouting, wailing, and fleecing. And they prayed. An old Indian stood playing a jew's-harp at the Reverend Jeremiah Porter's door, unaware that he was interrupting a religious service. When the payment was concluded, high winds and a driving rain sent the traders fleeing back into their cabins. The Indians went back to their camp at the Aux Plaines with $30,000 in silver. Porter thought that someone's prayer had been answered.[94]

In the months to come, the numerous mixed-blood residents of Chicago wrenched their hearts over whether to remove with their Potawatomi kinsmen or stay. Many wanted to remain: the sacred ground in which their grandfathers

---

politics and the treaty of 1833, see miscellaneous fragment, n.d., Alphabetical File: James Herrington, Chicago Historical Society; Frank R. Grover, *Antoine Ouilmette* (Evanston, 1908), pp. 12-16; Conway, pp. 410-418; Clifton, "Captain Billy Caldwell."

91. Andreas, pp. 126-128; Porter, pp. 71-73; *Chicago Democrat* (Dec. 10, 1833).
92. Andreas, pp. 126-128; Kappler, ed., pp. 402-410.
93. Porter, pp. 73-74.
94. *Ibid.*

Hamilton-educated, the mixed-blood Madore Beaubien was one of Chicago's "golden youngsters." Courtesy of State Historical Society of Wisconsin.

were buried meant more to people of native extraction than to the Yankees who were about to gain the territory. But the breach was irreparable. Indians and mixed-blood settlers willing to forgive were treated like some ghastly sore, too horrible to look at. The sore would not heal. It festered because the source of the disease was inside the Yankee eye. In time the Indian became the real evil in people's minds.[95]

Typical of the educated "mixed-bloods," Madore Beaubien was no fool. One of Chicago's "golden youngsters," he had wanted his share of power. Years later, as he wasted away on a reservation in Kansas, he explained that he had yearned for recognition in the white world. Denied that, he sought prestige within the tribe. Beaubien and most of his cohorts joined the local Potawatomi bands in 1835. Painted in the colors of death, they made their final turn through

95. Gale, p. 154; Madore Beaubien Papers.

the streets already covering the ancient trails and fields, dancing their way out of the Americans' vision, their shrieks sticking in the Americans' ears.[96]

In 1835 the land sales — and one of the most incredible heights of speculative fancy the West had ever seen — began. Chicago was again a one-horse town. Everyone dealt in lots. But the land bore a stigma: by 1838 the majority of Chicago's newer residents, as well as a few old ones who had managed to keep their heads long enough to see the six-figure totals, were bankrupt.[97]

It would be easy to suggest that William B. Ogden was elected the first mayor of Chicago, incorporated in 1837, because wealth was the measure of power. However, it seems just as likely that residents could not stand to face someone more familiar in their midst. New blood, clean blood, a new family, a new community might root and bloom in the desecrated land and make it whole once more.

---

96. In his old age, Madore Beaubien said that he wanted his children to honor his name and lamented the fact that Chicago had not remembered him. See interview in *Chicago Times,* May 16, 1882, in "Beaubiens of Chicago," Frank Gordon Beaubien Papers. See also John Dean Caton, *The Last of the Illinois and a Sketch of the Pottawatomie* (Chicago, 1876), pp. 26-30; Wentworth, *Early Chicago,* pp. 35-36.

97. Pierce, pp. 57-69. See also John D. Haeger, *Men and Money: The Urban Frontier at Green Bay, 1815-1840* (Mt. Pleasant, Mich.: Clarke Historical Library, Central Michigan University, 1970) for a comparable takeover by Eastern speculators of another fur-trading town.

CHAPTER 2

Irish Chicago:
Church, Homeland, Politics, and Class —
The Shaping of an Ethnic Group, 1870-1900

MICHAEL F. FUNCHION

The country has survived the Irish emigration — the worst with which any other country was ever afflicted. The Irish fill our prisons, our reform schools, our hospitals. . . . Scratch a convict or a pauper and the chances are that you tickle the skin of an Irish Catholic . . . made a criminal or a pauper by the priest and politician who have deceived him and kept him in ignorance, in a word, a savage, as he was born.

Chicago Evening Post, 1868

We are a distinctive historic people, and we have done the Americans a great deal of good by coming to this country.

John Fitzgibbon, Chicago Irish Businessman

The Irish first came to the Chicago region in large numbers in 1836, one year before the incorporation of the city.[1] Lured by promises of decent pay and steady employment, scores of Irishmen — some with experience on canal projects in the East, others fresh off the boat — came to build the Illinois and Michigan Canal, an ambitious project designed to link Lake Michigan with the Illinois River. By the time the canal was completed in 1848, thousands of Irish laborers had left their picks and shovels and had moved to Chicago or to Bridgeport, the northeastern terminus of the canal which was at that time a village separate from Chicago. There, along with other Irish immigrants, they worked mainly as unskilled laborers in meat-packing plants, brickyards, and

---

1. Unless otherwise stated, the word "Irish" in this essay refers to Irish Catholics. Although no exact statistics are available, it appears that the number of Irish Protestants in Chicago was small.

TABLE 2.1
Irish-Born in Chicago, 1870-1900

	Number of Irish-born Population	Percent of Foreign-born Population	Percent of Total
1870	39,988	27.66%	13.37%
1880	44,411	21.68%	8.83%
1890	70,028	15.54%	6.37%
1900	73,912	12.59%	4.35%

Source: U.S., *Ninth Census, 1870,* Vol. I, "Population," pp. 386-391; *Tenth Census, 1880,* "Population," pp. 538-541; *Eleventh Census, 1890,* "Population," Part I, pp. 670-673; *Twelfth Census, 1900,* Vol. I, "Population," Part I, pp. 796-799.

the like. By 1850, 6,096 — or about 20 percent — of Chicago's inhabitants were Irish immigrants. During the next twenty years, as Chicago grew by leaps and bounds and emerged as the transportation, manufacturing, and commercial mecca of the Midwest, thousands more Irishmen arrived in the city seeking jobs and a better life than they had had back home. By 1870, almost 40,000 Irish natives were living in the city.[2]

During the last three decades of the nineteenth century, the Irish-born population continued to grow, although far more slowly than before. Between 1870 and 1900, the number of Irish immigrants in the city rose from 39,988 to 73,912, or by some 85 percent (see Table 2.1), a substantial increase but not nearly as dramatic as the jump of 556 percent that had occurred in the twenty years prior to 1870.

The Irish-born, of course, were not the only Irish in Chicago. During the three decades after the Great Fire of 1871, the American-born Irish population expanded rapidly as well. By 1890, the first year in which the federal census listed the number of Chicagoans of foreign parentage, the Irish population, first and second generations included, totaled 183,844 (see Table 2.2).[3] Of these, only 38 percent were immigrants; and ten years later the

2. George J. Fleming, "Canal at Chicago" (Ph.D. diss., Catholic University of America, 1950), pp. 103, 126-129, 256; Bessie Louise Pierce, *A History of Chicago,* 3 vols. (New York, 1937-1957), I: 179-181, 226, 418; II: 13, 151, 482; Ruth M. Piper, "The Irish in Chicago, 1848-1871" (M.A. thesis, University of Chicago, 1936); George Potter, *To the Golden Door: The Story of the Irish in Ireland and America* (Boston, 1960), pp. 173, 184, 318, 320; Frederick F. Cook, *Bygone Days in Chicago: Recollections of the "Garden City" of the Sixties* (Chicago, 1910), pp. 179-180; William J. Onahan, "Irish Settlement in Illinois," *Catholic World* 33 (1881), 158-159; Joseph Hamzik, "Gleanings of Archer Road" (MSS, Chicago Historical Society), pp. 37-41; Charles S. Winslow, "Historic Goose Island" (MSS, Chicago Historical Society), pp. 1-13; Local Community Research Committee, "Chicago Communities" (MSS, Chicago Historical Society), Vol. III, Doc. No. 23; Vol. VI, Doc. Nos. 1-3; Chicago *Tribune,* Apr. 19, 1874.

3. Although the vast majority of these had both parents born in Ireland, the figures also

TABLE 2.2
First- and second-generation Irish in Chicago, 1890-1900

	Number	Percent of Total Population
1890	183,844	16.72%
1900	237,478	13.98%

Source: U.S., *Eleventh Census, 1890*, "Population," Part I, pp. 708, 714, 720, 726, 728; *Twelfth Census, 1900*, Vol. I, "Population," Part I, pp. 874-875, 882-883, 890-891, 898-899, 902-903.

Irish-born represented even fewer — 31 percent of the 237,478 Irish in the city. Among the adult population, it appears that until sometime during the 1890s, Irish immigrants outnumbered their American-born kinsmen.[4]

Nonetheless, from the 1870s on, when a number of them began to reach maturity, the American-born children of immigrants played a significant role in the institutional life of Irish Chicago. Indeed, one of the factors that distinguishes the last three decades of the century from the previous period was the emergence of the second-generation Irish.[5] No statistics are available for the third generation; but considering the years of Irish immigration to the United States, it appears that up until 1900 the overwhelming majority were children. After that date, as a number of these children reached adulthood, Irish Chicago became a community dominated by three instead of two generations.

Compared to that of other cities, the Irish population of Chicago was impressive in size. In 1890, for example, only three American cities — New York, Philadelphia, and Brooklyn — had more Irish than did Chicago.[6] Yet within Chicago the Irish were a minority, and one that was declining relative to the

---

include those with only one Irish-born parent. It should be noted that since these figures are based on parentage and not on nativity, they include a small number of persons born in a foreign country (mainly Britain and Canada) other than Ireland, and exclude the minuscule number of Irish immigrants both of whose parents were not born in Ireland.

4. In 1900 there were 72,591 adult males in Chicago who had either both parents born in Ireland or one Irish-born and one native-born parent. Of these, 34,250 or 47.2 percent were immigrants. See U.S., *Twelfth Census, 1900*, Vol. I, "Population," Part I, pp. 940, 954-955. Although such statistics are unavailable for the years before 1900, it seems reasonable, considering the ratio in 1900, to conclude that the Irish-born outnumbered the American-born until sometime in the 1890s.

5. I also chose 1870 as the point to begin this study because of certain changes that occurred in the church and the Irish nationalist movement at about that time. The arrival of Bishop Thomas Foley in 1870 helped to bring greater stability to the Chicago diocese, which had suffered some disruption during the administration of the mentally unstable Bishop James Duggan (1859-1869). And it was in the early 1870s that the Clan na Gael replaced the Fenians as the premier Irish nationalist organization in Chicago.

6. U.S., *Eleventh Census, 1890*, "Population," Part I, pp. 670-673, 708, 714, 720, 726, 728. Although its total Irish population was smaller than Chicago's, Boston had more Irish immigrants.

total population (see Tables 2.1 and 2.2). Both Germans and Americans of native parentage outnumbered the Irish; toward the end of the century, the ratio of Germans to Irish was more than two to one in Chicago. And while other groups — Scandinavians, Poles, Czechs, and Italians — were less numerous than the Irish, they were increasing at a faster rate.[7]

A minority in the city as a whole, the Irish were also a minority in most of the neighborhoods where they lived. In the decades after the Great Fire, most Irish lived on the South and West sides; except for a small area on the near North Side, they were only sparsely settled in the northern sections of the city. But despite their concentration on the South and West sides, relatively few Irish lived in authentic ethnic ghettos. The school census of 1884, for example, reveals that out of 303 census canvass districts in the city, the Irish formed a majority of the population in only eleven. And since these eleven districts contained only about 14 percent of the city's Irish, it meant that 86 percent of them lived in areas where they were in a minority.[8] Similarly, a study of the school census of 1898 reveals that the Irish were the most dispersed of the ten ethnic groups studied.[9] The historian, of course, must be careful not to exaggerate the significance of such dispersal. Geographical proximity to other groups, for example, did not necessarily lead to social interaction with them. This was particularly true when neighboring groups spoke different languages and attended different churches and schools. In fact, one could argue that proximity had the opposite effect: rubbing shoulders with people of a different national background could often lead to increased resentment.

Though few lived in true ethnic ghettos, the late nineteenth-century Chicago Irish nonetheless formed a highly visible and relatively cohesive ethnic community. Like other immigrants, the Irish derived their sense of unity from a common religious and ethnic heritage, a heritage they preserved through certain key institutions. And like other immigrants, their basic cohesiveness was further strengthened by certain forces and conditions they encountered in Chicago.

Most important in preserving a distinct Irish identity was their Catholicism, which, like the Polish variety, was inextricably intertwined with their national consciousness. Ever since the Protestant Reformation, the ancient Anglo-Irish struggle has been religious as well as national. Even though recent

7. U.S., *Eleventh Census, 1890,* "Population," Part I, pp. 670-673, 704, 708, 714, 720, 726, 728; U.S., *Twelfth Census, 1900,* Vol. I, "Population," Part I, pp. 796-799, 866, 874-875, 882-883, 890-891, 898-899, 902-903.

8. City of Chicago, Board of Education, *School Census of the City of Chicago, Taken May, 1884. Total Population of the City over 21 Years and under 21 Years of Age. By Ward and Division of the City* (Chicago, 1884), pp. 20-31.

9. Edward R. Kantowicz, "Polish Chicago: Survival through Solidarity," in Melvin G. Holli and Peter d'A. Jones, eds., *The Ethnic Frontier: Essays in the History of Group Survival in Chicago and the Midwest* (Grand Rapids, 1977), p. 183.

research has shown that the pre-Famine Irish did not practice their religion as devoutly as we have commonly assumed,[10] centuries of religious oppression had left them with a strong attachment to the Catholic Church, an attachment that usually remained strong after their arrival in America. And since the United States was an overwhelmingly Protestant nation, Catholicism was one of the chief factors that distinguished the Irish from other Americans.

Although the first Catholics in the frontier town of Chicago were mainly of French and French-Indian origin, they were overwhelmed in the late 1830s and 1840s by the large influx of Irish as well as German immigrants. And until the 1870s, the Catholic Church remained a predominantly Irish and German institution, with the Irish outnumbering the Germans.[11] Toward the end of the century, as the "new immigrants" arrived from southern and eastern Europe, the church became increasingly multiethnic, though as late as 1900 the Irish still formed the largest bloc of Catholics.

Because of their numerical superiority, and because the American hierarchy looked favorably on English-speaking prelates, the Irish dominated the ecclesiastical administration in Chicago throughout the nineteenth century. From the appointment of the first bishop, William Quarter, in 1844 until the death of Archbishop James Quigley in 1915, all the bishops of Chicago were either Irish-born or of Irish parentage, with the one exception of Bishop James Van De Velde, a Belgian who presided over the diocese from 1849 to 1854. The Germans, the French, and later immigrants naturally resented this Irish domination. They demanded a greater voice in the administration of the diocese, and at times they even demanded the creation of separate dioceses for the various foreign-language groups. And yet, except for a relatively minor schism among the Poles, these various immigrant groups did remain within the Irish fold of Roman Catholicism.

For this the Irish bishops, whatever their shortcomings, deserve some credit. They did much to quell ethnic tensions in the church by permitting the establishment of separate or national parishes for the Germans and other non-English speaking immigrants. Begun in the 1840s by Bishop Quarter, a native of County Offaly, this practice of creating national parishes was faithfully followed by his successors. By 1870, Chicago had nine national parishes besides the sixteen territorial ones that served English-speaking Catholics. And during the next thirty-odd years, when Bishop Thomas Foley (1870-1879) and Arch-

10. Emmet Larkin, "The Devotional Revolution in Ireland, 1850-75," *The American Historical Review* 77 (1972), 625-652.

11. Although throughout most of the century there were more Germans than Irish in Chicago, only about a quarter or a third of them were Catholics. See Charles H. Shanabruch, *Chicago's Catholics: The Evolution of an American Identity* (Notre Dame, 1981), pp. 8, 43. For a discussion of the problems with Catholic statistics, see John Patrick Walsh, "The Catholic Church in Chicago and Problems of an Urban Society, 1893-1915" (Ph.D. diss., University of Chicago, 1948), pp. 8-12.

Bishop William J. Quarter, the first bishop of the Chicago Diocese. Beginning with Quarter in 1844 until the death of Archbishop James E. Quigley in 1915, all of the bishops (with one exception) were either Irish born or of Irish parentage. Courtesy of the Chicago CATHOLIC.

bishop Patrick Feehan (1880-1902) presided over the diocese, sixty-three national churches, in addition to forty-seven territorial churches, were established. Feehan, an Irish immigrant from County Tipperary and the former bishop of Nashville, strongly emphasized the need for national parishes, believing that they were one of the best means of protecting the faith of non-English-speaking immigrants. The Germans and others obviously agreed with Feehan and praised him for his sensitivity to their needs.[12] One German Catholic editor

12. For the history of Catholicism in nineteenth-century Chicago, see Shanabruch, *Chicago's Catholics*, pp. 1-104; Ellen Skerrett, "The Catholic Dimension," in Lawrence J. McCaffrey, *et al.*, *The Irish in Chicago* (Urbana, IL, 1987), pp. 22-60; Gilbert J. Garraghan, *The Catholic Church in Chicago 1673-1871* (Chicago, 1921); James J. McGovern, ed., *Souvenir of the Silver Jubilee in the Episcopacy of His Grace, the Most Rev. Patrick Augustine Feehan, Archbishop of Chicago* (Chicago, 1891). For short histories of the various parishes, see Joseph J. Thompson, ed., *The Archdiocese of Chicago* (Des Plaines, 1920); Harry C. Koenig, ed., *A History of the Parishes of the Archdiocese of Chicago*, 2 vols. (Chicago, 1980). For Feehan, see Cornelius Kirkfleet, *The Life of Patrick Augustine Feehan, Bishop of Nashville, First Archbishop of Chicago, 1829-1902* (Chicago, 1922). For a discussion

Archbishop James E. Quigley and his Irish-American predecessors had eased ethnic tensions in the church by permitting the establishment of separate — or national — parishes for non-English-speaking immigrants. Theoretically, this should have resulted in non-ethnic territorial parishes, but in reality they were predominantly Irish, since virtually all English-speaking Catholics in nineteenth-century Chicago were Irish. Courtesy of the Chicago CATHOLIC.

remarked that "he has proven himself a truly Catholic prelate, guided by principle and zeal, regardless of national consideration."[13] And when he died in 1902, the *Chicago Tribune* lauded Feehan for his "diplomatic handling of the Irish, German, Polish, Bohemian, French and Italian elements in the diocese."[14]

The system of national parishes not only helped to diffuse the potential ethnic powder keg in the church; it also separated the Irish from other Catholics. Although in theory territorial parishes were not necessarily Irish, in practice they were, since the overwhelming majority of English-speaking Catholics in Chicago were Irish. An Irishman attending mass or a parish function might occasionally meet a non-Irish Catholic, but by and large the only people with whom he associated were fellow Irishmen. Thus membership in a universal church did little — at least at this time — to undermine Irish ethnic solidarity.

Just as in Ireland, the local parish played a central role in the lives of the

---

of the ethnic tensions in the church, see James W. Sanders, *The Education of an Urban Minority: Catholics in Chicago, 1833-1965* (New York, 1977), pp. 40-71.

13. *The Review,* Aug. 15, 1895, cited in Walsh, "The Catholic Church in Chicago," p. 20.

14. Cited in Sanders, *The Education of an Urban Minority,* p. 54.

people. Not only did it serve their religious needs, it also provided a host of other services. Most pastors took a vital interest in the lives of their parishioners. For example, Father Maurice Dorney, pastor of St. Gabriel's parish in the stockyards district from its establishment in 1880 until his death in 1914, was an extremely active figure in his community. He often provided food and fuel to the needy, found jobs for the unemployed, and at times served as an arbitrator in settling strikes and other labor disputes at the stockyards. Keenly aware of the particular evil of alcohol among his Irish flock, he campaigned against its abuse and was, in fact, successful in getting saloons removed from a small area of the Stockyards District.[15] Other priests might not have been as well known or as flamboyant as Dorney, but most shared with him a concern for the material as well as the spiritual welfare of their parishioners.

Affiliated with each parish was a variety of societies designed to meet the spiritual, social, and material needs of the parishioners. Some of these were linked with similar groups in other parishes through central organizations. Among the more common organizations were the St. Vincent de Paul Society, which tried to put the teachings of Christian charity into practice by helping the poor; the Catholic Total Abstinence Union of America, whose members completely abstained from alcohol; and the Catholic Order of Foresters, a mutual aid fraternity that provided assistance to its members in time of need.[16] Most parishes also had various sodalities, youth clubs, and the like. And, of course, there were the inevitable christenings, weddings, and funerals, where old friends could reminisce about the past or gossip about the present. All of these organizations and events helped to lighten the burdens of urban life and to bring the Irish into closer contact with one another.

Of all the institutions attached to a parish, probably the most important was the parochial school. Traditionally, the Catholic Church taught that religious instruction should be an integral part of a general education. To prepare a child for this life and forget about the next was, from the Catholic point of view, morally undesirable, to say the least. Throughout the nineteenth century the Catholic hierarchy in the United States had emphasized the need for Catholic schools. At the Third Plenary Council in Baltimore in 1884, for example, the bishops directed that every Catholic parish have a parochial school and that parents send their children to it.[17]

Yet Catholic educational philosophy was not the only reason behind the

15. Charles Ffrench, ed., *Biographical History of the American Irish in Chicago* (Chicago, 1897), pp. 796-801; "The Untold Story of Catholic Chicago," *Chicago Daily News*, Special Supplement, Dec., 1966; Local Community Research Committee, "Chicago Communities," Vol. VI, Doc. Nos. 1a, 1b, 7; *Chicago Inter Ocean*, Mar. 16, 17, 19, 1914; Charles J. Bushnell, *The Social Problem at the Chicago Stock Yards* (Chicago, 1902), p. 44; Thompson, *Archdiocese of Chicago*, p. 477.

16. Walsh, "The Catholic Church in Chicago," pp. 5-6, 62-73, 79-81, 332-335; Ffrench, *American Irish in Chicago*, pp. 175, 297, 372.

17. Sanders, *The Education of an Urban Minority*, pp. 12-14.

decision to build a parochial school system in Chicago. During the decades before 1870 the public schools in Chicago were not simply secular institutions; they were in fact quasi-Protestant schools: practically all members of the Board of Education were Protestants; Protestants held a virtual monopoly on teaching positions; and the King James Bible was read in the classroom.[18] One Catholic newspaper no doubt typified the view of many Irish parents when it complained that Catholic children "are taught to feel ashamed of the creed of their forefathers."[19]

In the decades after 1870 this public school situation improved somewhat. Despite a storm of protest, Catholics, liberal Protestants, and others succeeded in getting the King James Bible banned from the classroom in 1875, and by the 1890s more and more Catholics were teaching in the public schools. Yet the schools continued to have a Protestant flavor. Protestants still dominated the Board of Education, and textbooks and other aspects of the curriculum seemed at times to present Catholicism in an unfavorable light.[20]

For these reasons the Irish developed their own parochial school system. By the late nineteenth century most Irish parishes had their own schools, which were attended by at least half of the Irish school-age children.[21] Staffed mainly by nuns and — to a lesser extent — brothers of Irish origin, these schools gave their students the standard elementary education and an understanding of the Catholic faith, and instilled in them a loyalty to the United States. It was not until after the turn of the century, however, that these schools provided some instruction in Irish history and culture.[22]

Clearly, the local parish, with its school and various societies, was the most important institution in Irish Chicago. It touched the lives of more Irish people than did any other institution in the Irish community, for the overwhelming majority of Irish remained practicing Catholics. And while support for the church was an expression of a sincere religious commitment, it was also a manifestation of Irish ethnic identity. Finally, the point bears repeating that while devotion to the church was a legacy of their Irish heritage, it in turn did much to preserve that very heritage; paradoxically, the universal church brought the Irish closer together, by separating them not only from Protestant Chicagoans but from other Catholics as well.

Besides Catholicism, the second major force in the lives of the late nineteenth-century Chicago Irish was Irish nationalism. Like those in other parts of the

18. *Ibid.*, pp. 18-24, 29.
19. *Western Tablet*, April 3, 1852, cited in Sanders, *The Education of an Urban Minority*, p. 21.
20. *Ibid.*, pp. 24-30.
21. *Ibid*, p. 5.
22. Skerrett, "The Catholic Dimension," pp. 35-37, 43-47, 55. Skerrett agrees with Lawrence J. McCaffrey that the Catholic school system played an important role in the Americanization of Irish-American youngsters.

United States, the Chicago Irish showed a deep and abiding interest in the political future of their homeland. As early as 1842, Chicago had a branch of Daniel O'Connell's Repeal Association, which sought to undo the union between Great Britain and Ireland through nonviolent agitation. After this movement collapsed, the Chicago Irish turned to various revolutionary groups. Of these, the most popular during the years before the Great Fire was the Fenian Brotherhood. Founded in New York in 1858, the Fenians sent money, arms, and men across the sea to the Irish Republican Brotherhood in an effort to help them overthrow British rule in Ireland. Although an uprising did take place in Ireland in 1867, it ended a dismal failure. Meanwhile, in America the Fenians had split into two factions: one group wished to concentrate on military activity in Ireland, while the other advocated an invasion of Canada. The latter faction, known as the "Senate Wing," hoped a Canadian invasion would cause an Anglo-American war, which might possibly lead to the liberation of Ireland. Most Chicago Fenians supported the "Senate Wing," and a number of them, in fact, participated in a series of quixotic raids on Canada. These, like the uprising in Ireland, were complete fiascos, and they brought public ridicule on Chicago's Irish.[23]

Rent by factionalism and failure, Fenian membership quickly dwindled in Chicago, as it did elsewhere. But if the Fenian Brotherhood was gasping its last breath, as an organization its spirit was very much alive. In 1867 a group of disgruntled New York Fenians established the Clan na Gael, a secret, oath-bound society that, like the Fenians, was committed to "the attainment of the complete and absolute independence of Ireland by the overthrow of English domination" by means of physical force.[24] Irish nationalists in Chicago quickly flocked to this new revolutionary society. In 1869, Chicago's first Clan na Gael "camp," as local branches were known, was established in the Bridgeport area.[25] Others soon followed, and for the rest of the century — and indeed beyond it — the Clan was to serve as the nucleus of Irish nationalist activity in Chicago. Led for much of the period by Alexander Sullivan, a crafty lawyer with a rather seamy past, the Clan numbered among its ranks some of the most influential Irishmen in the city: John M. Smyth, a prominent Republican politician and large furniture dealer; Daniel Corkery, a wealthy coal merchant and Democratic

23. Piper, "The Irish in Chicago, 1848-1871," pp. 18-27; *Chicago Times-Herald,* Oct. 20, 1895; Mary Onahan Gallery, ed., "The Diaries of William J. Onahan," *Mid-America* 14 (1931), 163. For the Fenians, see William D'Arcy, *The Fenian Movement in the United States, 1858-1886,* (Washington, 1947).

24. *Gaelic-American,* Nov. 29, 1924; "Constitution of the United Brotherhood [Clan na Gael], 1877," reprinted in *Special Commission Act, 1888. Reprint of the Shorthand Notes of the Speeches, Proceedings, and Evidence Taken before the Commissioners,* 12 vols. (London, 1890), IV: 493. For a brief history of the Clan, see Michael F. Funchion, ed., *Irish American Voluntary Organizations* (Westport, CT, 1983), pp. 74-93.

25. Clan na Gael Notebook, Devoy Papers, MS 9824, National Library of Ireland.

leader; John F. Finerty, a one-term congressman and publisher of the *Citizen*, an Irish weekly; and John P. Hopkins, first Irish Catholic mayor of Chicago (1893-95), among others.[26]

Although the Clan was never large in numbers, its doctrine of revolutionary republicanism seemed to permeate the Irish community, and it exerted considerable influence over other larger Irish nationalist organizations. Clan na Gaelers or individuals sympathetic to their aims dominated the leadership of the Ancient Order of Hibernians and the local branches of the Irish National Land League, the Irish National League, and the Irish National Federation. As affiliates of the Irish Parliamentary party, these latter three groups were ostensibly dedicated to achieving Irish self-government through nonviolent means alone.[27] In practice, however, their members followed the Clan's policy. Although willing to lend moral and monetary support to the Irish Parliamentary party's peaceful efforts on behalf of home rule, they were more than eager, should the opportunity arise, to back a full-scale rebellion to secure an independent Irish Republic.

The Clan also managed to spread its message of revolutionary nationalism to the Irish community at large. Each week Finerty's *Citizen* informed its readers of the latest English misdeeds in Ireland and reminded them of the need for militant action. Furthermore, thousands of Irish Chicagoans, many of whom were probably not members of any nationalist group, attended rallies either sponsored or cosponsored by the Clan na Gael. In addition to St. Patrick's Day, major Irish gatherings were held on March 4, the birthday of the patriot Robert Emmet; on August 15, the feast of Our Lady Day in Harvest; and on November 23, the date three Fenians, known as the Manchester Martyrs, were executed by the British in 1867. Orators at these rallies rekindled the embers of Irish nationalism — if indeed they needed rekindling — among their audiences, recounting the long history of English misrule in Ireland. Though they had kind words for English leaders who were sympathetic to Irish grievances, they often harped on the theme that words alone would never change the hearts of most English people. English deafness to Irish problems, they argued, could only be cured by the bullet and the bomb.[28]

26. For a list of prominent Clan na Gaelers, see *Chicago Inter Ocean*, July 14, 1889. More detailed biographies of some of these can be found in Ffrench, *American Irish in Chicago*. For Sullivan's background, see Michael F. Funchion, *Chicago's Irish Nationalists, 1881-1890* (New York, 1976), pp. 45-46.

27. A list of the officials of these groups and others was usually printed each week in Finerty's *Chicago Citizen*, which began publication in 1882. For brief histories of these organizations, see Funchion, ed., *Irish American Voluntary Organizations*, pp. 50-61, 183-200. The Irish Parliamentary Party was founded by Isaac Butt in the 1870s and led by Charles Stewart Parnell during the 1880s. After the Parnell-O'Shea divorce scandal in 1890, the party split into Parnellite and anti-Parnellite factions, but it was reunited in 1900 under the leadership of John Redmond.

28. These speeches were usually reprinted in the *Citizen*. The gatherings on March 4, August 15, and November 23 were run by the United Irish Societies, an umbrella organization established

However, if many Irish Chicagoans seemed to support the Clan's revolutionary philosophy, the organization was not without its problems. During the last fifteen years of the century the Clan was plagued by factionalism. During the mid-1880s a relatively small group of Chicago Clan na Gaelers broke with the parent organization run by Alexander Sullivan, claiming that he was a thief who used the Irish cause for his own selfish ends. Though small in numbers, the dissidents carried on a vigorous campaign against Sullivan and his cronies. This campaign became intensely bitter after 1889, when one of the dissident leaders, Dr. Patrick Henry Cronin, was murdered by a few of Sullivan's supporters, an event that brought shock and disgrace to the city's Irish.

While these events undermined some of its popularity, Irish nationalism remained a viable movement in Chicago simply because its underlying causes continued to survive. Concern for the political future of Ireland was a way of reaffirming one's Irishness, a way of keeping in touch with one's roots. Yet there was more behind Irish-American nationalism than the simple need to reinforce a common ethnic bond. Irish-American nationalism was probably characterized by a more intense hatred of England than was the movement in Ireland itself. After all, the majority of the late nineteenth-century Chicago Irish had either emigrated from Ireland during or in the decade immediately following the Great Famine, or they were the children of such emigrants. Since few returned for any length of time, their memories of Ireland were frozen at a time when British rule was — or at least seemed to be — at its worst. They neither could nor would forget the hunger, the evictions, and the poverty, and they took up the cause of Irish nationalism not only in the hope of seeing an independent Ireland but also as an expression of vengeance on England. Indeed, sheer hatred of England does much to explain phenomena like the reckless and futile dynamite campaign that the Clan launched against Britain in the early 1880s. Although it did nothing to bring the dream of an independent Ireland any closer to reality, it served at least to give "Mother England" a few sleepless nights.[29]

Furthermore, as Thomas N. Brown has argued, the fires of Irish-American nationalism were fueled by a need for respect. Coming from a land ruled by authorities who had shown little but contempt for their way of life, and coming to a nation where — at least in the beginning — they had been scorned for their poverty, religion, and culture, the American Irish had developed a collective sense of inferiority. Perhaps nothing intensified these feelings so much as the

---

in 1876, which had Clan camps among its affiliates. See John Corrigan, "United Irish Societies of Chicago," in Funchion, ed., *Irish American Voluntary Organizations,* pp. 276-282. My thoughts on the impact that Irish nationalist organizations could have had on the general Irish-American population were influenced by Margaret Sullivan, "Where Have All the Irish Gone? St. Louis's Irish-Americans, 1900-1925," a paper delivered at the annual convention of the Organization of American Historians, St. Louis, 1976.

29. For the dynamite campaign, see Funchion, *Chicago's Irish Nationalists,* pp. 82-86.

Dr. Patrick H. Cronin, a critic of the financial irregularities of Chicago's Clan-na-Gael, was the victim of a ghastly and sensational murder in 1889. The Clan used both violence and non-violence in its efforts to win independence for Ireland, and was an important force in the lives of Chicago's Irish. Courtesy of Chicago Historical Society.

fact that their homeland was still in the hands of a foreign power.[30] John Finerty probably typified the sentiments of most Irish Chicagoans when he claimed (forgetting the Jews) that "all other foreign elements in this country, with, perhaps, the exception of the Poles, have strong governments behind them, and they are held in more respect than the Irish who have no government of their own to boast of."[31] Thus, Ireland's gaining self-government would lead to a greater respect for the American Irish.

Finally, Irish-American nationalism helped to meet some of the social and economic needs of the community. Nationalist organizations and rallies provided excellent opportunities for Irish Americans to mingle with their own kind. The August 15 picnic in particular was a major social occasion attended by thousands of men, women, and children from various parts of the city. Furthermore, membership in nationalist groups like the Clan na Gael often led to economic rewards in the form of jobs. And nationalist connections were particularly useful for advancement in local politics.

The forces sustaining Irish nationalism were much the same in Chicago as elsewhere in Irish America. Yet Irish nationalist activity in Chicago differed

30. Thomas N. Brown, *Irish-American Nationalism, 1870-1890* (Philadelphia, 1966), pp. 21-24.
31. *Chicago Citizen,* July 11, 1885; see also *Citizen,* Oct. 26, 1895.

in one respect, and that was in the complete absence of any true constitutional nationalist movement. Chicago did have branches of constitutional organizations like the Irish National League, but behind these there always lurked the shadow of the gunman. In several other cities, however, mainly those in New England and the state of New York, constitutional groups were often what they claimed to be, and a number of their leaders were quick to denounce the revolutionary brand of Irish nationalism.

The differences between the Irish nationalism of Chicago and of cities in New York and New England can be largely explained, I believe, by the respective attitudes of the church toward nationalism in those areas. The bishops and clergy in New York and New England were for the most part strongly opposed to secret revolutionary organizations. They agreed with traditional Catholic teaching that membership in such groups was sinful because their required oaths conflicted with one's religious and civic obligations, and because their revolutionary aims violated the conditions for a just war.[32] As a result, they encouraged their flocks to turn away from revolutionary societies and to support instead the nonviolent nationalism espoused by the Irish Parliamentary party. In fact, a number of priests, such as Father Thomas Conaty of Worcester, Massachusetts, and Father Lawrence Walsh of Waterbury, Connecticut, provided some of the leadership for constitutional Irish-American nationalism during the 1880s and 1890s.[33]

Of all the clerical opponents of revolutionary Irish nationalism, none were as bitter as Archbishop Michael Corrigan of New York and Bishop Bernard McQuaid of Rochester. During the late eighties and early nineties they did their utmost to have the Clan na Gael officially condemned by the Committee of Archbishops, which had ecclesiastical responsibility for such matters. That action, however, was continually blocked by three "liberal" archbishops — James Gibbons of Baltimore, John Ireland of St. Paul, and Feehan of Chicago. These prelates believed it was best to interfere as little as possible in the political activities of the laity, for to do so might needlessly alienate otherwise loyal Catholics.[34] Feehan, who had grown up in one of the more nationalist areas of Ireland, went even further than that.[35] Though never publicly condoning violent

32. For the traditional attitude of the church toward secret societies, see Fergus MacDonald, *The Catholic Church and the Secret Societies in the United States* (New York, 1946), pp. 1-62.

33. For relations between the Clan na Gael and the constitutionalists, see Brown, *Irish-American Nationalism,* pp. 104-106, 109, 112, 121-124, 155-156, 168-171, 176; see also Funchion, *Chicago's Irish Nationalists,* pp. 62-64, 73-74, 77-79, 92-93, 95, 98-100, 119-120.

34. McQuaid to Corrigan, Mar. 15, 25, 1886; Feb. 1, 1887; May 6, 1890; Nov. 29, 1891, Archives of the Archdiocese of New York, photostat copies in the University of Notre Dame Archives; Frederick J. Zwierlein, *The Life and Letters of Bishop McQuaid,* 3 vols. (Rochester, 1925-1927), II: 336, 378-379, 383-385, 436, 462; MacDonald, *Secret Societies,* pp. 63-184; Kirkfleet, *Feehan,* pp. 234, 238-240; Robert D. Cross, *The Emergence of Liberal Catholicism in America* (Cambridge, MA, 1958), pp. 170-171.

35. Feehan was born and reared in Killenaule in the eastern part of County Tipperary, where

methods, he freely associated with Clan na Gaelers and was particularly friendly with Alexander Sullivan and his wife, Margaret, a journalist active in Irish affairs. He also gave a donation to the Clan's burial plot in a local Catholic cemetery. Obviously, Feehan believed that one could be a good Catholic and still belong to the Clan na Gael.[36]

Considering the archbishop's friendly attitude toward the Clan, it is not surprising that most Irish priests in Chicago felt and acted similarly. Father Dorney, the stockyards priest, was active in the inner circles of the Clan. Other priests often attended Clan demonstrations as honored guests and permitted the Clan as an organization to attend special masses or other church services. While some priests chose sides after the Clan na Gael split into factions, criticizing the opposing faction, I have found no Chicago priests who condemned revolutionary activities as such.[37]

The amicable relationship between clerics and Clan na Gaelers was clearly the major reason Chicago lacked a constitutional nationalist movement. There was no encouragement from the Chicago pulpit to leave the Clan and support nonviolent Irish nationalism, as there was in New York and Rochester. There were a few constitutional nationalists like W. P. Rend, a wealthy coal dealer, and William Onahan, a long-time Democratic politician; but without the church pushing people in their direction, they were voices crying in the wilderness. Although Irish Chicago suffered from a certain degree of factionalism, no split ever developed between the church and the Clan, nor did the nationalist movement ever divide along constitutional-extremist lines. In this respect, at least, the Irish in Chicago manifested a level of solidarity absent in cities in New York and New England.

Unlike Catholicism and Irish nationalism, which had their origins in the

---

the abortive Young Ireland Uprising of 1848 took place. Furthermore, Feehan had a relatively liberal seminary education. Although he completed part of his seminary training at Maynooth, he left there for St. Louis in 1848, a year before Archbishop Cullen arrived in Ireland determined to spread the rigid, ultramontane views of the reactionary Pope Pius IX. Archbishop Corrigan, on the other hand, was one of the first graduates of the North American College in Rome, a bastion of ultramontanism. For Feehan's early life, see Kirkfleet, *Feehan*, pp. 1-23; for Cullen and the Irish church, see Larkin, "Devotional Revolution," pp. 625-652.

36. Diary of John Devoy, Devoy Papers, MS 9820, National Library of Ireland; McQuaid to Corrigan, Feb. 1, 1887, Archives of the Archdiocese of New York, photostat copy in the University of Notre Dame Archives; *Chicago Citizen*, Jan. 3, 1885; Mar. 19, Oct. 15, 1887; *Chicago Inter Ocean*, May 20, 1889; *New World*, Oct. 7, 1893; Kirkfleet, *Feehan*, pp. 123, 129, 134-135, 143-146, 277, 280-282, 294-295; Thompson, *Archdiocese of Chicago*, p. 397; Francis E. Croarkin, *Ninety Years: The Autobiography of Francis E. Croarkin* (Chicago, 1952), p. 47.

37. Ffrench, *American Irish in Chicago*, pp. 796-801; John F. Finerty, *The People's History of Ireland*, 2 vols. (New York, 1904), II:928-929; T. P. O'Connor, *Memoirs of an Old Parliamentarian*, 2 vols. (London, 1929), II: 194-195; "The Untold Story of Catholic Chicago"; *Gaelic-American*, Sept. 15, 29, 1923; *Chicago Citizen*, Jan. 3, Dec. 5, 1885; *New World*, Sept. 9, 16, Nov. 25, Dec. 9, 1893; Jan. 13, Mar. 10, 17, April 14, 21, 1894; Mar. 9, 1895; *Chicago Tribune*, Oct. 28, 1889; Mar. 5, 1895; Sept. 25, 1896; *Chicago Inter Ocean*, Mar. 5, 1895.

Irish past, the third important force in Irish Chicago — the local political system — was primarily an American institution. Perhaps because of its rapid growth rate, or perhaps because of a confusing set of overlapping local governmental jurisdictions, late nineteenth-century Chicago had a fragmented system of politics. Neither the Republicans, who dominated the city council, nor the Democrats, who occupied the mayor's office more often than the GOP did, were controlled by a centralized political machine like New York's Tammany Hall. Instead, each party was divided into a motley array of factions, or "mini-machines," which were continually involved in making deals with one another. In fact, on the local level at least, deals frequently were made across party lines: the spoils of office took precedence over party loyalty. Unlike the relatively small group of mainly middle-class Protestant reformers, who emphasized honest and efficient government, most Chicago politicians looked upon politics as a business designed to bring power and financial rewards to its practitioners. "Boodle" aldermen voted to give contracts and franchises to businessmen willing to pay handsome kickbacks. Local precinct captains and policemen took bribes from owners of gambling and prostitution establishments and in return protected them from the law. But the system also had its positive aspects: machine politicians provided jobs and other needed services to their constituents.[38]

Although their influence was not as extensive as some contemporary newspapers and journals would have us believe, there is little doubt that the Irish played a significant role in Chicago politics. In 1890, for example, when they made up just 17 percent of the city's population, the Irish held at least twenty-three of the sixty-eight seats on the city council. Of these twenty-three councilmen, nineteen were Democrats.[39] The Chicago Irish, like those in other cities, gave the bulk of their support to the Democratic party because it had been traditionally more sympathetic to their needs than had the Republicans. Not only were most Irishmen Democrats, but most Democrats were Irish. In 1885, for instance, the Irish occupied fourteen of the eighteen seats on the Democratic City Central Committee,[40] and in 1890 they accounted for about

38. The following are helpful for an understanding of late-nineteenth-century Chicago politics: Joel Arthur Tarr, *A Study in Boss Politics: William Lorimer of Chicago* (Urbana, 1971); Lloyd Wendt and Herman Kogan, *Lords of the Levee: The Story of Bathhouse John and Hink Dink* (New York, 1944); C. O. Johnson, *Carter Henry Harrison I* (Chicago, 1928); Willis J. Abbot, *Carter Henry Harrison: A Memoir* (New York, 1895); Carter H. Harrison II, *Stormy Years: The Autobiography of Carter H. Harrison, Five Times Mayor of Chicago* (Indianapolis, 1935); Carter H. Harrison II, *Growing Up with Chicago* (Chicago, 1944); F. O. Bennet, *Politics and Politicians of Chicago, Cook County, and Illinois, Memorial Volume, 1787-1887* (Chicago, 1886); Perry R. Duis, *The Saloon: Public Drinking in Chicago and Boston, 1880-1920* (Urbana, 1983), pp. 114-142. For the view that "the state party system inhibited both Republicans and Democrats from constructing a Chicago machine in the nineteenth century," see Steven P. Erie, *Rainbow's End: Irish-Americans and the Dilemmas of Urban Machine Politics, 1840-1985* (Berkeley, 1988), pp. 43-45.

39. *Chicago Daily News Almanac for 1890*, p. 84. Two other aldermen may also have been Irish, but since their names are common to both Ireland and Great Britain, I did not include them.

40. Chicago *Tribune*, Mar. 25, 1885.

two-thirds of the Democratic aldermen. Furthermore, most of the major Democratic bosses during the period were Irishmen: Dan O'Hara in the seventies; Mike McDonald and "Chesterfield" Joe Mackin in the eighties; and John Powers, "Bathhouse" John Coughlin, and "Hinky Dink" Kenna in the nineties.[41] A handful of Irishmen, of course, became Republicans, either for practical political reasons or because they felt the national Democratic party had not properly rewarded the Irish for their loyalty. Two of the more prominent of these were John M. Smyth, the furniture dealer, and Martin B. Madden, owner of a large stone company. Smyth and Madden, who both served as aldermen for a time, wielded considerable power in local Republican affairs.[42]

But whether Republicans or Democrats, Irish politicians generally played the game of machine politics. Like some others on the city council, many Irish aldermen took payoffs from businessmen seeking municipal franchises and contracts. Irish politicians also successfully mastered the art of election fraud. Several owned saloons where they supplied the party faithful with ample refreshments on election days, encouraging them to vote early and often. Itinerants, illegally naturalized citizens, and even the dead were often duly registered as voters. Frequently, party toughs would pound the heads of opposition voters, or friendly policemen would jail them. And if all else failed, the ballots of a rival faction occasionally landed in the Chicago River.[43]

There is no doubt that the Irish were successful practitioners of urban politics. But why? For one thing, their past experience in Ireland preconditioned them to participate in a political milieu that flaunted the law. The English legal system as practiced in Ireland was anything but just. It often discriminated against Catholics and favored the mighty landlord over the lowly tenant farmer. As a result, the Irish immigrant had developed little respect for the law; instead, he tried to evade it as much as possible and was thus more easily able to adapt himself to a political system that skirted legal refinements.[44] Secondly, the Irish

41. For a biographical sketch of O'Hara, see Michael L. Ahern, *The Great Revolution: A History of the Rise and Progress of the People's Party in the City of Chicago and County of Cook* (Chicago, 1874), pp. 123-125. Colorful accounts of the others can be found in Wendt and Kogan, *Lords of the Levee.*

42. *Gaelic-American*, Jan. 10, 1925; Ffrench, *American Irish in Chicago*, pp. 10-15, 713-714; Harrison II, *Growing Up with Chicago*, pp. 209-211; Tarr, *Boss Politics*, pp. 34, 43, 55, 58-59, 74-77, 90-91, 98. For a study of Madden, see Thomas R. Bullard, "From Businessman to Congressman: The Careers of Martin B. Madden" (Ph.D. diss., University of Illinois, Chicago Circle, 1973).

43. See Wendt and Kogan, *Lords of the Levee;* Tarr, *Boss Politics*, pp. 10-12, 65-88; Duis, *Saloon*, pp. 128-140. Reports in the daily press provide some of the best information on the shenanigans of Irish politicians. For example, see Chicago *Tribune*, Mar. 22, 23, 26, April 3, 7, 10, 1885. For an interesting account of the activities of Irish politicians in the Town of Lake, which was annexed to Chicago in 1889, see Louise Carroll Wade, *Chicago's Pride: The Stockyards, Packingtown, and Environs in the Nineteenth Century* (Urbana, 1987), pp. 169, 172, 294-297, 303-305, 331-351, 354-357.

44. Edward M. Levine, *The Irish and Irish Politicians* (Notre Dame, 1966), pp. 32-36, 47-48; William V. Shannon, *The American Irish*, 2nd ed. (New York, 1966), p. 11.

were culturally far more Anglo-Saxon than they liked to admit. A knowledge of English gave them an edge over foreign-speaking immigrants like the Germans, while a familiarity with British election procedures provided them with a better understanding of the workings of American politics. From the 1790s to the 1820s they had watched the landlords organize tenant farmers into effective voting blocs, and in the 1820s they had participated in O'Connell's successful political campaign to gain Catholics the right to sit in the British parliament. The Irish clearly came to the United States well schooled in political organization and electioneering tactics.[45]

If their past experiences in Ireland prepared the Chicago Irish to operate effectively in the political arena, employment opportunities provided the immediate incentive that drew them into it in such large numbers. Several leading Irish politicians, who were also lawyers and businessmen, used their political connections to increase their incomes. Lawyers sometimes served as judges or represented companies with municipal franchises, while building contractors made handsome profits from city contracts. And for many of the party faithful who had neither the education nor financial resources to launch professional or business careers, political patronage jobs on the police force, in the water department, and the like provided them with their only source of livelihood. The federal census of 1900, for example, reported that 43 percent of "watchmen, policemen, firemen, etc." were either Irish immigrants or their children, even though they represented only 14 percent of the city's male labor force.[46] Besides municipal employment, the Irish also held what might be termed indirect patronage jobs, that is, jobs in companies holding city franchises and contracts. In 1900, 58 percent of all gas works employees were first- or second-generation Irish Americans.[47] And employment was not the only economic service Irish politicians rendered to their constituents; they occasionally helped widows, the unemployed, and the destitute, providing them with modest handouts of food, fuel, and other services.

It was largely for economic reasons that the Clan na Gael participated in Chicago politics from the 1870s onward. Though most Irish politicians were probably not Clan na Gaelers, virtually all Clan na Gaelers — except for the relatively small group of dissidents — were deeply entrenched in machine politics. In fact, with a decentralized political system, the Clan had an excellent chance to act as a "mini-machine," wheeling and dealing with various Democratic and Republican factions. Several Clan na Gaelers held influential political positions (mainly in the Democratic party) and were able to provide their fellow members with countless patronage jobs. For example, Daniel Corkery was a Democratic leader in Bridgeport during much of the period;

---

45. Levine, *The Irish*, pp. 36-37; Shannon, *The American Irish*, pp. 15-16, 52, 60; Lawrence J. McCaffrey, *The Irish Diaspora in America* (Bloomington, IN, 1976), p. 138.
46. U.S., *Twelfth Census, 1900*, "Special Reports: Occupations," pp. 516-520.
47. *Ibid.*

Chicago's police department, symbolized here by the Haymarket Riot statue, was predominantly Irish by the 1890s. The policeman, the priest, and the politician formed the trinity of occupations dominated by the Irish in many cities such as Chicago.
Courtesy of the Chicago Police Department.

Frank Agnew, a building contractor from the near North Side, served for a time as chairman of the Cook County Democratic Central Committee; and Michael McInerney, owner of a large undertaking establishment, was the Democratic boss of the Stockyards District during the 1880s and 1890s. Besides getting jobs through its own members, the Clan also made deals with other politicians. In the early 1880s, Alexander Sullivan supported Mayor Carter Harrison I's successful bid for re-election as mayor and as a reward was given the opportunity to name several Clan na Gaelers to positions in the police department. He also obtained positions for Clan na Gaelers in other city and county offices, so that the Clan na Gael could be found everywhere — from lofty judicial chambers to the city sewer system.[48]

48. For documentation and a more detailed discussion of the Clan in Chicago politics, see Funchion, *Chicago's Irish Nationalists,* pp. 42-55.

TABLE 2.3
Occupational distribution of Irish-born Chicagoans, by percentage, 1870-1890

	1870 (M & F) (N=32,482)	1880 (M & F) (N=8,552)	1890 (Male) (N=22,337)	1890 (Female) (N=23,918)
Professional	0.52	0.97	1.60	0.93
Owners and Officials of Large Businesses	—	—	1.11	—
Owners of Small Businesses	3.98	4.21	1.83	2.89
Other White-Collar Workers	3.67	4.56	7.48	4.71
Manual Workers	76.76	74.08	75.41	88.06
Unclassifiable	8.90	9.48	4.09	1.22
Unlisted	6.17	6.70	8.47	2.19

Source: U.S., *Ninth Census, 1870*, Vol. I, "Population," p. 782; *Tenth Census, 1880*, "Population," p. 780; *Eleventh Census, 1890*, "Population," Part II, pp. 650-651.

Politics, then, played an important role in the lives of many Irish Chicagoans. While the church and Irish nationalism primarily filled their spiritual and emotional needs as Irish Catholics, politics helped to satisfy their practical needs as urban Americans by providing them with jobs and other economic benefits. Since in one way or another these jobs and services were obtained through Irish connections, the political system helped to reinforce rather than lessen their sense of Irishness, and thus helped to strengthen community cohesiveness. The politician, with jobs and other favors at his disposal, was undoubtedly a leading figure in Irish Chicago. Along with the priest and patriot, he formed part of an important trinity that gave direction and stability to the community.

If the church, Irish nationalism, and politics served to strengthen community ties, so did the fact that most Irish Chicagoans were members of the same general socio-economic class. As Table 2.3 shows, from 1870 to 1890 the overwhelming majority of Irish immigrants were manual workers, probably over 85 percent, since it is more than likely that most of those in unclassifiable and unlisted occupations held blue-collar jobs as well. (Indeed, in the case of the Irish female labor force in 1890, where over 96 percent could be classified, 88 percent were manual laborers.) Of these blue-collar workers, about half of the men were unskilled laborers, while about three-fourths of the women were domestic servants.[49] The number of Irish immigrants in the professions or in big business, by contrast, was minuscule.

The statistics for 1900 (see Table 2.4), unlike those for 1870 through 1890, include the second-generation Irish; unfortunately, they lump them together

49. Based on U.S., *Eleventh Census, 1890*, "Population," Part II, pp. 650-651.

TABLE 2.4
Occupational distribution of first- and second-generation Irish Chicagoans, by percentage, 1900

	Male (N=75,695)	Female (N=25,016)
Professional	4.01	8.51
Owners and Officials of Large Businesses	2.19	0.10
Owners of Small Businesses	4.80	3.35
Other White-Collar Workers	16.58	25.19
Manual Workers	69.78	59.90
Unlisted	2.64	2.95

Source: U.S., *Twelfth Census, 1900*, "Special Reports: Occupations," pp. 516-523.

with the Irish-born, thus precluding any exact comparison between the two. Yet it seems clear that the American-born Irish had more white-collar workers among their ranks than did the immigrants, because the percentage of non-manual workers, which had hovered around 10 percent from 1870 to 1890, jumped rather substantially in the 1900 census, when the second generation was included. In 1900, over 25 percent of Irish men and about 60 percent of Irish women were business proprietors, professionals, or in other white-collar jobs. It would seem that, had the second generation been included in the labor statistics prior to 1890, one would have seen a gradual increase in the number of Irish white-collar workers from 1870 onward, as the children of Irish immigrants entered the work force.

Nonetheless, even at the turn of the century most Irish Chicagoans were still manual workers. Furthermore, one would suspect that the gulf between them and white-collar workers was not too great, since the latter had grown up mainly in working-class environments and probably still had one or more members of their families among the blue-collar ranks. For example, biographical sketches of the leading Irishmen in Chicago in 1897 show that virtually all had come from rather humble backgrounds and that a number had worked as manual laborers before achieving success in business, politics, or the professions. Some, particularly the politicians, continued to live in working-class neighborhoods; and though others were members of the elite Columbus Club, many were also active in religious and nationalist societies made up of individuals from all classes. Relatively few joined the select groups dominated by upper- and upper-middle-class Protestant Americans.[50] Although there were some

50. Based on a survey of the biographies of 245 Irish Catholic laymen in Ffrench, *American Irish in Chicago*. Included in the book but omitted from the survey were the biographies of priests, Irish Protestants, and deceased Catholic laymen.

TABLE 2.5
Percentage of manual workers of selected groups in the labor force, Chicago, 1890*

	Male	Female
Native White of Native Parentage	53.56	55.59
British-born	72.40	71.73
German-born	85.85	90.48
Irish-born	86.24	91.17
Swedish- and Norwegian-born	90.39	95.10
Danish-born	86.02	91.44

*These percentages are based on the total labor force *less* the number in unlisted and unclassifiable occupations. (Compare percentages of Irish manual workers in this table with those in Table 2.3.) The percentage of workers in unlisted and unclassifiable occupations ranged from a high of 19.5 percent for native white males of native parentage to a low of 2.25 percent for Swedish- and Norwegian-born females.

Source: U.S., *Eleventh Census, 1890,* "Population," Part II, pp. 650-651.

signs of class differences, particularly during the 1890s, late-nineteenth-century Irish Chicago had a predominantly working-class flavor.[51]

In this respect, of course, the Irish were not unique. During the late nineteenth century, blue-collar workers dominated Chicago's work force as a whole. Until the 1890s, when the "new immigration" began to change the composition of the city's labor force, the Irish were on the lower rung of the occupational ladder. As Table 2.5 shows, they had a greater percentage of blue-collar workers than did either Americans of native parentage or the British-born; and although they had roughly the same percentage of manual workers as the German-born did and a somewhat smaller percentage than the Scandinavian-born did, they had a greater percentage of unskilled workers than did either of these two groups.[52] In the last decade of the century, however, the Irish began

51. For example, Finley Peter Dunne's "Mr. Dooley" columns occasionally refer to the differences between the lace-curtain and working-class Irish during the 1890s. See Charles Fanning, *Finley Peter Dunne and Mr. Dooley: The Chicago Years* (Lexington, KY, 1978), pp. 77-79. For a brief account of a parish with affluent as well as low-income parishioners, see Ellen Skerrett, "The Development of Catholic Identity among Irish Americans in Chicago, 1880 to 1920," in Timothy J. Meagher, ed., *From Paddy to Studs: Irish-American Communities in the Turn of the Century Era, 1880 to 1920* (Westport, CT, 1986), pp. 122-123.

52. In 1890, 35.8 percent of all Irish-born male workers were unskilled laborers, compared to 19.6 percent of German-born males and 18.4 percent of Swedish- and Norwegian-born males. Based on U.S., *Eleventh Census, 1900,* "Population," Part II, pp. 650-651. If the second generation, which as a whole ranked higher on the occupational ladder than immigrants, had been included, it seems probable that the Irish would have been at least on a par with the Scandinavians. Unlike the Germans and Irish, relatively few Scandinavians came to Chicago before the 1870s; thus the percentage of second-generation Scandinavians in the labor force would have been far smaller than the percentage of second-generation Germans and Irish.

TABLE 2.6
Percentage of manual workers of selected groups in the labor force, Chicago, 1900.
(Statistics for ethnic groups include immigrants and their children)*

	Male	Female
Native White of Native Parentage	43.16	39.18
British	56.07	45.53
Germans	69.03	70.03
Irish	71.67	61.72
Scandinavian	78.02	80.54
Poles	90.67	87.66
Italians	83.99	80.03

*These percentages are based on the total labor force *less* the number in unlisted occupations. (Compare percentages of Irish manual workers in this table with those in Table 2.4.) Unlike the 1890 census, all listed occupations could be classified, and the percentage of unlisted occupations was less than 5 percent for most groups.

Source: U.S., *Twelfth Census, 1900,* "Special Reports: Occupations," pp. 516-523.

to move up the economic ladder (see Table 2.6). Definitely better off than the "new immigrants," such as the Poles and Italians, they were slightly ahead of the Scandinavians and had narrowed the gap between themselves and the Germans. They still trailed Americans of native parentage and the British.[53]

The economic position of the Irish relative to these last two groups no doubt helped to reinforce their sense of inferiority, for it mirrored the long-standing economic disparity between the Saxon and the Celt. Group inferiority complexes are difficult to quantify, and it is quite conceivable that many Irish, particularly the uneducated and unskilled laborers, never gave the matter much thought. But it certainly bothered the educated middle-class Irish who sought respectability and who often rubbed shoulders with Anglo-Saxons in the workaday world. Much as they liked to talk about the lack of materialism among Celts, they measured success in terms of economic and social mobility; and when they looked at their fellow countrymen, they saw that they fell short of the mark. John Finerty probably expressed the attitudes of many of these "respectable" Irish when he advised Irishmen to stay in Ireland, claiming that in America the Irishman "is nothing but a poor emigrant, who is left to paddle his own canoe as best he may, and who, however delicately nurtured at home,

53. Although the Irish had a smaller percentage of manual workers than did the Scandinavians, a greater percentage of their male labor force was made up of unskilled workers (23.4 percent compared to 16.7 percent for the Scandinavians). In all respects, however, Irish women fared better than their Scandinavian counterparts. Slightly over one-third of Irish female workers were employed as unskilled laborers, compared to about one-half of Scandinavian women. Based on U.S., *Twelfth Census, 1900,* "Special Reports: Occupations," pp. 516-523.

must take, at last, to the pick and shovel, perhaps to the recruiting office, or become a charge upon the country."[54] Such sentiments did not die easily; they lingered on well into the twentieth century, albeit in more subtle ways.

In addition to feeling inferior to Anglo-Americans, the Irish also felt the sting of the anti-Catholic and anti-Irish attitudes of others. Such prejudice was not simply a source of irritation to the Irish; it also played an important role in reinforcing their sense of group consciousness, for it reminded them that they were a people somewhat apart from the mainstream of American life.

As an infant city, where all groups — native and foreign — were relative newcomers facing the common problems of a semifrontier environment, Chicago did not offer the more rampant anti-Catholic nativism that plagued several eastern cities during the two or three decades before the Civil War. Nonetheless, anti-Irish and, to a lesser extent, anti-German sentiment did exist. Some Americans resented the Irish for their political power, for their support of liberal drinking laws, for their sometimes squalid living conditions, and most of all for their Catholicism, which they felt posed a threat to the very fabric of American life. They often viewed Irish attempts to get public monies for their schools or to ban the King James Bible in the common schools as part of a concerted Roman attack on free American institutions. Only once during the decades before the Civil War, however, did nativism score a major triumph in Chicago: in 1855, after capturing the city council and the mayor's office, the nativist and xenophobic Know-Nothing party passed legislation requiring that all persons hired by the city be native-born Americans. They also increased the cost of beer licenses, which led to the Lager Beer Riots, in which the Germans and Irish teamed up to battle the nativist authorities. But the Know-Nothing victory, caused as much by a disruption in the two-party system over the slavery issue as by anti-Catholicism, proved to be short-lived. The following year the Know-Nothings were defeated, and their legislation was promptly repealed.[55]

Although the xenophobic incidents of 1855 were never repeated again, anti-Catholicism continued to survive in Chicago. In the years after the Civil War, certain Protestant ministers repeatedly warned their congregations that

54. *Chicago Citizen*, July 11, 1885.

55. Charles Cleaver, "Extracts from Articles Which Appeared First in the *Chicago Tribune*," in Mable McIllvaine, ed., *Reminiscences of Chicago during the Forties and Fifties* (Chicago, 1913), pp. 55-56; Pierce, *History of Chicago*, II:232-233, 377-378, 381-383, 398; 2:211-214, 379-381, 437-439; Fleming, "Canal at Chicago," pp. 131, 152-153; Bennett, *Politicians in Chicago*, pp. 59, 97-100; Charles M. Thompson, *The Illinois Whigs before 1846* (Urbana, IL, 1915), pp. 78-80, 82, 87-88, 128-129; Solomon Wills to James B. Campbell, Aug. 12, 1838, James B. Campbell Papers, Chicago Historical Society; John P. Senning, "The Know-Nothing Movement in Illinois, 1854-56," *Illinois State Historical Society Journal* 7 (1914), 18-21; John F. Flinn, *History of the Chicago Police* (Chicago, 1887), pp. 71-74; William Kirkland and John Moses, *History of Chicago*, 2 vols. (Chicago, 1895), I: 130-131; Chicago *Tribune*, April 19, 1874; Sanders, *The Education of an Urban Minority*, pp. 19-24; Piper, "The Irish in Chicago," pp. 8, 45-46; M. E. Thomas, *Nativism in the Old Northwest, 1850-1860* (Washington, D.C., 1936), p. 163; Shanabruch, *Chicago's Catholics*, pp. 19-30.

the "demon of Romanism" was prowling about, seeking to undermine the democratic institutions of America.[56] Several Protestant newspaper editors and political reformers attacked the Irish for polluting municipal politics. Although most were sincere reformers and not really bigots in the true sense of the word, they often seemed to be more alarmed at the number of Irish politicians than about the actual corruption they were responsible for.[57]

During the late 1880s, anti-Catholicism, which had been relatively low-keyed and somewhat sporadic since the Know-Nothing period, became more blatant and organized. This new wave of nativism was, of course, a national as well as a local phenomenon. Partially caused by the steady increase in Irish political power — city after city seemed to be electing Irish Catholic mayors — and by the immense growth of the Catholic Church and its parochial school system, it also arose from the alienation of middle Americans, or "in-between-ers," as John Higham has described them. Made up mainly of small businessmen and white-collar and non-unionized blue collar workers, the "in-betweeners" felt lost in an increasingly industrialized and urbanized America, where giant corporations, labor unions, and political machines rather than individuals seemed to be controlling the nation's destiny. Wishing to return to an earlier and less complex America, they lashed out at the foreign element, which in one way or another seemed to be connected with these new forces.[58] When they spoke of the foreign element, they really meant Catholics, not Protestant immigrants. In fact, in many areas foreign-born Protestants actively participated in nativist groups; and in Chicago a number of British and Protestant Irish newcomers were in the forefront of the anti-Catholic crusade.[59]

Of the various anti-Catholic groups active in Chicago during the late 1880s and early 1890s, the most prominent were the United Order of Deputies, founded there in 1886, and the American Protective Association, which opened its first branch in Chicago in 1888 and eventually made its national headquarters there. Among other demands, these groups advocated immigration restriction, encouraged employers to fire Catholics, campaigned to defeat Catholic political candidates, and supported school laws like the Edwards Law (passed in 1889), which gave local public school boards some control over parochial schools.[60] Besides anti-Catholic organizations, Chicago also had a few short-lived nativist

56. For example, see the sermon of Rev. M. M. Parkhurst, pastor of the Michigan Avenue Methodist Church, in Chicago *Tribune*, Aug. 14, 1876.

57. For example, see editorial in Chicago *Tribune*, April 1, 1886.

58. John Higham, *Strangers in the Land: Patterns of American Nativism, 1860-1925* (New York, 2nd ed., 1969), pp. 53, 58-60.

59. H. J. Desmond, *The A.P.A. Movement* (Washington, D.C., 1912), pp. 45-46; Higham, *Strangers in the Land*, pp. 61-62; Rowland T. Berthoff, *British Immigrants in Industrial America, 1790-1950* (Cambridge, MA, 1953), p. 201; Chicago *Tribune*, Nov. 4, 1888.

60. *Chicago Citizen*, Jan. 5, 1889; Oct. 4, 1890; Higham, *Strangers in the Land*, p. 61-63, 80-87. For the A.P.A., see Donald L. Kinzer, *An Episode in Anti-Catholicism: The American Protective Association* (Seattle, 1964).

newspapers, including the *Weekly Native Citizen* and *America*, whose editor, Slason Thompson, claimed that "the civilization of Ireland [was] a hissing and a reproach in the ears of history for the past 300 years."[61]

One must be careful not to overemphasize the extent of anti-Irish bigotry in late nineteenth-century Chicago. The more virulent form lasted only a decade, roughly from 1886 to 1896, after which nativists began to ease up on their anti-Irish and anti-German attacks and concentrate their opposition more fully on the large numbers of Catholic and Jewish immigrants arriving from eastern and southern Europe. Even at the height of its popularity, the power of anti-Irish prejudice was quite limited, a fact perhaps most forcibly demonstrated by the election of John P. Hopkins as Chicago's first Irish Catholic mayor in 1893. After all, outright bigots formed only a small minority of the city's population. In fact, several Protestant leaders, including a number of ministers, spoke out in defense of the Irish and other Catholics.[62] Nonetheless, anti-Irish sentiment was a fact of life for the Irish in Chicago; it constantly forced them to defend their own traditions, as well as their loyalty to the United States, and, in the process, reinforce their ethnic identity.

In the eyes of anti-Catholic bigots not only, but of most non-Irish Chicagoans, Irish Americans were a monolithic group. And yet, though they certainly formed a relatively cohesive community, the Chicago Irish were by no means a homogeneous lot. Like any other ethnic group, they exhibited a degree of diversity and disunity. First of all, despite a common Irish Catholic heritage, their geographical backgrounds were far from identical. The most obvious difference, of course, existed between those born in Ireland and those born in America. The former had grown up in a predominantly Catholic, rural, and old-world environment, the latter in one that was more Protestant, urban, and industrialized. There is no doubt that this resulted in a great many different experiences in their formative years. Since the American-born Irish ranked higher than the immigrants on the occupational ladder, there may also have been certain class differences between the two. Yet the gap between the Irish immigrant and his American-born cousin must not have been as great as it was among the non-English-speaking ethnic groups; for both the Irish immigrant and the "narrowback" (a term used for an American-born Irishman) had been exposed to Anglo-Saxon influences in their youth, and both spoke the same language with equal fluency, albeit with different accents. Although immigrants associated more with other immigrants, and American-born with other American-born, and although tensions could arise between them, I have found that relations between the two were harmonious for the most part. Immigrants and "narrowbacks," for example, seemed to mingle quite well in organizations like the Clan na Gael and the Ancient Order of

61. *America*, May 30, 1889.
62. For example, see *New World*, Dec. 30, 1893; April 21, 1894.

Hibernians.[63] The only major dispute between the two groups occurred in the church, when, at the turn of the century, a band of Irish-born priests tried to block the appointment of the American-born Father Peter Muldoon as an auxiliary bishop of Chicago, claiming that he was prejudiced against Irish-born priests. But even this was not a simple generational conflict. The dissident priests had other reasons for opposing Muldoon, and support for and opposition to Muldoon align imperfectly between the two groups: it is noteworthy that the Irish-born Feehan had nominated Muldoon, and that — for a time at least — the disgruntled priests received the support of the American-born bishop of Peoria, John Lancaster Spalding.[64]

If those born in Ireland and the United States came from somewhat different backgrounds but generally got along well together, the same can be said for groups within these two major categories. The native Irish population in Chicago was made up of individuals from every Irish county, though most of them seem to have come from counties in the western provinces of Munster and Connacht. While it is true that in the early days of Chicago, brawls frequently occurred among men from different parts of Ireland, such rampant factionalism had declined by 1870.[65] Immigrants arriving in the years after 1870 came from an Ireland where better communications and a more fully developed national system of education had significantly reduced provincialism. Still, the Chicago Irish were quite aware of county differences. Good-natured rivalries prevailed among people from different counties, and there probably was a tendency for those from the same localities to fraternize more with one another than with other Irish people.[66]

Far less noticeable than the differences among those of Irish birth were the diverse origins of the American-born Irish. Although the published censuses do not break down the second-generation Irish by state, county, or city of birth, it is apparent that a considerable number of them had spent their formative years in places other than Chicago. Of the 126 American-born Irish Catholics listed in Charles Ffrench's *Biographical History of the American Irish in Chicago*, 69 were born outside the city, and of these the majority arrived there as adults.

63. Occasionally, generational conflicts did arise among the ranks of the nationalists. For example, in 1883, when Sullivan, who was born either in Maine or Canada, became president of the Irish National League of America, the Irish-born Finerty complained that non-Irish natives were taking over control of the Irish nationalist movement in America. At this time, however, Finerty was at odds with Sullivan over a number of issues; later on, when he was reconciled with Sullivan, such complaints ceased. Diary of John Devoy, Devoy Papers, MS 9820, National Library of Ireland.

64. "The Untold Story of Catholic Chicago"; Shanabruch, *Chicago's Catholics*, pp. 98-102; Jeremiah J. Crowley, *Romanism: A Menace to the Nation* (Aurora, MO, 1912), pp. 29-52.

65. Chicago *Tribune*, April 19, 1874.

66. F. P. Dunne's "Mr. Dooley" columns make reference to county rivalries. See the columns reprinted in Fanning, *Dunne*, pp. 45, 47. Dunne, however, probably tends to overemphasize the intensity of these rivalries.

Most came from the Midwest and the East, some from large and middle-sized cities, others from small towns and farms.[67] It is difficult to know exactly how these individuals differed from the native Chicago Irish, but it seems likely that they tended to blur the distinction between immigrant and "narrowback." They held a sort of intermediary position between those reared in Chicago and those in Ireland, sharing with the former an American upbringing and with the latter the experiences of adjusting to an unfamiliar city.

Chicago's Irish, therefore, came from diverse origins, although it must be emphasized that this diversity rarely led to any serious dissension. Similarly, the class distinctions we have already mentioned never posed any serious threat to community solidarity. However, more research is needed before one can fully grasp the nuances of Irish life in Chicago. Of course, some of the necessary research material is unavailable. No sociological surveys on the Irish of this period exist; virtually all of those who might have been interviewed are dead; and the records of many organizations have been lost forever. Yet an intensive study of the census manuscripts, parish records, and the like, may yield some additional insights. Interviews with the children of the late nineteenth-century Irish, some of whom are still alive, would also be valuable.

In any event, the sources that are available indicate that differences in background and class caused relatively little friction among the Chicago Irish. The community experienced discord from other quarters. Machine politics, for example, was a perpetual source of trouble. Although Irish "boodle" politicians usually cooperated with one another, no election seemed to pass without dissension on the part of one faction or another. Since political power and patronage jobs were at stake, the struggles were usually bitter and at times led to violence.[68] If Irish machine politicians sometimes fought among themselves, they also had to contend with opposition from a small group of reform-minded Irish. These individuals came from a variety of backgrounds but shared a common feeling that the existing political system was demeaning to the Irish. Rarely successful, they did manage to score a few upsets, most notably in 1882, when the then Independent Democrat John Finerty defeated Henry F. Sheridan, the regular Democratic candidate, in the Second Congressional District race.[69]

The most visible split in Irish Chicago occurred among the ranks of the Irish nationalists. The trouble started shortly after Alexander Sullivan was elected chairman of the national executive committee of the Clan na Gael in August 1881. Sullivan and two other members of the committee, who were

67. Of the 69 born outside of Chicago, only 12 arrived there before the age of eleven; of the 57 who arrived in Chicago after the age of ten, 51 had spent their pre-Chicago years entirely in the East and/or Midwest.

68. For colorful accounts of the struggles among local politicians, see Wendt and Kogan, *Lords of the Levee*. Reports in the daily press also provide ample evidence of the often bitter nature of these struggles.

69. Funchion, *Chicago's Irish Nationalists*, pp. 47-50.

collectively known as "the Triangle," pursued some rather questionable practices and policies that disgusted a number of Clan na Gaelers. They ran the organization in a high-handed and dictatorial manner, launched a futile two-year dynamite campaign in England against the express wishes of the Irish Republican Brotherhood, their affiliate in Ireland and Great Britain, and apparently pilfered nationalist funds for their own use.

As a result of this, during the winter of 1884-1885 a group of New York Clan na Gaelers, led by the former Fenian John Devoy, began a national campaign to oust Sullivan and his cronies from the Clan. Devoy picked up support in Chicago from a small but vocal band of Clan na Gaelers, including Patrick Dunne (the father of a future Chicago mayor and governor of Illinois, Edward F. Dunne), who as early as 1882 had publicly complained that Sullivan was using nationalist monies to speculate on the Chicago Board of Trade; William J. Hynes, a local Democratic politician and former congressman from Arkansas; and the ill-fated Dr. Patrick Cronin, who had recently arrived in Chicago from St. Louis.

For fifteen years, up until 1900, when the Clan was finally reunited, the Devoyites waged a relentless crusade against Sullivan and his followers, a crusade that took a tragic turn in May 1889, when a group of Sullivan's followers assassinated Dr. Cronin in a lonely Lake View cottage. Setting up their own Clan na Gael and joining the Ancient Order of Hibernians, Board of Erin, which was separate from the Sullivanite-dominated A.O.H., the Devoyites held rival demonstrations on all the major Irish holidays, where they denounced Sullivan and his gang as phony patriots who were using the Irish cause to advance their own political ambitions. Since Finerty, a Sullivan supporter since 1885, generally denied them access to the columns of the *Citizen,* they used the pages of the daily press to inform the public about the seamier activities of their enemies. They also joined forces with political reformers in an attempt to undermine Sullivan and the political system in which he was so intimately involved. Yet, as Devoy himself admitted, the anti-Sullivan forces gained the allegiance of only a small minority of Chicago's Irish nationalists. The majority remained loyal to the Sullivanites, for not only did the latter cater to their nationalist aspirations as Irishmen but, by playing the game of machine politics, they also met their economic needs as Chicagoans. If they wondered at times about Sullivan's more dubious activities, the Irish were willing to give him the benefit of the doubt because he was one of their own kind, and he had enough detractors in Protestant America. Besides, they probably reasoned, could a man who was the friend of so many priests and of Archbishop Feehan be all that bad?[70]

If the anti-Sullivanites received the support of only a minority of Chicago's Irish, their presence nonetheless points to the fact that the Irish community

70. For documentation and a more detailed account of the Clan na Gael split and the Cronin murder, see Funchion, *Chicago's Irish Nationalists,* pp. 82-123.

had its fissures and cracks. Although such factionalism — whether among nationalists, clerics, or politicians — failed to destroy the essential unity of Irish Chicago, it at least tended to weaken it, and it certainly belied any claims that the Irish were a monolithic people. Furthermore, if not a monolith, neither was Irish Chicago cut off from the rest of the city: every day, in varying ways, the Irish came into contact with the larger urban community.

One of the major ways the Irish encountered other peoples was through their jobs. Whether working in packing houses, in the stockyards, or on street railways, most Irish labored alongside other Chicagoans. And labor unions like the Knights of Labor had a good mixture of Irish and non-Irish members.[71] Of particular importance in bringing the Irish into contact with the outside world were the large numbers of Irish women who worked as domestic servants in the homes of upper- and upper-middle-class Americans. No doubt they were influenced to some degree by the manners and customs of their employers, and since many of them later married, their families were also probably affected by their experiences, although in what way and to what extent is a matter of speculation.

If contacts made at work helped to break down some of the isolation between the Irish immigrants and the wider society, so did the fact that virtually all Irish Chicagoans spoke the English language. Having English as a mother tongue undoubtedly made their adjustment to American life much less complicated than it would have been had they still spoken Gaelic, the common language of much of Ireland until the early nineteenth century.[72] English helped to make them feel more American, more a part of the society in which they lived. And while it did not put them on the higher rungs of the economic ladder, knowledge of English gave them an advantage in certain areas, such as politics. Furthermore, it meant that the ethnic newspaper was far less important to the Irish than to non-English-speaking immigrants. Unlike these groups, the Irish never had a daily newspaper of their own, and their one successful weekly, the *Citizen*, did not begin publication until 1882. Like the Americans and the British, the Irish kept up on the world around them by reading the regular daily newspapers, most of which, incidentally, gave rather detailed coverage of Irish events on both sides of the Atlantic. Reading the English-language dailies, of course, brought the Irish into more direct contact with the Anglo-American

71. Pierce, *History of Chicago*, 3: 537.

72. No doubt some of the immigrants from the west of Ireland were fluent in both English and Gaelic/Irish. There may even have been a few who could only speak Irish. It is interesting to note that, although Irish-language classes were held regularly in Chicago from 1884 on, they attracted only a handful of students. Apparently, few Chicago Irish were interested in spending time studying the language of their ancestors. For the Irish language movement in Chicago, see *Chicago Citizen*, Nov. 5, 1892; Jan. 5, 26, April 13, 1895; *New World*, June 16,1894; *Irish World*, April 20, 1895.

world, but it did not necessarily lead to better relations with it, for the local press could often be quite hostile to the Irish, particularly to Irish politicians.

Jobs and a knowledge of the English language were not the only factors that promoted interaction between the Irish and non-Irish. Each of the three main institutions in Irish Chicago — the church, the Irish nationalist movement, and the local political system — helped to link the Irish with other Chicagoans in varying degrees. Most important was politics, in which the Irish constantly had to deal with Americans, Germans, and Scandinavians, and later on with immigrants from southern and eastern Europe. True, political factions often divided along ethnic lines, but there was also a good deal of interethnic cooperation. In the early 1870s, Irish politicians teamed up with Germans and machine-minded Americans to form the People's party, a coalition of Democrats and Republicans which defeated the reformist Fire Proof Ticket in 1873.[73] Throughout the 1880s and 1890s, Irish politicians had to deal with American politicians like Mayor Carter Harrison I and Alfred Trude, and with Germans like Washington Hessing and John Peter Altgeld. And although the "new immigrants" had few influential political leaders during this period, the Irish had to cater to their needs, since they supplied an ever-increasing bloc of votes. Alderman Johnny Powers, for example, kept a hold on the Nineteenth Ward long after most Irish had left by providing jobs and other favors to the Italians who moved in.[74] Powers was typical of most Irish bosses in Chicago. With a relatively small proportion of the city's population, the Irish knew that cooperation with other groups was essential to their political survival. Friction often occurred when other ethnics saw the Irish take more than their fair share of the prizes. But the Irish usually allowed their non-Irish political allies enough of the patronage to keep their allegiance. As a result, they managed to exercise a degree of political power out of all proportion to their numbers. If in the present century, Chicago politics — to use John Allswang's words — indeed became "a house for all peoples,"[75] it was one in which the Irish generally seemed to occupy the best rooms.

Although it failed to bring the Irish into contact with the larger community to the same extent that politics did, the church served as a catalyst in linking the Irish with other Catholics in the city. This is not to deny what I have said above: the Irish were indeed separated from other Catholics by language, customs, and the system of national parishes. Yet running through the motley fabric of Chicago Catholicism was the single thread of a common faith. A shared religious belief probably gave the Irish a better understanding of other Catholic groups than they might otherwise have had. And there is a great deal of truth

73. Ahern, *The Great Revolution*; Pierce, *History of Chicago*, III: 342-344.
74. Humbert S. Nelli, *Italians in Chicago, 1880-1930: A Study in Ethnic Mobility* (New York, 1970), pp. 92-112.
75. John M. Allswang, *A House for All Peoples: Ethnic Politics in Chicago, 1890-1936* (Lexington, KY, 1971).

in the claim that a common religious background was one of the reasons Irish politicians were able to deal more effectively with the "new immigrants" than were their American counterparts. While ethnic rivalries often overshadowed the universality of the church, there was a degree of Catholic solidarity that could become formidable in periods of anti-Catholic nativism. In the early 1890s, for instance, the Irish supported German Catholics in their campaign to repeal the Edwards Law, which threatened to undermine their parochial schools.[76] Of course, as the non-English-speaking groups lost their native languages and became more Americanized over time, ethnic differences among Catholics would decrease significantly.

At first glance, it may seem that Irish nationalism would have only served to isolate Chicago's Irish from the larger urban community. Yet in certain respects the opposite is true: it helped make them more open-minded in some matters. Since Irish nationalists played down the Catholic element in Irish identity and emphasized that all Irish people, be they Catholics, Anglicans, or Presbyterians, were true children of Erin, and since some of the more notable nationalist leaders — like Charles Stewart Parnell — were Protestants, the creed of Irish nationalism tended to dilute Irish Catholic prejudice against Protestants. Of course, more often than not, Irish Protestants were the objects of Catholic scorn, since most of them supported the British connection; but it must be emphasized that Catholics generally disliked their Protestant fellow countrymen because they were pro-British, and not because of their religion. Let any Irish Protestant wave the green flag, and he immediately became a hero to Irish Catholics. Arthur Dixon, an Ulster-born Protestant and long-time Republican alderman who supported Irish Home Rule, was revered by Irish nationalists in the city.[77] Two of the most popular out-of-state speakers at Irish meetings in Chicago were George Betts and George Pepper, the former an Episcopalian clergyman from St. Louis, the latter a Methodist minister from Ohio. A correspondent writing to the *Citizen* after hearing Pepper speak at an August 15 rally expressed the feelings of many Irish Catholic Chicagoans when he declared: "It was indeed a happy sight to observe the Rev. Dr. Pepper, a Methodist minister, and the Rev. Father Hayes, a Catholic priest, standing on the same platform. Such a scene augurs well for the future of Ireland."[78]

Secondly, the nationalist tradition helped to give at least some Chicago Irish a sense of empathy for the problems of other peoples. *Citizen* editor Finerty, for example, championed Cuban independence, defended the "new immigration," advocated the teaching of German and other foreign languages

---

76. Sanders, *The Education of an Urban Minority*, pp. 54, 108; Walsh, "The Catholic Church in Chicago," pp. 278-279; Shanabruch, *Chicago's Catholics*, pp. 59-77. German Lutherans were also strong opponents of the Edwards Law.

77. For Dixon's biography, see Ffrench, *American Irish in Chicago*, pp. 16-22.

78. "Observer," Letter to the Editor, *Chicago Citizen*, Aug. 27, 1887.

in the public schools, and condemned anti-Semitism in the United States and Great Britain.[79] Similarly, Alexander Sullivan professed concern for the plight of American blacks. Though many Irish opposed the antislavery movement, Sullivan recalled, after the death of the New England abolitionist Wendell Phillips, that the latter "was one of the first men whose utterances aroused in my blood hatred of human slavery, and gave my tongue some of its little power to denounce bondage even before I reached manhood."[80] The Irish nationalist experience clearly failed to wipe out Irish prejudice toward other groups, but it probably helped to diminish it. Anyone who spent time condemning English misrule in Ireland must have had some pangs of guilt when he acted in a bigoted manner toward others. Certainly the frustration of seeing a foreign power control their Irish homeland helps to explain why bishops like Foley and Feehan were willing to grant a certain degree of autonomy in the form of national parishes to the various Catholic ethnic groups.

Finally, and perhaps most important, the Irish were linked to other Chicagoans by a common loyalty to and faith in the United States. Most Irish immigrants came to America to stay, and of these the overwhelming majority became citizens.[81] They were no doubt only too anxious to renounce their legal allegiance to the British crown. But they became citizens more importantly out of a commitment to their adopted country, the country that was to be their home and the home of their children and grandchildren. On meeting with economic hardships or anti-Catholic prejudice, they might grow despondent; but by and large they looked on America as a good land, a land that certainly offered them a better future than Ireland had.

Indeed, the Irish identified very closely with the United States. As one Chicago Irishman remarked, "They're none of them foreigners when they come here, for their hearts and love were in America long before they thought of sailin' for America."[82] Irish-American apologists continually pointed out that the Irish had made significant contributions to the United States. Noting the number of Irish troops in the Revolutionary War, they claimed that the Irish had played a major role in America's struggle for independence, though they failed to mention that most of these troops were of Ulster Protestant origins. Far more justifiably, they noted the numbers of Irish soldiers who had fought to preserve the Union during the Civil War. Similarly, they recalled that several Irish policemen were wounded (one fatally) in the Haymarket Square Riot of 1886 as they were trying to protect the American democratic system from the alleged anarchists. And to charges that their commitment to Irish nationalism proved they were Irish first and Americans second, the Irish responded that

79. *Chicago Citizen,* Sept. 17, 1892; April 15, 29, 1893; July 6, Aug. 31, 1895.

80. Sullivan, Letter to the Editor, *Irish World,* Feb. 16, 1884.

81. In 1890, for example, there were only 5,777 Irish-born males in Chicago who were not American citizens. U.S., *Eleventh Census, 1890,* "Population," Part II, pp. 288-289.

82. J. J. McKenna, *Stories by the Original "Jawn" McKenna* (Chicago, 1918), pp. 62-63.

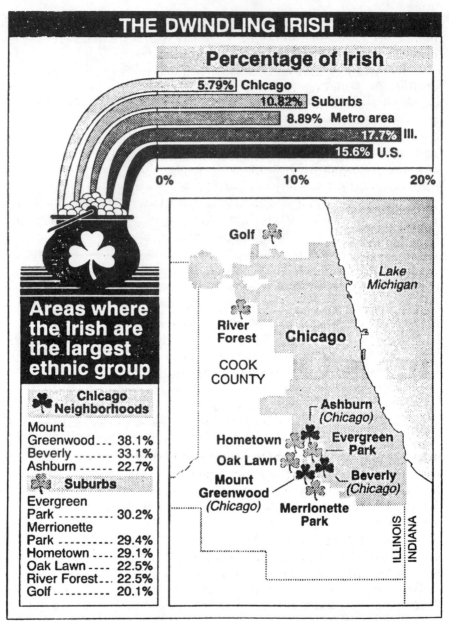

THE DWINDLING IRISH

Percentage of Irish

- 5.79% Chicago
- 10.82% Suburbs
- 8.89% Metro area
- 17.7% Ill.
- 15.6% U.S.

0%   10%   20%

Areas where the Irish are the largest ethnic group

Chicago Neighborhoods

Mount
Greenwood ... 38.1%
Beverly 33.1%
Ashburn 22.7%

Suburbs

Evergreen
Park 30.2%
Merrionette
Park 29.4%
Hometown 29.1%
Oak Lawn 22.5%
River Forest ... 22.5%
Golf 20.1%

Golf

Lake Michigan

River Forest

Chicago

COOK COUNTY

Ashburn (Chicago)

Hometown   Evergreen Park

Oak Lawn

Mount Greenwood (Chicago)   Beverly (Chicago)

Merrionette Park

ILLINOIS
INDIANA

SOURCE: 1990 U.S. Census   SUN-TIMES/Don Klappauf

Ethnicity was determined for the 1990 Census by taking the first and second groups that people wrote down on their census forms.
Courtesy Chicago SUN TIMES.

their concern for Ireland in no way diminished their love for America. After all, they argued, in fighting to overthrow British rule in Ireland, were they not following the example set by America a century before?

Nineteenth-century Irish Chicago, then, was not an isolated enclave cut off from the rest of the city. While they formed a highly self-conscious and relatively cohesive ethnic community, the Irish also came into contact with other Chicagoans. In the present century, of course, the Irish have become more totally integrated into the larger urban society. Much of their cohesiveness vanished as the factors that had sustained it changed. The ties that bound third-, fourth-, and fifth-generation Irish Americans to Ireland were naturally weaker than those that bound the immigrants and their children. The creation of the Irish Free State in 1922 did much to undermine the raison d'être of Irish-American nationalism, though, of course, some Irish Chicagoans continued to show an interest in ousting the British from Northern Ireland. Increased social and economic mobility tended to fragment what had once been a predominantly working-class community. Intermarriage with other ethnic groups (mainly Catholic), the decline of anti-Irish prejudice, and an increasing solidarity with other white groups against a growing black population tied the Irish more closely to other Chicagoans of a European background.

Yet it would be premature to sound the death knell for Irish Chicago. Among the nearly three quarter million persons of full or partial Irish ancestry living in Chicago and suburban Cook County today, there is a solid core of highly ethnic-conscious individuals who support a wide variety of Irish cultural, athletic, and nationalist organizations in the area.[83] In the last few years this solidly Irish core has been strengthened by the arrival of significant numbers of new Irish immigrants (many illegal), who have come to Chicago in search of jobs, which have been hard to find in Ireland since its economy went sour in the early 1980s. Although accurate figures for the number of Irish-born in the Chicago area are unavailable at present, it appears that the 1980s were the first decade in this century in which the Irish-born population of Chicago has increased.[84]

Besides the highly ethnic-conscious Irish, there are countless others who are aware of their Irish heritage in varying degrees. Indeed, during the past two decades or so, in view of the new interest in ethnicity, a number of

83. In 1980, 225,672 persons in Cook County (including Chicago) claimed Irish ancestry only and another 504,911 claimed partial Irish ancestry. For Chicago alone the figures were 105,430 for those of Irish ancestry only and 172,277 for those of partial Irish background. U.S., *1980 Census of Population,* Vol. 1: "Characteristics of the Population," Chapter C: "General Social and Economic Characteristics," Part 15: "Illinois," Section 1: Table 60, pp. 69-83. For present-day Irish activities in Chicago, see *The Irish American News,* a monthly published in Hoffman Estates, a Chicago suburb, and the Chicago columns of the *Irish Echo,* a weekly published in New York.

84. *Irish Echo,* Sept. 19, 1987; Maeve Kelleher's columns, *Irish Echo,* Dec. 3, 1988, March 10, 1990, April 18-24, 1990, May 30-June 5, 1990.

once-marginal Irish have begun to rediscover their Irish past. Young men and women whose great-grandparents came from Ireland study Irish history and literature at colleges and universities which once spurned these subjects as too parochial for an institution of higher learning. In the last three decades, increasing numbers of Irish Americans have visited Ireland, thanks to the fast and relatively cheap transatlantic travel available in this jet age. On the whole, it is probably easier for these Irish Americans to get back to their roots than it is for the descendants of non-English-speaking immigrants. Unlike them, Irish Americans speak the language of their immigrant ancestors and the language of present-day Ireland. Ironically, the English, of course, are responsible for this.

CHAPTER 3

German American Ethnic and Cultural Identity from 1890 Onward

MELVIN G. HOLLI

Without a doubt the brightest gem in Chicago's German-American musical heritage is the Chicago Symphony Orchestra and its founder Theodor Thomas.

No continental foreign-born group had been so widely and favorably received in the United States as the Germans or won such high marks from their hosts . . . before World War I.

Melvin G. Holli

The United States census released in 1980 showed that 28 percent of the American population traces its ancestral roots through one or both parents to Germany. Some 52 million Americans consider themselves to be at least partially German, which makes them the single leading nationality group, surpassing the Irish and English, the next two in rank order. In another measure of ethnicity, "mother tongue," Germans also ranked high, being the second largest in the non-English-speaking category — behind only Spanish. Five million German Americans claim the language of their forefathers as the language used in their childhood homes. The census indicates that German Americans, demographically and statistically, comprise an exceedingly large segment of America's ancestry.[1] Yet public expression of that ancestry is very scarce and difficult to locate.

Public expression of German ethnicity is nowhere proportionate to the number of German Americans in the nation's population. Almost nowhere are German Americans as a group as visible as many smaller groups. Two examples suffice to illustrate this point: when one surveys the popular television scene of

1. I would like to thank Dr. Hans A. Schieser of DePaul University for a critical and helpful reading of an early draft of this chapter.

the past decade, one hears Yiddish humor done by comedians; one sees Polish, Greek, and East European detective heroes; Italian-Americans in situation comedies; and blacks such as the Jeffersons and Huxtables. But one searches in vain for quintessentially German-American characters or melodramas patterned after German-American experiences. When Germans do appear, they are often cast in sinister roles as cruel-visaged and monocled Prussian Junkers, amusingly stupid prison camp guards, or diabolical submarine captains about to sink hospital ships or innocent passenger liners. A second example of the virtual invisibility is that, though German Americans have been one of the largest ethnic groups in the Chicago area (numbering near one-half million between 1900 and 1910), no museum or archive exists to memorialize that fact. On the other hand, many smaller groups such as Lithuanians, Poles, Swedes, Jews, and others have museums, archives, and exhibit halls dedicated to their immigrant forefathers.

Why is there so little German-American ethnicity in the slipstream of public consciousness? Is it a kind of ethno-cultural amnesia or historical forgetfulness? The answers to these questions lead us back to an examination of the great waves of German immigrants who came to the United States and Chicago between 1850 and 1900, and what happened to the cultures they brought with them.

The Germans who came to Chicago after the 1850s were predominantly artisans, skilled craftsmen, and men from the handicraft trades. They were, as one scholar wrote, "refugees from change." They were fleeing overpopulation, the extension of economic freedom into the German states, and the new factory methods of production that undermined the wages, the prosperity, and the traditional ways of life the guilds had protected. The guild system that had preserved the lifestyle of the German craftsman was breaking down. Competition was ruinous, prices plummeted, and thousands of German handicraft workers closed their businesses and sold their shops, packed their bags, and set out for America and Chicago.[2]

They arrived in the New World and Chicago at the right time. American cities were just beginning to industrialize and modernize and could use the crafts and skills that Germans brought. They fit well into the new industrializing economy. Chicago was in a transition stage from preindustrialism, and its labor force was not fully mechanized or modernized. In addition, there was a high demand for craftsmen especially in the building trades; Chicago's central business district burned down in 1871. Thereafter, the city's population doubled every decade up to 1890, when it reached one million. Both factors created enormous demand for carpenters and craftsmen in the building trades. Germans could grow up with Chicago and benefit in the process.

---

2. U. S. Census, 1980. Mack Walker, *Germany and the Emigration, 1816-1885* (Cambridge, MA, 1964).

Radical Phase

Although German Americans would later become the highest-paid ethnic group among foreign-born workers, they nonetheless passed through a phase of their history that might be called the anarchist-radical chapter of Deutschtum. German Americans' impact on the labor movement and immigrant radicalism was larger than life and bigger than usual in late nineteenth-century Chicago. They were on the cutting edge of importing new ideas from Europe, such as socialism, and making attempts to graft them onto the Chicago labor movement. The Chicago labor movement that flowered in the 1880s was shot through with radicalism and often led by German radicals. For example, the Socialist Labor Party of the time was dominated by German leaders, and German was one of the two official languages the party used at its meetings and in its publications; by 1890 the Chicago group was a German-speaking and German-thinking party.

Other indexes of the German-American presence on the political left can also be adduced: the names of the arrestees of the anarchist-radical-inspired Haymarket Riot of 1886 include a disproportionately large share of German names. One careful student of that decade of labor violence discovered that 63 percent of the anarchists were German and another 16 percent were Bohemians, many of whom spoke and read German and shared German working-class ideas.[3] Among the craft unions, Germans also exerted a potent influence: one of the strongest of the craft unions formed in the 1890s was the German carpenters, which unified the other nationalities under a single union and won a long-sought eight-hour day and higher wages.

But change was in the air. By 1900, German-American visibility in radical circles was a fading phenomenon and in a state of precipitous decline. "Where are they gone, the many who only a few years ago helped build . . . a new working class movement?" asked the Chicago editor of a radical German-language paper. His answer was, "many have turned bourgeois."[4] What had happened in Germany was that Bismarck had repealed the anti-socialist laws, thus drying up the flow of emigrant radical editors and agitators to Chicago and the nation. In addition, living standards among German-American workers in the 1880s and 1890s in terms of food and housing were superior to those of their brothers, sisters, mothers, and fathers who remained behind in the old country. In Chicago, German workers could enjoy the advantages of abundant food and livable housing without sending their children into the street trades and factories, as would the Italians, Poles, and other newcomer nationalities.

Higher living standards seemed to undercut the basis for radicalism and

3. Bruce Nelson, "Counting Anarchists: The Numbers and Patterns . . . Chicago, 1880-1886," paper presented at the conference "Working-Class Immigrants and Industrializing Chicago, 1880-1920," October 9-12, 1981, Chicago.
4. Bruce Nelson, *Beyond the Martyrs: A Social History of Chicago's Anarchists, 1870-1900.* (New Brunswick, NJ, 1988), p. 233.

socialism, so that their appeal to German workers after the turn of the century seemed both faintly anachronistic and increasingly incompatible with their high levels of achievement. The increasing embourgeoisiement of German-American workers seemed to result from their solid domination of higher-paying skilled crafts and their assimilation into the ideology of American labor unions. Heinrich Bartel, the radical editor of Chicago's *Arbeiter Zeitung*, excoriated German proletarians in 1908 for their social aspirations that "stop short at their stomach, a feed trough, a bankbook, a house being their highest ideals," and for whom "the labor question boils down to a question of knife and fork."[5] German workers by then had fully accepted the "bread and butter" unionism of their American and Irish counterparts in the American Federation of Labor. American unions have historically been nonpolitical, interested primarily in higher wages and less work. This job consciousness began to replace the class consciousness that had permeated an earlier generation of workers.

Finally, if one tests this thesis and looks at the ethnic radicalism in the 1920s in Chicago, one is immediately struck by the conspicuous absence of German-American names in either the leadership or the membership of radical groups. Other nationalities drawn from more recent immigrant groups had moved into the cadres and leadership. One example suffices to make the point: the American Communist Party, which was founded in Chicago in 1919, was composed of Russians, Ukrainians, Lithuanians, Finns, and other eastern Europeans.[6] Unlike 1886, when Germans comprised 63 percent of the anarchist membership, by the 1920s they were almost totally absent and virtually unrepresented in this new form of radicalism. Obviously, a great metamorphosis had taken place: the embourgeoisiement of German-American labor, or its large-scale entry into the middle classes and a broad sharing of American-based values.

Middle Class

Other factors would help to speed up the middle classification of Chicago's Germans. The city's Germans and German Jews were the most successful foreign-language immigrants to settle in Chicago, as well as in her sister cities of Milwaukee, St. Louis, and Detroit. No group but the English made such an easy economic, behavioral, and social adjustment to America as did nineteenth-

5. Heinrich Bartel, chief editor of the *Arbeiter Zeitung*, cited in K. Ensslen and H. Ickstadt, "German Working-Class Culture in Chicago," In H. Keil and J. Jentz, eds., *German Workers in Industrial Chicago, 1850-1910* (Dekalb, IL, 1983), pp. 241, 249; Hartmut Keil, "Chicago's German Working-Class in 1900," in *German Workers in Industrial Chicago*, p. 27.

6. Auvo Kostiainen, *The Forging of Finnish-American Communism, 1917-1924* (Turku, Finland, 1978), pp. 126, 127, 142; Werner Sombart, *Why There Is No Socialism in the United States* (White Plains, NY, 1976), 15, 74, 97.

century Germans. Propelled by a large artisan migration, they became the butchers, bakers (no candlestick makers), brewers, leather workers, coopers, and so forth, of America's rapidly growing cities. Their timing was perfect: American cities were in an early stage of economic and industrial takeoff, and German handicraft skills and artisan crafts fit admirably into this early stage of industrial takeoff. German occupational patterns in Chicago illustrate their dominance of the middle ranks of the job ladder. Although Chicago Germans in 1900 constituted 29 percent of the population (first and second generation), they monopolized skilled jobs in several categories and composed 50 percent of the bakers, 41 percent of the butchers, 74 percent of the brewers, more than one-third of the saloonkeepers and barkeepers, 44 percent of the brick, stone, and tile makers, 38 percent of the coopers, 39 percent of the cabinet makers and upholsterers, 37 percent of the machinists, 37 percent of the sweetshop owners, 35 percent of the tinners, and so forth. If one studies the entire German working population of Chicago in 1900, it appears that 57 percent were classed as skilled craftsmen.[7] No continental group came remotely close to the Germans in their skills. They were the nineteenth-century success story.

Chicago Germans also did extraordinarily well at the upper ranks of business. Before the guns of August sounded in 1914, the first generation of millionaires and wealthy Germans was in the making. Conrad Seipp, Jacob Rehm, Peter Schoenhofen, Charles Wacker, and others had amassed sizable family fortunes brewing beer. In addition, Germans made fortunes in carriage making, wagon manufacturing, and lumber dealerships. Meat packers such as Oscar Mayer and sausage king Nelson Morris had turned their packing skills into fortunes. In 1889 the *Illinois Staatszeitung* listed eleven Chicago German businessmen who were worth more than $1 million. The paper probably missed at least four or five others.

Chicago's German Jewish community, which was closely associated in language, culture and education, and recreation to Chicago's Germans, also added luster to German-American business success. The Harts, Schaffners, and Marxes put together ready-made clothing enterprises; the Florsheims did the same for shoes; and the Mandels for department stores. Julius Rosenwald reached the acme of Mammon's mountain when he bought an obscure watch company named Sears and Roebuck and turned it into a multimillion-dollar mail-order house. In 1913, when the federal tax laws became effective, Rosenwald paid the largest tax of any Chicago businessman — on a reported income of $1,320,000.[8] Rosenwald was a second-generation ethnic born of Jewish parents who emigrated from Germany in 1854. So pleased were Chicago Germans with their adopted city that immigrant Eugen Seeger, writing an appre-

---

7. Thomas Bullard, "Chicago's German Businessmen, 1871-1914" (M.A. Thesis, University of Illinois at Chicago, 1969). The count of German-American craftsmen includes first and second generation.

8. Hofmeister, *The Germans of Chicago* (Champaign, IL, 1976), p. 130.

ciative history of Chicago in 1893, called it *Chicago; Die Geschichte Einer Wunderstadt.* For Chicago Germans it had indeed been a wonder city. Even in politics, thought to be the natural province of the Irish, Germans began to make their mark: in 1907, Chicago elected its first German-American mayor, Fred Busse.

Music

Chicago's Germans have played a prominent role in the city's musical education and entertainment almost from the beginning of the city's history. Chicago's first professional musician, it is claimed, was Nicholas Berdell, who emigrated from his native Bavaria to Chicago in 1836. He organized a German band with his compatriots and would later open a dancing school on the North Side. Thereafter innumerable bands, orchestras, and choral groups would follow his initiative. Among those early pioneers was Julius Dyhrenfurth, a schoolmaster, businessman, and banker who began the first significant musical entertainment in 1850 with the Dyhrenfurth Philharmonic Society, putting subscription concerts on a sound financial footing and providing them for a number of years. Chicago's favorite nineteenth-century chronicler, A. T. Andreas, asserts that the city owes a "large part of its musical culture" to the influence of ethnics such as Dyhrenfurth who inaugurated concerts on a regularized basis. Other German-American bandsmen over the years put on light, popular, and some classical concerts on weekend afternoons in various halls and in Lincoln Park. A German-born musical educator who bears mention is Florence Ziegfeld, father of the Ziegfeld follies. The elder Ziegfeld had come to Chicago in 1863 and established the Chicago Academy of Music in 1867, which would attract more than 3,000 students by the turn of the century.[9] Choral music was also a part of the immigrant cultural baggage that would bring spectacular and memorable music festivals to the city.

Chicago Symphony Orchestra

Yet the brightest gem in Chicago's German-American musical heritage is without doubt the Chicago Symphony Orchestra. The orchestra (which renowned music critic Claudia Cassidy called "the world's best symphony") has a rich and distinctive German-American heritage. Its founder, Theodor Thomas, was born in the Oldenburg region of Germany in 1835 and came to America with his family when he was ten years old. Thomas was already a budding virtuoso, having given his first violin concert at the age of 6; and though he had

9. *Ibid.*, 217-219.

German-born Theodor Thomas, founder of the Chicago Symphony Orchestra and Music Director, 1891-1905, was a figure of enormous importance in the development of American culture and, according to one authority, the "sacralization of Highbrow aesthetic tastes" in the nation.   Courtesy of Chicago Symphony Orchestra Association.

Without doubt the brightest gem in Chicago's German-American heritage is the Chicago Symphony Orchestra, which one contemporary critic called "the world's best symphony." Here the Chicago Symphony Orchestra can be seen performing on the stage of the Auditorium Theatre with Theodor Thomas conducting, December 1897.   Courtesy of Chicago Symphony Orchestra Association.

THE CHICAGO ORCHESTRA.

First Violins.
BENDIX, M. (Principal.)
SCHNITZLER, J.
KNOLL, E.
KRAUSS, A.
HILDEBRANDT, CH.
HUMAN, TH.
OZERNG, J.
BRAUN, H.
SEIDEL, R.
RISSLAND, R.
TROLL, C.
MARUM, L.
BERESINA, F.
SCHMIDT, O.
MITTELSTÁDT, F.
NÜRNBERGER, H.

Second Violins.
POLTMANN, R. (Principal.)
ZEISS, A.
SCHMITZ, P. R.
STARKE, G.
HEILAND, F.
LIEFKE, A.
DONATI, R.
ULRICH, A.
ZETTELMANN, J.
WAGNER, E.
DU MOULIN, S.
KATSCK, TH.
BUSSE, H.
SEIFERT, L.
NÜRNBERGER, L.
BUSSE, L.

Violas.
WIGGER, A. (Principal.)
LÆNDNER, J.
MEYER, G.
RIEDELSBERGER, C.
MEIGROSS, J.

DIETRICH, W.
MAURER, A.
FITZEK, G.
HOFFMANN, C.
KRAUSS, PH.

Violoncellos.
STEINDEL, B. (Principal.)
UNGER, W.
CORELL, L.
AMATO, L.
SCHIPPE, E.
SACHLEBEN, A.
EICHHEIM, M.
HESS, F.
METZDORF, A.
CLUSSMANN, E.

Double Basses.
WIEGNER, A. (Principal.)
BECKEL, J.
KLEMM, L.
DRIEBRODT, F.
HELM, R.
HELLEBERG, A.
GLASS, R.
KRAMER, A.
KRETLOW, J.

Harp.
SCHUECKER, E.

Flutes.
ANDERSEN, V.
VALCK, F.

Piccolo.
BALLMANN, M.

Oboes.
BOUR, F.
FRIEDRICH, L.

English Horn.
SCHŒNHEINZ, E.

Clarinets.
SCHREURS, J.
QUITSON, A.

Bass Clarinet.
MEYER, C.

Bassoons.
LITKE, H.
FRIEDRICH, L.
KIRCHNER, A.

Contra Bassoon.
FRIEDRICH, L.

Horns.
DUTSCHKE, H.
SCHÜTZ, A.
DE MARE, L.
WALKER, A.

Cornets.
RODENKIRCHEN, CH.
DIETZ, F.
ULRICH, A.
BRAUN, W.

Tenor Trombones.
GEBHARDT, O.
ZELLER, W.
NICOLINI, J.

Bass Trombone.
HELMS, CH.

Tuba.
HELLEBERG, A.

Kettle Drums.
LŒWE, W.

Bass Drum.
KATSCH, TH.

Small Drum.
ZETTELMAN, J.

Cymbals.
WAGNER, E.

Librarians.
McNICOL, TH.
BAIRSTOW, W.

As this roster of musicians' names shows, the orchestra in its natal
years had so many German-born and German-American musicians that the
conductor often addressed them in the German language.
Courtesy of Chicago Symphony Orchestra Association.

had no formal education in music, he was an accomplished musician, playing with several orchestras before he was in his teens. In 1862 the twenty-seven-year-old Theodor formed the Thomas Orchestra in New York City and toured the country. But he had a hard time making ends meet as an itinerant musician. In 1889, Thomas was approached by a number of wealthy benefactors and asked if he would consider locating permanently in Chicago if they provided financing for his orchestra. Thomas answered that he "would go to hell" if someone would provide him with an orchestra. Chicago may not have been Bayreuth (Thomas was America's foremost proponent of Wagner) but neither was it hell. The Chicago Symphony Orchestra prospered under Thomas's baton and that of his illustrious German-born successor, Frederick Stock. Sometime later a leading music critic maintained that "Thomas literally taught us how to listen to beautiful music from Bach to Richard Strauss." Professor Lawrence Levine, in perceptive study of what he calls the "sacralization of Highbrow aesthetic tastes in the nation," says that "Thomas was a figure of enormous importance in the development of American culture."[10] During those early years the orchestra had so many German-American musicians that the conductor often addressed them in the German language.

German Theater and Literary Life

Although the German-American chapter in theater and literature would not be as brilliant as the one in classical music, it is worth recounting. The Teutons who came to Chicago generally had a literacy level of about 95 percent. By contrast, other ethnic newcomers had lower literacy rates: about 50 percent for Ruthenians, Italians, and Lithuanians, and about 60 percent for Russians and Yugoslavs, for example. Among the German scribes were many 48ers who had fled unsuccessful revolutions in the fatherland and wrote polemics for the German-American press. Others such as Caspar Butz, Lorenz Brentano, and Emil Dietzsch were of a literary bent and wrote passable verse and essays here about their adopted land as well as their ancestral homeland in papers such as the *Illinois Staatszeitung*. Perhaps equally important, the high literacy levels of German Americans gave them access to German classics that were widely circulated in the German community. Chicago's German-American theaters also had a lively existence: playwrights poured out a prodigious volume, which was performed in such local theaters as the Vorwarts Hall, the various Turner halls, and Volkstheaters. These were often plays that were written, staged, and acted in by local talent, and they enlightened and entertained community audiences.

---

10. Theodore Thomas, *A Musical Autobiography* (New York, 1964), pp. a-27; Claudia Cassidy, "The Years of Splendor," *Chicago History* (Spring 1972), 4f.; Lawrence Levine, *Highbrow/Lowbrow: The Emergence of Cultural Hierarchy in America* (Cambridge, MA, 1988), p. 112.

In addition to this vernacular and popular theater, classical theater could also be seen; Schiller's play *Wilhelm Tell* and Goethe's *Faust*, for example, were favorites that graced the boards of these exhibition halls for more than half a century. Theater buildings such as the Deutsche Haus, the Globe, and the Schiller provided suitable venues for such performances and played a role in introducing German classics to Chicago audiences. World War I brought increasing problems for the use of the German language in performances, but the theater managed to survive the wartime hysteria. It turned out to be the Depression of the 1930s and the competition of the motion picture that would spell its demise. Still, during its life of eighty years, Chicago's German theater presented not only the amateur works of New World playwrights but also the classics from Schiller, Goethe, and others from the Old.[11] No ethnic theater in Chicago glittered with such a classy repertory as did the German-American theater, or served to introduce so many European classical works to American audiences.

Most Favored Nationality Status

From the Great Fire of 1871 to the Great War of 1914, Chicago's Germans waxed in numbers, confidence, economic success, and cultural acceptance. With the exception of the British, no ethnic group was so numerous in Chicago or the nation or had made such rapid and solid economic progress, dominating and monopolizing in many cases the middle rungs of the occupational ladder. They also did well at the upper ends of the job ladder, and as entrepreneurs and businessmen.

One of the results of of this was that they won high marks from the host culture and were perceived as the most desirable of the newcomers. Public opinion came to accept Germans as one of America's most reputable immigrant groups. Repeatedly, old-stock Americans praised German ethnics as being law-abiding, stolid, patriotic, and hard-working citizens. They made the fields bloom and the shops prosper. In 1903 a Boston sociologist declared the Germans the best ethnic type in the city; in 1908 a group of professional people rating the traits of various immigrants ranked Germans above the English and in some respects superior to native-born Americans. In 1916 a college professor in New York City published a paper called "Rating the Nations," which ranked ethnic groups by various desirable traits. His poll of professional people noted that in such measures as efficiency, leadership, and intellect, German-American students appeared to have higher ranking than Americans. No one today would claim that these polls were scientific, but they underscore the larger point: that

11. Hofmeister, *Germans in Chicago*, pp. 227f.; Esther M. Olsen, "The German Theater in Chicago," *Deutsch-Amerikanische Geschichtsblatter* 33 (1937), 66f.

German-Americans had become the country's "most favored nationality." No immigrant group had won such high marks from their hosts and were perceived to be such desirable newcomers. German Americans could bask in the reflected glory of their own achievements. They had become the favored adopted son of Uncle Sam.

Not only were there German-American achievements to celebrate, but the German fatherland overseas was becoming a major scientific, industrial, and military power. German Americans were also aware of a rich cultural heritage, a brilliant scientific community, and the world-class literature, philosophy, and music of their ancestral homeland. The names of Bach, Haydn, Mozart, and Beethoven in music; Leibniz, Kant, and Hegel in philosophy; Munsterberg and Freud in psychology; and a host of inventors and industrial scientists were broadly known to Americans and lent luster to the German-American reputation. In addition, some 10,000 American graduate students had studied in Germany and brought back to America the idea of the German seminar and the research university. As noted earlier, Germans not only basked in their own achievements but also shared vicariously in the triumphs of the sciences and arts in Germany.[12] German Americans then seemed secure among all of the nationalities that had come across the Atlantic: their fatherland was powerful and progressive, and their own achievements were solid and noteworthy.

World War I

That would change. The fury that broke upon German Americans during World War I represented the most spectacular reversal of judgment of an ethnic group in American history. The coming of the war spread a pall of gloom and dire foreboding. German American leaders with a sizable following publicly sought to prevent the U.S. Congress from declaring war on Germany and the Central Powers in April 1917. Anti-war "specials" and delegations from German organizations across the nation streamed into Washington, D.C. in that fateful week before the war to insist on American neutrality. This divisive effort rose to a crescendo just as Congress made its decision. War was declared, and in the following months the American public was seized with convulsions of patriotic hysteria.[13] That patriotic hysteria was fixed on the German element as potentially seditious and possibly treacherous to the American war effort. Incredibly,

12. Howard B. Woolston, "Rating the Nations: A Study in the Statistics of Opinion," *American Journal of Sociology* 22 (November 1916), 381-390; John Higham, *Strangers in the Land: Patterns of American Nativism, 1860-1925* (New York, 1963), p. 196; B. Simek, "More About Americanization," *Czechoslovak Review* 3 (August 1919), 231.

13. Illinois *Staats Zeitung*, March 26, 1917; F. Britten, Biographical File, Chicago Historical Society; P. Holbo, "They Voted Against War: A Study of Motivations" (Ph.D. dissertation, University of Chicago, 1961), p. 264.

the German American, the "most favored nationality," now found himself the detested outsider in American life. In 1917 the German American was viewed as the brother of the Hun, the ancestor of those who destroyed the Lovain, pillaged Belgium, took civilian hostages, the blood brother of those who sank passenger liners such as the *Lusitania* with no provision for the innocent. The whole image of German Americans took the most abrupt "volte-face" that history has seen. No group fell from such high favor to such low disregard as did German Americans during the period of World War I.

Everywhere they went in 1917, German Americans felt the sting of being the outsider. Their culture, language, customs, and even food came under attack. Nothing seemed to escape the frenzied attack of Americanizers. German sauer-kraut was renamed "liberty cabbage" by Americanizers; even the *frankfurter* (reminiscent of a German city) was renamed the "hotdog." *Hamburgers* (sounding too much like the German city Hamburg) were re-christened "Salisbury steaks," the name of an English city. Even man's best friend did not emerge unscathed from the Americanization movement: that stately Teutonic canine, the German shepherd, was renamed the Alsatian. The experiences of German Americans during the war was one of the greatest trials endured by any European-born minority up to that time. Even the language of their ancestors came under attack: the teaching of German was forbidden in twenty-six states (though Illinois was not one of them[14]). German high culture took its share of attacks: the *Saturday Evening Post* declared that anyone who defended German music must be either woolly minded or radical. Famous German-American writers such as Theodore Dreiser and H. L. Mencken were charged with being "amoral" and filled with nihilism, "Herrenvolk" with anti-democratic attitudes and Teutonic-Oriental pessimism.

By 1918 all the stops had been pulled, and the Americanization crusade steamrollered forward, running down all forms of Germanism whenever or wherever they were found. In Chicago the Schiller statue got a coat of coward's yellow paint, and the Goethe monument was threatened with destruction but removed to storage for safety during the war period. Amid charges of lack of patriotism, the Chicago Symphony Orchestra's German-born conductor, Frederick Stock, stepped down from the podium to complete the naturalization process for citizenship. The designated choral director of the Illinois Bicentennial pageant, William Boeppler, was pressured into resigning in 1918 because of his German antecedents. The Chicago Athletic Club began firing its alien German employees in May, and employers in vital war industries began to scrutinize their payrolls with an eye to extirpating potential subversives.[15] Ger-

14. Melvin G. Holli, "Teuton vs. Slav: The Great War Sinks Chicago's German *Kultur*," *Ethnicity* B (1981), 431; B. Simek, "More About Americanization," p. 231. For the national picture, see Frederick C. Luebke, *Bonds of Loyalty: German Americans and World War I* (Dekalb, IL, 1974).

15. *Free Poland*, July 2, 1917; Hofmeister, *Germans of Chicago*, pp. 73f.; Holli, "Teuton vs.

man Americans began to protest the violation of their civil liberties by the Americanization campaign, but their protests went unheard.

In fact, the opprobrium intensified as the war moved forward. Some groups, fearing the worst, made voluntary efforts to comply with the new patriotism before they were forced to do so. Chicago's Germania Club became the Lincoln Club on May 9, 1918, and days later the Bismarck Hotel was rechristened Hotel Randolph and the Hotel Kaiserhof was renamed the Hotel Atlantic. The imperial-sounding Kaiser Friedrich Mutual Aid Society became the George Washington Benevolent Aid Society, and the city's German Hospital was redubbed with an American-sounding Grant Hospital. Even private citizens found it prudent to change their names: according to the *Abendpost* of August 20, 1918, a Harry Feilchenfeld became H. H. Field, Hans Kaiser became John Kern, Emma Guttman became Goodman, Berta Griescheimer became Gresham, which is a partial sample of one day's parade of name changes. More than 1,000 Chicagoans petitioned the city council to abolish such German street names in their district as Berlin, Hamburg, Frankfurt, Coblenz, Lubeck, and Rhine. The council complied.[16]

Smitten by the new patriotism, old-stock Gold Coast citizens joined the crusade in December 1918, requesting that Goethe Street be renamed. They denied any anti-German animus, saying merely that they could not pronounce the name Goethe properly and wanted instead the name Boxwood Street. Alderman "Bathhouse" John Coughlin suggested in jest that it be renamed "Busse Place" in honor of the city's only German American mayor; two German American aldermen then suggested it be called "Nutwood Street" to properly characterize the mental state of the petitioners. German fraternals and civic-minded citizens protested any name change, and Goethe Street remained Goethe Street.[17]

Such an occasional small victory could not, however, conceal the generalized and widespread collapse of Germanism in Chicago and the nation. Already in April, for example, the most powerful and influential ethnic and fraternal lodge the nation had ever seen, the National German American Alliance and its Chicago chapter, disbanded voluntarily in the face of fierce Congressional pressure and before the federal government could revoke its charter. Indexes of "Deutschtum's" demise in Chicago and the nation abounded: a leading German-language daily, the Illinois *Staatszeitung*, lost subscribers and was on the road to extinction; German-language instruction in the public

---

Slav," pp. 438f.; A. L. Levy, "The American Symphony at War: German-American Musicians," *Mid-America* 71 (January 1989), 9.

    16. Holli, "Teuton vs. Slav," pp. 444f.; Hofmeister, *Germans of Chicago*, pp. 69f.; A. J. Townsend, "Germans of Chicago," in *Jahrbuch Deutsch Amerikanischen Historischen Gesellschaft* (XXXII), 107.

    17. Hofmeister, *Germans of Chicago*, 76.

schools collapsed for a lack of students and never recovered its prewar position in Chicago. In 1917 the Missouri Synod's Lutheran Church conference minutes appeared in English for the first time, and the synod's new constitution dropped its insistence on using the language of Luther only and instead suggested bilingualism. Dozens of Lutheran schools also dropped instruction in the German language. English-language services also intruded themselves into parishes where German had been the *lingua franca*. Whereas only 471 congregations nationwide held English services in 1910, the number preaching in the tongue of Albion in the synod skyrocketed to 2,492 by 1919. The German Evangelical Synod of Missouri, Ohio, and other states also anglicized its name by dropping German from the title. A key indicator of the decline of "Deutschtum" in Chicago was the census: the number identifying themselves to the census-taker as German-born plummeted from 191,000 in 1910 to 112,000 in 1920. This drop far exceeds the natural mortality rate or the number who might be expected to move. Self-identifiers had found it prudent to claim some nationality other than German. To claim German nationality had become too painful an experience.[18]

No continental foreign-born group had been so widely and favorably received in the United States, or had won such high marks from its hosts as had the Germans before World War I. Some public opinion surveys conducted before the war showed German Americans were even more highly regarded than immigrants from the mother culture, England. After the Great War it became clear that no ethnic group was so de-ethnicized in its public expression by a single historic event as German Americans. While Polish Americans, Lithuanian Americans, and other subject nationalities underwent a great consciousness raising, German ethnicity fell into a protracted and permanent slump. The war damaged public expression of German ethnic, linguistic, and cultural institutions almost beyond repair. Even today it is clear that Chicago's "Deutschtum" never experienced a third-generation revival; and no resurrection seems to be in the offing. While Chicago has museums and cultural exhibit halls and archives for Lithuanians, Ukrainians, Poles, Swedes, Jews, African Americans, and others, no museum or permanent public exhibit of German America is anywhere to be found. Being on the wrong side in two wars had a devastating and long-term negative impact on the public celebration of German-American ethnicity.

Without positive public recognition, German ethnicity was bound to go

---

18. P. T. Dietz, "The Transition from German to English in the Missouri Synod from 1910 to 1947," *Concordia Historical Institute Quarterly* XXII (October 1949), 102-103; D. W. Kolhoff, "Missouri Synod Lutherans and the image of Germany, 1914-1945" (Ph.D. dissertation, University of Chicago, 1973), p. 93; Holli, "Teuton vs. Slav," pp. 446f. On the national aspect of the decline, see LaVern Rippley, "Ameliorated Americanization: The Effects of World War I on German-Americans in the 1920s," in Frank Trommier and J. McVeigh, eds., *America and the Germans* (Philadelphia, 1985), pp. 224, 228, 17.

into a slump. It would never regain its prewar public acclaim, its larger-than-life public presence, with its symbols, rituals, and, above all, its large numbers of people who took pride in their Teutonic ancestry and enjoyed the role of Uncle Sam's favored adopted son.

After the Great War

The wartime anti-German hysteria had been such a searing experience for Chicago Germans that much of their hitherto visible cultural presence vanished from public view. Although several scholars have pointed out that subcultures under oppression can survive hidden and virtually underground, that has rarely been the case in the United States. Here public celebration of ethnicity has been an important sustaining and reinforcing ritual. The larger-than-life prewar presence in the public life of Chicago almost vanished with no fraternal or political leaders to replace those who had been discredited by what Americanizers perceived to be disloyalty.

One result of this lowered profile has been that scholars studying German-American public behavior have turned to adducing German-American social history and attitudes from voter patterns at the polls. Chastened by the war, Germans learned to keep their heads down and to express their public views only in the privacy of the secret ballot at election time. A keen student of that subject, Professor Frederick C. Luebke, describes this behavior as the "politics of revenge." Chicago Germans turned away from the Democrats, the party of war; already in 1918 they were voting against Democrats in Congressional elections. In 1920, "it was not that they were for Harding," the Republican Luebke writes, but "it was that they were against Wilsonianism" and the Democrats.[19] That year Chicago Teutons gave a record-high 82 percent of their votes to the Republican presidential candidate; the 1924 election registered a similar anti-Democratic vote. At that time the German American press and many lodge spokesmen endorsed a politically progressive presidential candidate, Robert LaFollette, not for his advanced reform ideas, but because he had been a firm supporter of German Americans during their time of trial. A third-party candidate with little hope of election, LaFollette drew a full third of Chicago's German vote, while the Democratic standard-bearer drew a mere 15 percent. The Republican presidential ticket, which supported the Dawes plan of loans to war-prostrated Germany, pulled half of the Windy City's German vote.[20]

Later in the decade (1927), the Republican Chicago mayoral candidate, William "Big Bill" Thompson, tapped a deep well of resentment among German

19. Frederick C. Luebke, "German-American Politics, 1870-1968," in R. Miller, ed., *Germans in America: Retrospect and Prospect* (Philadelphia, 1984), p. 69.

20. Leslie Tischauser, *The Burden of Ethnicity: The German Question in Chicago 1914-1941* (New York, 1990), p. 82.

voters when he vigorously campaigned against three of their bete noires: the League of Nations and the World Court; he promised not to enforce the national Prohibition law; and he promised to root out Chicago public school textbooks that lionized the British and cheated ethnics such as Germans from their fair share of credit for building America. He called his platform "America First." Big Bill handily took 63 percent of the German vote.[21]

The 1928 presidential election was more complicated by the issues of religion and Prohibition, which exerted cross-pressures on German voters. The normally powerful anti-Prohibition sentiment among German Lutherans was offset by Democratic candidate Al Smith's Catholic religion, and they voted mostly Republican. German Catholics, on the other hand, were doubly attracted to the "wet" candidate Smith and gave the Democrat a majority of their votes. The pain that caused the "politics of revenge" had not ceased; it was simply temporarily muted by two other sensitive issues, Prohibitionism and religion.[22]

By 1930, some German American leaders in Chicago felt, as Dr. Leslie Tischauser put it, "the damage done by the wartime experience had been largely repaired." The German language was being taught in the schools again; the German theater still survived; and German Day celebrations were drawing larger and larger crowds. Although the assimilation process had taken its toll of pre–1914 German immigrants, a smaller group of newer postwar arrivals had developed a vocal if not impolitic interest in the rebuilding process in Germany under National Socialism. As the 1930s moved on, Hitler's brutality and Nazi excesses made Germanism once again suspect. The rise of Nazism, as Luebke notes, "transformed German ethnicity in America into a source of social and psychological discomfort, if not distress. The overt expression of German-American opinion consequently declined, and in more recent years, virtually disappeared as a reliable index of political attitudes. . . ."[23]

The pain increased during the late 1930s and early 1940s, when Congressman Martin Dies held public hearings about the menace of Nazi subversives and spies among the German Americans. In 1940 the Democratic party's attack on anti-war elements as disloyal and pro-Nazi, and the advent of the war itself, made German ethnicity too heavy a burden to bear. As Professor Tischauser wrote, "The notoriety gained by those who supported the German government between 1933 and 1941 cast a pall over German-Americans everywhere. Leaders of the German-American community would have great difficulty rebuilding an ethnic consciousness. . . . Few German-Americans, however, could defend what Hitler . . . had done to millions of people in pursuit of the 'final solution,' and

21. Douglas Bukowski, "Big Bill Thompson," in P. Green and M. G. Holli, eds., *The Mayors: The Chicago Political Tradition* (Carbondale, IL, 1987), pp. 61f.

22. John Allswang, *A House for all Peoples; Ethnic Politics in Chicago, 1890-1936* (Lexington, KY, 1961), pp. 42, 192; Tischauser, *Burden of Ethnicity,* p. 174.

23. Tischauser, *Burden of Ethnicity,* p. 133; Luebke, "German-American Politics," pp. 70, 71.

the wisest course for German-Americans was to forget any attachment to the German half of their heritage."[24]

By the end of World War II, they were ethnics without any visible national or local leaders. Not even politicians would think of addressing them explicitly as an ethnic constituency as they would say, Polish Americans, Jewish Americans, or African Americans. They could take some comfort in the nation's discovery in the postwar period that Soviet Russia and communism were then the great enemies of freedom. This helped transform some pain into patriotism: a few leaders now pointed out that it was not Germanism but Sovietism that had all along been the greater enemy of free peoples.

By 1976, one of the city's most venerable and highly regarded (among Germans) clubs and landmarks, the Germania Club, had failed to attract young blood and new membership and was on its last legs. Hoping to leave a monument to Deutschtum's past, the club sought landmark status from the Chicago city council. But this request served only to resurrect the nightmares of the past. Critics charged that the building had been used by Bundists and Nazis and that some of its officers had been pro-Hitler before World War II. The council refused Germania landmark status, and the small collection of German American artifacts and art was dispersed. Germania was no more.

More recently — and beginning in 1966 — the German Day Association resuscitated a German Day parade but renamed it the Steuben Day parade. Although small by Chicago ethnic standards, such as those set by the St. Patrick's Day, Bud Billiken, and Columbus Day parades, it nonetheless has continued into the 1990s. The officers of the group have been mostly post-1945 immigrants with little link to the nineteenth century or the interwar German colonies.[25] The Turner and singing societies have also experienced a modest, quiet renaissance. Yet there is surprisingly little public awareness or public display of nineteenth-century German America's great impact on labor organization, the craftsmen and shopkeeper subculture, and the high culture of Chicago as exemplified by its symphony orchestra. No museum archive or exhibit hall memorializes one of the nineteenth century's most illustrious immigrant groups and its contributions to building the city and its cultural institutions.

24. Tischauser, *Burden of Ethnicity*, p. 254.

25. Interview with Carl Lashlet, January 17, 1991; Tischauser, *Burden of Ethnicity*, pp. 259-260. See also Hans A. Schiesser, "German *Kultur* in America: Has it Disappeared?" *Der Monat* (Vol. 2, No. 1, 1986), 25f.

CHAPTER 4

A Community Created:
Chicago Swedes, 1880-1950

ANITA R. OLSON

*We do not want to form a state within a state; but we want the Swedes
to be a salt in America that has a savor.*

Vilhelm Lundstrom (1922)

By 1880 the presence of Swedish immigrants had been evident in the city of
Chicago for nearly forty years. Countless early immigrants passed through
Chicago on their way to the rich farmland in the Midwest, but an increasing
number began to realize the opportunities that Chicago offered and remained
in the city. As Chicago grew in population and in area, its Swedish population
likewise increased. In 1880, Chicago — a city only forty-three years old —
boasted half a million inhabitants, nearly thirteen thousand of whom were born
in Sweden. Most of these Swedes lived in centralized enclaves, but this pattern
of settlement changed in subsequent years. By 1920 the number of Swedish
immigrants and their children in Chicago had reached 121,326.[1] As Swedish
immigrants moved to Chicago's newly developing suburbs, they brought strong
ethnic organization affiliations with them. These voluntary associations — both
religious and secular — gave the city greater personal meaning and provided a
means of uniting the immigrants' past in Sweden with the reality of living in
urban Chicago.

Ulf Beijbom has provided the most comprehensive analysis of Swedish
settlement in Chicago. His book *Swedes in Chicago*, delving into the early
Swedish community in Chicago between 1846 and 1880, breaks down the
settlement pattern of Swedes in Chicago into three distinct periods: the squatter
period, the formation of three main enclaves, and the era of the suburb. During

---

1. Statistics drawn from *The People of Chicago: Who We Are and Where We Have Been*
(Chicago: Department of Development and Planning, 1970).

the early squatter period, slum conditions predominated and life was marred by poverty and epidemics of cholera. By 1860, as Swedes became a bit more economically secure, they were moving to newly developing ethnic enclaves. The largest enclave became known as Swede Town and was located on the near North Side of the city. The other enclaves, numerically less significant, were found on Chicago's South and West sides. When Beijbom leaves the Swedes in 1880, they are living largely in these three main ethnic clusters.[2]

The era of Swedish suburbanization, however, was at hand. From 1880 to 1920, Swedes settled in suburban regions throughout the greater Chicago area. Better economic conditions and the changing ethnic composition of the city encouraged Swedes to move to these new regions, where they could build and own their own homes. And movement to suburban regions was accompanied by a proliferation of Swedish churches and clubs, institutions that provided the means for them to transfer their ethnic affiliations to new, scattered areas of Chicago, adding continuity to their lives and reaffirming their ethnicity.

The decade of the 1880s witnessed the merging of two separate trends: a surge in the number of people immigrating to the United States from Sweden and an explosive growth in the physical size and population of Chicago. Between 1879 and 1893, nearly half a million Swedes arrived in the United States, an average of over thirty-two thousand per year. A number of economic conditions created this mass exodus from the homeland, including crises in the timber and iron industries and the devastation of Sweden's agricultural sector.[3] By contrast, Chicago was a boomtown, offering jobs and plenty of space in which to live. During the 1880s alone, Chicago's population doubled, reaching a total of a million people; in that decade the number of Swedes living in the city more than tripled. This population explosion occurred simultaneously, with significant changes in the structure of the city of Chicago. The trend of population movement away from central Chicago, which had begun with the Chicago Fire in 1871, continued with the great influx of people during the 1880s and led to the ultimate annexation of these areas to the city in 1889. In this process, the size of the city grew by 125 square miles. Chicago's inhabitants lived in widely scattered areas, and population hubs remained interspersed with small truck farms often isolated from each other and removed from the city.[4]

The 1884 Chicago school census shows that Swedes were only beginning

2. Ulf Beijbom, *Swedes in Chicago: A Demographic and Social Study of the 1846-1880 Immigration* (Chicago: Chicago Historical Society, 1971).

3. Sten Carlsson, "Why Did They Leave?" in *Perspectives on Swedish Immigration*, ed. Nils Hasselmo (Chicago: Swedish Pioneer Historical Society, 1978), 25-35; Carlsson, "Chronology and Composition of Swedish Emigration to America," in *From Sweden to America: A History of the Migration*, ed. Harald Runblom and Hans Norman (Minneapolis: University of Minnesota Press, 1976), 114-29.

4. *The People of Chicago; Historic City: Settlement of Chicago* (Chicago: Department of Development and Planning, 1976); *Residential Chicago: Chicago Land Use Survey* (Chicago: Chicago Planning Commission, Works Progress Administration, 1942).

to respond to this trend in outward migration. This census gives a comprehensive listing of population by ethnic group, making it possible to analyze the density of Swedes and other ethnic groups in wards and in smaller districts within those wards. According to the 1884 census, 23,755 Swedes lived in Chicago: 58 percent on the North Side, 26 percent on the West Side, and 16 percent on the South Side. On the North Side the Swedish population centered around the area designated as Swede Town, concentrating most heavily in the region bordered by Division, Superior, Franklin, and Larrabee streets, and the North Branch of the Chicago River. Other important areas of Swedish settlement on the North Side surrounded this core; only one ward district as far north as Lincoln Park reflected any significant Swedish settlement. On the West Side, no such tight clustering of the Swedish population existed. The heaviest density of Swedes occurred in the southeast portion of North Lawndale, with other significant areas located on the near West Side, and in German and Norwegian sections of West Town. On the South Side, no census district held more than three hundred Swedes; the largest concentration of Swedish population occurred in an east-west corridor through Armour Square, McKinley Park, Bridgeport, and Douglas. On the whole, in 1884, Swedes most often settled in regions of Chicago with other immigrants, usually those from Germany, Ireland, and Norway. No Swede could be sheltered from interacting with other ethnic groups in the city.[5]

After this time, both the Swedish population and the population of the city of Chicago continued to grow. In 1890, when the number of people in Chicago reached the million mark, Swedish-born inhabitants and their American-born children represented nearly 6 percent of Chicago's entire population, ranking as the third largest ethnic group — behind the Germans and the Irish. Although immigration from Sweden declined during the American economic problems in the 1890s, it resumed from 1900 until the beginning of World War I. During the 1890s, the *Swedish-born* population in Chicago increased 14 percent, and from 1900 to 1910 it grew another 30 percent, to a peak of sixty-three thousand people. By the end of the next decade, this pattern of growth reversed itself, as the Swedish-born population actually declined by 7 percent. In 1920, over fifty-eight thousand American-born Swedes lived in Chicago. By this time, Chicago's incorporated area was fully integrated into the

5. *Report of the School Census, City of Chicago* (Chicago: Board of Education, 1884). The neighborhood boundaries were determined by sociologists at the University of Chicago in the 1930s and published in Ernest W. Burgess, ed., *Community Factbook* (Chicago: Chicago Recreation Commission, 1938). The 1884 census lists the "Nationality of White Persons by Wards"; African Americans and Asians are not included in these population figures. The census categorizes "Americans" as a separate ethnic group, and thus includes native whites only. Nationalities are not given for inmates of orphan asylums, hospitals, "Homes for the Friendless," and penal institutions, but these people are included in total population figures.

metropolitan region by a public transportation network that linked the outlying neighborhoods to the central business district.[6]

A look at the 1920 United States census reveals how the Swedes living in Chicago distributed themselves, reflecting an overall process of outward migration and population dispersal. Previously important regions of habitation, such as Swede Town, West Town, and the area on the South Side between 21st and 39th streets, reflected a remarkable decline in their importance to Swedish settlement. These areas came to be dominated largely by immigrant groups from southern and eastern Europe and by African Americans. By 1920 most Swedes lived in a ring outside the city's core, away from industrial areas along the North and South branches of the Chicago River. The primary areas where Swedes were the largest single ethnic group included the North Side neighborhoods of Lake View near Belmont Avenue and Clark Street, Andersonville at Clark Street and Foster Avenue, and North Park, located farther west on Foster Avenue. In western Chicago, Swedes dominated the Austin and Belmont-Cragin communities. In the southern part of Chicago, primary areas included one census tract in Armour Square — an old Swedish neighborhood — and several areas on the far South Side of Chicago: Hyde Park, Woodlawn, Englewood and West Englewood, South Shore, Greater Grand Crossing, East Side, Morgan Park, and Roseland. A number of other areas on the outskirts of the city held significant Swedish settlements. On the whole, despite the influx of immigrants from southern and eastern Europe, Swedes were least likely to settle in census districts dominated by Greeks, Czechs, Hungarians, Russians, Poles, Yugoslavians, and Italians; instead, they continued to settle near Germans, Irish, and Norwegians.[7]

The creation of the Swedish community in Chicago occurred in the context of this outward movement of the Swedish population. Although clusters of Swedish people were a necessary ingredient of institutional life, the community itself went beyond the purely territorial dimension of enclave settlement patterns. The voluntary associations created by the immigrants in the form of churches and social organizations transcended neighborhood boundaries, creating a complex institutional web throughout the city. From 1880 to 1920, the Swedes built more than 72 churches and more than 130 secular clubs. The variety of churches established — Augustana Lutheran, Mission Covenant, Free Church, and the Swedish branches of the Methodist and Baptist churches, among others — reflected the particular denominational interest of the Swedish people. Secular societies tended to develop in neighborhoods after the estab-

---

6. Cf. Carlsson, "Why Did They Leave?" and "Chronology and Composition of Swedish Emigration to America." See also *The People of Chicago; Land Use Survey,* 5; and "From Intramural to L," Chicago Historical Society Pamphlet Collection, 1923.

7. All 1920 census data extracted from Ernest W. Burgess and Charles Newcomb, eds., *Census Data of the City of Chicago, 1920* (Chicago: University of Chicago Press, 1931). In this census study, American-born are considered separately, thus ethnic groups reflect only the foreign-born. Americans dominated nearly all the census tracts.

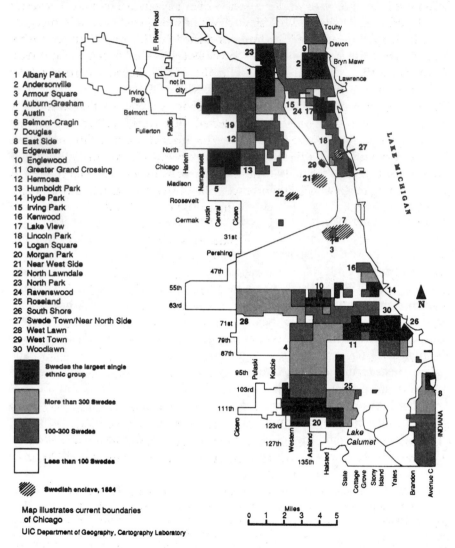

SWEDISH NEIGHBORHOODS IN CHICAGO, 1920

1 Albany Park
2 Andersonville
3 Armour Square
4 Auburn-Gresham
5 Austin
6 Belmont-Cragin
7 Douglas
8 East Side
9 Edgewater
10 Englewood
11 Greater Grand Crossing
12 Hermosa
13 Humboldt Park
14 Hyde Park
15 Irving Park
16 Kenwood
17 Lake View
18 Lincoln Park
19 Logan Square
20 Morgan Park
21 Near West Side
22 North Lawndale
23 North Park
24 Ravenswood
25 Roseland
26 South Shore
27 Swede Town/Near North Side
28 West Lawn
29 West Town
30 Woodlawn

Swedes the largest single
ethnic group

More than 300 Swedes

100-300 Swedes

Less than 100 Swedes

Swedish enclave, 1884

Map illustrates current boundaries
of Chicago

UIC Department of Geography, Cartography Laboratory

lishment of the mainline Swedish churches at a point when the Swedish population was large enough to sustain a variety of organizational interest. The result was the creation of diverse Swedish enclaves in widespread areas of Chicago.[8]

In 1880, thirteen Swedish churches existed in Chicago; all but one were located in Swedish enclaves in Swede Town, Douglas-Armour Square, and West Town. Since transportation networks in the city of Chicago were not fully developed, members of these older churches who moved to new suburbs of Chicago could not easily reach their old congregations, so they built new churches closer to their homes that reflected their particular denominational persuasion. Once built, these churches became magnets for first-time members. Swedes organized at least twenty-seven churches in Chicago during the 1880s alone, more than tripling the 1880 number. These churches were built in regions just beginning to show their importance to Swedish settlement: South Chicago, South Shore, Pullman, Roseland, and Englewood on the South Side; the Lower West Side, Austin, and Humboldt Park on the West Side; and Lake View, Logan Square, and Ravenswood on the North Side. Growth continued during the 1890s and the first decade of the twentieth century, when the number of Swedish churches grew by forty-two. Additional neighborhoods where Swedish churches were built included the Summerdale-Andersonville area, North Park, Irving Park, Edgewater, Portage Park, Hyde Park, and West Englewood. From 1910 to 1920, the number of new Swedish-speaking churches established in Chicago dropped sharply — only three new churches were founded. The era of rampant institutional expansion drew to a close as the number of native-born Swedes in Chicago dropped and an American-born, English-speaking generation took their place.[9]

Swedish organizational life, in its infancy in 1880, matured in the subsequent decades. According to Beijbom, forty Swedish organizations existed in Chicago prior to 1880, varying in purpose from general social interaction aimed at the middle class to trade societies and sports and recreation clubs.[10] Most of

8. Church addresses and listings derived from Tom Hutchinson, comp., *The Lakeside Annual Directory of Chicago* (Chicago: Chicago Directory Company, 1880, 1889, 1899, 1910, 1915, 1917).

9. Statistics and locations of Lutheran churches derived from *Protokoll hallet vid Skandinaviska Evangeliska Lutherska Synodens arsmote (1880-94); Referat ofver Evangelisk Lutherska Augustana-Synodens arsmote (1895-1920); Almanack* (Rock Island: Augustana Book Concern, 1920). For Covenant Church statistics, see *Protokoll. Svenska Evangeliska Missions-Forbundet i Amerika* (Chicago, 1885-1920); for Baptist information, see *Arsbok for Svenska Baptist-forsamlingarna inom Amerika* (Chicago, 1908, 1909); for Methodist churches, see *Protokoll ofver forhandlingarna vid Nordvestra Svenska arskonferensen (1877-93); Protokoll fordt vid forsta arliga sammantradet af Metodist Episkopal Kyrkans Svenska Central Konferens (1894-1920)*. Free Church information is found in *De forsta tjugo aren eller begynnelsen till Svenska Evangeliska Frikyrkan i Nord Amerikas Forenade Stater enligt protokoll inforda i Chicago Bladet (1883-1903); Protokoll ofver Svenska Evangeliska Fria Missionens arsmote (1904-20)*.

10. Beijbom, *Swedes in Chicago;* Beijbom, "Swedish-American Organizational Life," in *Scandinavia Overseas: Patterns of Cultural Transformation in North America and Australia,* Harald Runblom and Dag Blanck, eds. (Uppsala: Centre for Multi-ethnic Research, 1986), 57f.

these associations were loosely organized and few survived beyond 1880. None exerted positions of leadership in Swedish associational life after that date. The newer organizations differed significantly from their predecessors. Functionally, many of them served purposes of social interaction, much like earlier associations. In the case of fraternal societies, however, that social agenda was balanced with a beneficiary system that provided sick and death benefits to workers and their families who were unprotected in their American work environment. This social insurance program broadened the appeal of many benevolent societies beyond the middle class to include many working-class individuals. Structurally, the new associations departed widely from earlier models, as groups such as the Svithiod and Viking orders created overarching grand lodges, with smaller, neighborhood lodges functioning as subordinated clubs. Upon moving to new areas of Chicago, many Swedish settlers laid the foundation of new associations in their neighborhoods. This expansion under the guise of central grand lodges created an umbrella effect that kept the structure of large organizations intact while allowing for branch lodges to follow the Swedish population into dispersed areas throughout the city.[11]

As Swedes abandoned their older ethnic enclaves for new neighborhoods, the neighborhoods themselves underwent a transformation from farmland to subdivision to ethnic enclave. Both small and large Swedish hubs that had begun as outlying farming regions subdivided into urban settlements on the outskirts of the city. New settlers moved to these areas to build their own homes and improve their living conditions. For example, Swedes living in Armour Square in the 1880s worried about their health: the factories springing up in the area, as well as the stockyards, polluted the air. When they had the opportunity to move farther south to new suburbs such as Englewood, many did so. Some economic stability was needed to afford a new home in Englewood, but as one son of Swedish immigrants remembered, "It was just as cheap in the long run to go to the newer sections and build a new home" as it was to upgrade an older home in Armour Square.[12] To Swedes who had any intention of staying in Chicago, conditions in Armour Square were not acceptable. This same man observed that "there were lawns and gardens to be found in the new places, whereas down in the old settlement the houses were built to the sidewalks, and no chance was given for any beautification. The people down there began to be nothing but foreigners who cared nothing for making the neighborhood attractive."[13] It is interesting that this comment came from a second-generation Swede, who apparently considered his family to be quite Americanized.

11. Axel Hulten, ed., *Swedish-American Participation in "A Century of Progress"* (Chicago: A.V.S.S. Festcommittee, 1933), in the Swedish American Archives of Greater Chicago, North Park College; *Runristningar: Independent Order of Vikings 1890-1915* (Chicago: Martenson, 1915).

12. Chicago Historical Society, *Documents: History of . . . Communities, Chicago,* research under the direction of Vivian Palmer, Chicago, 1925-30, vol. 6, part 1, doc. 9e.

13. *Ibid.*

Swede Town continued to be the largest single hub of Swedish population during the 1880s, after which time its relative importance to Swedish settlement began to decline. Church membership in that region peaked during 1887 at Immanuel Lutheran Church and in 1892 and 1893 in the Covenant and Methodist churches respectively.[14] A German grocer living in the district during this period noted that "it was an Irish, German and Swedish neighborhood then. The people didn't live in segregated groups but did live altogether harmoniously."[15] The nature of Swede Town, however, soon began to change. A Jewish business leader observed that the coming of the elevated train (the "L") changed the neighborhood dramatically: "It became a poorer district and more commercialized. The 'L' was noisy and people did not like to live near it, consequently, rents decreased."[16] A Swedish woman attributed falling rents to "the factories [that] have been encroaching upon the district."[17] Swedes were also unhappy with demographic changes, as Italians and African Americans moved into the area. "Before the Italians came," claimed this same Swedish woman, "the district was much better and cleaner." She noted that the "Swedish people sold two of their churches to the Negroes very cheaply."[18] The Free church and Baptist church moved to new locations on the North Side in 1910 and 1911, and Immanuel Lutheran relocated in Edgewater in 1920. A number of people believed that the "coming of Italians has . . . caused the Swedish and Irish to move north."[19] This may have been partially true, but to many Swedes the possibility of building new homes in attractive neighborhoods proved to be the most powerful incentive for moving to new areas of the city.

In the 1870s, Lake View was largely a rural community where truck farming and livestock trading dominated local affairs. Gradually, the area began to assume the characteristics of an urban neighborhood. In the next decade — known as the "Golden Years" in Lake View — building boomed and the population soared. *The Chicago Land Use Survey,* conducted in 1940 and published in 1942, estimated that 43 percent of all homes in Lake View were built between 1880 and 1894.[20] Churches of a variety of denominations and ethnic persuasions were established in Lake View during this time, including five Swedish churches. From 1890 to 1919, Swedes established eleven lodges in the area. Although the Trinity Lutheran Church continued to grow after 1920, membership in Lake View's Methodist church peaked in 1908, and in the Covenant church in 1913. By this time, a University of Chicago student observed that "the

14. *Protokoll* from Lutheran, Mission Covenant, and Methodist denominations.
15. Palmer, vol. 3, part 2, doc. 18.
16. *Ibid.,* doc. 21.
17. *Ibid.,* doc. 22.
18. *Ibid.*
19. *Ibid.,* doc. 23, interview conducted by Mr. Zorbaugh, 1923.
20. *Land Use Survey;* Stephen Bedel Clark and Patrick Butler, *The Lake View Saga, 1837-1985* (Chicago: Lakeview Trust and Savings Bank of Chicago, 1985), pamphlet collection, Chicago Historical Society.

Belmont Avenue-Clark Street neighborhood had definitely taken on the aspect of a temporary stopping place for immigrants. Since then the older residents have moved farther north."[21] Lake View continued to be an important Swedish enclave, but it was beginning to relinquish its prominence to Andersonville, its neighbor to the north.

The development of a Swedish enclave in the Summerdale-Andersonville area demonstrates the persistence of ethnicity in a new suburb. Before 1890, this region was mostly rural, inhabited by a handful of American, German, and Swedish settlers who operated truck farms, blacksmith shops, or earned some kind of livelihood from the traffic passing through on its way to the city. Developers subdivided the land in 1890, but the boom in settlement came after 1908, when transportation links to the city improved and made Andersonville a viable residential option for those people who commuted to work. Fred Nelson, a Swede who moved to Summerdale in 1892, observed that at the time only a few Swedish families lived there, most of them arriving after 1890: "The influx [of Swedes] was always gradual. . . . I would say the reason Swedish people came here was because lots were cheap. They came from Swedish settlements further south."[22]

The Ebenezer Lutheran Church, formed in 1892, was the first Swedish church in Andersonville. Before that time, Swedes had not migrated to the area in any significant numbers, and the Swedish population could not sustain ethnic institutions. Many of the earliest Swedish settlers, therefore, attended American churches since no ethnic options existed. A pastor of the Summerdale Congregational Church reminisced about the time when his church was truly a community church, drawing in its neighbors regardless of their ethnic persuasion. "There were some Scandinavians in the locality when the church was started in 1890. . . . But after 1900 with the increase in the Scandinavian element in our population, the membership decreased, for the Scandinavians very naturally and properly went to their own religious organizations as they were organized. In 1914, then, when the Swedish influx assumed its largest proportions, our little church was nearly in a state of insolvency."[23] A member of another Congregational church in the area remembered that "when the Swedish churches came and took the Swedish members away from us we couldn't make the church pay."[24] Swedes who had had no alternative but to join American churches attended their own ethnic institutions once they were built, demonstrating the strength of Swedish affiliations even after a period of interaction with non-Swedes.

By 1920, Swedish arrivals in Chicago were greeted by a complex ethnic community fundamentally different from the community of 1880. The city of

21. Palmer, vol. 3, part 1, doc. 10.
22. *Ibid.*, vol. 2, part 1, doc. 19, 1.
23. *Ibid.*, doc. 28, 1, interview with Rev. Silas Meckel.
24. *Ibid.*, doc. 6, 4, interview with Walter H. Baxter.

Chicago had grown and expanded, and its population had become more ethnically diverse. The Swedish enclaves, no longer as centralized as they had been in
1880, spread throughout the city. Swedes coped with this dispersion by creating
institutions that allowed for continuity of expression in terms of their ideological,
religious, and social values, and which mitigated the possible dislocating and
alienating effects of migration. Instead of shaping Swedish American behavior by
loosening ethnic ties, the newly developing suburban regions allowed Swedish
immigrants to exert power over their environment and recreate their community
affiliations. While reflecting the diversity within the Swedish community, the
existence of these institutions strengthened ethnic consciousness in areas removed
from central Chicago and asserted the Swedish presence in the city.

*   *   *

After 1920, the Swedish-born population of Chicago diminished dramatically,
from 65,735 in 1930 to 7,005 in 1970. The population of Swedes and their
American-born children dropped during these same years from 140,913 to
26,988. Between 1930 and 1950, Swedish immigrants and their children still
ranked as the city's fifth largest group, behind Poles, Germans, Russians, and
Italians; but the *Swedish-born* proportion of Chicago's population had shrunk
considerably, from 1.95% in 1930 to only 0.86% in 1950. The decade of the
1960s marked a turning point in the ethnic composition of the city: Swedes
went from the seventh largest group in 1960 to the fourteenth in 1970, only
0.21% of Chicago's population. By that time, many more groups had surpassed
the Swedes, including those from Mexico, Greece, Yugoslavia, Ireland, Lithuania,
Cuba, Austria, Czechoslovakia, and the Philippines.[25]

The primary reason for the decline in the Swedish population in Chicago
was the overall drop in the number of Swedish immigrants arriving to American
shores. Swedish immigration never again reached the levels of the 1880s, and
after a brief surge in the 1920s, it flattened out during the Depression. Despite
the declining numbers, Chicago itself remained a favorite destination of Amer-
ican-bound Swedish immigrants well into the 20th century: in 1940, Chicago
was still the largest Swedish-American city in the United States, with nearly
twice as many inhabitants of Swedish stock as the second largest city, Minneapolis.[26] Furthermore, as Harald Runblom points out, the Swedish population in Chicago was younger than in most other American cities, thus Chicago
"received much stronger impulses from Sweden during the last phase of mass
migration," resulting in a strong Swedish cultural life.[27]

25. *The People of Chicago.*
26. Sture Lindmark, *Swedish America, 1914-1931: Studies in Ethnicity with Emphasis on
Illinois and Minnesota* (Upsala: Studia Historica Upsaliensia, 1971), p. 31; also see Lars Ljungmark,
Swedish Exodus (Carbondale and Edwardsville: Southern Illinois University Press, 1979).
27. Harald Runblom, "Chicago Compared: Swedes and Other Ethnic Groups in American

After 1920, social organizations continued to serve as important centers of Swedish ethnicity. Mirroring the decline in Chicago's Swedish population, organizational membership also diminished, particularly after 1930. Membership in the Svithiod lodges, for example, reached its peak in 1927, and after that time the lodges began to struggle with their role within the Swedish-American community. As different generations of immigrants grew older, became well-adapted to life in Chicago, and were not replaced by as many new immigrants from Sweden, older fraternal orders no longer filled a necessary function of helping the newcomers adapt to the city. Instead, they served as a means of promoting ethnic identity within the city of Chicago.[28]

Membership in the two largest Swedish denominations, the Augustana Lutheran and Covenant churches, continued to grow after 1920. Perhaps more than any other organizations, the churches realized the importance of reaching out to a largely English-speaking second generation. The Swedish churches gradually converted their official language to English, a task that was hotly debated but was officially complete by the end of the 1920s. After that time, many churches supported only one Swedish-language service a month in order to satisfy the older immigrant generation. Even as these ethnic institutions embraced the English language, they continued to serve as important cultural centers for the Swedish American community in Chicago by perpetuating their Swedish ethnic heritage through forms of worship, music, and traditional celebrations.[29]

As the Swedish neighborhoods of the 1920s diversified, diminishing in their Swedish character, ethnic organizations continued to serve as important sources of identity and pride. In fact, the Swedish Americans themselves were strongly aware of the importance of preserving their own particular heritage — not only their Swedish roots, but their Swedish American legacy. The Swedish presence in Chicago had reached its centennial year when the Swedish Pioneer Historical Society was formed in 1948 to "record the achievements of the Swedish pioneers and to stimulate and promote interest in Swedish and Swedish-American contributions to the development and life of the United States of America. . . ."[30] In the first issue of the Swedish Pioneer Historical Quarterly that appeared in 1950, Vilas Johnson, the society's president, noted: "The Americans of Swedish background hold the keys to unlock the doors to a full appreciation of the achievements of the Swedish pioneers, the Swedish immigrants and their descendants. This vital chapter in the history of America

Cities," in Philip J. Anderson and Dag Blanck, eds. *Swedish-American Life in Chicago: Cultural and Urban Aspects of an Immigrant People, 1850-1930* (Urbana and Chicago: University of Illinois Press, 1992), 71-72.

28. Timothy J. Johnson, "The Independent Order of Svithiod: A Swedish-American Lodge in Chicago," in *Swedish-American Life in Chicago*, 343-363. See also Lindmark, pp. 304-320.

29. See Lindmark.

30. Christopher Olsson and Ruth McLaughlin, eds., *American-Swedish Handbook* (Minneapolis: Swedish Council of America, Eleventh Edition, 1992), p. 115.

This Chicago Swedish restaurant advertised authentic Swedish smorgasbord dinners
for 90 cents and luncheons for 45 cents in 1942.   Courtesy Perry Duis collection.

that concerns the Swedes must be written without delay before priceless records
are forever lost; before the memory of our many leaders and their great accomplishments have dimmed."[31]

By the 1950s, Sweden-born Chicagoans lacked the numerical strength to
dominate Chicago's Swedish American community and no longer numbered
among the city's largest ethnic groups. Although the Andersonville neighborhood
remained an important Swedish American center, with shops, churches, and
nearby North Park College and Swedish Covenant Hospital, it lacked the dense
clustering of Swedish residents of an earlier time. Other ethnics and Americans
were moving in. But even today some Swedish flavor can be experienced there. As
third- and fourth-generation Swedes dispersed residentially, the work of Swedish
fraternals, churches, and foundations such as the Swedish Pioneer Historical
Society, which did not depend upon residential clustering, became even more
important in reminding Chicagoans of a Swedish American presence in Chicago.
By mid-century and after, the ethnic identity of Chicago's Swedes was decidedly
Swedish American. The descendants of the immigrants and pioneer settlers saw
themselves as Americans, but with a unique Swedish-American heritage.

31. Vilas Johnson, "The Challenge to Americans of Swedish Background," *Swedish Pioneer
Historical Quarterly 1* (1950), 5-6.

CHAPTER 5

The Jews of Chicago:
From Shtetl to Suburb

IRVING CUTLER

Jews came to Chicago from almost every country in Europe. By 1930 there were some 275,000 Jews in the city, comprising 8 percent of its population. Chicago had the third largest Jewish population of any city in the world at the time — exceeded only by New York and Warsaw.

Like the members of other immigrant groups, Jews left Europe because of economic, political, and religious difficulties. For Jewish immigrants, however, these difficulties were often compounded by a virulent anti-Semitism and even sporadic massacres. The most affluent and educated members of other immigrant groups often remained in their homelands, where they occupied secure and respected positions. But Jews of all economic strata and educational levels welcomed the opportunity to emigrate from most central and eastern European communities. Because of the harsh treatment they had suffered and because they were usually considered aliens in their homelands, even though they may have lived there for centuries, Jews were less interested in returning to Europe than were any other immigrant groups, despite some lingering sentimental attachments.

Most of the European Jewish immigrants to America settled along the East Coast, especially in New York City; but large numbers also made their way westward to the relatively accessible and thriving Chicago area. Although the opportunities for those who came to Chicago were at times limited by covert discrimination on the job, in housing, and in education, especially during the earlier years, the opportunities of a free nation enabled them to flourish. Despite their varied homelands and backgrounds, Jews in time overcame periods of internal discord and achieved a degree of unity based on a common heritage, the problems of being a minority in a gentile world, and most recently by a common desire for the success of Israel.

The First Wave: The German-Speaking Jews

Unlike the early Jewish settlers of colonial New York, who were mainly Sephardic Jews from the Mediterranean — with their distinct liturgy, religious customs, and pronunciation of the Hebrew language — the Jews who first settled in Chicago were Ashkenazim of central and eastern Europe. There were no Sephardim among Chicago's Jewish pioneers, although small numbers of Sephardim did come to the city later.

The Ashkenazic Jews of Chicago fell into two relatively distinct groups. The first to arrive were German-speaking Jews from Central Europe — from Bavaria, the Rhenish Palatinate, Prussia, Austria, Bohemia, and the Posen part of Poland that was occupied by the Germans. Many of these Jews had experienced some of the political, intellectual, and economic benefits of the French Revolution during the decades that preceded the Congress of Vienna (1814-1815). Subsequently, however, there was some retrogression in the position of the Jews. In 1816 the Prussian minister of finance said:

> It would be desirable not to have any Jews at all among us. Since we have them, however, we have to put up with them; but we must strive incessantly to render them as powerless as possible. The conversion of Jews to the Christian faith must be facilitated; all civil rights flow from that. But as long as the Jew remains a Jew, he cannot obtain a position in the state.[1]

Despite restrictions such as that in their homelands, the German-speaking Jews were more secular and urbane and more well-to-do than the second group, the Eastern European Jews who came in much larger numbers later. The latter were Yiddish-speaking Jews who came mainly from Russia, Poland, Romania, and Lithuania — areas where Jews suffered political and economic handicaps and were often subjected to especially severe persecution. They were a poor, deeply religious people, and most of them lived in small towns and villages (shtetls).

Among the earliest settlers in Chicago were small numbers of German Jews, mainly from Bavaria, who began to trickle into the area in the late 1830s and early 1840s. Among those who arrived in 1841 was Henry Horner, a Bohemian Jew who later became an organizer of the Chicago Board of Trade and a founder of a major wholesale grocery company, originally established at the western fringes of settlement at Randolph and Canal streets. His grandson of the same name served as governor of Illinois from 1933 to 1940.

In 1845 the Jews of Chicago held their first religious service on the Day

---

1. Bildarchiv Preussischer Kulturbestz, *Jews in Germany Under Prussian Rule* (Berlin, 1984), p. 33.

of Atonement. That same year they organized the Jewish Burial Ground Society, and in 1846 they purchased an acre of land for forty-six dollars (in what is now Lincoln Park) for use as a Jewish cemetery. In 1847, above a dry goods store owned by Rosenfeld and Rosenberg on the southwest corner of Lake and Wells, about fifteen men formed Kehilath Anshe Mayriv (Congregation of the People of the West), or K.A.M., Chicago's first Jewish congregation — an Orthodox one. In 1851 the congregation, at an estimated cost of $12,000, erected a small frame synagogue on Clark Street just south of Adams Street (a site now commemorated by a plaque on the Kluczynski Federal Building).

The *Daily Democrat* of June 14, 1851, reported the dedication of the synagogue as follows:

> The ceremonies at the dedication of the first Jewish synagogue in Illinois, yesterday, were very interesting indeed. An immense number had to go away, from inability to gain admittance. There were persons of all denominations present. We noticed several clergymen of different religious denominations.
>
> The Jewish ladies cannot be beaten in decorating a church. The flowers, leaves and bushes were woven into the most beautiful drapery that Chicago ever saw before. The choir, consisting of a large number of ladies and gentlemen, did honor to the occasion and the denomination. . . .

As for any possible prejudice or anti-Semitism in Chicago, the newspaper went on with considerable enthusiasm:

> No person that has made up his mind to be prejudiced against the Jews ought to hear such a sermon preached. It was very captivating and contained as much real religion as any sermon we ever heard preached. We never could have believed that one of those old Jews we heard denounced so much could have taught so much liberality towards other denominations and earnestly recommended a thorough study of the Old Testament (each one for himself) and entire freedom of opinion and discussion. . . .
>
> The Jews in our city are not numerous, but are wealthy, very respectable and public spirited.
>
> The Jewish Sabbath is on Saturday, and a very interesting service takes place today. The whole Mosaic law written on parchment (they never have it printed for church services) will be unrolled from a large scroll and read from.
>
> Gentlemen are requested to keep their hats on, and to take seats below. The ladies will take seats upstairs, according to the Jewish custom of separating the sexes.

In 1853 the congregation organized a day school. Two of its best-loved teachers were Irishmen who taught the first-born Jewish generation in Chicago not only the grammar school curriculum but also some rudimentary Hebrew. Early Chicago was a city of many immigrants, without an ingrained social structure. Unlike in Europe, Jews were accepted in the social milieu as well as in civic affairs, with a few of the German-Jewish immigrants holding political office, including those of alderman and city clerk.

The defeat of the revolutionary movements that swept central Europe in 1848 increased Jewish immigration to the United States, and by 1860 there were approximately 1,500 in Chicago. Most of them lived around Lake and Wells streets, the business center, where a few owned clothing and dry goods stores. Such stores were often established by Jews who had started out as virtually penniless backpacking peddlers. The owners usually lived behind or above the stores. Later, large-scale retailers such as Mandel Brothers, Goldblatts, Rothschilds, Maurice B. Sachs, Polk Brothers, Aldens, and Spiegels grew from similarly modest beginnings, as did manufacturers like Hart, Schaffner & Marx, Kuppenheimer, and Florsheim.

By 1870 the Chicago Jewish community, enlarged by further immigration, had spread out somewhat, the largest concentration settling between Van Buren Street (north), Polk Street (south), the Chicago River (west), and Lake Michigan (east). By then there were a number of B'nai Brith fraternal lodges, the United Hebrew Relief Association, women's organizations, literary and dramatic groups, a hospital, and seven synagogues that were scattered throughout what is today's central business district. Chicago's second congregation, B'nai Sholom, was founded in 1849 by a K.A.M. splinter group that wished to be more Orthodox. B'nai Sholom's first building was on Harrison and Fourth Avenue (Federal Street). Today B'nai Sholom is back with its parent congregation as part of K.A.M. Isaiah Israel in Hyde Park.

The third oldest Jewish congregation in Chicago, Sinai Temple, was first located in a former Christian church on Monroe Street just east of La Salle. It was founded in 1861 as Chicago's first Reform congregation by twenty-six men who had seceded from K.A.M. because they considered it too Orthodox. The secessionists wanted a more westernized prayerbook, head coverings to be removed in the temple, and the maintenance of decorum and uniformity in prayer instead of each man being more or less on his own. Developed earlier in the century in Germany, Reform Judaism emphasized the progressive nature of Judaism. Sinai Temple is now in Hyde Park. Other early congregations that are still in existence include Zion Congregation (today's Oak Park Temple), established in 1864 on Des Plaines between Madison and Washington streets, and North Chicago Hebrew Congregation (today's Temple Sholom on north Lake Shore Drive), established at Superior Street near Wells Street in 1867.[2] In time, all of these temples adhered to Reform Judaism, though some practiced a more traditional kind of Judaism when they were first founded.

In 1869 a number of prominent Jews, reflecting their growing numbers and affluence, organized the Standard Club, mainly as a social and recreational

2. Morris A. Gutstein, *A Priceless Heritage* (New York, 1953), pp. 25-34.

gathering place; it later became active in civic and communal affairs and supported many worthy causes. Its earliest members included individuals who were
or would become very successful, such as Dankmar Adler, architect; Judge Philip
Stein; Nelson Morris, meat packer; Elias, Michael, and Henry Greenebaum,
bankers; Abraham Kohn, city clerk; Simon Florsheim, Charles Schwab, Bernard
Kuppenheimer, and Emanuel Mandel, manufacturers and merchants.

An 1870 city business directory showed that people believed to be Jews
were engaged in almost fifty different occupations at the time. The leading
occupations and the number engaged in each were as follows:[3]

Dry Goods	80	Hardware	10
Cigar and Tobacco	66	Carpenters	9
Clothing	59	Lawyers	9
Boots and Shoes	43	Second Hand Stores	8
Distillers and Saloons	34	Architects	7
Tailors	32	Books	7
Meat Markets	22	Real Estate	7
Furniture	17	Upholsterers	6
Variety Stores	16	Boarding Houses	6
Furriers	15	Crockery	6
Jewelers	13	Druggists	6
Physicians	11	Livery Stables	6
Commissioned Merchants	11	Vinegar	5
Bakers	11	Bankers	5
Barbers	11	Dentists	5
Flour and Feed	11	Blacksmiths	5
Dressmakers	10		

The table indicates that a high percentage of Jews were merchants either in the
retail or wholesale trade, with smaller numbers being professionals or skilled
craftsmen.

The Great Fire of 1871, as well as another one on the near South Side in
1874, destroyed most of the homes and businesses of the Chicago Jewish community, and most of the synagogues. Immediately after the Great Fire of 1871,
Jewish organizations sent out a national appeal for additional aid, and relief
soon came pouring in from many parts of the nation, even from overseas. After
the fire, the *Chicago Times* noted with approval: "Not one Jew has been sent to
ask for the aid of the general or special relief committee of the Gentiles."[4] The

3. *Edwards 13th Annual Directory of the Inhabitants, Incorporated Companies, and Manufacturing establishments of the City of Chicago embracing a Complete Business Directory for 1870*
(Chicago, 1870). As classified by Michael Charney in 1974.
    4. Ron Grossman, "Touring Chicago's Older Jewish Neighborhoods." *Jewish Chicago* (Sep-
tember, 1982), 45.

fire of 1874 inflicted major damage, especially on the poor Russian-Polish Jewish community. This time there was only limited local response to an appeal for aid, for many of the German Jews had been financially drained by the first fire and because they did not take kindly to the newer, culturally different Russian-Polish Jewish immigrants, who, they feared, lowered the status of all the local Jews. The highly respected Rabbi Liebman Adler of K.A.M. was asked to help in the raising of funds and to try to dispel the narrow sectionalism among the Jewish groups in Chicago. His message read as follows and had the desired effect:

> Scarce two decades have elapsed since all the Israelites of this city were living as in the bonds of one family circle. Each knew the other. All worshipped harmoniously in one temple and shared others' woes and joys.
>
> How great is the change! Thousands scattered over a space of nearly thirty miles, in hundreds of streets, divided by pecuniary, intellectual and social distinctions, provincial jealousies, and even religious distinctions and differences. Separation, division, dissolution, estrangement, repeated and continual, are the words which characterize the history of our brothers in faith until now. Dissolved in the mass of our population, we are losing the consciousness of homogeneity and the strength gained for each individual by concerted action.
>
> Let us also consider the oft-heard complaint that Poles and Russians absorb a disproportional large share of the means of this Association.
>
> Brothers and Sisters: Are these poor ones less to be pitied, are they less poor, are they less Israelites because Poland or Russia is the land in which they first saw the light, or rather the darkness of the world? The poor of those countries are doubly poor. These unfortunates came to us from a country which is the European headquarters for barbarism, ignorance, and uncleanliness. In these countries, thousands of Israelites are densely crowded into small towns and villages, and they become singular and peculiar in their customs, manners, and ideas. In conferring charity, it is the duty of the Israelite first to look to the needs and then to the deserts of the recipient.[5]

After the fires the German Jews, who were increasing rapidly in number, moved out of the expanding business area and settled one or more miles south of the downtown area along such streets as Michigan, Wabash, and Indiana. Eventually they moved into the Grand Boulevard, Washington Park, Kenwood–Hyde Park areas, and later into South Shore. As they moved, they built numerous synagogues and institutions to take care of the needy. After World War I, the South Side Jewish community also included many persons of Eastern European descent.

The southward movement of German Jews can be traced by the relocations of the K.A.M. Congregation: in 1875 it moved from the downtown area

5. Hyman L. Meites, ed., *History of the Jews of Chicago* (Chicago, 1924), p. 133.

Prominent German-Jewish club women at a social-political event in
Chicago in 1900.   Courtesy of the University of Illinois Library, Chicago.

to 26th and Indiana Avenue; in 1891 it occupied a beautiful temple at 33rd and
Indiana Avenue, built by the renowned architect Dankmar Adler (whose father
was a rabbi of K.A.M.); in 1920 it moved to 50th and Drexel Boulevard; and it
is now part of K.A.M. Isaiah Israel, located at 1100 Hyde Park Boulevard. This
is the congregation's seventh synagogue home in its 144-year history; its average
tenure per site has been about twenty years.

Similarly, Sinai Congregation moved to 21st and Indiana Avenue in 1876,
to 46th and what is now King Drive in 1912, and to Hyde Park in 1950. The
congregation was headed from 1880 to 1923 by the nationally prominent Rabbi
Emil G. Hirsch (1851-1923), who was born in Luxembourg. Rabbi Hirsch
helped to bring about or solidify numerous radical reforms in his congregation,
including the controversial and temporary elimination of the traditional ark.
In addition, he curtailed Hebrew reading and prayers at the congregation's
services, which were held on Sunday instead of Saturday. In forceful sermons
and numerous articles in Reform journals, Rabbi Hirsch strongly defended the
evolutionary concept of Judaism. He generally opposed Jewish Zionist-nation-
alism, and he championed the rights of organized labor and the inauguration

of pioneering welfare reforms in Chicago. He edited Jewish Reform periodicals, was one of the original faculty members of the University of Chicago, where he taught rabbinic literature and philosophy, and served as president of the Chicago Public Library Board. More than half a century later, Edward Levi, one of his grandsons, served as president of the University of Chicago and as Attorney General in President Gerald Ford's cabinet.

The German Jews were on friendly terms with the non-Jewish Germans of Chicago and identified quite closely with them: they spoke the same language, and in many instances they had been forced by common political views to leave Germany after the collapse of the revolutions of 1848. The German Jews read German newspapers, attended German theaters, and belonged to German organizations. Even with their good relations with the German non-Jews, however, they built their own welfare facilities and took care of their own. They founded the Michael Reese Hospital on the South Side in 1880, the Chicago Home for the Jewish Aged in 1893, and the Chicago Home for Jewish Orphans in 1899.

During the Civil War, some Jews belonged to army units that were made up predominantly of Germans. Other Jews quickly formed a volunteer company of Jewish troops known as the Concordia Guards, and the Jewish community helped finance its expenses. On August 16, 1862, the *Chicago Tribune* published the following tribute to the Jews of Chicago:

> Our Israelite citizens have gone beyond even their most sanguine expectations. Their princely contribution of itself is a record which must ever redound to their patriotism. The rapidity with which the company was enlisted has not its equal in the history of recruiting. In barely thirty-six hours' time they have enlisted a company reaching beyond the maximum, of gallant, strong-armed, stouthearted men, who will make themselves felt in the war. The ladies have set an enduring example by their contributions, their earnest work, and their encouragement of the recruits. In two days, the Israelites have paid in over $11,000; in a day and a half they have raised more than a full company and mustered it in; in one day the ladies have subscribed for and made a beautiful flag. Can any town, city, or state in the North show an equally good two days' work? The Concordia Guards have our best wishes for their future and our hopes that victory may always crown their aims.

As part of the 82nd Illinois Volunteer Infantry Regiment, the company participated in a number of Civil War encounters, including Gettysburg and Sherman's march to the sea. When the war ended, the regiment returned home to a huge welcoming reception, where Mayor John Wentworth's speech included the following:

> A few years since, there was a cry raised that "foreigners" could not be trusted, and an attempt was made to disenfranchise you, but when at last the time came that tried men's souls — when native-born Americans proved false to

their allegiance to their flag, and tried their utmost to tear down and trample under foot the noble structure their fathers fought and died to rear up, then you "foreigners" came forward and showed yourselves true men. You have done honor to your native and to your adopted countries. I say it: you have proved that this country owes its existence to foreign immigrants.[6]

As some of the Jews prospered, they also became generous donors to numerous non-Jewish institutions, including the University of Chicago, where many facilities have been funded by Jewish contributors. A gift of $28,350 in 1892 by the Standard Club members helped rescue the university at its very inception.

Efforts were also made by some Jews in the community to set up an educational program to instill a knowledge and love of Judaism into the growing number of Jewish youth. The Jewish Educational Society was organized in 1876, and its aims were expressed in the following appeal:

Israelites of Chicago:

What have you done for preserving our faith and transmitting the noble bequest of ages to posterity? True, you have in the different parts of this city formed congregations and erected beautiful houses of worship, redounding to the honor of the God of our Fathers. You have ministers preaching to you every Sabbath and Festival Day, well accredited by the surrounding world. You have Sabbath schools and teachers, besides, to imbue the youth with all elements of Jewish religion and history. But are you satisfied that thereby you have done all in your power to maintain the religion of our Fathers in its pristine glory and purity? True, you have raised your children as Jews, but do you believe that they, after having attended the Sabbath school up to the time of their confirmation, will be able to expound and to defend Judaism around the world? Or do you know of any one of them desirous of pursuing the study of Jewish lore and history, in order to know what Judaism is, and what it has accomplished in its wonderful march? And suppose there are such people, what opportunities have they of studying Hebrew and acquiring the knowledge indispensable for a thorough understanding of Judaism? Where are the schools from which you expect your future rabbis and teachers and well-read laymen to come? The latter can certainly not be imported from the old country for the purpose of upholding our Jewish institutions.

Indeed, indifference and dissension, ignorance and shallowness have long enough eaten the very marrow and root of our sacred inheritance. Compare the zeal and devotion, the generosity and sympathy manifested in Christian churches by young and old, with the indolence and lethargy which have estranged the young, particularly to our holy cause, so as to make every attempt of enlisting their interest fail at the very outset. Christian mission societies send forth their soul-hunting agents to ensnare Jewish young men

6. Ibid., p. 97.

Founded in 1847, Chicago's first Jewish congregation, Kehilath Anshe Mayriv (Congregation of the People of the West), occupied this building at 33rd and Indiana Avenue from 1891 to 1920 before it moved farther south to the Hyde Park–Kenwood area. Today the building houses the Pilgrim Baptist Church.
Courtesy of Irving Cutler.

and tear them away from the breast of their religion, while the Jewish community, for want of religious education and protection, leaves them to spiritual starvation.[7]

However, the reasoned appeal did not arouse the various, often divergent, elements in the community to any immediate action.

The Second Wave:
The Eastern European Jews of the Maxwell Street Area

In the old country, the world of the "shtetl" Jews of Eastern Europe differed greatly from the more cosmopolitan life of the Jews in Germany; in Chicago, at least initially, the differences between the two groups were probably even greater. When Eastern European Jews began to arrive in large numbers in

7. Pamphlet, Jewish Educational Society of Chicago, September 15, 1876, as quoted in Louis Wirth, *The Ghetto* (Chicago, 1928), pp. 176-77.

Chicago during the last quarter of the nineteenth century, the German Jews were for the most part well established and accepted. They mingled quite freely with the general populace, held respected positions in a number of business fields and in the professions, and had even brought their religious practices into closer conformity with those of their Christian neighbors. The throngs of Eastern European Jews who arrived rather suddenly differed markedly from their German brethren in dress, demeanor, economic status, religious beliefs and rituals, and language.

The Eastern European Jews had come from an area much more backward and autocratic than had the German Jews. In the Russian Empire, the Jews had been restricted to living in certain parts of western Russia — the Pale of Settlement, where their life in the shtetl revolved around the synagogue, the home, and the marketplace. There were numerous restrictions of their economic activities, and there was the ever-present scourge of military conscription for young boys that lasted as long as twenty-five years.

Another terrifying experience that fostered immigration to America was the periodic outbreak of pogroms (organized massacres of Jews). That pogroms were often encouraged by the government is disclosed in the following letter from the great Russian writer Leo Tolstoy regarding the infamous Kishinev Pogrom of 1903, which had resulted in the killing or wounding of over six hundred Jews:

> My opinion concerning the Kishinev crime is the result also of my religious convictions. Upon the receipt of the first news which was published in the papers, not yet knowing all the appalling details which were communicated subsequently, I fully realized the horror of what had taken place, and experienced simultaneously a burning feeling of pity for the innocent victims of the cruelty of the populace, amazement at the bestiality of all these so-called Christians, revulsion at all these so-called cultured people who instigated the mob and sympathized with its actions. But I felt a particular horror for the principal culprit, our Government with its clergy which fosters in the people bestial sentiments and fanaticism, with its horde of murderous officials. The crime committed at Kishinev is nothing but a direct consequence of that propaganda of falsehood and violence which is conducted by the Russian Government with such energy.[8]

On arrival in Chicago, many of the Jewish immigrants from the small Eastern European villages found it difficult to adjust to the sudden change of living in a large American city. Articles in such Chicago Yiddish newspapers as the *Jewish Daily Courier,* the voice of Orthodox Jewry, reflected these feelings (as reported by S. J. Pomrenze):

8. S. M. Dubnow, *History of the Jews in Russia and Poland,* Vol. 3 (Philadelphia, 1916), p. 76.

The "hurry up" spirit of the city overwhelmed him at first. The strangeness of the city left him lonely; and the longing to return "home" increased. "What kind of memories could the immigrant fleeing from a land of persecution have?" asked a *Courier* writer. Why was it that something reminding the immigrant of the old home, like a pouch of tobacco, tea, or a European utensil brought forth a sigh and a tear? How could one compare the little village with the straw-bedecked houses and its crooked streets of dirt with the great American cities where noise, turmoil, hustle and bustle reigned, he quoted older immigrants querying the "greenhorn". Furthermore how could one help but scoff at the longing of the immigrant for his old home when here in a city like Chicago he found himself in the center of a civilization that was prepared to offer him everything with a broad hand? The writer answered these questions in a typical Jewish manner. When one digs a little deeper, he said with a Talmudical flourish of his hand, he will see that there were certain values in the little town that are still lacking in the big city. In a small town everybody knew everybody else. In the big city the houses are "cold" inside, no matter how much better built, and how superior in other ways they may be to the little cottages. Moreover, the social recognition given to men of learning and of honorable ancestry was lacking in the city.[9]

But while they may have had warm feelings for the milieu and traditions of the shtetl, they did not feel the same for the *country* they had fled. A Russian Jew's account in his diary showed how the masses of Eastern European Jewish immigrants probably felt about Russia:

> Sympathy for Russia? How ironical it sounds! Am I not despised? Am I not urged to leave? Do I not hear the word *Zhid* (Jew) constantly? Can I even think that someone considers me a human being capable of thinking and feeling like others? Do I not rise daily with the fear lest the hungry mob attack me? . . . It is impossible . . . that a Jew should regret leaving Russia.[10]

In 1880, Eastern European Jews comprised only a small number of Chicago's 10,000 Jews. But when Russia's especially brutal pogroms of 1881 were followed by the repressive May Laws of 1882, expelling many Jews from their homes and towns, a wave of emigration began that lasted for nearly half a century. By 1900, Chicago's Jewish population had reached almost 80,000, of whom an estimated 52,000 were from Eastern Europe, 20,000 were of German descent, and the remaining 8,000 were largely northwest European and Near Eastern in origin. Although the availability of census data on Jews is often limited, by 1930, when the Jewish population of the Chicago area was estimated at about 275,000, over 80 percent were Eastern European.

9. Seymour Jacob Pomrenze, "Aspects of Chicago Russian-Jewish Life, 1893-1915," in Simon Rawidowicz, ed., *The Chicago Pinkas* (Chicago, 1952), pp. 130-31.
10. Irving Howe, *The World of Our Fathers* (New York, 1976), p. 27.

The Russian-Polish Jews crowded into the area southwest of the down-town area, a district that had previously been occupied by communities of German, Bohemian, and Irish gentiles. The Russian-Polish Jews moved south along Canal and Jefferson streets, westward to Halsted Street, and then farther westward as new immigrants increased the congestion. By 1910, Eastern European Jews occupied a ghetto that stretched approximately from Canal Street westward almost to Damen Avenue, and from Polk Street south to the railroad tracks at about 16th Street. Of the estimated 50,000 immigrant Jews who arrived in Chicago during the last two decades of the nineteenth century, most settled in this area of cheap rents and poor housing not far from the maze of railroad facilities with not much more than their small bundles of belongings. A 1901 housing survey noted that almost half of all dwellings there were "dangerous."

The Russian-Jewish immigrant Bernard Horwich arrived in Chicago in 1880 as a youth of seventeen. From the railroad station he was directed to the West Side, where the "greenhorns" were to be found. At the time, he had no idea that Jews lived elsewhere in Chicago. He began to earn his living by selling stationery in the streets, and later he became the president of two banks and one of the most prominent leaders in Chicago Jewish charitable, community, and Zionist organizations. In his later years he recalled the hardships of Chicago's Eastern European Jews at the time of his arrival.

> Jews were treated on the streets in a most abhorrent and shameful manner, stones being thrown at them and their beards being pulled by street thugs. Most earned their living peddling from house to house. They carried packs on their backs consisting of notions and light dry goods, and it was not an unusual sight to see hundreds of them who lived in the Canal Street district, in the early morning, spreading throughout the city. There was hardly a streetcar where there not to be found some Jewish peddlers with their packs riding to and from their business. Peddling junk and vegetables, and selling various articles on street corners also engaged numbers of our people. Being out on the streets most of the time in these obnoxious occupations, and ignorant of the English language, they were subjected to ridicule, annoyance and attacks of all kinds.[11]

Horwich later also recalled the early relationship of German and Eastern European Jews:

> The relationship between the Russian and Polish Jews and the German Jews was anything but amicable. The latter group, with their background of German culture, speaking the German language, engaged in more worldly and sophisticated business enterprises, and practicing Reformed Judaism, were

11. Meites, pp. 150-151.

looked upon as Germans rather than as Jews. The Russian and Polish Jews maintained that the reformed religious ideas of the German Jews made them really "substitute" or "second-hand" Jews, and that their rabbis were almost like Christian ministers. Some even asserted that they regarded the Christian ministers more highly than the Reformed Rabbis, since the former were believers and preached their religion truthfully and faithfully, while the latter tried to deny their Judaism, so as to ingratiate themselves with the non-Jews. . . .

The attitude of the German Jews towards their Russian and Polish brothers was one of superiority and unpleasant pity. They tolerated them only because they were Jews, and one would often hear the German Jews bewailing their fate — that they, Americanized businessmen, had to be classed in the same category with the poor, ignorant, ragged Jewish peddlers on the other side of the river, on Canal Street. . . .[12]

The focal point of the ghetto was around the corner of Halsted and Maxwell streets. In the blocks around this intersection the population was about 90 percent Jewish. The community in many ways resembled a teeming Eastern European ghetto. It housed kosher meat markets and chicken stores, matzo bakeries, groceries, dry goods stores, tailor and seamstress shops, bathhouses and peddlers' stables.

Its colorful outdoor market on Maxwell and on Jefferson streets, with its pushcarts, stands, and stores, was filled with people from dawn till past dark. Jewish merchants matched wits not only with other Jews but with Poles, Lithuanians, Galicians, Russians, Bohemians, and others who felt much more at ease in their familiar ghetto market than in modern department stores. In turn, the multi-lingual Jewish merchants (some could speak a half dozen or more languages) knew the needs, tastes, and prejudices of their customers.

> The smell of garlic and of cheeses, the aroma of onions, apples, and oranges, and the shouts and curses of sellers and buyers fill the air. Anything can be bought and sold on Maxwell Street. On one stand, piled high, are odd sizes of shoes long out of style; on another are copper kettles for brewing beer; on a third are second-hand pants; and one merchant even sells odd, broken pieces of spectacles, watches, and jewelry, together with pocket knives and household tools salvaged from the collections of junk peddlers. Everything has value on Maxwell Street, but the price is not fixed. It is the fixing of the price around which turns the whole plot of the drama enacted daily at the perpetual bazaar of Maxwell Street. . . . The sellers know how to ask ten times the amount that their wares will eventually sell for, and the buyers know how to offer a twentieth.[13]

12. Bernard Horwich, *My First Eighty Years* (Chicago, 1939), pp. 131-132.
13. Wirth, pp. 232-233.

The other Jews: life and trade near Maxwell Street.
Courtesy of Chicago Historical Society.

Halsted Street, a major transportation artery, had basically one-price stores, including two department stores. It had some decorum in selling, and some of its merchants were graduates of Maxwell-Jefferson street selling. Its rich and varied religious and cultural life included synagogues, Hebrew schools, book stores, Hebrew- and Yiddish-speaking literary organizations, the offices of the Yiddish newspapers, and a number of Yiddish theaters. At the beginning of the twentieth century, a boy named Muni Weisenfreund (1895-1967) performed various roles in his father's playhouse, a Yiddish theater on Roosevelt Road near Halsted Street. Decades later he won an Academy Award as Paul Muni, the stage and screen star.

Dominating the scene were more than forty Orthodox synagogues, for the Orthodox synagogues had to be within walking distance. The synagogues were usually small, sometimes in the rabbi's home or in converted Christian churches, with only a few having more than a hundred members; and the members of each congregation consisted largely of immigrants from the same community or region in Europe.[14] In religious matters most of the Eastern European Jews tried to cling to the old traditions, while the German Jews

14. Ibid., pp. 205-206.

espoused new ideas. The Orthodox were devoted to the Torah and its study, daily attendance at the synagogue if possible, and strict observance of the Sabbath, religious holidays, and dietary and other laws prescribed in the *Schulchan Aruch,* the codification of Jewish religious law and practice.

Eastern European Jews, with their strict Orthodoxy, did not feel at home in the Reform atmosphere of German-Jewish synagogues, and the German Jews did not make them feel overly welcome either. Like the German Jews, however, the Eastern Europeans experienced factionalism within their own ranks, and synagogue splits resulted from personal and ritualistic strife, often based on conflicting local customs. One such split started on a hot summer Sabbath afternoon when a member was ejected from prayer services at Congregation Beth Hamedrosh Hagodol for wearing a straw hat. He was soon followed out by his countrymen from the town of Mariampol, Lithuania, and before the year was over they had organized Congregation Ohave Sholom Mariampoller.

Most Eastern European Jews found it imperative to belong to a synagogue and to provide religious instruction for their children, as this 1905 description reveals:

> They know that the public school will attend to their secular education, so out of their scant earnings they pay synagogue and Talmud Torah (religious school) dues. The synagogue plays a very important part in the daily life of the Orthodox Russian Jew, for his life and religion are so closely interwoven that public divine worship is to him a duty and a pleasure. The synagogue is the religious and social center around which the activity of the community revolves and it has now become, since the formation of auxiliary loan societies, a distributing agency for its various philanthropies where "personal service" is not a fad, but has always been recognized in dealing with the unfortunate. Small wonder is it that the Orthodox Russian Jew clings to his synagogue. It is open not only "from early morn till dewy eve," but far into the night, and in some cases the laboring man can attend services and yet be in time for his work. There are morning, afternoon, and evening services — seldom attended by women. Often the peddler's cart can be seen standing near the entrance while the owner is at prayer within. On Sabbaths and holy days services are always well attended by men and women, the latter occupying a gallery set apart for their use.

For older Jews especially, the synagogue offered intellectual and spiritual sustenance:

> Connected with the synagogue is the *beth hamedrash,* or house of learning, where students of religious literature are always welcome, and Bible and Talmud are studied and discussed. Many take advantage of the opportunity thus afforded, and form study circles or meet for devotional reading. There is much to attract and hold the older generation, who are continually receiving

accessions from abroad, and in their lives the synagogue means much, if not all worth striving for.

The beginning of a congregation is generally a *minyan* or gathering of at least ten men for divine worship. This is held in rented quarters. As soon as a sufficient number of members are gained they resolve to form an organization and when funds are forthcoming a house of worship is bought or built.

But with the younger generation of East European Jews there were already problems, and the pressures of acculturation were strong:

> Expense is not spared in making the exercises interesting to the older people, but little is done to attract the younger generation. The beautiful Hebrew language, which they do not understand, is used exclusively in the services. And when there is a sermon it is in Yiddish, and rather tedious and uninteresting for young people, who are almost starving for that religious food which would satisfy the heart and mind.[15]

Consequently, the younger, less religious Eastern European Jews were usually crowded into the neighborhood public schools, and soon such elementary schools as Washburne, Garfield, Smythe, and Foster were more than 80 percent Jewish. For these children, public education became an important vehicle for becoming Americanized and moving upward socially and economically, and often away from the world of their parents.

Jane Addams' Hull House was another agency that helped educate and Americanize the East European Jewish immigrants of the Maxwell Street area, as it also helped other ethnics. Founded in 1889 at 800 South Halsted Street, this pioneering social settlement complex fought for better conditions for the various peoples of the area and helped them to adjust to their new environment. Among the more famous Jewish students at Hull House were Sidney Hillman, Benny Goodman, Studs Terkel, and Arthur Goldberg.

Other major concerns that required the attention of the Jewish immigrants were the disputes arising over *Kashrut* (kosher practices), which eventually came under rabbinical supervision, and also the need to help the large number of newly arriving Jewish immigrants, who were aided especially by the Hebrew Immigrant Aid Society (HIAS) and by the *landsmanshaften*. Besides synagogues of *landsleit* (fellow townsmen) from the same Eastern European community, Jews organized *landsmanshaften* or *vereins*. Some supported the synagogue and its educational functions, but most served as social clubs, loan associations, sick-benefit and cemetery agencies, help sources for the unemployed, places to meet old friends and reminisce about the old country, and the

---

15. Charles Bernheimer, *The Russian Jew in the United States: Studies of Social Conditions in New York, Philadelphia, and Chicago with a Description of Rural Settlements* (Philadelphia, 1905), pp. 173-174 (citation covers two previous quotations).

Upper class German Jews at a charity show.
Courtesy of University of Illinois Library at Chicago, Manuscripts Division.

means for aiding those who had been left behind. One *verein* was initially organized to raise $25 for a landsman peddler so that he could buy a horse to replace his horse which had died.

During World War I, Chicago *landsleit* from numerous towns in Russia, Poland, Romania, Lithuania, and Galicia formed relief committees to aid the war victims in the communities of their origin. During World War II there were about 600 *landsmanshaften*. The Holocaust wiped out virtually all of the Jewish communities of Eastern Europe, and with them millions of the relatives and friends whom the *landsmanshaften* had tried to aid through the years. The *landsmanshaften* then directed their efforts to aiding Israel. In time, however, as the immigrant population began to diminish, the *landsmanshaften* declined rapidly in membership, and one by one they disappeared.

The first branch of the Arbeiter Ring (the Workman's Circle) was established in Chicago in 1903. The Arbeiter Ring was a Jewish socialist fraternal organization, generally hostile to religion and to Jewish nationalism. At its peak it had many thousands of members in Chicago. It ran secular Yiddish-language schools and camps, and its members read the influential Yiddish daily news-

Unemployed men marching along 14th Street in the Maxwell Street area en route to
City Hall, 1914. Courtesy of Chicago Historical Society.

paper *The Forward,* which presented local and world news of Jewish interest
while at the same time giving a basic education in Americanization.

In the Maxwell Street area even the dress was largely that of the Eastern
European ghettos. Bearded Jews who wore long black coats, and Russian caps
and boots were a common sight. Absent from this area were the many saloons
found in other ethnic areas. An account in the *Chicago Tribune* of July 19, 1891,
described the ghetto of the near West Side:

> On the West Side, in a district bounded by Sixteenth Street on the south and
> Polk Street on the north and the Chicago River and Halsted Street on the east
> and west, one can walk the streets for blocks and see none but Semitic features
> and hear nothing but the Hebrew patois of Russian Poland. In this restricted
> boundary, in narrow streets, ill-ventilated tenements and rickety cottages,
> there is a population of from 15,000 to 16,000 Russian Jews. . . . Every Jew
> in this quarter who can speak a word of English is engaged in business of
> some sort. The favorite occupation, probably on account of the small capital
> required, is fruit and vegetable peddling. Here, also, is the home of the Jewish
> street merchants, the rag and junk peddler, and the "glass puddin" man. . . .
> The principal streets in the quarter are lined with stores of every description.
> Trades with which Jews are not usually associated such as saloonkeeping,

קלאוק מאכער דרעס און רעגען קוים מאכער ליידעם טיילערס

דיו יניאן איז אין געפאר!

א מאסטען מיטינג פון אלע אינטערנעשאנאל מעמבערס וועט אפגעהאל־
טען ווערען מאנטאג נאוועמבער דעם 15־טען, 1926, 8 אוהר אבענד אין לייבאר
לייסעאום, אגדען קארנער קעדזי עוועניוס.

שוועסטער און ברידער:—

עם איז פון דער גרעסטער וויכטיגקייט אז איהר זאלט אנוועזענד זיין בײ דיזען
מאסטען פאראזאמלונג וואו וויכטיגע פראגען וואם שטעלען אין געפאר דעם עקזיסטענץ
פון אונזער יוניאן וועלען באשפראכען ווערען.

שוועסטער און ברידער:—

עם האט גענומען לאנגע יאהרען פון שוועערע ארבעט לײדען און נויט ביז אונזער
יוניאן איז אויפגעבויט געוואָרען צו זיין א ווירקזאמע וואפען גענען די אנדלונגען און
אטאקעם פון די באליבאטים.

ווילט איהר דערלאזען אז אונזער יוניאן זאל צוכראכען ווערען?

אויב נים קומט צום **מאסטען מיטינג.**

מים גרוס,

וו. דיילי, סעם לעדערמאן, מענדע פיינבערג, דזש. האפמאן
פיליפ דייווידם

דזשאינט באארד דעלעגאטען

CLOAK, DRESS, RAIN COAT MAKERS AND LADIES TAILORS

The Union is In Danger!

A MASS MEETING of all International members will be held ON
MONDAY EVENING, NOVEMBER 15th, 1926, 8 P. M. sharp, at the Labor
Lyceum, Ogden and Kedzie Avenues.

Sisters and Brothers, it is of the utmost importance that you be present
at this meeting.

Questions that is now up in our Union and that treatens the existance
of our Union will be discussed.

COME IN MASSES.   PROTECT YOUR UNION.

Brotherly yours.

W. DAYLY, SAM LEDERMAN, MANDY FINEBERG, J. HOFFMAN
and PHILIP DAVIDS

Joint Board Delegates

562

Union poster, in Yiddish and English, announcing a mass meeting at
the Workmen's Circle Labor Lyceum, 1927.   Courtesy of Irving Cutler.

shaving and hair cutting, and blacksmithing, have their representatives and Hebrew signs. . . . In a room of a small cottage forty small boys all with hats on sit crowded into a space 10 × 10 feet in size, presided over by a stout middle-aged man with a long, curling, matted beard, who also retains his hat, a battered rusty derby of ancient style. All the old or middle-aged men in the quarter affect this peculiar head gear. . . . The younger generation of men are more progressive and having been born in this country are patriotic and want to be known as Americans and not Russians. . . . Everyone is looking for a bargain and everyone has something to sell. The home life seems to be full of content and easygoing unconcern for what the outside world thinks.

To support themselves, many Jewish immigrants from Eastern Europe worked in the sweatshops of the clothing industry and in cigar-making factories. Others became peddlers, tailors, butchers, bakers, barbers, small merchants, and artisans of every variety. As the immigrants became more Americanized, they organized to fight for better working conditions. In 1886, a day after the Haymarket Riot, thousands of Jews marched from the ghetto toward the downtown area to protest the intolerable conditions of the sweatshop. At the Van Buren Street bridge they were beaten and routed by club-swinging police.

Jews comprised about 80 percent of the 45,000 workers who participated in the prolonged and successful garment strike of 1910. The strike, largely an action of Jewish workers against a Jewish-owned concern, was led by Sidney Hillman and Bessie Abramowitz (who later became husband and wife). It resulted in the organization of the Amalgamated Clothing Workers of America under Hillman's leadership. In addition, Jews rose to leadership in the other two major needle trade unions — the International Ladies' Garment Workers' Union and the United Hat, Cap and Millinery Workers' Union. All three unions became well known for the progressive benefits they won for their members and for their social democratic philosophy.

The more affluent and established German Jews of the South Side "Golden Ghetto" continued to be embarrassed by the old-world ways and beliefs of the newly arrived Eastern European Jews of Maxwell Street. To the middle-class, Americanized German Jews, the Eastern European immigrants were a frightening apparition. Their poverty was more desperate than German-Jewish poverty had ever been, their piety more intense that German-Jewish piety, their irreligion more violent than German-Jewish irreligion, and their radicalism more extreme than German-Jewish radicalism.[16] The German Jews founded a number of community facilities to speed up the Americanization of their Eastern European brethren. Julius Rosenwald (1862-1932), for example, who was of German-Jewish descent and the president of Sears, Roebuck and Company, was a generous philanthropist who gave great sums for such charities as well as for other causes, including housing and education for blacks, the University of

16. Nathan Glazer, *American Judaism* (Chicago, 1957), p. 66.

The Hart, Schaffner and Marx men's clothing factory, about 1930, where many of the immigrant Jews worked.   Courtesy of Hartmarx Corporation.

Chicago, and the famous Museum of Science and Industry. Rosenwald helped fund the Chicago Hebrew Institute (later the Jewish People's Institute), the forerunner of today's community centers, which opened in 1908 on the six-acre grounds of a former convent at Taylor and Lyle Streets. The Institute contained classrooms, playgrounds, clubrooms, a library, gymnasiums, assembly halls, and a synagogue and offered a very wide variety of educational, social, cultural, and recreational activities. Another of its founders, the attorney Nathan Kaplan, spoke of its purposes as follows:

> The younger generation speaking English and mixing with English-speaking people loses its interest in things Jewish, and the older people speaking nothing but their native language live always in a foreign atmosphere. We hope the Institute will give both an opportunity to meet on common ground and so, while making the Orthodox tolerant and the younger element better fitted to sympathize, preserve all that is best in the race and its faith.

The German Jews were willing to give their Eastern European coreligionists financial and educational assistance, but not social equality. For many years the two Jewish communities lived separately and had separate synagogues, fraternal organizations, and community centers. Having been excluded from the gentile downtown clubs, German Jews formed their own club, the Standard Club, whose membership consisted mainly of South Side Jewish "aristocracy." Initially it excluded Eastern European Jews. In 1917 the Eastern European Jews organized their own Covenant Club. Both clubs served both social and philanthropic goals.

In addition to the Chicago Hebrew Institute, other community service centers in the Maxwell Street area were largely supported by German Jews. These included the Jewish Training School, one of the first vocational training schools in the United States; the Mandel Clinic (one of whose founders was the merchant Leon Mandel), a modern facility that provided free medical care and medicine for the poor immigrants; the Maxwell Street Settlement; and the Chicago Maternity Center, a facility which provided free prenatal and obstetric care. The Chicago Maternity Center was founded and supervised by one of the world's leading obstetricians and pioneers in the field, Dr. Joseph De Lee (1869-1942).

The Russian-Polish immigrants sometimes resented the paternalistic attitude of their more worldly German brethren. But they accepted the help extended to them because ghetto life was hard and living conditions were deplorable. The crowded wooden shanties and brick tenements of the area usually had insufficient ventilation and light, few baths, and were usually surrounded by areas of poor drainage and piles of garbage. Recreational facilities were grossly inadequate. Many ghetto families took in lodgers to help defray expenses; sometimes the same bed would be used by a baker during the day and a butcher during the night, which was called the "hot bed" system. The wives and children often had to work. Yet crime was low on Maxwell Street in those days, and the alcoholism and disease rate of the Jewish ghetto was lower than that of most immigrant concentrations. Jews of the Maxwell Street neighborhood exhibited a physical and mental vitality that was sustained by a long tradition of hard work and learning. They strove for success, if not for themselves then for their children.

A surprising number of people with roots in the Maxwell Street area became well known:

> Joseph Goldberg was one of these immigrants. He came to America from Russia and eventually landed on Maxwell Street. He bought a blind horse, the only horse he could afford. He became a fruit-and-vegetable peddler; his son, Arthur, would serve in President Kennedy's cabinet and become a Supreme Court Justice of the United States.
>
> Samuel Paley became a cigar maker in America, as did Max Guzik. Samuel's son William, born in the back room of the modest family cigar store near Maxwell Street, is founder, president and chairman of the board of the

Columbia Broadcasting System. Mr. Guzik's son Jake, known as "Greasy Thumb," became the brains behind the Capone gang. . . .

Eastern European immigrants David Goodman and Abraham Rickover took jobs in Chicago as tailors. Their sons were Benny Goodman and Admiral Hyman C. Rickover.

The father of Barney Ross, onetime world lightweight boxing champion, and the father of Barney Balaban, the late president of Paramount Pictures, each owned a tiny grocery store in the Maxwell Street area.

Paul Muni's father owned a Yiddish theater near Maxwell Street. Jack Ruby's father was a carpenter there.

John Keeshin, once the greatest trucking magnate in America, is the son of a man who owned a chicken store on Maxwell Street, as did the father of Jackie Fields, former welterweight champion of the world. The father of Federal Court Judge Abraham Lincoln Marovitz owned a candy store near Maxwell Street.

Colonel Jacob Arvey, once a nationally prominent political power broker, was the son of a Maxwell Street area peddler.[17]

Others from the area include author Meyer Levin; heavyweight boxing contender King Levinsky; community organizer Saul Alinsky; and con artist Joseph "Yellow Kid" Weil.

By 1910 improvements in their economic status, the encroachment of industry and the railroads, and the influx of blacks caused the Jews to start moving out of the Maxwell Street area — first toward the areas around Ashland and Damen avenues and then to more distant parts. By the 1930s only a small remnant of Jewish businessmen and older Jews remained in the Maxwell Street area. Today the neighborhood is almost wholly black, and the bazaarlike Maxwell Street commercial strip has been reduced to a few short blocks, the result of changing shopping patterns, a changing neighborhood, and the construction of the Dan Ryan Expressway on the eastern fringe and of the University of Illinois at Chicago campus on the north. But on Sundays throngs of curiosity-seekers and shoppers still crowd Maxwell market, which moved in 1994 to Canal Street, looking for bargains and odd merchandise that can range from used toothbrushes, rusty nails, and questionably obtained hubcaps to valuable antiques.

Ironically, in an otherwise solidly Orthodox neighborhood, Temple B'nai Jehoshua, the last surviving synagogue in the area (it closed in 1965) was a Reform congregation. This sole non-Orthodox congregation, at 19th and Ashland Avenue on the fringe of the Maxwell Street area, was organized by Bohemian Jews who wished to live near their small stores on 18th and 22nd streets in the Gentile Bohemian neighborhood of Pilsen. Like German Jews, Bohemians

17. Ira Berkow, *Maxwell Street* (Garden City, N.Y., 1977), pp. 10-11.

often favored Reform Judaism. Among the members of B'nai Jehoshua were the Bohemian Jewish immigrants Judge Joseph Sabath (1870-1956) and his brother, the liberal congressman Adolph Sabath (1866-1952), who served in the U.S. House of Representatives for twenty-three consecutive terms, the second-longest continuous service of any U.S. congressman. Also members were the family that owned the chain of Leader Department Stores, which catered to Eastern European neighborhoods and sold, among other items, thousands of *perinas* (comforters) annually to their largely non-Jewish Bohemian and Polish customers. In 1965, B'nai Jehoshua merged with Congregation Beth Elohim of Glenview. The proceeds from the sale of its building on Ashland Avenue helped pay for the new site of the merged congregations.

During the almost half century that Jews lived in the Maxwell Street area, major changes in the community had taken place there. Help from the German-Jewish community was being increasingly replaced by self-help. Secular agencies eventually took over many of the social services from the synagogue; economic advancement and diversity increased; participation in union and other workingmen's groups accelerated; some important changes took place in the quality of Jewish education; many of the older religious, cultural, and social practices began to change or even disappear. And while the older generation generally kept to its old-world ways, their children, while keeping some of the traditions, were also rapidly adopting the ways of the new world.

The Dispersion

The World War I period brought a frenzy of activity to the Jewish community. Some 20,000 Chicago Jews served in the armed forces, and a number, including Julius Rosenwald and Judge Julian Mack, held high government positions in Washington. One of the mightiest efforts of the Chicago Jewish community during the war and postwar periods was the raising of millions of dollars for overseas war relief. While money was raised for a variety of needy causes, the effort was especially concentrated on helping the Jews of central and eastern Europe who were caught in the war zone between invading and retreating armies.

It was during the war that the British government issued the Balfour Declaration stating that it viewed "with favor the establishment in Palestine of a national home for the Jewish people." The declaration produced a surge of Jewish interest in Zionism, although by that time there already were a number of active Zionist organizations in Chicago. The first organized Jewish Zionist group in the United States had been established in 1896 in Chicago, mainly by members of the Hebrew Literary Society located in the Maxwell Street area. Most of the early Zionists were Eastern European Jews. Most Reform Jews initially opposed the Zionist movement for a variety of reasons, including the belief that Jews were a religious group and not a nationality; that they were American citizens and the United States was their home; that striving for a Jewish state might be misconstrued as being disloyal and unpatriotic and give more strength to anti-Semitic elements. Nevertheless, Zionism continued to grow rapidly: a variety of new Zionist organizations representing a wide spectrum of Jews was organized; drives raising funds for Palestine were greatly expanded; and during the war, 212 Chicago Jewish men joined the Jewish Legion organized by the British for the purpose of freeing Palestine from Turkish rule. And in the ensuing years the problems of the Jews in Europe culminating in the Holocaust brought about almost unanimous support and aid from Chicago Jews for a Jewish state and then for the survival of Israel.

In 1923 a major step was taken toward bringing together the German Jews and Eastern-European Jews with the merger of their two separate charity organizations into the Jewish Charities of Chicago (now the Jewish Federation of Metropolitan Chicago). The combined organization helped support two hospitals, two homes for the aged, two orphanages, two dispensaries, a tuberculosis sanitarium, a number of Jewish schools as well as numerous other organizations that ministered to the needy.

By the 1920s most of the Jews of Maxwell Street had scattered — in a number of directions. A small number joined the German Jews in the Golden Ghetto of the South Side. After some settlement in the Grand Boulevard, Washington Park, Englewood, and adjacent community areas, until the region began changing racially, the bulk of the German-Jewish community — who by this time had been joined by an increasing number of Eastern-European Jews — became concentrated in the Hyde Park-Kenwood and South Shore areas near the lake. The nearby University of Chicago was an important influence in these communities, and many Jews contributed to the university, some financially and others intellectually, such as Nobel Prize winners Albert Abraham Michelson (physics), Milton Friedman (economics), and Saul Bellow (literature).

Bolstered by an influx of survivors from Nazi Germany before and after World War II, each of these two South Side areas had about a dozen synagogues — a mixture of the usually small Orthodox congregations and the generally large Reform and Conservative congregations. The newer Conservative Judaism, like Reform Judaism, was conceived as a developmental religion that was needed to adjust to contemporary conditions; but it adhered more to the traditional practices and spirit of historical Judaism than did the Reform, including the greater use of the Hebrew language and fuller adherence to the time-honored liturgy and religious holidays. However, some modifications or changes from the traditional were allowed, including mixed seating of men and women during worship services, confirmation of girls, and broader interpretation of the Code of Jewish Law. Conservative Judaism was not only a modification of strict Orthodoxy, but a reaction against the many major changes instituted by Reform Judaism. Conservative Judaism in time attracted many of the American-born

The Museum of Science and Industry, Chicago's most popular tourist attraction, was established in 1933 by Julius Rosenwald, prominent Chicago businessman, civic leader, and philanthropist. His brother-in-law, Max Adler, had founded the Adler Planetarium in 1930.   Courtesy of the Chicago Convention and Tourism Bureau.

children of Eastern European Jews, who were reconciling their attachments to the traditions of their youth and their acculturation in America. Many of Chicago's Conservative synagogues started out in the Orthodox fold.

The Jewish population and the number of synagogues started to decline rapidly in the 1950s as the racial composition of Hyde Park–Kenwood and South Shore began to change. Because of the more stable racial balance that has been attained in Hyde Park, the community still has a substantial Jewish population, concentrated largely in its eastern section, which is served by three large synagogues. South Shore is now devoid of synagogues, although Agudath Achim Bikur Cholem, on South Houston Avenue in adjacent South Chicago, still occupies the city's oldest continuously used synagogue building (since 1902) and is supported largely by members coming from somewhat distant areas. The South Side communities of South Chicago, Roseland, and Jeffery Manor no longer have Jewish residents.

A small number of Jews moved north into the lakefront communities of Lake View, Uptown, and Rogers Park. One of Chicago's most beloved rabbis was the Russian-born Solomon Goldman (1893-1953), who served the Lake View area's Conservative Anshe Emet Synagogue from 1929 to the time of his death. Rabbi Goldman was a gifted speaker, a prolific writer and scholar, and an ardent Zionist, in fact, the first president of the Zionist Organization of

America who did not come from the eastern United States. His synagogue, like other large lakefront area congregations such as Temple Sholom and Emanuel Congregation, was founded in the last century just north of the Loop and was located at its present site after a series of northward moves that followed the Jewish population. Some other early Jewish facilities were also located north of the Loop. Near the first Jewish cemetery in that area was also the first Jewish hospital, built in 1867 on La Salle Street near Schiller Avenue (1400 north) and destroyed by the Chicago Fire of 1871.

A large number of Jews moved to the Northwest Side; many were from Hungary, Ukraine, and Galicia (mainly northeastern Poland). There the nucleus of a Jewish community had been established in the late 1800s in the West Town area of Milwaukee Avenue and along Division Street. The first synagogues in the West Town area were built in the 1890s, and eventually about twenty served a Jewish community that in time spread to the western side of Humboldt Park. And there were a number of Hebrew schools, including the large Jabneh, sponsored by four Orthodox synagogues of the area. Many of the local Jews were inclined to emphasize Yiddish culture and somewhat radical philosophies rather than the religious Orthodoxy of the near West Side. The area was known for its activists and intellectuals, some fervently espousing various causes and philosophies and others pursuing the arts and literature. Ideologically, the area was split among adherents of socialism, secularism, Zionism, and Orthodoxy. But these differences declined markedly among the more Americanized children.

On Division Street, the principal commercial artery of the West Town–Humboldt Park area, were numerous Jewish stores and the Deborah Boys Club. Although Jews were a minority in the West Town area, which included large numbers of Poles, Ukrainians, and Russians, this was the childhood home of such well-known Jews as comedian Jackie Leonard (Fats Levitsky), movie impresario Michael Todd, composer and play producer Jule Styne, columnist Sydney J. Harris, and novelist Saul Bellow. The last two, both of whom were alumni of Tuley High School, were part of a distinguished group of Chicago writers of Jewish descent (though Bellow was born in Canada of Russian-Jewish parents and initially brought up in Montreal), which included Edna Ferber, Ben Hecht, Herman Kogan, Albert Halper, Maxwell Bodenheim, Meyer Levin, Isaac Rosenfeld, Leo Rosen, Studs Terkel, and Louis Zara. Henry Crown and A. N. Pritzker, who were to become giants in the business world, also had their roots in this area.

Some Jews moved beyond the West Town–Humboldt Park neighborhood farther northwest into Logan Square and Albany Park; but the vast majority of the Jews who left Maxwell Street leapfrogged over the railroad and industrial area and settled some three miles to the west in the Lawndale–Douglas Park–Garfield Park area, which became the largest and most developed Jewish community that ever existed in Chicago. At its peak in 1930, this Greater Lawndale area contained an estimated 110,000 Jews of the city's total Jewish population of about 275,000.

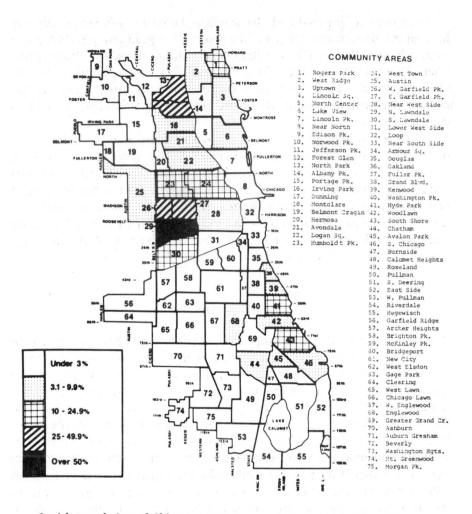

COMMUNITY AREAS

1.	Rogers Park	24.	West Town
2.	West Ridge	25.	Austin
3.	Uptown	26.	W. Garfield Pk.
4.	Lincoln Sq.	27.	E. Garfield Pk.
5.	North Center	28.	Near West Side
6.	Lake View	29.	N. Lawndale
7.	Lincoln Pk.	30.	S. Lawndale
8.	Near North	31.	Lower West Side
9.	Edison Pk.	32.	Loop
10.	Norwood Pk.	33.	Near South Side
11.	Jefferson Pk.	34.	Armour Sq.
12.	Forest Glen	35.	Douglas
13.	North Park	36.	Oakland
14.	Albany Pk.	37.	Fuller Pk.
15.	Portage Pk.	38.	Grand Blvd.
16.	Irving Park	39.	Kenwood
17.	Dunning	40.	Washington Pk.
18.	Montclare	41.	Hyde Park
19.	Belmont Cragin	42.	Woodlawn
20.	Hermosa	43.	South Shore
21.	Avondale	44.	Chatham
22.	Logan Sq.	45.	Avalon Park
23.	Humboldt Pk.	46.	S. Chicago
		47.	Burnside
		48.	Calumet Heights
		49.	Roseland
		50.	Pullman
		51.	S. Deering
		52.	East Side
		53.	W. Pullman
		54.	Riverdale
		55.	Hegewisch
		56.	Garfield Ridge
		57.	Archer Heights
		58.	Brighton Pk.
		59.	McKinley Pk.
		60.	Bridgeport
		61.	New City
		62.	West Elsdon
		63.	Gage Park
		64.	Clearing
		65.	West Lawn
		66.	Chicago Lawn
		67.	W. Englewood
		68.	Englewood
		69.	Greater Grand Cr.
		70.	Ashburn
		71.	Auburn Gresham
		72.	Beverly
		73.	Washington Hgts.
		74.	Mt. Greenwood
		75.	Morgan Pk.

Under 3%

3.1 - 9.9%

10 - 24.9%

25 - 49.9%

Over 50%

Jewish population of Chicago, 1931. Courtesy of the Jewish Charities of Chicago.

Other areas with significant Jewish populations in 1930 included the Lake View–Uptown–Rogers Park area (27,000), West Town–Humboldt Park–Logan Square (35,000), Albany Park–North Park (27,000), and on the South Side the Kenwood–Hyde Park–Woodlawn–South Shore area (28,000). The Jews of the South Side had the highest economic status, followed by those of the North Side and the Northwest Side. Small Jewish communities were situated in Austin (7,000), Englewood–Greater Grand Crossing (4,000), and Chatham–Avalon Park–South Chicago (3,000). Small numbers of Jews also lived on the near North Side, the Southwest Side, and in other communities of the Northwest Side.

Geographic dispersal and German–East European differences were not the only divisions among the Jews. The Eastern European group included Jews from Lithuania, Poland, Ukraine, Bessarabia, Galicia, Latvia, and other regions. There were religious divisions along the lines of Orthodox, Conservative, Reform, and secular Jews. There were Zionists and anti-Zionists, radicals and conservatives, employees and employers, and aspiring assimilationists and ardent Yiddishists.

The Jews continued to be involved in business, and after World War I they moved increasingly into such professions as law, medicine, teaching, writing, accounting, music, and art. Jews often had to overcome restrictive provisions and quotas to move ahead. Not only were they barred from higher positions in many industries, but they were also often excluded even from lower-level positions, such as secretarial jobs. Some institutions of higher learning limited the enrollment of Jews by quotas, and until recent decades most North Shore and other suburban realtors severely restricted the sale of homes to Jews.

Greater Lawndale

Whether they live today in Chicago or its suburbs, many Jews can trace their roots to the Greater Lawndale area; during the first half of the century, as many as 40 percent of the Jews of Chicago lived there. Jews began moving out of the crowded Maxwell Street area in the first decade of this century to the Chicago community of North Lawndale and — to a lesser extent somewhat later — into the adjacent communities to the north, East Garfield Park and West Garfield Park (the combined communities forming the Greater Lawndale area). This was a quieter residential area whose comparatively spacious streets, yards, and parks were largely encircled by the belt railroads. The German and Irish residents initially tried to stem the influx of Jews by refusing to rent to them. But many Jews then bought the one- and two-family brick homes of the area and also built numerous three-story apartment houses there. By 1920 the neighborhood had become largely Jewish. Yiddish spoken in various dialects could then be heard throughout the community.

The population of the Greater Lawndale area more than doubled between 1910 and 1930, to become one of the most densely populated communities in the city. In 1930 its proportion of foreign-born inhabitants — mainly from Russia and Poland — was higher than that of any other community in Chicago (about 45 percent). The area at its broadest delineation stretched approximately from California Avenue west to Tripp Avenue (4232 west) and from Washington Boulevard south to 18th Street.[18] The greatest

18. Leonard C. Mishkin, "Orthodoxy: Saga of Chicago's Great West Side," *The Sentinel's History of Chicago Jewry, 1911-1961* (Chicago, 1961), p. 127.

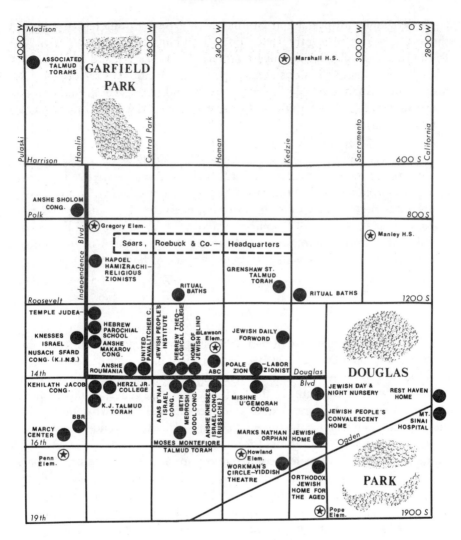

Jewish facilities along Douglas and Independence boulevards, 1948.
Courtesy of Irving Cutler.

concentration in this area was in North Lawndale, south of Arthington Street, the street along which Sears Roebuck's huge mail order and headquarters complex was aligned for more than half a mile. There was also a small spin-off to the west into the Columbus Park–Austin area, which contained about 8,000 Jews in 1946. In the central core of the area, south of Roosevelt Road, the Herzl, Penn, Howland, Bryant, and Lawson public schools each averaged about 2,000 Jewish students by 1933. This probably was more than 90 percent of each school's enrollment. The students from these elementary schools went mainly to Marshall and Manley high schools, which were located slightly north of North Lawndale.

Its almost solidly Jewish population led to the neighborhood being referred to as the "Chicago Jerusalem." However, to those Orthodox Jews still living in the Maxwell Street ghetto area, Greater Lawndale was sometimes disparagingly referred to as "Deutschland," its inhabitants as the "Maxwell Street Yankees of Douglas Park," because the Orthodox saw in the newer Jewish neighborhood a relative desertion of the old customs and religious beliefs, and the aspiration to emulate the German Jews with their "goyishe" ways.[19]

The heart of the area was the L-shaped Douglas Boulevard (1400 south) and Independence Boulevard (3800 west), parkways whose wide central grass malls separated one-way roads. These boulevards were about a mile long and were flanked by Douglas Park on the east end and by Garfield Park on the north. Both parks were beautifully landscaped, with flower beds, lagoons, and woodlands. Many of the major Jewish institutions of the community were built along Douglas and Independence boulevards, including about a dozen synagogues, many of imposing classical architecture, all but one of which were Orthodox; a huge community center, the Jewish People's Institute; the Hebrew Theological College, headed for many years by Rabbi Saul Silber, whose students came from all over the world; a home for the Jewish blind; and a number of other religious, Zionist, and cultural organizations.

Theodore Herzl Junior College, which had large enrollments of Jewish students, was located on Douglas Boulevard near its junction with Independence Boulevard at Independence Square. Just to the west was the beautiful Kehilath Jacob Synagogue, which maintained the largest Talmud Torah (Hebrew School) in the area. It had a band whose membership included the young Benny Goodman. There were a number of other Hebrew schools on the two boulevards and more on the side streets, including the large Grenshaw Street Talmud Torah near Kedzie Avenue (on the street where the future Admiral Hyman Rickover lived), and the Moses Montefiore Talmud Torah on St. Louis (3500 west) south of 15th Street. This area created a Jewish cultural life that was perhaps without parallel except for that on the East Side of New York.

Among the earliest (1913) larger synagogues on Douglas Boulevard was Congregation Anshe Kneseth Israel, known as the "Russishe shul." It had a seating capacity of 3,500, and some of the prominent Eastern European Jewish families were members. Some of the best cantors in the world were invited from Europe to conduct its services. The synagogue remained open almost twenty-four hours a day so that scholars, often supported by the congregation, could continue their Hebrew studies. For almost half a century the rabbi of Anshe Kneseth Israel was Ephraim Epstein (1876-1960), a renowned Talmudic scholar who furthered the cause of Jewish education and

19. Wirth, p. 191.

Banquet at the Orthodox Jewish Home for the Aged, Albany Avenue near 18th Street, about 1925.   Courtesy of Chicago Historical Society.

helped rescue many Jews from Europe during the Nazi period. Another large synagogue on Douglas Boulevard was the First Romanian Congregation. In 1926 its members gave Queen Marie of Romania a royal welcome when she visited the synagogue on her tour of the United States — although many of them had fled her country because they could not tolerate her country's policy regarding Jews. The congregation, like most in Lawndale, was formerly in the Maxwell Street area.

On the Jewish High Holy Days, Douglas and Independence boulevards were thronged with people in holiday dress. Almost everyone went to the synagogue on those particular days, and local automobile traffic virtually ceased. On the side streets were about four dozen more synagogues, all Orthodox, many of which bore the names of the communities in Russia, Poland, Lithuania, or Romania from which their founders had come. Some synagogues were organized by occupational groups and consequently were referred to as the laundryman's synagogue or the carpenter's synagogue. As late as 1944, about half of the synagogues of the Chicago area were located in Greater Lawndale. Friday night was very special among the Orthodox Jews, with the synagogue services, the lighting of the Sabbath candles, and the festive Sabbath meal, which was usually followed by singing and religious discussions. Jewish teenagers ex-

Sam's Fruit Store at 3509 West 16th Street in 1937 was typical of the small mom and pop stores in Lawndale.   Courtesy of Rose Pollack.

changed "Good Sabbath" greetings on Douglas Boulevard and often gathered at Independence Square to dance the *hora* late into the night.

On Kedzie at Ogden Avenue was the large Labor Lyceum building, which contained the educational and administrative facilities of the Workmen's Circle. The building also housed Chicago's last Yiddish theater (1938-1951). Farther north on Kedzie Avenue was the building of a Jewish daily newspaper, the *Forward*. On both sides of Douglas Park, on California Avenue and Albany Avenue (3100 west), were aligned an imposing array of social service institutions supported by the Jewish community. These included a rehabilitation hospital, a convalescent home, a day-and-night nursery, a large orphanage, a home for the Orthodox Jewish aged, and Mount Sinai Hospital. The hospital was established for a number of reasons, including the need to serve the new growing Jewish community and because Michael Reese Hospital served no kosher meals and originally discriminated against Jewish doctors of Eastern European origin.

The main commercial street bisecting Greater Lawndale was Roosevelt Road, to which Jews would come from all over the city to shop. In the mile stretch from about Kedzie Avenue to Crawford (Pulaski) Avenue were a half-dozen movie houses (where such performers as Sophie Tucker, the Marx Brothers, and Benny Goodman appeared in vaudeville acts). Jewish bookstores,

A campaign poster in Yiddish urging the voters to register in order to
elect Judge Henry Horner governor. Horner served as governor of
Illinois from 1933 to 1940. His grandfather, also named Henry Horner,
was one of the first Jewish immigrants to Chicago in 1841, an organizer
of the Board of Trade, and owner of a large wholesale grocery company.
Courtesy of Irving Cutler.

funeral chapels, restaurants, delicatessens, Best's and Lazar's kosher sausage establishments, groceries, fish stores (with elderly horseradish grinders and their machines on the sidewalk outside), meeting halls, and political organizations.

The 24th Ward, led by Alderman Jack Arvey, was the top Democratic stronghold in Chicago. In the 1936 presidential election Roosevelt received 29,000 votes to Landon's 700, and FDR called that ward "the number one ward in the Democratic Party." In addition to politics, Roosevelt Road was also known for such well-remembered and homely institutions as "Zookie" the bookie and Davy Miller's pool hall–boxing gym–gambling–restaurant complex, which had originated on Maxwell Street. Jewish youths who hung around Davy Miller's establishment on Roosevelt Road near Kedzie served a community function of a special sort: they took on the gentile youth gangs that harassed Yeshiva students and stuck gum in the beards of the elderly Jews. In the 1920s the Miller boys also fought the young gentiles of Uptown for the territorial right of Jews to make free use of the newly created Clarendon Beach, just as in earlier days they had fought for the right of Jews to use Humboldt Park and Douglas Park. In later years such Jewish youths battled members of the Nazi Bund.

The Greater Lawndale community was alive with outdoor activity, especially in the warmer months. Through the alleys came a constant procession of peddlers in horse-drawn wagons, hawking their fruits and vegetables in singsong fashion. Mingled among them were the milkmen and the icemen. Occasionally fiddlers would play Jewish melodies in the yards, and the housewives would throw them a few coins wrapped in paper. The area was also traversed by the "old rags and iron" collector, the knife sharpener, the umbrella man, and the organ grinder with his monkey. Soul-hunting Christian missionaries canvassed the area often, going from house to house, but they made very few converts.

In the evenings most people would sit on their front porches conversing with their families and neighbors as a procession of ice cream, candy, and waffle vendors passed. People would go to the parks in the evening. There they would rent rowboats, attend occasional free band concerts, and sometimes sleep at the park all night during the most stifling summer weather. Various groups met in special sections of the parks where they sang to mandolin music or danced the *hora*. Some of the intellectuals congregated outside Silverstein's restaurant on Roosevelt and St. Louis to debate the issues of the day with the soapbox orators — communists, socialists, anarchists, atheists, Zionists, and so on.

Many of the boys of Greater Lawndale participated in the activities, mainly athletic, of three youth centers in the area: ABC (American Boys' Commonwealth), BBR (Boys' Brotherhood Republic), and the Marcy Center. All three had been located in the Maxwell Street area. While the ABC and BBR were Jewish-sponsored youth centers, Marcy Center was engaged in Christian missionary work and was not welcomed by the Jews it hoped to convert. Although it had a well-equipped dispensary, people injured nearby usually refused to be taken to the Marcy Center for treatment.

In the Lawndale area the Jewish People's Institute (left), on Douglas Boulevard and St. Louis Avenue, was a major social, cultural, and recreational center of Chicago Jewry from 1926 to 1955. The Hebrew Theological College (right) was located here from 1922 to 1956. It now occupies a 16-acre site in Skokie, to which it attracts students from all over the world. These two buildings are now the Julius Hess Elementary School.   Courtesy of Irving Cutler.

Other Jewish youths, including the future Judge Abraham Lincoln Marovitz, Stuart Brent, Barney Ross, and Maurice Goldblatt joined in the athletic, educational, and social activities of the Jewish People's Institute on Douglas Boulevard (declared a national landmark in 1979). They could eat there at the Blintzes Inn, vote for delegates to Jewish congresses, dance under the stars on the roof garden on Sunday evenings, attend lectures, listen to the institute's own orchestra, see Jewish museum exhibitions, watch plays by Chekhov and Turgenev in English or Yiddish, attend Herziliah Hebrew School or Central Hebrew High School, and study at the library. Here Leo Rosen taught English to immigrants, an experience that inspired his book *The Education of H*Y*M*A*N K*A*P*L*A*N*. Its hero was an indomitable Russian Jewish night school student who insisted that the Atlantic's opposite ocean was the "Specific," that the sixteenth president was Abram Lincoln, that "laktric" lights "short soicused," and that the three pilgrims who followed the star to Bethlehem were the "Tree Vise Guys."

In the summer those Jewish families who could afford it rented cottages in the Indiana Dunes or in the Union Pier and South Haven areas of Michigan, to which the husband of the family would usually commute on weekends. The largest Jewish resort area was South Haven, situated on the eastern shore of Lake Michigan and accessible by boat, train, bus, and auto. It contained summer camps, cottages, and especially resort hotels, most of them kosher and some with entertainment. The South Haven area was a miniature borscht belt — without the mountains.

While the Jews of the Maxwell Street area had been almost a direct transplant of the poor, isolated European ghetto Jews, the Jews of Greater Lawndale were people who lived in pleasant physical surroundings and were working hard to achieve middle-class status. Despite the universally severe hardships caused by the Great Depression of the 1930s, upward mobility continued among the Jews, and old-world cultural patterns were slowly modified by the "American way." This was especially true among younger Jews, usually American born, who often preferred baseball to Hebrew school, basement social and athletic club "hangouts" to synagogue, and careers in the professions to careers in merchandising. Despite the prejudice that restricted opportunities in certain spheres, more opportunities existed for Jewish youth in Chicago than ever before.

Almost as rapidly as Greater Lawndale had changed from gentile to Jewish earlier in the century, it changed from Jewish to black during the late 1940s and early 1950s. Other choice areas in Chicago and its suburbs had begun to open up for the Jews, and they leapfrogged over intervening zones to reach them. The Jews started to leave this area of their second settlement even though Greater Lawndale had not deteriorated physically, despite its very dense population. They left because of few opportunities for home ownership, relatively high income that allowed them to move readily from the changing neighborhood, the desire to own single-family homes in areas with more amenities and higher status, and because of the improved mobility provided by the automobile. Jews have been on the move for 2,000 years, and even in Greater Lawndale they had frequently moved from one apartment to another. Relatively few members of the new generation of Jewish adults were interested in clinging to the great institutional structures that their parents and grandparents had built. Old-world traditions, religious intensity, and the Yiddish language meant much less to those raised in the more secular environment of the new world. So they moved to the better and more prestigious areas of the North Side — some to Albany Park and Rogers Park, but more to West Rogers Park (West Ridge) and part of the northern suburbs — areas that were being built up after World War II. A smaller number went to Austin and the western suburbs.

Most of the Jewish institutions that once dotted the Lawndale area were transferred to other uses, though some were demolished and others abandoned. Mount Sinai Hospital still serves the community. The ABC and BBR facilities were turned over to a community organization for use by the new youths of the area. Most of the former synagogues are now black churches. The Jewish People's Institute was sold in 1955 to the Chicago Board of Education for a nominal fee; it is now a public elementary school, as is the former Herzl Junior

College. Most of the facilities formerly occupied by Hebrew schools have been torn down. The eastern part of the Roosevelt Road commercial strip is largely barren, its structures burned down in the 1968 riots. This vacantness exposes to view the giant Sears Roebuck mail order complex just to the north. It has outlasted the numerous immigrant groups that have passed through the area, but has now been phased out.

Many of the Jewish institutions of Greater Lawndale were rebuilt on the North Side, especially in the California Avenue area of West Rogers Park. Some synagogues of Lawndale liquidated completely, usually donating a portion of their assets to a congregation in a new neighborhood that would perpetuate their name and memorials and another portion to the Hebrew Theological College, which had moved from Douglas Boulevard to Skokie.

The North Side

Jews began to move into the Albany Park area a few years after the completion of the Ravenswood elevated line in 1907 to its terminal at Lawrence and Kimball (3400 west) avenues. The first Albany Park synagogue was the Reform Temple Beth Israel, founded in 1917. One of its members, Shimon Agranat, later became one of the chief justices of Israel. By 1930, Albany Park contained about 23,000 Jews, almost half of the community's total population. Many came from the older and less affluent Jewish areas of the West and Northwest sides. For them Albany Park represented a movement upward into a more Americanized community as well as a transitional middle ground between the Orthodoxy of the West Side and the Reform Judaism of the South Side. The area developed Orthodox, Conservative, and Reform synagogues and other institutional facilities, including a Hebrew day school, a rabbinical college, a boys' club, a Yiddish school, and a home for the Jewish blind. A strong concentration of Jewish institutions clustered around Kimball Avenue, on which the two major public high schools, Roosevelt and Von Steuben, were also situated. Lawrence Avenue, the main business street, was somewhat similar in character to Lawndale's Roosevelt Road, from which some of its stores had been transplanted. Albany Park was an active Jewish community with about fifty fraternal, social, communal, and political organizations in addition to those associated with the synagogues.

During the post–World War II exodus from Lawndale, many Jewish families, including numerous Orthodox ones, settled in Albany Park and adjacent North Park, and at the same time some of the more affluent earlier Jewish settlers of Albany Park moved still farther north. The Jewish movement out of Albany Park accelerated during the 1960s, and by 1990 only an estimated 2,000 Jews remained, most of them elderly and of limited means. The Ark, with its more than 200 professional and lay volunteers, and other organizations, ministered to their needs. Following the shifting Jewish population, the Ark moved

One of Chicago's most beloved rabbis was Solomon Goldman, noted scholar and speaker, president of the Zionist Organization of America, and Conservative rabbi of Anshe Emet Synagogue for almost a quarter of a century. He is seated here with Zionist leader Rabbi Stephen S. Wise of New York (left) and Albert Einstein (right). Courtesy of Irving Cutler.

from Albany Park to West Rogers Park. Just to the north of Albany Park, several thousand Jews still live in the higher income North Park community.

Until the extension of the elevated line to Howard Street in 1907, Chicago's most northeastern community, Rogers Park, was largely an area of single-family frame houses. With the improvement of transportation, numerous large apartment buildings and apartment hotels were built in Rogers Park, especially in the eastern portion adjacent to Sheridan Road and Lake Michigan. Jews, mainly from Eastern Europe, started to move into this area after 1910, and by 1930 about 10,000 lived there. After World War II the area contained about 20,000 Jews, making up about one-third of the population. At that time a majority of the students at Sullivan High School were Jewish. Thereafter, the Jewish population in the area gradually declined to an estimated 10,000 or fewer now. Most of the Jews who now live in Rogers Park are elderly — retirees, widows, and widowers. Some are residents of the numerous nursing homes along Sheridan Road. There are very few Jewish children; the average age of the Jewish population of Rogers Park is about sixty.

Since the early 1970s, more than 12,000 Soviet Jewish immigrants have settled in Chicago, most initially living in small apartments in the Rogers Park area, with smaller numbers in adjacent communities. Chicago, with about 4 percent of the country's Jewish population, has taken in over 9 percent of the

A protest against Soviet policy toward Jews, during an appearance by the Bolshoi
Ballet at the Civic Opera House in the 1970s. A change in Soviet policy later allowed
thousands of Russian Jews to come to Chicago.
Couresty Jewish Federation of Metropolitan Chicago.

Soviet Jews settling in the United States, and these recent immigrants already
comprise about 5 percent of Chicago's Jewish population. They are typically
well-educated professional couples with a couple of children and often an
elderly parent or two.[20] Many are doctors, scientists, lawyers, and engineers;
they constitute one of the best educated immigrant groups of recent years.

On their arrival in Chicago, they were welcomed by Jewish organizations who helped find them living quarters and jobs, and helped them with
finances and language problems. Some twenty-one organizations participated
in the resettlement program. In less than a year 80 percent were considered
self-sufficient and over 90 percent were working.[21] Only 25 percent had received
any public assistance, and most of those for less than three months.

Adjustment to the American way of living was not easy for many of the
Russian-Jewish immigrants. They had come from a land of enormous
bureaucracy where they were fearful of a government that usually made the

20. Donald J. McKay. "Soviet Jewish Emigration to Chicago, 1970-1980" (Ph.D. dissertation,
University of Illinois at Chicago, 1986), p. 135.
21. *Ibid.*, p. 140.

decisions regarding apartments, schooling, medical care, jobs, and vacations — where petty bribery and aggressive behavior were necessary to obtain hard-to-get goods. In democratic America they had to fend for themselves. How they fared in America often depended on their age, profession, English language knowledge, and adaptability to a new system. Those in the more needed professions became successful; others had to settle for jobs below their skills. Some experienced culture shock and complained, for example, of a vulgarity in American culture and the "pandering to common tastes which they found repulsive."[22] One irate mother even protested that her daughter in the nursery school was sleeping on a floormat "like a dog."

Many Jewish organizations, especially those with strong Orthodox ties, reached out to the immigrants to educate them about Judaism. Some of the immigrants were amenable to these efforts; but others were indifferent: many had come here mainly for the possibility of a better life and also for more opportunities for their children. Most of them had little religious background or knowledge of Jewish traditions. Their general lack of involvement in Jewish life in Chicago was a cause of concern for some in the Jewish community. Some felt that the Russian-Jewish immigrants were not like the "teeming masses," Zionist zealots, or Torah scholars who had come from Russia almost a century earlier. Some of the immigrants had never even heard of the Torah. The hope was that the immigrants would not "go native" and forget their identity as Jews.[23] The efforts of the various Jewish organizations were meeting with increasing success. Although the Russian-Jewish immigrants still socialized mainly among themselves and had set up their own facilities, such as delis and restaurants, many were using the facilities of the Jewish Community Centers, sending their children to Jewish schools, undergoing circumcision, and when they had become financially successful, as many have, were moving out of declining areas in Rogers Park and into predominantly Jewish areas of the northern suburbs.

Thousands of Jews live in the vicinity of Lake Shore Drive southward from Rogers Park to near the downtown area. They live mainly in relatively high-priced condominiums, cooperatives, and rental apartments in an unbroken array of high-rises that extend along Lake Shore Drive. They include many retirees as well as many young professionals. Included are a sizable number of singles, widows, and widowers but not many small children. These lakeshore Jewish residents are interested and active in numerous Jewish organizations and causes, and are supportive of some of the largest congregations in Chicago.

Since World War II, the big intracity movement of Jews who have left their former communities on the South, West, and Northwest sides has been into the area of West Ridge. This neighborhood, generally coinciding with what is popu-

22. *Ibid.*, p. 155.
23. *Ibid.*, p. 146.

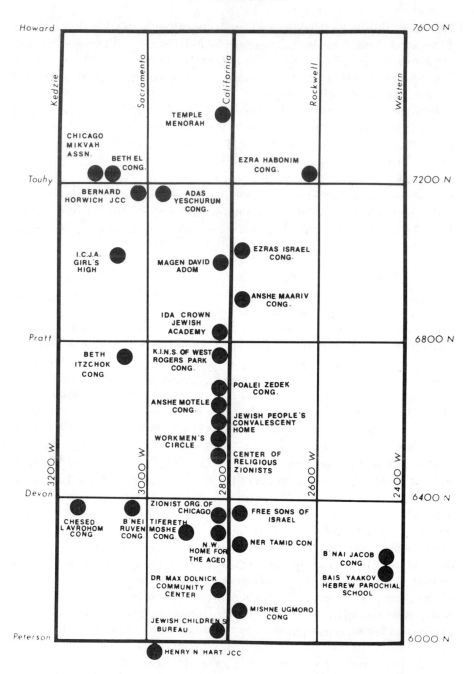

Jewish facilities in the heart of West Rogers Park, 1979: 18 such facilities are aligned along a two-mile stretch of California Avenue. West Rogers Park has Chicago's greatest concentration of Jews today. Courtesy of Irving Cutler.

larly referred to as West Rogers Park, lies between Rogers Park and the Albany Park–North Park area. Its approximate boundaries are Ravenswood Avenue (1800 west) on the east, the North Shore Channel (3300 west) on the west, Bryn Mawr Avenue (5600 north) on the south, and Howard Street (7600 north) and the Evanston border on the north.

There were fewer than 2,000 Jews in the area in 1930; by 1950 the number had reached about 11,000. In the 1950s the Jewish population of West Rogers Park quadrupled, and in 1963 it reached an estimated 48,000, or about three-fourths of the total population of the community. Most of the Jews of West Rogers Park are of Russian-Polish descent and are mainly second- and third-generation Americans. They came especially from Lawndale and Albany Park, and they purchased single-family homes in the northern part of West Rogers Park. Many Jews also moved into the new Winston Towers condominium complex south of Touhy Avenue.

Today West Rogers Park is the largest Jewish community within the city of Chicago. A number of its synagogues were founded almost a century ago in the Maxwell Street area and reached West Rogers Park via Lawndale. Most of its approximately twenty synagogues are Orthodox. Many are aligned along California Avenue, between Peterson and Touhy avenues, in a way that is reminiscent of Douglas Boulevard in Lawndale. On or near California Avenue are a religiously oriented high school, a large Jewish community center, a home for the Jewish aged, a Jewish convalescent home, and the offices of various Jewish organizations. Devon Avenue is the main business street of West Rogers Park; many of its merchants were previously located on Roosevelt Road or Lawrence Avenue.

The Jewish population of West Rogers Park is older and has a higher median income and a higher median educational level than the rest of Chicago's population. But like the population of the city as a whole, it has been declining in numbers — to about 35,000 Jewish residents at present. While the Conservative and Reform Jewish population of the area is declining, Orthodox Jews, including many young families, continue to move in and try to maintain their strength and institutions in the area where the services they require exist. It is the last Jewish area in Chicago where the rhythm of Orthodox life is still evident from the dress of some of the populace to the daily synagogue prayer services to the closing of the stores for the Sabbath. But increasingly, Greeks, Asians, Slavs, and others have been moving into the community. Devon Avenue has become a street of many nations.

The Exodus to the Suburbs

The major Jewish population movement in recent years has been out of Chicago into the northern and northwestern suburbs, where over 80 percent of the

154,000 Jewish suburbanites live. Small numbers of Jews, mainly descendants of the early German immigrants, moved into North Shore suburbs such as Glencoe and Highland Park shortly after World War I. The first synagogue in the North Shore area was the "branch" of the Sinai Congregation (Reform) of the South Side of Chicago, established in Glencoe in 1920. It soon became the independent North Shore Congregation Israel. But as late as 1950 only about 5 percent of the Chicago area's Jews were living in the suburbs. The 1950s saw a rapid general movement to the suburbs by many groups of people for a variety of reasons, such as changes in city neighborhoods, increases in the number and size of young families, the desire for better schools, the removal of restrictive covenants, and improved transportation.

By the early 1960s, some 40 percent of Chicago Jews were living in the suburbs, and today the proportion exceeds 62 percent.[24] It is estimated that today more than 80 percent of the 248,000 Jews of the entire Chicago metropolitan area, now live north of Lawrence Avenue (4800 north). In Chicago, about 80,000 of the city's 85,000 Jews live in the north lakefront communities (from the Loop north to Rogers Park) or the contiguous communities inland, especially West Rogers Park (West Ridge). Other Jews live in the Hyde Park–Kenwood area, and a few are scattered in other Chicago communities. There are also small numbers of Jews in most of the western and southern suburbs, with some concentration to the west in the Oak Park–River Forest–Westchester area and to the south in the Glenwood–Homewood–Flossmoor–Olympia Fields–Park Forest area. Small and often declining Jewish communities exist across the state line in the larger cities of northwest Indiana, such as Hammond, Gary, East Chicago, and Michigan City. Small numbers have moved into the growing cities of Highland, Munster, and Merillville, Indiana. The Jews of these areas, as well as in the southern and western suburbs, because of their small numbers and lack of certain services such as kosher butcher shops, bakeries, delis, and other organizations, often feel removed from the mainstream of Chicago Jewry which is concentrated dozens of miles to the north. Efforts to overcome the feeling of isolation have resulted in the establishment of a few Jewish educational and community facilities in these areas, supplementing the synagogues that have been the focus of Jewish life in these areas.

The first major move of Jews to the suburbs was into Skokie and adjacent Lincolnwood, with the first synagogue of these two suburbs, Niles Township Jewish Congregation, being founded in 1952. Skokie and Lincolnwood were not far from the Jewish concentrations in Rogers Park, West Ridge, Albany Park, and North Park. The opening of Edens Expressway in 1951 made them readily accessible. Furthermore, unlike the North Shore suburbs, Skokie and Lincolnwood contained a good deal of vacant, relatively low-priced land, some of which

24. Jewish Federation of Metropolitan Chicago, *A Population Study of the Jewish Community of Metropolitan Chicago* (Chicago, 1985), p. 19.

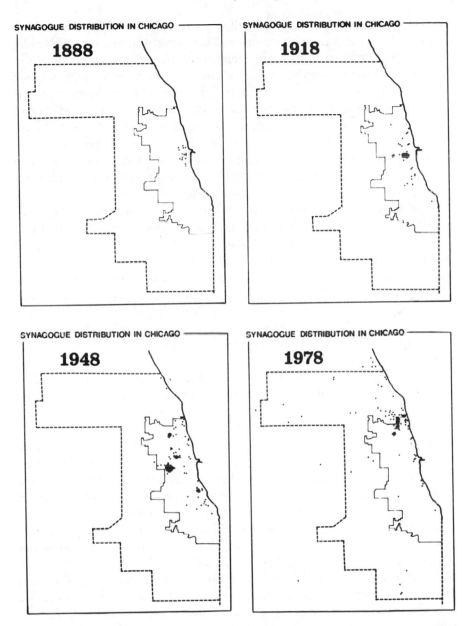

The changing pattern of synagogue distribution in the Chicago area, by 30-year periods, reflects the changing residential locations of the Jews in the area.
Courtesy of Irving Cutler.

had been prematurely subdivided during the 1920s — before the Depression and World War II halted construction. Thousands of mainly single-family dwellings were built in Skokie and Lincolnwood, often by Jewish builders who advertised in Jewish neighborhoods, and by the 1960s these suburbs were about half Jewish. In 1975 the Jewish Federation of Metropolitan Chicago estimated that about 40,000 of Skokie's almost 70,000 residents were Jewish. At present the two suburbs contain about a dozen congregations, most of which adhere to the Orthodox-Traditional or Conservative ritual, in contrast to the greater concentration of Orthodox synagogues in West Rogers Park, with its much larger numbers of elderly and foreign-born, and the preponderance of Reform temples in the more distant North Shore suburbs. Skokie also has a large rabbinical college.

After World War II, many Jews also moved into most of the other northern suburbs, with a few exceptions, such as Lake Forest and Kenilworth, which had long been largely closed to Jews. The population of the northern suburbs of Niles, Evanston, Wilmette, Glenview, Winnetka, Morton Grove, and Northbrook is now believed to be 10 to 25 percent Jewish. Skokie, Lincolnwood, Deerfield, Glencoe, Highland Park, and Buffalo Grove have a population now estimated at over 25 percent Jewish, with Glencoe, Highland Park, Skokie, and Lincolnwood estimated as close to 50 percent Jewish.[25] Most of the Jewish population of these suburbs moved into the new subdivisions developed after World War II. Some of the Jews who have been moving there in recent years come from Chicago. However, there has also been intersuburban movement among Jews, especially from Skokie, whose Jewish population has declined in recent years, partly because its post–World War II children have grown up and moved out. The Jewish population of Northbrook and Deerfield has increased especially rapidly in recent years.

The latest Jewish settlement pattern has been for young Jewish families to move into the still further outlying suburbs to the northwest, where there is vacant land and more reasonably priced housing. Serving these newer Jewish communities are synagogues in Hoffman Estates, Des Plaines, Wheeling, Buffalo Grove, and Vernon Hills. Buffalo Grove, some thirty miles northwest of the Loop, has a large and growing Jewish population, with six synagogues in the area. Unlike in Chicago, where the Jewish population has become largely concentrated in fewer neighborhoods, the suburban population continues to be dispersed over a widening geographic area, thus making it more difficult to supply certain services desired by Jews.[26]

25. *Ibid.*, p. 21.

26. For an overall geography of the Chicago region, which pays close attention to social and ethnic changes, see Irving Cutler, *Chicago: Metropolis of the Mid-Continent,* 3rd ed. (Dubuque, Iowa, 1982). (Eds.)

Chicago Area Jewry Today: Problems and Progress

The Jewish population of the Chicago metropolitan area has declined in recent years, to an estimated 248,000 in 1982, or about 4 percent of the total population. The decline has been due mainly to a low birthrate, movement to the sunbelt states, assimilation due to intermarriage, lack of Jewish identity and alienation among some youth, and the elimination of most immigration — though some European-Jewish survivors after World War II, and more recently thousands of Russian-Jewish immigrants, have come to the area.

The Jewish population of Chicago has aged: there are fewer children and more but smaller households reflecting more singles, elderly, and childless couples. The Jews have made advances educationally, professionally, and in relative influence, and are now accepted in most fields of endeavor. Their high median income compared to the general population reflects the fact that about twice as many Jews attend college compared to the general population; nevertheless, there are still more than 20,000 Jews in the area whose incomes are below the poverty level.[27]

Like American society as a whole, the Jews of the suburbs increasingly are faced with problems dealing with their youth, family relationships, and changing values. Maladies of society, such as alcoholism, drugs, and divorce, all of which had been rare in the Jewish community in the past, are now also increasing, though still below the national level. The lack of adequate Jewish education and religious involvement in a free, open society has led to an increase in cult membership and in the rate of intermarriage. Still, the residual effects of their culture and immigrant experience have helped to soften some of the effects of these problems. Irving Howe takes a long-range, and on the whole an optimistic, view of the future survival of Jewish culture. He believes that "cultures are slow to die," and "sometimes they survive long after their more self-conscious members suppose them to have vanished," a view that certainly seems to fit many of America's ethnic groups besides Jews. On the general suburbanization of his own people, Howe comments:

> A great many suburban Jews no longer spoke Yiddish, a growing number did not understand it, some failed to appreciate the magnitude of their loss; but their deepest inclinations of conduct, bias, manner, style, intonation, all bore heavy signs of immigrant shaping. What Jewish suburbanites took to be "a good life," the kinds of vocations to which they hoped to lead their children, their sense of appropriate conduct within a family, the ideas capable of winning their respect, the moral appeals to which they remained open, their modes of argument, their fondness for pacific conduct, their view of respectability and delinquency — all showed the strains of immigrant Yiddish culture, usually blurred, sometimes buried, but still at work. Like their parents,

27. Jewish Federation of Metropolitan Chicago, p. 15.

many were still enamored of that mystery call "education," still awestruck by the goods of culture. . . .[28]

And suburban Jews are no different in many respects from those who stay in the American big city environment:

> . . . the suburban Jews remained a crucial segment of the cultural audience in America: the operagoers, the ballet supporters, the book buyers. If Jewish socialism had almost vanished, it took on a second, less impassioned life in the liberalism prevailing among suburban Jews. And the tradition of tsedaka — charity, in the larger sense of communal responsibility — remained powerful, lashing the suburban (and urban) Jews to feats of self taxation that could not be matched in any other American community.

Jews are increasingly concentrated in the high-status northern suburbs and are moving out from there over a wide geographical area. This broader dispersal reflects economic success and also the decreasing dependence of Jews on totally Jewish institutions and support systems. However, in many cases the abandoned communal institutions of the city have been replaced by new ones, scattered mainly in the northern fringes of the city and suburbs. About a dozen city and suburban Jewish community centers operate under the aegis of the Jewish Federation of Metropolitan Chicago. This model umbrella-like community organization supports sixty community, social welfare, cultural, religious, and educational services and organizations, plus giving overseas help, mainly from funds raised through contributions by many thousands to the Jewish United Fund. The Jews have traditionally "taken care of their own" with zeal and dedication. This successful united effort is spurred on by memories of the Holocaust, care for new immigrants, and the strong feeling of the urgent need for a Jewish state that is secure.

The long-established afternoon Hebrew schools, most of which are synagogue-sponsored, have experienced enrollment losses because of the decline in the Jewish school-age population. However, there has been a growth of all-day Jewish elementary schools and high schools, both Orthodox and non-Orthodox, many of them newly organized, as some parents try to upgrade their children's secular education as well as instill in them their cultural heritage. Jewish study courses for adults have also been experiencing a recent resurgence that stems from a renaissance of interest among many Jews in their heritage and from their concern about Israel's future.

The hundreds of *landsmanshaften* that banded together *landsleit* from the same town in Europe have declined sharply with the passing of most of the Jewish immigrants from the scene. The Workman's Circle has experienced a

28. Howe, pp. 618-619.

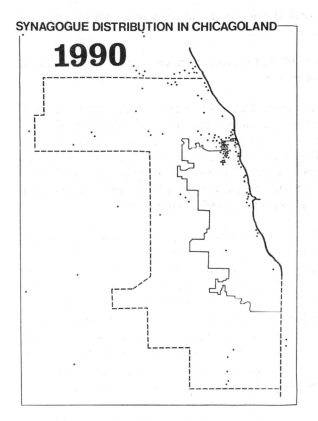

SYNAGOGUE DISTRIBUTION IN CHICAGOLAND

1990

The number of synagogues in 1990, about 120, has been about the same for the last few decades, but their size, religious affiliation, and location have undergone some change. A major change has been the increase of synagogues in southern Lake County, Illinois, to seventeen, more than double the number there a dozen years ago.
Courtesy of Irving Cutler.

similar decline. In their places are a broad range of local, regional, and national organizations that have been formed to aid various institutions in Israel.

Today there is a great diversity in religious feeling among Jews, ranging from the religious fervor of the Orthodox Hassidic to the humanistic Reform congregations, as well as an estimated 56 percent of Jewish households that are no longer synagogue affiliated.[29] Religious convictions are no longer always the chief motivation for joining a particular congregation; the social, cultural, and locational attractions are often just as important. The change in religious behavior that has accompanied the rapid decline of earlier immigrant groups and the movement of Jews to the suburbs is shown by the fact that there are now about 50 Orthodox-Traditional, 35 Conservative, and 30 Reform congregations in the Chicago metropolitan area, compared to 84 Orthodox, 8 Conservative, and 13 Reform congregations in 1930. The Conservative and Reform congregations of today usually have larger memberships than do the Orthodox. It is estimated that of those Jews who remain religiously affiliated, 30 percent are

---

29. Jewish Federation of Metropolitan Chicago, p. 40.

Orthodox and the remaining 70 percent are about equally divided between the Conservative and Reform movements.

The once tripartite division of virtually the entire Jewish community into North, South, and West Side neighborhoods in Chicago with certain social, economic, national, and religious implications has long been erased as the Jews dispersed into many communities, especially into the north and northwest suburbs. The literally extended family may now have the grandparents living in West Rogers Park, their children in Wilmette, and their grandchildren in Buffalo Grove.

The once-sharp dichotomy between German and Eastern European Jews has largely disappeared as the process of acculturation has progressed rapidly. The transition from European shtetls to Chicago suburbs took less than a century to complete. But despite some lingering problems, it is a remarkable American — and Jewish — success story, though it was not written without hardship, persistence, and toil.

CHAPTER 6

Polish Chicago:
Survival through Solidarity

EDWARD R. KANTOWICZ

What precisely is a Polish American? The question is not as thorny as that perpetual puzzler, what is a Jew? But it occasionally causes confusion. At the first Chicago Consultation on Ethnicity in 1969, a noted urbanologist, expounding on a series of census maps and tables, concluded that the most heavily Polish neighborhood in Chicago was Rogers Park. But this far north side neighborhood is populated largely by Polish and other Eastern European *Jews* and is never considered a "Polish neighborhood" by Chicagoans. A meaningful definition of Polish Americans includes only Polish Christians.[1]

It is true that the Polish Commonwealth during its heyday in the late Middle Ages was a multinational state, remarkably tolerant of the many Jews who fled from persecution in Western Europe. But when, after the decline and partition of the Polish state, Polish nationalism arose in the nineteenth century, it was linked very closely with traditional Roman Catholicism. Romantic nationalist writers like Adam Mickiewicz made a mystic, messianic fusion between God and Nation.

In the United States, Polish-American historians have occasionally beefed up their filiopietistic lists of great Poles in America with the names of Polish Jews, like Haym Salomon, a financier of the American Revolution.[2] But for the

---

1. The best introductions to the Polish experience in America are: Victor Greene, "The Poles," in *Harvard Encyclopedia of American Ethnic Groups*, Stephan Thernstrom et al. (eds.) (Cambridge, 1980), pp. 787-803; John J. Bukowczyk, *And My Children Did Not Know Me* (Bloomington, 1987); and Helena Znaniecki Lopata, *Polish Americans: Status Competition in an Ethnic Community* (Englewood Cliffs, 1976). Three books have been published about Poles in Chicago: Victor Greene, *For God and Country: The Rise of Polish and Lithuanian Ethnic Consciousness in America* (Madison, 1975); Edward R. Kantowicz, *Polish American Politics in Chicago, 1888-1940* (Chicago, 1975); Joseph John Parot, *Polish Catholics in Chicago, 1850-1920: A Religious History* (DeKalb, 1981).

2. See, for instance, Joseph Wytrwal, *Poles in American History and Tradition* (Detroit, 1969), pp. 75-79.

TABLE 6.1
Polish-Americans (1st and 2nd generations)

	United States	Chicago
1890	250,000	40,000
1910	1,663,808	210,000
1930	3,342,198	401,316

most part, though Poles and Polish Jews often lived close by in American cities, their community histories were separate. No anti-Semitism, simply analytical precision, is intended in excluding Jews from the definition of Polish Americans.

Counting Polish Americans is excruciatingly difficult and imprecise. The United States Census Bureau changed its method of enumerating immigrants nearly every ten years, sometimes counting only the foreign-born, at other times including the second generation, "native-born of foreign parentage." No census data includes the third or subsequent generations of Poles in America. Furthermore, many of the tables in the 1900 and 1910 censuses, when immigration was at its peak, contain no listing at all for Poles, counting them instead by their origin in the partitioning countries of Germany, Austria, and Russia. Yet by supplementing the federal censuses with other sources, such as school censuses, it is possible to produce the population estimates listed in Table 6.1. The 400,000 Poles in Chicago in 1930 formed 12 percent of the city's population of 3,376,438. Contemporary guesses place Chicago's Polish population today at about 600,000, or roughly 20 percent of Chicagoans. Since at least 1930, Polish Americans have been Chicago's largest white ethnic group, but they have never approached a majority in the city.[3]

Settlement Patterns: Ethnic Clustering

Polish peasants left the land in the late nineteenth and early twentieth centuries and journeyed to cities in Poland, Germany, and the United States in a search "for bread" (*za chlebem*, in the words of the novelist Sienkiewicz). Their settlement patterns in the United States were largely determined by that search. Most Poles and other turn-of-the-century immigrants settled in the northeastern quarter of the United States, where industry was crying for manpower. But

3. No one should take too seriously any population estimates for Polish-Americans, including my own. Censuses probably underestimate the numbers of Poles and other immigrant and racial minorities; Polish sources overcompensate by giving inflated estimates. My own figures are on the conservative side and are drawn from the following sources: 1890, U.S. and Chicago — extrapolations from U.S. census totals of foreign-born; 1910, U.S. — census totals for "foreign stock"; Chicago — extrapolations from the population of minors in the 1910 school census; 1930, U.S. and Chicago — census totals of foreign stock.

Caroline Golab has shown in a survey of fifteen cities from 1870 to 1920 that Polish immigrants, who had only their peasant strength to offer industry, were very selective even within this quadrant. Poles avoided semi-southern cities like Baltimore, Cincinnati, and St. Louis, where large black populations took up the unskilled jobs; they settled sparsely in other cities like Boston and Philadelphia, where light industry demanded mainly skilled labor; but they poured into new, raw cities of heavy industry like Buffalo, Chicago, and the numerous mine and mill towns of Pennsylvania.[4]

Within the city of Chicago, both the search for bread and a desire to find relatively familiar neighbors determined the sites of Polish neighborhoods. By 1890 five large Polish colonies had been settled in Chicago. Each was in an area of heavy industry: Polish Downtown on the northwest side, just west of the Goose Island industrial complex; the Lower West Side, adjacent to many factories along the Burlington Railroad and the ship canal; Bridgeport and Back of the Yards, circling the Union Stock yards; and South Chicago, hard against the steel mills. In at least three of these areas the Poles settled among Germans and Bohemians, with whom they were familiar in the old country.[5]

It has been a truism that Poles and other immigrants lived in ethnic clusters or "ghettoes" in American cities; but the term "ghetto" is imprecise and merits a closer look. The Polish settlement pattern was both segregated and decentralized. The segregation can be indicated by a statistical measure, the index of dissimilarity. This index measures the general unevenness of a group's distribution throughout a city. For instance, if Poles were 30 percent of a city's population, a perfectly even distribution would find them forming 30 percent of the population of every ward. This situation would produce an index of zero (0). At the opposite extreme, if all the Poles resided in one ward with no non-Poles present, this situation of perfect segregation would produce an index of 100. The intervening values of the index from 0 to 100, which are the only ones found in reality, give a rough indication of the extent of segregation. In 1898, the Polish index of dissimilarity by wards was fifty-nine; as late as 1930 that index still stood at fifty-five. By way of comparison, Table 6.2 gives the index of dissimilarity for most of Chicago's ethnic groups in 1898.

Two of the major Polish settlements were overwhelmingly Polish in population. Polish Downtown, near Division and Ashland Avenues, was a classic ghetto. In 1898, eleven precincts in this neighborhood formed a contiguous area, about three-quarters of a mile long and a half mile wide, which was 86.3 percent Polish. One precinct in the heart of this area was 99.9 percent Polish with only one

4. Caroline Golab, *Immigrant Destinations* (Philadelphia, 1977), pp. 3-27.
5. See Kantowicz, *Polish American Politics,* pp. 12-22, for details on these five settlements. Greene, *For God and Country,* pp. 31-33, stresses the mediating effect of established German and Bohemian communities in lessening the culture shock for incoming Poles.

TABLE 6.2
Indexes of dissimilarity, by wards, 1898[6]

Russian (Jews)	67	Norwegian	55
Bohemian	64	Danish	43
Italian	61	Swedish	34
"Colored"	60	German	29
Polish	59	Irish	27

non-Pole among 2,500 inhabitants. A total of 24,374 Poles — 25 percent of all the Poles in the city — lived in just these eleven precincts. Two of the largest Catholic parishes in the world, St. Stanislaw Kostka and Holy Trinity, served the Poles of this neighborhood. Headquarters for three Polish-language daily papers and the two largest Polish fraternal organizations were located here. Polish Downtown was to Chicago Poles what the Lower East Side was to New York's Jews. The Polish area near the steel mills of South Chicago also had a high Polish population dominance: four precincts forming an arc around the gates of the mills were 72.4 percent Polish in 1898. The other three Polish clusters were not as heavily dominated by Poles; each was less than 50 percent Polish.

But if Poles were segregated in clusters, the clusters themselves were decentralized and scattered. Slightly fewer than half the Poles lived on the northwest side of Chicago; the rest resided in the four other large colonies on the west and south sides, or in several smaller clusters which formed along railroad lines near industries.[7]

Demographic mixing, where it took place, did not generally lead to social mixing. The process of community-building in Polish neighborhoods produced a social and cultural ghetto.[8]

6. Population data for this table was obtained from the Chicago Board of Education School Census, 1898. The data for calculating the 1930 index came from Ernest W. Burgess and Charles Newcomb (eds.), *Census Data of the City of Chicago, 1930* (Chicago, 1933). Burgess and Newcomb used "community areas" as a base; these were generally about the same size as a city ward. The index of dissimilarity is explained most fully in Karl and Alma Taeuber, *Negroes in Cities* (Chicago, 1965), pp. 28-31, 195-245.

7. Kantowicz, *Polish American Politics*, pp. 23-24; Edward R. Kantowicz, "The Ghetto Experience: Poles in Chicago as a Case Study" (Paper delivered at the National Archives Conference on State and Local History, May, 1975).

8. Historians like Humbert Nelli and Howard Chudacoff, who have argued that the ethnic neighborhood was not so common an experience as supposed, fail to take sufficient account of the social and cultural aspects of the ghetto. See Nelli, *The Italians in Chicago, 1888-1930: A Study in Ethnic Mobility* (New York, 1970), p. 45; Chudacoff, "A New Look at Ethnic Neighborhoods," *Journal of American History*, LX (June, 1973), 77.

Building a Polish Community

The process of community-building is probably the best-known aspect of Polish-American history, thanks to the monumental sociological work by William I. Thomas and Florian Znaniecki in *The Polish Peasant in Europe and America*.[9] Polish immigrants built a complex of community institutions at the neighborhood level, recreating in part the milieu of the peasant village they had left behind. The Polish communities in Chicago approached very closely what one sociologist has called "institutional completeness."[10] This meant that the Polish ethnic group supported such a wide range of institutions that it could perform nearly all the services its members required — religious, educational, political, recreational, economic — without recourse to the host society.

The process of community-building generally began, ironically, with thoughts of death. The Polish peasant who was uprooted in Chicago, far from the village churchyard where his ancestors lay, worried about his own final resting place. The first mutual aid societies formed by Polish immigrants were mainly death-benefit societies. A tiny yearly payment of a dollar or two ensured that when an industrial worker succumbed to disease or occupational hazard, his wife would receive a payment sufficient to bury him properly.

These local mutual-aid societies, often composed of individuals from the same village in Poland, quickly proliferated and took on additional functions. They provided social life for the immigrants, many had religious overtones, and others formed to promote specific activities like community singing or needle work. A particularly important form of mutual aid was provided by the building and loan associations. Land hunger, a prime motive force in Polish peasant communities, was translated into the urge to buy one's own home in Chicago. While the Bohemians made the most extensive use of building and loan associations, these cooperative institutions were significant in the Polish communities as well. An association member made regular payments of fifty cents or a dollar per week for a number of years to build up a down payment, and the association supplemented this accumulation with a low-interest loan when the member actually purchased his home. By 1900, Polish building and loan societies held assets approaching one million dollars.[11]

A local society usually took the next step in the community-building process by founding a Catholic parish. The Catholic Poles worshipped at first in Bohemian or German churches, like St. Wenceslaus on the west side, or St. Michael's on the north; but before long the Poles organized churches of their

9. Consult the original five-volume edition (Chicago, 1918), but also read the lengthy introduction by Eli Zaretsky, in the new, abridged edition (Urbana, 1984).

10. Raymond Breton, "Institutional Completeness of Ethnic Communities and the Personal Relations of Immigrants," *American Journal of Sociology*, LXX (1964), 193-205.

11. Jakub Horak, "Assimilation of Czechs in Chicago" (Ph.D. diss., University of Chicago, 1924), pp. 74-75; Greene, *For God and Country*, pp. 54-56.

Community building: Polish thrift encouraged in bank ads.
Courtesy of the Polish Museum, Chicago.

own. A society of laymen formed under the patronage of some Polish saint obtained contributions from their countrymen in the neighborhood, purchased a piece of property, and then asked the bishop to help them find a Polish-speaking priest. Thus the first Polish community in Chicago, which had been pioneered by Anton Smarzewski-Schermann in 1851, organized the St. Stanislaw Kostka Society in 1864 under the leadership of Smarzewski-Schermann and Peter Kiolbassa. They formally petitioned the bishop for a

Kościół, Hala, Dom Sióstr i Szkoła

St. Stanislaw Kostka, one of the largest Polish parishes in the world.
Courtesy of University of Illinois Library at Chicago, Manuscripts Division.

priest in 1867, and St. Stanislaw Kostka parish built a small frame church and received a resident pastor in 1869. This process of lay initiative and episcopal approval was repeated in every settlement of Poles; but after this pioneering effort the time lag between the founding of a church-building society and the actual foundation of a parish was generally only a year or two. Eventually, forty-three Polish-Catholic churches were founded in the city of Chicago and eighteen more in the suburbs and outlying cities included in the Archdiocese of Chicago.[12]

Local societies were both the cause and effect of the parish-building process. Once a Polish church arose in a neighborhood, some pre-existing societies affiliated with it and numerous others organized. Thomas and Znaniecki counted seventy-four parish societies at St. Stanislaw Kostka in 1919, ranging from the needlework Club of St. Rose of Lima to the Court of Frederic Chopin.

The most important adjunct of a Polish parish was the parochial school. At the Third Plenary Council of Baltimore in 1884, the American bishops had

12. *Ibid.,* pp. 58-63; Kantowicz, *Polish American Politics,* pp. 14-22, 165-168.

decreed that every church should be accompanied by a school. In Chicago, under Archbishops Feehan, Quigley, and Mundelein, the school was often built first, with church services held in the basement until a more suitable house of worship could be built later. Yet not every parish responded to the Church's call for parochial education. In particular, Italian Catholics saw little reason not to utilize the free public schools. In 1910 only one of the ten Italian parishes in Chicago had a school. But the Poles responded more enthusiastically than most. The Resurrectionist Fathers, who administered St. Stanislaw and several other Polish parishes, not only built large elementary schools but also founded St. Stanislaw College in 1890 as a collegiate preparatory school. By the 1920s every Polish parish in the city and suburbs had its accompanying school. Attendance at Polish parochial schools in 1920 was 35,862, roughly 60 percent of Polish youth between the ages of seven and seventeen. No other Catholic ethnic group in Chicago equaled this percentage of parochial school attendance.[13]

The Polish Catholic Church in Chicago attained a remarkable institutional completeness. Of the estimated 213,000 Poles in Chicago in 1910, 140,000 were members of Polish-Catholic churches. The criterion of membership used by the various Polish pastors was generally more than baptism but less than regular Sunday attendance. Probably anyone who at least performed his Easter Duty and made some financial contribution to the parish was counted as a member. Thus about two-thirds of Chicago's Poles were part of the Polish-Catholic complex, with the remainder not church members, members of the schismatic Polish National church, or communicants in non-Polish-Catholic parishes. In 1930 the proportion of Chicago Poles attending Polish parishes was still nearly 60 percent.[14] In addition to churches, elementary schools, and St. Stanislaw College, Chicago Poles also supported St. Hedwig's Orphanage and Industrial School, Holy Family Academy for girls, four cemeteries, two day nurseries, an old-age home, and a hospital.

After the creation of local societies and parishes, the final step in the building of a mature Polish-American community was the federation of many local societies into a number of national, superterritorial Polish fraternal organizations. National fraternals emerged in the late nineteenth century, such as the Polish Falcons (a gymnastic union on the order of the German Turners), the Polish Alma Mater (which specialized in youth work), and the Alliance of Polish Socialists (not really very socialist, but rather a nationalist organization linked to Pilsudski's party in Poland). But the two most important Polish-

13. James W. Sanders, *The Education of an Urban Minority: Catholics in Chicago, 1833-1965* (New York, 1977), pp. 56-71; Francis Bolek, *The Polish American School System* (New York, 1948), p. 5.

14. These figures were calculated from the annual reports submitted by the pastor of each parish to the archbishop, Archives of the Archdiocese of Chicago. The proportions of other ethnic groups in ethnic parishes in 1930 were: Lithuanians, 38%; Italians, 36%; Yugoslavs, 33%; Czechs, 19%.

American fraternals, both of which had their headquarters in Chicago after 1880, were the Polish National Alliance and the Polish Roman Catholic Union.

An individual immigrant did not belong to one of these fraternals directly but rather as a member of some local society affiliated with it. The key to each society's mass membership was its ability to provide greater insurance benefits through large organization. But in addition to providing practical advantages, both the PNA and the PRCU pursued definite ideological goals. The PNA was a nationalist organization, directed by political *emigrés* from Poland who worked as a sort of Polish "Zionist" force for the liberation of the motherland from the partitioning powers. PNA leaders considered the American Polish colonies to be a "fourth province of Poland." The Alliance's leaders were laymen, its policies at least mildly anticlerical, and its membership open to Polish Jews, schismatics, and nonbelievers as well as Catholics. The PRCU, as its name implied, was a religious organization, open only to Catholics, dominated by the clergy, and dedicated primarily to the strengthening of Catholicism among the immigrant Poles.

The two organizations were bitter rivals for membership and influence. PNA leaders considered the PRCU insufficiently nationalistic, whereas the PRCU leaders thought the PNA godless. Yet this polarization can be exaggerated. The rank and file members of both organizations were overwhelmingly Catholic; they joined primarily for social and economic benefits, and because they usually belonged to several local societies, they often found themselves affiliated with both PNA and PRCU. The two organizations worked closely together during World War I. Once Poland was liberated, no ideological issue separated the two fraternals.

The national fraternals published Polish-language newspapers and other literature. Each had an association organ that appeared weekly. The PNA's *Zgoda* (Harmony) was started in 1880; the PRCU began publication even earlier, went through several titles, and finally in 1897 settled on *Narod Polski* (Polish Nation) as its main propaganda arm. Both papers are still published in Chicago today. The two organizations later moved into the daily newspaper field in Chicago, the PNA with *Dziennik Zwiazkowy* (Alliance Daily News) in 1908, and the PRCU with *Dziennik Zjednoczenia* (Union Daily News) from 1923 to 1939. The Alliance's *Zwiazkowy* remains today as the last of Chicago's Polish language dailies.[15]

The PNA-PRCU rivalry reflects an important division in the leadership class of Polish Americans, a division into two camps that Victor Greene has termed "nationalists" (PNA) and "religionists" (PRCU).[16] Division into two ideological groupings was a common experience for all the East European immigrants. The

15. Joseph Wytrwal, *America's Polish Heritage* (Detroit, 1961), pp. 148-259, presents a fascinating, and still useful, description of the PNA-PRCU rivalry. Donald E. Pienkos has written an exhaustive official history of the Polish National Alliance, *PNA: A Centennial History* (Boulder, 1984). There is no modern history of the Polish Roman Catholic Union in English.

16. Greene, *For God and Country*, pp. 61-68.

nationalist-religionist dichotomy that troubled the Polish community actually split the Bohemians into two mutually exclusive groups. Bohemian nationalism harks back to the Protestant followers of Jan Hus in the fifteenth century, who were ruthlessly suppressed by the Catholic Austrian emperor. When it re-emerged in the nineteenth century, Bohemian nationalism was not only anti-Catholic but secularist. Though Bohemia was a nominally Catholic country, the leading nationalist intellectuals were self-styled atheists and "free-thinkers." In the United States the free-thought movement broadened its base and embraced a large number of uprooted Bohemian peasants and workers as well. Free-thought had all the trappings of a secular church and engaged in its own drive for institutional completeness. The largest Bohemian fraternal organization, the Czech-Slovak Protective Society, identified itself with free-thought; the *Slovenska Lipa* organized as a national cultural center on Chicago's west side; nineteen free-thought schools taught Bohemian language and the principles of free-thought outside regular school hours; and the Bohemian National Cemetery became the final resting place of those who disdained consecrated ground.

Though Bohemian religionists, led by the Benedictines of St. Procopius Abbey, counter-organized with a full panoply of eleven national parishes, parochial schools, an orphanage, and a Catholic cemetery (shared with Polish Catholics), the free-thinkers greatly outnumbered Bohemian Catholics in Chicago. An estimated 70 percent of the Bohemians in Chicago avoided religion altogether. Compared with this Bohemian split into two completely separate cultural communities, the religionist-nationalist rivalry among Poles was mild. Nationalists and religionists formed two tendencies within one community of Polish Americans, rather than two separate communities.[17]

This interpretation of the community-building process may seem too monolithic to those who lived through the fierce internal quarrels in Polish Chicago. Just how fierce the quarrels were is illustrated in the next section. Yet those divisions remained for the most part within the Polish family, which prayed together and stayed together.

Polish-Catholic Factions

The main theme of Polish-Catholic history in Chicago was the community-building drive for institutional completeness. But as this drive unfolded, three stages of fierce controversy ensued. The first stage, which began as soon as the first Polish parish was organized in 1869 and continued until about 1900, was a struggle for control of the finances and administration of the parishes. The

17. *Panorama: A Historical Review of Czechs and Slovaks in the USA* (Cicero, 1976), pp. 31-32; Horak, "Assimilation of Czechs," p. 84; Eugene R. McCarthy, "The Bohemians in Chicago and Their Benevolent Societies" (M.A. thesis, University of Chicago, 1950), pp. 35-38.

second stage witnessed a campaign, running from about 1900 to 1920, to obtain Polish bishops in America. The final stage was a holding action, to preserve the institutional separateness of Polish Catholics and prevent absorption by the rest of the Church in Chicago. This stage began with the arrival of Cardinal Mundelein in 1916 and still continues today.

The first phase of controversy surrounding the Polish parish dealt not with dogma or belief but rather with church polity, the structure of church government. In the late nineteenth century, Poles, Slovaks, Lithuanians, and other recent Catholic immigrants reopened a fundamental question that had troubled the American Church from the beginning: who held legal title to Catholic Church property? The hierarchy had always maintained that legal title to all parish property must rest with the local bishop. Ultimate authority over parish finance would then be vested in him or in his direct representative, the pastor. But in the early years of the American republic, a more democratic polity, akin to American congregationalism, appealed to many lay leaders. In such a system, repeatedly condemned by the bishops as "lay trusteeism," a board of lay trustees would hold title to parish property, administer the parish finances, and hire and fire the pastor.[18]

The Polish nationalist faction in America revived the demands for lay trustee control, for they viewed the Irish bishops in Chicago and elsewhere as foreigners. Furthermore, the European church custom of *jus patronatus* (right of patronage) seemed to support their position. In Europe a noble patron often founded a local church, retained title to the property, and hired the pastor — all with Vatican approval. Polish lay leaders in America tried to transform this custom into a collective right of patronage by the whole local congregation, expressed through the board of trustees. In order to get a parish founded, the Poles usually surrendered title initially to the bishop; but if a particular pastor's personality or financial management later displeased them, they reasserted demands for lay, nationalist control.[19]

In Chicago the nationalist dissenters were opposed by the Resurrectionist Fathers, and especially by Rev. Wincenty Barzynski, C.R., pastor of St. Stanislaw Kostka from 1874 to 1899. In 1871, Bishop Thomas Foley made an agreement with the Resurrectionists whereby legal title to all church property would be vested in the bishop, but the Resurrectionists would exercise administrative supervision over all Polish parishes in Chicago as the bishop's representatives. The nationalists resented the Resurrectionists' "sellout" to the Irish bishop and

---

18. Patrick J. Dignan, "A History of Legal Incorporation of Catholic Property in the United States, 1784-1932" (Ph.D. diss., Catholic University of America, 1933); Patrick W. Carey, *People, Priests, and Prelates: Ecclesiastical Democracy and the Tensions of Trusteeism* (Notre Dame, 1987).

19. Greene, *For God and Country,* pp. 70-71; William Galush, "The Polish National Catholic Church," *Records of the American Catholic Historical Society of Philadelphia,* LXXXIII (Sept.-Dec., 1972), 132-133; Mark Stolarik, "Lay Initiative in American Slovak Parishes, 1880-1930," *Records of the American Catholic Historical Society of Philadelphia,* LXXXIII (Sept.-Dec., 1972), 151-158.

chafed under their authoritarian control of church affairs. In 1873, when over-crowding at St. Stanislaw necessitated the building of another church, a lay society founded Holy Trinity church three blocks away and tried to retain title and find a pastor more to their liking. The bishop and the Resurrectionists wanted the church to be merely a mission of St. Stanislaw. This Holy Trinity–St. Stanislaw dispute dragged on for twenty years. Several persons were excommunicated, and Holy Trinity was closed by the bishop for long periods of time. Finally, in 1893 a papal representative, Monsignor Francis Satolli, visited Chicago and personally ended the dispute. The dissidents had to yield the formal question of legal title, which was finally ceded to the bishop. But Satolli also ended the special relationship of the Archdiocese of Chicago with the Resurrectionist Order and brought in Rev. Casimir Sztuczko, a Holy Cross Father from South Bend, Indiana, and a strong nationalist priest, as pastor of Holy Trinity. This was a compromise solution that worked. Fr. Sztuczko was the pastor at Holy Trinity for the next sixty years.[20]

Controversy broke out again a year later in a new location. A few miles to the northwest of St. Stanislaw, the Resurrectionists had founded a new parish, St. Hedwig. Fr. Wincenty Barzynski unwisely gave ammunition to his opponents by appointing his brother, Joseph Barzynski, to be pastor of St. Hedwig's. When Fr. Anthony Kozlowski came to St. Hedwig as an assistant priest in 1894, he formed an anti-Barzynski faction of parishioners. Noisy disturbances broke out whenever the pastor said mass. On a cold February day in 1895, a mob of dissatisfied parishioners stormed the rectory and had to be driven back by the police. Though the bishop quickly brought in a new pastor, the dissidents would not settle for less than total control. So in June 1895, Fr. Kozlowski and about one thousand families seceded from St. Hedwig and formed a new parish of All Saints.

Over twenty years of nationalist battles with the Resurrectionists and the presence of a willing leader in Fr. Kozlowski had heightened the intensity of the St. Hedwig's conflict. Unlike the Holy Trinity affair, no reconciliation occurred. The dissident parishioners still considered themselves Roman Catholics at first; but when Kozlowski was consecrated a bishop in 1897 by the schismatic Old Catholic Church in Switzerland, and subsequently excommunicated by the Pope, they found themselves outside the Roman Church.[21]

These two church quarrels should not be viewed as freak occurrences, caused only by personality conflicts or the special position of the Resurrectionist

20. The only surviving record of the Resurrectionist-episcopal agreement is in the memoirs of the Resurrectionist Superior General, Jerome Kajsziewicz, *Pisma: Rosprawy, Listy z Podrozy, Pamietnik o Zgromadzenia* (Berlin, 1872), III, 350. Joseph Parot mounted a search for firmer evidence, but was unsuccessful. See Parot, *Polish Catholics,* pp. 49-51, 246-247. For the Holy Trinity controversy, see Greene, *For God and Country,* pp. 74-82; Parot, *Polish Catholics,* pp. 62-82.

21. Greene, *For God and Country,* pp. 103-109; Parot, *Polish Catholics,* pp. 109-119; Galush, "Polish National Catholic Church," pp. 133-134.

Order in Chicago. Trustee quarrels with bishops and pastors broke out in numerous Polish, Slovak, and Lithuanian communities throughout the United States in the late nineteenth century. Among Poles they resulted in three separate federations of independent, non-Roman parishes, headed by Kozlowski in Chicago, Fr. Stephan Kaminski in Buffalo, and Fr. Francis Hodur in Scranton, Pennsylvania. After Kozlowski's death in 1907 and Kaminski's in 1911, Fr. Hodur obtained Old Catholic consecration as a bishop and consolidated all the schismatic churches into one denomination, the Polish National Church. This church maintains nine parishes in Chicago and embraces an estimated 5 percent of Polish-Americans in the United States.[22]

The first stage of Polish-Catholic controversy had many causes. High handed pastors, financial mismanagement, the release of pent-up emotions in the free air of America — all contributed to the turbulence. But fundamentally the rebelliousness of the Polish parishioners was rooted in a desire for national autonomy within the American Catholic Church. The majority of Polish Catholics remained within the Roman church, and title to church property was ceded to the Irish bishops; but the struggle for the greatest possible national independence continued at a higher level with the launching of a drive for Polish bishops after the turn of the century.

During the second stage of Polish-Catholic controversy, initiative shifted from laymen to the clergy. This shift has been little noted and never studied in detail, but it is significant. It was part of a general damping down of lay activity in the American Catholic church as bishops and clergy slowly consolidated their administrative control in the twentieth century. What probably happened among the Poles was that the most outspoken lay leaders departed into the Polish National Church, leaving the Roman Catholic clergy in firmer control. It is also significant that at this stage the conflict was purely between Poles and outsiders. Though many Polish priests held aloof from the campaign for Polish bishops, none actually opposed it. Unlike the first stage of controversy, the new campaign united Polish Americans.

The primary leader in the drive for Polish bishops was Rev. Waclaw Kruszka, a priest of the Milwaukee archdiocese stationed in Ripon, Wisconsin. Fr. Kruszka, one of the first historians of Polish America, was a journalist and publicist of great talent. His brother, Michael Kruszka, edited an influential Polish-Catholic newspaper in Milwaukee. Fr. Kruszka opened the campaign with an article entitled "Polyglot Bishops for Polyglot Dioceses" in the July 1901 issue of the New York *Freeman's Journal*. He carried on the fight at two Polish-Catholic Congresses in 1901 and 1903 and made two trips to Rome. In Chicago

---

22. John P. Gallagher, *A Century of History: The Diocese of Scranton, 1868-1968* (Scranton, 1968), pp. 154-223; Theodore Andrews, *The Polish National Catholic Church in America and Poland* (London, 1953), pp. 18-25; Paul Fox, *The Polish National Catholic Church* (Scranton, n.d.), pp. 139-140.

he was supported by most of the diocesan Polish clergy, though the Resurrectionists remained aloof.[23]

The watchwords of the new campaign were equality and recognition. The
appointment of Polish bishops would recognize both the numerical importance
and the special cultural needs of Polish Catholics, which were neglected by the
Irish, German, and Anglo-American bishops who ruled virtually all American
dioceses in 1900. Ideally, the Polish clergy would have liked a reorganization of
the American church completely along ethnic lines. Instead of the existing
territorial dioceses, where all Catholics in a given area were subject to one
bishop, they desired the creation of purely Polish, Lithuanian, German, and
Irish dioceses irrespective of territorial location. Ukrainian Catholics in the
United States actually obtained this goal in 1913, over the protests of the
American bishops. Since Ukrainians worshipped in a separate rite and used Old
Slavonic as their liturgical language, Rome removed them completely from the
jurisdiction of American bishops and established a separate exarchy, or diocese.
But Rome held firm against any jurisdictional separation within the Latin rite.[24]

Failing to obtain separate dioceses, Poles tried to secure the appointment
of a fair share of Polish bishops to rule over American dioceses. At the very
least, they wanted Rome to appoint Polish auxiliary bishops in dioceses like
Chicago, where Poles were numerous. This would give symbolic recognition to
Polish Catholics and ensure that the ruling bishop had a Polish advisor. The
result of the Kruszka campaign was Rome's concession to the minimum
demand, the appointment of a Polish auxiliary in Chicago in 1908 and in
Milwaukee in 1914. Paul Rhode, the pastor of St. Michael's Polish church in
South Chicago, was chosen auxiliary bishop of Chicago by the Polish priests of
the archdiocese in a special election called by Archbishop Quigley. When Rome
ratified his selection, he became the first bishop of Polish ancestry in the United
States.[25]

Bishop Rhode proved a popular, energetic, and diplomatic leader of Chicago's Polish clergy. As Archbishop Quigley's Polish lieutenant, he had more
influence than an auxiliary bishop usually does. Besides making the rounds of
Polish parishes for confirmations and ordinations, he determined the assignments of Polish priests in the archdiocese. As the only Polish-American bishop
until 1914 and an organizer of the Association of Polish Priests in the United
States, his influence extended outside Chicago as well. Yet his appointment was

23. Parot, *Polish Catholics,* pp. 142-160; Anthony J. Kuzniewski, *Faith and Fatherland: The
Polish Church War in Wisconsin, 1896-1918* (Notre Dame, 1980), pp. 45-47.

24. Bohdan P. Prosko, "Soter Ortynsky: First Ruthenian Bishop in the United States, 1907-
1916," *Catholic Historical Review,* LXIII (Jan., 1973), 513-533; Gerald R. Fogarty, "The American
Hierarchy and Oriental Rite Catholics, 1890-1907," *Records of the American Catholic Historical
Society of Philadelphia,* LXXXV (Mar.-June, 1974), 17-28.

25. Parot, *Polish Catholics,* pp. 158-160; Greene, *For God and Country,* pp. 141-142. The
Polish auxiliary in Milwaukee was Edward Kozlowski, no relation to the schismatic Anthony
Kozlowski.

Paul P. Rhode, the first bishop of Polish ancestry in America. Courtesy of Chicago Historical Society.

essentially a form of tokenism. Without jurisdiction over a diocese, an auxiliary bishop's importance is largely symbolic. Rhode was not even a member of the diocesan consultors, the bishop's financial council. But the Polish clergy were satisfied for the moment.[26]

The recognition drive heated up again after Rhode was transferred from Chicago in 1915 to become Bishop of Green Bay, Wisconsin. In a sense this was a promotion, for Rhode now became the first Polish Ordinary, or ruling bishop, of a diocese in America. But Green Bay was a very small see, and the Poles were deprived of their symbolic leader in Chicago. When George Mundelein, a German-American, was appointed Archbishop of Chicago shortly after Rhode's departure and he failed to appoint a Polish auxiliary, the Polish clergy suspected a conspiracy. In the overheated atmosphere of World War I, friction developed between the Poles and their German bishop.

The campaign for Polish bishops climaxed in 1920, when the Polish clergy in the United States joined the newly formed Polish legation at the Vatican in drawing up a thirteen-page memorial. All the Polish nationalist rage against the

---

26. Greene, *For God and Country*, p. 142, misconstrues the significance of Rhode's appointment, picturing it as a successful conclusion of the Polish recognition drive and ending his book at that point. He implies that Rhode, as auxiliary bishop, shared in the archbishop's corporate, financial authority, which is erroneous.

neglect and insensitivity of "Americanizing" bishops — Archbishop Mundelein in particular — came out in this memorial. Specifically, the Polish priests requested that Bishop Rhode be transferred to a more important see, that Polish auxiliaries be appointed in a number of cities, and that the Poles be allowed a largely separate development of their Catholicism in the United States. The American hierarchy, in their annual meeting of September 1920, formed a three-bishop committee, including Archbishop Mundelein, to draft a strong rebuttal to the Polish memorial. Cardinal Gibbons of Baltimore forwarded the committee's reply to the Vatican, and Rome apparently accepted the American bishops' explanation. No action was taken on the Polish memorial.[27]

Waclaw Kruszka in Wisconsin had still not given up. In 1923 he wrote to Pope Pius XI:

> A nation . . . is part of nature. A nation is of divine origin, not human invention. . . . As a rule, even in the fourth and fifth generation . . . families are purely Polish in America. . . . Parishes of mixed nationalities in America are generally considered a necessary evil. . . . Therefore, as both families and parishes are regularly purely Polish . . . consequently dioceses also should be purely Polish. . . .[28]

Despite the token victories and many defeats of the previous twenty years, Kruszka was reiterating the maximum demand, purely Polish dioceses. But this issue was dead, and even the lesser demands of the Polish recognition drive were ignored. Chicago remained without a Polish auxiliary until 1960; few Polish bishops were appointed elsewhere in the United States.

Previous studies of Polish-Catholic controversies in Chicago have not given adequate attention to the third stage of the struggle. Victor Greene ends his book on a note of triumph with Rhode's appointment in 1908; Joseph Parot and Charles Shanabruch end their studies in the early 1920s on a note of defeat for the Poles. Since none of them explores fully the successful holding action of the third stage, they miss much of the significance of the struggles.

By the second decade of the twentieth century, Polish Catholics had suffered notable defeats in their movement for a purely ethnic Catholicism. The right of parish councils to hold church property in their own name had been denied; the desire for purely Polish dioceses had been rejected; and the demand for Polish ordinaries and auxiliaries in existing dioceses had been met with tokenism. Yet Polish Catholics in Chicago retained a remarkably complete complex of churches, schools, and welfare institutions, which, though technically part of the archdiocese of Chicago, were quite separate. Polish language predominated in the churches and schools, Polish priests served exclusively in their

---

27. Parot, *Polish Catholics,* pp. 188-214; Charles Shanabruch, *Chicago's Catholics: The Evolution of an American Identity* (Notre Dame, 1981), pp. 217-223.

28. Kruszka to Pius XI, June 9, 1923 (Archives of the Archdiocese of Chicago: 7-1923-P-21).

own churches and institutions, and a lively Catholic press was printed in Polish. Furthermore, the existence of an alternative church in the schismatic Polish National denomination gave the Roman Catholic Poles a secret weapon against any Americanizing bishop who might try to break down this institutional complex. If the Polish clergy yelled loud enough, a bishop's hand could be stayed by the fear of further defections. This secret weapon did not prove sufficient to make further gains, such as the appointment of Polish bishops; but it helped the Poles protect what they already had.

The coming of Archbishop George William Mundelein (Cardinal Mundelein after 1924) to Chicago in 1916 made necessary a Polish holding action to preserve their institutional complex. Mundelein ruled the Chicago arch diocese like a Renaissance prince from 1916 to 1939. He was a vigorous centralizer, a consolidating bishop in the mold of Cardinal O'Connell in Boston, Cardinal Dougherty in Philadelphia, and Cardinal Spellman in New York. Furthermore, he prided himself on his fourth-generation Americanism and was determined to break down the ethnic separatisms within the church in Chicago. Besides opposing the wishes of Poles, Slovaks, and Lithuanians for auxiliary bishops of their own nationalities, he initiated three policies in the first years of his reign that seemed to threaten the institutional completeness of Polish Catholics: he declared a moratorium on the building of purely national parishes; he initiated a standardization of the curriculum in the parochial schools and a policy of English only for teaching most school subjects; and he began to assign newly ordained priests of Polish and other East European ancestry to Irish or mixed parishes. But by vigorous protests and a tacit use of their secret weapon, the Polish clergy deflected the impact of the first two policies and completely defeated the third.[29]

As Polish-Americans and other ethnic groups moved out of their original neighborhoods into more middle-class areas on the Southwest and Northwest sides, Mundelein was reluctant to establish new national parishes for them, preferring territorial parishes open to all. The revision of canon law in 1918, which required Vatican permission for any new national parishes, supported his position; but he acted largely from his own motives. The expense and inefficiency of building many separate parishes in new areas bothered him; besides, he wished to expose the younger generation of Poles to a more mixed environment. The Poles were numerous and cohesive enough to defeat his purposes. Mundelein founded new parishes that were technically territorial, but in many cases he assigned only Polish priests to them. Parishes like St. Bruno,

29. Edward R. Kantowicz, *Corporation Sole: Cardinal Mundelein and Chicago Catholicism* (Notre Dame, 1983); Kantowicz, "Cardinal Mundelein of Chicago and the Shaping of Twentieth-Century American Catholicism," *Journal of American History,* LXVIII (June, 1981), 52-68; Kantowicz, "Cardinal Mundelein of Chicago: A 'Consolidating Bishop'", in David J. Alvarez (ed.), *An American Church* (Moraga, Cal., 1979), pp. 63-72.

St. Camillus, and St. Turibius on the Southwest Side and St. Constance on the North Side were just as Polish as any technically national parish.

Mundelein's establishment of the first diocesan school board in 1916, to coordinate the heretofore independent parochial schools, to standardize the curriculum, and to mandate English-language instruction, evoked much favorable comment in the Chicago daily papers and a storm of protest from the Poles, Lithuanians, and even the French-Canadian Catholics. But the centralization implied in this policy extended only to choice of textbooks, and languages other than English were still permitted for the teaching of catechism and reading. In what was perhaps an overreaction to Polish protest, Mundelein made sure that both the school board chairman and one of the two superintendents were always Polish priests throughout the whole of his administration. Through the teaching of the Felician Sisters and other Polish orders of nuns in the elementary schools, and that of the Resurrectionist Fathers, who expanded St. Stanislaw College into two modern high schools, Weber High and Gordon Tech, Polish leaders ensured a distinctively Polish education for most of their youth.

Finally, when Mundelein assigned three newly ordained Polish priests to non-Polish parishes in 1917, sixty-eight Polish priests signed a letter of protest against this attempt to denationalize the Polish clergy. Mundelein fumed and wrote testy letters in response. He later fired one of the protest leaders, Fr. Louis Grudzinski, from his post on the board of diocesan consultors, replacing him with one of the few Polish pastors who had not signed the letter, Rev. Thomas Bona. But despite this retaliation, the incident was one of Mundelein's most stinging defeats. Within two years the newly ordained priests in question were back in Polish parishes; and for the rest of his jurisdiction, Mundelein never assigned a single Polish priest to a non-Polish parish, even though he continued to assign priests of other ethnic groups to territorial parishes when the supply of priests permitted. The Polish clergy had succeeded in their holding action against one of the most authoritarian of archbishops.[30]

Despite the losses at the first two stages of Polish-Catholic controversy, the underlying process of community-building and the holding action against Archbishop Mundelein were so successful that the "Polish League" has remained a largely separate component of the Catholic Church in Chicago. Polish pastors acted like feudal barons throughout much of the twentieth century, answerable only to the Polish "boss," Monsignor Thomas Bona, whom Mundelein and his successor left in nearly complete control of Polish clerical affairs. When Mundelein built his new major seminary of St. Mary of the Lake, one of its purposes was to unify the clergy and instill *esprit de corps*. Accordingly, ethnic divisions were slight at the seminary; but after ordination, young Polish priests were assigned to the Polish League, indoctrinated by the pastor, and often forbidden

30. Kantowicz, *Corporation Sole*, pp. 72-83.

to attend class reunions or to go on vacations with Irish priests. In 1934, Cardinal Mundelein organized a mission band of diocesan priests to preach missions of spiritual renewal in the parishes of the archdiocese; but he had to arrange for a separate Polish mission band since the Polish pastors would not accept the ministrations of outsiders. As late as 1960, students of Polish descent at the minor seminary were required to study the Polish language, whereas all other seminarians could choose any modern language.

This victory of the Polish League was a pyrrhic one in several ways. For the priests themselves, assignment only to Polish parishes meant a longer than average wait to become a pastor. A Polish priest ordained in Chicago in 1926 or 1927 waited an average of twenty-four years until a pastorate in the Polish League opened up, whereas the average waiting time for an Irish priest was sixteen years, and the average for all priests in the diocese was eighteen years.[31]

More important, the Polish commitment to separate Catholic development meant a lack of influence in the affairs of the archdiocese as a whole. Polish priests had influence on the school board, and Monsignor Bona and one other Polish pastor sat on the board of consultors. But none of the newer archdiocesan agencies established by Mundelein and his successors, such as Catholic Charities or the Society for the Propagation of the Faith, had Polish directors. The crucial positions in the chancery office were completely devoid of Polish names. Even today, a glance at the Chicago clergy directory shows very few Polish priests in influential church positions.

Polish Catholics today often decry this lack of influence as discrimination, and discrimination there may have been. But the choice of separate development largely predestined this result. Polish Catholics could not have it both ways — separate development and influence in wider circles. Confined to their own community, Polish priests did not develop the contacts, the political skills, or the diversity of experiences necessary to forge ahead in internal church politics. Cardinal Mundelein offered the Polish clergy a beginning on the road to greater influence in Chicago Catholicism, but the Polish priests chose to stay with the path of separate development. Their choice was thoroughly consistent with the process of community-building that had been going on for half a century in Polish Chicago, but it closed off new options in church politics. Polish leaders made a similar choice in secular politics.

---

31. These figures were obtained by tracing the "cohort" of priests ordained in 1926 and 1927 through their entire careers by means of the official announcements of appointments in *The New World* and the yearly listings in *The Official Catholic Directory*. The 1916-17 cohort showed a similar disparity; 22 years waiting time for Polish priests, 15.4 for Irish. However, the cohorts of 1936-37 and thereafter shows a different pattern. By this time, Mundelein's seminary was producing such a supply of clerics that all priests of the archdiocese, Polish and non-Polish alike, had to wait between 25 and 30 years for a pastorate.

Polish-American Politics

The voting record of Chicago Poles in American politics can be summarized briefly: Poles voted Democratic from the beginning. In eighteen
mayoral elections from 1889 to 1935, the identifiably Polish voting precincts
gave a majority of their votes to the Democratic candidate in every instance.
In thirteen Presidential elections from 1888 to 1936, the Polish precincts
produced a Democratic majority in all but two cases. This political allegiance
was rooted in a perception of the Democrats as the party of average working-
men and of broad-minded toleration for the Poles' religion and customs. The
Republicans, on the other hand, were perceived as puritanical, aloof, and
plutocratic. These perceptions and their attendant voting patterns were not a
product of Franklin Roosevelt's New Deal, as is sometimes supposed, but of
the nineteenth century.[32]

More significant, perhaps, than the voting record is the political strategy
pursued by Polish Democratic leaders, a strategy of solidarity politics. Polish
politicians organized their bloc vote around in-group concerns, constantly tried
to perfect the unity and solidarity of the bloc, and neglected the building of
coalitions with other political blocs. The high point of this solidarity strategy
came in the 1930s, with the organization of the Polish American Democratic
Organization (PADO) as a political service agency and an ethnic lobby within
the Democratic party. This strategy parallels the separate development of Poles
within the Catholic Church during the same period.

Polish leaders were misled by the fact of their large numbers into thinking
that political power would fall to them like a ripe fruit if only they could perfect
the solidarity of their group. Since Polish voters never formed a majority of the
electorate in Chicago, however, such a strategy was doomed to failure. Despite
their large numbers, Polish Americans never elected a Polish mayor of Chicago
and they remained weak in the councils of the Democratic central committee.
With the death of Mayor Richard J. Daley in the winter of 1976, Polish candidates were passed over to succeed him, and a special post of vice-mayor was
created as a consolation prize for the Poles.

Anton Cermak, the Bohemian political boss, rose to power in Chicago
politics in the 1920s by pursuing a different strategy. Through such organizations as the United Societies for Local Self Government, an anti-Prohibition
lobby, Cermak allied a great number of ethnic blocs behind him. Polish leaders,
on the other hand, organized around specifically in-group concerns, like having
the name of Crawford Avenue changed to Pulaski Road. This won them no
allies. At the time of Mayor Cermak's death, the influential *Dziennik Chicagoski*
seemed to understand the lesson of his political career:

---

32. See Kantowicz, *Polish American Politics*, for all references in this section.

A Pole will be mayor of Chicago, only if we continue the politics of the dead mayor Cermak, i.e., if we make alliances with other groups. . . . Unfortunately, the majority among us is now playing at Pan-Slavism and forgetting that Mayor Cermak practiced a different kind of politics. In his organization were found next to the Czechs, Jews; next to the Poles, Irish; next to the Germans, Swedes.[33]

However, neither the *Chicagoski* nor other Polish spokesmen took this advice to heart. As in the Roman Catholic Church so in the Democratic party, Polish leaders continued to nurture separate development and internal solidarity. They did not engage in bridge-building, coalitions, or broker politics.

A Wider Solidarity

Through their numbers and the success of their community-building process, Poles in Chicago attained a large measure of institutional completeness. Within the Catholic Church and the Democratic party they achieved a cohesive, largely separate existence. Yet such success has been purchased at the expense of wider influence in Chicago Catholicism and city politics.

One important area of Polish-American life, economic development, escaped this centrifugal tendency of Polonia. The overwhelming majority of Polish immigrants worked as laborers in large industries, owned and managed by others. A shop-owning and business class did develop in Polish neighborhoods, made up mainly of saloon and grocery-store owners. Indeed, the Polish-language press constantly implored its readers to follow a policy of *"Swoj do Swego,"* or *"*support your own,*"* whenever they went shopping. These Polish businesses were not insignificant economically. One study found that they employed about 30,000 persons in the 1920s.[34] Yet there were at least 80,000 Polish heads of households in Chicago at that time, so the majority of workers still earned their livelihood outside the Polish institutional complex. The factory floor was the major arena in which a Polish immigrant made contact with members of other ethnic groups.

At first, this contact was incidental and superficial. Factory owners mixed the ethnic groups together at work in order to divide and control them more effectively; so Poles worked cheek by jowl with Germans, Irish, blacks, and Latinos. Yet, when the job was over, immigrants would retreat to their own families, neighborhoods, churches, and saloons. As Polish Americans put down deeper roots in the working-class world, however, they built crucial alliances with other immigrant groups in labor unions and community organizations.

33. *Dziennik Chicagoski*, March 14, 1933, p. 4.
34. Sr. Lucille Wargin, C.R., "The Polish Immigrant in the American Community, 1880-1930" (M.A. thesis, DePaul University, 1948), pp. 54-55.

Polish solidarity extends to the business world.
Courtesy of the Polish Museum, Chicago.

Without abandoning their fierce communal loyalties, Poles reached out in a wider solidarity to control their economic destiny.

In the early days of trade unionism, union leaders badly misread the Poles' clannishness and considered them unorganizable. Polish peasants had come primarily as temporary laborers, intending to stay only long enough to earn a nest egg and buy land back home. Many got their first job in the steel mills or stockyards as strikebreakers. They willingly worked the longest hours, for any wage, and tried to save every penny. Under normal circumstances, then, their limited aspirations in the New World and their peasant submissiveness and dedication to hard work put them at cross purposes with the militant aims of union organizers. Yet a peasant remained submissive only up to a point. If he felt his fundamental rights were being violated, he would resist fiercely; and in such cases, his communal solidarity proved a tremendous asset in a strike situation.[35]

By World War I, Polish workers in Chicago were receptive to arguments for union solidarity across ethnic lines. John Kikulski, a fiery Polish socialist, headed the largest local in the Amalagamated Meat Cutters' Union and was a key leader of the Stockyards Labor Council. Under Kikulski's leadership, one historian has concluded, "by far the best union men and women were the Poles."[36]

When the stockyards workers went out on strike in 1921, the whole Polish community threw themselves into the struggle. Father Louis Grudzinski, pastor of St. John of God, Packingtown's largest parish, openly supported the strike. Pitched battles broke out between Polish strikers and the packers' strikebreakers at the 43rd and Ashland gate to the Chicago Stockyards. When mounted police charged the strikers, like so many Cossacks in the old country, the Polish women threw red pepper and paprika in the eyes of both the police and their horses.[37]

The packinghouse strike failed in 1921; John Kikulski had been murdered under mysterious circumstances the year before. The major industries in Chicago remained unorganized until the 1930s. Polish workers, however, joined the industrial unions of the CIO en masse when a Packinghouse Workers' Organizing Committee finally organized the stockyards and the United Steelworkers of America overcame the power of U.S. Steel in South Chicago. Union solidarity built upon a firm foundation of ethnic solidarity.[38]

Polish Americans also reached outside their own ethnic group in two working-class community organizations, the Back of the Yards Neighborhood Council and the Russell Square Community Committee. Back of the Yards was a ramshackle, dispirited neighborhood in the 1930s: nearly everyone was a Catholic immigrant, but ethnicity divided the neighborhood into separate enclaves, with eleven Catholic churches of seven different nationalities. In the late 1930s, Saul Alinsky, a community organizer from the University of Chicago,

35. Victor Greene, *The Slavic Community on Strike* (Notre Dame, 1968), was the first to study Polish labor attitudes in detail. John J. Bukowczyk, "Polish Rural Culture and Immigrant Working Class Formation, 1880-1914," *Polish American Studies*, XLI (Autumn, 1984), 23-44, has described the complexities of these attitudes.

36. James R. Barrett, *Work and Community in the Jungle: Chicago's Packinghouse Workers, 1894-1922* (Urbana, 1987), pp. 195-196.

37. Dominic Pacyga, *Polish Chicago: The Making of an Urban Working Class Community* (Columbus, Ohio, forthcoming). I have benefited greatly from conversations with Professor Pacyga and from readings of an advance copy of his book.

38. Barbara Wayne Newell, *Chicago and the Labor Movement: Metropolitan Unionism in the 1930s* (Urbana, 1961), pp. 163-168; Robert A. Slayton, *Back of the Yards: The Making of a Local Democracy* (Chicago, 1986), pp. 194-205.

sought out natural leaders and local institutions as the base for what he called a "people's organization." On July 14, 1939, representatives of every organization in "Packingtown" met to form the Back of the Yards Neighborhood Council. Two-thirds of the 185 groups allied in the Council were parish societies, representing all the ethnic groups of the neighborhood. An Irish Catholic, Joseph Meegan, guided the organization as executive director; but Father Edward Plawinski, Grudzinski's successor at St. John of God parish, worked closely with Meegan as the first president of the council. The Back of the Yards Council checked the community's decay into a slum. It instilled pride in the residents, organized fix-up campaigns, and pressured business and government to provide jobs, relief money, and better services for the neighborhood.[39]

Similarly in South Chicago, Clifford Shaw, a University of Chicago sociologist, served as catalyst for a community-organizing effort in the Polish community around the steel mills. Shaw had written a classic study of immigrant juvenile delinquency called *The Jack Roller* in 1930, and he chose South Chicago as an experiment for his Chicago Area Project to counteract youth crime. Shaw formed an alliance with Father John Lange, the pastor of St. Michael's Polish Catholic Church, which dominated the neighborhood. Lange and Shaw frankly used each other. Shaw needed a base for his project, Lange needed something to keep his parish youth off the streets and away from the YMCA or other Protestant organizations. Their alliance resulted in the formation of the Russell Square Community Committee in 1933. The Committee organized recreational activities in Russell Square Park, across the street from St. Michael's, and it pressured the city into renovating the park. It worked closely with the police to have juvenile offenders released into its custody and also established an Adult Parole Program to supervise older criminals.[40]

In the CIO industrial unions, in the the Back of the Yards Neighborhood Council, and in the Russell Square Community Committee, Polish Americans cautiously reached across ethnic lines to combat unemployment, neighborhood blight, and crime. These efforts proved successful in surmounting some of the problems of the Depression era and raising the standard of living of the Polish communities.

Polish Chicago and the Success Myth

Once the Great Depression ended, the steady factory work of the Poles and their wholehearted embrace of union solidarity produced immediate benefits in higher earnings and job security. Poles in Chicago were less likely to become

39. Saul Alinsky, *Reveille for Radicals* (New York, 1969); Robert Bailey, Jr., *Radicals in Urban Politics: The Alinsky Approach* (Chicago, 1972); Slayton, *Back of the Yards*, pp. 189-223.

40. Dominic Pacyga, "The Russell Square Community Committee: An Ethnic Response to Urban Problems," *Journal of Urban History*, XV (February, 1989), 159-184.

self-employed, independent businessmen than were the Italians, and much slower to join the professions than were Jews. Various studies by Andrew Greeley in the 1970s revealed that Polish Americans did not generally hold prestigious jobs; but they did make more money than the average.[41]

Polish Americans have generally pursued a different dream of success from the standard American ideal of an individualist rise to the top in a profession or business; their success dream has valued family, religion, and community more highly. They opted for monetary success in unionized jobs and for economic and psychological security in home-owning rather than for risk-taking in business and the professions. Though they did not achieve separate development in the economic realm, a process similar to the trend in the church and politics seems to have been in operation. Poles pursued and attained a working-class variety of success at the expense of wider influence.

If Polish immigrants came to America seeking primarily bread, a home, and a better standard of living for their families, and at the same time they tried to preserve their communal lifestyle as much as possible, the conclusion is inescapable that they got what they wanted and have been successful on their own terms.

Yet the Polish-American communities have been changing. Despite the economic boom after World War II and the efforts of community organizations to improve living conditions, the working-class neighborhoods near the stockyards and steel mills have remained tired, dirty, and crowded. Many Polish-Americans continued working in the yards or the mills but bought homes in the suburbs or on the semisuburban fringes of the city. Some reversed the process by remaining in the old neighborhood but reverse-commuting to jobs in the suburbs. Either way, the traditional working-class link between job and neighborhood was broken. Blacks and Latinos took the places vacated by Poles both in the factories and the neighborhoods.

Then suddenly, the heavy industries that had given birth to these neighborhoods collapsed. Under the pressure of low-wage, foreign competition, the industrial heartland of the Northeast and the Midwest changed into the "Rust Belt." The stockyards closed forever on August 1, 1971; Wisconsin Steel, in South Chicago, shut down in 1980; then, four years later, U.S. Steel closed its massive South Works plant. Both Packingtown and the South Chicago steel mills became ghost towns. The other three primary Polish neighborhoods fared little better.[42]

Having lost their economic base, the original Polish working-class neighborhoods are also losing their symbolic centers. The Polish Roman Catholic Union is still headquartered in Polish Downtown, but the Polish National Alliance moved to the far northwestern edge of the city in the late 1970s. The Polish churches remained for a time after most of the Polish parishioners had

---

41. Andrew M. Greeley, *American Catholics: A Social Portrait* (New York, 1977), pp. 63-65.
42. Dominic Pacyga, "Polish America in Transition: Social Change and the Chicago Polonia, 1945-1980," *Polish American Studies*, XLIV (Spring, 1987), 38-55.

left the neighborhoods, typically offering three different masses on Sundays, one in Polish, one in English, and one in Spanish. Then on January 21, 1990, Cardinal Joseph Bernardin announced that at least 37 churches and schools would be closed or consolidated in a major cost-cutting drive. Polish parishes in Polish Downtown, Bridgeport, and Back of the Yards were among those shuttered. In a separate development, the cardinal also announced the closing and probable destruction of Polonia's largest and most magnificent church, St. Mary of the Angels, despite a vigorous fundraising drive by parishioners to renovate the Renaissance-style edifice.[43]

Polish Americans in Chicago, no longer tightly clustered around church steeple and factory smokestack, are more diverse today than they have ever been. Some older Poles remain isolated in the original five neighborhoods. Many recent immigrants from Communist Poland, who have come in increasing numbers since the revision of American immigration laws in 1965, have settled in the traditional areas of second settlement, particularly Avondale and Belmont-Cragin on the Northwest Side. Though many of the women work as cleaning ladies and some of the men have taken factory jobs, most of the recent immigrants come from the business and professional classes and have experienced more rapid economic mobility than the earlier peasant immigrants. The descendants of those turn-of-the-century peasants live primarily on the far Northwest and Southwest sides and in suburbs such as Niles and Park Ridge to the northwest and Calumet City and Lansing to the south. Increasing numbers of third- and fourth-generation Polish Americans have severed their working-class roots and entered medical, dental, and law schools. Yet many more remain in working-class jobs, often as foremen or supervisors.[44]

Having long employed the survival strategies of ethnic and working-class solidarity, Poles in Chicago and elsewhere in America recently swelled with pride as their homeland was freed from Communism by a movement named Solidarity. Yet many face a future in the Chicago area nearly as uncertain as that of Poland itself. One historian has concluded: "In a way Poles . . . were seduced and abandoned by industrial America. . . . Polish Americans are in a sense migrating once again, not necessarily to another country, but through the educational system to other forms of employment in the professions or newer technologies."[45]

Not even a cohesive group like the Polish Americans is immune to the powerful forces of industrial change and the American success myth. Poles in Chicago lived on their own terms for a long time, but those terms are changing rapidly. Polonia's second century in Chicago will be far different from its first.

---

43. The mass church closings were announced in *Chicago Tribune*, January 22, 1990, p. 1, and explained in more detail in *The New World*, January 26, 1990, pp. 9-16.

44. Pacyga, "Polish America in Transition," pp. 43-48.

45. *Ibid.*, p. 53.

CHAPTER 7

Ukrainian Chicago: The Making of a Nationality Group in America

MYRON BOHDON KUROPAS

The United States is the only country in the world where, when one becomes a citizen, one does not betray his own nation.

— *Sich*, January 1, 1930

Basic to any understanding of the nature of the Ukrainian experience in Chicago is an appreciation for the persistent need of Ukrainian Americans, wherever they settle, to maintain their ethno-national integrity. Denied an opportunity to develop their unique heritage in a homeland free of foreign rule, Ukrainian immigrants have created a second homeland in the United States and have nurtured it for over one hundred years. It is here in America that Ukrainian institutions have flourished, and it is here that Ukrainian traditions have survived for four generations. If one were asked, therefore, to summarize the Ukrainian-American experience in a brief statement, that statement would be "the development and preservation of Ukrainianism."

Chicago's First Emigrés from Ukraine

The first emigrés from Ukraine to settle in Chicago were probably living in the city and environs as early as the 1880s. According to Dr. Volodymyr Simenovych, a physician who settled in Chicago in 1893, there was a Russian Orthodox church already in existence at Madison and Racine when he arrived. Most of the parishioners, Simenovych believed, were from Carpatho-Ukraine,[1] having been con-

---

1. Stephen Kuropas, "Shikago" (Chicago), *Propamyatna Knhla Vidina z Nahody Soroklithnoho Yuvileyu Ukrayinskoho Narodnoho Soyuzu* [*Jubilee Book of the Ukrainian National Association in Commemoration of the Fortieth Anniversary of its Existence*], Luka Myshyha, ed. (Jersey City, New Jersey, 1936), p. 541.

verted to Orthodoxy in all probability during Fr. Alexis Toth's visit to the city in 1892. Upon learning in 1895 that Bishop Nicholas planned to build a Russian cathedral in the city, *Svoboda* protested against this new "russification":

> During his visit to St. Petersburg, Bishop Nicholas convinced the so-called Synod and the Czar that the time was ripe to energetically develop the area because the "material" here happens to be more than ample. That "material" happens to be our poor Rusin people from Galicia and Hungarian Rus. Already the poor Rusin nation has far too many unsolicited protectors. In the old country they tried to take away our nationality and to make us Poles, Hungarians, and Slovaks; here in America they wish to take away our faith. Difficult will be the road of our adversaries. We are equal to the struggle and we are confident that our people will not sell their souls to Judas.[2]

Ultimately, the Russian czarist regime allocated $4,000, with a per annum 600 gold rubles as collateral for the building loan.[3] Designed by the famous Chicago architect Louis H. Sullivan, Holy Trinity Russian Orthodox Cathedral was completed at Leavitt and Haddon in 1903. Those Carpatho-Ukrainians who remained with the church were eventually absorbed into the Russian ethno-national stream, but the church remains as a reminder of the non-Russian origins of the Cathedral's founding members.[4]

A second group of Rusins, also from Carpatho-Ukraine, settled on Chicago's South Side. A parish was organized in June 1903, and in 1905 a church was constructed on the corner of 50th and Seeley, with Fr. Victor Kovaliczki as the first pastor. Naming their new edifice "The First Greek Catholic Church of St. Mary's of Chicago," the parishioners steered clear of Russian Orthodoxy and eventually became part of the Rusin-Ruthenian ethno-national stream.[5]

The Ukrainian stream in Chicago began with the arrival of Dr. Simenovych. Once a third-year law student at the University of Lviv, a personal friend of Ivan Franko, Ukraine's leading poet during this period, and an energetic activist in Ukrainian ethno-national organizations in eastern Galicia, Simenovych came to America in 1887 at the request of a priest who was responding to Fr. Volansky's plea to "send me an intelligent young man to assist me with my work in America." Settling in Shenandoah, Pennsylvania, Simenovych was made editor of *Ameryka*, a Ukrainian-language newspaper that Volansky had established in 1886. A man of many and varied talents, Simenovych soon came to manage a Ukrainian cooperative store and to organize a drama troupe, a reading room for illiterates, and an evening school for adults and children. Leaving the co-op following a disagreement

---

2. *Svoboda*, December 12, 1895.
 3. Theodore Turak, "A Celt Among Slavs: Louis Sullivan's Holy Trinity Church," *The Prairie School Review* (4th Quarter, 1972), 7.
 4. *Ibid.*, pp. 19-20.
 5. *St. Mary's Greek Rite Catholic Church Golden Jubilee Book,* October 2, 1955.

with Volansky's successor, Simenovych enrolled in medical school and, with financial assistance from a Lithuanian doctor friend, completed his studies and moved to Chicago in 1893, where he practiced medicine until his death in 1932.[6] Chicago's Ukrainian community could not have had a more distinguished and nationally dedicated founder.

Chicago's First Ukrainian Community

Emigrants from Ukraine continued to come to Chicago in ever-increasing numbers, settling for the most part in an area bounded by Division Street on the north, Racine on the west, Roosevelt Road on the south, and Orleans on the east.[7] At a baptismal party in 1905, Fr. Kovaliczki agreed to help immigrants from Carpatho-Ukraine and Galicia to establish a (Rusin) parish on the North Side.[8] Thus a Chicago Ukrainian community came into being on December 31, 1905, when fifty-one Rusins gathered at 939 Robey (now Damen) to establish the St. Nicholas Ruthenian Catholic Church. Learning that a Danish Lutheran Church located at Superior and Bickerdicke was on the market, they purchased it for $8,000, with a 6 percent loan from a bank. A twelve-member board of trustees was elected, with Kovaliczki as chairman and Dr. Simenovych as secretary, and passed a motion to prevent the church from falling into "alien" (Latin-rite or Irish) hands by stipulating:

> . . . all the property of said church which may hereafter be acquired be held in the name of its incorporated name but under no conditions shall said church or its priests or pastors be ever under the jurisdiction of bishop or bishops except those of the same faith and rite.

Some thirty-three individuals pledged $295, while six others promised to loan the parish a total of $350.[9]

The new church had not only a "religious-moral" aspect but also a "national-educational" goal:

> To elevate ourselves through the support of a school, a reading room, political clubs, and whatever else is deemed necessary.

The pastor, of course, was expected to "live up to the religious-moral and national-educational purposes of the parish," and he was to be respected as the

---

6. Volodymyr Simenovych, "Z Moho Zhyttya" [From My Life], *Calendar of the Ukrainian National Association for 1931* (Jersey City, New Jersey, 1931), pp. 69-71. See also Bachynsky, pp. 360, 375, 443.

7. Stephen Kuropas, *op. cit., Svoboda*, September 5, 1900.

8. *Sitch,* December 1, 1931; interview with May Olenic, June 23, 1979.

9. St. Nicholas Church Council Minutes, December 31, 1905.

"head of the community; he must be consulted in all matters pertaining to the community and he must be obeyed."[10]

The Strutinskys and the Growth of Ethno-National Consciousness

Fr. Kovaliczki left St. Nicholas parish in the spring of 1907, and he was succeeded by Fr. L. Beseha, who remained for less than six months.[11] By the middle of November, St. Nicholas had a new pastor, one Nicholas Strutinsky, who, at the first church council over which he presided, was able to convince the members to consider deeding all church property to Bishop Ortynsky, the newly arrived Ukrainian prelate, and to pledge 5 percent of all church income to the bishop's office.[12] Given the resistance of other Ukrainian parishes to relinquishing ownership to the bishop — in the minds of many Rusins, loss of local ownership meant loss of local control — Strutinsky's early success in this regard was no small accomplishment. But then Strutinsky was no ordinary person. A tall, dynamic, no-nonsense Ukrainian cleric who was not averse to taking an occasional punch at a Polish editor who wrote what Strutinsky believed was an anti-Ukrainian editorial,[13] he remained at St. Nicholas until 1921. It was during his — and his equally energetic wife's — stay in the city that Chicago's Ukrainian community grew, prospered, and became irrevocably Ukrainian in ethno-national thinking, feeling, and action.

Saints Peter and Paul Church

On Chicago's South Side, meanwhile, a second Ukrainian community was beginning to coalesce in Burnside. Served initially by a priest from Whiting, Indiana — where *Svoboda* reported a functioning Rusin church as early as 1899[14] — the Burnside community came into its own when Bishop Ortynsky assigned Fr. Volodymyr Petrovsky to the parish in 1909. By the end of that year, a Ukrainian Catholic Church, Saints Peter and Paul, was standing at the corner of 92nd and Avalon.[15]

---

10. St. Nicholas Church Council Minutes, February 11, 1906.

11. *Sitch,* December 1, 1931.

12. St. Nicholas Church Council Minutes, November 17, 1907.

13. Interview with Rev. John Hundiak, February 16, 1969. Now Bishop Mark of the Ukrainian Orthodox Church of America, Hundiak was once a Ukrainian Catholic priest who served for a brief period as Strutinsky's assistant at St. Nicholas.

14. *Svoboda,* October 26, 1899.

15. "The History of Sts. Peter and Paul Ukrainian Orthodox Church, 1909-1959," *Fifty Years of Service to God and Country, A Jubilee Book,* 1959.

The Nativity of the BVM Church

At about the same time, another Ukrainian community was being organized in the working-class Back of the Yards area. A UNA branch, the Nativity of the Blessed Virgin Mary, was established by Emil Skorodinsky in 1909, and its members became the initiators of Chicago's third Ukrainian parish. Fr. Michael Prodon came to serve the community in 1910, and with seed money from St. Nicholas he established a small chapel in an apartment at 47th and Hermitage.[16] When this facility proved too small, the parish moved temporarily to St. Michael's Roman Catholic Church at 47th and Damen. Finally, in 1912 a church hall was constructed at 49th and Paulina, and the parishioners of the Nativity of the Blessed Virgin Mary had their own Ukrainian house of worship.[17]

The New Rus

Ukrainians on the North Side were also experiencing a substantial population increase, and by 1911 it was obvious that a new, larger church was needed. "Let us move west where much land is still available," urged Dr. Simenovych at a parish meeting in March. "We can build a glorious new church, we can all purchase lots near the church, we can eventually build our homes on these lots and, with God's help, we can have our own, new Rus right here in Chicago."[18]

Simenovych's "new Rus" concept was enthusiastically accepted, and after much discussion during the next few council meetings over possible sites, Fr. Strutinsky announced that twenty lots had been purchased on Rice Street between Oakley and Leavitt for $12,000.[19] The cornerstone of the new church was blessed by Bishop Ortynsky on November 27, 1913, following a construction delay of two years. Finally, after more delays, the magnificent edifice — a Byzantine-Slavonic masterpiece — was completed. On Christmas Day, January 7, 1915, the first divine liturgy was celebrated in what was then, and is still for many today, America's most beautiful Ukrainian church.[20]

Fr. Strutinsky's role in the "making" of Ukrainians in Chicago went far beyond writing articles, normal parish responsibilities, and even building churches. He was one of a dying breed of Ukrainian priests: he was a patriot, a person who, if forced to choose between being a Catholic and being a Ukrainian, would probably have chosen the latter. Few priests then and now could have matched his devotion to his people and to the Ukrainian stream.

16. St. Nicholas Church Council Minutes, January 30, 1910.
17. Mary Troc, *Nativity of the Blessed Virgin Mary Church School, Dedication Book*, 1956.
18. St. Nicholas Church Minutes, March 9, 1911.
19. *Ibid.*, May 28, 1911.
20. *Sitch*, December 1, 1931.

St. Nicholas Ukrainian Catholic Cathedral was constructed
in 1913 on Rice and Oakley Streets and is considered by many
to be America's most beautiful Ukrainian church.
Courtesy of M. B. Kuropas.

Ridna Shkola

An ethnic school for the purpose of "perpetuating the Rusin heritage" was first
discussed at a St. Nicholas council meeting as early as 1906,[21] but it was not
until the arrival of Fr. Strutinsky that a *Ridna Shkola* (national school) was
formally established.[22] By 1909 the parish was willing to pay fifty dollars a

---

21. St. Nicholas Church Council Minutes, February 11, 1906.
22. Semen Kochy, "Pochatkc i Rozvyto Tserkvy i Shkole Sv. O. Mykolaya v Shikago" [The
Founding and Development of St. Nicholas Church and School in Chicago], *Ukrayinske Zyttya*
[Ukrainian Life], March 7, 1960.

month for a *diak-uchytel* (cantor-teacher)[23] who, in addition to his duties as a cantor-respondent during the divine liturgy, was also expected to take responsibility for a variety of cultural activities, such as the organization and direction of a choir, of a drama group, and, most important of all, of an ethnic school for the youth. As might be expected, the approach of the *diak-uchytel* toward American-born youngsters was crucial in determining his effectiveness. If he could establish rapport — a difficult task for some European-born teachers — his efforts to Ukrainianize the younger generation would be generally successful. If he was like some teachers, for whom, unfortunately, as *Svoboda* once complained, "the only pedagogical tool was the stick," the school often did more harm than good.[24] As the church council minutes point out, St. Nicholas had its share of incompetent educators.[25] Under Strutinsky's firm hand, however, the parish finally assembled a relatively competent teaching staff, and Chicago's *Ridna Shkola* blossomed. In its modest inception in 1907, St. Nicholas had one teacher and ten students who attended Ukrainian school one day per week, Saturday from 10:00 to 12:00 a.m. By 1922 there were four teachers, some 300 students, and a Ukrainianization program that was in operation five days a week — Monday through Friday from 4:00 to 6:00 p.m.[26]

Inspired by the American feminist movement then sweeping the country, as well as by her personal acquaintance with Jane Addams of Hull House, Mrs. Emily Strutinsky helped organize a national congress of Ukrainian women in hopes of forming a national Ukrainian mutual benefit insurance society for women. Held in Chicago in 1917, the congress gave birth to the Ukrainian Women's Alliance of America, an organization with headquarters in the rectory of St. Nicholas Church. A year later the alliance began publishing *Ranna Zorya* (Morning Star), which outlined the purpose of the organization: to help in the hard task of creating a new "free, independent state of ours, Ukraine."[27] Despite the great hope expressed by its founders, the alliance had a short history. It organized classes for illiterates in Chicago and managed to publish a few more issues of *Ranna Zorya*. But in the end it disappeared from the Ukrainian-American scene, to be replaced in 1925 by the Ukrainian National Women's League of America (UNWLA), which has survived until the present day.

23. St. Nicholas Church Council Minutes, January 3, 1909.

24. *Svoboda*, September 21, 1905.

25. See St. Nicholas Church Minutes, 1907-1922.

26. Kochy, *op. cit.*

27. "Where We Aim," *Ranna Zorya*, January-February 1918; "A Call," *Ranna Zorya*, March-April 1918, pp. 60-62.

Simenovych and the Ukrainian Independence Movement

Of the three ethno-national streams that prevailed in the Rusin-American community prior to 1914, the most radical politically was the Ukrainian. Adopting a posture that was essentially socialist (occasionally anti-capitalist), the early editors of *Svoboda*, most of whom were members of the American Circle of Galician priests, advocated labor union organization in America and revolutionary activity in Ukraine. "Washington was a revolutionary who mobilized the American people to overthrow the English yoke," wrote *Svoboda* in 1903:

> We must be revolutionaries, agitators on the order of Washington. . . . The Poles and Magyars who agitated against the dictatorship of the emperor now have strength and significance. Today the world is such that only those who have wisdom and strength mean anything. And those who lick the hand and feet of aristocrats will be rewarded with spittle in their soup and a kick by the same aristocrats they venerate.[28]

Throughout 1906, *Svoboda* promoted fund-raising activities for the support of three political parties in Galicia: the National Democrats, the Radicals, and the Socialists.[29] "Take up donations at every opportunity," urged *Svoboda*, "at meetings, concerts, even at weddings and baptisms. . . ."[30]

When the long-anticipated war in Europe finally erupted in 1914, *Svoboda*, with guarded optimism, dreamed of an independent Ukrainian state.[31] The cataclysmic train of events during World War I, including the collapse of the Russian Czarist regime; the Bolshevik overthrow of Kerensky's provisional government; Ukraine's declaration of independence (January 22, 1918); President Wilson's promulgation of "The Fourteen Points" underscoring America's commitment to national self-determination; the demise of the Austro-Hungarian empire; the proclamation of a Republic of Western Ukraine (October 1918); and finally, the formal unification of Western and Eastern Ukraine (January 22, 1919) — all these events had a profound and electrifying impact on America's Ukrainians especially when the situation in Ukraine seemed to be changing so quickly and dramatically.

During its brief and stormy history, the Ukrainian National Republic had three separate governments: a socialist government headed by Michael Hrushevsky (May 1917 to April 1918); a conservative monarchist government headed by "Hetman" Pavlo Skorapadsky (April 1918 to December 1918);[32] and a coali-

---

28. *Svoboda*, February 26, 1903.
29. See commentary by Michael Lozynsky in *Svoboda*, May 26, 1904; *Svoboda*, May 10, 1906.
30. *Svoboda*, May 24, 1906.
31. *Svoboda*, September 15, 1914.
32. "Hetman" is a kozak title meaning commander-in-chief. Since Ukrainians had no royal

tion government headed by Simon Petlura (December 1918 to November 1920). None of the Allied powers recognized Ukraine because of their hope that Russia would remain in the war and their fear that a dismembered Russia would weaken the war effort. Germany and Austria, on the other hand, needed the grain that Ukraine could provide, and they favored Russia's withdrawal from the war and a weakening of the empire. They recognized Ukraine because it was in their interests, but when the Hrushevsky government could not deliver promised food supplies, it was overthrown by the Germans and replaced by the Skoropadsky regime. Skoropadsky was toppled by Petlura after the war ended and the German forces had left Ukraine.

In Chicago, meanwhile, the indefatigable Simenovych could now rely on the financial and intellectual support of two recent immigrants to the city, Dr. Stephen Hrynevetsky, also a physician, and Cyril Bilyk, a university student. Born in Ukraine, Hrynevetsky completed his medical studies at the University of Vienna, where, according to one source, he once flirted with the communist political ideology of Nikolai Bukharin, the theorist who later rose to power in Russia and was executed by Stalin in 1938. Hrynevetsky practiced medicine in Austria, spent time as a doctor on a German cruise ship traveling around the world, met and married Natalie Pidlyashetko, a singer with the Vienna State Opera, immigrated to Chicago sometime between 1903 and 1907, and established a highly successful medical practice there. He and his wife were members of the Erie Street National Church, where Natalie Hrynevetsky eventually organized and directed a choir. Both were elected to the twenty-two-person executive board of the Federation in 1915.[33]

Cyril Bilyk arrived in Chicago as a young man, enrolled at the University of Chicago, and, along with Simenovych and Emily Strutinsky, helped organize the Ukrainian Self-Education Club, an enlightenment society with a socialist flavor. Graduating from Rush Medical College in 1917, Dr. Bilyk became a member of the UWA leadership and in time replaced Simenovych as chairman of the Federation.[34]

Given its somewhat shaky development, the Federation was hard pressed to realize its ambitious program. Undaunted, a delegation consisting of Simenovych, Bilyk, Emily Strutinsky, and the UWA president visited the White House on January 4, 1917, to urge President Wilson to proclaim a national "Ukrainian Day," an effort which also had the support of the rival Ukrainian

---

blood line, those who supported Hetman rule in Ukraine came the closest to being monarchist in political orientation within the Ukrainian stream.

33. Osyp Nazarak, "Po Rokakh Prachi v Amerytsi" [After Years of Work in America], *Sich*, March 26, 1926; Toma Laphychak, "D-r Stepan Hrynevetsky" [Dr. Stephen Hrynevetsky], *Medical Almanac, op. cit.*, pp. 42-44; interview with Philip Wasylowsky, September 26, 1968.

34. Interview with Philip Wasylowsky, September 26, 1968; Toma Lapychak, "D-r Kyrylo Bilyk" [Dr. Cyril Bilyk], *Medical Almanac, op. cit.*, p. 51; Stachiw, pp. 102-107.

National Council. With legislative approval in both the House and the Senate, President Wilson responded on March 16 with a proclamation that recognized "the terrible plight" of "at least one million Ruthenians (Ukrainians) in dire need of food, clothing, and shelter," and designated April 21, 1917, "as a day upon which the people of the United States may make such contributions as they feel disposed for the aid of the stricken Ruthenians (Ukrainians) in the belligerent countries."[35] As a result of the proclamation, the Federation and its branches collected a total of $32,217.17 for Ukrainian relief, while the Alliance reported collecting $53,189.32.[36]

On May 19, 1917, Simenovych and Hrynevetsky established *Ukraynia*, Chicago's first Ukrainian-language newspaper, which attempted to accommodate all segments of the Ukrainian community and unite them in a general nationalist effort.[37]

> We are not going to attack any party, sect or individual. Our newspaper is not that of any privileged class in America. . . .
>
> We are publishing *Ukraynia* for Ukrainians in order that Ukrainian nationalism can be elevated to its highest possible level. Our greatest ambition in editing our *Ukraynia* is to acquaint such powerful nations as England, America and France with the Ukrainian question. . . .[38]

The new publication provided a flattering and detailed report on the successful "Ukrainian Day in Chicago," a fund-raiser approved by the city council. The Ukrainian celebration, which raised more than $8,000, had been aided significantly by Chicago's Poles and Lithuanians.[39]

35. A photostat copy of the resolution can be found in *Shisdesyat Lit Organizatsinoho Zhittya Ukrayintsiw v Filadelfiyi* [Sixty Years of the Ukrainian Community in Philadelphia], *A Jubilee Book*, p. 67.

36. *Svoboda*, September 22, 1917; Stachiw, p. 103.

37. V. Simenovych, "Nova Ukrayinska Hazeta" [A New Ukrainian Newspaper], *Ukrayina*, May 19, 1917.

38. *Ibid.*, May 19, 1917.

39. A brother of Emily Strutinsky, Miroslav Sichynsky, had assassinated the anti-Ukrainian Polish governor of Galicia, Count Andrew Potocki, in 1908. Sentenced to a long prison term for his crime, Sichynsky soon became a national martyr, a living symbol of Ukrainian independence. The UNA organized a legal fund on his behalf in 1909 and began efforts to obtain or engineer his release. With the help of Ukrainian supporters in Galicia, who succeeded in bribing his Polish guards with money sent from America, Sichynsky escaped from prison on November 3, 1911. After living for a time in Scandinavian countries, he arrived to a hero's welcome in America on October 21, 1914. A radical socialist his entire life (he died in Michigan in 1979 on the eve of the arrival of another Ukrainian symbol of freedom, Valentyn Moroz), Sichynsky was active with the Federation, Defense of Ukraine, a socialist organization, and the UWA; Stachiw, pp. 102-107. See also Volodymyr Lotocky, "Yak Osvobody Sya Myroslav Sichynsky" [How Miroslav Sichynsky Freed Himself], *Calendar of the Ukrainian National Association for 1916* (Jersey City, New Jersey, 1915), pp. 36-43.

A year later, on May 30, 1918, at the initiative of Simenovych and Hry-nevetsky, a mass rally was held at Pulaski Park (Noble and Blackhawk), which attracted some 10,000 persons.[40] A reporter described numerous floats and placards with proclamations such as "Let Democracy Live" and "Down with the Kaiser and His Regime." The description of the day's events concluded with comments relating to the manifestation that followed the parade. Held at the Pulaski Park auditorium, where 3,000 people sat and thousands more stood outside listening to the loudspeakers, the gathering was addressed by a number of distinguished guests.

Pulaski Park in 1918 proved to be a high point in the ethno-national development of Chicago's Ukrainian community. No Ukrainian gatherings before and few after have been as successful, both in terms of the number of Ukrainians involved and the unifying spirit that prevailed.

The Old and New Left

Ukrainian ethno-national aspirations for the permanent establishment of a free and sovereign Ukrainian state after World War I were never realized. With the fall of the Ukrainian National Republic to the Bolshevik Red army, and as a result of agreements reached by the peacemakers, Ukraine was eventually partitioned among four nations and swallowed up: Carpatho-Ukraine, referred to as "Subcarpathian Ruthenia," became a part of the newly created Republic of Czecho-Slovakia (Treaty of St. Germaine-en-laye, 1919);[41] the province of Bukovina was annexed by Rumania (Treaty of St. Germaine-en-laye); Eastern Ukraine came under Russian control (Treaty of Riga, 1921) as the Ukrainian Soviet Socialist Republic (UkSSR), and on December 29, 1922, the UkSSR was incorporated into the Union of Soviet Socialist Republics; Western Ukraine became a part of the new Polish state (Decision of the Council of Ambassadors, 1923). Thus, despite a monumental effort and the raising of hundreds of thousands of dollars by the Ukrainian-American community between 1914 and 1923, a united and free Ukraine was not to be.[42]

---

40. See "Slavs Combine to Fight German Agents in Russia," *Chicago Tribune,* May 31, 1918.

41. On November 12, 1918, at a meeting of the American Carpatho-Rusin Council in Scranton, Pennsylvania, a Rusin-American plebiscite was organized to determine the future of Carpatho-Ukraine. Each religious, fraternal-benefit, and civic society in the Rusin stream was entitled to one vote. Ballots were mailed, returned, and tabulated on December 24 with the following results: union with Czecho-Slovakia (735); union with Ukraine (310); total independence (27); union with Galicia-Bukovina (13); union with Russia (10); union with Hungary (9); union with Galicia (1). Peter Stercho, *Diplomacy of Double Morality: Europe's Crossroads in Carpatho-Ukraine, 1919-1939.*

42. Peter Poniatyshyn, "Ukrayinska Sprava v Amertysi Pid Chas Pershoyi Svitovoyi Viny" [The Ukrainian Situation in America During the First World War], *Jubilee Almanac of Svoboda, 1893-1953* (Jersey City, NJ, 1953), p. 74.

Angry and confused by the turn of events in Europe, Ukrainians in America began to search for answers, alternative perspectives, new leaders who could satisfy their recently crystallized and now badly bruised national consciousness. A new era was beginning, a period during which Ukrainian-American awareness would be tempered — hardened as it were, to a new, more sophisticated level of ethno-national assertiveness. Between 1920 and 1939 three new ethno-national political models presented themselves and were accepted by substantial segments of the increasingly pluralistic Ukrainian stream. The first to emerge were the Ukrainian Bolsheviks.

Of the many Ukrainian political ideologies that existed in America during the war, the one that came closest to being called a "party" was socialism. Capitalizing on the radical tradition and left-leaning bias of America's pioneer Ukrainian leaders, the socialists had established the Ukrainian Federation of Socialist Parties of America (UFSPA) in 1915. Within a year the UFSPA leadership had split between the "social patriots," who felt the party's first priority should be national reform in Ukraine, and the Bolsheviks, or as they preferred to be called, the "internationalists," who argued that social reform should be the primary concern.[43]

The Bolsheviks gained ground rapidly, and in 1919, at the third UFSPA convention, they recognized the Third International, a move tantamount to full acceptance of Soviet rule in Ukraine. Ejected from membership in the Socialist Party of America for its action, the UFSPA joined other expelled socialist groups to give birth that same year to the Communist Party of America.[44] The UFSPA's journal, *Robitnyk* (Worker), explained that the organization was, after September 1, 1919, the Ukrainian Federation of Communist Parties of America.[45] So sweeping was the enthusiasm of Ukrainian Bolsheviks during this period, and so convinced were they that the victory of the proletariat was just around the corner — "a few more days, weeks, months and not one trace of the old order will be found," wrote one *Robitnyk* correspondent — that they viewed all other Ukrainian organizations and American institutions as anachronistic.[46]

Ukrainian Communists in Chicago and elsewhere never wavered in their support of Soviet rule in Ukraine: "Sovereignty," they argued in 1939, was guaranteed by the Stalinist Constitution, which made it possible for all Soviet republics, "of their own free will," to belong to "the brotherly family of Soviet nationalities which exists on the basis of full equality and mutual faith."[47]

43. M. Nastasiwsky (Michael Tkach), *Ukrayinska Imigratsiya v Spoluchenykh Derzavakh* [The Ukrainian Immigration in the United States] (New York, 1934), pp. 85-89.

44. *Ibid.,* pp. 174-175.

45. *Robitnyk,* September 13, 1919; cited in *ibid.,* p. 176.

46. Cited in Robert E. Park, *The Immigrant Press and Its Control* (New York, 1922), pp. 235-236.

47. See "Shcho Take Suverennist" [What is Sovereignty?], *Narodni Kalendar na rik 1939,* p. 106.

Adopting the Popular Front posture in 1936 that the major world struggle was not that of capitalism versus communism but rather of democracy versus fascism, the Communists advanced the notion — accepted at the time by many American liberals — that whatever was "antifascist" was automatically "democratic." Since the Soviet Union was "democratic," only "fascists" could be against it. And included in this latter group were, of course, nationalists of every stripe and hue. Thus the First Congress of the Ukrainian National Front in September 1936 issued a proclamation that declared:

> Let there be unity everywhere under the motto — "Away with Fascism,
> Fascism is our enemy! . . .
> Away with war, it only hurts the poor. . . .
> Away with the chains of nationalism and socialism.
> We want liberty, bread and peace!"[48]

Hrynevetsky and the Rise of Ukrainian Monarchism in America

The political organization with the greatest strength and influence in the Ukrainian-American nationalist camp all through the 1920s and the early 1930s was the Ukrainian Athletic Association, Sich — later known as the Hetman sich — the first branch of which was organized by Fr. Strutinsky in 1902. Originally a gymnastic society patterned after the Czech Sokol, Sich gradually evolved into a paramilitary organization that recognized Pavlo Skoropadsky, the former head of the Ukrainian National Republic, as the only legitimate representative of the Ukrainian government-in-exile. As the sole Ukrainian political organization in America that could count on the tacit support of the Ukrainian Catholic Church, Sich was by the early 1930s the most effective political opponent of the Ukrainian Communists.

The metamorphosis of Sich from a nonpartisan athletic society to an ideologically oriented paramilitary organization began in 1918, when Dr. Hrynevetsky, Dr. Simenovych, Fr. Strutinsky, and others managed to convince the U.S. Congress to pass a bill authorizing the creation of a Slavic Legion of "Jugo-Slavs, Czecho-Slovaks, and Ruthenians (Ukrainians) belonging to the oppressed races of the Austro-Hungarian or German empires. . . ."[49] The Ukrainians who supported the legislation were confident that this legion would

48. Leon Tolopko, "Na Shklakhu Nevpynoyi Borothy" [In the Unfinished Struggle], *Ukrayinski Visti*, January 29, 1970, pp. 6, 7. See also Frank A. Warren, III, *Liberals and Communism: The "Red Decade" Revisited* (Bloomington, IN, 1966).

49. See Memorandum for Colonel Conrad from the Military Intelligence Division of the War Department, September 11, 1918; photostat copy in Peter Zadoretsky, "Korotki Narys Istoriyi Sichovoyi Organizatskiyi v Z.D.A." [A Short History of the Sich Organization in the U.S.A.], *Hei Tam Na Hori, Sich Ide* [Hey, On the Hill, Sich is Coming] (Edmonton, 1965), p. 361.

be the beginning of a Ukrainian liberation army. They were disappointed. Rallies called for the purpose of gaining popular support in the Ukrainian-American community were a failure, resulting in only a handful of recruits, at least one of whom, as Dr. Simenovych once wrote, "was probably trying to get away from his wife." Opposition to the legion came mainly from the Bolsheviks, who at the time had begun to infiltrate the Sich organization. So popular were the Bolsheviks at this time that two Sich branches elected to designate themselves as "Soviet" Siches.

The first Sich branch in Chicago was established in 1917 by Fr. Strutinsky and Dr. Bilyk, and it was here that the dream of a Ukrainian liberation army continued to live.[50] By 1920, Bolshevik influence had been eliminated. That same year the Sich Supreme Executive, headed by "Supreme Ataman" P. Novodvorsky, and the Sich newspaper, Sichovy Visti, were moved to Chicago.

Late in 1923, Dr. Osyp Nazaruk arrived in Chicago to become editor of Sichovi Visty. In the period that followed, Nazaruk convinced Hrynevetsky that the next logical step in the evolution of Sich was for the organization to accept the idea of monarchy — a Ukrainian Hetman. As Nazaruk later admitted, both he and Hrynevetsky were aware that, given the poor reputation of the monarchists in America (monarchism was viewed as antidemocratic among most Ukrainians, as well as among Americans in general), the political transformation would not be an easy task.[51]

Despite the ideological crisis precipitated by the monarchists, the Hetman Sich survived and in the years that followed flourished, especially among that segment of the nationalist Ukrainian-American community that was weary of political bickering, was desperate for a charismatic leader to point the way, and still believed that a future Ukrainian army could be trained in America. So potent was the Sich call for order and discipline that even Dr. Simenovych succumbed. Agreeing to serve as interim editor of its organ, Sich, the venerable Ukrainian-American agonized over "the lack of program . . . lack of authority . . . lack of direction . . . lack of goals" and told his conationals that, "in order to emerge from chaos, we must accept a clear idea. . . . There is absolutely nothing left but to support the Hetman monarchist idea." Democracy and self-rule "will lead Ukrainians nowhere," Simenovych warned, for "first we must get our liberty" and then the people will decide what comes next.[52] The call for unity by Sich promoted the monarchist "one idea" to overcome the cacophony of confusion.

For many Ukrainian-Catholic priests, then under attack from Com-

---

50. Zadoretsky, p. 363; Stephen Musiychuk, "Prychyny Opadku Sichovoyi Organizatsiyi v Z.D.A." [Reasons Behind the Decline of the Sich Organization in the U.S.A.], Hei Tam Na Hori, Sich Ide, pp. 373-374; Sich, December 10, 1932.

51. Nazaruk, op. cit.; see also Stephen Hrynevetsky, "Shcho Musit Bute" [What Must Be], Sich, March 15, 1916.

52. Sich, March 15, 1926.

A group of commissioned and non-commissioned Sich officers pose for a picture at Chicago's St. Nicholas picnic grove in 1931.   Courtesy of M. B. Kuropas.

United States military authorities, concerned about the poor state of their forces in the 1930s, encouraged the formation of Sich units. Here is a group of Sich Guards near St. Nicholas church.   Courtesy of M. B. Kuropas.

munists, Socialists, the Orthodox, and a growing number of nationally concerned Catholics, the growth of the Hetman Sich was a welcome development. Fr. Tarnowsky, a pastor of St. Nicholas Ukrainian Catholic Church, condemned the "infection of socialism" and praised the need for obedience, authority, and discipline by Chicago Ukrainians.[53]

The Hetman Sich also realized its dream of a Ukrainian army, at least in part. Soon after the Hetman takeover, great efforts were made to completely militarize the organization, even to the point of wearing uniforms. In addition, separate female Sich companies were organized as Red Cross units and taught first-aid techniques. Initially, only military drills and gymnastics were practiced, but later, as the Sich membership grew, field maneuvers were held in various forest preserves, wooded areas, and farm fields. Speaking at one of the early field maneuvers in Chicago, Dr. Hrynevetsky lauded America,

> in which we are permitted to cultivate our national spirit and to even have army exercises with our uniformed Sich soldiers without a special police permit.

Sich military maneuvers soon became one of the most exciting aspects of being a Sich member, especially for the youth. In time, maneuvers were being held throughout the country, and later still joint maneuvers, involving companies from two or three cities, became a regular part of the Sich summer program. Every able Sich member participated, the men as "combatants," the women as field nurses. A full day's program was usually planned, beginning with a field divine liturgy in the morning, military activities in the afternoon, and a gala outdoor dance and social in the evening.

The activities of the Hetman Sich also won favorable attention from the U.S. government authorities. Hoping to bolster what was then a sagging militia, American military officials suggested that Ukrainians form separate militia units of their own, a proposal that was eagerly seized. Among the first to enlist were a number of Chicago Sich members who formed Company B of the 33d Division of the 132d Infantry.[54] Ecstatic with such good fortune, *Sich* bubbled with excitement:

> The United States is the only country in the world where when one becomes a citizen one does not betray his own nation . . . and that is because the American nation is composed of many nations which have joined together to form a common state. . . . There is no other country in the world where when one becomes a citizen one can continue to be a son of his European Fatherland and actively help and fight for it. . . . By joining the American militia, we shall realize the main aim. i.e., to be the base and the beginning of the new Ukrainian army.[55]

53. *Sich*, January 1, 1928; February 1, 1928; January 1, 1932.
54. *Sich*, October 20, 1926; October 1, 1929; July 15, 1930; March 1, 1930.
55. *Sich*, January 1, 1930.

The next step in the development of a Ukrainian fighting force was the creation of a Ukrainian "air corps." During the 1930s the Hetman Sich obtained three airplanes — two biplanes, and a four-passenger, single-wing model — naming them, in order of purchase, "Ukraina," "Lviv," and "Kiev."[56] With the purchase of these planes, Sich "air corps" companies and aviation schools were established in Chicago, Cleveland, and Detroit, where the Hetman movement had its largest membership.[57]

Chicago's Ukrainian community meanwhile continued to organize rallies and political protest marches, which in the 1930s condemned Soviet and Polish rule in Ukraine. One such march was held on December 17, 1933, to protest the Soviet-induced famine during which seven million Ukrainians eventually perished. Gathering at St. Nicholas, some 3,000 Ukrainians began to march toward Plumber's Union Hall (1340 W. Washington), where a manifestation was scheduled. Along the way they were attacked by Communists who were throwing rocks and wielding lead pipes and brass knuckles. "100 HURT IN W. SIDE RED RIOT," declared the Chicago *Tribune* headline the next day. The nature of the protest was given full coverage in the headline story, which added: "Mainly with the aid of the Ukrainian siege [*sic*] guards who used clubbed rifles, police within five minutes routed the Reds and quelled the fighting."[58] Allowed to continue, the marchers arrived at their destination and called upon the U.S. President, "in view of the recent recognition of the present Russian government," to use his good offices "to alleviate the unbearable suffering and deliberate starvation now prevailing in Ukraine. . . ."[59]

Despite the best efforts of the new leaders to maintain the viability of the UHO, however, Sich began to decline. The primary reason for the loss of strength in the monarchist camp was the emergence of another nationalist model, a different approach being articulated by the Organization of Ukrainian Nationalists (OUN).

The Organization of the Rebirth of Ukraine (ODWU)

The political group that experienced the most phenomenal growth during the 1930s was the Ukrainian Nationalists, who, despite a relatively late organizational start, were by 1938 the largest Ukrainian political group in the anti-Communist camp and in firm control of the largest Ukrainian fraternal organization, the UNA.

56. See *Za Ukrayina* [For the Ukraine: The Tour of His Highness Hetmanych Danylo Skoropadsky Through the United States of America and Canada] (Chicago, 1938), pp. 54-57.

57. *Sich*, April 21, 1934; *Nash Styakh*, September 15, 1934; interview with Nicholas Olek, August 8, 1970.

58. *Chicago Tribune*, December 18, 1933.

59. *Sich*, December 23, 1933.

The rise of the Ukrainian Nationalists in America began in 1928 with the arrival of Colonel Evhen Konovalets, a former Ukrainian army commander and head of the Ukrainian Military Organization (UVO). His trip, arranged largely through the efforts of Dr. Luka Myshuha, who was to become the editor of *Svoboda* in 1933, had a twofold purpose: to acquaint Konovalets with the Ukrainian-American community, and to create an effective fund-raising vehicle for UVO activities in Western Ukraine. Konovalets succeeded in his mission. Before his departure, UVO branches were established in a number of American cities, including Chicago.

In 1929, soon after UVO had been transformed into the Organization of Ukrainian Nationalists (OUN) in Europe, Konovalets returned to America to establish a Ukrainian Nationalist organization with broader community appeal than UVO. It was during his second visit to this country that the idea of a new nationalist society, the Organization for the Rebirth of Ukraine (ODWU), came into being. ODWU branches were soon formed throughout the United States, and by the IVth ODWU convention in 1934, some fifty were in existence.[60]

Ukrainian-American Communists, as well as other left-leaning Ukrainian-American groups, were fond of labeling the Ukrainian Nationalist camp as fascist-inspired, undemocratic, and even subversive. Given the American climate, these allegations proved to be increasingly threatening, especially during the late 1930s, when the unrelenting Communist barrage first began to have a decided effect on the future development of this segment of the Ukrainian-American community. Especially vulnerable were ODWU and its affiliates, a self-proclaimed nationalist alliance.

In an attempt to counter Communist allegations and to promulgate their political approach, ODWU executives began a concerted effort to reach the American public. Beginning in 1939, ODWU took over the publication and editorship of *The Trident,* an English-language publication begun in Chicago by the Young Ukrainian Nationalists (MUN). At the IXth ODWU convention that same year, the delegates loudly professed their support for democratic freedoms, condemned the Soviet oppression of their kinfolk, and repudiated the "baseless" smear that they engaged in "un-American activities and ideas." Denouncing the "Hetmanci" (monarchists), the "Social Radicals," the "Russian Socialists," and the "Stalinist expositors" as groups that "have recorded themselves in the history of the Ukrainian immigration in the United States as enemies of the Ukrainian Liberation Movement," the delegates also turned their attention to foreign affairs and passed a number of resolutions, including one denying entanglements and asserting that

---

60. Volodymyr Riznyk, "Pochatky ODWU i Rozbudov Yi Merezhi: Nashi Uspixy i Trudnosohi" [The Beginnings of ODSU and the Development of Its Affiliates: Our Successes and Problems], *Samostiyna Ukrayina* (October-November, 1968), 6-7, 8.

the Ukrainian Independence Movement is based on no foreign ideologies, or international blocs, and especially it has nothing in common with the ideologies which now predominate in Germany and Italy.[61]

The Dies Committee and Its Aftermath

The unceasing Communist attack on the Nationalists and the UHO finally took its toll when both organizations came under the investigation of a special House Un-American Activities Committee headed by Congressman Martin Dies (Democrat, Texas). Called to testify concerning Ukrainian-American organizational life was Emil Revyuk, an associate editor of *Svoboda*, who confirmed that both the UHO and ODWU were associated with Ukrainian organizations in Germany; wore uniforms, had leaders who once attended a German *Bund* meeting in America, and had members who received letters from Germany and had praised Mussolini's Italy in 1933; had airplanes, and were once under the national leadership of reserve officers in the U.S. Army (Siemens of UHO and Gregory Herman of ODWU); had members who worked in munitions plants in the United States; and had publications that occasionally published articles criticizing the "democratic process." After hearing only one witness — and despite numerous attempts to lead the witness, improper translations of OUN communiqués, contradictory testimony, and largely hearsay evidence (most of Revyuk's replies began with "People told me that . . ." or "I believe that . . ." or "He told me that . . .") — Congressman Dies concluded that all of the testimony fit into a neat and tight pattern. At the end of Revyuk's appearance before his committee, Dies declared:

> Here are organizations that have shown to be nothing in the world but agencies of foreign powers. That is all they are under their own admission. They provide an elaborate espionage system in this country. . . .[62]

The Chicago *Daily News* reported on the testimony with a headline that read: "NAZI GROUPS WOO UKRAINIANS . . . KING ALREADY CHOSEN."[63] And so another era in Chicago's Ukrainian history came to an end.

61. "The Ninth ODWU Convention," *The Trident* (July-August 1939), 58, 60.
62. U.S. Congress, House of Representatives, Investigation of Un-American Propaganda Activities in the United States: Hearings Before a Special Committee on Un-American Activities, 76th Congress, 1st Session, 1939, pp. 5259-5322.
63. *Chicago Daily News,* September 28, 1939.

The Religious Response

Political debates were not the only source of friction within the Ukrainian-American community during this period. A related conflict — also tied to the preservation of Ukrainianism in America — emerged in the religious arena when a viable national alternative was offered Ukrainian Americans in the form of the Ukrainian Orthodox Church.

The establishment of Ukrainian national churches, begun after the founding of the Erie Street Church, proceeded slowly after 1915. By 1919, there were only six such churches functioning in the United States, leaving most Ukrainians well within the Catholic fold. In 1922, Deacon Paul Korsunowsky of the Ukrainian Autocephalous Orthodox Church in Ukraine — an independent church created during the halcyon days of the republic — arrived in America and, in a series of meetings with the national church leadership, convinced them to accept Ukraine's newly established church and to petition Kievan Orthodox Metropolitan Vasyl Lypkiwsky for a bishop. The request was made, honored, and on February 13, 1924, Bishop John Theodorovich was formally installed as America's first Ukrainian Orthodox bishop in June. At the time, his diocese consisted of eleven parishes, 8,500 faithful and fourteen priests.[64] Later, as the number of Ukrainian Orthodox parishes increased, Bishop Theodorovich moved his episcopal seat to Philadelphia.

The Holy See, meanwhile, decided to formalize an earlier decision to split the late Bishop Ortynsky's eparchy into two jurisdictions — one for the Carpatho-Ukrainians (who continued to call themselves Rusins) and one for the Ukrainians — and appointed two bishops to serve Uniate Catholics in America. On September 1, 1924, Bishop Basil Tkach arrived in the United States to take charge of a Rusin eparchy consisting of 155 parishes, 129 priests, and 288,290 faithful. He was accompanied by Bishop Bohachevsky, whose Ukrainian eparchy included 144 parishes, 102 priests, and 237,445 faithful.[65]

Within two years after his arrival, Bohachevsky found himself in the center of one of the most prolonged and bitter controversies in the history of the Ukrainian-American community. Believing that the introduction of certain Roman Catholic traditions was essential to the survival of the Ukrainian Catholic Church in America, Bohachevsky decided to enforce a recent Rome-ordained celibacy decree for Uniate Catholic clergy in America and to encourage the adoption of the Gregorian calendar, the stations of the cross, the rosary, May devotions of the Blessed Virgin Mary, and other purely Latin rite practices by Ukrainian Catholics throughout America. Angered by what they perceived

64. Interview with Stephen Kuropas, June 5, 1970. Stephen W. Mamchur, "Nationalism, Religion and the Problem of Assimilation Among Ukrainians in the United States" (unpublished Ph.D. diss., Yale University, 1942), pp. 101-111.

65. Sohocky, p. 275; Walter E. Warzeski, "Religion and National Consciousness in the History of the Rusins" (unpublished Ph.D. diss., University of Pittsburgh, 1964), pp. 246-248.

to be a conscious attempt on the part of their bishop to denationalize their church, a group of lay and clerical leaders convened in Philadelphia and on December 26, 1926, formed the so-called "Committee for the Defense of the Greek Catholic Church in America."[66] The first resolution passed at the conclave was a demand of Rome to recall Bohachevsky.[67] Supporting the dissidents was *Svoboda*, which praised the Philadelphia congress:

> Ukrainian Catholics demonstrated that they have learned much from the democratic principles they have seen in operation in this country, a land in which they have found not only a piece of bread but knowledge and a new outlook on life and the world as well. The congress demonstrated that no longer can an autocratic church, which recognizes only blind obedience, count on the Ukrainian serf.[68]

Rome, of course, supported Bohachevsky, and after all the smoke had cleared, most of the twenty-six priests who had initially resisted Bohachevsky recanted their opposition and reaffirmed their fidelity.[69] A minority group of priests, however, decided to leave the Catholic Church and form a second Ukrainian Orthodox diocese. On April 9, 1929, nine clergy and thirty-four lay representatives met in Allentown, Pennsylvania, to form the "Ukrainian Orthodox Diocese of America" under the leadership of Rev. Joseph Zhuk, who became bishop-elect.[70] Both Orthodox groups grew as a result of Catholic defections during the next few years. By 1939, Bishop Theodorovich's Autocephalous Orthodox Diocese consisted of 24 parishes and 22 priests,[71] while the Ukrainian Orthodox Diocese of America that same year claimed 43 parishes and 36 priests.[72]

Chicago, like other Ukrainian-American communities, was deeply affected by the religious turmoil that erupted during the late 1920s. The most serious rift occurred at Sts. Peter and Paul in Burnside, which had a history of dissension dating back to 1917, when some seventy Ukrainian families had left to form a fourth Ukrainian Catholic parish in the Chicagoland area — St. Michael's — in West Pullman. In 1928, largely as a result of the Bohachevsky controversy, Sts. Peter and Paul became a Ukrainian national church and, in time, joined the Ukrainian Orthodox Diocese of America.[73] Another Ukrainian Catholic church, St. Basil's, was eventually established in Burnside by those parishioners who had elected to remain Ukrainian Catholic.

66. Mamchur, *op. cit.*, pp. 68-72.
67. *Svoboda* (December 31, 1926).
68. *Svoboda* (January 3, 1927).
69. *Svoboda* (June 24, 1927).
70. Mamchur, *op cit.*, pp. 126-131.
71. *Ibid.*
72. *Ibid.*, pp. 105-106.
73. *Sich* (December 15, 1931). See also *Fifty Years of Service to God and Community.*

Not all Ukrainian Christians in Chicago became embroiled in the Catholic-Orthodox debate. A small Ukrainian Baptist community had been formed in the city in 1915 and remained totally isolated from the religious struggle that erupted in later years.[74]

Ukrainian Organized Life

There is an old Ukrainian saying that "when two Ukrainians get together, there are three political parties represented, and when three meet, one has the beginnings of a choir." Never reluctant to form, as Ukrainians say, *"shche udnu organizatsiyu"* (one more organization), Chicago's Ukrainians could list a total of 113 separate organizations, societies, and clubs in 1935. When one considers that there were, according to statistical data compiled by Dr. Simenovych in 1930 and updated by Stephen Kuropas in 1935, approximately 41,000 first- and second-generation Ukrainians living in Cook County at that time and that some 57 percent, according to Kuropas, were not members of any Ukrainian organization, then only 17,630 were what Ukrainians would call "organized."[75]

While many organized Ukrainians in the city were intimately involved with the political and religious life of their community, many more were not. The typical Ukrainian attended the church of his choice and belonged to one of the fraternal societies — the UNA, the UWA, the Providence Association, or the Ukrainian National Aid Association *(Narodna Pomich)*. Concerned about the future of Ukraine and their community in America, they tended nevertheless to remain on the periphery of the turmoil and conflict that many community leaders seemed to relish. The majority of Chicago's Ukrainians preferred to cultivate and express their Ukrainianism in other ways, most often in activities that were culturally oriented.

The Cultural Response

Ukrainian cultural life developed early in Chicago. Two choirs already existed by 1909: the Nicholas Lysenko Singing Society and the Ukrainian Singing Society "Sitch," the former organized by Fr. Strutinsky and Michael Kostiuk and associated with St. Nicholas Church, and the latter organized by Natalie Hrynevetsky and affiliated with the Ukrainian National Club, "Sitch." During the 1920s, Ukrainian cultural life continued to evolve under the leadership of such talented choir directors as Dymtro Atamanec — who also developed drama

74. Anatol Hornysky, "Ukrayinska Baptyska Tserkva v Shikago" [The Ukrainian Baptist Church in Chicago], *The Evangelical Kalendar,* "Good Friend" for 1956 (Toronto, 1956), pp. 59-65.
    75. Stephen Kuropas, *op. cit.,* p. 543.

One of the cultural highlights of Chicago's Ukrainian community was the famed
Lysenko Chorus, which won first place in a 1930 choral contest sponsored by the
Chicago *Tribune.* Courtesy of M. B. Kuropas.

troupes in his role as *diak uchytel* at St. Nicholas — and by the 1930s, Chicago's
Ukrainian community could boast of numerous choral ensembles, dance
groups, drama clubs, bands, and orchestras that enhanced the cultural life of
the community. Performing at various *sviatos* (commemorative assemblies)
honoring Ukraine's Declaration of Independence (January), the birthday of
Taras Shevchenko (March), Western Ukrainian Independence Day (November),
as well as at carnivals, balls, picnics, and other festivals, these groups helped
sustain the ethno-cultural traditions of Chicago's maturing Ukrainian society.

Ukrainian musicals such as "Kateryna,"[76] "Zaporozhets Za Dunayem,"[77]
and "The Fair at Soroschintzi"[78] became annual events, along with art exhibits,[79]
band concerts under the direction of John Barabash[80] and Stanley Sabor,[81] and
dance festivals under the leadership of M. Darkowicz[82] and the famed Vasili
Avramenko, the "father" of Ukrainian dance in America. Arriving in the United
States in 1928, Avramenko dedicated his life to the establishment of dance
groups in various Ukrainian-American communities as well as in Canada. His

76. *Ukrayina* (August 8, 1930).
77. *Ukrayina* (October 16, 1931).
78. *Program Book* (October 14, 1934).
79. *Ukrayina* (November 14, 1930).
80. *Ukrayina* (July 11, 1930).
81. *Sich* (March 31, 1934).
82. *Ukrayina* (August 8, 1930).

most notable achievement in Chicago was a Ukrainian Festival he helped to organize at the Civic Opera House on November 8, 1932, during which some 200 young dancers, all local talent, performed.[83] Dramas such as "Marusia Bohuslavka,"[84] Gogol's "Inspector General,"[85] and "Verkhouynchi"[86] were also part of the cultural fare offered Chicago's Ukrainians.

Ukrainian cultural life in Chicago reached a high point during the early 1930s when the Ukrainian Chorus of Chicago was established. Entering the choral competition associated with the Chicagoland Music Festival, the Ukrainian Chorus won first place three times, twice under the direction of Leontyn Sorochinsky (1931).[87] The chorus came to be known throughout Chicago, performing at Soldier's Field, the Chicago Stadium, the Studebaker Theater, and Kimball Hall, as well as over the national NBC radio network.[88]

The Chicago World's Fair

The zenith of Chicago's pioneer Ukrainian history, however, the one effort that more than any other united all segments of the nationalist community, was the planning and construction of a Ukrainian pavilion at the Chicago World's Fair in 1933. Plans to celebrate Chicago's 100th anniversary with a "Century of Progress" fair and exhibition were greeted by Chicago's Ukrainians as a rare opportunity to better acquaint America with Ukraine and her people. Forming a bipartisan committee headed by Dr. Myroslaw Siemens, Stephen Kuropas, Taras Shpikula, and Jurij Nebor, Ukrainians in Chicago went to work early in 1932 and on June 25, 1933, opened a pavilion that included a restaurant, an open-air theater, an entrance hall, and two larger halls, one devoted to history, the other to culture.[89] The highlight of the cultural section — divided into folk and modern art — was the exhibition of the world-famous Ukrainian sculptor Alexander Archipenko.[90] To the delight of the Ukrainian community, the pavilion attracted some 1,800,000 visitors,[91] many of whom presumably learned

83. *Sich* (November 15, 1932).

84. *Ukrayina* (November 28, 1930).

85. *Ukrayina* (August 28, 1931).

86. *Sich* (May 1, 1932).

87. *Ukrayina* (August 29, 1930); *Sich* (September 1, 1931); newspaper clippings in scrapbook of Katherine Domanchuk-Baran; see also *Ukrainians in the United States* (Chicago, 1937), pp. 136-138.

88. *Chicago Daily News* (May 9, 1932).

89. Luka Myshuha, "Ukrayinska Uchast v Dvokh Svitovykh Vystavakh" [Ukrainian Participation in Two World Fairs], *Golden Jubilee Almanac of the Ukrainian National Association, 1894-1944* (Jersey City, NJ, 1944), pp. 215-216.

90. Wasyl Halich, *Ukrainians in the United States* (Chicago, 1937), p. 142.

91. Stephen Kuropas, *op. cit.*, p. 545.

Ukrainian women exhibit cultural objects at the Chicago World's Fair of 1933.
Courtesy of M. B. Kuropas.

much about a people still waiting for the day when their national will could be realized once and forever.

Summary and Conclusion

The seven decades between 1884 and 1950 were years of ethno-national maturation for the Ukrainian people both in Ukraine and in the United States. It was during this crucial period that Ukraine's Rusins were transformed from a religio-cultural people to a politically conscious nationality. In America the national metamorphosis occurred in two phases. Prior to World War I, the emphasis was on the preservation of a religio-cultural heritage that was uniquely and irrevocably Ukrainian. This end was achieved when an autonomous Ukrainian Catholic eparchy was established in 1913. The tempering of the Ukrainian identity took place during the 1920s and 1930s. Three major ideological groups — the Communists, the Monarchists, and the Nationalists — emerged to compete for the political loyalty of Chicago's Ukrainians. Each camp presented its own reasons for the rise and fall of the Ukrainian National Re-

During the period of 1884 to 1939 the Ukrainian people matured from
an ethno-cultural group into a politically self-conscious nationality.
The Ukrainian Pavilion at the World's Fair in 1933 sharply symbolizes
their national self-consciousness.   Courtesy of M. B. Kuropas.

public, and each offered a different plan for the realization of Ukrainian national
aspirations.

Having established a new ethno-national identity in America, Ukrainians
were determined to preserve it. Perceiving their church to be a symbol of their
national identity, they were incensed by the introduction of certain external
changes in the Ukrainian Catholic Church during the 1920s, which they believed
were designed to "Latinize" their faith. A number of Catholic parishes, including
Sts. Peter and Paul in Chicago, joined the Ukrainian Orthodox Church in
protest.

Following World War II, a third Ukrainian immigration arrived in Chicago, and the community experienced a cultural and national revival. The
Communists and Monarchists all but disappeared from the Ukrainian political
scene, and the Nationalists, now divided among three rival factions of the
Organization of Ukrainian Nationalists (OUN), became the dominant force.

An increase in Chicago's Ukrainian population resulted in the need for
new parishes. In 1956 the indefatigable Fr. Joseph Shary arrived in the city,
mobilized a number of second- and third-generation Ukrainian Chicagoans,
and established St. Joseph's Ukrainian Catholic parish on the Northwest Side.

Sts. Volodymyr and Olha Ukrainian Catholic Church. Courtesy of M. B. Kuropas.

A magnificent new church that combines traditional and modern trends in current Ukrainian church architecture was completed in 1977 on Cumberland Road near Lawrence. Meanwhile, within five years of establishing that new parish in the city, Fr. Shary organized the Immaculate Conception parish in Palatine, Illinois, to meet the spiritual needs of the increasing number of Ukrainian families who were purchasing homes in the Northwest suburbs.

In 1961, Chicago's prestige as a center of Ukrainian-Catholic life in America was greatly enhanced when the Holy See established an episcopal seat in the city. Msgr. Jaroslaw Gabro, who was born and raised in the city, became the first bishop of the newly created Ukrainian Catholic eparchy.

But religious controversy erupted again when a group of parishioners at St. Nicholas Cathedral objected to the introduction of the Gregorian calendar into their parish. When the change was supported by the bishop, the dissidents, choosing to believe that the change was yet another attempt to undermine their ancient religio-cultural heritage, left St. Nicholas and in 1974 erected Sts. Volodymyr and Olha Church at Oakley and Superior. The new church cost in excess of $2,500,000, and despite neighborhood opposition from non-Ukrainians and *Chicago Magazine,* a new cultural center was erected at the corner of Oakley and

Chicago by the parishioners of Sts. Volodymyr and Olha in 1988 to commemorate the millennium of Ukrainian Christianity. These events, combined with the official designation of the neighborhood as "Ukrainian Village" by Mayor Jane Byrne, assured the future of this unique Ukrainian enclave. An article in the Chicago *Sun-Times* on April 9, 1989, described Ukrainian Village as a neighborhood that saved itself from extinction: "Construction of the church in the old neighborhood," wrote Phil Franchine, "was a signal that community institutions would stay put."

Bishop Gabro died in 1980 and was succeeded the following year by Bishop Innocent Lotocky. Much of the original animosity that existed between St. Nicholas and Sts. Volodymyr and Olha parishes has healed during the past few years, culminating in an All-Catholic jubilee manifestation in 1988 that commemorated the millennium of Christianity in Ukraine.

Chicago's Ukrainian-Orthodox community also experienced a period of growth and expansion following World War II. A new church was purchased at Cortez and Oakley in 1946 and rededicated in honor of Saint Vladimir. Three new Orthodox parishes — Saint Sophia's at 6655 W. Higgins, Saint Mary the Protectoress at Iowa and Washtenaw, and Holy Trinity at 1908 N. Humboldt — have been established within recent years. Saints Peter and Paul Ukrainian Orthodox Church moved from Burnside in Chicago to Palos Park in 1977, where a new church was erected two years later. Another Ukrainian Orthodox parish, St. Andrew's, was established in Bloomington, where a magnificent Byzantine-style church was completed in 1987. A memorial to the victims of the Ukrainian Famine of 1932-33 was also erected on the premises.

In 1969, St. Vladimir's became a cathedral with the creation of a Chicago Ukrainian Orthodox diocese and the appointment of Father Alexander Nowecky as the first bishop. Thus, after a hiatus of almost fifty years, the Ukrainian Orthodox in Chicago once again had a bishop. Bishop Nowecky died unexpectedly and was succeeded by Bishop Constantine Bagan in 1972.

Ukrainian Baptists have prospered as well. Under the leadership of the Reverend Olexa Harbuziuk, Chicago's Ukrainian Baptists purchased church property at 1042 N. Damen Avenue in 1952. In 1985 the Ukrainian Baptist Church moved to newer, larger facilities in Berwyn. In 1968, Ukrainian Evangelical Christians purchased a house of worship at 5004 W. Wellington.

The year 1991 was a banner year for Chicago's Ukrainian community. In the spring, Chicago and Kiev, Ukraine's capital, became sister cities. And on December 1, 1991, the hopes, dreams, and aspirations of Chicago's Ukrainians were finally realized when the people of Ukraine held a referendum and 91 percent of the population voted for total independence. What had often seemed an impossible dream was now a reality. Ukraine was free and the community rejoiced. In 1992 the newly formed Ukrainian government established a consulate in Chicago, the first American city to be so honored.

Today, Chicago's metropolitan-area Ukrainian community, now more than eighty years old, is flourishing, with a population of about 65,000. The rich cultural tradition initiated by Chicago's Ukrainian pioneers was continued by the third immigration. Ridna Shkola, the heritage school system interrupted during World War II, was resurrected at Saint Nicholas School in 1950 and at Saint Joseph's Church in 1956; a heritage school was also inaugurated at Saint Vladimir's Church Hall in 1949. Thousands of young Ukrainians have attended these three schools, which offer classes in the Ukrainian language as well as Ukrainian history, religion, culture, geography, and literature, beginning in the first grade and ending in the eleventh.

A number of new youth organizations were established by the third immigration soon after their arrival. The largest is the Ukrainian American Youth Association (SUMA), which has three branches in Chicago and one in Palatine. SUMA sponsors a soccer team ("Wings") as well as a youth choir ("Vatra") and a dance ensemble ("Ukraina"). Ukraina has performed throughout the United States, including a nine-day booking at the Epcot Center. SUMA also sponsors a ballet school at St. Joseph's Church Hall and a summer camp and resort in Baraboo, Wisconsin. The Ukrainian American Scouting Association (Plast) was founded in Chicago in 1949 and operated a summer camp for youth in Westfield, Wisconsin, from 1967 to 1987. The Organization of Ukrainian Youth (ODUM) was established in 1950 and the organization has sponsored a bandura ensemble and a mandolin orchestra for youth.

Saints Volodymyr and Olha parish sponsors a dance ensemble, "Hromovytsia," as well as a ballet school and a mixed choir, "Bayda." Saint Nicholas School has a children's choir, which performs at various functions along with "Moloda Dumka," another children's choir. A number of adult choirs are also thriving in Chicago's Ukrainian community, including SURMA, a male chorus; SLAVUTA, the Saint Nicholas mixed chorus; IRMOS at Saints Volodymyr and Olha; BOYAN at Saint Vladimir's; the Saint Joseph Church Choir and the Saint Andrew Church Choir. The Lions, a Ukrainian-American sports club in Chicago, sponsors an athletic program for the younger generation that includes soccer, volleyball, and tennis.

Chicago is the home of two outstanding Ukrainian museums: the Ukrainian National Museum located at 2453 W. Chicago Avenue was established in 1952, and the Ukrainian Museum of Modern Art at 2320-24 W. Chicago opened its doors in 1975.

A significant contribution to Ukrainian Chicago's cultural life is being made by various professional societies, almost all of which were created after World War II. Medical doctors, pharmacists, veterinarians, engineers, lawyers, and business leaders all have their own separate organizations. Younger professionals established the so-called "Chicago Group" in 1989 to serve as clearinghouse for Ukrainian professionals and business people interested in networking with other Ukrainians with different professional and business interests. It is also worth noting that the community supports a weekly newspaper, *New Star,* eight weekly radio programs, and a weekly television show.

Perhaps the most significant contribution of the third Ukrainian immigration has been in the economic arena. The Ukrainian Federal Credit Union, "Selfreliance," was founded in 1951 with thirteen members and $300 in assets. By 1989, Selfreliance, headquartered at 2351 W. Chicago Avenue, had over 10,000 members and $101 million in assets. Today there are Selfreliance branches on Chicago's South Side (Nativity of the BVM), the Northwest Side (Saint Joseph's), Bloomingdale (Saint Andrew's), Palos Park (Saints Peter and Paul), and Saint Josephat (Munster, IN). The First Security Federal Savings Bank at 936 N. Western Avenue was established as a savings and loan institution in 1964 and as a bank in 1984; in 1989 the bank had assets of over $136 million.

Ukrainians in Chicago are proud of the vitality of their community, its many achievements, and the fact that the original Ukrainian neighborhood, still centered around Chicago and Oakley, has managed to survive as an urban oasis within Chicago's deteriorating west side.

CHAPTER 8

Chicago's Italians:
A Survey of the Ethnic Factor, 1850-1990

DOMINIC CANDELORO

Italians have been in Chicago since the 1850s. Up until about 1880, the group consisted of a handful of enterprising Genoese fruitsellers, restaurateurs, and merchants with a sprinkling of Lucchese plasterworkers. These were joined in the 1870s by a group of itinerant musicians. Except for the last group, they were generally well accepted and economically successful, establishing themselves in the central city and the near North Side.[1]

Most Chicago Italians, however, trace their ancestry — with some important and notable exceptions — to the central and southern parts of Italy and the poor and illiterate country folk displaced by the land and economic policies of an uncaring government. This wave of unskilled southern immigrants came to the United States between 1880 and 1914. Most of them were young men, birds of passage, who intended to work for a season or two and return to their families. Many did just that. Others became part of intricate chains of migration that re-established villages and towns in Chicago's neighborhoods and suburbs. The culture they brought with them, while not quite the culture of the Roman Empire or the Italian Renaissance, was richly textured, agrarian, peasant, Christian, and family oriented. One writer has gone so far as to describe the South Italian culture as being so exclusively family centered (amoral familism) as to discourage the development of healthy relationships and trust in government, the economic and education system, and voluntary associations outside the family.[2] Though most immigrants came before World War I broke out, the

1. Rudolph Vecoli, "Chicago's Italians Prior to World War I" (unpublished Ph.D. diss., University of Wisconsin, 1963), p. 52.
2. Edward Banfield, *The Moral Basis of a Backward Society* (Glencoe, IL, 1958).

The author wishes to thank the following who read this essay in manuscript form and made valuable suggestions: Carol Candeloro, Dino Dalpiaz, Fred Gardaphé, Anthony Scariano, and Anthony Sorrentino. Lorretta Calcaterra printed the photos.

Italians in Chicago
Number and percentage of foreign born in the city[3]

1920	59,215	7.30%
1910	45,169	5.76%
1900	16,000	2.73%
1890	5,685	1.26%
1880	1,357	.66%
1870	552	.38%

ethnic community has been almost continuously renewed by additional immigrations in the 1920s and during the period between the end of World War II and the 1980s.

As a rail center, an industrial center, and America's fastest-growing major city, Chicago offered opportunities for immigrants from all nations. In the mid-nineteenth century it was the mecca for German and Irish migration; in the early twentieth century, Italians, Russian Jews, and, most importantly, Poles found a place in Chicago. Later, blacks from America's South, Mexicans and Asians, and a steady stream of others added their presence to the city, making it today the home of sizable colonies of over eighty different nationalities. Chicago's black population is second only to that of New York City; at one time or another it has been the largest Lithuanian city, the second largest Polish city, the second largest Bohemian and Ukrainian city, and the third largest Swedish, Irish, Polish, and Jewish city in the world.[4] But it has never been claimed that Chicago had enough Italians to be one of the largest *Italian* cities of the world.

As in most older American cities, ethnic identities have persisted well beyond the "melting pot," and a sophisticated understanding of the economic, political, social, and cultural dynamics of the city is impossible without a careful consideration of ethnic factors.[5] Being part of the complex interaction and outnumbered by the Irish, Poles, blacks, and Hispanics, Italian aspirations for power and prestige have often been thwarted. Efforts at developing internal unity and at building coalitions with other ethnic groups have not offset their numerical weakness. And while Italians have played a significant role, they have never been as important in Chicago's mix of ethnics as they have been in New York, for instance.

3. Ernest Burgess and Charles Newcomb, eds., *Census Data of the City of Chicago 1920* (Chicago, 1931), p. 21. Quoted in Vecoli, p. 463.

4. Irving Cutler, *Chicago: Metropolis of the Mid-Continent* (3rd ed., Dubuque, IA, 1982), pp. 43-116.

5. Nathan Glazier and Patrick Moynihan, *Beyond the Melting Pot: The Negroes, Puerto Ricans, Jews, Italians, and Irish of New York City* (Cambridge, MA, 1963).

Early Settlement

Typical chain migration patterns prevailed with families and villages gradually re-forming in Chicago neighborhoods as workers accumulated savings with which to send for their relatives and buy homes. The 1911 Dillingham Report showed about 10 percent of their Italian sample as homeowners.[6] Throughout the early twentieth century there continued to be a good deal of residential mobility among the Italians, as newcomers arrived and earlier immigrants bought homes in different zones. Nevertheless, their major colonies, as outlined by Rudolph Vecoli, shaped up as follows:

The original Genoese/Lucchese neighborhood in the shadow of today's Merchandise Mart produced the first Italian-Catholic Church of the Assumption in 1881, staffed by Servite priests.

Toward the south end of the Loop, near the Polk Street Station, the Ricilianesi (Salerno) lived. Men and boys from Ricigliano eventually monopolized the Loop area news vending stands. Over the years the colony moved further south into what is now known as Chinatown, where they were joined by Sicilians from Nicosia. The Scalabrinian Church of Santa Maria Incoronata (patron saint of Ricigliano) remained the focal center for the community until the 1980s, when it became the Chinese mission of St. Theresa.

On the near West Side, in a neighborhood made famous by Jane Addams and Hull House, the largest Italian colony grew up. This Taylor Street area contained about one-third of the city's Italians — a mixture of people from Naples, Salerno, Bari, Messina, Palermo, Abruzzo, Calabria, Basilicata, the Marche, and Lucca. A multiethnic zone, they shared the neighborhood with Russian Jews to the south and Greeks to the north. For the most part, this area could be considered a slum in the pre-1920 era. The Scalabrinian churches of the Holy Guardian Angel and Our Lady Pompeii, plus a hospital founded by Mother Cabrini, served the area. Tina De Rosa has written a superb fictionalized account of family life there in the 1950s entitled *Paper Fish.*[7]

On the near Northwest Side a varied community of Baresi, Sicilians, and others grew up around still another Scalabrinian church, Santa Maria Addolorata.

Perhaps the most colorful Italian sector was in the 22nd Ward on the city's near North Side. Known alternately as "Little Sicily" and "Little Hell," this neighborhood was home to some 20,000 native-born Italians and Italian Americans by 1920. Most originated from the small towns surrounding Palermo, but important contingents from Catania, Vizzini, and Sambuca-Zabat were also there. The Dillingham Commission reported only one northern Italian family,

---

6. U.S. Immigration Commission, *Reports,* Vol. 26, "Immigrants in the Cities," p. 302. Hereafter cited as *Dillingham.*

7. Tina De Rosa, *Paper Fish* (Chicago, IL, 1980).

compared to 155 southern families, in the Gault Court block of this area.[8] The Servite Church of St. Philip Benizi provided the backdrop for a score of patron saint street processions each summer sponsored by *paesani*-based mutual benefit societies.[9] The neighborhood was the focus of Harvey Zorbaugh's classic sociological study of 1929, *The Gold Coast and Slum.*

In addition to these major inner-city Italian enclaves, a number of outlying and suburban colonies formed in the pre-1920 period. Closest in was the settlement of Toscani, where many worked at the McCormick Reaper plant, a few miles southwest of the Loop at 24th and Oakley Avenue. Major towns of Italy contributing to this zone were Ponte Buggianese, Bagni di Lucca, and Montecatini. The Dillingham Commission showed sixty-seven northern Italian families and only one southern Italian family in a two-block sample of this neighborhood.[10] Historically socialist in politics and virtually crime-free, this northern enclave was in 1990 perhaps the best preserved Little Italy in the city. The remnants of this colony are served to this day by a dozen northern Italian restaurants and shops, and the Scalabrini St. Michael the Archangel (patron saint of Lucca) Church, which eventually overcame leftist anti-clericalism to assert effective community leadership. Sociologist Peter Venturelli has written a dissertation and several articles about this, his home neighborhood.[11]

At 69th Street and Hermitage and in the Grand Crossing area were two minor settlements of migrants from Salerno and Calabria respectively. St. Mary of Mt. Carmel served the former. Also to the south, in the famous planned company town established by George Pullman, there was a colony of Italian brickmakers and others from the Altopiano Asiago area of the Veneto region. The nearby Roseland neighborhood was also home to a contingent of Piedmontese and Sicilians. The Scalabrinian Church of St. Anthony of Padua served this group.

The town of Blue Island at the southwest border of the city was heavily settled by railroad workers from Rippacandida (Basilicata).[12] They worshipped at the diocesan church of San Donatus.

Chicago Heights, 30 miles to the south of the Loop, had a population that was 50 percent Italian stock by 1920, most hailing from San Benedetto del Tronto (Marche), Caccamo (Sicily), Amaseno (Lazio) and Castel di Sangro.[13] Their church, San Rocco, was founded in 1906 and was one of the many ethnic parishes ordered closed by Cardinal Bernardin in 1990.

---

8. *Dillingham*, p. 256.

9. Harvey Zorbaugh, *The Gold Coast and Slum* (Chicago, IL, 1929).

10. *Dillingham*, p. 261.

11. Peter Venturelli, "Acculturation and Persistence of Ethnicity in a Northern Italian District" (Ph.D. diss., University of Chicago, 1981; "Institutions in an Ethnic District," *Human Organization* 41 (1982), 26-35.

12. Harry Jebsen, Jr., "Blue Island, Illinois: The History of a Working Class Suburb" (Ph.D. diss., University of Cincinnati, 1971).

13. See the author's article "Suburban Italians: Chicago Heights, 1890-1975," in Melvin Holli and Peter d'A. Jones, *Ethnic Chicago* (revised and expanded edition, Grand Rapids, 1984).

Neighborhood Italian family, proprietors of the Gonnella Bakery, in front of their
bakery and store on Sangamon Street just east of Halsted,
circa World War I.   Courtesy of University of Illinois at Chicago: Special Collections.

The ethnic store was often an important element in the lives of newcomers. Here
they could purchase familiar foods, tobaccos, and condiments, and transplant a part
of the Old World into the New. Above is Joe Cipriani (left), in his Chicago Heights
store in the 1920s.   Courtesy of Nick Zaranti.

Melrose Park, sixteen miles to the west of the central city, was a place of second settlement attracting Riciglianesi, Trivignesi, and others from the inner city to the wide open spaces of the western suburbs. The growth and development of the feast of Our Lady of Mount Carmel (established in 1894) attracted increased numbers of Italians and eventually saw Melrose Park become identified as the quintessential Italian suburb in the Chicago area.

The Highwood community, twenty-eight miles north of the Loop, developed after the turn of the century when migrants from the Modenese towns of Sant' Anna Peligo and Pievepeligo settled there after venturing into the coal-mining towns of downstate Illinois. As explained by Adria Bernardi in her *Houses with Names*, they made their way in the world "working for some rich people."[14]

The pattern that emerges from the post-pioneer settlement (1880-1920) is a varied one. Mostly *contadini* (small farmers) from dozens of towns in Italy, both north and south, they settled around the core of the central city and in selected suburbs. They practiced *campanilismo*, living near others from the same village or region. The inner-city colonies were considered slums, and their inhabitants were the object of intensive efforts by social workers to make them middle class and of masterful maneuvers by political ward bosses to get their votes.

Work

Deprived of decent opportunities to earn a living in Italy, immigrants came to Chicago for *pane e lavoro* (bread and work) and evinced an enormous work ethic. As grueling as were their unskilled jobs, as unpleasant and dirty as they might be, the toil brought results and enabled the immigrants to reconstitute their families in Chicago. The occupations pursued by the immigrants fell into the usual categories: railroad laborers, construction workers, small-scale fruit and vegetable peddlers, shoemakers, and barbers. Both men and women were engaged in the needle trades at such establishments as Hart, Schaffner and Marx; Italian socialists such as Emilio Grandinetti were among the leaders in several Chicago strikes by the Amalgamated Clothing Workers Union in the pre–World War I period. According to Rudolph Vecoli, however, during that prewar era it was unusual to find Italian employees indoors, in factories. Only a minuscule number worked in the meatpacking plants.[15] And even though they preferred outdoor work, there were few, if any, engaged in agriculture in the Chicago area, despite efforts by reformers to return the former *contadini* to the land. About 10 percent were listed by the Dillingham Report as being businessmen.[16] The same 1911 source showed 19 percent of southern Italian women and 13 percent

14. Adria Bernardi, *Houses with Names* (Urbana, 1990).
15. Vecoli, chapter 7.
16. *Dillingham*, p. 309.

Teenage Italian onion pickers from Chicago Heights pose for a
photo in a South Holland onion field, about 1930. Even in the
hot summer the girls wore enough clothing to protect
themselves from the blowing dust in the fields.
Courtesy of the Italians in Chicago Project, University of Illinois at Chicago.
Funded by a grant from the National Endowment for the Humanities.

of northern Italian women working outside the home, a surprisingly high
number compared to the much lower rate reported by Yans-McLaughlin in her
study of Italian women in Buffalo.[17] Only about 10 percent of all Italian women
in the sample were reported to be English-speaking.[18]

Especially in the period before 1900, Italian immigrants found work
through the *padrone* system. Among the more entrepreneurial early immigrants
there developed a class of labor agents who also often served as merchants,

17. *Dillingham*, p. 324; Virginia Yans-McLaughlin, *Family and Community: Italians Immigrants in Buffalo, 1880-1930* (Ithaca, NY, 1977), p. 173.
18. *Dillingham*, p. 333.

saloonkeepers, travel agents, and landlords. These men found work for their countrymen on the railroad construction gangs and in other unskilled employment — at a price. The "padrone system," as it was called, was open to enormous abuses because sharp operators could take advantage of illiterate greenhorns. It was a practice that also existed among other immigrant groups such as the Greeks. Exploitation of the immigrant workers was especially severe during the long spells of high unemployment in the 1890s, but it seems to have diminished after 1900 as the immigrants built family and *paesani* networks to perform functions previously handled by the *padroni*.

Early Newspapers

The institutions created among Italians in Chicago included Italian-language newspapers, such as *L'Unione Italiana* (1867-68), *Il Messagero Italo-Americano* (1888-1890), *L'Italia* (1886-1950s), *La Parola dei Socialisti* (1908-82), *La Tribuna Transatlantica* (1910-1920s), and other shortlived ventures.[19] The newspapers provided the news of the day in Italian. They kept alive links with Italy, promoted the political or religious causes of the editors, and drew Italians into political participation, the citizenship process, and voting. And the papers served as advertising vehicles for Italian businesspeople and as a social register for Italian-American *prominenti*. In urging Italian immigrants to learn English and become citizens, however, the papers were sowing the seeds of their own destruction. There is currently no exclusively Italian-language newspaper published in Chicago. Most fell victim to growing English-language literacy and the strictures of censorship connected with World War II.

Egidio Clemente, socialist, OSS Officer, and printer, kept alive *La Parola dei Socialisti* as a bimonthly (renamed *La Parola del Popolo*) until his death in the 1980s. Clemente and *La Parola* represented the strong radical tradition of Italian immigrants and remind us of the fact that, from 1900 to the 1930s, Chicago was a focal center for a movement of Italian radicals and union organizers among coal miners, garment workers, and laborers.[20] Although few in number, the Italian radicals worked to establish unions, joined the IWW to overthrow capitalism, fought to save Sacco and Vanzetti, and struggled to defeat fascist influences among Italian Americans.[21] Today, socialist ranks have

19. Humbert Nelli, *The Italians in Chicago: A Study in Ethnic Mobility* (New York, 1970), pp. 165ff.

20. Files of *La Parola del Popolo* are available at the University of Illinois at Chicago Library; Clemente's papers are at the Immigration Research Center of the University of Minnesota.

21. Eugene Miller and Gianna Sommi Panofsky, "The Beginnings of the Italian Socialist Movement in Chicago," in Joseph Tropea, James Miller, and Cheryl Beattle-Repettl, eds., *Support and Struggle: Italians and Italian Americans in a Comparative Perspective,* Proceedings of the Seventeenth Annual Conference of the American Italian Historical Association (New York, 1986), 55-70.

Pupils at Assumption School at the turn of the century. Assumption
parish was located near the present-day Merchandist Mart and
was the first Italian parish in the city. Courtesy of Dominic Candeloro.

dwindled and they have become almost forgotten as ethnic historians and
publicists accentuate the positive success story of immigrant mobility.

The Church

Early immigrants were often disaffected from the church. The papacy in Italy
had been a stumbling block to Italian unification, and the church had usually
sided with wealthy landlords. The radical vocal minority of Italian immigrants

was strongly anticlerical. At first few priests emigrated. The reception that immigrants received from the Irish and other Catholic groups was disheartening; sometimes they were relegated to the church basement or considered semi-pagan because of their veneration of local saints. The Servite Fathers were the first to establish Italian parishes: Assumption (1881) and St. Philip Benizi (1904). In 1903, Scalabrini Fathers began coming to Chicago. Missionaries who were inspired by Bishop Giovanni Battista Scalabrini of Piacenza, the mostly northern Italian order dedicated itself to the religious, social, and cultural needs of Italian immigrants in North and South America.[22] Established in 1903, the Province of St. John the Baptist (midwestern and western parts of the United States) grew to include almost a dozen Italian parishes that the Scalabrini Fathers either founded or took over in the Chicago area: Holy Guardian Angel (near West Side, 1899), Santa Maria Addolorata (near Northwest Side, 1903), Santa Maria Incoronata (Chinatown, 1904), St. Callistus (near West Side, 1919), Our Lady of Pompeii (near West Side, 1910), St. Frances Cabrini (West Side, 1939), St. Anthony of Padua (Roseland, 1904), St. Michael the Archangel (24th and Oakley, 1903), Our Lady of Mt. Carmel (Melrose Park, 1905), and St. Charles Boromeo (Stone Park, 1943). These parishes, their schools, sodalities, and charitable groups were nurtured by the efforts of dozens of Scalabrini priests, whose letters back home attest the enormous difficulties of their tasks. Dealing with often illiterate and sometimes anticlerical southern peasants, while at the same time trying to make personal adjustments to the American church hierarchy and American society, placed the early Scalabrini priests under considerable stress.[23]

The relationship between the Chicago cardinals and the Scalabrinians, however, seems to have been a smooth one, and the chancery office rather willingly left the spiritual care of the Italian population to them. Scalabrinians learned fast and built and rebuilt churches, schools, and voluntary social networks necessary for fundraising. After the establishment of the parishes and schools came Sacred Heart Seminary (founded in 1935, now the Italian Cultural Center) in Stone Park. In the early 1950s the order opened the Villa Scalabrini Home for the Aged, and in 1961 came the *Fra Noi* newspaper — both major pillars of the contemporary Chicago Italian community. The conversion of the Sacred Heart Seminary building to the Italian Cultural Center in the 1970s is perhaps the capstone in the Scalabrinian program.

By the 1990s, however, the role of the Scalabrini Fathers in the administrative leadership of Villa has diminished. Fr. Larene Cozzi, Pierini's successor, resigned in 1993, after more than 10 years as administrator and the operation reverted to the direct control of Catholic Charities. In addition, the *Fra Noi* has

22. See Tina De Rosa, *Bishop John Baptist Scalabrini: Father to the Migrants* (Chicago, IL, 1987).

23. Manlio Cinfoletti to the Scalabrini Headquarters, July 1, 1924, Archives of the Centro Studi Emigrazione Roma.

broken its financial ties with the Villa and is currently being published with no change in editor or format by the Friends of the Needy. While the residents of the Villa remain overwhelmingly Italian-American and the chaplain is a Scalabrinian, there is considerable concern that contributions from the Italian community of money and volunteer time might fall off. In early 1994 it appeared problematical as to whether the Villa will continue to be the shining jewel of Italian American unity that it has been since the 1950s.

Through it all, the Scalabrini Fathers provided leadership and focus and helped to create a sense of community among the Italians despite challenges from the anticlericals, the Protestants, and a renegade independent Catholic movement.[24] In a word, the Scalabrini Fathers *saved* the faith of the Italians in Chicago, while providing them with major institutions for nourishing and maintaining the Italian language, culture, and identity. Thus, while the Italian immigrant attachment to the Roman Catholic Church could be described as weak and sometimes anticlerical in 1900, by the 1930s it was strong, and by the 1990s it has become difficult to distinguish between Italian Catholicism and that of the Poles and Irish of Chicago. Thus, after an unpromising start, the rapport between the immigrant and the church has warmed into a nurturing relationship for the preservation of Italian ethnic life in Chicago.

The Italian communities of Chicago were also enriched by a phenomenon all too rare in their towns of origin — an abundance of voluntary associations. By the 1920s mutual benefit associations, parish clubs and school organizations, marching bands, settlement house clubs, and even Protestant vacation Bible schools grew up on the near West Side to complement the extended family social networks of the Italian community. According to Humbert Nelli, the Americanizing influence of this participation and the general prosperity of the 1920s went far toward assimilating Italian Americans.[25] Though Nelli has perhaps claimed too much for the assimilation process, his point about the importance of voluntary associations is well taken.

Early Politics

By the 1920s, the Italian communities apparently had not yet matured to the point where they could produce important political leaders; the 19th Ward

24. Into the 1930s there was quite an active Protestant group on the near West Side under the leadership of Reverend Di Carlo. A renegade pseudo-Catholic movement in the 1920s and 1930s focused on the Celestial Messenger, Giuseppe Abbate, a former barber who dressed like the Pope and posed for photographs with a young girl, described as "the Virgin Mary at age 14." The photo is in one of Abbate's publications on file at the Italian American Collection at the University of Illinois at Chicago Library. The anticlerical aspect of Italian immigrant life in Chicago is best described in Rudolph Vecoli's "Prelates and Peasants," *Journal of Social History* 2 (Spring 1969), 217-68.

25. Nelli, p. 200.

A favorite summertime diversion for Italian families was the Sunday picnic in the forest preserve (1930s). Courtesy of the Italians in Chicago Project, University of Illinois at Chicago. Funded by a grant from the National Endowment for the Humanities.

continued to be represented by Irishman John Powers ("Johnny De Pow" to the Italians). Historian Giovanni Schiavo, writing in the mid-twenties, touted the contributions and progress of Italians in Chicago and highlighted the promising future of a Judge Barasa as a mayoral hopeful, apparently to no avail.[26] Anti-Wilson sentiment stemming from the failure of the Versailles Treaty to support Italian territorial claims in Yugoslavia pushed most Italians into the Republican party.[27] Evidence that Italians were able to extract their fair share of benefits from the multiethnic coalition crafted by Democrat Anton Cermak in the early 1930s is not overwhelming. Italians remained numerically underrepresented in both Republican and Democratic regimes.

The Capone Legacy

No treatment of Chicago's Italians would be complete without some discussion of the city's most famous Italian American, Al Capone. The image of this gangster who for twenty years operated a vice, gambling, and illegal

---

26. Giovanni Schiavo, *The Italians in Chicago: A Study in Americanization* (Chicago, 1928).
27. John Allswang, *A House for All Peoples: Ethnic Politics in Chicago, 1890-1936* (Lexington, KY, 1971), p. 116.

liquor empire under the bribed consent of the city's non-Italian political leadership has besmirched the name not only of Italians in Chicago but of the city itself. The universal reaction in any foreign land to the announcement that one is from Chicago is the rat-tat-tat of the machine gun and the knowing mention of the most notorious gangster in world history. There is more. Capone and his kind had an economic impact on the Italian community. Sociologists Daniel Bell and Francis Ianni have detailed the allure that organized crime has had for underprivileged ethnics as an avenue of social mobility.[28] And Humbert Nelli, in outlining the integration of organized crime in the political and economic structure of Chicago, has emphasized that the members of criminal syndicates were *American*-born practitioners of the *American* ethic of success at any cost: "Turning to crime was not a denial of the American way of life, but rather comprised an effort by common laborers who lacked skills to find 'success.' They used the most readily available means at their disposal."[29]

Indigenous efforts to combat delinquency were conducted by the Near West Side Community Committee, with such young leaders as Anthony Sorrentino using as a model the Chicago Area Project developed by sociologist Clifford Shaw.[30] Nelli further points out that Chicago politicians had been using underworld elements to win elections long before the Italians came to the city.[31] Though the numbers directly involved in syndicate crime were less than 1 percent of the Italian American people, the Capone mob did share some of its wealth by employing compatriots and relatives for both the legal and illegal aspects of their business. A showoff, Capone fancied himself a Robin Hood, passing out cash at social functions and establishing soup kitchens for the destitute during the Depression. Many of his associates used their ill-gotten fortunes as a base to launch subsequent generations into the professions. Others simply launched future generations into the same kind of business, bequeathing the Italian community a substratum of organized crime that to this day lurks in and out of political affairs affecting both the Italian and the larger communities.

The Image

On the whole, public opinion of the Italian immigrant in the 1920s was a negative one. Poverty, ignorance, black-hand crime, and prohibition-related violence were the chief ingredients in the public image of Italians during that

28. Francis Ianni, *Black Mafia: Ethnic Succession in Organized Crime* (New York, 1974); Danie Bell, "Crime as an American Way of Life: A Queer Ladder of Social Mobility," in *The End of Ideology: On the Exhaustion of Political Ideas in the Fifties* (New York, 1962).

29. Nelli, *The Business of Crime* (New York, 1976).

30. Anthony Sorrentino, *Organizing Against Crime: Redeveloping the Neighborhood* (New York, 1977).

31. Nelli, *Business*, p. xi.

A legendary racing car driver of the "Roaring '20s," Sonny Talamonte
(Talamont) was the most famous celebrity of the Chicago Italian community.
Courtesy of Nick Zaranti.

decade. Even the most sympathetic saw Italians in the city as suitable objects
for social work, charity, and rehabilitation — perhaps a more negative image
than the criminal stereotype. Nevertheless, in the mid-1920s the Italians in
Chicago still maintained their *Italianitá:* they retained their language, their
family patterns, and their religious practices in the old neighborhoods even
while they were becoming Americanized by their daily contacts with non-
Italians (mostly immigrants themselves).

Mussolini came to power in Italy in 1922 and led Italy into fascism and
a disastrous alliance with Hitler in World War II. Initially, Mussolini and fascism
reinforced *Italianitá* among Chicago's Italians. In fact, the proudest moment in
the history of the Chicago colony came in July 1933, when Italo Balbo's squad-
ron of planes completed their transatlantic flight, landing in Lake Michigan as
part of the World's Fair activities. The event and the hoopla surrounding it put
Italians on the front pages of *The Tribune* — in a positive light for a change.[32]
The glory of Balbo reflected well on the Italian community, welding them close
to the Mussolini regime even while elevating their status in Chicago society.
The lone dissenters were a small group of socialists who dropped leaflets from
airplanes condemning Balbo and fascism; they also sent an embarrassing "con-
gratulatory" telegram to Balbo: the bogus message was read aloud at a banquet
and was signed "Don Minzoni," the name of the priest whom Balbo was accused
of murdering in the early days of fascism.[33]

32. *Chicago Tribune,* July 16, 1933, p. 1.
33. Related to the author by Egidio Clemente in a videotaped interview for the Italians in
Chicago Project, 1979, on file in the Italian American Collection, UIC Library.

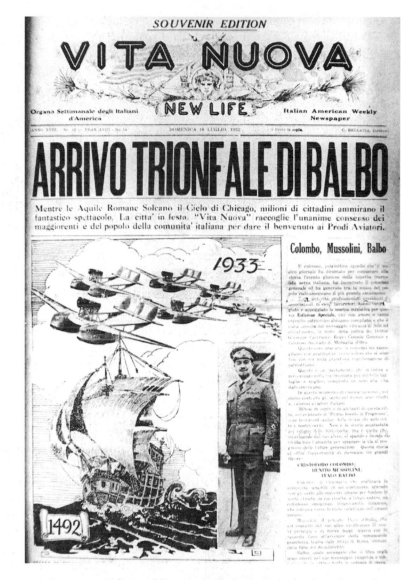

A Protestant Italian publication hails the arrival of Italo Balbo at the
1933 Chicago World's Fair and compares the famous aviator to
Benito Mussolini and Christopher Columbus. Balbo's arrival on
July 15 was a proud day for Italian-Americans.
Courtesy of Dominic Candeloro.

In addition to the Balbo flight, the Mussolini government made the usual efforts — invitations to Italy, awards of merit, the sponsorship of Balilla (Boy Scout type) organizations — to woo the Italian-American leadership. The consulate diligently sent back reports on "subversive" anti-fascist Italian Americans. Until the declaration of war between Italy and the U.S. in 1941, support for Mussolini in the Italian community was high. Then things changed: the second generation marched off to war, and vocal support for the fascist regime died out. Only a handful of Italian fascists throughout the United States were arrested during the war, apparently none of them from Chicago.

World War II

Roughly speaking, what might be called the second generation emerged in the period 1920-1940. Born in Chicago, educated according to American and/or Catholic standards, influenced by the Prohibition of the twenties, tempered by the Depression, and tested by service in World War II, this group was often ambivalent about ethnicity. Though they had experienced the joys of Italian family life, middle-class America had always frowned on their parents' language and customs. Then came the war with Italy as an enemy.

World War II changed everything. It Americanized the second generation. Military experience exposed them to a wider range of life's possibilities. The G.I. Bill opened up the first opportunities for a college education or suburban housing. Other governmental policies such as urban renewal, public housing projects, and the creation of the interstate highways and urban expressways combined to destroy the inner-city neighborhoods. It is doubtful that any Chicago ethnic community was damaged as greatly by government policies during that period as was the Italian American. First there was the building of the Cabrini-Green housing project, which helped drive the Sicilians out of the near North Side in the 1940s and 1950s. Then came the construction of the expressway system on the near South, West, and Northwest sides, which dislodged additional Italian (and other ethnic) families and institutions, including the church and the new school of the Holy Guardian Angel at the Dan Ryan Expressway and Forquer Street. The exodus of Italians was west to Austin and along Grand Avenue, eventually reaching Harlem Avenue. In the early 1960s, the first Mayor Daley determined to build the new Chicago branch of the University of Illinois in the Taylor Street neighborhood. This meant that approximately one square mile of the heavily Italian community, including thirteen buildings of the Hull House complex, had to be razed. Almost simultaneously, the Roseland-Pullman Italian community fell victim to residential change accelerated by real estate block busters who profited from the expansion of the black South Side by scaring Italian-American residents into abandoning their neighborhood and their new Church of St. Anthony of Padua.

Communities of Interest

The overall result of all the positive and negative urban forces at work during the post–World War II era was that, except for a few noteworthy pockets of Italian settlement, Chicago's old Little Italies were destroyed. With them have gone the sentimental sense of identity and security that the continuity and customs and familiar faces of the old neighborhood offered. And whatever political power the Italians could muster on the basis of geographic concentration was also undermined. Henceforth there could be no geographic base for the community. The community identity that survived had to be based instead on a community of *interest* based almost entirely on voluntary associations and self-conscious identification with Italian-ness.

One of the first to perceive the change and to plan for it was Fr. Armando Pierini. Easily the most productive leader in the history of Chicago's Italian community, Pierini began serving at the Scalabrinian Santa Maria Addolorata Church in the early 1930s. Within a year he organized a seminary to train Italian-American priests to minister to their own. The base for this project was the city-wide community rather than a single neighborhood or parish. Sacred Heart Seminary was a success into the 1960s. In addition to preparing future priests, the suburban Stone Park Institution educated young men for community leadership both within and outside the priesthood.

Pierini used the same city-wide approach for his next project: An Italian Old People's Home. Proposed in 1945, Villa Scalabrini opened in 1951. From that time forward it has been the focus of a continuous and intense campaign to create an Italian community and to unite that community behind a common noble cause — the Villa Scalabrini. In the forty-five years since the Villa was first proposed, Italians from various parishes and various parts of the metropolitan area have cooperated to stage carnivals, dinner dances, stage shows, fashion shows, spaghetti suppers, golf outings, cocktail parties, raffles, and picnics, over and over as a result of their identification with Italian-ness unto the third and fourth generations. The $20-million institution stands today as a proud testimonial to what Chicago Italians can accomplish if they are united. And it is the raison d'etre of the Italian community.[34]

The campaign to support the Villa also resulted in the establishment of L'Ora Cattolica (an Italian-language radio program), and in 1960, *Fra Noi*, an English-language monthly. *Fra Noi* began as a house organ for the Villa Scalabrini. The paper's major function was to give favorable publicity to major contributors to the Villa, usually by running a picture of the prominent supporter handing a check to a beaming Fr. Pierini. Over the years, *Fra Noi* became

34. Dominic Candeloro, "*Fra Noi* and the Italian American Community in Chicago," unpublished paper presented at the 1985 Annual Conference of the American Italian Historical Association, Washington, D.C., 1985; see also Dominic Candeloro, "Villa Scalabrini: Citadel of Italian American Culture in Chicago," unpublished paper, 1984.

the Italian community newspaper, mirroring a sense of community even as it was helping to create a nongeographic sense of community. Featuring local articles on politics, people, organizations, dinners, meetings, sports, recipes, cultural and religious topics, in its 360 issues since 1960 the newspaper has reinforced a sense of Italian-ness among its 15,000 subscribers and their families. In March 1985, *Fra Noi* passed from Pierini into the hands of third-generation professional journalists, who widened the intellectual scope, the circulation, and the advertising revenues of the paper. They even expanded the Italian-language section. After three or four years of this direction, Fr. Lawrence Cozzi, who succeeded Pierini as director of the Villa and the paper, shifted the focus of the paper back on the organized Italian community. Building on Pierini's base, Cozzi added retirement apartments, the Casa San Carlo, located adjacent to the Villa, creating a community concept that he calls "Scalabrini Village." In any case, the *Fra Noi* and the Northlake complex continues to function together as a community "maker" and as an agent for the retention of ethnic identity.

Another city-wide Scalabrinian institution that addresses itself directly to the retention of the Italian heritage is the Italian Cultural Center. Fr. August Feccia in the 1970s converted the old seminary building in Stone Park into a center that now features a library, historical and art exhibits, classrooms for Italian-language instruction, a radio studio, immigrant pension counseling, and a 1:100 miniature of St. Peter's Square. With a budget of approximately $150,000, the current Director, Ft. Gino Dalpiaz (a product of the original Sacred Heart Seminary), leads a program that blends the religious and the artistic with emphasis on radio broadcasting and youth groups.

Recent Statistics

A brief demographic analysis of the Italians in the city in recent times yields some varied conclusions. Illinois in 1980, with 640,304, ranked sixth among the states in the number of residents of Italian ancestry in its population. That amounts to 5.3 percent of the state's population. The 1980 census also showed 44,756 *Italian-born* persons in the Chicago area and classified 12,618 of them as noncitizens. The census figures for 1970 and 1980 show Italian Americans in the city to have above-average incomes, but to be slightly underrepresented in the professions.[35] Andrew Greeley's survey of 1975 showed Italians in third place, behind Jews and Irish Catholics in income.[36] Other studies have shown Chicago Italians along with blacks, Poles, and Hispanics to be woefully underrepresented on the boards of directors of

---

35. City of Chicago Department of Planning, *General Profile of the Chicago Italian Foreign Stock Population* (Chicago, 1970), pp. 29-30.
36. *Chicago Tribune*, October 19, 1975, section 1, p. 6.

corporations.[37] Though recent trends have shown Italian Americans to be attaining educational levels in proportion to their percentage in the population, small business rather than education has been the traditional means of social and economic mobility for Italians in Chicago.

Statistics from 1980 show the highest concentration of people of Italian ancestry in the Dunning, Montclare, and the Belmont-Cragin area in the northwest corner of the city; approximately 20,000 of the 138,000 city Italians live there. This forty-block area is shared with second- and third-generation Poles but contains hardly any blacks.[38] The look of the neighborhood reveals the ethnicity of the district. It features large grocery stores specializing in Italian imports (Gino's, for example) and several genuine Italian-style bars (like the Bar San Francesco) complete with espresso, gelato, and cardplayers in the backroom. So many of the stores and businesses on Harlem Avenue are owned by Italians, many of them recent immigrants, that there is a movement to organize a Harlem Avenue Italian Chamber of Commerce.

Both statistical and impressionistic evidence points unmistakably to the fact that the era of the poor Italian is gone. Italian Americans are financially comfortable as a result of success in family business, the acquisition of skilled trades, or through unionized factory work. Moreover, the underconsumption of previous generations, their thrifty cultivation of enormous vegetable gardens, their slow accumulation of real property, and family economic cooperation reinforce their economic status. They have achieved the American Dream, except for one thing — respect.

The Search for Respect

Attaining that final goal of respect is the stated or unstated purpose of the hundreds of voluntary associations that Italians have formed. Pre-eminent among these is the Joint Civic Committee of Italian Americans (JCCIA). It was established in 1952 in a response to an effort by the Democratic party of Cook County to drop a respected Italian-American judge from the electoral ticket. An important part of the Capone legacy is the assumption in the public mind (and among Italian Americans) that every successful Italian American is somehow "connected" with organized crime. The party feared at the time that a newspaper exposé on the mob, though not involving the candidate in any way, would nevertheless bring down the whole slate. To combat this gross injustice,

37. Russell Barta, et al., "Representation of Poles, Italians, Hispanics, and Blacks in the Executive Suites of Chicago's Largest Corporations," Minority Report 2, Institute for Urban Life (Chicago, 1984).

38. Chicago Fact Book, *Local Area Community Fact Book, Chicago Metropolitan Area, Based on the 1970 and 1980 Censuses* (Chicago, 1984), pp. 380-81.

leaders from a variety of organizations formed the JCCIA as a federation to fight the major Italian-American problem: defamation.

Among the early presidents of the JCCIA were attorney Joseph Barbera (1952-1960), wine merchant Anthony Paterno, shoe-repair magnate Joseph Tolitano, and union leader James Coli. Since its founding, the JCCIA has maintained a downtown office with a director, a secretary, and volunteers on a current budget of about $150,000. Despite some flaws in its claim to be a federated umbrella organization, the JCCIA is generally conceded to be *the* speaker for the Chicago Italian-American community. Of key importance to the success and continuity of the JCCIA was the thirty years of diligent work of its executive director Anthony Sorrentino (one-time director of the Illinois Department of Delinquency Prevention) and the group's secretary, Marie Pallelo. Its Anti-Defamation Committee has used an effective combination of quiet influence, outraged protest, and award-giving flattery to nudge the news media toward more objective coverage of Italian Americans. Their major achievement has been the cessation of the use of Italian words such as "Mafia" and "Cosa Nostra" in favor of the more neutral term "organized crime."

Oriented toward the regular Democratic party, the officially nonpartisan JCCIA derives a good deal of its clout from the fact that its major patron is Congressman Frank Annunzio. The most important annual function of the JCCIA is the Columbus Day Parade which attracts almost every politician in the state regardless of race, ethnicity, or party — jostling each other for positions in the front row. Like the old May Day Parades in Red Square, the Columbus Day event shows off the Italian community's "big guns," its power and its influence. The other major event sponsored by the JCCIA for the past twenty years has been the spring dinner-dance, a hotel banquet attended by two thousand in honor of such luminaries as Mayor Jane Byrne, Alderman Edward Vrdolyak, and various powerful Italian-American labor leaders. In some years the proceeds from these extravaganzas have been as high as $50,000.

In the early 1960s, the JCCIA forged an alliance with Villa Scalabrini and the *Fra Noi* that gave increased credibility to all concerned. Together, the agencies have sponsored a dizzying array of cultural, folkloric, and social events ranging from Italian language classes to debutante balls.

Organizational Life

The Italian-American horizon in Chicago is filled with hundreds of clubs and organizations that reinforce and promote Italian identity. A sampling will serve to illustrate their range and depth: the Mazzini-Verdi Society of mostly Lucchesi businessmen has a Franklin Park clubhouse with carpeted bocce courts; the Maroons Soccer Club draws big crowds at 7 a.m. on Sunday mornings to view soccer matches live from Italy via satellite; at the monthly meetings of the

Amaseno Society in Chicago Heights the debate is conducted in four languages — standard Italian, the Amasenese dialect, standard English, and broken English; the JCCIA Young Adults Division plans Wisconsin ski trips and candlelight bowling parties; the Italian American Executives of Transportation organize evenings at the hockey games; the Italo American National Union presents "David Awards" to young professions based on the *promise* in their work; the Italian American Chamber of Commerce (established in 1907) conducts an annual summer convention/retreat at a Wisconsin resort; the Piedmontese Association plans exchange trips to northern Italy and to California to visit colonies of other Piedmontese; the Italian American Sports Hall of Fame regularly calls on Tommy La Sorda as its banquet emcee; the Order Sons of Italy Illinois Grand Lodge holds its annual dinner in an airport hotel on the weekend before Columbus Day; each Labor Day weekend sees the descendants of immigrants from Alta Villa Milicia celebrate the Feast of Santa Maria Lauretana at Harlem and Cermak, complete with a procession and the "flight of the angels" (children suspended on thirty-foot high pulleys above the shrine); Gino and Maria Nuccio of the Italian Radio Theatre have mounted Italian-language plays each year for the past two decades that draw large crowds of adults and children; a dozen Italian-language broadcasts and one English language program, "Ciao, South Suburbia!" hit the airwaves each week from a variety of high- and low-powered AM and FM stations; and the Italian Cultural Center each year mounts an art and history exhibit at the Daley Civic Center to mark Columbus Day.[39]

These activities and organizations do good: they contribute funds to the Villa Scalabrini and they offer small scholarships to young people. More important than the good they do is the recognition these organizations bring to their leaders and their members. For it is in this kind of manageable social matrix that ethnics and nonethnics alike can find the fellowship, recognition, prestige, and respect that most people find so elusive in the larger social arena of the metropolis with its seven million inhabitants.

Though most of the major Italian-American organizations are city wide, a relatively new neighborhood-based organization has emerged in the mid 1980s that has creatively combined ethnic identity with other urban forces, such as political patronage, fear of neighborhood racial change, professional public relations tactics, and *paesani*-type loyalty, to produce the Old Neighborhood Italian American Club (ONIAC). The group is focused on the Chinatown, Bridgeport, and Armour Square areas of the near South Side. Using the slogan "Basta!" (enough), the group has picketed the local NBC-TV affiliate, sponsored a parade and free picnic, organized a multi-saint *festa*, sponsored city-wide "unity" dinners, and generally injected militant rhetoric into what is usually regarded as an "Uncle Tommaso" (Uncle Tom) Italian-American style. In the

---

39. The last part of this essay is drawn largely from the author's experience as a participant-observer on the Italian-American scene in Chicago from 1978-1990.

late 1980s, ONIAC seemed to be challenging the JCCIA for the leadership of the Italian community, but after one of its leading members was imprisoned on racketeering charges, ONIAC's activities seemed to be confined to the neighborhood, and prospects of organizing the entire community on the militant model of ONIAC diminished sharply.

Street Feste

The most dramatic evidence of the retention of ethnicity among Chicago's Italian Americans has historically been demonstrated in the religious street festivals. Italians' parading the graven images laden with money pinned to their garments through the streets of America was shocking to American Protestants, and not a little disturbing to the Irish hierarchy and even some Italian priests. One would have thought that such maudlin folk practices would have been an early casualty of Americanization. And indeed, twenty years ago the number of such feasts had dwindled to a handful. But in recent times there has been a resurgence in the number and intensity of these celebrations. In the 1920s one could attend a different festa each Sunday in the summer at the Sicilian St. Philip Benizi Church; in the 1980s one could still attend a festa each Sunday, but one would have to travel around the whole Chicago metropolitan area to do it. The July 1987 *Fra Noi* contained a pull-out section detailing some twenty feasts, big and small, in the Chicago area. The Feast of Our Lady of Mt. Carmel, which has been celebrated in mid-July in Melrose Park since the 1890s, and the Feast of Santa Maria Lauretana, which originated at St. Philip Benizi in 1900 and is now celebrated at Harlem and Cermak, are the two largest feasts, drawing upwards of 100,000 people each. Also notable are the smaller feasts that have either been revived or established in the past few decades, such as the San Lorenzo Feast in Chicago Heights and the Feast of San Francesco di Paola, sponsored by the Calabresi and held at the Italian Cultural Center. Religious events, these *paesani*/clan/neighborhood activities have mixed charitable and commercial purposes, but few who attend can fail to appreciate the symbolism, the tradition, and the sincerity of the faithful. Ethnicity is nothing if not symbolic, and the *feste* themselves, laden with ancient symbolism, proclaim a convincing challenge to all who would dismiss the authenticity of Italian-American ethnicity in Chicago today.

In Chicago, as in other cities for the past decade, the commercialized Festa Italiana has featured big-name Italian-American entertainers, food, art, and Sunday mass on the lakefront. The organizers, Anthony Fornelli and his Amerital Unico, each year attract up to 100,000 people and have used the proceeds to encourage and support Italian-American cultural and charitable activities, intensifying and perpetuating the identification of all participants with things Italian. Between the neighborhood *feste* and the downtown Festa Italiana, Chi-

A St. Joseph's Day celebration about 1930 at All Saints Church
on the South Side. Courtesy of Dominic Candeloro.

The Devotees of Santa Maria Incoronata bear the statue of the Madonna through the
neighborhood streets in the mid-1940s. Note the cash offerings pinned to the
streamers flowing from the Madonna's right hand.
Courtesy of the Italians in Chicago Project, University of Illinois at Chicago.
Funded by a grant from the National Endowment for the Humanities.

A 1933 bilingual poster beckons Italian Chicagoans to the Feast of
Our Lady of Mount Carmel in Melrose Park. The Italian language
text warns that no one is to collect funds for the celebration without
the written authorization of the pastor. Courtesy of Dominic Candeloro.

cago Italians have a summer full of opportunities to express their ethnic identity. Below is a partial list of *feste* celebrated in the late 1980s in the Chicago area:

Feast	Approximate Date	Location
San Antonio	June 13	St. Anthony of Padua
Santa Liberata	June 10	St. Ferndinand Church
Our Lady of Mount Carmel	July 15	Melrose Park
Our Lady of Mount Carmel	July 15	Chicago Ridge
Tutti Santi	July 20	Armour Square
St. John Bosco	July 26	Italian Cultural Center
San Rocco Di Modugno	August 26	Santa Maria Addolorata Church
San Donatus	August 10	Blue Island
San Fancesco di Paola	August 10	Italian Cultural Center
San Lorenzo	August 10	Chicago Heights
San Rocco di Potenza	August 12	Holy Rosary Church
Santa Maria del Pozzo	August 26	Villa Scalabrini
Santissima Maria Lauretana	September 5	Harlem & Cermak
Santa Maria Incoronata	September 12	Chinatown
San Gennaro	September 19	Our Lady of Pompeii
Crosifisso di Rutgliano	September 23	St. Ferdinand Church

A New Italy Encourages *Italianitá*

An important impulse for the survival and growth of *Italianitá* in Chicago is the policy of the Italian government. Since 1887, Italy has maintained a counsular office in Chicago. Consul General Giuseppe Castruccio was largely responsible for organizing the spectacular Balbo flight in 1933 that enhanced Italian (and fascist) prestige in the city. During that same era, the consulate spent a good deal of time spying on immigrant anti-fascists. In more recent times, the official envoys of Italy in Chicago represent the new Italy, a major prosperous industrial power. And political forces in Italy are reaching out to the fifty million Italian immigrants and their descendants in all parts of the world to maintain cultural links and to enhance the worldwide political and economic prestige of Italy. COEMIT (Committee of Italian Emigrants) has been formed at the initiative of the Italian government in Chicago; the group consists mainly of Italian citizens who live in Chicago. Regional associations with heavy support from Italy are especially strong among the Calabresi, Baresi, Veniti, and Piedmontesi. Chicago is the regional headquarters for a consulate and branches of the Italian Trade Commission, the Italian Government Travel Office (ENIT), the Istituto Italiano di Cultura (Italian Cultural Institute), and several important Italian banks. Employing perhaps a hundred Italian nationals, these agencies promote the Italian image in trade, travel, and culture. Under the direction of the current consul general, Leonardo Baroncelli, their initiatives provide leadership, direction, and financial resources to the Italian-American community. In fact, the prestige of being in the same building with the consulate and other government offices played a big role in the 1988 decision of the Joint Civic Committee of Italian Americans to relocate to 500 N. Michigan Avenue. The Italian agencies sponsor social events, lectures by visiting Italian scholars (like Umberto Eco), receptions for film stars (like Gina Lollabrigida), major design exhibits, conference junkets to Rome, travel promotion, and sister-city receptions in a steady flow of stimulating events that keep and bring Italian Americans in touch with the mother country. Thus, Italian-American leaders are influenced and encouraged in promoting and developing their ethnic identity by agents of the newly-prosperous old country. And the identity that they are cultivating is one that relates to modern Italy as much as it does to the immigrant heritage of their ancestors or the neighborhood culture of their parents.

Recent Politics

While there may be an abundance of symbolic ethnic identification at the feasts, and an upsurge in activity from Italian government agencies, until recently this phenomenon did not extend to the field of elective politics. Italian Americans have not been successful in getting elected to major posts in Chicago or in the state of Illinois. There has never been an Italian-American candidate for mayor of Chicago. Ward-based Italian aldermen began to appear in the 1880s (Stephen Rovere, 1885-1897, and Frank Eazzolo, 1892-1913).[40] The most colorful of Chicago Italian politicians, Vito Marzullo became a precinct captain in 1920, was elected state representative in 1940, and became alderman from the near Southwest Side 25th Ward in 1953. Fiercely loyal to the Democratic machine, Marzullo put into practice the maxim that "all politics is local politics." He was a powerful ally of the first Mayor Daley and in the 1980s was referred to as the dean of city council. Lionized at Harvard University, where he lectured in nonstandard English, Marzullo, perhaps unconsciously, symbolized the limited ambitions of his generation of ethnic politicians.

Down from six a decade ago, in the mid-nineties there were only three Italian-Americans in the city council. Several of the members of the Cook County Board are Italian Americans and Aldo DeAngelis and Aldo Botti have played prominent roles in Cook and DuPage county politics, respectively. But until 1978, no Italian American had ever been slated for a *statewide* elective office. In that year Jerome Cosentino was the first to break the barrier when he ran successfully as the Democratic candidate for state treasurer. Though he was defeated in his bid for secretary of state four years later, he was again elected

40. Nelli, *Italians*, p. 113.

Three well-known Chicago Italian Americans, U.S. Congressman Frank Annunzio, Alderman Vito Marzullo, and Cardinal Joseph Bernardin, gather outside of Our Lady of Pompeii Church after a Columbus Day mass in the mid-1980s.
Courtesy of Dominic Candeloro.

state treasurer in 1986, and was once more the Democratic candidate for the patronage-rich position of secretary of state.

Italians have been more fortunate getting elected to a smaller district office, such as state legislators, county judges, and suburban mayors. Historically, the number of Italians in the larger electoral units has never been great enough to successfully challenge other more populous ethnic groups.[41] However, in electoral units such as suburbs like Chicago Heights, a base of 10,000 co-ethnics and a little coalition building can bring success, as it had for Mayor Charles Panici. In the past dozen years Panici built up the most powerful Republican organization in the state, and his town was rewarded for that by a visit from President Reagan in 1986. In the mid-1980s there were Italian-American mayors in Chicago Heights, Blue Island, Evergreen Park, Stone

41. Illinois population is about 11 million; 640,304 (5.3%) are reported by the 1980 census to be of Italian ancestry.

Park, Melrose Park, Elmwood Park, Lincolnwood, and Highwood, among others.

The dominant political figure among Chicago Italians for the past thirty years has been Democratic Congressman Frank Annunzio. Annunzio began his career in the mid 1930s as an industrial arts and history teacher at Schurz High School, became legislative and educational director of the United Steel Workers of America, chair of the War Rations Board in Illinois, and in 1949 director of the Illinois Department of Labor in the administration of Adlai Stevenson. In the 1950s he allied himself with the Joint Civic Committee of Italian Americans' campaign to support the Villa Scalabrini, bringing together the two most dynamic groups in the city. The personal alliance between Annunzio and Fr. Pierini was a powerful and a lasting one. In the 1964 Lyndon Johnson landslide, Annunzio was elected to Congress from the 7th District on the near West Side. In Washington, Annunzio has fashioned for himself the role of "the leading Italian-American congressman." He was a major protagonist in getting Columbus Day proclaimed a national holiday. He spearheaded earthquake relief funding for Italy in 1978, and he has used his influence to develop the Washington-based National Italian American Foundation. He is the champion fundraiser for Villa Scalabrini and for the Joint Civic Committee, and he is responsible each year for attracting a top political celebrity to be the grand marshall in the Chicago's Columbus Day Parade.[42]

Italian names seem to be overrepresented in the judiciary. This is a result of several factors. There are thousands of Italian-American lawyers in the city, and every lawyer wants to be a judge. Most judicial careers begin by appointment, which can be arranged through political influence. The existence since the 1920s of an effective Italian-American lawyers' association, the Justinian Society, is another factor reinforcing this overrepresentation on the bench. Moreover, the judiciary offers a political career without the necessity of enduring an all-out political campaign and the inevitable Mafia smears and innuendoes that are mounted against any candidate with an Italian name. On the other hand, in retention voting, several experienced, well-respected Italian-American judges have been knocked off by unknowns with Irish names. Though there are several Italian Americans who sit on the State Appellate Court, none has ever been appointed or elected to the Illinois Supreme Court.

Political issues do not seem to matter. At a Chicago conference of Italian-American elected officials, participants were hard pressed to identify specific

---

42. In 1992 old age and redistricting prompted Annunzio's retirement and the loss of his district for Italian Americans. In that same year, Congressman Marty Russo lost the primary for his redistricted seat, leaving the Illinois Congressional delegation with no Italian Americans.

Foreign-born and foreign-stock Italians in Chicago 1850-1985
(excludes suburbs)

Year	Foreign born	Foreign stock
1850	4	N.A.
1860	104	N.A.
1870	552	N.A.
1880	1,357	N.A.
1890	5,685	8,405
1900	16,008	27,250
1910	45,169	74,963
1920	59,215	124,184
1930	73,960	181,861
1940	66,472	N.A.
1950	54,954	171,549
1960	N.A.	134,963
1970	32,539	97,642
1980		138,000
1990		119,697

Year of immigration of Italians to Chicago and suburbs

Year of immigration	Chicago	Suburbs
1965-1969	12.4%	10.0%
1955-1964	21.8	16.1
1945-1954	11.5	16.9
1935-1944	1.8	1.2
1925-1934	11.0	10.0
1915-1924	17.2	15.7
Before 1917	23.9	29.3
Not reported	0.4	0.8

Source for both of the above tables: city of Chicago, Department of Planning, *General Profile of the Chicago Italian Foreign-Stock Population,* Chicago, 1970, p. 6.

Italian-American issues or causes that shaped their politics, except, of course, for the antidefamation issue. All Chicago politics is based on place and influence. The one time that an Italian issue did emerge in the 1960s — when Mayor Daley decided to tear down the Italian neighborhood to make way for the University of Illinois Chicago Circle — the Italian elected officials supported him, leaving only a heroic housewife, Florence Scala, to lead a fruitless battle to save the near West Side Italian community.

Litany

If Italian Americans have been sometimes thwarted in their political ambitions, as individuals they have compensated in other fields. The litany of contemporary and historic ethnic achievers and overachievers gives a clear sense of the dynamic roles played by Italian Americans in Chicago society. The list also provides some role models for emerging leaders who will influence the future of the community.

The saintly Mother Cabrini died in the Chicago hospital that she founded. The previously mentioned Capone distinguished himself in his field and has become a role model to all too many of his co-nationals. Enrico Fermi was a Chicago Italian. The legendary Serafina Ferrara helped plan thousands of Italian American weddings in the back room of her Taylor Street bakery. More recent stellar achievers include Dominick De Matteo, who parlayed a small North Side grocery into the gigantic supermarket chain that bears his first name. Cardinal Berardin is an Italian American who grew up in North Carolina. Anthony Scariano served in the Office of Strategic Services in Italy, as a popular independent liberal Democrat in the state legislature, and currently sits on the Illinois Appellate Court. Dino D'Angelo, born in Castel di Sangro in the 1920s, conquered mental illness, then created a real estate empire that includes the Civic Opera House. D'Angelo's philanthropy toward various universities and hospitals approaches the $10 million mark.

Our list continues with Federal Judge Nicholas Bua, whose courageous decisions have outlawed political coercion of city and county employees. Virginio Ferrari, a Veronese minimalist sculptor, is the creator of one of the most visible art works in the city, "Being Born," which is located on State Street near Marshall Field's. Theresa Pettone is a member of the State Board of Elections. Professor Robert Remini of the University of Illinois at Chicago was the winner of the American Book Award for nonfiction for his three-volume biography of Andrew Jackson. Dominick Bufalino is the former chair and current member of the Board of Governors, which runs some five universities in the state. Leonard Amari is executive director of the Illinois Bar Association. Fred Gardaphé's play "Vinegar and Oil" was staged in 1987. Joseph Marchetti, a patron of the arts and Ferrari automobiles, is head of the family that runs one of Chicago's most popular restaurants, the venerable Como Inn. Several Italian-named persons read us the evening news and sports on major Chicago TV stations, and "Holy Cow!" Harry Caray, baseball announcer for the Cubs, is an Italian American. The list is longer, but the point is clear that there is an abundance of Italian Americans achieving at the very highest levels of Chicago society. And to varying degrees, each of these current leaders maintains a sense of *Italianità* that they transmit to the public and — more importantly — back to the Italian-American community. In their lifestyles and through ethnic media such as *Fra Noi*, these *prominenti*, along with the more humble community-based organizations, reinforce Italian-American ethnicity in Chicago.

Conclusion

There are in the Chicago area about 300,000 Italian Americans of various generations, which is the population of a medium-sized Italian city. Economically, they have entered the American mainstream and are solidly middle class, with incomes higher than that of most urban ethnic groups. Although probably fewer than 5 percent of them use Italian as their first language, most Italian Americans know a few phrases in the language, and the registration of third- and fourth-generation young people in high school and college Italian classes is slowly increasing. And despite the exogamy rate (outmarriage to non-Italians) of about 50 percent, a solid sense of Italian-ness still persists. The typical Chicago Italian American is now in the third or fourth generation and has given up the inner city for suburban locations. Strong family bonding and family orientation are still highly cherished values even in the third generation. Though the group has been represented in the city for over a century, it continues to maintain a lively array of social, cultural, and religious institutions and organizations that provide a sense of ethnic identification and recognition in a manageable arena within the large metropolis. Because the institutions perform the psychic function of allocating recognition, they will not die or fade quickly from the scene. New initiatives on the part of the Italian government will enhance the "high culture" aspect of Italian-American ethnicity. Moreover, the tolerant cultural climate for all ethnicities in the city, and the increased interest among third and fourth generation in ethnic roots and travel to Italy will maintain Italian-American ethnic presence in Chicago.

CHAPTER 9

Greek Survival in Chicago

ANDREW T. KOPAN

The Greek school will train children to be Greeks so that they will not be digested in the vastness of America.

—Peter Lambros, editor of the *Greek Star*

Every ethnic group must be seen against the background of the social order of which it is a part. To get the proper perspective, then, one must see the early Greek immigrants to Chicago as descendants of Hellas (as the Greeks call their country) and as Hellenes (Greeks), the proud inheritors of their nation's long and illustrious history. This "Hellenism" was reflected in the nearly 3,000 years of Greek achievement in the arts, science, philosophy, politics, and governance, in education and religion, the bedrock of Western civilization.

Historically, they came from a small country in southeastern Europe, a poor nation about the size of Illinois, with less than one-fifth of its land arable though it was basically an agricultural nation. The mountainous terrain of Greece, with its 3,000-mile rugged seacoast and its proximity to the sea, has made the Greeks a nation of emigrants from time immemorial. It was the constant seeking for better conditions, coupled with political exigencies of the times, that led to the Greeks' emigration from their country to many parts of the world and later to the United States. A continuous pattern of emigration has been responsible for the spread of Greek immigrant culture from ancient times to the modern period.

Immigration to the United States

The Greek presence in America begins with the first voyage of Columbus, who had a number of Greek crew members.[1] The largest colonization attempt took place much later in 1767, when some 500 Greeks, along with Italians and Minorcans, landed on Florida's Atlantic coast. They had been recruited as indentured laborers by a Scottish entrepreneur who had secured a British land grant. This first episode of Hellenism in America was abandoned ten years later, after they had encountered enormous difficulties.[2]

The Greek War of Independence (1821-1828) provided another episode of Hellenism in America, a wave of "philhellenism" that swept the United States in support of the Greek cause.[3] Meanwhile, another group of Greeks appeared on the American scene during the nineteenth century. These were merchants who were establishing their import-export business in American port cities. It was these merchants who in 1864 established the first Greek Orthodox church in the United States in New Orleans.

The poor and illiterate but energetic and resourceful immigrants who began a mass exodus from the villages of Greece to the United States near the end of the nineteenth century came from a world of desperate poverty. Crop failures, poor soil conditions, floods, earthquakes, oppressive taxation, family debts, political turmoil, and political harassment — especially for those still living in the unredeemed parts under Turkish control — forced many to look elsewhere for the land of opportunity. This was especially the case in the Peloponnese during the 1890s, when the price of currants, the main money crop, dropped drastically, forcing a massive departure of young and middle-aged males from the villages of this area and leaving them bereft.

America was a beckoning symbol, the land of "gold in the streets," where money could be made quickly, which would enable Greek emigrants to return home with sufficient capital to pay off the family debt, provide dowries for sisters, and live in comfort. Thus, nine out of every ten Greeks immigrating to the United States were male at that time. It has also been estimated that at least one-third of those who immigrated to the United States returned to Greece.

---

1. Some speculation has existed that Columbus himself was a Greek. See Seraphim G. Canoutas, *Christopher Columbus: A Greek Nobleman* (New York, 1943).

2. For an excellent account of this little-known episode in American colonial history, see E. P. Panagopoulos, *New Smyrna: An Eighteenth Century Greek Odyssey* (Gainesville, Fla., 1966). Contemporary testimony of this colonization is to be found in *Virginia Gazette*, Sept. 29, Oct. 6, 1768.

3. For an account of the "Greek fever" that swept America at the time, see Stephan A. Larabee, *Hellas Observed: The American Experience of Greece, 1775-1865* (New York, 1952), Chs. 3-7; William St. Clair, *That Greece Might Still Be Free: The Philhellenes in the War of Independence* (New York, 1972); Edward M. Earle, "American Interest in the Greek Cause, 1821-1827," *American Historical Review* 33 (Oct. 1927), 44-63; and Harris J. Booras, *Hellenic Independence and America's Contribution to the Cause* (Rutland, Vt., 1934).

TABLE 9.1
Immigration from Greece by decades, 1821-1980

Decade	Number	Decade	Number
1821-1830	20	1901-1910	167,579
1831-1840	49	1911-1920	184,201
1841-1850	16	1921-1930	51,084
1851-1860	31	1931-1940	9,119
1861-1870	72	1941-1950	8,973
1871-1880	210	1951-1960	47,708
1881-1890	2,038	1961-1970	85,969
1891-1900	15,979	1971-1980	102,000*

U.S. total for 160 years: 675,158

*Immigration figures for 1977-1980 estimated at 9,000 annually.

Source: Immigration and Naturalization Service, *1965 Annual Reports* (U.S. Government Printing Office), pp. 47-49; Department of Commerce, Bureau of the Census, *Statistical Abstract of the United States, 1972* (U.S. Government Printing Office), p. 92; and Immigration and Naturalization Service, *1976 Annual Reports* (U.S. Government Printing Office), pp. 87-88.

Greek immigration became largely a male phenomenon, with one of the highest rates of repatriation.[4]

According to the United States Census, more than 15,000 Greeks immigrated to the United States during the 1890s. But during the next two decades, 1900 to 1920, the greatest number of Greek immigrants arrived — some 400,000. After that, the figures are drastically reduced because of the passage of the Immigration Restriction Act of 1924, the Depression, and World War II; but they increased again following the war, especially as a result of the reformed Immigration Act of 1967. The total number of Greeks immigrating to the United States, from the time immigration records were begun in 1820 to the present time, is said to be 675,158 (Table 9.1). Of course, these are only official figures; they do not reflect Greeks who immigrated from Turkey, Cyprus, Rumania, Egypt, and other parts of the Mediterranean world.

Chicago was the city that attracted the largest number, and it remained until after World War II the largest community of Greeks in the United States — containing approximately 10 percent of the Greek population in the United States. The 1890 census shows only 245 Greeks in Chicago, but by 1900 this figure had increased to 1,493, by which time the organized Greek community of Chicago had come into existence.[5]

---

4. For a descriptive analysis of this movement, see Theodore Saloutos, *They Remember America: The Story of Repatriated Greek-Americans* (Berkeley, 1956).

5. Compiled from the 1970 *Census: General Social and Economic Characteristics, Illinois* (U.S. Gov't Printing Office, 1972), Table 40, p. 325.

The Greek population of Chicago never reached more than 75,000 persons, considerably less than the 125,000 to 250,000 usually claimed by the Greek press and community leaders. But from its initial stages to the present, it has been one of the most viable Greek communities in the United States and the first to respond to the need for ethnic survival and educational adjustment.

Origin of the Greek Community in Chicago

Historically, it all began in the 1840s with the arrival of a few pioneer Greek traders in Fort Dearborn from New Orleans by way of the Mississippi and Chicago rivers. Some returned to their homeland with glowing tales of the Midwest and came back with relatives. One of these was Captain Nicholas Peppas, who arrived in 1857 and lived on Kinzie Street for more than fifty years. Another early pioneer was Constantine Mitchells, who, while a Confederate soldier, was taken prisoner by the Union armies during the Civil War and brought to Chicago. At the end of the war he settled in Chicago permanently. During the same period, "Uncle" Thomas Combiths moved to Chicago, and in 1869 his son Frank became the first child of a Greek father to be born in the city. Frank Combiths' mother was not of Greek descent, nor were there any Greek women in Chicago until many years later.

It was not until after the Great Fire of 1871 that Greek immigration to Chicago accelerated. One of those who settled there after the fire was Christ Chakonas, who became known as the "Columbus of Sparta" for his successful effort in encouraging Greeks to settle in Chicago. When he first arrived in 1872, Chakonas saw the opportunities the growing city offered and returned to his native city of Sparta to urge his friends to immigrate to Chicago. When they did, many of these early Greek settlers worked on construction jobs, rebuilding the city after the fire. Others became fruit peddlers or merchants along Lake Street, then the city's main business artery. News of their "success" reached the homeland, and a new wave of Greeks arrived to seek their fortunes. This time people from the neighboring villages in the province of Laconia and the adjoining province of Arcadia joined the immigration movement, and by 1882 the Greek community was a settlement of several hundred people who resided in the vicinity of Clark and Kinzie streets on the near North Side. Chicago soon became the major terminal point for Greek immigrants to the United States, making the city the largest Greek settlement in the country, with a distinctive Peloponnesian composition — mostly of men from Laconia and Arcadia.

The first Greek woman in Chicago is said to have been Mrs. Peter Pooley, who came with her sea-captain husband from the Greek island of Corfu in 1885. Mrs. Pooley became active in the minuscule community, organizing a benevolent society together with the Slavic Orthodox community for the purpose of forming a common house of worship. In 1887 the first purely Greek

Mr. and Mrs. Peter Pooley (Panagiotis Poulis), the first Greek family known to settle in Chicago, shown shortly after their arrival from Corfu, Greece, in 1885. Mr. Pooley was a sea captain who had visited Chicago several times. Impressed with the city, he returned to his native island of Corfu, married Georgia Bitzi, and brought her to the Windy City. A well-educated and aggressive woman, Mrs. Pooley organized the Greco-Slavonic Brotherhood — the first Greek voluntary association in Chicago. Mr. Pooley died in 1914 and his wife in 1945. They had seven children, all born in Chicago. Courtesy of Andrew T. Kopan.

benevolent society, Therapnon, was organized, followed in 1891 by a second society, Lycurgus, organized by immigrants from Laconia.[6] By 1892 the Greek community had acquired its first resident pastor, Rev. Peter Phiambolis, who officiated at the first Greek Orthodox church in a rented upper-level warehouse on the northeast corner of Randolph and Union streets, near the produce market where most Greeks worked.[7] On March 25, 1893, the church was consecrated by the first Greek Orthodox hierarch to visit the United States, Bishop Dionusius Lattas of Zante, who had come to represent the church of Greece at the Columbian Exposition. Later, the Annunciation Church (as it was named) in cooperation with the Lycurgus Society relocated the church in more appropriate quarters at 60 East Kinzie Street. The contemporaneous American press described religious services in this early church as follows:

6. *Greek Star* (Chicago), April 9, 1937. Founded in Chicago in 1904, this Greek ethnic newspaper remains today the oldest of its kind in continuous publication in the United States.

7. *The Chicago Herald,* May 10, 1887; *Chicago Daily Journal,* April 22, 1924; see also *Chicago Herald and Examiner,* May 2, 1938; Canoutas, *Hellenism,* pp. 184-186.

Greek service is said at a church on the second floor of an unpretentious building in Kinzie near Clark Street. Here come regularly 3,000 members of the Greek colony of Chicago to hear bearded Father Phiambolis clad in canonical robes. The mass is said in the Greek tongue like it has been sung in Greece for nearly 2,000 years. It is, for the time being, a part of ancient Greece, transplanted and set down in the heart of a busy, bustling community, where the rattle of wagon wheels and the clang of street car bells break in with striking rudeness on the holy intonation of the priest. To the casual visitor who knows the Greeks in a business way and is conversant with their quickness in adapting themselves to American methods and manners, the impression thus given is a forceful one.[8]

The newly relocated church became a source of tension and discord. One account claims that a few influential Spartans of the Lycurgus Society wanted to place a tax on "certain Halsted Street Greeks," namely the Arcadians, who were beginning to settle there in greater numbers. The feud brought about a split in the organized community, forcing the Arcadians to organize their own association, Tegea, followed by a parish of their own. This was accomplished in 1897, when they purchased a former Episcopal church at 1101 South Johnson Street (later renamed Peoria Street) and obtained an Arcadian priest. The new parish, Holy Trinity Church, became the focal point of a new "Greektown" on the near West Side.

A profile of Greek population dispersion before 1900 indicates that in the early 1890s the first Greek shops were found at Clark and Kinzie streets, just north of the Loop. It was here, as we have seen, that the city's first "Greektown" was located with the first organized church community. By 1895 newer Greek immigrants, predominantly from the province of Arcadia, began to move to the new West Side. A newspaper account observes:

> The better class of Greeks is to be found on South Water Street, while the poorer class is sandwiched in the settlements of Italians, Syrians, and Slavonians [sic] on the west side. West Polk Street from the river to Blue Island Avenue is thickly populated with Greeks.[9]

A later newspaper account indicates three areas of Greek concentration: Fifth Avenue (Wells) and Sherman Street between Van Buren and 12th Street; the north side of Kingbury, Kinzie, and Illinois streets; and the "vicinity of Tilden Avenue, Taylor Street and Center Avenue on the west side."[10]

The Greek population of Chicago grew rapidly at the beginning of this century. In 1904 there were reportedly 7,500 Greeks, and by 1909 about 15,000, of whom 12,000 came and went according to their work in the city or on the

8. *Chicago Tribune*, February 21, 1897.
9. *Chicago Tribune*, April 7, 1895.
10. *Chicago Tribune*, February 15, 1897.

Typical of the growing stream of Greek immigrants to the United States during
the early part of the twentieth century was this group of 13 young men who
emigrated from a small village near Olympia (site of the ancient Olympic games)
in 1910. Arriving in New York, they boarded a train and took it to the end of the
line — Chicago, where they posed for this photograph to send back to their
relatives in the village.   Courtesy of Andrew T. Kopan.

railroad lines in states further west. As the Greeks became more numerous on
the West Side, they invaded the Italian section, gradually displacing Italians from
the area. The district was surrounded by Halsted, Harrison, Blue Island, and
Polk streets, and was just north and west of the famed Hull House and the
present location of the University of Illinois at Chicago campus. It became
Chicago's famous "Greektown," also called the "Delta," the oldest, largest, and
most important settlement of Greeks in the United States. By 1930 the area had
a foreign and native-born population of 12,000 to 18,000 Greeks.

The first permanent Greek community consisting of a church and a school
was organized in the Delta. In this transplanted piece of Greece emerged the
first Greek-language newspapers, offices of benevolent, fraternal, and social
organizations, and new businesses that soon surpassed those on Lake Street.
According to Fairchild, an early writer on Greek immigration to the United
States, the district became more typically Greek than some sections of Athens.

Practically all stores bear signs in both Greek and English, coffee houses
flourish on every corner, in the dark little grocery stores one sees black olives,
dried ink-fish, tomato paste, and all the queer, nameless roots and condiments

which are so familiar in Greece. On every hand one hears the Greek language, and the boys in the streets and on the vacant lots play, with equal zest, Greek games and baseball. It is a self-sufficient colony, and provision is made to supply all the wants of the Greek immigrant in as near as possible the Greek way. Restaurants, coffee-houses, barber-shops, grocery stores, and saloons are all patterned after the Greek type, and Greek doctors, lawyers, editors, and every variety of agent are to be found in abundance.[11]

While the Delta was to remain the largest concentration of Greek immigrants in Chicago, a second concentration of Greek newcomers developed on the South Side. After 1904, Greek shops and stores appeared in the Woodlawn district, mainly along 63rd Street between Wentworth and Cottage Grove. Subsequently, a second church community was organized with the assistance of a dissident group from the original Delta community. It became known as the Church of Saints Constantine and Helen, and a building was erected in 1909 at 61st and Michigan Avenue, followed by a parochial day school in 1910.

Similarly, Greek immigrants began moving to the North Side, some coming from the first area of settlement at Clark and Kinzie. A third church and school community was organized and erected independently at LaSalle and Oak streets in 1910, dedicated to the Annunciation of the Virgin Mary. Gradually, as Greek immigrants dispersed to other parts of the city, fed by increasing immigration, additional church communities were organized. By 1930, Greek immigrants had established eleven formal communities in Chicago. Today persons of Greek descent are dispersed throughout the metropolitan area and clustered around twenty-one Greek Orthodox parish churches, thirteen of which are located in the suburbs. Each parish church represents a *koinotis,* or community, named after its patron saint; and the church as the nucleus of such a *koinotis* serves as a multifunctional center for religious, educational, social, and cultural activities.

The Role of the Church

The church is an ecological concept for Greek Orthodox Christians. If asked where he lives, a Greek is most likely to use the name of the church as a place of reference. Generally, church parishes in the central city, which were the original establishments, tend to be oriented to recent immigrants, especially those coming after World War II, while parishes toward the northern and southern outskirts of the city tend to be oriented to first- and second-generation

---

11. Henry Pratt Fairchild, *Greek Immigration to the United States* (New Haven, 1911), pp. 123-124. For a colorful description of Chicago's Greektown at Halsted and Harrison streets, see Edward A. Steiner, *On the Trail of the Immigrant* (New York, 1906), pp. 282-291; see also Theano P. Magaris, *Chroniko tou Halsted Street* [Chronicle of Halsted Street] (Athens, Greece, 1962) and her *Etchings of Chicago* (Athens, 1967).

Holy Trinity Church, 1897, was the first permanent Greek Orthodox
parish in Chicago. It was located in the Greek Delta at Halsted and
Harrison Streets, the largest Greektown in the United States.
Courtesy of Andrew T. Kopan.

Greek stock. Suburban parishes are all postwar phenomena, representing the
movement of second and third generations to the suburbs.

The church of Greece is governed by a synod of bishops, with the archbishop of Athens as president. It is from this church that Greek emigrants began
arriving in America at the turn of the century.[12] The significance of the institution of the Greek Orthodox Church within the structural cohesiveness of the

12. Information about the religious affairs of Greek people has been secured from standard
sources, which, unless otherwise noted, are in agreement with matters cited: Ernst Benz, *The Eastern
Orthodox Church: Its Thought and Life* (New York, 1963); Thomas J. Lacey, *A Study of the Eastern
Orthodox Church* (2nd rev. ed., New York, 1912); John Meyendorff, *The Orthodox Church: Its Past
and Its Role in the World Today* (New York, 1962); Basil K. Stephanides, *Ecclesiastiki historia*

Greek community in Chicago is paramount. Along with the family, it was and is the enduring force in keeping the Greek ethnic group together. A leading theologian once said that "church and society are one in their essential nature: for the substance of culture is religion and the form of religion is culture."[13] The prototype of formal organization among the Greek immigrants was, as we have already seen, the *koinotis*, which grew out of the *paroikia*, or "colony." The latter was a term applied to any group of Greek immigrants in a given locality; the former was a specialized term designating a regularly organized community centered in a church organization and usually called "the Orthodox Greek Community."[14] All Greek immigrants were considered members of the *paroikia* (colony), but when the *koinotis*, or "community," was organized, membership was increasingly limited to those who paid dues in support of the community. The purpose of the *koinotis* was to raise enough money to establish and maintain a local Greek Orthodox church. A general assembly of the entire dues-paying membership (consisting only of males) would then be called to elect a *symboulion*, or "board of trustees," which governs the affairs of the community by electing officers headed by a president.

The first task of the *symboulion* was the formal organization of the community by renting or purchasing property for religious services and obtaining a charter of incorporation from the state in which the community was located. The next task was to apply for a priest from either the Patriarchate of Constantinople (Istanbul) or the Church of Greece. Once this had been achieved, the new community would then proceed to establish a school. Thus every community would possess a church and school. The Greek immigrants of Chicago were the first to organize such a community in 1892, followed later in the same year by New York.[15] As noted above, Chicago now has twenty-one such communities.

Greek Orthodox communities in the United States originated from the action of the immigrants themselves and were not instituted by ecclesiastical authorities in Constantinople or Athens. Unlike the hierarchial situation in the old country, priests in America were hired directly by the *koinotis* rather than assigned by bishops. The governance of the church community was in the hands of the *symboulion*, which often served as a barometer of community opinion. The members disputed about priestly qualifications and role expectations, educational concerns, teachers, and board members, political affiliations and rival

---

[*Ecclesiastical History*] (Athens, 1948); Frank Gavin, *Some Aspects of Contemporary Greek Orthodox Thought* (Milwaukee, 1923); Timothy Ware, *The Orthodox Church* (Baltimore, 1963); and Panagiotis Bratisiotis, *The Greek Orthodox Church*, trans. Joseph Blenkinsop (Notre Dame, IN, 1968).

13. Paul Tillich, "The Interpretation of History," *Chicago Tribune*, July 5, 1970.

14. The distinction is made by Canoutas in *Hellenism*, pp. 162-163 (fn.), and in Burgess, pp. 52-53.

15. Holy Trinity Church, *Forty Years of Greek Life in Chicago, 1897-1937* (Chicago, 1937), pp. 19-22.

Greek Orthodox Church Communities of
Chicago and Suburbs (1890-1980)

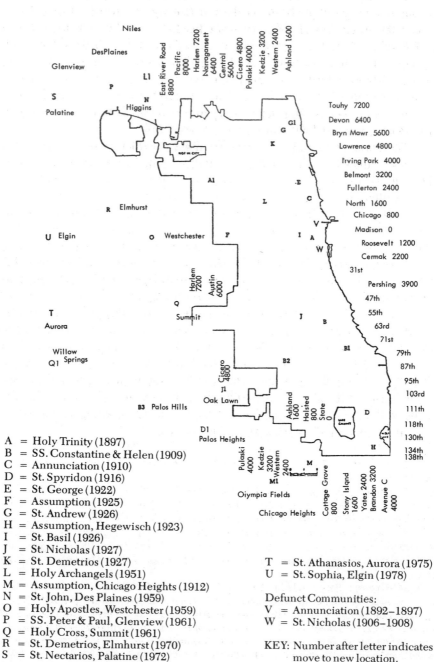

A = Holy Trinity (1897)
B = SS. Constantine & Helen (1909)
C = Annunciation (1910)
D = St. Spyridon (1916)
E = St. George (1922)
F = Assumption (1925)
G = St. Andrew (1926)
H = Assumption, Hegewisch (1923)
I = St. Basil (1926)
J = St. Nicholas (1927)
K = St. Demetrios (1927)
L = Holy Archangels (1951)
M = Assumption, Chicago Heights (1912)
N = St. John, Des Plaines (1959)
O = Holy Apostles, Westchester (1959)
P = SS. Peter & Paul, Glenview (1961)
Q = Holy Cross, Summit (1961)
R = St. Demetrios, Elmhurst (1970)
S = St. Nectarios, Palatine (1972)

T = St. Athanasios, Aurora (1975)
U = St. Sophia, Elgin (1978)

Defunct Communities:
V = Annunciation (1892–1897)
W = St. Nicholas (1906–1908)

KEY: Number after letter indicates
move to new location.

leaders, use of church funds for projects, community policies, the use of the English language, and kindred concerns.

The early Greek Orthodox churches in America, though independent in all reality, were by canon law under the spiritual aegis of the Ecumenical Patriarchate of Constantinople in Turkey, world headquarters of the Orthodox Catholic Church.[16] However, for practical purposes during this early period of Greek migration, the churches were placed under the spiritual jurisdiction of the Russian Orthodox bishop at San Francisco. The Russians were the first to introduce Orthodoxy into the United States and had the only resident bishop.[17] For the Greeks, however, this dependency meant humiliation; they were proud, nationalistic, and owed allegiance to a state church.[18]

The Patriarchate officially transferred the jurisdiction of its immigrant churches to the Church of Greece in 1908 for composite reasons. Numerous editorials in Greek-language newspapers demanded the establishment of an American diocese, but no action was taken other than the special assignments of Greek bishops to visit and return to the homeland. This situation was somewhat parallel to that of the colonial Anglican Church, which was forced to fend for itself prior to the American Revolution due to the lack of a resident bishop.

The outbreak of the Russian Bolshevik Revolution and the Venizelist-Royalist dispute, a political issue in Greece, radically altered Greek church development in this country. In 1922 the Patriarchate of Constantinople reassumed control of American Orthodox churches to remove them from the political factionalism that intensified in the communities. Along with this jurisdictional change came the formation of the Archdiocese of North and South America, and Chicago received its first bishop in 1923, when the area made up a diocese. Unfortunately, fierce turmoil persisted within the newly formed archdiocese, with two political factions — Venizelist and Royalist — each establishing its own hierarchy and parishes.[19] Finally, in 1930, with the nomination of Athenagoras as archbishop for the United States, the wounds and the schism gradually healed.

16. See Theodore Saloutos, *The Greeks in the United States* (Cambridge, Mass., 1964), pp. 118-120.

17. On September 24, 1794, eight Russian Orthodox monks landed on Kodiak Island. In succeeding years, thousands of Aleuts were baptized, and in 1824 the mission was run by John Veniaminov, who translated the gospel into Aleutian, created schools, and constructed an Aleutian grammar. When, in 1867, Alaska was sold to the United States, a separate diocese was created with the episcopal residence in San Francisco and later in New York. A detailed missionary account appears in the *Encyclopedia Britannica*, 1955 ed., s.v. "Orthodox Eastern Church," by Matthew Spinka.

18. Burgess, p. 54; *Saloniki Greek Press* (Chicago), December 12, 1931.

19. A list of "canonical" and "uncanonical" clergymen based on the political division engendered by the Royalist-Liberal controversy is to be found in the *Monthly Illustrated National Herald* 11 (April, 1925), 299-301. In Chicago three of the four Greek churches were Royalist. In 1924 a national meeting was called by the Royalist churches to force the Greek government to rescind the Patriarchal Tome of 1922 and again place the American churches under Greece. See *E en eti 1924 en Sikago laikokleriko syneleusis* [The Chicago Laity-Clergy Conference in the Year 1924] (printed minutes of proceedings in possession of this writer), pp. 8-11.

The interior of Annunciation Cathedral, the seat of the Greek Orthodox Bishop of
Chicago, founded in 1910 and still in existence at 1017 North La Salle Street. The
elaborate Byzantine decor is typical of the ornamentation in Greek Orthodox
churches.   Courtesy of Andrew T. Kopan.

The erratic action of the church community in these years of dramatic
political upheaval in Europe created modifications in the statutes: the archdiocese was now called "Hellenic" and was composed of churches using only
Greek as the liturgical language. All other Orthodox Christians were formally
excluded.[20] This exclusivity and linguistic nationalism is another reminder that
Hellenism and Greek Orthodoxy were deeply intertwined: they kept the immigrant attached to the mother country, nourished his patriotic appetite, and
helped to preserve his faith and the language of his parents. The thought of
never being able to return home to his ancestral origins and the fear of dying
in a strange land caused him for a time to embrace his religion with a fervor
unknown in Greece itself.

Thus a compelling aggressiveness characterized the American *koinotis,*
with its determined, lay-elected *symboulion.* Many imbroglios resulted, since
the *symboulion* managed church finances and paid the priest and teachers.[21]

20. *Orthodoxy 1964* (Athens, 1964), pp. 350-354.
21. The *symboulion* of the Association of the Community of Holy Trinity Church, the first
Chicago *koinotis,* was often at odds with the parish. On several occasions it became involved in
court litigations. See Gregory A. Papiliou v. Demetrios Manousos et al., 108 Illinois Appellate Court
272 (1903).

After 1922 the *koinotis* remained singularly autonomous in internal matters, controlling communal property and making parish policy. The hierarchy was left with only spiritual jurisdiction and the task of assigning clergy to the *koinotis*.[22] Membership in the *koinotis* was open to all baptized Orthodox Christians, but only those males who paid dues could vote. Some Greek immigrants could not understand why it was necessary in America to support the church by fees and contributions. The strict separation of church and state in the United States was to them a fresh concept, difficult to grasp at first: at home in Greece all baptized persons were automatically church members, and no dues had to be paid to the state church. They gradually learned this lesson, however, and one other American lesson as well: women were allowed to vote in parish affairs and serve on the parish council after World War II.

The clergy were trained in ecclesiastical colleges in Greece or in territories considered Greek. The early priests sent to Chicago were highly educated and dedicated. They exerted leadership in organizing the parish, the voluntary, philanthropic, and mutual-aid societies, as well as the parish schools, and they often assumed teaching functions.[23] However, there were other clergy without official credentials; as opportunists, they seized the chance to establish rival parishes in order to secure a job. And there came clerics from the Greek districts of the Ottoman Empire who kept their parishioners in a perpetual state of nationalistic excitement by accusing them of being remiss in their patriotic mission.[24]

The role of the priest was not regarded as separate from the community. He was, by special training and ordination, an ambassador of the sacred church, as well as a mortal by nature and existence. The priestly character was thus described:

> As although [the Greeks] may sometimes despise the man for his lack of education or his worldly-mindedness, they nevertheless respect the priest and treat him with the proper marks of courtesy, as doffing their hats, or rising when he enters the room.[25]

Because of deep-rooted democratic Greek traditions, the priest had no formal control but had considerable informal influence, if he cared to exercise it. And some exercised it extensively. These "empire builders" led the uphill battle for the promotion of ethnic education. Often they faced direct confrontation with the *koinotis*, which resented control of communal schools by clergy.

---

22. For a description of the democratic organization of the Greek church as a *koinotis*, see W. Lloyd Warner and Leo Srole, *The Social System of American Ethnic Groups* (New Haven, 1945), pp. 176-192.

23. *Ibid.*

24. Canoutas, *Hellenism*, pp. 228, 330, 326; Mary S. Economidou, *E Hellenes tis Amerikis opos tous eida* [The Greeks in America as I Saw Them] (New York, 1916), pp. 151-163.

25. Burgess, p. 108.

The *symboulion* leaders were often anticlericals who found such priestly involvement incompatible with the immigrant's former experiences in Greece.

An example of this stance appeared in an editorial at the time the Chicago Greek community was debating the establishment of a communal school.

> With our Greek schools in America springing up like mushrooms beside Greek churches, the Greeks in Chicago and elsewhere are warned to bear in mind the futile efforts of the church in the past to dominate public instruction. And we Greeks of America, for our own interest, the interest of coming generations, the interest of our adopted country, and the interest of the church itself must accept this great American educational system which is free from any ecclesiastical domination. Church is an imperative necessity for a nation, but school is the nation's whole life, and public schools which are free from theocracy are the real bulwarks of the country. Let us profit by the pitfalls into which others have fallen and maintain freedom of education if we wish to produce good, useful, broad-minded citizens whose knowledge and enlightenment will promote and protect the welfare of the church.[26]

A Greek was born into his religion and nationality; it was thus unthinkable to be anything else. Yet some evangelical groups succeeded in making inroads in converting Greeks away from the Orthodox faith.[27] Strong opposition set in, with Greeks blaming the chaotic conditions on quarreling parish councils and partisan clergy failing to minister to the needy and distressed. Others had little sympathy for "traitors" who embraced a strange faith. In their patriotic estimation, a man who renounced the Greek Orthodox church was not Greek.[28]

All of these vexing problems — dissension within church communities, unqualified priests, evangelization — underscored the long-recognized need for a workable central authority. Chicago's Greeks awaited a bishop who could function with a stern hand; but none came because of the difficult political conditions in Greece.[29] So the Greek church communities floundered on their own.

Conditions in Chicago from 1914 to 1917 revealed the low opinion the *koinotis* held of the clergy and local ecclesiastical administrations. The Greek press continued its attack on allegedly greedy, grasping priests who, in league with conscienceless members of parish councils, trampled on the dignity of the church and integrity of the communities. Lengthy court trials, criminal waste, and extravagant use of church funds for litigation and fees became a disgrace.[30] Clerical commercialism was a common journalistic theme. Priests were accused

26. *Greek Star* (Chicago), October 21, 1904 (Chicago Foreign Language Press Survey, WPA Project, 1942).

27. *Greek Star* (Chicago), February 26, 1909; *Saloniki* (Chicago), June 19, July 17, 1915.

28. *Greek Star* (Chicago), March 5, 1909; *Saloniki* (Chicago), July 10, 15, 17, 1916.

29. Theodore N. Constant, "The Religion of the Hellenes," *Athene* 6 (March 1945), 12; *Atlantis* (New York), July 12, December 17, 1908.

30. *Saloniki* (Chicago), February 18, 1914; November 13, 1915.

of neglecting pastoral duties in order to officiate at sacramental events for lucrative fees.[31] Additional complaints involved their failure to adjust and relate to new surroundings, furnish relevant educational programs, and meet basic concerns of parishioners.[32]

Frequent pleas were voiced for unifying the parishes of Chicago. In the autumn of 1915 the United Greek Parishes of Chicago announced the formation of a committee designed to bring order out of confusion. It was comprised of local priests, council presidents, and representatives, and it called for a thorough auditing of financial records, a public listing of debts, purchase of a communal cemetery, maintenance of a consolidated school, establishment of a high school with dormitories for all Greek students in the United States, creation of special funds for the needy, and the building of a hospital.[33]

This ambitious plan for unification floundered, as usual, on the factionalist feud over the Venizelist-Royalist political issue in Greece. Even the formation of the diocesan structure of 1923 failed to effect a real union of the Greek community. The damage had been done, and they were unable to agree to unite.[34] Greek individualism and divisiveness would remain, despite the attempt to superimpose a formal church structure.[35] The precepts of Hellenism would, however, be taught and transferred to ensuing generations through the ethnic community schools.[36] But down to the 1980s, each community attacked its local concerns independently.

Economic Status

In view of the Greek immigrants' peasant background, it is noteworthy that in America they should have such business skill and resourcefulness. At home, few of the emigrants had ventured beyond their native villages or made contact with other ethnic groups. They arrived in the New World with no liquid capital or experience in the world of work in which they were to become so conspicuous.[37]

31. *Saloniki* (Chicago), December 4, 1915; December 15, 1917; *Loxias* (Chicago), March 4, 1911.

32. *Saloniki* (Chicago), December 4, 1915.

33. *Saloniki* (Chicago), October 16, 1915.

34. Two communities, Annunciation and Saint Demetrios, managed to unite into a consolidated community in 1942.

35. For detailed accounts of the role of the church in the Greek community, see Warner and Srole, pp. 156-219; Saloutos, *Greeks in the United States*, pp. 118-137; Burgess, pp. 87-122; Thomas James Lacey, *A Study in Social Heredity as Illustrated by the Greek People* (New York, 1916), pp. 37-39; J. Mayonne Stycos, "Community Cohesion Among the Greeks of Bridgetown," in Arnold Caroline Rose, ed., *Minority Problems* (New York, 1964), pp. 255-256.

36. For an insightful look into the role of the Greek Orthodox Church in ethnic identity and the encroachment of assimilation, see Theodore Saloutos, "The Greek Orthodox Church in the United States and Assimilation," *International Migration Review* 7 (Winter 1973), 395-407.

37. *Saloniki* (Chicago), September 7, 1918.

Pan Orthodox Day at the Chicago World's Fair in 1933. Symbolic of the large
multiethnic Orthodox population in Chicago is this rare gathering of Greek, Russian,
Serbian, Ukrainian, and Syrian clergymen who participated in services at the city's
100th birthday celebration — "A Century of Progress" exposition.
Courtesy of Andrew T. Kopan.

Unskilled Greeks found work in the textile mills and shoe factories of New
England and in diverse industries in New York, Philadelphia, and Chicago. Labor
agents persuaded many to take heavy labor on railroad and waterfront construction jobs in Utah, Nevada, Oregon, and Washington. But many newcomers
underwent mental and physical suffering on such jobs, and as soon as possible
they ventured into business on their own.

Business appealed to the Greek immigrants for many reasons, in addition
to the typically American desire to be "one's own boss." Some, desiring wealth
and status so that they could return to their native villages and flaunt their
success in front of their detractors, believed that independent business was the
surest way to economic success, and it certainly was preferable to working for
others for wages. Wherever one turned in America, the admonition was to work
hard, save, invest, succeed, and become independent.[38] In short, the Greeks —
unknowingly perhaps — were practicing the "Protestant ethic" of hard work
and success, the American Dream ideology.

38. *Greek Star* (Chicago), January 19, 1906.

Marked individualism was obviously one of the innate traits of Greek immigrants. An early writer commented on the dominant characteristics of the Greek *Zeitgeist:*

> We noted as characteristic of ancient Hellas an extreme individual freedom. The same individualism is as marked today as in ancient times. Jealousy, rivalry, restiveness, factiousness, self-assertion, inherent in the national character.[39]

These traits had a profound impact on Greek business success and economic failures. They were, for the most part, unable or unwilling to work cooperatively and harmoniously with one another. But in time, through exposure, interaction, and acculturation with the dominant American culture, these traits were somewhat modified.

In their early years in Chicago, many Greek immigrants became peddlers. It was not long before Greek peddlers, fighting for control from the Italians, achieved a large share of the banana and fruit business, and began moving into the wholesale business. The *Chicago Tribune* noted:

> . . . the Greeks have almost run the Italians out of the fruit business in Chicago not only in a small retail way, but as wholesalers as well, for the big wholesale fruit houses on South Water Street are nearly all owned by men from the isles of burning Sappho. As a result, there is a bitter feud between these two races, as deeply seated as the enmity that engendered the Graeco-Roman wars.[40]

Two years later the same newspaper described the proclivity of Greek immigrants toward economic independence by saying that the ". . . true Greek will not work at hard manual labor like digging sewers, carrying the hod, or building railways. He is either an artisan or a merchant, generally the latter."[41]

The successful Greek fruit and vegetable peddlers were confronted with numerous problems besides the confrontations with Italians. One was the neighborhood merchant who resented their competition. In 1904 the Grocers' Association accused the peddlers of being the parasites of the trade and asked the city council to prohibit them from selling in alleys and streets — or else to impose a heavy tax. The struggle between the established grocers and the peddlers was fierce. In some cases it was even a Greek grocer versus a Greek peddler. The peddlers, by insisting that they rendered a public service to housewives who preferred produce that was cheap and fresh, won a temporary victory and were

---

39. Lacey, *Social Heredity,* p. 27.
40. *Chicago Tribune,* April 7, 1895.
41. *Chicago Tribune,* February 21, 1897.

Greek-American peddlers with a horse-drawn wagon about the time of World War I.
The Greek immigrants who began in vending, peddling, pushcart, and other street
trades would soon move into permanent locations and come to dominate some
businesses such as restaurant trade, more than one-half of which today are owned
and operated by Greeks in Chicago.   Courtesy of Andrew T. Kopan.

thus encouraged to organize a fruit and vegetable dealers' association to ward
off future attacks from grocers.[42]

The peddlers also suffered from the effects of graft-ridden law-enforce-
ment agencies. They were often intimidated and forced to pay a small fee to
dishonest policemen. Their ignorance of the law, a passive attitude, or a lack of
necessary funds to acquire a license often invited unscrupulous police officers
to threaten them with prosecution for the violation of municipal ordinances.[43]
On the basis of such alleged legal violations, Greeks were arrested in large
numbers. The Abbott study indicates that in 1908 alone there were 1,157 Greek
arrests, of which 891 were for city ordinance violations. Based on the Greek
population in the 1908 school census, it claimed that twenty-seven out of every
hundred Greeks in Chicago had violated the law; for the rest of the city's
populace the ratio was only four per hundred. The Abbott study suggests that
these figures were further distorted because there were probably three to four
times more Greeks in Chicago than revealed by the 1908 census.[44]

42. *Greek Star* (Chicago), April 1 and 22, 1904.

43. *Greek Star* (Chicago), September 25, 1908; interviews with Pericles Orphanos, George
Damolaris, et al., May 21, 1968.

44. See Grace Abbott, "A Study of the Greeks of Chicago," *American Journal of Sociology* 15
(Nov. 1909), 382-384.

This meat market was located on Halsted Street in Chicago's Greektown (or "Delta").
By 1920 Chicago's entrepreneurial Greeks operated more than 10,000 stores,
meat markets, bakeries, flower shops, confectioneries, restaurants,
shoe repair and shine shops, and other small businesses.
Courtesy of the Jane Addams Memorial Collection, University of Illinois at Chicago.

In 1909, when the City of Chicago attempted to raise the peddlers' license
fee from $25 to $200 a year, the anger of the Greeks and other nationality groups
was aroused. The Greeks had special reason to believe that this legislation was
aimed at them, because they had a firm grasp on the peddling business. These
legal maneuvers made clear to them the need to become American citizens and
reinforce their protests through the power of the vote.[45]

45. *Loxias* (Chicago), February 12, June 4, 1910.

Other ventures undertaken by Greek immigrants met with similar obstacles and discrimination. The restaurant business, which became a major economic enterprise for them, began with their selling "red hots" and "hot tamales" from pushcarts and lunchwagons throughout the city. Then, under the administration of Mayor Carter H. Harrison II, the city-county, responding to pressure from native restaurateurs who feared Greek competition, passed an ordinance prohibiting the sale of food on the streets.[46] At first, Greek merchants organized to fight the ordinance, but finally they agreed to abandon their street vehicles. All those who could scrape together enough money, often by mortgaging the homestead in the old country, rented stores and opened restaurants. Their apparent success aroused increased resentment from rivals, from Americans who opposed foreigners, and from an unsympathetic press.

Eventually, Greek restaurant owners organized to defend their growing trade against the antiforeign attitudes and measures of native businessmen. They formed the Greek Restaurant Keepers' Association, but typical factionalism among the Greeks made the association almost impotent.[47] Nonetheless, Greek immigrants began to realize that they could compete with Americans, and their restaurants became an important part of the Chicago commercial establishment.

Similarly, Greek merchants entered the shoeshine and shoe repair, florist, confectionery, ice cream, and hotel businesses. Beginning meagerly with small stands, they expanded their respective industries and in some cases became pioneers in the field. In fact, the first soda fountain was established in a Greek ice cream parlor, and the first sundae reputedly was invented by Greeks in Chicago.* Fairchild predicted that if immigration from Greece were to continue at its rate of that time, the candy, soda, and perhaps the fruit businesses of the country would be a Greek monopoly after twenty years.[48]

By the 1920s, in fact, Greek immigrants were among the foremost restaurant owners, ice cream manufacturers, florists, fruit and vegetable operators, and confectionery merchants in Chicago. A metropolitan newspaper declared:

> Chicago Greeks operated more than 10,000 stores — 500 of them in the Loop — an aggregate monthly rental that exceeds $2,500,000. These stores, it is estimated, do business of more than $2,000,000 a day.[49]

46. *Chicago Herald and Examiner,* November 6, 1927.

47. *Loxias* (Chicago), May 21, October 15, 1910.

*The origins of the *sundae* remain obscure, though it seems agreed that the strange spelling derives from "Sunday," and that the ice cream, fruit, and nuts concoction was sold on that day — a response to the sabbatarianism of the Women's Christian Temperance Union, headquartered in Evanston, Illinois, a northern suburb of Chicago.

48. Fairchild, p. 171. At one time, Chicago had as many as one thousand Greek-owned candy stores. It still remains the Greek-American center of the candy industry. In 1947 an estimated 350 to 400 shops and eight to ten candy manufacturers were located in the city. See *Greek Star* (Chicago), June 15, 1906.

49. *Chicago Herald and Examiner,* November 6, 1927.

The attitude of the Greek immigrant community toward that success was expressed in 1907, in an editorial in a Chicago Greek-language newspaper, the *Greek Star.*

> The Greek with his active mind and his American-acquired scope of operations, enhanced by the greatness of the American spirit, has flooded America with confectioneries, restaurants, flower shops, fruit stores, commission houses, shoe repair shops, shoe shine stands, grocery stores and many other businesses. . . . And this handful of Greeks in America have made themselves known to the whole country as a progressive element in the United States, and have made themselves a locomotive power pushing Mother Greece. . . . The phenomenal superiority of the American-Greeks over all Greeks, according to our reasoning, is attributed to the spirit of America which the Greek immigrant to America has accepted, adopted, and injected into his being.[50]

Despite obstacles, many climbed the socioeconomic ladder, and by 1919 it was estimated that 10,000 of the 18,000 men owned their own establishments.[51]

Later the Greeks moved into the coffee and fur business, real estate, and the entertainment field. They gained holdings in the movie industry and became operators of theater chains and ballrooms, such as the famed Aragon and Trianon. An indication of their economic progress was reflected in the large sums of remittances they sent back to the homeland. As dutiful sons, they lived abstemiously and frugally, usually saving half of the profits. They sent sizable portions back home to pay off mortgages and family debts, buy real estate, and provide dowries for unmarried sisters or relatives. Between 1903 and 1908, these remittances amounted to approximately $5 million annually — an average of $50 per capita. According to American consular officials in Greece, it was the highest average remittance of any ethnic group surveyed.[52] Between 1919 and 1928, they averaged $52 million annually, the peak being $121 million in 1920;[53] not until 1963 was this amount surpassed, with a figure of $126 million.[54] These remittances formed one of the chief invisible imports of Greece.

The role of Greek women in the American labor force was another story. For the most part, rigid tradition forbade their entrance into the labor market, especially after marriage. If they worked, it was usually in industries that also

---

50. *Greek Star* (Chicago), June 8, 1907. For the Horatio Alger stories, see *Monthly Illustrated National Herald* 11 (April 1925), 333-353.

51. *Greek Star* (Chicago), November 14, 1919.

52. Other ethnic groups contributed per capita as follows: Germans, $4.05; English and Irish, $7.14; Italians, $30; Slavs, $28.10; Russians, $14.80, as quoted in Fairchild, pp. 191-192.

53. Eliot Grinnell Mears, *Greece Today: The Aftermath of the Refugee Impact* (Stanford, 1929), pp. 195-197.

54. This was due to the resurgence of Greek immigration following the Displaced Persons Act of 1948. See E. N. Botsas, "Emigration and Capital Formation: The Case of Greece," *Balkan Studies* 10 (1969), 127-134.

employed Polish, Bohemian, Russian, and Italian females. To be a domestic was frowned upon. With some exceptions, domestic work was done by Swedish, Norwegian, Irish, German, Canadian, and Scotch women.[55] Only 5 of 246 Greek women and girls over fifteen years of age were gainfully employed in about 1910, according to the Abbott investigation. And because the Greek male considered it a disgrace to have a wife or a sister working outside the home, many families suffered financially.[56] This "sacred tradition" was part of the Greek immigrant's cultural baggage inherited from his agrarian background.

That the Greek immigrant had finally achieved status as a successful entrepreneur was revealed in 1952 at the hearings of the Truman Commission on Immigration and Naturalization. The argument in favor of liberalizing the quota for immigrants from Greece claimed that the contemporary professional, commercial, and intellectual prominence of Greeks was "impressive." The Greeks had come to America and "carved successful niches in the business and professional worlds. They were on their way to a new status . . . the immigrant of yesteryear had established sobriety, industry, and integrity."[57] This was also underscored by a well-known study in 1959 which found that Greek immigrants and their offspring had the highest achievement motivation in a sample of white Protestant Americans and other ethnic groups in America.[58] This conclusion was supported by United States census data, a further corroboration of the social and economic attainments of Greeks. An analysis of the 1960 census reveals that second-generation Greek Americans possessed the highest educational levels of all and were exceeded only by Jews in average income.[59] The same pattern was confirmed in the 1970 census, which showed that among twenty-four second-generation nationality groups, Greeks trailed only Jews in income levels and continued to rank first in educational attainment.[60]

The economic wealth of Greek immigrants helped reinforce their ethnic pride and provided the means for them to give financial assistance to the Greek community for ethnic schooling. Successful businessmen provided leadership by becoming members of church boards of trustees and school boards.

55. Florence J. Chaney, "The Social and Educational Protection of the Immigrant Girl in Chicago" (M.A. thesis, University of Chicago), p. 31.

56. G. Abbott, "Study of the Greeks," p. 388.

57. U.S. Congress, House of Representatives, *Hearings before the President's Commission on Immigration and Naturalization*, 82nd Cong., 2nd sess., 1952, pp. 216-218, 431-433, 536-537.

58. Bernard C. Rosen, "Race, Ethnicity and the Achievement Syndrome," *American Sociological Review* 24 (Feb. 1959), 47-60.

59. Leonard Broom, Cora A. Martin, and Betty Maynard, "Status Profiles of Racial and Ethnic Populations," *Social Science Quarterly* 12 (Sept. 1971), 379-388.

60. U.S. Bureau of the Census, *Census of the Population: 1970*, Subject Reports, National Origin and Language, Final Report PC(2)-1a.

Hull House

The Chicago Greeks formed a plethora of mutual aid and burial societies, business and trade groups, professional, religious, and educational organizations, athletic, theatrical, and musical associations. Many were organized under the protective concern of Hull House and the benevolent influence of Jane Addams, who had an immeasurable impact on their lives. In commenting on these kinds of societies, Park states:

> These organizations are not, in fact, pure heritages, but the products of the immigrants' efforts to adapt their heritage to American conditions. The immigrant, therefore, comes to a society of his own people, and this non-native American society is the matrix which gives him his first impression. The character of this society . . . is the primary influence in determining the desire and capacity of the immigrant to participate in American life.[61]

The Hull House Theater, the first of its kind in the nation, was inaugurated in December 1899 with a presentation of the classical Greek tragedy *The Return of Odysseus*. The actors were Greek immigrants and they attracted wide attention in the city; it was the first public recognition for Greek immigrants in Chicago. The success of *The Return of Odysseus* prompted the Greek community to work on another theatrical production, Sophocles's *Ajax* in December 1903.[62]

The special attention given by Jane Addams to Greek immigrants and her espousal of Greek culture, which is indicated by these activities and the many others she sponsored, quickly endeared her to the Greek community as a patroness of Hellenic arts and ideals. She did much to help solidify ethnic solidarity and pride among the Greek immigrants of Chicago. A regular participant in the activities of Hull House in the early days remembers the phillhellenic attitude of Jane Addams, which encouraged Greeks to center around Hull House.[63] The Greeks had more and larger clubs than the other ethnic groups using Hull House[64]; in fact, Greeks began to think of it as their own institution, often trying to keep other ethnic groups from using the facilities.[65] Many began to engage in amateur wrestling and won national and regional titles for Hull House.[66]

Ironically, in view of Jane Addams' leadership of the pacifist movement, the gymnasium was allowed to be used by young Greeks for military training

61. Robert E. Park and Herbert A. Miller, *Old World Traits Transplanted* (New York, 1921), p. 121.

62. *Chicago Record*, December 13, 1899; *Hull House Bulletin* 6 (1903-1904), 18.

63. S. N. Soter, "Jane Addams, the Hull House, and the Early Greek Immigrant," *Greek Star* (Chicago), November 25, 1964.

64. *Hull House Yearbook*, January 1, 1916, p. 33.

65. G. Abbott, "Study of the Greeks," p. 385.

66. Jane Addams, *Twenty Years at Hull House* (New York, 1910, 1961), pp. 268-269; see also *Hull House Yearbook*, January 1, 1913, pp. 23, 26-27; January 1, 1921, pp. 9-10.

in preparation for the Balkan Wars (as we shall see later), a matter that was cited against Addams before she was awarded the Nobel Peace Prize.[67] Even the boards of trustees of Greek church parishes used the Hull House facilities, and the numerous educational activities of the settlement house served as springboards for subsequent educational designs by the Greeks. They availed themselves of every opportunity to attend night classes to study the English language, learn music, dancing, and handicrafts, and hear lectures on various topics. The staff made a concerted effort to accommodate the Greeks, since they were the most immediate neighbors of the settlement.[68] Hull House, located on Halsted Street, was in the approximate center of Chicago's great immigrant colonies. Immediately adjoining it to the north was the Greek community; immediately to the south was the Italian colony, followed by the Jewish, German, Polish, Russian, and Bohemian neighborhoods.[69]

The Greeks complained constantly about the hostility and discrimination they encountered from the "native" American population. The *Hull House Bulletin* lists the following grievance:

> In the last five years, since Greeks have been coming in large numbers to Chicago, they found that Americans made no distinction between them and other more ignorant immigrants from southern Europe. As the modern Greek is devoted to his own country and race, the Greek immigrant bitterly resents the criticism of his manners and habits in America by Americans who, he believes, disregard his historical background and tradition.[70]

Therefore, Greek leaders arranged with Miss Addams to host a meeting "in which Americans should speak in English of the glorious history of Greece, and the Greek speakers should tell their countrymen in their native tongue some of the duties and requirements of their adopted country."[71] This first of a series of sessions was held on January 3, 1904, to a capacity crowd, which viewed a cultural program, listened to speeches by Jane Addams, Professor Paul Shorey, classicist from the University of Chicago, and Mayor Edward Dunne of Chicago, who received a standing ovation. Miss Addams describes the event as follows:

> As the mayor of Chicago was seated upon the right hand of the dignified senior priest of the Greek Church and they were greeted alternately in the national hymns of America and Greece, one felt a curious sense of the possi-

---

67. Addams, *Twenty Years,* pp. 304-305; *Hull House Yearbook,* January 1, 1913, p. 23; and *Forty Years of Greek Life,* p. 57.

68. *Hull House Bulletin* 5 (Autumn 1904), 23-24.

69. A detailed description of social conditions on Halsted Street is to be found in Addams, *Twenty Years,* pp. 80-83.

70. *Hull House Bulletin* 6 (Autumn 1904), 23-24.

71. *Ibid.*

bility of transplanting to new and crude Chicago some of the traditions of Athens itself, so deeply cherished in the hearts of this group of citizens.[72]

Due to Jane Addams's ceaseless dedication, Hull House became the spiritual and cultural hearth of the Greek immigrants — their veritable second home. A young arrival who aspired to be a poet wrote:

> We had problems and Jane Addams was always there to straighten them out for us. She was like a mother to us; she was our protector and our advisor. It was a great alliance based on nobility and understanding. What's more, Jane Addams admired Greek culture, and felt that the modern Greeks who had come here to make America their home, possessed many of the virtues of their ancestors.
>
> I used to go to Hull House quite often. One day I showed Jane Addams some of my poetry, some verses I had published here and there. She became interested. She was always ready to give advice and I learned to appreciate her judgment. And when in 1930 my sonnets were about to be published, under the title "Sonnets of An Immigrant," she wrote the foreword to the book. . . .[73]

In 1930, in recognition of Addams' meritorious work on behalf of the Greek immigrants, the Greek Consul of Chicago awarded her a medallion.[74]

The Greek immigrants' apogee at Hull House was reached on February 12, 1911, when former President Theodore Roosevelt, while visiting the world-famed settlement, was informed that the young men in the gymnasium were Greeks. Seizing this opportunity, the president addressed the assembled immigrants and said that they, unlike other ethnic groups who were expected to abandon old-world loyalties and look toward a new life in America, were exempt because of their own illustrious history.[75]

Those who had an intimate association with Hull House, when interviewed, described the settlement house as epitomizing humaneness toward fellow men — a lone outpost of succor in a bewildering metropolis. The "soul" of Hull House is commemorated in this example:

> I remember the red brick Hull House well. My mother used to press three pennies in my hand and send my sister and me two blocks to the House, where we were showered, cleaned, and sent to an "open air" room to dry off. Later, we spent our three pennies for a bowl of lentil soup, a bologna sandwich, and a glass of milk.[76]

72. Addams, *Twenty Years*, p. 184.

73. Demetrios Michalaros, "1960: Jane Addams Centennial," *Athene 21* (Autumn 1960), 3.

74. *Greek Star* (Chicago), May 23, 1930; November 25, 1964.

75. *Forty Years of Greek Life*, pp. 55-56; Malafouris, p. 141.

76. Constantine D. Orphan, "Goodbye Greektown," *Inlad: The Magazine of the Middle West* (Spring 1963), 20.

It is a small wonder that, at the death of Jane Addams in 1935, a Chicago Greek newspaper editorialized:

> Her death has stirred in us memories that go back . . . to those days when in the buoyancy of our youth we would walk into Hull House as though we walked into our own house, there is absolute freedom to enjoy the House, not in its physical aspects but in that nurturing warmth that animated every-thing and all . . . there sound in our ears the soft words and sentences of the women of the House, the only soft and kind words we immigrant boys heard in those days . . . for we of foreign birth have lost our best friend and the only one who understood us.[77]

In short, the arrival of Greek immigrants during the 1890s and 1900s coincided with one of the most colorful eras of Chicago's multifaceted history. And it was amid such surroundings that they found their "home-away-from-home" at Hull House and thus were assisted in coping with problems in the areas of economic sufficiency, socialization, and educational adjustment.

Education and Ethnic Survival

What was the general educational situation in Greece at the turn of the century, when Greeks began immigrating to the United States? The vast majority had no schooling, or at best a minimal amount of schooling. Indeed, according to immigration records, the average Greek illiteracy rate for the period 1900-1908, during the height of Greek immigration to America and particularly to Chicago, was approximately 27 percent, higher than most immigrant groups (except for southern Italians) who were arriving at the same time. In 1910, 24 percent were unable to read and write; but by 1920 the illiteracy rate had dropped to 3.2 percent. This dramatic change was probably due to the compulsory education laws that were beginning to be enforced in Greece.[78]

Thus Greek immigrants arriving in Chicago had a limited amount of schooling and were mostly of peasant stock. Despite this paucity of formal training, however, Greek immigrants were knowledgeable about their illustrious past and the achievements of their people, possibly because of a long oral tradition in Greece. In this respect they considered their language a binding force. They valued education and were interested in learning more about their 4,000 years of continuous history and linguistic accomplishments. They recog-nized the fact that Greek stood as the oldest living spoken language in Europe

---

77. As quoted in James Weber Linn, *Jane Addams: A Biography* (New York, 1935), p. 111.

78. U.S. Department of Labor, Bureau of Immigration, *Annual Report of the Commissioner-General of Immigration, 1910* (Washington, D.C., 1910), table 8, pp. 20-21; *Annual Report of the Commissioner-General of Immigration, 1920,* table 7, pp. 95-97.

and that it embodied essential aspects of the Greek way of life. In fact, ethno-centric Greeks felt that the Greek tongue made possible the achievements of their people. Twentieth-century Greeks felt kinship with Homer and Plato and with the Byzantine accomplishment; nor could they forget that the New Testament and the development of the Christian Church were Greek accomplishments. A further link with the past was the church's liturgical language, which had remained unchanged through the centuries.

Perpetuation of the Greek language became a prime concern of the early Greek immigrants, and they demanded that their children learn the language that "gave light to the world." The intensity of this universal feeling manifested itself every time a new Greek community was organized. After the establishing of a church, the Greek school received top priority. Every facet of the community, from voluntary associations to the Greek-language press, was used to promote formal and informal schooling for language preservation. This preoccupation with learning the mother tongue probably accounts for the fact that the vast majority of children born in the United States of immigrant Greek parents knew Greek as their first language until the 1930s. Greek immigrants were among the most successful ethnic groups in transmitting their language and cultural heritage to their progeny.[79] They were conditioned by upbringing and history to regard Greek culture as inferior to none. Much to their surprise and chagrin, they found in coming to the United States that many Americans did not share this view. And in the American public schools the Greek legacy, as well as any other non-American culture, except the Anglo-Saxon, was not openly appreciated or even readily tolerated. The public schools appeared to be "destroyers" of ethnic culture; they attempted to do away with the indigenous culture of the immigrants and replace it with an "instant" American way of life — a difficult if not impossible task.

The schools' formal attempts to bring about the enforced Americanization of Greek immigrants were demeaning to the newcomers. They could not understand why learning the English language and American ways required them to abandon loyalty to their homeland and betray their ethnic and religious identity. In many instances, public school policy had the effect of alienating the Greek child from the immigrant parent culture and contributed to tension among family members, especially in the area of language maintenance.

For most Greek students, however, the public school was crucial to their external adjustment and acculturation to mainstream American society. But nearly all Greek children attending public schools were also enrolled in supplementary Greek schools and other private educational arrangements. Public

79. A sociological study of three generations of Greeks residing in San Antonio, Texas revealed that 100 percent of the families interviewed spoke Greek. See Helen Capanidou Lanquier, "Culture Among Three Generations of Greeks," *American Catholic Sociological Review* 22 (1961), 224. See also *Encyclopedia Britannica*, 1955 ed., s.v. "Orthodox Eastern Church," by Matthew Spinka.

schools in Chicago lacked adequate provisions to accommodate immigrants and their children, and thus naturally judged their performance by American cultural standards and conduct. School records and documents, along with available testimony, indicate that Greek children did actively attend public schools; but their actual number is unknown since the schools did not list pupils according to ethnicity. A comparison of the Chicago school census of 1908 with the survey of the Immigration Commission made in the same year reveals that fewer than half of all Greek children were known to be enrolled.[80] The majority were either not attending school at all or were gainfully employed.

Most Greeks immigrated to America, as we have seen, to make money in order to pay off family debts, provide dowries for sisters, and return to Greece with a sufficient amount of money to live comfortably. Consequently, working rather than schooling was the top priority of young boys. The reports of the Immigrants' Protective League describe many accounts of young men engaged in diverse occupations and often exploited.[81] Another reason for their nonattendance in Chicago schools was the fact that these boys were alone, without kinship guidance, as Abbott's study indicated.[82] Still, there were a few young men who exerted great effort and sacrifice in order to attend school.

Following World War I, the profile of Greek children attending public schools began to change. As more immigrants arrived and moved into all sections of Chicago, Greek children began to be regularly enrolled in the city's public schools — for a number of reasons: (1) Greek communal schools were not conveniently located in all the neighborhoods in which immigrants settled; (2) tuition fees for Greek schools made attendance prohibitive for some; (3) the erosion of Hellenic sentiment along with the acculturative process induced many parents to send their children to public schools; and (4) the state's compulsory education law was increasingly being enforced.

Greek children enrolled in the public schools were generally placed in "retarded" classes, as was the custom of the time with children having insufficient knowledge of English. Most were in the primary grades, with heavy attrition after the fifth grade. Very few completed elementary schools, and few indeed went on to high school. By the 1930s, however, because of a number of factors, most Greek children were attending public schools. By that time, children beginning primary grades had a knowledge of English acquired from older siblings or from the broader community; few were placed in "retarded" classes, most finished elementary school, and a large number entered high schools,

80. When the Dillingham Commission made its investigation in Chicago in 1908, it found 193 Greek children (and 5 Turkish children) enrolled in the public schools of Chicago and 34 Greek children attending a Greek parochial school. See *Abstract of Report on Children of Immigrants in Schools* (Washington, D.C., 1911), pp. 66-67.

81. See Immigrants' Protective League, *Seventh Annual Report for Year Ending January 1, 1916;* see also Grace Abbott, *The Immigrant and the Community* (New York, 1917), p. 39.

82. G. Abbott, "Study of Greeks," p. 104.

many graduating. By the 1940s and 1950s, third-generation children (grand-children of the original immigrants) were part of the general American pattern of public school attendance.

The pattern was entirely different with evening public schools, in which young Greek adults were avid participants. From 1902 to 1922 the Greeks were the seventh largest ethnic group in Chicago enrolled in evening programs. During the 1907-1908 school term, one out of every five Greeks officially residing in Chicago attended evening school — one of the highest ratios of all ethnic groups in Chicago.[83] The large attendance of Greek immigrants at evening school can be attributed to their desire to learn English for economic competence and the convenience of evening hours for workers. Most attended school from six to ten months, then dropped out when they felt they had learned enough.

Chicago's Greek immigrants were also heavy patronizers of Americaniza-tion classes; the most successful were those organized at Hull House exclusively for Greeks. Others were held in Greek churches and at people's places of em-ployment — the factory, the railroad, and other areas. Government statistics reveal that the Greek immigrants' incidence of participation in Americanization or citizenship programs was one of the highest of all ethnic groups. Yet they were reluctant to acquire full American citizenship itself, and in Chicago, both in 1910 and 1920, the majority did not hold citizenship.[84] This unusual attitude is explained by the fact that, according to the mentality of the Greek immigrant, acquiring American naturalization was tantamount to betrayal of the homeland. And many Greeks still intended to return home. Attendance at citizenship programs was motivated solely by the desire to acquire greater facility in English for improving job opportunities.

To counteract the alienating influence of the public schools, Greek parents persisted in the transmission of the Hellenic heritage to their offspring by organizing various informal and formal education agencies, especially com-munal schools. But education in the home was also intense, as the following excerpt indicates:

> When I was very young my father used to read Homer to me. While other kids were getting Mother Goose, I was getting Thucydides. The Peloponnesian Wars became exceptionally meaningful to me, and I remember how I dreamt of being a Spartan. (Father was from Sparta and came to Chicago in 1893.) I also remember many sleepless nights when I felt a restless spirit and wondered if strange and mythological gods, somehow controlled my destiny. . . . I felt different because I was proud that my forefathers were warriors who helped shape the history of mankind.[85]

83. Data compiled from a review of the Annual Reports of the Chicago Board of Education for the period 1902 to 1922.

84. See Ernest W. Burgess and Charles Newcomb, *Census Data of the City of Chicago, 1920* (Chicago 1931), p. 26.

85. C. Orphan, "Goodbye Greektown," p. 23.

The pervasive impact of the home is also seen in the following Chicago testimony:

> Father was always telling us about the greatness of Greece and her contribution to world culture and civilization. He ran our home like a school, conducting quizzes at the dinner table, asking us questions from our Greek lessons on the great men and events of Greek history. We enjoyed these sessions as he rewarded us with money. . . . But we were dismayed and hurt by the attitude of our teachers in the public school who kept telling us that we should forget about Greece and become good Americans. . . . We wanted to be good Americans but we were also very proud to be Greeks. I, for one, looked forward to the Greek school which we attended after American school. Here, the teacher was always telling us about the glory of Greece and I enjoyed my Greek textbook. I marvelled that I was reading about the great men of Greece in the Greek language and I dreamed of the day when I would go to Greece to visit the land of Plato, Pericles, and Alexander the Great. When I finally did many years later, I felt that I had come home. . . . Hellenic culture has been a lifelong obsession with me and for this I am indebted to my father and the Greek school.[86]

Meanwhile, the Greek community of Chicago began to exert direct pressure on the Chicago Board of Education. This took the form of the establishment of the Hellenic Education League in 1935 by Greek educational leaders charged with the task of language maintenance. The Greeks had become concerned that, with the passage of the years and the erosion of Hellenic sentiment about the military dictatorship in Greece in 1935, the dream of returning to the ancestral homeland was weakening.[87] They became alarmed at the prospect of their offspring's becoming alienated from the Greek heritage, especially in high school. Hoping to counteract the acculturative influence of high school and to legitimate Greek language and culture in the public sector, the Hellenic Educational League petitioned the Board of Education to introduce the study of Greek into the high school curriculum. The League cited the precedent of the German community's successful petition for the inclusion of German in the city's public schools during the previous century. Furthermore, it contended that Greek had been part of the curriculum of Chicago schools from 1856 until 1883, when it was discontinued.[88] The League also hoped that it could prevail on the Board of Education to restore the study of Greek not only because it

86. Cited in Andrew T. Kopan, "Education and Greek Immigrants in Chicago, 1892-1973: A Study in Ethnic Survival" (Ph.D. diss., University of Chicago, 1974), p. 209.

87. For the erosion of Hellenic sentiment among Greek immigrants, see Saloutos, *Greeks in the United States,* pp. 310-325.

88. Hannah B. Clark, *The Public Schools of Chicago* (Chicago, 1897), p. 74; the Greek text of the petition is to be found in the *Greek Star,* January 24, 1936.

was one of the world's greatest historical and literary languages but also because the Greek citizens of Chicago were now demanding it.

Despite some characteristic factionalism within the Greek community concerning the plan, it was accepted by the Board of Education with the stipulation that a minimum of one hundred students would have to be enrolled. The Greeks responded enthusiastically, and the first Greek-language course was instituted at Austin High School on the city's west side in the fall of 1936. Other courses were begun at Amundsen and McKinley high schools on the North Side and at Englewood High School on the South Side. The Hellenic Educational League had established as its ultimate goal the introduction of Greek studies in at least ten Chicago high schools. In appreciation for the support of Superintendent of Schools William Johnson, the league sponsored a testimonial dinner in his honor, which was well attended by Greeks, and the Greek government awarded Johnson a medallion through its consul general in Chicago.[89]

The Greek instructional program lasted for twenty-five years, avidly supported by the community, which saw to it that Greek students of high school age enrolled. Additional Greek instructors were hired by the public schools to staff the growing number of classes, and thousands of Greek youngsters from all parts of the city attended.[90] Part of this success, aside from the concerted thrust of the community, stemmed from the authorized permissive transfer plan adopted by the Board of Education, which allowed students to leave their school districts in order to pursue Greek studies in districts that offered them. The permissive transfer was inaugurated to permit flexibility for those Greek families who lived outside such districts. This plan, however, proved to be the downfall of the Greek instruction program years later. Its initial purpose was gradually supplanted when non-Greek students began enrolling in Greek courses at these high schools in order to avoid attending schools in neighborhoods that were racially changing. Finally, in 1961, despite protests from the Greek community, Superintendent Benjamin Willis decreed the end of the permissive transfer, and the program collapsed.

Nevertheless, for the period that the program was in operation, it succeeded well in fostering knowledge of Greek, especially among the American-born generations. In the first place, it helped to reinforce the knowledge of Greek among those coming from homes where Greek was spoken. In the second place, it provided advanced knowledge for those who were products of the Greek communal afternoon schools, and it introduced those who had not attended Greek schools to the formal study of Greek. Finally, it legitimated and gave status to the study of the Greek language by its very inclusion in the public curriculum.

89. Interview with Paul Demos, a founder of the league, July 19, 1970.
90. Interview with George Drossos, veteran Greek-language educator of Chicago, November 17, 1967.

The second time the Greek community applied formal pressure on the Board of Education was as late as 1971, but for different reasons. An ethnic survey of Chicago public schools revealed that next to Spanish-speaking pupils, the largest ethnic group in the schools whose mother tongue was something other than English were the Greeks.[91] The large number of Greek children with inadequate knowledge of English were enrolled primarily in the public schools of the Ravenswood, Albany Park, and Belmont-Cragin districts of Chicago's North Side. The postwar Greek immigrants had settled in these areas, creating new "Greek-towns." Children of these immigrants who were enrolled in local public schools were unable to benefit from instruction due to a lack of knowledge of English.

Interestingly, a generation after the first successful attempt was made to introduce Greek studies in the Chicago public schools by the Hellenic Educational League in the 1930s, a similar attempt developed in the 1970s. However, this time the venture was promoted primarily by second- and third-generation Greek Americans who perceived it as part of the current ethnic revival movement, and it involved more than simply the teaching of Greek in public schools. On December 10, 1971, educators from public and private schools organized the Hellenic Council on Education in order to promote and coordinate the educational concerns of the Greek community of Chicago in light of the new ethnicity awareness.[92] One of the first projects of this new group was to encourage the assignment of Greek-speaking teachers and administrators in schools with large enrollments of Greek-speaking pupils. Their pressure on the Board of Education succeeded in bringing this about.[93] Later the Hellenic Council encouraged Greek parents in these schools to develop bilingual education proposals for the teaching of Greek. With the help of the council and the assistance of Dr. Michael Bakalis, then state superintendent of public instruction, and Dr. Angeline P. Caruso, then associate superintendent of Chicago public schools, both of whom were children of Greek immigrants and products of Greek communal schools, several bilingual programs were established, funded by federal grants from Title VII — the Bilingual Education Act of 1967.

But like the earlier attempt in the 1930s, this movement had its detractors in the Greek community. Many resented the creation of such bilingual programs as insulting to the Greek community, implying that it was unable to take care of its own and that Greeks were in need of the federal aid associated with low-income groups, something the Greeks were definitely not. The resulting controversy received national attention in the Greek press as well as in the local metropolitan press.[94] Indeed, the dispute had all the marks of a social class conflict between

91. Chicago Public Schools, "A Comprehensive Design for Bilingual Education" (Chicago Board of Education, 1972), mimeographed, p. 3.

92. *Greek Star* (Chicago), December 23, 1971.

93. Letter of Superintendent James F. Redmond to Hellenic Council on Education, September 5, 1972.

94. See *Greek Press* (Chicago), April 27, 1973; *Chicago Tribune*, July 8, 1973; and *Hellenic Chronicle* (Boston), October 10, 1973.

foreign-born and native-born Greek Americans. But the programs prevailed and are still part of the educational scene in the Greek community of Chicago.

Similarly, the Hellenic council on Education embarked on the development of Greek ethnic studies units for inclusion in social studies classes in those public schools with large Greek enrollments. This too was achieved as an attempt to provide ethnic and cultural identity for those pupils in keeping with state legislation (Ethnic Studies Bill, H.B. 19H), which required local school districts to develop material for acquainting school children with ethnic groups that make up the American population.[95] The Greek material, one of the first of its kind in Chicago, was written by Greek educators in the Greek community with cooperation from the Hellenic Council on Education and was subsequently approved for use in the public schools by the Board of Education.[96] The establishment of this new voluntary association of Greek educators, therefore, represents a new commitment on the part of second- and third-generation Greeks to speed the successful adjustment of recently arrived immigrant children in the city's public schools, and to perpetuate the Greek identity and way of life in the culturally pluralistic society that is America.

However, there is no evidence that those who attended public schools were brought into mainstream culture more quickly than those who attended Greek communal day schools. And while public schools did provide for avenues of acculturation, they did not, in the main, obliterate Greek culture. This was true because of the high priority Greek immigrants placed on transmitting that cultural heritage to their children at home, and the strong structural cohesiveness of the Chicago community with its supportive informal and formal educational agencies. Furthermore, revisionist studies of American schooling show that most immigrant groups did not achieve the upward social mobility that Greeks, Japanese Americans, and Eastern European Jews did.[97] The Greeks achieved this upward mobility not because of their attendance at public schools but because of the heavy emphasis their ethnic culture placed on personal achievement, and the fact that they were among the first of the so-called new immigrants to achieve middle-class status.[98] This process was perhaps hastened by informal educational adjustments that took place among the Greek inhabitants of Chicago via business endeavors, the factory, the church, the playground, and even their limited participation in politics.

95. See *Ethnic Studies Process* (Chicago, 1972), pp. 1-46.

96. *Ibid.*

97. Cited in Charles E. Silberman, *Crisis in the Classroom* (New York, 1970), p. 58; see also Colin Greer, "Public Schools: The Myth of the Melting Pot," *Saturday Review* 52 (November 15, 1969), 84-85; and especially his later work, *The Great School Legend. A Revisionist Interpretation of American Public Education* (New York, 1972).

98. For an explanation of this phenomenon, see Bernard C. Rosen, "Race, Ethnicity and the Achievement Syndrome," *American Sociological Review* 24 (Feb. 1959), 47-60.

Greek Response to Educational Needs: Communal Schools

The Greek immigrants to Chicago, though latecomers to the American scene, are part of the historical framework of responding to the educational concerns of the ethnic group. Every ethnic group has certain knowledge, skills, folkways, and mores that it regards as indispensable to its survival. In order to regularize the transmission of these forms, it sets some sort of educational system. The informal educational system carried on in the home, church, and voluntary associations is not as easily discernible as a formal school system. With the Greek immigrants of Chicago, the formal ethnic school system did not materialize until the first decade of this century, even though its Chicago community was formally established in 1892. The delay apparently was due to agitation over the kind of school to organize, the paucity of families, and their inability to cooperate toward a collective goal. When early communal attempts to establish ethnic schools proved abortive, family men took matters into their own hands and established the first Greek school in Chicago in 1904. This was organized by the Mutual Benevolent Society of Family Men, which broke away from the Greek Orthodox parish of Holy Trinity over educational concerns, and established the abortive parish of St. Nicholas on State Street south of the Loop.[99] Shortly thereafter, another school was organized by another voluntary association of "family men," the "School of Hellenism."

The local Greek newspaper promoted the fact that Chicago's Greeks not only founded the first organized Greek community in the United States but also the first Greek school. Peter Lambros, editor of the *Greek Star,* spoke of the school as being "the organ that will save our language, and the means by which Greek letters will be taught along with our glorious history." Accordingly, the "Greek school will train children to be Greeks so that they will not be digested in the vastness of America."[100] The school principal announced that church and school were "the two pillars which support our national aspirations . . . and they must become our two anchors if we are to maintain our ethnicity in America and remain Greek and Christian Orthodox. . . . We must depend on the church and school."[101]

Much editorializing took place in the Greek press concerning the importance of the church and school in perpetuating ethnic heritage in America. One editorial pointed out that ethnic institutions were needed to combat the "fanatical efforts of Protestants missionaries" to alienate the Greek from his ancestral patrimony.[102] These first schools were short-lived; they did, however, serve as catalysts for the establishment of the first permanent Greek communal day school by the organized *koinotis* of Chicago. This school, named after the philosopher Socrates, was established in 1908 by the oldest Greek Orthodox

99. See *Forty Years of Greek Life,* pp. 52-53; *Greek Star* (Chicago), March 8, 1904.
100. *Greek Star* (Chicago), February 9, 1906.
101. *Greek Star* (Chicago), February 16, 1906.
102. *Greek Star* (Chicago), February 15, 1906.

parish in the city, Holy Trinity Church, but only after overcoming a serious internal feud.[103] The school is still functioning today. After 1908 a variety of educational institutions catering to different segments and age levels of the Greek populace were formed, most of them ephemeral but still illustrative of the Greek immigrant's commitment to education.

Ethnic Education at Hull House

One of the greatest assets to the Greek community in its task of providing educational facilities was, of course, Hull House. Its services to the nearby Greek community helped organize a number of private educational enterprises to take care of needs in two major areas: adjustment to the urban American milieu for the immigrant and his wife, and the transmission of the cultural heritage to his children. Hull House became the educational center for guidance, fellowship, and adjustment for the many Greek immigrants living in the Delta. All kinds of helpful services were available, from finding employment to tracing lost immigrant girls. So important was the work of the social workers, especially that of Jane Addams herself, that the young immigrants looked upon her as their "mother." When she died, as we have seen, the Greek community mourned and Greek businesses were closed on the day of her funeral. She was eulogized as the "Saint of Halsted Street."[104]

The People's School was, in fact, one of the enterprises held at Hull House. One of the most effective endeavors there was the Greek Educational Association, chartered by the State of Illinois on February 9, 1909. A group of young men organized this association to promote the "educational, spiritual, and physical development" of young Greek immigrants, and it was popularly known in Greek as the "Hellenic League for the Molding of Young Men." The organization had hundreds of active members and sponsored scholarships and athletic activities along with military drills, in which young men met regularly at the Hull House gym for strenuous workouts under the direction of former Greek army officers. In her memoirs Jane Addams speaks of this group as follows:

> It was in this connection with a large association of Greek lads that Hull-House finally lifted its long restriction against military drill. If athletic contests are the residuum of warfare first waged against the conqueror without and then against the tyrants within the State, the modern Greek youth is still in the first stage so far as his inherited attitude against the Turk is concerned. Each lad believes that at any moment he may be called home to fight this

103. *Greek Star* (Chicago), July 3, 1908. Full details of the controversy are to be found in *Forty Years of Greek Life*, pp. 61-62.
104. *Orthodox Observer* 1:14 (June 9, 1935), 5; *Athene* 12:1 (Spring 1951), 34.

The Executive Council of the League for the Development of Greek Youth in
Chicago, 1910. The League was organized at Hull House in 1908 to provide
paramilitary and athletic experiences for young Greek men in Chicago. During the
Balkan Wars of 1912 and 1913, thousands of young men trained by the League
returned to Greece to fight the Turks.   Courtesy of Andrew T. Kopan.

longtime enemy of Greece. With such a genuine motive at hand, it seemed
mere affection [sic] to deny the use of our boys' club building and gymnasium
for organized drill, although happily it forms but a small part of the activities
of the Greek Education Association.[105]

When Theodore Roosevelt visited Hull House in 1911, he was greeted by
young Greek men in full-dress uniform who escorted him through the premises.
The following day a Chicago newspaper described the event and quoted Roosevelt
as saying that he "came to Hull House not to teach, but to learn."[106]

With the approaching Balkan Wars, a quasi-military group, the Greek
Volunteers of America, was organized by the Greek Educational Association.
Larger quarters were procured to maintain military preparedness, and in 1912,
five thousand Chicago Greeks volunteered to help Greece "liberate her subjugated
sons and daughters in Macedonia, Epirus and Thrace."[107] The first contingent of

105. Addams, *Twenty Years at Hull-House,* p. 305.
106. *Chicago Tribune,* February 21, 22, 1911.
107. Interview with Aristotle Collias, an original member of the group, July 24, 1969.

Pacifist and Nobel Peace Prize winner Jane Addams (right) with
Mary McDowell (left) not only tolerated but permitted training at
Hull House for Greek Americans preparing to fight in the
Balkan Wars (1912-13). Later, however, she opposed American
intervention in World War I against Germany and the
Austro-Hungarian Empire.
Courtesy of the Jane Addams Memorial Collection,
University of Illinois at Chicago.

300 men embarked for war after attending religious ceremonies at Holy Trinity Church and civic ceremonies at Hull House: with an accompaniment of Greek organizations, a military band, and unfurling banners, they departed triumphantly from Union Station.[108] The civic ceremony was held in Bowen Hall of Hull House, where a Greek priest blessed the group of young men prior to their departure, and it was attended by Miss Addams, who was subsequently awarded the Order of the Phoenix by the Greek government for her "help" in training young immigrants for the Greek army. Unfortunately, receiving that award hindered her peace efforts during World War I, much to her chagrin, and the incident was raised against her when she was considered for the Nobel Peace Prize.[109] Another 3,000 Greek immigrants left later to participate in the wars; many remained in Greece, but others returned to America with wives.[110] It is estimated that as many as 42,000 Greek immigrants returned to Greece from the United States to fight in the Balkan Wars.[111]

The military phase of the Greek Educational Association was only one aspect of its active program. The nightly gymnastic program was well attended because the young men, bereft of families, found it friendly and educational. Many became amateur and professional fighters who won regional and national championships, achievements which contributed to the Greek ethnocentrism of the immigrant.[112] Others were persuaded to attend the craft shops of Hull House, where useful trades became their life's work. And for many, the efforts of the association served as a catalyst for them to enter the professions and broader American society.[113]

But perhaps the most enduring contribution of the Greek Educational Association to perpetuating ethnic identity was its sponsorship of patriotic programs associated with the ancestral homeland. Numerous such events were held, including the annual observance of Greek Independence Day on March 25th. Others commemorated milestones of Greek history and current affairs, such as the one held at Chicago's Blackstone Theatre on June 27, 1918, which observed Greece's one-year participation in World War I, with utility magnate Samuel Insull serving as chairman. Indeed, the celebration of patriotic events became an integral part of Greek community ritual, and when the association ceased to function in the 1920s, the Greek churches collectively assumed the sponsorship of such events. From the 1930s to the 1950s, elaborate festivities observing Greece's Independence Day were held at Chicago's Civic Opera House

108. *Chicago Tribune,* October 10, 1912, with photograph.

109. See *Hull House Yearbook,* January 1, 1913, p. 23; *Forty Years of Greek Life,* p. 57; see also Addams, *Twenty Years at Hull-House,* pp. 304-305.

110. *Chicago Tribune,* September 27, 1913.

111. Saloutos, *Greeks in the United States,* p. 114.

112. *Hull House Yearbook,* January 1, 1913, pp. 23, 26-27; January 1, 1927, pp. 9-10.

113. Interview with Dr. S. N. Soter, an original member of the association, October 12, 1967.

Transmitting ethnic heritage continues today as newer Greek Orthodox parochial schools replace older buildings. Koraes Elementary School of the Saints Constantine and Helen parish in suburban Palos Hills has educated thousands of Greek children since its inception in 1910. Its curriculum provides for instruction in the Greek language and Greek Orthodox faith along with the typical elementary school program.   Courtesy of Andrew T. Kopan.

or Medinah Temple. From the 1960s, a city-wide organization representing parishes, schools, and voluntary associations assumed the sponsorship of such events, including the now elaborate annual Greek Independence Day parade on the city's main thoroughfares. These events have grown into expensive enterprises and serve once again to reinforce ethnic pride and identity for the Greeks of Chicago.

The Broader Greek Community

With the dispersal of Greek immigrants to all parts of the city and the establishment of new communities or parishes, additional Greek communal schools were organized. Up to World War II, eleven organized communities, or parishes, each with its own kind of school, made up the Chicago Greek community. Following the war, the influx of new Greek immigrants and the relocation of second-generation descendants to the suburbs increased the number to twenty-one in the metropolitan Chicago area. Not all were day schools; the large expense necessary to operate such schools made them prohibitive to many parishes. Only three such schools survived through the years: Socrates, of Holy Trinity Church (1908); Koraes, of Saints Constantine and Helen Church (1910); and Plato, of Assumption Church (1952). As a result, a supplementary school — the afternoon Greek school — evolved, meeting several times a week after public school hours. For the most part, these schools, like the day schools, bore the names of eminent ancient Greeks — Solon, Aristotle, Pythagoras, Artage — and a commitment to Byzantine tradition.

The governance of these communal day and afternoon schools was usually under the control of the parish *symboulion,* or under a special appointed or elected school committee. This body generally determined curriculum, the hiring of teachers, and the setting of fees, since they all charged tuition. Because each community or parish was organized independently, each made its own educational arrangements, giving rise to the congregational nature of these religio-ethnic schools.

Another kind of ethnic school that evolved was the private Greek school, maintained by voluntary associations, parental groups, and individuals, which also met after public school hours and sometimes on Saturdays; organized by professional teachers, most of these met in rented quarters and were short-lived.[114] In addition, many youngsters received their Greek education at home with private tutors, especially in areas where Greek schools were not close at hand. The tutorial practice has endured because of its flexibility.

Still another form of communal school was the Sunday school, which every parish organized after the 1920s (despite its Protestant origins). Ostensibly religious in nature, it was nonetheless ethnically oriented and was utilized as another vehicle to inculcate youngsters with the Greek Orthodox faith and culture, initially using Greek as the medium of instruction. For the most part, communal Greek schools were patterned after the provincial primary schools of Greece. All ethnic education was at the elementary level (it was not until the 1970s that a private secondary Greek school was established in Chicago — the Hellenic Lyceum). Initially, Greek was the language of instruction, and it was not until after World War I that English was introduced into the day schools, and not until the 1960s that English began to replace Greek as the language of instruction.

The objective of these schools (and indeed the objective of all ethnic Greek education) was to transmit the Greek language and cultural heritage to children born of Greek parents, while religion had a somewhat secondary role. Unlike in Roman Catholic parochial schools, religion did not permeate the total curriculum but was taught as part of Greek ethnic education. The curriculum itself

114. Interview with Mrs. Bessie Spirides, a long-time observer and archivist of the Chicago Greek scene, September 21, 1970.

was closely patterned after the six-grade primary schools of Greece. A core curriculum included the Greek language, Greek classical and modern literature, Greek history, geography of modern Greece, church history, and catechism. These were taught by professional teachers who received their training at pedagogical institutes in Greece. In time, the day schools were "accredited" by the Chicago Board of Education, and their graduates were admitted into the city's high schools.

The multiplicity and variety of Greek educational facilities in Chicago made them accessible to Greeks residing throughout the city — poorly organized, for the most part, and often inadequate and ill-equipped though they were. Every child born of immigrant parents was exposed to one or another of these educational arrangements. The Greek immigrant's commitment to education and his insistence that children learn the Greek language and heritage probably account for the fact that the vast majority of second-generation Greek Americans had a fluent command of Greek (indeed, often better than did their immigrant parents), and remained active participants and expositors of the Greek ethos, despite alienation and indifference by some. To a great extent, these educational arrangements served members of the third generation and are now serving those of the fourth. According to one product of the system,

> The Greek Orthodox parish in which I was reared had, since 1910, a bilingual day elementary school, whose graduates went straight into the Chicago public schools. For those parents whose children attended the "American" school, an afternoon Greek language was available. I attended this school on Mondays, Wednesdays, and Fridays from 4:00 p.m. to 6:00 p.m. for six years. I graduated from this school. From native Greek-trained teachers I learned both katharevousa and demotiki types of Greek. The textbooks were imported school books from Greece. The curricular content was literary, historical, religious, and grammatical. From that experience in Greek language study and with a couple of courses in classical Greek. . . . I am now able to converse in modern demotic Greek, read a newspaper, write a letter with the aid of a grammar and dictionary, and read technical materials and Koine Greek with a dictionary. At the doctoral level, I passed a reading translation test in modern Greek. . . . I grew up in the shadow of the Greek Orthodox Church and its schools, the Greek language school, the Sunday school, the several youth groups of the church, and several public service Greek-speaking national groups. It is in this church environment that I still live, albeit in another city and state today.[115]

Greek Ethnic Survival

The meaning of Greek-American ethnicity has been a striving to perpetuate and appreciate the best in the Greek heritage and the American nationality. The Greek immigrants of Chicago attempted to preserve their ethnic identity through the use of educational agencies, both formal and informal. Despite Greek individualism and factionalism, they succeeded in the mission of transmitting the cultural legacy by way of the family, voluntary associations, church, school, and communication media.

Naturally, acculturative influences are apparent in the daily lifestyles of Greek Americans. Nonetheless, the retention and expansion of cultural activities and schooling arrangements today indicate a renewed determination to perpetuate ethnic traditions without necessarily using the Greek language to maintain the classic heritage. New problems, however, are arising for Greek ethnic survival. Greek nationalism is favored by the more recent Greek immigrants, while the American-born generations favor preservation of religious and cultural legacies.[116] Perhaps, like the Greeks of the Byzantine period, they are oppressed by the weight of their own history; the continuity of their culture is too strong for alteration.

In this respect, the Greek experience in Chicago has been a blend of ethnic pride and resourceful participation in American life. It was the story of the children and grandchildren of those immigrants, most of whom enjoy levels of education and income surpassing that of the average American, and a disproportionate number of whom have been extraordinarily successful in the country of their birth.[117] And it is the still-evolving story of the new immigrants from Greece who have been coming to America in large numbers over the past decade and a half. But this Greek experience has also had an underside: exploitation of Greek by Greek, old immigrant men whose lives were drained away in poverty and loneliness, fights between contending political and church factions, conflicts between generations, and misunderstanding between the older and newer immigrants.

---

116. Increasingly, Greek ethnicity is being defined by Greek Orthodoxy rather than the Greek language, especially by native-born generations; see Kopan, "Education and Greek Immigrants," pp. 415-420.

117. A rather complete list of Greek achievers in business, politics, education, etc., is to be found in Charles C. Moskos, Jr.'s excellent study *Greek Americans: Struggle and Success* (Englewood Cliffs, NJ, 1980), pp. 111-122. It is interesting to note that in the area of education the two highest ranking officers in Illinois have been Michael J. Bakalis, who served as State Superintendent of Public Instruction from 1970 to 1975, and Angeline P. Caruso, currently Superintendent of Chicago Public Schools, both products of the Chicago Greek community and its communal school system.

CHAPTER 10

African-American Migration to Chicago

JAMES R. GROSSMAN

Farewell, We're Good and Gone,
Bound for the Promised Land

> — chalk writing on railroad cars bound for Chicago

I never see a city that big.
All those tall buildings.
I thought they were universities.

> — Louis Armstrong, arriving in Chicago, 1922

James Reese, a black Floridian "looking for a free state to live in," set out for Chicago in 1917. A new generation of black southerners had begun to turn to industry, to the city, and to the North for access to the perquisites of American citizenship.[1] World War I and the economic boom that accompanied it created the conditions that made possible this new option. Until then, immigrants had been arriving from Europe at an annual rate that surpassed the North's total black population, providing employers with a pool of labor that they considered preferable to black Americans. The outbreak of war in 1914 abruptly halted the flow of European immigrants. By 1916, increasing orders both from abroad and from a domestic market stimulated by military preparedness raised prospects for spectacular profits in most major industries. Confronted with the loss of their traditional source of additional labor, northern employers looked to pre-

---

1. James D. Reese [to Chicago Urban League?], April 24, 1917, in a folder marked "Migration Study, Negro Migrants, Letters Fr.," Box 86, Series 6, National Urban League Records (NULR), Library of Congress (hereafter cited as Migration Letters, NULR).

The long journey to the North often began by leaving a sharecropper's shack with all of the family's belongings which would be sold in a nearby Southern town to buy railroad tickets to Chicago. Courtesy of the Mayor's Committee on Race Relations.

viously unacceptable alternatives: they opened the factory gates to white women and black southerners, although only as a temporary measure. The mobilization of the armed forces in 1917 exacerbated the labor shortage and created still more opportunities for newcomers to the industrial labor force.[2]

A white Alabaman who wrote in the Montgomery *Advertiser* that "it's plain as the noonday sun the Negro is leaving this country for higher wages" may have simplistically overstated his case, but he was aware of the most obvious attraction of the North. A Hawkinsville, Georgia, black laborer, unable to afford a railroad ticket, concurred: "The reason why I want to come north is why that the people dont pay enough for the labor that a man can

2. "Immigration During September and October, 1915," *Monthly Labor Review* 2, no. 1 (Jan. 1916), 10; "Work of Federal, State, and Municipal Employment Offices in the United States and of Provincial Employment Bureaus in Canada," *Monthly Labor Review* 5, no. 1-6 (July-December, 1917), 164, 372, 559, 728, 966, 1188; U.S. Department of Labor, Division of Negro Economics, *Negro Migration in 1916-17* (Washington, D.C., 1919), 11-12 (hereafter cited as USDL, *Negro Migration*); Chicago Commission on Race Relations (CCRR), *The Negro in Chicago*, 83; *Iron Age* 99 (June 28, 1917), 1563-64. For a more systematic discussion of the inverse relationship between white immigration and black migration to northern cities, see Brinley Thomas, *Migration and Urban Development: A Reappraisal of British and American Long Cycles* (London, 1972).

Black migrants from the South often came from sharecropper cabins such as this one. Courtesy of University of Illinois at Chicago: Special Collections.

do down here." A South Carolinian was even more succinct: "There is no work here that pays a man to stay here."[3]

These men believed they could do better in the North. Readers of the popular Chicago *Defender* learned that anyone could find a job "if you really want it." Chicago daily wages in 1916 started in the $2.00 to $2.50 range for men; most workers earned at least $2.50. The minimum in the packinghouses, soon to be increased by 50 percent, was 27 cents per hour in March 1918. Women reportedly earned $2.00 per day as domestics — as much as many earned in a week in the South — and could earn even more in factories. Southerners could not help but be impressed. Even unskilled laborers supposedly could earn as much as an astronomical $5.00 per day. By 1919 the average hourly manufacturing wage in Chicago was 48 cents, a rate unheard of in the South. Although many were aware of Chicago's high cost of living, they expected these "big prices for work" to be more than adequate.[4] "Willing to do most ennery kind of Work," prospective migrants did not expect "to live on flowry Beds of

3. Montgomery *Advertiser*, quoted in CCRR, *Negro in Chicago*, 81; Emmett J. Scott, comp., "Additional Letters of Negro Migrants of 1916-1918," *Journal of Negro History* 4 (Oct. 1919), 424, 421.

4. *Defender*, March 20, 1915, January 1, 1916, February 24, 1917, November 1, 1919; Scott, "Additional Letters," 437; CCRR, *Negro in Chicago*, 80-81, 366-67; USDL, *Negro Migration*, 22; United States Administrator for Adjustment of Labor Questions Arising in Certain Packing Houses, *Findings and Award* (Feb. 15, 1919), 7-8, pamphlet in File 33/864, FMCS, RG 280; folder marked [Charles S. Johnson], "Chicago Study, Migration Interviews," pp. 1, 4, Box 86, Series 6, NULR (hereafter cited as Johnson, "Interviews," NULR).

ease." But they were confident they could earn high wages, even if that required learning new skills.[5]

Most contemporary examinations of the migration emphasized the primacy of wage differentials, along with the economic setbacks caused by the boll weevil, natural disasters, and low cotton prices in 1914 and 1915. James H. Dillard, Emmett J. Scott, and George E. Haynes, whose studies dominated the discussion of the "Great Migration" for many years, regarded economic considerations as "primary," "fundamental," and "paramount." Charles S. Johnson, who was responsible for much of Scott's monograph and analyzed the exodus for the Urban League and the influential Chicago Commission on Race Relations, emphasized "the desire to improve their economic status." Twenty years later, sociologists St. Clair Drake and Horace Cayton, in their classic *Black Metropolis*, drew on these studies and others to conclude that the migration's "basic impetus has remained economic."[6] Recent quantitative studies have reiterated the conventional wisdom that persecution had long plagued black southerners and therefore could not have "caused" the migration.[7]

Racial oppression cannot, however, be dismissed quite so easily, even if the impossibility of quantifying either its incidence or impact renders it difficult to

5. Emmett J. Scott, comp., "Letters of Negro Migrants of 1916-18," *Journal of Negro History* 4 (July 1919), 297, 313; Scott, "Additional Letters," 421, 425, 427. This sentiment is evident throughout both collections of letters.

6. USDL, *Negro Migration*, 11-12, 118; Emmett J. Scott, *Negro Migration during the War* (New York, 1920), 6; George E. Haynes, "Migration of Negroes into Northern Cities," *Proceedings of the National Conference of Social Work* 44 (1917): 495; Charles S. Johnson, "How Much of the Migration Was a Flight From Persecution," *Opportunity* 1, no. 9 (Sept. 1923): 272-74; St. Clair Drake and Horace R. Cayton, *Black Metropolis: A Study of Negro Life in a Northern City* (New York, 1945), 99-100. Three often-cited Columbia studies reached the same conclusion. See Dean Dutcher, *The Negro in Modern Industrial Society: An Analysis of Changes in the Occupations of Negro Workers, 1910-1920* (Lancaster, Pa., 1930); Edward Lewis, *The Mobility of the Negro: A Study in the American Labor Supply* (New York, 1931); Louise V. Kennedy, *The Negro Peasant Turns Cityward: Effects of Recent Migrations to Northern Centers* (New York, 1930). See also Henderson H. Donald, "The Negro Migration of 1916-1918," *Journal of Negro History* 6, no. 4 (October 1921), 389-90, 410ff., for conclusion that the migration was economically motivated, based on his survey of migrations in general, which demonstrated that "the economic causes of migration are primal." A notable exception to this narrow framework is Clyde Vernon Kiser's insightful study of migration from St. Helena in the South Carolina Sea Islands to northern cities, especially New York. Rejecting the search for "one or two operative causes," he examined a variety of social, economic, and environmental factors, along with "changes and alterations in the personal attitudes of individuals." See Kiser, *Sea Island to City: A Study of St. Helena Islanders in Harlem and Other Urban Centers* (New York, 1932), 85-113.

7. Florette Henri reviews much of the sociological and historical literature in *Black Migration: Movement North, 1900-1920* (Garden City, 1975), 51-59, and in contrast to most other analyses, sees these studies as slightly overstating their case. For the quantitative studies, see William E. Vickery, "Economics of Negro Migration, 1900-1960" (Ph.D. diss., University of Chicago, 1969); Robert Higgs, "The Boll Weevil, the Cotton Economy, and Black Migration: 1910-1930," *Agricultural History* 50, no. 2 (Apr. 1976). Both, most egregiously Vickery, dismiss "discrimination" as a "constant."

measure as an "input" into an equation of causation. Along with sporadic violence, continuous discrimination did stimulate the exodus. One black church elder in Macon, Georgia, pointed to "unjust treatments enacted daily on the streets, street cars and trains . . . driving the Negro from the South." It was this kind of day-to-day indignity that led Jefferson Clemons, "tired of bein' dog and beast," to leave his DeRidder, Louisiana, home. In a South permeated with an "atmosphere of injustice and oppression," the *AME Church Review* observed, migration had become the only solution for those who sought to "stand erect as men."[8]

Most analysts of the migration grouped these "causes" of the exodus under the general category of "social" or "sentimental" factors. Also included among these were disfranchisement, inferior educational facilities (sometimes included under economic factors), unfair treatment in the courts, peonage, and "poor treatment" in general. Usually this group fell into the "secondary" category of explanations for the exodus. Some commentators assigned to them an order of relative significance; others simply recited a list, best summarized as "conditions were bad."[9]

Beyond negative aspects of the South, analysts also examined the *appeal* of the North — the "pull" forces — and compiled innumerable lists, citing high wages, equality, bright lights, "privileges," good schools, and other attractions describing the obverse of what the migrants were fleeing in the South. Indeed, as Richard Wright would later learn, southern black images of Chicago, and the North in general, "had no relation whatever to what actually existed." Wellborn Jenkins of Georgia thought that "when white and black go into the courts of the north they all look alike to those judges up there."[10] Misinformed or not, southern blacks were certain they could find racial justice and opportunities for improvement in Chicago.

Regardless of how much priority is placed on which factor, lists of "push" and "pull" forces suggest mainly the range of injustices and privations driving blacks from the South. No simple list can weave together its various components to compose an image of the fabric of social and economic relationships that drove black southerners to look elsewhere for a better life. Nor can lists communicate the fears, disgust, hopes, and goals that combined to propel blacks from the South and draw them northward.[11]

8. CCRR, *Negro in Chicago*, 85-86; Charles S. Johnson, "The New Frontage on American Life," in Alain Locke, ed. *The New Negro: An Interpretation* (New York, 1925), 281; "The Exodus," *AME Church Review* 33, no. 3 (Jan. 1917), 149.

9. For comprehensive lists of "social" causes, see Scott, *Negro Migration*, 18-22; CCRR, *Negro in Chicago*, 84-86; Thomas J. Woofter, *Negro Migration: Changes in Rural Organization and Population of the Cotton Belt* (New York, 1920; reprint, New York, 1969), 121; Eric D. Walrond, "The Negro Migration to the North," *International Interpreter* 2, no. 20 (Aug. 18, 1923), 628-29.

10. Wright, *Black Boy*, 147; Wellborn Victor Jenkins to *Atlanta Constitution*, October 10, 1916, in Migration Letters, NULR.

11. For an insightful critique of both the "push-pull" framework and the separation of individual dissatisfactions from a general pattern of social relations, see Neil Fligstein, *Going North: Migration of Blacks and Whites from the South, 1900-1950* (New York, 1981), 65-66.

The simplest explanation of the cause of the Great Migration is that it happened because of the impact of the war on the labor market. With northern jobs available at wages considerably higher than what a black southerner could earn at home, migration represented a rational response to a change in the labor market. Simultaneously, a series of economic setbacks drove blacks from the rural South. Boll weevils, storms, floods, the tightening of credit — all made farming more tenuous. Changes in northern and southern labor markets thus coincided, and the major question for labor economists has been whether the push was stronger than the pull. More sociologically oriented observers have emphasized the push of racial discrimination in the South and the pull of less oppressive race relations in the North, along with the attractions of the urban environment. Analysis of the changes occasioned by the onset of World War I can tell us why the Great Migration happened when it did, but cannot fully explain why people decided to leave. Causes are not the same as motivations.

An explanation of motivation, of the decision to move North, lies in the continuity of southern black life, as much as in the changes caused by the wartime economy. A Mississippian tried to explain the problem:

> Just a few months ago they hung Widow Baggage's husband from Hirshbery bridge because he talked back to a white man. He was a prosperous Farmer owning about 80 acres. They killed another man because he dared to sell his cotton 'off the place.' These things have got us sore. Before the North opened up with work all we could do was to move from one plantation to another in hope of finding something better.[12]

All the exploitation — legal, social, economic — was bound together within his use of the impersonal "they." This reference to a web of social relations has broad implications for both the causes and meaning of the Great Migration, especially when considered within the context of the tradition of black migration and persistence in the South.

The Great Migration both constituted a stage in the long-term process of African-American urbanization and accelerated a northward trend that had begun in the 1890s. Urbanization had started before the guns of the Civil War had quieted and has continued into the 1980s. In absolute terms, the approximately three million blacks who left the South between 1940 and 1960 formed an exodus twice as large as that of 1910-30.[13] The Great Migration, however,

12. Charles S. Johnson, "General," 1-2, in folder marked "Migration Study, Mississippi Summary," Box 86, Series 6, NULR (hereafter cited as Johnson, [title], "Mississippi Summary," NULR).

13. U.S. Bureau of the Census, *Historical Statistics of the United States, Colonial Times to 1970* (Washington, D.C., 1975), part I: 95. Jack T. Kirby has observed that the Great Migration must be considered partly responsible for the direction and volume of the larger migration that followed because it established "interregional networks of family and friends." See "The Southern Exodus, 1910-1960: A Primer for Historians," *Journal of Southern History* 44, no. 4 (Nov. 1983), 592.

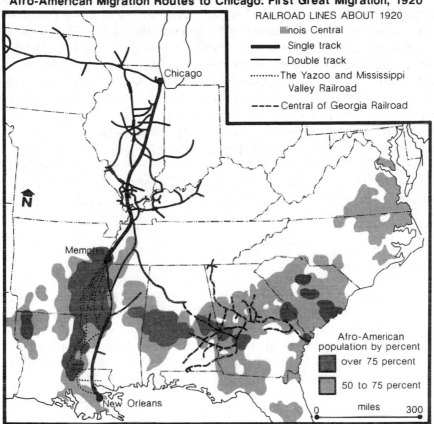

Afro-American Migration Routes to Chicago: First Great Migration, 1920

RAILROAD LINES ABOUT 1920

Illinois Central

━━━━ Single track

──── Double track

·········· The Yazoo and Mississippi Valley Railroad

──── Central of Georgia Railroad

Chicago

N

Memphis

New Orleans

Afro-American population by percent

■ over 75 percent

□ 50 to 75 percent

miles 0 —————— 300

represents an important shift in direction, with the center of black population moving northward, rather than toward the south and west as it had in previous decades. It also marks an important transformation in outlook among a growing minority of black southerners. Since emancipation, both migration and persistence had usually involved strategies directed toward a degree of autonomy based on land ownership. The Great Migration, by contrast, drew upon black southerners who looked to urban life and the industrial economy for the social and economic foundation of full citizenship and its perquisites. It was, as observers noted then and since, a "second emancipation," and accordingly it must be considered within a historical context anchored by the first emancipation and as a similarly transforming event.[14]

Upon being emancipated, ex-slaves seized on spatial mobility as one of

14. *Defender,* October 18, 1916; E. Franklin Frazier, *The Negro Family in Chicago* (Chicago, 1932), 80.

the most meaningful components of their newly won status. Subsequently, they and their children moved within the rural South, to southern cities, and finally to northern cities, in a frustrating quest for equality and opportunity. Neither stability nor geographic mobility, however, enabled very many blacks to fulfill the promise of emancipation. Even those who had followed all the rules and had lived (at least outwardly) according to the values preached to them ever since white missionaries had followed the Union armies south had nothing to show for it. Most black southerners were well aware of the "Dixie limit," beyond which no African American could advance. Black sharecropper and occasional lumber hauler Ned Cobb later recalled how whites reacted to his ambitious ways: "Whenever the colored man prospered too fast in this country under the old rulins, they worked every figure to cut you down, cut your britches off you. . . . Weren't no use in climbin too fast; weren't no use in climbin slow, neither, if they was goin to take everything you worked for when you got too high."[15]

But if southern blacks realized that the American success ethic had offered them nothing but false promises in the South, they did not dismiss the ethic itself as invalid. Tenancy rates for farmers of both races in the South were steadily increasing, but the higher average age of black tenants suggests a continuing difference in the likelihood of ownership. The number of white farmers who were able to move up the "agricultural ladder" did make it appear that while whites could "leave the tenant class entirely," most blacks could move merely "from one class of tenancy to another."[16] The problem seemed to be essentially racial. Success in America through hard work was possible, but not for blacks in the South.

Voices from the North reinforced black southerners' belief in the possibility of success, while convincing them that they could open the door of opportunity by moving North. The *Defender* had long preached the virtues of patience and hard work, reminding its readers that blacks did face obstacles, "perhaps a few more than their white brother, but none they could not surmount." In 1916, the *Defender* began to emphasize that such homilies pertained only to the North, "where every kind of labor is being thrown open." As proof, it publicized biographies of southerners who had "made it" in Chicago. These men had traveled the road to success in Chicago earlier, when fewer occupations

15. Theodore Rosengarten, *All God's Dangers: The Life of Nate Shaw* (New York, 1974), 27, also 192-93, 213; Leon F. Litwack, "Ordeal of Black Freedom," in Walter J. Fraser, Jr., and Winfred B. Moore, Jr., eds., *The Southern Enigma: Essays on Race, Class, and Folk Culture* (Westport, 1983), 15-18; Janet S. Hermann, *The Pursuit of a Dream* (New York, 1981), 228; and John Dittmer, *Black Georgia in the Progressive Era, 1900-1920* (Urbana, 1977), 25.

16. Rupert B. Vance, *All These People: The Nation's Human Resources in the South* (Chapel Hill, 1945), 215, 242; U.S. Bureau of the Census, *Thirteenth Census, Bulletin, Age of Farmers, By Color of Operator, Character of Tenure and Size of Farm* (Washington, D.C., 1914), 14; Gavin Wright, *Old South, New South: Revolutions in the Southern Economy since the Civil War* (New York, 1986), 120-21; Fligstein, *Going North*, 127; Scott, *Negro Migration*, 24-25.

had been open to blacks. For the mass of the race, the newspaper announced, "our chance is now."[17] Migrants' letters, written on the eve of their departures, suggest that they shared both the values and the optimism expressed in the *Defender*.

Most migrants who left oral or written testaments to the migratory impulse conflated economic and social stimuli into the goal of "bettering their position." Variants of this theme abound: "Better his Standing"; "better my conditions in the business world"; "aspire to better my condition in life"; "elevate myself"; "better my condishion in as much as beaing asshured some protection as a good citizen"; "chance for advancement."[18] They moved North in search of many of the same things black Americans had once hoped would accompany emancipation: good schools, equal rights before the law, and equal access to public facilities. Those black men and women who decided to leave the South saw all of these, as well as the numerous other "privileges" they expected in Chicago, as the foundation of freedom and citizenship. A New Orleans woman was typically attracted to "the great chance that a colored parson has in Chicago of making a living with all the priveleg that the whites have and it mak me the most ankious to go."[19]

The opportunity of industrial employment for African Americans that was opening as a direct result of World War I made it possible to translate these goals into a decision to leave the South and the agricultural economy that had once promised their fulfillment. Unlike their parents and many who remained behind, northbound migrants looked to industrial occupations rather than to landed independence as the means of attaining these goals. After two generations of economic, educational, social, and political stultification in the South, it appeared that northern factories and cities offered a final chance to obtain what other Americans supposedly had — the opportunity to better their condition by hard work. "All I ask is give me a chance," wrote one Louisiana man, "and I will make good."[20]

To black writer Alain Locke, commenting on this "new vision of opportunity," the migration represented "a spirit to seize . . . a chance for the improvement of conditions."[21] The vision was new, because blacks had never before anticipated economic security or social mobility through mass entrance into American industry. But of equal importance was Locke's choice of the verb *seize*. The migrants acted to better their condition by seizing control over their

---

17. *Defender*, October 23, 1915, August 19, 1916, July 10, 1915.

18. Scott, "Letters," 298-99, 303, 306, 315, and passim; Scott, "Additional Letters," 439 and passim; Haynes, "Migration of Negroes into Northern Cities," 496. See also CCRR, *Negro in Chicago*, 80-84, 95-98.

19. Scott, "Additional Letters," 426.

20. *Ibid.*, 428. On the importance of these perquisites of citizenship to emancipated slaves, see Leon F. Litwack, *Been in the Storm So Long: The Aftermath of Slavery* (New York, 1979), 547.

21. Locke, "The New Negro," in Locke, ed., *New Negro*, 6.

own destiny. The southern system had rested on their dependence on whites and its ability to restrict their options. To those like the Kentuckian who migrated to Chicago because he "was tired of being a flunky," migration constituted a rejection of that dependence. "Negroes are not so greatly disturbed about wages," a black leader in Florida commented. "They are tired of being treated as children; they want to be men."[22] "Pushes" and "pulls" might be abstractly separable, but they operated together in the minds of black southerners comparing one place to another. To the ambitious men and women venturing North to seek independence and mobility, the Great Migration represented a new strategy in the struggle for the full rights of American citizenship, including the right to equality of opportunity.

But if leaving the South promised new vistas, it could also be fraught with tension and ambivalence. Even as they left, some shared Richard Wright's recognition that he "was leaving the South to fling myself into the unknown." The *Defender* reflected on "black workmen [who] left the South with trembling and fear. They were going — they didn't know where — among strange people, with strange customs. The people who claimed to know best how to treat them painted frightful pictures of what would befall the migrators if they left the land of cotton and sugar cane."[23] Despite the uncertainties, many, like Wright, expected that in Chicago they "could live with a little less fear." Migrants riding the Yazoo and Mississippi Railroad one Friday morning in February 1921 were readily reminded of those anxieties when they saw the body of a black man swinging lifeless from a tree alongside the railroad track. These migrants must have shared Gordon Parks' reaction as he left southern Kansas a few years later, aware that he was leaving behind "a doom. . . . For although I was departing from this beautiful land, it would be impossible ever to forget the fear, hatred and violence that Negroes had suffered upon it. It was all behind me now."[24]

Many migrants were unable to leave it all behind immediately. Although some journeyed directly to the North, others stopped in southern towns and cities. Rural people might move to a nearby town after cotton picking ended in November or December and prepare to leave for the North in the spring. Many

22. CCRR, *Negro in Chicago,* 385; USDL, *Negro Migration,* 107. For the same theme, see the Oklahoma City *Black Dispatch,* October 10, 1919, quoted in Robert Kerlin, *The Voice of the Negro* (New York, 1920; reprint, New York, 1968), 63. A view of urban industrial life as a modern and promising alternative to dependency relationships in rural areas was hardly unique to northbound black southerners. A recent study of eastern European Jewish women observes that to immigrating Jews, "factories had a mysterious, almost forbidden quality, in part because industrial jobs had been restricted mainly to gentiles." See Susan A. Glenn, "The Working Life of Immigrants: Women in the American Garment Industry, 1880-1920" (Ph.D. diss., University of California, Berkeley, 1983), 249.

23. Richard Wright, *Black Boy* (New York, 1937), 228; *Defender,* April 20, 1918.

24. Wright, *Black Boy,* 181; Chicago *Whip,* February 12, 1921; Gordon Parks, *A Choice of Weapons* (New York, 1966), 6-7.

migrants, especially those living in areas served by the Illinois Central Railroad, were able to board Chicago-bound trains in the deep South, but the majority had to make their way to a railroad hub. At Grand Central Station in Memphis, for example, a migrant headed for Chicago could transfer from any one of eight southern railroads to the Illinois Central.[25] In the Mississippi Delta the migratory chain was lengthened by blacks from the nearby hill country moving onto plantations to replace tenants who had gone to towns or directly to the North. Some of these "hill people," too, would eventually make their way north.[26] The longest trail might start on a one-mule farm in the hill region and include stays of varying lengths in a plantation settlement, southern town, southern railroad center, and finally the North.

Migrants who tarried in a southern town or city usually did so because they could afford to go no farther. In the earliest stages of the exodus, when free passes were thought to be available in large cities, many migrants made their way to such places as Birmingham, Jackson, Memphis, or New Orleans in hopes of securing a free ticket to Chicago. Trying to arrange transportation at these points was considered by most to be safer than sending and receiving letters on a plantation or in a small village. With free transportation disappearing long before black southerners ceased believing in its existence, many found themselves stranded in cities, unable to proceed until they could accumulate enough money to finance the rest of the journey. Others were less naive, but considered a southern city — especially one in a border state — a convenient stopping place where they could either earn enough to continue north or learn the ways of the city and acquire some urban job skills.[27]

Work was not difficult to find in most southern cities, which had already begun losing their black labor force to northward migration. Hattiesburg, Mississippi, a large lumber center and by 1917 the site of a United States Army cantonment, had been "almost depopulated of Negroes and repopulated again." Newcomers had little trouble finding jobs that would pay enough to allow them

25. Johnson, "Jackson, Mississippi," 9, "Mississippi Summary," NULR; USDL, *Negro Migration*, 53, 55; [John F. Merry], *About the South on Lines of the Illinois Central and Yazoo and Mississippi Valley* (Chicago, 1905), 40. Peter Gottlieb has argued that step migration was most likely among young, single males. See Gottlieb, *Making Their Own Way: Southern Blacks' Migration to Pittsburgh, 1916-1930* (Urbana, 1987), 43-47.

26. *Defender*, December 30, 1922; Charles Johnson to Robert Park, November 19, 1917, Folder 6, Box 1, Robert Park Papers, Regenstein Library, Univ. of Chicago; Johnson, "Greenwood," 2, "Jackson, Mississippi," 5, "Greenville," 2, "Mound Bayou and Boliver Co.," 1, "Clarksdale, Mississippi," 1, all in "Mississippi Summary," NULR.

27. Johnson, "Gulfport," 2, "Mississippi Summary," NULR; Johnson, "Interviews," 1, NULR; Johnson, "The Course of the Movement," 1, in folder marked "Migration Study, Draft (Final) Chapters 7-13" [1917], Box 86, Series 6, NULR (hereafter cited as "Draft," NULR). Most of the letters in the collection published by Emmett Scott (Scott, "Letters" and "Additional Letters") have datelines from southern cities or large towns, possibly because migrants from more rural areas went to the larger places to send the letters safely. See also Glenn N. Sisk, "Negro Migration in the Alabama Black Belt — 1875-1917," *Negro History Bulletin* 17 (Nov. 1953), 33.

to follow the twenty-five hundred blacks who had already left the city for Chicago by late 1917. In Nashville, a convenient way station for migrants from most parts of the South, a severe shortage of young and middle-aged black males created job opportunities for even the most unskilled laborers; by June 1918 most of the city's black workers were recent arrivals from rural areas.[28]

For many that first move, entailing an intermediate adjustment to a southern city, rendered the final step less intimidating. Yet what migrants learned in southern cities would be of only limited help in Chicago. Except in a few cities — notably Nashville and Birmingham — they could not secure jobs similar to those they would find in Chicago's packinghouses and steel mills. Even the border cities were sufficiently southern in their racial mores to offer little preparation for the impersonal, uncertain patterns of a northern city. In addition, most southern cities confined their black population to areas that were more rural than urban. Paved streets, running water, electric lights, sewers, and police and fire protection were either nonexistent or meager. The number of families with livestock further suggests the rural aspects of such neighborhoods. In small cities such as Pass Christian, Mississippi, where one observer noted that the railroad "does not disturb the country-like quiet," streets were unnamed and houses unnumbered. Even in larger cities in the South, blacks often lived amid what Monroe Work described as late as 1923 as "country conditions."[29]

Whether a migrant had stopped in a southern city or migrated directly to the North, a Jim Crow train framed lasting memories. Limited to whatever space was available in the "Negro car," migrants rode great distances standing in crowded aisles. As a rule, these cars were attached either to the tender or baggage car, with the accompanying fumes and dirt, or to the end of the train. Even the more privileged migrants who were able to afford first-class Jim Crow fares suffered what Arthur Mitchell in 1919 described as "a horrible night ride."[30] Nor was there any place on the train (or in some of the stations) for

28. Johnson, "Hattiesburg," 1, "Mississippi Summary," NULR; Paul F. Mowbray to George E. Haynes, August 31, 1917, Folder 25, Box 2; Mowbray to L. Hollingsworth Wood, June 13, 1918, Folder 18, Box 3; both in Haynes Papers. Mowbray was the field secretary of the Nashville Public Welfare League.

29. Monroe N. Work, "Research With Respect to Cooperation between Urban and Rural Communities," *Opportunity* 1, no. 2 (Feb. 1923): 8; George E. Haynes, "Negro Migration," *Opportunity* 2, no. 21 (Sept. 1924): 273; ? Curran, "Negro Quarter, Pass Christian, Mississippi," April 1, 1919, field report for a study of labor in Gulf Coast canneries, File 20-21-7, Box 980, Central Files of the U.S. Children's Bureau, U.S. Department of Labor, RG 102, NA. The presence of livestock is documented in Cost of Living Schedules for Memphis, Atlanta, Birmingham, Mobile, and New Orleans [1919], Boxes 625, 666, 671, 687, Records of the U.S. Bureau of Labor Statistics, Record Group (RG) 257, National Archives (NA). See also Johnson, "Vicksburg," 3-4, Johnson, "Hattiesburg," 1, both in "Mississippi Summary," NULR; John Dittmer, *Black Georgia in the Progressive Era, 1900-1920* (Urbana, 1987), 10-12; Lester C. Lamon, *Black Tennesseeans, 1900-1930* (Knoxville, 1977), 137; Woofter, *Negro Migration,* 139-40.

30. St. Luke *Herald* (Richmond, Va.), September 29, 1917, quoted in U.S. House of Representatives, Committee on Interstate and Foreign Commerce, *Return of the Railroads to Private*

black people to eat. Louis Armstrong, who came from New Orleans to Chicago in 1922, later recalled that "colored persons going North crammed their baskets full of everything but the kitchen stove." People were crammed as well. Mary Fluornoy, traveling to Chicago from Anniston, Alabama, found it difficult to breathe. "You couldn't get no air. . . . It was crowded." Nevertheless, migrants did all they could to maintain their spirits, including chalking on the side of the railroad cars such slogans as "Farewell — We're Good and Gone," "Bound for the Promised Land," and "Bound to the Land of Hope."[31]

As their trains sped northward, migrants looked forward to their first opportunity to put aside the way of life symbolized by the very conditions they experienced during the trip. Seventeen-year-old Matthew Ward, from southwest Tennessee, hoped that he would be able to see the Mason-Dixon line, which he and his traveling companion had expected to be marked by a row of trees. Although he was disappointed, he moved from the Jim Crow car when someone told him they were crossing into the North; he searched until he found a seat beside a white man. A party of migrants from Handsboro and Gulfport, Mississippi, celebrated the event by enjoying a meal in the dining car. Others were more demonstrative. While crossing the Ohio River, many migrants prayed and sang songs of deliverance. A woman from Hattiesburg claimed that the atmosphere changed as they crossed the river, that the air was "lighter," allowing her to breathe more easily. Having crossed what the *Defender* referred to as the Styx, these and other migrants felt that they were embarking on a new life.[32]

As the train approached Chicago, hope and excitement began to mix with awe, trepidation, and sometimes disappointment. Most railroad routes passed through the steel towns lying south and east of Chicago, offering initial views dominated by the gray pall that usually hung over the mills and the rickety houses of Gary and South Chicago.[33] To those arriving at night, the sight must have been particularly impressive and disorienting, as the fiery smokestacks never rested, denying the natural rhythms of night and day that ruled agricultural labor.

Finally, the train rolled into one of Chicago's railroad depots. Migrants

Ownership, Hearings on H.R. 4378, Part 12, 66th Cong., 1st sess., 1919, p. 2027; also p. 2014. See also "Memorandum on Exodus from the South" [1917], File No. 13/65, Files of the Chief Clerk, U.S. Department of Labor, RG 174, NA.

31. Louis Armstrong, *Satchmo: My Life in New Orleans* (New York, 1954), 229-30; Myra Young Armstead, interview with Mary Fluornoy, Chicago, May 1, 1985 (tape in possession of author); Arna Bontemps and Jack Conroy, *They Seek a City* (Garden City, 1945), 136.

32. Matthew Ward, *Indignant Heart* (Detroit, 1957), 27; *Defender,* September 23, 1916, June 16, 1917; Scott, *Negro Migration,* 45-46; Frazier, *Negro Family in Chicago,* 80.

33. Mary F. Adams, "Present Housing Conditions in South Chicago, South Deering, and Pullman" (master's thesis, University of Chicago, 1926), 20; Richard Wright, *American Hunger* (New York, 1977), 1.

fortunate enough to have someone to meet them might have been unsettled by the crowds but were soon reassured by the sight of a familiar face. The same network that stimulated and facilitated migration by sending information South now assisted migrants upon their arrival. "Let me know what day you expect to leave and over what road, and if I don't meet you I will have some one there to meet you and look after you until I see you," wrote one woman to a member of her former church in Mississippi. Some migration clubs timed their departures so as to arrive in Chicago on a Sunday, when a working person would be able to come to the station.[34] Members of these clubs could not only count on someone to guide them through their first hours in the city but could enjoy the comfort of numbers as well.

Those who were not met at the train by a friend were immediately faced with the problem of finding their own way, usually to the South Side. A redcap at the Illinois Central station later recalled the confusion evinced by many of the newcomers, who had little idea of where they were going. "They knew somebody in Chicago. The only directions they had were when you get to the station you go two blocks this way or go this way, things like that." One migrant remembered being "completely lost. . . . I was afraid to ask anyone where to go." Louis Armstrong, arriving from New Orleans in 1922, was terrified when he was unable to locate his friend Joe Oliver in the crowd at the station:

> I saw a million people, but not Mister Joe, and I didn't give a damn who else was there. I never seen a city that big. All those tall buildings. I thought they were universities. I said, no, this is the wrong city. I was fixing to take the next train back home — standing there in my box-back suit, padded shoulders, double-breasted wide-leg pants.

Whatever their problems immediately upon arrival, migrants experienced a series of shocks as they emerged from the railroad station. Those without warm clothing received a chilling introduction to Chicago's climate, which could be daunting in the early spring, when migration tended to peak.[35] Like the characters in Alden Bland's *Behold A Cry*, many newcomers gazed at the immense structures, the seemingly ubiquitous concrete and iron materials, and the swift motion of people, automobiles, and trolleys. Richard Wright was taken aback by the "towering buildings of steel and stone" and by elevated trains which occasionally shook the ground. The screeching of streetcars and honking of horns augmented the awesome sights. Scurrying residents seemed oblivious

34. Johnson, "Stimulation of the Movement," 17, "Draft," NULR; Johnson, "Interviews," 2, NULR. See also Chicago *Daily News*, March 14, 1917.

35. Johnson, "Early Manifestations of the Movement," 6, and "Gulfport," 2, both in "Mississippi Summary," NULR. Most migrants told interviewers for the Chicago Commission on Race Relations that their most difficult adjustment was to the climate; see CCRR, *Negro in Chicago*, 101.

not only to their environment, but to other people as well, and their "clipped speech" was incomprehensible to Wright.[36]

But if the urban landscape was disorienting, it was exciting as well. Migrants generally headed straight for Chicago's famous South Side ghetto, where the bright lights and commotion introduced them to the rhythms of their new home. Langston Hughes recalled the thrill of his arrival in 1918: "South State Street was in its glory then, a teeming Negro street with crowded theaters, restaurants, and cabarets. And excitement from noon to noon. Midnight was like day."[37] The Chicago *Whip*, a black newspaper, described the district as a cosmopolitan "Bohemia of the Colored folks," where "lights sparkled, glasses tinkled," and one could find bootblacks and bankers dressed in finery. The center of activity, the heart of "The Stroll," was at Thirty-fifth and State streets, where crowds of people milled about day and night. Looking east from the busy corner, a newcomer with an eye for the symbolic might have compared past and future: five blocks away the Plantation Cafe's bright neon sign suggested dissonant images of the rural South and urban North.[38]

Unfortunately, the crowds, lights, and attractions could also be dangerous to a newcomer fresh off the train. On his first night in town, James Parker of Alabama picked up an eighteen-year-old girl at Thirty-fifth and State, and they spent the evening cabaret-hopping. The next morning Parker awoke in a hotel room, with neither the girl nor his money in sight. James Hill from Burnette, Texas, also arrived in Chicago "with plenty of cash in his jeans." Some "old friends," scenting a free night on the town, offered to show him the bright lights. Not only did he foot the tabs, but unaccustomed to city dangers, he repeatedly displayed his wad of bills. At the end of the night he was relieved of his remaining $102.60 by three muggers.[39] An even more naive rube walked into a grocery store and handed the owner a twenty-dollar bill, telling him that he would return for it in a few hours. The police recovered his money, leaving him more fortunate than the numerous newcomers who fell victim to pickpockets preying on the crowds at busy street corners.[40]

Even before they experienced the excitement and perils of State Street, however, migrants confronted what had been on their minds ever since they had contemplated the journey — the absence of the despised southern racial code. In the railroad station, Richard Wright searched for the familiar FOR WHITE and FOR COLORED signs.

36. Alden Bland, *Behold a Cry* (New York, 1947); Wright, *American Hunger,* 1.

37. Langston Hughes, *Big Sea: An Autobiography* (New York, 1945), 33.

38. *Whip*, August 15, 1919; Chicago *Broad Ax,* November 22, 1919; Photograph of the corner of 35th and Calumet streets [c. 1915-25], in "35th St." file, Graphics Dept, CHS.

39. *Defender,* August 20, 1921, October 20, 1917.

40. *Defender,* May 19, 1917. See also *Whip,* October 9, November 20, 27, December 4, 1920, April 2, 1921.

It was strange to pause before a crowded newsstand and buy a newspaper without having to wait until a white man was served. And yet, because every-thing was so new I began to grow tense again, although it was a different tension than I had known before. I knew that this machine-city was governed by strange laws and I wondered if I would ever learn them.[41]

Migrants reacted to this sudden change in racial protocol in diverse ways. Many, perplexed like Wright, avoided racial contact and continued their accus-tomed patterns of cautious behavior. On the streetcars these men and women sat toward the rear; in stores they asked merchants "can a Colored man buy this or that here."[42] Such fears were hardly irrational. Chicago had its own racial rules, but they were unwritten and ambiguous. An imaginary "dead line" sep-arating the South Side's "Black Belt" from an Irish neighborhood symbolized the problem; to cross it could have violent consequences for the transgressor. Teenager Langston Hughes painfully learned that lesson when he ventured to explore the city his first Sunday in town. "Over beyond Wentworth," he "was set upon and beaten by a group of white boys, who said they didn't allow niggers in that neighborhood."[43]

Other newcomers quickly set out to test and assert their rights. These individuals deliberately sat next to whites on the streetcar, if only to prove to themselves that freedom was real. Coming from a region where a black person's sole privileges were described by one observer as "ter pay his taxes and ter git out o' de road," many migrants wasted so little time learning and testing the new rules that the normally militant *Defender* chided them not to "mistake privilege for right."[44] Most migrants, however, were probably more tentative. A Mississippi man moved to the front the first time he boarded a streetcar but "would not sit beside a white person at first." One woman recalled that when she boarded a streetcar for the first time and saw black people sitting alongside whites, "I just held my breath, for I thought any minute they would start something. Then I saw nobody noticed it, and I just thought this is a real place for Negroes."

Many black southerners arriving in Chicago knew where to go once they walked out of the train station. Like their counterparts in New York who asked in Pennsylvania Station how to get to Harlem, most black migrants to Chicago, upon alighting at the Illinois Central terminal, requested directions to the South Side or to State Street. People whose friends, relatives, or townspeople had

41. Wright, *American Hunger*, 1-2.

42. CCRR, *Negro in Chicago*, 302; *Defender*, February 16, 1918.

43. CCRR, *Negro in Chicago*, 115; Hughes, *Big Sea*, 33. The imaginary boundary along Wentworth Avenue became increasingly real during the following decade; in 1929 a black man crossed the line and was beaten to death. His wife had retreated to the "black side" of the street and was left alone to watch the assault. See Associated Negro Press News Release, March 20, 1929, Box 1, Barnett Papers.

44. CCRR, *Negro in Chicago*, 169, 302; Frazier, *Negro Family in Chicago*, 82; Haynes, "Negroes Move North, I," 119; *Defender*, February 10, 1917.

preceded them sought out specific addresses; those who had no idea where to go were likely to be directed simply to the South Side. Whites would assume that all blacks "belonged" in the ghetto; blacks would reason that bewildered newcomers might obtain assistance from black institutions while avoiding the danger of straying into hostile white neighborhoods. The logic of such advice suggests the significance — if not the visibility — of Chicago's color line, as well as the importance of various aspects of community within black Chicago. Shaped by both the circumscribing influences of the white city that surrounded it and the demands of the migrants and "Old Settlers" who inhabited it, the emerging "Black Metropolis" on the South Side divided along lines of class, region, and even age. But it remained a community nevertheless, unified by the conventions of racial taxonomies.[45]

In 1910, prior to the Great Migration, 78 percent of black Chicagoans lived on the South Side in a narrow strip of land known to whites as the "Black Belt." Beginning at the edge of an industrial and warehouse district just south of Chicago's central business district, black Chicago stretched southward along State Street for more than thirty blocks, remaining only a few blocks wide except at its northern end. The 1910 census counted 34,335 black residents in this growing ghetto, which was expanding slowly along its southern and eastern boundaries. Another 3,379 black Chicagoans lived on the West Side, while most of the remaining 6,389 lived in smaller enclaves in Englewood, the near North Side, and scattered other districts. Only 1,427 lived on the city's North Side. Because of the lingering presence of some whites in black neighborhoods, especially those on the edge of the Black Belt and the smaller enclaves, some black Chicagoans lived in what might loosely be called an integrated setting; but with black people virtually restricted to certain areas of the city, the housing market was actually segregated.[46]

This residential pattern had evolved during the previous quarter century, during which Chicago's black population had increased from 6,480 in 1880 to 44,103 in 1910. As late as 1898, only slightly more than one-fourth of Chicago's black residents lived in precincts in which blacks constituted a majority of the population; more than 30 percent inhabited precincts at least 95 percent white.

---

45. For the conceptualization and classic description of the "Black Metropolis" on Chicago's South Side, see Drake and Cayton, *Black Metropolis*. The term "Old Settler" specifically identifies members of an extremely exclusive Old Settlers Social Club formed in 1902, closed even to members of "many of our oldest families" (Franklyn A. Henderson to Helen Buckler, September 18, 1947, Folder 79, Box 7, Daniel Hale Williams Papers, Moorland-Spingarn Research Center, Howard University, Washington, D.C.). The club was open only to residents of thirty years or more and their descendants, but Drake and Cayton (p. 66) indicate that the term customarily designated any blacks living in Chicago prior to World War I, and I have used the term in that manner. See "History of Chicago Old Settlers Club 1902-1923," 4, pamphlet in Dunmore Family Collection, DuSable Museum of African American History, Chicago.

46. CCRR, *Negro in Chicago*, 107-8.

Yet black enclaves were already emerging, mainly on the South and near West Sides.[47]

The color line separated more than residences. State legislation prohibiting racial discrimination in schools, municipal services, and public accommodations was seldom enforced, and except on the streets and in the streetcars, blacks and whites seldom mingled. Black children attended schools with whites, but only because by 1915 the emerging ghetto was still neither compact nor homogeneous enough to enable the Board of Education to draw district lines that would go beyond merely assuring that as few schools as possible would have black students. Municipal institutions often segregated black clients or discriminated in the provision of services.[48]

Blacks occupied a similarly limited place in Chicago's booming economy. Fewer than one black male in twenty — and virtually no black females — worked in an occupation that might be described as managerial, professional, or proprietary; and many of that small number operated marginal businesses. Most workers were unskilled, and few worked in industry. If Chicago was the "City of the Big Shoulders," with an economic base of heavy industry, construction, and transportation, black workers found themselves relegated to marginal roles. White immigrants from southern and eastern Europe had to accept the worst jobs in the city's industries, but blacks lacked access even to those positions. Sharing the racial attitudes of other Americans, industrialists in Chicago and other northern cities saw no reason to hire blacks when they had thousands of white immigrants to fill their factories. Blacks were considered useful as strikebreakers on occasion, but generally they were discharged once the strike ended. Industrial managers drew upon a series of commonly held assumptions about work habits and aptitudes of various "races," and if most Eastern European groups suffered from images that kept them in unskilled positions, at least they were white. Where foremen controlled access to industrial jobs, black workers lacked access to the networks of community and kin that were central to recruitment patterns. Chicago and other northern cities offered mainly service jobs to blacks: between 1900 and 1910 the number of black servants in Chicago increased by six thousand, nearly half the city's increase in black population. Men were likely to work as porters, waiters, servants, janitors, or elevator operators; two-thirds of all employed black women in 1910 were

47. Allan H. Spear, *Black Chicago: The Making of a Negro Ghetto* (Chicago, 1967), 11-27; Thomas L. Philpott, *The Slum and the Ghetto: Neighborhood Deterioration and Middle-Class Reform, Chicago 1880-1930* (New York, 1978), 119-30. Philpott demonstrates that Spear and others have understated pre-1900 housing segregation. But even his argument does not preclude a decrease in residential proximity between the races after 1900.

48. Spear, *Black Chicago*, 29-49; CCRR, *Negro in Chicago*, 232-33; Philpott, *The Slum and the Ghetto*, 301-8. For school boundary lines, see Michael Homel, "Negroes in the Chicago Public Schools, 1910-1941" (Ph.D. diss. University of Chicago, 1972), 36-43, 50-51.

either servants or hand laundresses, with most of the others performing some other type of service.[49]

Despite this apparent homogeneity, however, black Chicago — like other urban black communities — was divided along class lines. Severely truncated at the top, this class structure rested less on wealth or contemporary white definitions of occupational status (except at the highest levels) than on notions of "refinement" and "respectability" maintained by the upper and middle classes. The few professionals, some with professional connections to the white community, tended to dominate the highest rungs, with businessmen close behind. Postal workers, Pullman porters, and servants employed by Chicago's wealthiest white families and best hotels constituted much of the solid middle class, which at its margins could include other workers with stable incomes and some education. Stable income was at least as important as accumulated wealth, an uncommon phenomenon in the black community. "Respectability" frequently depended upon property ownership, membership in the appropriate organizations, and leisure habits. Church, club, or lodge activities conferred as well as signified status: symbols of respectability could include affiliation with one of the larger Baptist or African Methodist Episcopal Churches, a YMCA membership, or a Masonic identification card. Upper-class blacks, who considered themselves "refined" rather than merely "respectable," joined Episcopalian, Presbyterian, or Congregationalist churches, entertained according to specific rules of etiquette, and socialized only within a limited circle of acquaintances.[50]

Until the late nineteenth century, this black upper class — largely businessmen with white clientele and professionals who had won the respect of their white colleagues — dominated black Chicago's leadership and resisted attempts to organize alternative institutions catering to blacks. To do so, they argued, would imply their acceptance of segregation. This elite not only opposed racial segregation in principle, but also feared its likely impact on their own social lives and institutional relationships. Disdaining association with blacks who lacked their refinement, members of this thin upper stratum recognized

---

49. U.S. Bureau of the Census, *Thirteenth Census of the United States Taken in the Year 1910,* vol. 4, *Population, Occupations* (Washington, D.C., 1914), 544-47; Spear, *Black Chicago,* 29-36. The often contradictory popular images of "races" and "nationalities" and their aptitudes and characteristics are discussed in Barry Karl, *The Uneasy State: The United States from 1915 to 1945* (Chicago, 1983), 63-64.

50. This discussion of Chicago's black community rests heavily on Spear, *Black Chicago.* For other especially insightful discussions of black social structure in pre-Great Migration northern cities, see David M. Katzman, *Before the Ghetto: Black Detroit in the Nineteenth Century* (Urbana, 1973), and Kenneth L. Kusmer, *A Ghetto Takes Shape: Black Cleveland, 1870-1930* (Urbana, 1976), 91-112. On the status of postal workers, see Henry McGee "The Negro in the Chicago Post Office," (master's thesis, University of Chicago, 1961), 70-71, 83; Claude Barnett, "Fly Out of Darkness" (unpublished autobiography, c. 1965), ch. 1, p. 1, typescript in Box 4, Section 14 ("Family"), Barnett Papers. For an example of the symbols of respectability, see *Defender,* January 15, 1916.

that segregation would force their social life inward toward the black community, rather than outward as they hoped.[51]

Between 1900 and 1915 a new leadership emerged in black Chicago, one with an economic and political base in the black community. The emergence of the physical ghetto coincided with widening racial discrimination in Chicago and other northern cities, which forced blacks to make decisions circumscribed by their exclusion from a variety of social and economic institutions. But increasing separation opened new opportunities for business, professional, religious, and political leadership. By the first decade of the twentieth century, a new middle class had begun to replace an older elite unwilling to sacrifice integrationist principles and therefore wary of separate black institutions and a ghetto economy.[52]

This new generation of black editors, politicians, business people, and ministers would dominate Chicago's black institutions during the Great Migration and construct the foundation of what by the 1920s would be known as a Black Metropolis. The southern origins of these prominent figures perhaps contributed to their continuing influence on newcomers. Robert Abbott, raised outside Savannah, Georgia, visited Chicago in 1893 as a member of the Hampton (Institute) Quartet performing at the Columbian Exposition. He returned four years later and in 1905 founded the Chicago *Defender*. Louis B. Anderson, born in Petersburg, Virginia, also was drawn to Chicago by the fair; by 1919, he was not only an alderman but also Mayor William Hale Thompson's floor leader in the city council. Born in Alabama, Oscar DePriest traveled to Chicago from Kansas in 1889 and worked his way up from house painter to election as Chicago's first black alderman in 1915. Thirteen years later he would climb even higher to become the first black congressman elected from a northern district. Reverend Archibald J. Carey, like DePriest the child of ex-slaves, came from Georgia in 1898 to serve as pastor of Quinn Chapel, the city's largest African Methodist Episcopal Church. Such notables provided an image — and a self-image — of a prewar generation of migrants who built institutions, shaped a self-conscious black community, and dominated Chicago's growing black middle class.[53]

51. Spear, *Black Chicago*, 51-70.

52. On the evolution of the "new middle class" in black Chicago, see Spear, *Black Chicago*, 71-89; since Spear's seminal study, scholars examining other cities have found similar patterns. See, for example, Kusmer, *A Ghetto Takes Shape*; Katzman, *Before The Ghetto*; Joe W. Trotter, *Black Milwaukee: The Making of an Industrial Proletariat, 1915-1945* (Urbana, 1985).

53. Roi Ottley, *Lonely Warrior: The Life and Times of Robert S. Abbott* (Chicago, 1955), 6, 76; *Defender*, July 10, 1915; Harold F. Gosnell, *Negro Politicians: The Rise of Negro Politics in Chicago* (Chicago, 1935), 163-95; Chicago *Record-Herald* [?], 1909, clipping in Archibald J. Carey, Sr., Papers, Chicago Historical Society (CHS); Joseph Logsdon, "Reverend Archibald J. Carey and the Negro in Chicago Politics" (master's thesis, University of Chicago, 1961), 9; Charles R. Branham, "Black Chicago: Accommodationist Politics Before the Great Migration," in Melvin G. Holli and Peter d'A. Jones, eds., *The Ethnic Frontier: Essays in the History of Group Survival in Chicago and the Midwest* (Grand Rapids, 1977), 218. On the general significance of black politicians who arrived between 1880 and 1915, see Charles R. Branham, "The Transformation of Black Political Leadership in Chicago, 1864-1942" (Ph.D. diss., University of Chicago, 1981), 50-94.

Adapting Booker T. Washington's doctrines of racial solidarity and self-help to the northern city, these business leaders and politicians deemphasized the fight for integration and dealt with discrimination by creating black institutions. Between 1890 and 1915 they established a bank, a hospital, a YMCA, an infantry regiment, effective political organizations, lodges, clubs, professional baseball teams, social service institutions, newspapers, and a variety of small businesses. The growth of the black community promised to multiply growing political influence and economic activity. Like Abbott, whose newspaper was partly responsible for the popularity of Chicago as a destination for black southerners, Chicago's black politicians and entrepreneurs saw the migrants as a source of votes and customers.[54]

Growth, however, also implied diversity, and neither the "old" nor "new" leadership in black Chicago was prone to tolerate those who did not measure up to their standards. The *Conservator*, Chicago's first black newspaper and the voice of prominent leaders in the late nineteenth century, had frequently criticized "the seamy side" of black Chicago during the 1870s and 1880s. The *Defender* picked up the mantle in the twentieth century, complaining about newcomers and degeneration even before the Great Migration. Both newspapers couched these criticisms within the context of appeals for improvement, providing lessons for proper behavior while they chided lower-class blacks for giving the race a bad image.[55] George Cleveland Hall, a prominent physician and personal friend of Booker T. Washington, typified the attitudes of many of his contemporaries. He served in official capacities in the NAACP as well as the Washingtonian National Negro Business League and later became one of the founders of the Chicago Urban League. In 1904, Hall voiced the attitudes of middle-class black Chicago concerning the need — and yet the impossibility — of maintaining the distance between classes in the black community:

> Those of the race who are desirous of improving their general condition are prevented to a great extent by being compelled to live with those of their color who are shiftless, dissolute and immoral. . . . Prejudice of landlords and agents render it almost impossible for [the Negro] to take up his residence in a more select quarter of the city . . . no matter . . . how much cultivation and refinement he may possess.[56]

Most black Chicagoans before the Great Migration, however, neither possessed Hall's "cultivation and refinement" nor lived "shiftless, dissolute and immoral" lives. Laboring long days in menial occupations, they returned home

54. Spear, *Black Chicago*, 11-126.

55. *Defender*, April 8, 15, 1916; The *Conservator* is discussed in Drake and Cayton, *Black Metropolis*, 47-49.

56. George C. Hall, speech before the Frederick Douglass Center, reprinted in the Chicago *Broad Ax*, December 31, 1904, quoted in Spear, *Black Chicago*, 73.

tired. Women, especially, spent most of their waking hours working, as they had to combine traditional household chores with other employment. Leisure activities offered respite from their backbreaking, low-status jobs. Enthusiastic worship and a lively night life earned the scorn of much of the middle class, but such activities already were central elements of what St. Clair Drake and Horace Cayton later would call "the world of the lower class" in black Chicago. By 1904 (if not earlier) the storefront churches later to be associated with the Great Migration had already begun to appear along State Street. Less spiritually inclined workers found release in petty gambling, the fellowship of the numerous saloons along the State Street "Stroll," or boisterous parties. By 1914 the rent party (later made famous in Harlem) had been improvised to leaven the struggle for subsistence with sociability and relaxation. These comforts drew upon the familiarity and relief of an African-American world. On the "Stroll," observed a black essayist in 1915, "for a minute or so one forgets the 'Problem.' It has no place here. It is crowded aside by an insistence of good cheer."[57]

Most migrants probably anticipated a warm welcome from this community. Much of what they knew about Chicago had been filtered through sources that emphasized race consciousness, along with individual and racial accomplishment. Class tensions and divisions within the black community seldom found their way into the *Defender*. Similarly, information from friends and relatives who only recently had arrived in Chicago highlighted instead the contrasts between South and North, rural and urban. Accustomed to middle-class disdain for poorer blacks, informants were unlikely to mention class tensions in letters extolling the wonders of the Windy City. Based on the information at their disposal, black southerners preparing to go to Chicago could logically envision a black community that was self-sufficient, fiercely militant, and eager to assist those of "the Race" in flight from southern oppression. Accordingly, many wrote hopefully to the *Defender,* the Chicago Urban League, and Bethlehem Baptist Association for train fare, suitcases, and prearranged employment and housing. Chicago's black institutional leadership could not provide these resources, but it did offer useful assistance and services. The same network that had stimulated and facilitated migration could now work toward smooth adjustment. As migration increased, the other part of the network, community and kin, would prove most useful to newcomers during their first days in the city.

It was fortunate that there were some black institutions to which migrants

---

57. Arthur P. Drucker, et al., *The Colored People of Chicago* (Chicago, 1913), 13-14; Richard Robert Wright, *87 Years behind the Black Curtain: An Autobiography* (Philadelphia, 1965), 105; *Defender,* May 8, 1915; Harold F. Gosnell, *Negro Politicians: The Rise of Negro Politics in Chicago* (Chicago, 1935), 129; Harry Haywood, *Black Bolshevik: Autobiography of an Afro-American Communist* (Chicago, 1978), 38; Drake and Cayton, *Black Metropolis,* 600-657. The quotation is from W. H. A. Moore, "In a Black Belt," *Journal of National Association of Negro Authors* [Chicago] (Aug. 1915), 3-4, copy in Dunmore Collection.

could turn in their search for interim lodging upon arrival, since they were denied access to the standard alternatives available to other newcomers to Chicago. Most lodging houses in the city, including the Salvation Army's Reliance Hotel, YMCA Hotel, Christian Industrial League, Dawes Hotel, and probably the Municipal Lodging houses, turned blacks from their doors despite stated policies of accepting anyone who could pay other than "inebriated" applicants. Even hotels sufficiently nonexclusive to accept the patronage of "quiet" drunks, rejected blacks. These institutions, like the Travelers Aid Society, preferred to refer blacks to the Urban League, using that organization — which defined itself as a "clearinghouse" for social service work among blacks — as a dumping ground for an undesirable clientele.[58]

Even black institutions, however, accepted transients only on an emergency basis, and few alternatives beckoned to newcomers. Single people might stop at one of black Chicago's hotels, such as the Pullman, which offered a range of accommodations at fifty cents to one dollar per day. At C. K. Smith's, all but the most impoverished migrants could afford the fifteen- to twenty-cent charge for a bed for the night.[59] By 1917 a migrant in search of more comfortable quarters could secure a room at the Idlewild Hotel — complete with steam heat and hot water. Although the number of hotels catering to blacks increased from six in 1917 to eleven in 1921, these establishments could not satisfy the demand. The Chicago Commission on Race Relations reported that between 1915 and 1920, "hundreds of unattached men and women" roamed the streets of Chicago's black neighborhoods until well after midnight looking for rooms.[60]

If housing constituted one measurement of "bettering one's condition," Chicago was at best a flawed promised land. Black migrants moved into houses and apartments in some of the city's most deteriorated neighborhoods. Among Chicago's decaying inner districts — many of which had been marked for extinction as residence areas by the city's planners — only those inhabited by blacks showed population increases between 1910 and 1920.[61] But Chicago did seem to offer many migrants, especially those who arrived before 1919, better homes than they had left behind in the South. Although

58. *Defender,* July 9, 1921; "Memorandum of Conference on Temporary Shelter, Housing and Care for Colored Women with Young Children," Chicago, July 9, 1926, Box 145, Records of the Welfare Council of Metropolitan Chicago (WCMC), CHS; Chicago Urban League, *Fifth Annual Report* (1921), 5; Philpott, *The Slum and the Ghetto,* 100. For the Urban League's self-image as a clearinghouse, see Chicago Urban League, *Second Annual Report* (1918), 7.

59. *Defender,* May 13, 1916; Ford S. Black, comp., *Black's Blue Book, Business and Professional Directory* (Chicago, 1917), 19-20.

60. *Defender,* March 26, 1921; "General Race News," *Half-Century Magazine* 3, no. 2 (Aug. 1917), 8; Ford S. Black, comp., *Black's Blue Book: Directory of Chicago's Active Colored People and Guide to Their Activities* (Chicago, 1921), 32; CCRR, *Negro in Chicago,* 165.

61. Elizabeth A. Hughes, *Living Conditions of Small-Wage Earners in Chicago* (Chicago, 1925), 9; Thomas W. Allison, "Population Movements in Chicago," *Journal of Social Forces* 2, no. 4 (May, 1924), 533.

Black migrants to Chicago often found only rundown housing such as the above available to them.   Courtesy of University of Illinois at Chicago: Special Collections.

many newcomers never escaped the dilapidated dwellings located west of State Street, others somehow managed to secure more space, if only temporarily. Even the ramshackle houses on some of the worst blocks were frequently quite roomy, especially compared to what had been available in the South. Migrants from towns or farms in the South had probably lived in crude cabins of perhaps three or four rooms. In such homes it was not unusual for as many as five members of a family to sleep in a single room. Traveling through Mississippi in 1917, Charles Johnson found "a stock accommodation: a two room cabin for a family in which they cook, sleep, eat and rear their children." A survey of North Carolina rural housing found cabins of three rooms — or smaller — that left inhabitants open to the vicissitudes of even the relatively mild climate. "Hot in the summer . . . [and] . . . almost impossible to heat" in the winter, these homes invariably had leaks that left floors damp after storms.[62] If many migrants ended up in Chicago

62. Hughes, *Living Conditions,* 21-24; Alice Q. Rood, "Social Conditions among the Negroes on Federal Street between Forty-Fifth Street and Fifty-Third Street" (master's thesis, University of Chicago, 1924), 28-30; Eva Boggs, "Nutrition of Fifty Colored Families in Chicago" (master's thesis, University of Chicago, 1929), 13-14; [Carrie A. Lyford], *A Study of Home-Economics Education in Teacher Training Institutions for Negroes,* U.S. Office of Education, Federal Board for Vocational

flats without hot running water, even cold tap water had been unavailable in their southern homes, which probably had lacked any plumbing or sewerage connections. And though the housing available to black newcomers to Chicago ranked among the worst in the city, utilities that were routine in Chicago had been a luxury in plantation cabins and even in many southern towns. A Floridian who was "not particular about the electric lights" could hardly have been aware before leaving the South that in Chicago a dangling light bulb characterized even the dingy "kitchenette." Although migrants soon would grow dissatisfied with their substandard housing, most found homes that seemed better than what they had left behind in the South.[63]

Although most migrants moved frequently after locating in Chicago, their ability to find better housing was limited. The small black ghetto grew rapidly in 1917, but resistance soon formed along its eastern and western borders. The ghetto expanded mainly to the south during the war, but it did so slowly and along a narrow corridor. Because landlords could extract higher — and rapidly increasing — rents from blacks excluded from the city's general housing market, recently "opened" blocks frequently commanded rates beyond the financial resources of most migrants. Black Chicagoans who moved into more expensive homes left behind buildings to be filled by newcomers; but this process did not create nearly enough vacancies to meet the demand. By 1919, despite a surplus of housing elsewhere in Chicago, including in working-class neighborhoods west of the ghetto, a severe housing shortage plagued black Chicago. This crisis contributed to the outbreak of the bloody race riot that year.[64]

Education Bulletin no. 79 (Washington, D.C., 1923), 2-3; Johnson, "Home Life in Mississippi," "Mississippi Summary," NULR; Rupert B. Vance, *Human Factors in Cotton Culture: A Study in the Social Geography of the American South* (Chapel Hill, 1929), 250. Another North Carolina survey cited by Vance (p. 230) found an average of 3.72 rooms per house for black farmers. See also Subcommittee on the Function of Home Activities in the Education of the Child, White House Conference on Child Health and Protection, "Family Relationships and Personality Adjustment" [c. 1920s], 9, typescript in Folder 2, Section 3, "Research," Ernest W. Burgess Papers, Regenstein Library, Univ. of Chicago. Hughes (p. 23) argued that "contrary to popular current opinion, the overcrowding among Negro households was of relatively infrequent occurrence."

63. Hughes, *Living Conditions*, 29-30; Dorothy Dickens, *Nutritional Investigation of Negro Tenants in the Yazoo Mississippi Delta*, Mississippi Agricultural Experiment Station Bulletin no. 254, 1928, 11; Scott, "Letters," 292. For a graphic description of blacks' homes in a Georgia village, see Clifton Johnson, *Highways and Byways of the South* (New York, 1904), 31. Peter Gottlieb found that Pittsburgh's migrants were relegated to housing that was worse than what they had left behind in the South, homes that failed "to meet migrants' customary standards, let alone their hopes for better conditions." Pittsburgh's black migrants lived near the steel mills or in barracks built by employers, facilities vastly different from the old residential neighborhood on Chicago's South Side. See Gottlieb, *Making Their Own Way*, 66, 69-76.

64. CCRR, *Negro in Chicago*, 93; Memoranda relating to availability of housing in Chicago in 1918-19, in Box 307, Records of the U.S. Housing Corporation, RG 3, NA; see especially Charles Bixby to James Ford, July 2, 1919; Bixby to William C. Graves, July 9, 1919; Fred D. McCracken

The interaction of discrimination and rapidly rising demand for housing not only fueled racial tensions and frustrated migrants' hopes of progressively improving their living conditions; it also had an impact on the physical environment of blacks who already lived in Chicago and contributed to their concerns about the effects of the Great Migration. Although most black Chicagoans recognized that the exodus from the South and the entrance into the industrial economy represented a step forward for black America, they were not necessarily eager to see the newcomers become their neighbors. Some of these Old Settlers tried to avoid the social consequences of the Great Migration by fleeing from neighborhoods affordable to newcomers. Housing discrimination, however, left most of the city inaccessible even to the few blacks whose incomes should have provided a wide range of alternatives. Unlike white immigrants and their children, who similarly worked to accumulate the resources to move to a "better" neighborhood, most black Chicagoans struggling for security, respectability, and an environment suited to raising children found their ambitions stymied.[65]

Middle-class black Chicagoans generally tried to insulate themselves by moving further south along the narrow strip that defined the gradually expanding South Side Black Belt. But the migrants inevitably followed. What had been the middle-class edge of the South Side ghetto in 1917 became a central part of that district by 1920. High rents and large houses in such areas inhibited, but could not prevent, their gradual transformation. Newcomers unable to afford large houses but wanting extra space or income frequently rented these buildings and took in lodgers. In addition, landlords — black and white — learned that they could increase profits by dividing a comfortable four-room flat into four "kitchenettes" by installing a gas burner in each room and renting to poor families by the week. Although newcomers tended to cluster in the older neighborhood west of State Street and north of Thirty-fifth Street, and the proportion of migrants decreased as one moved south, no black neighborhood lacked a significant number of migrants. Caught in the vise of the dual housing market, the middle class could not escape. One black professional man, who moved from Thirty-seventh Street to Fifty-first Street trying to keep ahead of the newcomers, complained in 1927 that "the same class of Negroes who ran

---

to Ford, July 10, 1919. On the efforts to exclude blacks from white neighborhoods, see Philpott, *The Slum and the Ghetto*, 146-200; William M. Tuttle, *Race Riot: Chicago in the Red Summer of 1919* (New York, 1970), 157-83.

65. In Philadelphia and Homestead, PA, blacks who had arrived before the Great Migration were able to maintain territorial distance from newcomers, even within the black working class itself. See Allen B. Ballard, *One More Day's Journey: The Story of a Family and a People* (New York, 1984), 184; Gottlieb, *Making Their Own Way*, 73-74. On the ability of Chicago's white immigrants to move to new neighborhoods, see Humbert S. Nelli, *Italians in Chicago 1880-1930: A Study in Ethnic Mobility* (New York, 1970), 36-54; Edward Mazur, "Jewish Chicago: From Diversity to Community," in Holli and Jones, eds., *The Ethnic Frontier*, 281-82.

us away from Thirty-seventh Street are moving out there. They creep along slowly like a disease."[66]

Few middle-class black Chicagoans, however, went so far as to liken the migrants to an army of infectious germs. Most received the newcomers ambivalently. "They didn't seem to open-arm welcome them," recalled one black Chicagoan, "but they seemed to welcome them."[67] Although the *Defender,* the Urban League, and other major black institutions had encouraged the exodus and invited black southerners to relocate in their city, the men and women who dominated these institutions perceived a potential threat in the influx. Fearful that the migrants, with their rural southern manners, would disrupt the community and embarrass the race, Chicago's black middle class tried to protect its respectability by instructing newcomers in acceptable behavior. Many migrants, in turn, sought to maintain their self-respect and way of life by forming their own institutions — mainly churches — and networks of associations. And many, especially the younger men and women who constituted the bulk of the newcomers, adapted too easily to urban life, noisily crowding the streets, night clubs, dance halls, and "cafes," to the chagrin of the more staid Old Settlers.

If many of the middle-class social clubs and their members continued to ignore the poor except for occasional contributions to charity and frequent moralizing about respectability, the Great Migration did stimulate social welfare activity on the part of black Chicagoans. Considering the limited financial resources of Chicago's black institutions and the widespread poverty in the community even before the influx of newcomers, black Chicago demonstrated a considerable commitment to aiding new arrivals. The centerpiece of both black and white efforts to assist and influence the newcomers was the Chicago Urban League, which provided the bulk of the services most important to recent migrants. Established five years after its parent organization's founding in 1911, the Chicago chapter immediately focused on the "adjustment or assimilation" of the city's black migrants.[68]

Chicago's black establishment encouraged and assisted migrants partly out of sheer self-interest. Politicians, businessmen, and newspaper publishers recognized that the newcomers represented voters, customers, readers, and a potential population boom that could swell the prestige of black Chicago both

66. Philpott, *The Slum and the Ghetto,* 197-98; Chicago Urban League, "Block Work," memorandum in Folder 6, Arthur Aldis Papers, Library of the University of Illinois at Chicago; Frazier, *Negro Family in Chicago,* 99-100; the quotation is on p. 112. Among these landlords who overcharged black newcomers for apartments recently vacated by whites was Oscar DePriest; see Gosnell, *Negro Politicians,* 169.

67. William M. Tuttle, Jr., Interview with Chester Wilkins, June 25, 1969, p. 1 (transcript in possession of Tuttle).

68. Chicago Urban League, *First Annual Report* (1917), 9; Dorothy Crounse, Louise Gilbert, and Agnes Van Driel, "The Chicago Urban League" ([Chicago], 1936), 5, typescript in Chicago Urban League File, Box 286, WCMC, CHS. On the establishment of the Chicago Urban League, see Arvarh Strickland, *History of the Chicago Urban League* (Urbana, 1966), 25-37.

in the city and in black America. Editor Robert Abbott foresaw the *Defender's* influence growing along with the exodus it spearheaded and the community it represented. By 1918 the *Defender* had increased its display advertisements by 93 percent over the three years since 1915.[69] But this self-interest transcended the personal ambitions of individual politicians and entrepreneurs; it included a racial component. The *Defender* voiced the hopes of much of black Chicago's business community and political leadership when it emphasized the progress that the migration could bring to the race. Abbott recognized that participation in the industrial sector of the economy constituted the linchpin of success for any ethnic group in the United States. "Our entrance into factories, workshops and every other industry open to man places us on an entirely different footing. . . . We become a factor in the economy to be reckoned with."[70] The relationship between individual accomplishments, community prosperity and power, and racial progress placed the migrants at center stage.

This optimism placed a great burden on the newcomers. "If you do well you will serve not only yourself but the entire race," the Urban League told them. Conversely, failure would discredit the race; "respectable" black Chicagoans recognized that even if they could avoid living among migrants they would still be associated with them. If some Old Settlers reacted like the "Old Philadelphians," who "secretly hoped that whites would recognize that they were different from the southerners and treat them accordingly," most more realistically appreciated the importance of race as a category central to white social attitudes. Like German Jews, who in the late nineteenth century feared that the influx of their coreligionists from eastern Europe would endanger their marginal but substantial foothold in gentile Chicago, black Old Settlers considered themselves vulnerable to stereotyped images dominated by visibly outlandish newcomers. It was essential to organize the community to handle the problem before it grew so large as to overshadow the community's respectable core. "We are our brother's keeper, whether we like it or not," the *Defender* reminded its readers. "It is our duty, if resolved to a selfish duty, to guide the hand of a less experienced one, especially when one misstep weakens our chance for climbing."[71]

Chicago's black middle-class residents assumed that the migrants had to be guided and controlled from the moment they stepped from the train. Mechanisms of social control in the South — church, lodge, gossip, and established customs — were weaker in Chicago, according to one Urban League official, and the migrants were thus more susceptible to dissolution and "disorganization." Ida B. Wells-Barnett lamented that migrants were first attracted to State Street, where "not a single uplifting influence" competed with the saloons,

69. See *Defender,* July 17, 24, 1915, August 3, 1918.

70. *Defender,* January 19, 1918.

71. Ballard, *One More Day's Journey,* 188; *Defender,* March 17, 1917, January 19, 1918. Urban League statement quoted in *Defender,* November 23, 1918. On German and eastern European Jews, see Mazur, "Jewish Chicago," 279-81.

poolrooms, and cabarets.[72] The attractions of State Street and the old vice district at the northern end of the Black Belt threatened the migrants' moral fiber and sobriety as well as the reputation of the community. For if the newcomers fell easily into degeneracy — as many Old Settlers feared, and whites expected — they would reflect poorly on the race. They would also be unable to serve as efficient industrial workers or respectable citizens. By inculcating restraint, the Old Settlers hoped to protect the migrants' souls and pocketbooks, while preserving the community's honor.

The Urban League and the *Defender,* assisted by the YMCA, the larger churches, and a corps of volunteers, fashioned a variety of initiatives designed to help — and pressure — the newcomers to adjust, not only to industrial work, but to urban life, northern racial patterns, and behavior that would enhance the reputation of blacks in the larger (white) community. The *Defender* repeatedly published exhaustive lists of "do's and don't's," calling attention to examples of unacceptable behavior:

- Don't use vile language in public places.
- Don't act discourteously to other people in public places.
- Don't allow yourself to be drawn into street brawls.
- Don't use liberty as a license to do as you please.
- Don't take the part of law breakers, be they men, women, or children.
- Don't make yourself a public nuisance.
- Don't encourage gamblers, disreputable women or men to ply their business any time or place.
- Don't congregate in crowds on the streets to the disadvantage of others passing along.
- Don't live in unsanitary houses, or sleep in rooms without proper ventilation.
- Don't violate city ordinances, relative to health conditions.
- Don't allow children to beg on the streets.
- Don't allow boys to steal from or assault peddlers. . . .
- Don't be a beer can rusher or permit children to do such service.
- Don't abuse or violate the confidence of those who give you employment.
- Don't leave your job when you have a few dollars in your pocket. . . .

The Urban League, through such activities as "Strangers Meetings," leafleting, and door-to-door visits, advised newcomers on their duties as citizens: clean-

---

72. Johnson, "New Frontage on American Life," 285; Alfreda Duster, ed., *Crusade for Justice: The Autobiography of Ida B. Wells* (Chicago, 1970), 303. See also Forrester B. Washington, "A Program of Work for the Assimilation of Negro Immigrants in Northern Cities," *Proceedings of the National Conference on Social Work* 44 (1917), 498. Although Washington was an Urban League administrator in Detroit when he wrote this article, it expresses a widespread sentiment; also, Washington had worked in Chicago for a short time, and his observations probably took this experience into consideration.

liness, sobriety, thrift, efficiency, and respectable, restrained behavior in public places. Under the League's auspices, hundreds of club women visited the homes of migrants in 1917, offering "messages emphasizing the necessity of being orderly citizens, efficient working-men and good housekeepers." Perhaps expressing greater confidence to a white audience than he would privately among others of his race and class, Dr. George Cleveland Hall predicted that newcomers would "rapidly adjust themselves to their changed surroundings if they are reached by the proper people and get the right tip."[73] Under the tutelage of the respectable citizens of black Chicago, migrants were to become urbanized, northernized, and indistinguishable from others of their race. At the very least, they would learn to be as inconspicuous as possible.

This campaign exposed cultural conflicts generated by tensions along lines of age, class, and region. "Respectability," the badge of middle-class status in black Chicago, defined the standards to which migrants were held, and manifestations of southern culture drew both attention and reproof. So also did boisterous leisure activities undeniably urban and not specific to any region. The middle-class sensibilities of the men and women who spoke for black Chicago's newspapers, the Urban League, clubs, and churches resembled those of settlement house reformers and others who sought to compete with streets, saloons, and other loci of popular culture for the souls and leisure hours of lower-class youth.

Mostly young men and women, the newcomers indulged in forms of public behavior characteristic of young urbanites, frequently antagonizing churchgoers with their apparent repudiation of conventional morality and their attraction to the "gay life." They hung out on street corners, threw loud parties, dressed in the latest risqué fashions, and enjoyed the bright lights of the city's night life. Like the black alderman who wanted to "forbid loitering on street corners," community leaders objected to the tendency of young men and women to converse loudly, in language not entirely within the bounds of genteel respectability. Spending evenings in dance halls, and "dancing in a rareback fashion entirely too close to her partner to be anything other than VULGAR," aroused the *Defender's* ire as quickly as wearing tight or "abbreviated clothes." Young blacks could make a better impression on whites and improve themselves by partaking in the "wholesome recreation" available in community centers,

---

73. *Defender*, August 17, 1918; USDL, *Negro Migration*, 23; Chicago Urban League, *First Annual Report* (1917), 11; *Daily News*, April 2, 1917. See also the leaflet reproduced in Annual Report of the National Urban League (1919), in *Bulletin of the National Urban League* 9, no. 1 (Jan. 1920), 20-21. *Defender* lectures on proper behavior can be found in almost any issue, 1917-20; this particular one appeared on October 20, 1917. By 1923, the NAACP, which had had very little visibility in Chicago during the war years, was distributing a three-page flyer issued by its Education Committee, and carrying a detailed message similar to that previously broadcast by other institutions. The notable differences lie in the NAACP emphasis on voting and citizenship and on its call for "refined and gentle manners," a standard not set by the Urban League, *Defender*, or YMCA. See "Chicago, Great City" (August 1, 1923), typescript in Box G-48, Group 1, Records of the National Association for the Advancement of Colored People, LC.

churches, and the YMCA and YWCA.[74] The migrants were, on the whole, considerably younger than the adult black population already living in Chicago; moreover, young blacks in Chicago were likely to be migrants, while older blacks were likely to have arrived before 1910. The importance of bright lights and leisure opportunities had been central to migrants' image of Chicago as a "freer" environment than the rural or small-town South.[75] It seemed logical to the older, settled residents that recent arrivals would be particularly susceptible to the temptations of city life because of their unfamiliarity with its dangers and their supposedly undeveloped sense of self-discipline.

Much of what offended and embarrassed those concerned with maintaining standards, however, was identifiably southern. The deep South origins of the wartime-era migrants distinguished them not only from native Chicagoans but also from those who had arrived earlier, usually from the upper South. The differences were obvious to black Chicagoans: there was no mistaking the regional provenance of streetside barbecue stands and such icons as watermelon and head rags. Old Settlers grew particularly upset when newcomers publicly displayed their southern backgrounds. Both the *Defender* and the *Whip* castigated women who were "frequently seen in their boudoir caps, house slippers and aprons around the corner in the grocery store," or who appeared in public wearing a head rag. "We are not in the Southland and there is no mark of servitude that must be placed on a man or woman of color in these climes," the *Defender* informed migrants who wore overalls and aprons downtown, on streetcars, and to places of amusement. An Urban League leaflet was equally stern, demanding that the migrants pledge "I WILL REFRAIN from wearing dust caps, bungalow aprons, house clothing and bedroom shoes out of doors."[76]

Unlike socially secure settlement-house workers, who valued the folk music, art, and material culture of their European immigrant clients, Chicago's

74. Charles E. Merriam and Harold F. Gosnell, *Non-Voting: Causes and Methods of Control* (Chicago, 1924), 211; CCRR, *Negro in Chicago*, 478; *Defender*, August 4, 1917, July 13, 1918, July 24, 1920, July 23, 1921, June 17, 1922; Bontemps and Conroy, *They Seek a City*, 142. On community centers, which were open "suitable evenings" in selected public school buildings, see Chicago Board of Education, *Proceedings*, October 22, 1919, p. 872, September 28, 1921, pp. 186-87; and Chicago Board of Education, *64th Annual Report of the Superintendent of Schools for the Year Ending 1918* (Chicago, 1919), 113-16.

75. For statistics on age, see U.S. Bureau of the Census, *Thirteenth Census, 1910*, vol. 2, *Population* (Washington, D.C., 1913), 480; and *Fourteenth Census, 1920*, vol. 3, *Population* (Washington, D.C., 1922), 248. For a comparison of the ages of Illinois-born black Chicagoans and migrants, see Appendix A. The calculation for the proportion of young black Chicagoans in 1920 who were migrants draws on the Forward Census Survival Ratios described in Lee, et al., *Population Redistribution and Economic Growth, United States, 1870-1950*, vol. 1, *Methodological Considerations and Reference Tables* (Philadelphia, 1957), 15-25.

76. *Whip*, October 9, 1920; *Defender*, October 20, 1917, May 25, 1918, October 30, 1920, August 13, 1921, September 3, October 22, 1921, June 3, 1922; see also leaflet reprinted in *Bulletin of the National Urban League* (1920), 21. For a comparison of the states of birth of Chicago's black population in 1910 and of those who came between 1910 and 1920, see Appendix B.

black middle class could see little redeeming value in southern black folk culture. Symbolizing the dependence and degradation of blacks in the rural South, it had no place in the modern northern city and only confirmed white stereotypes, thereby tarnishing the image that Chicago's black community wished to project. Although the image of the "golden age" of race relations before the migrants arrived, as later recalled by some Old Settlers, represented a view distorted by time and open conflict, black Chicagoans had worked long and hard to attain what civil rights they had won. Many feared that the already tenuous racial peace in Chicago would dissolve as whites reacted against crude peasants unaccustomed to the proper exercise of those rights. Kathryn Johnson, the associate editor of the *Half-Century*, a black middle-class women's magazine published in Chicago, feared "an aggravation of the segregation problem which has been so prevalent with us since Mr. Wilson became president. Many of those who are coming will be imprudent and will take their newly found liberty for license." A member of one of "the first colored families in Chicago" worried about what "to do with all of these Negroes from the South coming in here. They look terrible. They sit down on the street car beside white people and I am sure that there is going to be trouble." When trouble came, in the form of a race riot in 1919, many long-time residents blamed the migrants. One native Chicagoan insisted in 1927 that until the Great Migration "we had been accepted as equals." Even the *Defender*, the champion of the exodus, commented (inaccurately) that "there was absolutely no friction until the advent of a handful of undesirables who 'felt their oats' and cut loose upon the slightest provocation."[77]

The reactions of migrants to these messages varied, especially according to class. Middle-class migrants sought acceptance into Chicago's black bourgeoisie and shared its attitudes toward street life, boisterous behavior, and the trappings of lower-class life. They no more wished to be associated with southern rural culture than did the Old Settlers. At least one newcomer not only

77. Kathryn M. Johnson, "Immigration and Segregation," *Half-Century Magazine* 2, no. 2 (Feb. 1917), 8; Frazier, *Negro Family in Chicago*, 82; Gunnar Myrdal, *An American Dilemma: The Negro Problem and Modern Democracy* (New York, 1944), 196; *Defender*, September 24, 1921; *Whip*, July 24, 1920. On "walking the narrow path of liberty and avoiding the precipice of license," see also George E. Haynes, "Effect of War Conditions on Negro Labor," *Proceedings of the Academy of Political Science* 8, no. 2 (Feb. 1919), 306. For examples of "golden age" perspectives, see Drake and Cayton, *Black Metropolis*, 73. Not all Old Settlers maintained this nostalgic image; see, for example, Wilhelmina Warfield, Interview with William C. King, October 28, 1937, in Box 95, "Music," IWP, "Negro in Illinois." On racial conflict before 1916, see CCRR, *Negro in Chicago*, 291; Charles E. Bentley, Address Delivered before Kenwood Congregational Church, Chicago, 1908, Folder 74, Box 5, Carter G. Woodson Collection, LC; Philpott, *The Slum and the Ghetto*, 146-56. While not suggesting a golden age, Allan Spear, *Black Chicago*, 29-49, argues that race relations in Chicago had seen better days in the nineteenth century and proposes the end of that century as the era of "Jim Crow's triumph," thereby placing the degeneration of race relations before the Great Migration but in an era characterized by a moderate increase in migration from the South. The interest of Chicago settlement-house workers in white immigrant folk culture is discussed in Philpott, *The Slum and the Ghetto*, 70.

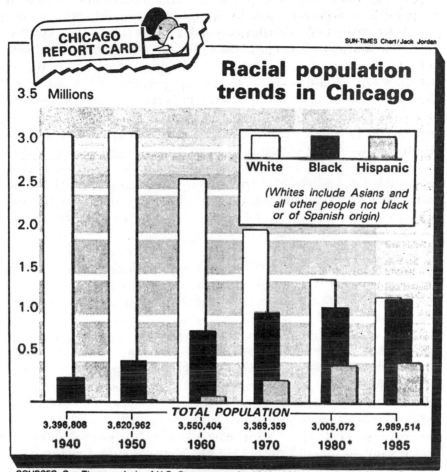

CHICAGO
REPORT CARD

SUN-TIMES Chart / Jack Jordan

Racial population trends in Chicago

3.5 Millions

White   Black   Hispanic

(Whites include Asians and all other people not black or of Spanish origin)

3.0

2.5

2.0

1.5

1.0

0.5

TOTAL POPULATION

3,396,808	3,620,962	3,550,404	3,369,359	3,005,072	2,989,514
1940	1950	1960	1970	1980*	1985

SOURCES: Sun-Times analysis of U.S. Census tracts for 1940-1960 figures. City of Chicago Dept. of Planning analysis of U.S. Census figures for 1970-1985 figures. *Asians represent 66,673 of the white population.

This graph clearly shows ethnic population changes in Chicago with a declining white population, a dramatic slowing of black population growth after 1975, and a steadily increasing Hispanic population.

Courtesy of City of Chicago, Dept. of Planning.

worried about what her new neighbors might think, but also made certain that "friends back home" would not open their weekly *Defender* and discover her name among those reprimanded for unacceptable behavior.[78]

Other newcomers, however, found the lessons condescending and either unnecessary, unwelcome, or impractical. Many had heard it all before: the Chicago Urban League's sermons on thrift, hygiene, and work habits differed little from the message emanating from Tuskegee. In Chicago, however, women encountered increased pressure to attend to the proper care of their homes. Many, especially those from rural areas, were in fact unaccustomed to the imperatives and standards of urban housekeeping. But the problem had less to do with race or geographic origins than with class. As one investigator discovered during the winter of 1919-20, working-class black women were as concerned as their white counterparts about "good housekeeping." Working-class women in general found it difficult to live up to standards set by middle-class women living in homes with proper plumbing facilities, more time for housework, and perhaps even a maid. More likely than whites to work outside the home, black women had even less time than whites facing similar obstacles.[79]

Misdirected criticism extended beyond the home. Black stockyards workers were, on the whole, more conscientious than their white coworkers about showering and changing clothes before heading home. Most white workers, of course, lived near the packinghouses and did not have to ride the streetcar, where black workers — unable to eradicate the stockyards stench — attracted criticism for carrying home the aroma from their workplaces. Similar reproofs about disorderly conduct on streetcars led one newcomer from Mississippi to complain that "the whites act just as disorderly on cars as the Negroes. . . . Nothing is ever said."[80]

Migrants were most active in resisting attempts to change aspects of their everyday life. Despite the pleas of Old Settlers to "give us more grand opera and less plantation melodies," the migrants did not leave their cultural baggage at the train station. "It's no difficult task to get people out of the South," the Chicago *Whip* remarked, "but you have a job on your hands when you attempt to get the South out of them."[81] Although they brought with them fewer "plantation melodies" than their fearful neighbors imagined, migrants did carry to Chicago a form of music equally disliked by many Old Settlers — the boogie-

78. E. Franklin Frazier, "Chicago: A Cross-Section of Negro Life," *Opportunity* 7, no. 3 (March 1929), 71.

79. Alice Q. Rood, "Social Conditions among the Negroes on Federal Street between Forty-fifth Street and Fifty-third Street" (master's thesis, University of Chicago, 1924), 42-43. On housekeeping standards in the rural South, see Jacqueline Jones, *Labor of Love, Labor of Sorrow: Black Women, Work, and the Family from Slavery to the Present* (New York, 1985), 86-89.

80. CCRR, *Negro in Chicago*, 177, 304.

81. *Whip*, October 23, 1920, March 4, 1922.

woogie, which probably had its origins in the Mississippi Delta and was closely related to southern revival music. Newcomers also continued to sing southern blues and work songs. One recently arrived huckster probably infuriated many staid Chicagoans with his products as well as his tone:

> Water-mel-lone, jes' like from down home; rosten' ears, tatoes-tatoes-tatoes; nice ripe toma-toes; tommy — tommy — tomatoes; o-o-o-ochree and dry ingyuns.[82]

Continuing to sing, sell, eat, and dress as they had "back home," migrants retained their cultural ties with the South. Many sustained these links by occasionally visiting kinsmen who had stayed behind. It was a relief to have left behind that region's oppression, but even years after coming North, many migrants retained a certain ambivalence about what came to be called "down home." Richard Wright, even before leaving the South, recognized what Chicago's Old Settlers would reluctantly learn: "I knew that I could never really leave the South, for my feelings had already been formed by the South, for there had been slowly instilled into my personality and consciousness, black though I was, the culture of the South."[83]

Along with retaining some of their southern customs, migrants also established their own institutions in Chicago. Many southern business and professional people followed members of their community to Chicago, hoping to retain their patronage. By 1919, approximately two-thirds of all black-owned businesses in Chicago were operated by what the *Whip* called "newcomers" and an Urban League spokesman called "migrants." The Southern Home Cooking and Southern Lunch Room restaurants appealed to the newcomers' affinity for "down home" cooking. Other businesses, such as Robert Horton's Hattiesburg Shaving Parlor, appealed to more specific loyalties. Even newcomers from regions sending relatively few migrants to Chicago could find continued identification with their southern roots at establishments such as the Florida East Coast Shine Parlor or the Carolina Sea Island Candy Store.[84]

The most important institutions founded by the migrants were their churches. At first, the city's established black churches exerted special efforts to recruit newcomers, and thousands of migrants readily accepted the invitations. During 1917-18, each week's *Defender* carried messages from churches claiming that "newcomers are welcome," "strangers welcome," or "everyone is welcome

82. "Boogie Woogie in Chicago," 1-4, Box 84 ("Music History"); and "Native Sons: Rhythm," 8, Box 85 ("Music History") — both in IWP, "Negro in Illinois"; *Defender*, July 22, 1922.

83. Wright, *Black Boy*, 228. On black ambivalence toward the South and the notion of "down home," see Lawrence Levine, *Black Culture and Black Consciousness: Afro-American Folk Thought from Slavery to Freedom* (New York, 1977), 364.

84. *Defender*, March 16, 1918, April 12, 1919; *Whip*, June 24, September 20, 1919; T. Arnold Hill to Walter F. White, November 14, 1919, "September-December, 1919" Folder, Box C-319, NAACP; Bontemps and Conroy, *They Seek a City*, 145.

and made to feel at home." Some of the larger churches, led by Olivet Baptist and Institutional AME, viewed the newcomers as a challenge to their expanded programs, which included such services as employment bureaus, housing directories, and day nurseries. Others advertised guidance, dynamic preaching, or "good singing."[85] The migrants responded enthusiastically. Olivet, which soon claimed to be the largest Baptist church in the world, added more than five thousand new members between 1916 and 1919. Arriving from Alabama in 1922, Mary Fluornoy went to Olivet her "first week here. We couldn't get in. We'd have to stand up. I don't care how early we'd go, you wouldn't get in." Smaller congregations grew as well. Walters AME Zion more than tripled its membership in three years, counting 351 newcomers by 1919. Such increases were not unusual: men and women coming from towns and rural areas where ministers passed through only once or twice each month to preach in crude buildings were impressed even with Chicago's more modest institutions.[86]

The enthusiasm, however, was often temporary. Many migrants felt distinctly uncomfortable in Chicago's churches, because of both the size of some congregations and the styles of acceptable worship. Migrants, especially those from the rural South, were accustomed to services accompanied by improvisational singing, "shouting," and other forms of active participation and demonstrative enthusiasm. These men and women reacted coolly to the intellectual sermons of such ministers as Rev. William Braddan of Berean Baptist Church, who refused to hold revivals and prohibited standing in his church during services. Even at such places as Walters AME Zion, where migrants apparently worshipped as they pleased, they hardly could be unaware that the pastor, Rev. W. A. Blackwell, considered "singing, shouting and talking being the most useless ways of proving Christianity." Most Chicago ministers permitted traditional "enthusiasm," and many of the most respected among them even matched southern preachers at driving a congregation to an emotional pitch. But these ministers generally did so only as a concession to some of the older members of the congregation and as an attempt to appeal as widely as possible; they also devoted a part of the service to a more sober sermon, which some migrants found uninspiring. One woman, who had joined Olivet when she arrived in Chicago, later recalled that she "couldn't understand the pastor and the words he used." She also soon realized, "I couldn't sing their way. The

85. For "invitations," see, for example, *Defender*, February 24, March 3, 17, 24, 31, July 7, September 1, 15, 22, October 20, 27, 1917, March 30, October 19, November 23, 1918, April 5, May 17, 1919. On Olivet and Institutional, see Black, *Black's Blue Book* (1921), 80; S. Mattie Fisher, "Olivet as a Christian Center," *Missions* 10, no. 3 (March 1919), 199; E. Jennings, "Institutional AME Church," Box 29 ("Churches"), IWP, "The Negro in Illinois."

86. Myra Young Armstead, interview with Mary Fluornoy; CCRR, *The Negro in Chicago*, 94; George E. Haynes, "Negro Migration," *Opportunity* 2, no. 21 (Sept. 1924), 273; Woofter, *Negro Migration*, 163; Jesse O. Thomas, *My Story in Black and White: The Autobiography of Jesse O. Thomas* (New York, 1967), 21-22.

songs was proud-like." She left to join a smaller church. Indeed, the majority of Old Settlers in most of the major churches considered "the old time religion" preferred by this woman and many other migrants to be outdated, unrefined, and embarrassing. One group of migrants from rural Alabama and Georgia told an interviewer in 1917 that they needed a church "where they can sing without appearing strange, and where they can hear somebody else pray besides themselves." A newcomer from Slidell, Louisiana, felt similarly uncomfortable at Pilgrim Baptist Church because "nobody said nothing aloud but there were whispers all over the place." Religious practice in such an atmosphere was not the communal experience that many southerners expected on Sunday mornings.[87]

Migrants not only objected to the general atmosphere and style of worship characteristic of Chicago's "old line" churches, but also found that they did not receive the individual recognition to which they were accustomed. One woman left the first church she joined because it was "too large — it don't see the small people. . . . The preacher wouldn't know me, might call my name in the book, but he wouldn't know me otherwise. Why, at home whenever I didn't come to Sunday School they would always come and see what was the matter." This experience especially offended men and women who had been influential members of their churches back home. In response, some chose to organize their own congregations, frequently joining with former townsmen or other dissatisfied migrants seeking an alternative.[88]

This process of joining churches, splitting off, and starting new institutions was part of the adjustment process for many newcomers. By first entering established, large churches, newcomers could receive assistance in finding jobs and homes, meet other southerners, and perhaps glean useful information from announcements during services. Eventually these migrants could decide whether to leave the large church for a more intimate congregation or try a different — but established — church.[89] That kind of shopping around would have been impossible for most migrants before they came to Chicago. Rural villages and towns in the South generally supported at most one church of any

---

87. William S. Braddan, *Under Three Banners; An Autobiography* (Nashville, 1940), 249; *Defender*, May 27, 1922; Scott, *Negro Migration*, 110; Drake and Cayton, *Black Metropolis*, 634; Joseph Bougere, interview with Robert Mays, Chicago, March 9, 1938, Box 77 ("Migration"), IWP, "Negro in Illinois." For ministers at "mainline" churches whipping congregations to a frenzy, see *Whip*, February 12, October 29, 1921, September 30, 1922. On ministers who tried to appeal widely by including both sober and emotional appeals, see Robert Lee Sutherland, "An Analysis of Negro Churches in Chicago" (Ph.D. diss., University of Chicago, 1930), 97. This ability to "swing easily" between styles dates back to the antebellum South; see Eugene D. Genovese, *Roll, Jordan, Roll: The World the Slaves Made* (New York, 1974), 268.

88. Frazier, *Negro Family in Chicago*, 74.

89. For a suggestive discussion of how churches helped migrants to adjust to urban life, see Vattel E. Daniel, "Ritual in South Side Churches for Negroes" (Ph.D. diss., University of Chicago, 1940), 90-91, 141-43, and *passim*.

given denomination; considering the importance of the church to community life, the limitation was significant. In Chicago, options were circumscribed by attitudes of Old Settlers, but migrants exercised considerable discretion over which church community they joined. Experimentation not only facilitated their adaptation to urban Chicago, but was in itself a form of adaptation.[90]

As a mode of adaptation to the new environment, choosing a church — or starting a new one — symbolized the hopes of many migrants. Migration not only had increased the number of available options; those options included the chance to adjust to the urban North while still retaining aspects of one's southern cultural heritage. In addition, many could realistically look forward to "bettering their condition" either by joining a more prestigious church or by organizing and leading a new congregation. And all this took place within institutions controlled by blacks, relatively insulated from oppressive race relations. "I goes every Sunday and Wednesday nights to prayer meeting," remarked one migrant who belonged to Olivet Baptist Church, "just to thank God that he let me live to go to a place of worship like that, a place where my people worship and ain't pestered by the white men."[91]

It is not surprising that a migrant might express in that way one aspect of the church's importance in her life. Olivet was dominated by Old Settlers — though not the elite of black Chicago — but it was still a black institution. Indeed, religious life in black Chicago suggests the complexity of the relationships between migrants and the city's established black community. If many migrants felt alienated from Chicago's black religious institutions, others did remain within the large churches. The hostility that existed in individual churches along lines of class and geographic origin was partially bridged by the fact of membership in a single institution and the leadership of the minister. The divisions both within and between churches existed alongside a significant degree of cohesion based on identification as part of Chicago's black community and its institutions. Although the fissures were significant, they were neither as deep nor as wide as the gap separating white and black. Migrants found a black community that seemed snobbish and condescending at times; nevertheless, the established community and the migrants shared one identity that set them all off from the rest of Chicago — race.

---

90. Gottlieb, *Making Their Own Way,* 201, offers a similar argument with reference to black migrants in Pittsburgh during this period.

91. CCRR, *Negro in Chicago,* 488; see also Gottlieb, *Making Their Own Way,* 198-203. On the importance of autonomy, control, and status in black religious life, see J. J. Watson, "Churches and Religious Conditions," *Annals of the American Academy of Political and Social Science* 49 (Sept. 1913), 120.

CHAPTER 11

Chatham:
An African-American Success Story*

WILLIAM BRADEN

Chatham is a bastion of Chicago's black middle class. It represents perhaps the largest concentration of middle-class blacks in America outside of Harlem and Atlanta, and it calls itself "a community of excellence." Its residents put a premium on hard work, discipline, education, family life, and keeping up their property. But the winds of change are blowing, and Chatham in 1986 is also now a community in transition.

There are comparable black communities in Chicago, including Pill Hill, West Chesterfield, and the Jackson Park Highlands. But they are relatively small in comparison. Chatham is populated by some 23,000 people who live in an area most locals agree is bounded by 75th and 87th Streets, the Dan Ryan Expressway, and Cottage Grove Avenue. And its residents epitomize the culture and values of the middle class that constitutes probably half of Chicago's black population.

You never hear about these people, says Northwestern University sociologist William A. Sampson. "Everybody writes about the elite and the underclass," he says. "Nobody writes about the fifty percent in the middle." Sampson estimates that about one-third of blacks in Chicago and the nation are poor, and about a third of those poor are underclass; about 20 percent are upper

---

*William Braden, "Making It: The Story of Chatham," *Chicago Sun-Times* (special supplement, June 1986).

EDITORS' NOTE: The editors did not want to leave the reader with the impression that the African-American experience in Chicago was and is solely the story of the social pathology of a black underclass. There was a black middle-class from the earliest times, and despite its growing size, urbanists generally ignore its existence. In an effort to offer a more balanced presentation, we have included here a short piece by a thoughtful city watcher and journalist, William Braden, which tells the story of a middle and upper-middle income Chicago neighborhood.

class; and the rest are middle class. But the press and academicians have focused their attention on the bottom third. "Therefore," Sampson says, "much of what we think we know about blacks in America is erroneous, because it's based upon the studies, essentially, of poor blacks."

"The Bill Cosby syndrome is alive and well in Chatham," says Governors State University political scientist Paul Michael Green. "The American dream is being lived out there." Sampson, an authority on the black middle class, has been studying Chatham for years. "Chatham is an anchor," he says. "The people in Chatham serve as role models for everybody else on the South Side. They are going about their lives in a decent, respectable way, every day. Mothers and fathers who are trying to get their kids to live the same kinds of lives in the surrounding neighborhoods can point to these people and say, 'You can do it. Look at that guy walking down the street. He's doing it. It can be done.'"

"There's a breakdown in social control in the underclass because there are not Chathams all over Chicago. There aren't older folks who are saying to young kids, 'Boy, if you do that, I'm going to break your head.' 'Girl, if you let that happen to you, don't you ever come back here.' These people are absolutely crucial."

Chatham today is virtually 100 percent black. Its residents include civil servants, schoolteachers, city workers, business people, politicians, and a growing number of young black urban professionals.

Some three decades ago, Chatham was 100 percent white. Groundwork for the change was laid in 1948, when the United States Supreme Court struck down restrictive covenants. There always had been a black middle class, says William J. Grimshaw, an Illinois Institute of Technology political scientist. But its members had lived in the city's Black Belt cheek by jowl with the poor, and they became visible only when the court ruling allowed them to break out of the ghetto. With savings accumulated during the war years, they began to move south into Chatham around 1955. The migration accelerated with demolition for the University of Illinois at Chicago and the Dan Ryan.

Chatham at that time was an attractive community occupied by middle-class and working-class ethnics, mainly Irish and Scandinavians. The whites resisted the incursion. But ultimately they fled, whipped into panic by block-busters who warned that property values were sure to plummet. Some of the whites who decamped come back now to visit, and find Chatham an upgraded community with greatly increased property values. It is a standard joke in Chatham that a motorist driving through would think he was in an upscale white neighborhood if the residents would hide in their homes.

"When friends from work come out here, they're just absolutely shocked," says Lee Nunery, thirty, an assistant vice president at the First National Bank of Chicago. "They say, 'Gee, you have grass and trees and squirrels. This is kind of like Wilmette, isn't it? It's kind of like Evanston, isn't it?' They say, 'Jeez, the house is nice.' I say, 'What did you expect, jungle vines?' We care a fig about trees. We care about the type of grass we're going to plant, and the way we're going to cut it. We added a garage, added carpeting, resodded the lawn, added another layer of insulation in the attic. In three years we've plowed almost a third of the purchase price back into the house."

"I bought my house from a Lithuanian in 1955," says Arthur N. Turbull, eighty, a retired vocational high school teacher who serves as treasurer of the Chatham Avalon Park Community Council. "Before I moved in, I asked him how the white people really felt about black people. He said, 'Hell, these Irishmen don't speak to me.' And his son comes back today. He's a grown man. But he almost cried in front of the house. They went out to Cicero and went to the dogs. They have problems out there. He looked at the house and said, 'Gee, I wish we were back.' He had so many fine memories."

"There were many schoolteachers among the original settlers," says real estate broker Jane Melnick. "There were post office workers and a sprinkling of Pullman porters. But the common denominator was these were people who were putting their money in the future. They were buying a house. And they were people who knew what it was to save that money every single paycheck, to pinch off and sock it away." They also were charged top dollar for their homes. The poor could not afford Chatham. And that is one reason it remained stable during the early years.

Drive through Chatham today and you will see block after block of large brick bungalows set far back from the street. Some north-south avenues stop short of Chatham, so lots run as much as 185 feet deep (compared with about 125 feet in the average city lot). You will see lawns that look as if they were trimmed by obsessed barbers. There are broad avenues with median parkways planted with flowers.

There are gaslights and wrought-iron fences that real estate broker Dempsey Travis said became the rage after he put up the first one on his property. (The fences cost $10,000 to $15,000, Travis said.) There is the Whitney M. Young Jr. Library that opened in 1973 at 79th Street and Martin Luther King Drive after the community council picketed to prevent construction of a filling station on the site. In her office, librarian Mae Gregory sits under a sign that quotes Young: "If we must march, let us march to the library." She does a brisk business in books on home repair, gardening, and computers.

Apartments are concentrated to the north and east and are mostly two-flats and three-flats, many of them owner-occupied. Residents picketed to prevent construction of high-rises on King Drive. The highest structure in the community is a new seven-story senior citizen building, the Chatham Park South Cooperative, approved by Chathamites at a mass community meeting.

The Chatham Park Village Cooperative looks like the residential quarter of an Ivy League college campus. Formerly a rental development for whites, it turned co-op on January 23, 1962, and now has 552 units in sixty-three buildings on twenty-three acres, says site manager Jack Seals. It is beautifully maintained and has a twenty-four-hour private control. "We had thirty-five people on the waiting list when we stopped the list more than six months ago," says duplex owner Herman O. Hamilton, seventy-four. "When the thirty-five are placed, we'll start taking more applications."

Travis says homes range in value from $40,000 to $500,000, and they include some veritable palaces constructed since the racial change. Melnick says that bungalows that sold for $17,000 in 1955 would sell for about $50,000 today without improvements, and improved basements have been added to almost every house. "As for more expensive homes," Melnick says, "the sky's the limit. I could sell block after block in Chatham. I don't even advertise. If I get a listing in Chatham, I call people on my list. And it will go. I'd give my eye teeth for more. I want them so much I can taste them." Travis says that he has a two-year waiting list. "I line up maybe twenty clients to look at a house," he said, "so I can pick and choose. It's that kind of market. I can sell anything that comes on the market in Chatham within forty-eight hours."

Streets and alleys are whistle clean. "Paper doesn't stand a chance in this community," says Keith Tate, thirty-seven, an accountant at the University of Illinois Medical Center. "We pick it up. We don't wait for the city to come by and sweep our curbs." "There's hardly a day we're not out picking up paper," says Clementine Skinner, seventy, retired assistant principal of South Shore High School. "People come by in cars and toss it out as if there's some magic person to come pick it up. We get out there and sweep that stuff ourselves."

William Garth, publisher of the *Chatham-Southeast Citizen,* estimates the average household income at $30,000. Travis says incomes range up to $500,000, and a substantial number of Chatham residents are in upper-income brackets. Well-known residents include millionaire Travis; Illinois Comptroller Roland W. Burris; Daryl F. Grisham, president of Parker House Sausage Company; Jolyn H. Robichaux, chief executive officer of Baldwin Ice Cream Company; William Abernathy, president of Jiffy Cab Company; and Fred Luster, Sr., president of Luster Products.

Chatham went up instead of down because its settlers inherited a viable community, had the money to maintain and improve it, came into the area with middle-class values, and banded together in block clubs and a community council that enforced rigid standards of construction, maintenance, and social behavior. Council members slap tow stickers on abandoned cars. Block clubs will not permit residents to wash or repair their vehicles on the street. Block-club signs admonish, "No littering. No loitering. No ball playing. Please drive carefully. Have a nice day."

The community has two major problems. One is the vitality of its shopping strips. A far more significant problem was summed up by Rev. Michael J. Nallen, pastor of St. Dorothy's Church and one of the few remaining whites in Chatham: "We just had six funerals in two weeks," he says. "And this is a small parish." It is the community's greatest challenge — "the graying of Chatham."

Chatham's pioneers are dying off, and it is an open question who will succeed them.

America has many dreams. And the seventy-three-year-old Judge Leighton suggests that one of them, integration, might now be eroding the original purpose of Chatham. He wonders aloud whether blacks still need such a community. "Something has happened," he says. "The younger people are moving out. They're moving into places like Lake Point Tower, Outer Drive East, Lincoln Park. They are quietly disappearing into the integrated community. And I have no doubt that Chatham will pay a price. But I think it's good. When I was active in civil rights, we were talking about an integrated America. At least that's what I understood. I thought we were struggling for the very thing that to some extent is happening now. And I have a great deal of difficulty mustering any feeling of regret about this."

Sampson and others fear the price could be painfully high — and that Chatham could go the way of Woodlawn, the blighted South Side community from which many Chathamites migrated in the 1950s. Although homes sell quickly, turnover at this point is still very low. And there is no guarantee that the exodus of Chatham's young people will be balanced in the future by an influx of middle-class young adults now living in integrated areas who will find Chatham an attractive place to settle when they decide to raise families. Low-income young people already are moving into rental units in Chatham and surrounding areas, and Sampson worries that the community ultimately could lose its middle-class character.

"If these middle-class folks disappear," he says, "then you leave the black community at the mercy of the pimps and the hustlers and the nogoodniks. If Chatham goes, then to a considerable degree, the whole South Side goes. The people in Beverly had better watch out if Chatham can't survive."

Many observers share Sampson's concern. But others believe a new generation of young blacks, and whites, will build a new and better Chatham.

CHAPTER 12

Latino Chicago

JORGE CASUSO AND EDUARDO CAMACHO

We thought we would go back, but . . . we're not going back. I know that, and my husband knows that. Still, I only became a citizen five years ago, and my husband still is not a citizen.

— Teresa Fraga in Chicago, 1985

There is a perception of success, an element of jealousy toward Cubans, which is dangerous. We are discriminated against (by other Hispanics) in the same sense as the Jews.

— Marcelino Miyares, President of OMAR

The Hispanic "Myth"

By the year 2,000, one of every four Chicago residents will be Hispanic, demographers predict. There are Hispanic politicians and Hispanic voter registration drives; and Hispanic advertising firms have cropped up as companies scramble to cash in on a mushrooming Hispanic market.

But Hispanics are not, like blacks, a single race with a common past. "Hispanic" is an umbrella term encompassing Spanish-speaking people of different races and twenty separate nationalities. Hispanics come from as far as Uruguay, at the edge of South America, or as near as Texas, once a part of Mexico. Some have been here since the First World War, while others arrived only yesterday. They include highly skilled professionals, political refugees trying to regain what they have lost, and peasants who never had much to lose. They share a language and a culture. "Hispanics share common ideas, attitudes and

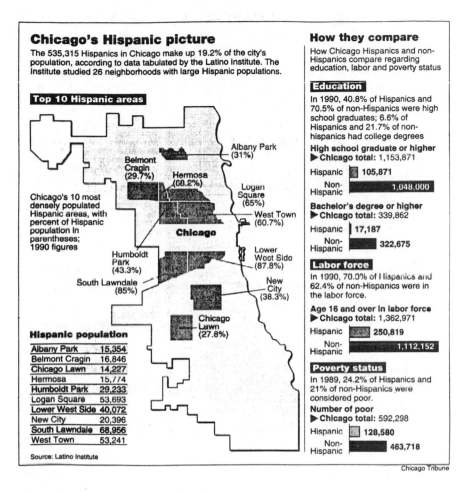

Chicago's Hispanic picture

The 535,315 Hispanics in Chicago make up 19.2% of the city's population, according to data tabulated by the Latino Institute. The Institute studied 26 neighborhoods with large Hispanic populations.

Top 10 Hispanic areas

Chicago's 10 most densely populated Hispanic areas, with percent of Hispanic population in parentheses; 1990 figures

Albany Park (31%)
Belmont Cragin (29.7%)
Hermosa (68.2%)
Logan Square (65%)
West Town (60.7%)
Chicago
Humboldt Park (43.3%)
Lower West Side (87.8%)
South Lawndale (85%)
New City (38.3%)
Chicago Lawn (27.8%)

Hispanic population

Albany Park	15,354
Belmont Cragin	16,846
Chicago Lawn	14,227
Hermosa	15,774
Humboldt Park	29,233
Logan Square	53,693
Lower West Side	40,072
New City	20,396
South Lawndale	68,956
West Town	53,241

Source: Latino Institute

How they compare

How Chicago Hispanics and non-Hispanics compare regarding education, labor and poverty status

Education

In 1990, 40.8% of Hispanics and 70.5% of non-Hispanics were high school graduates; 6.6% of Hispanics and 21.7% of non-hispanics had college degrees

High school graduate or higher
▶ Chicago total: 1,153,871

Hispanic 105,871
Non-Hispanic 1,048,000

Bachelor's degree or higher
▶ Chicago total: 339,862

Hispanic 17,187
Non-Hispanic 322,675

Labor force

In 1990, 70.0% of Hispanics and 62.4% of non-Hispanics were in the labor force.

Age 16 and over in labor force
▶ Chicago total: 1,362,971

Hispanic 250,819
Non-Hispanic 1,112,152

Poverty status

In 1989, 24.2% of Hispanics and 21% of non-Hispanics were considered poor.

Number of poor
▶ Chicago total: 592,298

Hispanic 128,580
Non-Hispanic 463,718

Chicago Tribune

values that come from Spain through our own countries," explains Rev. Daniel Alvarez, the Cuban-born director of Casa Central, the city's largest Hispanic social service agency. "We share a strong belief in God, the importance of the family, respect for the elderly and a special care for children. Then, there is also the 'machismo.'"

But Hispanics are separated by vast socio-economic differences, widely varying concerns, and strong prejudices. These stem from their birthplaces as well as why and when they came to the United States. Chicago is one of the few U.S. cities containing large populations of each of the major Hispanic groups. In 1990, Chicago was home to 352,000 Mexicans, 120,000 Puerto Ricans, 10,000 Cubans, and 63,000 other Hispanics.

The term "Hispanic" has been popularized in the local press. Community-based organizations no longer call themselves Puerto Rican or Mexican, but rather Hispanic or Latino. But the term implies a unity that does not exist. "An organization will call itself Hispanic when putting together a proposal. But it is Mexican or Puerto Rican when that proposal is implemented," says Samuel Betances, a Puerto Rican who is a professor of sociology at Northeastern Illinois University. "There is no such thing as the Hispanic community in that overall, arching, cosmic way," says Siobhan Oppenheimer-Nicolau, president of the Hispanic Policy Development Project, a national Hispanic research and policy group based in Washington, D.C. "You can't think that by dumping everybody into the same category you can expect them to act the same. It's just not going to work." In 1984 the market research firm of Yankelovich, Skelly and White published a survey indicating that 50 percent of Hispanics found "a great deal of difference or some important differences among Hispanic nationalities."

Special Concerns

As a result of its migration history, each Hispanic group holds deeply felt concerns and attitudes not shared by the others. For example, many Cubans share a strong anticommunist sentiment reflected in several organizations formed to oppose Cuban leader Fidel Castro. Cubans, therefore, are suspicious of communist influences in the community-based development efforts that are prevalent in Mexican and Puerto Rican areas. Many Mexicans, on the other hand, are concerned with immigration issues, which do not affect Puerto Ricans, because they are citizens, or Cubans, because they are political refugees. In a 1983 survey conducted for the Washington, D.C.-based Federation for American Immigration Reform, 58 percent of Hispanics polled believed that illegal immigrants take jobs away from Americans who want them, and 46 percent considered that to be a major problem.

The lack of understanding among groups is reflected in the negative stereotypes they impose on one another — the same kinds of stereotypes invoked by non-Hispanics. "My cousin can't find work because illegals are getting all the jobs," said a Puerto Rican factory worker when asked what he thought of Mexicans. In turn, a Cuban store owner who was asked about Puerto Ricans replied, "Almost all the Puerto Ricans who come in here use food stamps. They just don't want to work." Meanwhile, Cubans are viewed by others as arrogant and self-serving. "Cubans never get involved in helping the community. All they think about is how to help themselves," said a Puerto Rican community organizer.

Immigrants from Cuba and South America, because many are affluent, are dismissed by some Mexicans and Puerto Ricans as not really Hispanic. For example, when former Mayor Jane M. Byrne announced that she would name Hispanics to prominent city posts, the Hispanic community applauded. But when she appointed Dr. Hugo Muriel, a Bolivian, to head the city's Department of Health, and Luis Salces, a Cuban, to sit on the Chicago Board of Education, Puerto Rican and Mexican leaders argued that they did not truly represent the Hispanic community.

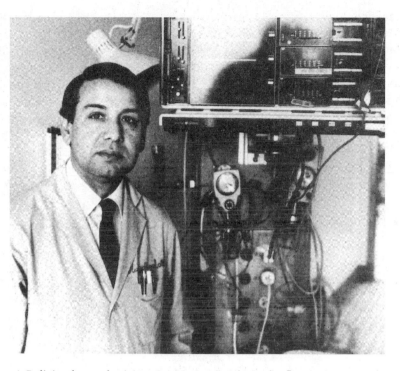

A Bolivian-born physician, Dr. Hugo Muriel was the first Latino named to a top city position when Mayor Jane Byrne appointed him Chicago Health Commissioner in 1979. Courtesy of Chicago Reporter.

Catching On

Hispanics were first officially acknowledged as a minority group by the federal government in 1969, when the Inter-agency Committee on Mexican-American Affairs was expanded to include, initially, Puerto Ricans and Cubans. When the 1970 census popularized the notion of Hispanic by creating a Spanish-speaking category, the media picked it up, and the concept caught on. In the Midwest, which for years had large Mexican and Puerto Rican populations, Latino became a common term in the 1970s, emerging naturally from the interaction of the different groups. Hispanic leaders have tried to make the term not only a label but also a force for community development.

In the early 1970s, for example, more than thirty Hispanic community groups from across the city formed the Spanish Coalition for Jobs, which successfully pressured City Hall and several large corporations to adopt affirmative hiring practices. More recently, thirteen Hispanic Chambers of Commerce, traditionally separated along ethnic lines, have joined together as the Federation of Hispanic Chambers of Commerce. They are currently lobbying big business for more contracts and jobs.

Mayor Martin Kennelly honors Toribio Tapia, president of the
Latin American Fraternal Society, November 16, 1947.
Courtesy of Calumet Industrial and Railroad Photographs.

In most successful organizing attempts, Hispanics have organized
around issues that are not exclusively of interest to them. In fact, apart from
language, there are few "Hispanic" issues. "There is policy for poor people,
policy for old people, policy for veterans. You don't need a Hispanic housing
policy, for example. You need a low-income housing policy that includes
Hispanics," says Opperheimer-Nicolau. "The question is, Are Hispanics invited to the policy table when the policy is being debated? Is there reasonable
access to the policy-making process?"

Hispanics in Chicago have organized naturalization drives and voter
registration projects to increase the number of Hispanics who sit at the table.
Before 1980, Cook County Commissioner Irene Hernandez, a Democratic
party loyalist, was the only Hispanic elected official in the city. Since then,
several Latino candidates have been elected to local office. But "we can never
reach the unanimity blacks have reached on identity and issues," said Ricardo
Tostado, Mexican-American researcher for the Chicago Department of
Economic Development.

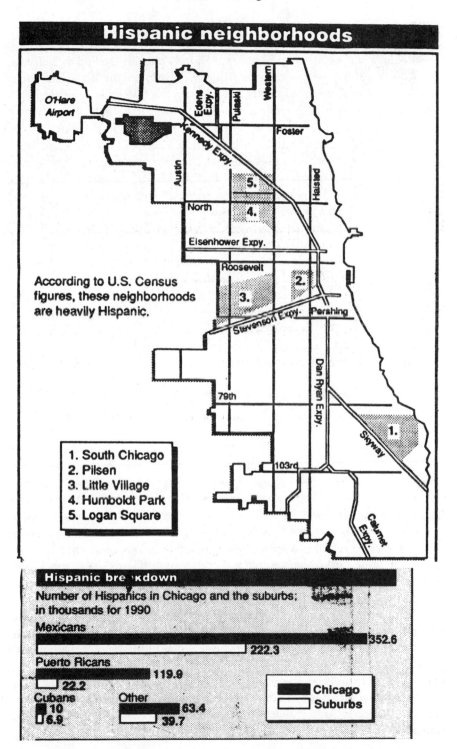

Hispanic neighborhoods

O'Hare
Airport

Edens Expy.

Pulaski

Western

Foster

Kennedy Expy.

Austin

5.

North

4.

Halsted

Eisenhower Expy.

Roosevelt

2.

According to U.S. Census
figures, these neighborhoods
are heavily Hispanic.

3.

Stevenson Expy.

Pershing

Dan Ryan Expy.

79th

1.

Skyway

1. South Chicago
2. Pilsen
3. Little Village
4. Humboldt Park
5. Logan Square

103rd

Calumet
Expy.

Hispanic breakdown

Number of Hispanics in Chicago and the suburbs;
in thousands for 1990

Mexicans

352.6

222.3

Puerto Ricans

119.9

22.2

Cubans   **Other**

10   63.4

6.9   39.7

■ Chicago
□ Suburbs

Worlds Apart

Statistically, Puerto Ricans and Mexicans share some compelling similarities: both groups are young, poor, and uneducated. And, for the first time, many are living in the same neighborhoods. During the last decade, as the city's population exploded and near South Side Mexican neighborhoods overflowed, more and more immigrants established enclaves in the North Side's heavily Puerto Rican communities. But young Puerto Ricans and Mexicans come from different backgrounds and move in different worlds. Many young Puerto Ricans were raised in Chicago and speak little Spanish. They have been absorbed into the American mainstream: they dance to pop music, watch American television, and keep up with the latest American fads. Puerto Rico is the homeland of their parents; Chicago is their home. In contrast, the young Mexican immigrants who have moved into the area are foreigners. They may be the same age as the Puerto Ricans, but they dress differently; they listen to Mexican music and watch Spanish-language television. Mexico is still their home.

"Even more important than the socio-economic rift is the rift between the foreign-born and those born and raised here. The first group is still trying to make up its mind whether to stay or return," declares Leo Estrada, a Mexican-American who is an assistant to the deputy director of the U.S. Census Bureau. As immigration from various countries continues, the differences that divide Hispanics are likely to remain intact, frustrating those who envision a united community.

Single Market

The only arena where Hispanics can be viewed as a group, experts contend, is the marketplace. According to the Yankelovich study, "Differences blurred when consumer behavior and media usage patterns were at issue." Jorge Caballero, who heads one of a half-dozen local Hispanic advertising firms, divides Hispanics not along national lines but according to similarities in attitude and lifestyle. "When you came (to the U.S.) and your socio-economic status will dictate where you live, what kind of car you drive, what clothes you wear. Hispanic factory workers want basically the same things, whether they're Puerto Rican or Mexican. The same is true of Hispanic professionals," says Caballero, a Peruvian whose firm lists the Commonwealth Edison Company among its major American accounts.

"I don't try to raise flags. Not that nationality isn't important, but you don't have to use it. You can't be too specific," he adds. Those national differences blurred temporarily in the marketplace will be blurred permanently among those Hispanics raised here, Hispanic leaders say.

The Mexicans

Seventy years ago, Justino Cordero came to Chicago from Mexico to work. A Mexican friend found him a job at U.S. Steel Corporation's South Works. Business was booming; day and night, smoke spewed from the tall stacks. "Those were good times. There were jobs, and the employers realized Mexicans were good workers," he said. The young Mexican community grew. "We built a church and a school, and organized parades and ball teams," recalled Cordero, who was eighty-one at the time of the interview. The steel mill area is a corroding ghost town today. Its smokestacks are still. Nearby, weeds poke from abandoned lots where bustling stores and taverns once stood. Yet new Mexican immigrants continue to come to South Chicago, attracted not by jobs but by the Mexican community that Cordero helped found.

For decades Mexicans have come to Chicago in the hope of escaping poverty in their homeland. Soaring unemployment, a sinking peso, and an uncontrollable population boom in Mexico City — seventeen million in 1984, up from five million in 1960 — are driving more and more Mexicans to escape by immigrating here. In 1910 there were about 1,000 Mexicans in the Chicago metropolitan area; the population leaped to 25,211 by 1930 and to 55,597 by 1960. The 1980 U.S. Census counted 368,981 Mexicans in Chicago and its suburbs, and by 1990 they had grown to 547,847. Mexicans are Chicago's largest Hispanic group, making up almost two-thirds of the metropolitan area's Hispanic population. As a result, statistics that describe Hispanics as a whole are often more reflective of Mexicans than any other group.

Mexicans differ significantly from Puerto Ricans and Cubans, the next largest Hispanic groups here. Unlike Puerto Ricans, Mexicans are not U.S. citizens by birth; many, in fact, are in this country illegally. And unlike Cubans, Mexicans are free to return to their homeland at will.

Uneducated Poor

The census shows:

- Mexicans are youthful: their median age in Cook County was twenty-two in 1980; about one-third were under fifteen years old. Mexicans are the least educated of the major Hispanic groups in the county: nearly half of those over eighteen years old had no more than an eighth grade education in 1980, and only 32.1 percent had completed high school. Mexicans are concentrated in lower-skilled occupations: 47 percent of Mexican workers held jobs as operators, fabricators, and laborers; only 6.4 percent of employed Mexicans held managerial and professional positions.

- Mexican per capita income was $4,735 in 1979 — slightly higher than that of Puerto Ricans, but much lower than that of Cubans. White per capita income was $9,700. On the other hand, relatively few Mexicans receive public assistance. In 1980, 9.9 percent of Mexican households reported they received public aid, compared with 27.3 percent of Puerto Ricans and 14.1 percent of Cubans. "Mexicans come from a society with no welfare. You have to hustle, period. You don't come expecting to get anything because you don't get it in your country," says Carlos Heredia, director of Por Un Barrio Mejor, a community organization in the predominantly Mexican Little Village neighborhood on the near South Side. Low income, poor education, and youthfulness are most characteristic of newer members of the Mexican community. They differ markedly from earlier immigrants like Justino Cordero who found a very different city when they came.

The earlier immigrants to Chicago found jobs in heavy industry. They made good money and entered the economic mainstream. Many have moved to the suburbs. Their children and grandchildren speak little or no Spanish. But as Chicago's more lucrative blue-collar jobs faded, they were replaced by lower-paying service and light manufacturing jobs. Many of the newer immigrants who have taken these jobs live in isolated barrios where they find comfort in their numbers. They have not assimilated, as earlier immigrants did, but cling to their native culture. "Socially, the transition for new immigrants is easier than for those who came in the twenties. You can live your whole life without speaking English. But economically it is tougher," says Ricardo Tostado, co-editor of a 1983 report on Hispanics prepared at the University of Chicago.

The contrasting experiences of the earliest immigrants, their children, and later immigrants make Mexicans the most diverse Hispanic group in Chicago. "Within the Mexican community, there are whole cliques who don't understand each other. There are big generation gaps, historical gaps, divisions depending on where you came from in Mexico or where you live here," says Ramiro Borja, a community activist in Pilsen, a predominantly Mexican community bordering Little Village on the near South Side. "You can no longer ask, 'What does the Mexican community say about [an issue]?' You have to ask, 'What do third generation Mexicans living in the suburbs, for example, say?'" says Manuel Gallvan, a Chicago-born Mexican-American reporter for the *Chicago Tribune*.

Population Boom

Mexicans are found throughout the Chicago area. Outside the city, their population skyrocketed from 113,179 in 1980 to 222,560 in 1990. The largest enclaves outside Chicago in 1980 were in Aurora, with more than 10,000 Mexicans, and

Mexican Americans in a Spanish-speaking meeting of the United Packing House Workers Union.　Courtesy of Chicago Historical Society.

in Joliet and Waukegan, with more than 5,000 each. The industry in those cities has long attracted Mexicans. The northwest suburb of Elk Grove Village, the western suburbs of Cicero and Melrose Park, and the south suburbs of Blue Island and Chicago Heights each had more than 2,000 Mexican residents.

"Everybody in the Mexican community wants to move to the suburbs. The minute he can jump the fence, he does," says Eusebio Arce, owner of Tropical Optical Corporation and president of the Little Village Chamber of Commerce. Arce, whose five stores are located in Chicago, moved south to suburban Bridgeview in 1968. But most Mexicans still live in the city. The largest Mexican populations are in the South Lawndale community area known as Little Village, with 69,000 Mexican residents in 1990, and the lower West Side community known as Pilsen, with 40,000. Between 1970 and 1990, the Mexican population in the near North Side community areas of West Town, Humboldt Park, and Logan Square also increased, although these areas tend to be heavily Puerto Rican. New enclaves also appeared on the far North Side.

Mexicans began coming to the city in the first quarter of this century. Fleeing the aftermath of a revolution at home, they were drawn to Chicago,

Mexican Americans learning English in adult education classes during the early
forties.   Courtesy of Chicago Historical Society.

then the nation's industrial hub. They first settled near the railyards of satellite
cities and the near South Side. Soon they were lured by better-paying jobs in
the meatpacking houses of "Back of the Yards" and the steel mills of South
Chicago. Those were predominantly white ethnic communities, and the immigrants were not welcome; so they formed tight-knit enclaves, with their own
organizations, newspapers, and festive events.

The most important institution was the Catholic Church. The great majority of Mexicans are Roman Catholics. But the immigrants were not welcomed
into existing Catholic parishes, so they formed their own congregations. The
church became a rallying point for the community. "The Church was seen as a
continuation of their lifestyle, not only religiously but culturally. It was a social
gathering place as well as a place to get help finding jobs," said Rev. Tomas
Paramo of Our Lady of Guadalupe Church in south Chicago. Built in 1928, it
is the oldest Mexican church in the city. The church remains a social and political
center for Mexicans. At least ten Catholic churches in Chicago have large Mexican congregations. Several of these form the core of the United Neighborhood
Organization (UNO), the only citywide Hispanic grassroots organizing effort.

After the Depression, heavy industry boomed and the Mexican community prospered. There was a second generation now, reared on the patriotism

In Chicago's Southwest Side Pilsen neighborhood, Mexican Americans have for years annually re-enacted the crucifixion of Christ in Good Friday processions similar to those in Mexican villages.   Courtesy of Chicago Reporter.

of the war years. It included union members, war veterans, loyal Democrats. By 1950, Mexicans in the city were earning as much as Italians and Poles were. The system had worked for them. "I've always considered myself an American. I was born and raised here. I fought in Korea. This is my country," says Lupe Valadez, former financial secretary of United Steelworkers of America Local 65. Valadez, fifty-one, was born in South Chicago. His father, who came from Mexico in the early 1920s, worked in the steel mills for forty years. Valadez worked there for thirty-three years, until his machine shop shut down in 1984. He has watched as the Mexican community his father helped to build slowly fades. He can afford to leave South Chicago, but he won't. All his past is there. "You look and see no smoke coming out of those stacks. I tell you, it makes you want to cry," says Valadez, whose two sons live in the suburbs and speak no Spanish.

While they are no longer major ports of entry for Mexican immigrants, South Chicago and Back of the Yards remain among the largest Mexican communities. In 1980, Back of the Yards, in the New City community area, had 17,234 Mexican residents and South Chicago had 15,960. The largest Mexican population increase in the past two decades occurred in the Pilsen-Little Village area, bordered by 17th Street on the north, the city's boundary on the west, and the southern branch of the Chicago River on the south and east. There the Mexican population exploded from 6,972 in 1960 to 83,385 in 1980 to about 109,000 in 1990. In the lively streets, taco stands and bodegas have sprung up, and street vendors roll their carts beneath Spanish-language store signs and colorful murals. The neighborhood draws visitors from across the city with its quaint south-of-the-border flavor. But behind the spicy facade lie pressing problems. Pilsen-Little Village is one of the most overcrowded areas in the city; its aged housing is decaying. Nearly one-fourth of the area's occupied housing units were overcrowded in 1980, compared with less than one-tenth of housing citywide.

The area's schools, also packed beyond capacity, are cultivating a generation of frustrated youth, many of whom drop out and join street gangs. Some 49.4 percent of the 467 Hispanic students in the class of 1982 at Benito Juarez High School, a predominantly Mexican school in Pilsen, dropped out, according to a study by the Chicago Panel on Public School Finances. Also, between 1978 and 1981, there were thirty-five gang-related homicides in Pilsen-Little Village, according to Chicago Police Department records analyzed in a 1983 study by Irving Spergel, professor of social work at the University of Chicago.

Port of Entry

When Teresa Fraga came to Chicago in 1966, Pilsen had become the leading port of entry for Mexican immigrants. Fraga, her husband, and two children had followed the harvests, taking the northbound path of earlier migrant workers who came from Mexico to fill a labor demand during World War II. For Fraga, Chicago was the name stamped boldly on the shipping crates she had filled for years. "Here we could find work that would last more than a month," she said. Her husband landed a construction job and Fraga had her third child. It was the era of civil rights, and community activism burgeoned. Fraga, appalled by the overcrowded, dilapidated condition of the school her son was attending, joined others to press the Chicago Board of Education to build Juarez High School, which opened in 1977 and offers bilingual instruction. "You can say, 'That's the way it is,' and cry about it. Or you can change it. I felt I could be a part of that change," says Fraga, forty-two, a member of the board of the Pilsen Neighbors Community Council.

The construction of Juarez temporarily alleviated school overcrowding. But facilities are not being built fast enough to keep up with the boom in the city's Mexican population, says Raul Villalobos, member and former president of the school board. The fight for Juarez planted the seeds for the city's first Hispanic independent political movement, which has already developed its own local heroes.

Mexican voters, traditionally regular Democratic organization stalwarts, elected Juan Soliz in 1984 as state representative of the 20th legislative district, which encompasses Pilsen-Little Village. Soliz had run an emotionally charged but unsuccessful campaign for that seat in 1982. Another independent, Jesus Garcia, was elected Democratic committeeman of the 22nd Ward in Little Village. Garcia was swept into office during a wave of sympathy following the murder of community activist Rudy Lozano, who had run an unsuccessful campaign for alderman of the ward in 1983. Lozano soon became a martyr for the local independent political movement.

The activism reflects the growing commitment of Mexican immigrants to a city long viewed by many as a temporary home. Fraga, like others, dreamed of returning to Mexico or the Southwest. For years she and her family went to Texas each winter, where they were building a house. They ended the trips when their oldest son entered high school. "We had invested money and time in our home in Texas. We thought we would go back, but it was empty for eleven years, just waiting for us. We're not going back. I know that, and my husband knows that. Still, I only became a citizen five years ago, and my husband still is not a citizen," Fraga says. Only 10.1 percent of Mexicans in Cook County were naturalized citizens in 1980; 37.7 percent were not U.S. citizens; the remainder were born in this country.

Border Life

While Fraga and other legal Mexican residents put down roots in Chicago, thousands of illegal immigrants live marginal lives. In 1981 the U.S. Immigration and Naturalization Service apprehended 7,591 undocumented Mexicans in the Chicago area. Estimates by the agency place the number of Mexicans here illegally at about 200,000 in 1984. Illegal immigrants represent the Mexican stereotype held by many. They live quietly, day to day, keeping mostly to themselves in an effort to avoid discovery and deportation. "Most of the Mexicans who come (now) are young, strong people who can work hard. Many of them are men who leave their families behind. They are running away from their country out of necessity. They are desperate and will work jobs nobody wants," says Olivia Barrera, former director of the Midwest Coalition in Defense of Immigrants. Carlos (not his real name) came to Chicago from Mexico in 1979, when he was nineteen years old. He came to work and to satisfy his curiosity. Chicago, he had been told by friends, was a good place to make money and start a new life. And there were many Mexicans there. Carlos saved the money he made working in a warehouse in his hometown of Tuxpan in southern Mexico and paid a "coyote" $750 to usher him across the border. He and forty others crossed the Rio Grande River in a small boat while the border patrol changed shifts. "Anyone who can afford it comes. Only the poorest stay behind with the women and children and the old men," he explained. Carlos got a job washing dishes in a North Side restaurant. Now the cook there, he earns $175 per week. He says he would make $10 for the same work back home.

But his illegal status takes its toll. "If you are here illegally," Carlos says, "you have to be more careful, you have to deprive yourself of many things. At first, I didn't go out much, occasionally to a movie. Now I go out often, but always by myself. It's harder to get into trouble that way. But it is lonely." Carlos lives in an Uptown apartment he shares with two Mexicans he met here. When he gets a vacation, he plans to bring his wife and son back from Mexico. To help stem the flow of illegal immigrants, the Simpson-Mazzolli law penalizes employers who knowingly hire undocumented workers. It also offers an amnesty plan for many of those who are here illegally.

But the stream of immigrants swells the barrios. Some older immigrants contend that the more Mexicans the barrios contain, the harder it will be for those who live in them to become a part of the American mainstream. "When I came from Mexico, I went to school at night to learn the language," says businessman Arce, who immigrated in 1948, when he was twenty-two. "But the people who come from Mexico now think they can make everybody speak Spanish. I don't believe in discrimination. If you're good people, you get along with good people. If you're honest, you try to live like a good American. You have to learn to live the American way."

The Puerto Ricans

When Puerto Ricans came to Chicago, they were like most immigrants. They spoke a foreign language, they settled in isolated inner-city enclaves, and they maintained the culture of their homeland. But Puerto Ricans are not immigrants. They are American citizens: their homeland is a territory of the United States. As a result, Puerto Ricans can vote, receive public assistance, and move freely to and from the island. Still, their status has been a mixed blessing. As citizens, Puerto Ricans expect more than immigrants do. But after more than three decades here, the Puerto Rican community has made little socio-economic progress.

Puerto Ricans are the poorest Hispanic group in the country. In fact, they are the poorest of all major racial and ethnic groups in Chicago. The census shows:

- Puerto Rican per capita income in 1979 was only $4,101. About one-third of Puerto Rican families had incomes below the poverty level; 27 percent of Puerto Rican households said they received public assistance, compared with 14.4 percent of all Hispanic households. Like most Hispanics, Puerto Ricans are youthful: their median age was twenty-one in 1980, and 59 percent were under the age of twenty-five. Some 37.7 percent of Puerto

Rican adults had no more than an eighth-grade education, and 64.5 percent had not completed high school. Forty-two percent of Puerto Rican workers were employed as operators, fabricators, and laborers, and 8.6 percent held managerial and professional positions.

Barrio Life

There were 126,700 Puerto Ricans in Chicago and its suburbs in 1980, making them the second largest Hispanic group after Mexicans. Most of them (112,074) lived in Chicago. By 1990, Chicago's Puerto Rican population has grown only to 119,800, and in the metropolitan area to 142,000. They experienced a much slower growth rate than did Mexicans. Puerto Ricans are concentrated in three adjoining near Northwest Side community areas — West Town, Humboldt Park, and Logan Square — where the Puerto Rican population skyrocketed from 8,780 in 1960 to 70,030 in 1980. That was the rapid growth period; the 1990 census shows a slower increase.

In the 1970s more than 100,000 white residents left those neighborhoods. The business strip along West Division Street in West Town now is almost deserted. Abandoned storefronts are gutted or leveled to rubble; many streets in the area are no longer safe to walk. "Puerto Ricans, like others, would like to get out of the barrio. They are constantly looking for improvement. Their dream is to find a better place, to purchase their own home. But for the majority, their financial reality holds them back," says Rev. Daniel Alvarez of Casa Central, a social service agency in the West Town area. Although 40 percent of all Mexicans lived in the suburbs, only about 15 percent of the 142,000 Puerto Ricans in the six-county metropolitan area lived outside the city in 1990; and most of these lived in satellite cities, where they were drawn by manufacturing jobs. Waukegan, Aurora, and Elgin each had more than 1,400 Puerto Ricans. Few Puerto Ricans resided in middle-class suburbs.

Like Mexicans, Puerto Ricans came to Chicago in search of opportunity. They too were unskilled farmers and laborers escaping poverty in their home-land. But Mexican immigrants who came in the 1920s found steady, well-paying industrial jobs. By the time Puerto Ricans came in the 1950s and 1960s, those jobs had become increasingly scarce. As a result, many Puerto Ricans took dead-end menial and light manufacturing jobs. "The jobs that allowed other groups to make it were not here for Puerto Ricans. As society continued to make technological advances, Puerto Ricans were not a part of that order. They remained on the periphery," says Felix Padilla, sociology professor at Northern Illinois University, who came here with his parents from the island in 1959.

Although they are American citizens by birth, Puerto Ricans are viewed by many as foreigners. "The Puerto Rican is not accepted by the Anglo. Nor are we accepted entirely by other Latin Americans. We are up in the air, and that has led to frustration," says Jose Salgado, director of the Chicago regional office of the Commonwealth of Puerto Rico. Adding to their difficulties is the constant movement to and from the island, which has kept many immigrants uprooted. A survey published in 1971 by the University of Chicago polled Puerto Ricans in West Town. It found that 60.7 percent of those who had been here more than ten years planned to return to the island; of those here less than five years, 87.5 percent planned to return. "Since Puerto Ricans have the doors wide open, they are always thinking of going back. They decided to make a little money and return when things got better on the island. But they never do, so they are left in limbo. They are neither here nor there," says Daniel Ramos, owner of Ramos Movers and a member of the Mayor's Advisory Commission on Latino Affairs. Ramos came here from Puerto Rico in 1952.

The children of the migrants are raised on the mainland and speak fluent English. But poverty, inadequate support for education at home, and a negative self-image have led to alarming school dropout rates and widespread street-gang activity. For example, 55.7 percent of the 855 Hispanic members of the class of 1982 at Roberto Clemente High School dropped out, according to a study by the Chicago Panel on Public School Finances. Clemente is a predominantly Puerto Rican public school in West Town.

Yet second-generation Puerto Ricans have higher expectations than their parents did. They are unwilling to take the jobs filled by the first generation. "Many Puerto Rican kids come out of school and can't find the work they expect, so they don't work. That's where the anxiety comes in. It comes from not being able to go beyond your parents," says Estrella Tudela, a Puerto Rican community activist who came from the island in 1956. The regional office of the Commonwealth of Puerto Rico estimates that almost one out of four working-age Puerto Ricans in Chicago is unemployed. This includes those not actively seeking employment.

Violent demonstrations have expressed the pent-up frustration of many in the Puerto Rican community. Puerto Ricans are the only Hispanic group in Chicago that has rioted — they have done so twice. And a series of bombings by the Fuerzas Armadas para la Liberacion Nacional (Armed Forces for National Liberation) has rocked government buildings in the Chicago area. Better known as the FALN, the small extremist group, many of whose members grew up in Chicago, ties the plight of Puerto Ricans here to the political status of the island.

Steady Work

The influx of Puerto Ricans to Chicago began after World War II and continued for two decades. During that period the population of the island soared, and the growing work force, much of it rural, could not be absorbed by the underdeveloped economy. "The first Puerto Rican migrants were simple country people. They still

The large waves of Puerto Rican and some Cuban immigrants often came by airline,
unlike the early immigrants at the turn of the century who came by boat.
Courtesy of Chicago Reporter.

held on to their traditional values. They were committed to their work and to their families," says sociologist Samuel Betances, who came to the mainland in 1948.

Like most of the early arrivals, Angelo Otero was young and poorly educated when he left the island in 1956. The son of a farmer from the small town of Vega Baja on the northern coast of the island, Otero was looking for a way out when he heard a radio ad for migrant workers on the mainland. The United States employer would pay for the trip, so Otero boarded the plane. "I would have cultivated tobacco my whole life if I had stayed. But I wanted something better. I was willing to try my hand at anything," he recalls. After the harvest season in a migrant camp in Glassboro, New Jersey, Otero joined his sister in New York, where he landed a job in a Brooklyn factory. In the crowded barrios of New York City the competition was stiff. When a cousin told him about the job opportunities in Chicago, Otero decided to move.

Chicago's Puerto Rican community, second in size to New York's, was growing rapidly. Lured here by the promise of steady work, Puerto Ricans found jobs in Loop restaurants and hotels and on assembly lines in factories across the city. In 1960 there were 32,371 Puerto Ricans in Chicago. Otero found work in a lumberyard and moved to the South Side Englewood community. "I came to make money and return. Then I got married and had kids, and I ended up staying. But I still sometimes think of returning. Most of my friends are back in Puerto Rico," he says. Otero has worked in lumberyards for twenty-seven years. Now a widower, he owns a home in Logan Square and has four grown children.

In the early 1950s, Puerto Ricans, most of whom are Roman Catholic, formed social and religious groups in several parishes. The most prominent was Los Cabelleros de San Juan, founded in 1955. Non-English-speaking Puerto Rican migrants were frequent victims of consumer fraud and also had trouble obtaining credit. In 1957, Los Cabelleros established a credit union, and by 1984 it had loaned Hispanics more than $25 million. "We were a group of simple men with little academic preparation. But we were committed to doing something for each other. We had many problems, and we saw the need for unity," says Cesar Rivera, a businessman who served as credit union president from 1959 to 1961.

As the Puerto Rican population increased dramatically, so did its problems. In 1970 there were 79,582 Puerto Ricans in the city. "By the late 1960s, it was starting to become difficult to find work of any kind. More and more families went on welfare. The men felt demoralized, their initiative broken. It became a vicious cycle," says Daniel Ramos. "There was widespread discrimination against Puerto Ricans," declares Alfredo Torres de Jesus, veteran Puerto Rican journalist and the former editor of La Raza, a Chicago weekly Spanish-language newspaper. "Puerto Ricans were underpaid and lived in dilapidated tenements. Those who tried to move to white ethnic communities were harassed," he alleges. There were also charges of police brutality.

Many Puerto Ricans are black or mulatto, which makes them more vulnerable to racial discrimination than members of other Hispanic groups. "By the mid-1960s, there was a lot of anger and frustration, but there was not community awareness. There was no sharing of the pain," says Mirta Ramirez, founder of the Chicago branch of ASPIRA, a national Puerto Rican educational service and advocacy group for youth.

During the summer of 1966 the frustration was violently released in a series of riots on Division Street in West Town. The riots were triggered by the police shooting of a Puerto Rican youth after the annual Puerto Rican parade, when ethnic pride was high. There were two successive nights of violence and looting. Shop windows were broken and police cars torched and overturned. More than 100 persons were arrested. "The riots were like a revolution that exposed all the grievances. A political awareness emerged on the part of both Hispanics and Anglos. The government began to pay more attention to services," says Torres de Jesus.

Getting Out

During the 1970s the mainland economy was in a recession, and many Puerto Ricans began to migrate back to the island, where the standard of living had improved. But the local population, with its high birth rate, continued to grow.

In 1980, there were 112,074 Puerto Ricans in the city, a 40.8 percent increase over 1970; but the 1990 figures showed a much smaller increase — to only 119,800.

It is the young Puerto Rican who represents the popularly held stereotype: a frustrated youth leading an often violent, dead-end existence. For years Angel "Figgy" Figueroa, twenty-four, lived the stereotype. "At first you join the gangs because you like the colors. Then you see the guy's house next door get blown up, or the baddest guy get his brains blown out, and it's not a game anymore. You stay in to save your ass," observes Figueroa, who joined his first gang when he was thirteen years old.

Between 1978 and 1981, there were seventy-three gang-related homicides in West Town, Humboldt Park, and Logan Square, according to the 1983 study by Irving Spergel. Together, those areas had the highest concentration of gang killings in the city. There is a theory that gang violence is perpetrated by those with high aspirations but insufficient means to carry them out. When the gap gets too great between the reality and aspirations, they look for a way to succeed. "These are usually kids raised in Chicago who don't get out of the area. They fear leaving the community, and gangs become their way to succeed," Spergel says.

For Figueroa, music was the way out of the barrio. As a child he had always banged on pots and pans around the house. When he turned twelve, his family bought him a set of bongos. "The music saved me," declares Figueroa, who for eight years played with "La Tipica '78," a local Salsa band. Figueroa has played on three record albums and is the director of the Percussion Artists Workshop, which offers percussion training to neighborhood residents. He is also completing training as an air traffic controller.

It was gang violence that set off the second Puerto Rican riots, about a mile west of the first, during the summer of 1977. Two policemen, allegedly trying to quell an outburst of gang activity after that year's Puerto Rican parade, shot and killed two Puerto Rican youths. Two days of violence ensued, with more than 100 arrests. A decade after the first riots, the same grievances were being aired. "There was a serious lack of communication between the community and the city. Puerto Ricans had no political representation. Our complaints had gone unanswered," says Torres de Jesus.

No Puerto Rican held local elective office until 1981, when Mayor Jane M. Byrne appointed Jose Martinez alderman of the 31st Ward, which encompasses West Town and Humboldt Park. In 1982, Joseph Berrios was elected state representative of the 9th District, made up of West Town, Humboldt Park, and Logan Square. He was re-elected in 1984, one year after Miguel Santiago was elected 31st Ward alderman, replacing Martinez. Berrios and Santiago are Democratic party loyalists who ran unopposed. Several others have been elected since.

Following the election of Mayor Harold Washington in April, 1983, three

Shown here is the annual observance of Puerto Rican week in Humboldt Park on Chicago's Northwest Side. Courtesy of Chicago Reporter.

Puerto Ricans were named to high-ranking city positions: Benjamin Reyes, assistant to the mayor; Maria Cerda, director of the Department of Employment and Training; and Miguel de Valle, one-time chairman of the Mayor's Advisory Commission on Latino Affairs. "For years, we had a lack of understanding of the system. But we are organizing a constituency, and because of this the powers that be are beginning to make some concessions," said de Valle, who was then executive director of Association House, one of the city's major Hispanic-oriented social service agencies.

Social service agencies began to emerge in the Puerto Rican community after the 1966 riots, as many of the older social clubs gave way. There are now about twenty-five agencies. Most are small and operate on shoestring budgets. Rosario (not her real name) was one of those who have been helped by the agencies. Once she dreamed of graduating from high school and becoming a nurse. But in eleventh grade she became pregnant and was expelled from public school. "The baby shattered everything," says Rosario, now thirty. Her parents had been poor farmers in Puerto Rico; they spoke no English and ran a strict, old-fashioned household. "They didn't understand me," complains Rosario, who came to the mainland with her family in 1958, when she was four years old.

Rosario married, but soon was divorced. She and her daughter joined the

31.2 percent of Puerto Rican families headed by single women. That compares with 19.1 percent of all Hispanic families. With no money for day care, Rosario was forced to stay at home and ended up on public aid. She applied for numerous jobs but was constantly rejected. For a time she worked on an assembly line and at an insurance company, but quit those jobs because they didn't compensate her enough for the day care and other costs. "I felt shattered, and the longer I stayed on public aid, the harder it was to get out of it," she says. "The motivation leaves you. After a while, you start feeling like a vegetable, like you're not thinking anymore. You get up, do housework, and then — nothing. But you're afraid to move out of that shelter. You don't know what to expect on the other side. It's not that you don't want to get out, it's that you're afraid to be turned down again and again."

Two years ago, after applying to a number of training programs at social service agencies, Rosario was accepted at Casa Central in a nurse's aid program for single mothers on public aid. "Someone from Casa Central actually came out to talk to me. It was the first time I had an answer," she says. After finishing the program, Rosario hoped to earn a high school equivalency diploma and look for work. Meanwhile, she was raising her twelve-year-old daughter. "I'm involving myself more with my daughter than my parents ever did with me. It's not that they were bad parents, but they just didn't communicate. I'm trying to fill the gap that was between us with my daughter," says Rosario. "Now I'm finally looking forward to something."

Rosario and other second-generation Puerto Ricans, unlike their parents, view Chicago as their home. But many are poor, uneducated, and victimized by discrimination. They lag far behind the changing demands of the economy. Some strides have been made. Puerto Ricans have taken the first steps toward political representation, and a new leadership is emerging. But the gap between Puerto Ricans and the rest of society remains large.

The Cubans

When Alberto Palomares came to Chicago from Cuba in 1960, he didn't expect to stay. He had fled Fidel Castro's year-old revolution, which had just confiscated the bank he managed. As soon as Castro was overthrown, he would return. "It was just a trip, a little vacation. I even drew up a shopping list of things to take back: some utensils, a white terrier, some Christmas lights," Palomares recalled. The following year the U.S.-backed Bay of Pigs invasion failed. "The revolution will last," Palomares thought. He got a job. Twenty-four years later, he still kept the shopping list as a memento. Penned on top are the words, "Return to Cuba."

Cubans are political refugees. That distinguishes them from other Hispanics here, many of whom fled poverty in their homelands in search of the American dream — a job, a home, an education. In contrast, many Cubans left that dream, unfulfilled, behind. They are bitter toward a revolution they say took everything they had, even their country. They are zealous anticommunists and staunch defenders of free enterprise. Unlike other Hispanics, they often vote Republican.

Cubans survived by their wits when they came. The early arrivals — many of them entrepreneurs and professionals — brought only their industriousness and a keen business savvy. To start from scratch in a strange country, to piece their lives together again, they had to rely on self-assurance, which was often interpreted as arrogance by other Hispanics. "There is a perception of success, an element of jealousy toward Cubans, which is a danger. We are discriminated against (by other Hispanics) in the same sense as the Jews," says Marcelino Miyares, founder and president of OMAR, Inc., a Hispanic-oriented advertising agency. OMAR had sales of $3.5 million in 1983. Miyares fought in the Bay of Pigs incursion and was subsequently jailed in Cuba. He is also president of WBBS-TV (Channel 60), a Hispanic-owned television station in Chicago.

"Cubans are more flexible than other Hispanic groups," says Jose Llanes, a sociology professor at California State University and author of a study of Cuban-Americans. "For the most part, we can pass for white and are able to fit in with the majority. Cultural biases exist, but Cubans seem willing to ignore the apparent prejudices."

Success Story

Socio-economically, Cubans are the most successful Hispanic group in Cook County, where 84.4 percent of Cubans in Illinois live. The census shows:

- Per capita income for Cubans was $8,169 in 1979, by far the highest of any Hispanic group; 71 percent of Cuban families earned $15,000 or more; 17 percent of employed Cubans worked as managers and professionals, almost twice the percentage of all Hispanic workers. Fifty-seven percent of Cuban adults had completed at least four years of high school, and 15.9 percent at least four years of college, compared with 37.2 percent and 4.9 percent, respectively, for all Hispanics. Forty-five percent of Cubans owned their own homes, compared with 35.8 percent for all Hispanics.

Cubans are more successful than other Hispanics, observers say, in part because they are older, have been here longer, and realize that there is no going back. Cuban households are also smaller, pushing Cuban per capita income higher, according to 1980 figures. With a median age of thirty-four, Cubans are significantly older than Hispanics as a whole, whose median age is twenty-two. In fact, 11.8 percent of all Cubans are at least sixty years old, compared with four percent of all Hispanics. About 70 percent of Cuban immigrants in Cook County came to the U.S. before 1970, compared with 38.1 percent of all His-

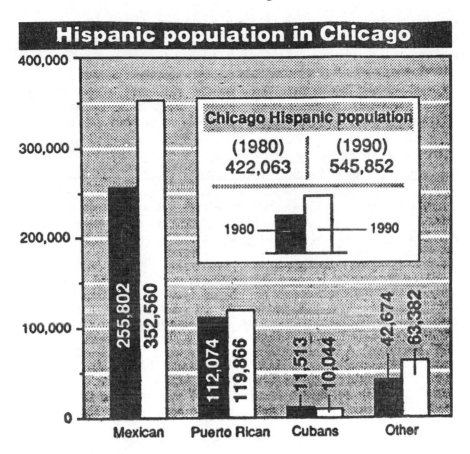

Hispanic population in Chicago

Chicago Hispanic population

(1980)	(1990)
422,063	545,852

1980 — 1990

	Mexican	Puerto Rican	Cubans	Other
1980	255,802	112,074	11,513	42,674
1990	352,560	119,866	10,044	63,382

panic immigrants. "Other groups have always had a foot here and another in their homeland because they knew they could return. But for the Cuban, all hope of returning was gone, so they established themselves here," says Rev. Samuel Acosta, Colombian-born pastor of the First Spanish United Church of Christ, which has a large Cuban congregation.

For most Cubans, it took years for the dream of returning to wane. It took building a new career, buying a house, becoming grandparents. They still yearn to regain their homeland; but even if the Castro government were overthrown, few say they would return. "There's no backing up. When you first come, you think about returning, but with the years you come to the conclusion that you will die here," commented Jesus Diaz, a grocery store owner in the Logan Square neighborhood, who came here from Cuba in 1969.

The six-county Chicago area had 17,780 Cubans in 1980; there were 15,961 in Cook County, 11,513 of them in Chicago. Cubans made up only 3.2 percent of the total Hispanic population in Cook County. The overall number of Hispanics jumped by 74 percent from 1970 to 1980, but the Cuban population dropped by 9 percent as immigration slacked off and many Cubans moved to Miami, which has the nation's largest Cuban population. By 1990, the Chicago-area Cuban population had declined by a few hundred to 16,900.

While Mexicans and Puerto Ricans have staked out neighborhoods in Chicago, Cubans are dispersed throughout the North Side and neighboring suburbs. The typical Cuban lives in a block with a population that is two-thirds white, while Mexicans and Puerto Ricans live on blocks that are one-third white, according to a study produced at the University of Chicago. "The assimilation process was extremely fast. [Cubans] wanted to live among Americans. They had a tremendous desire to regain what they had lost and to be accepted," says Rev. Daniel Alvarez, executive director of Casa Central, who came from the island in 1960.

The largest Cuban enclaves in 1980 were in Logan Square, on the near Northwest Side, with 1,590 Cuban residents, and Edgewater, along the lakefront on the north side, with 1,441. In both neighborhoods, Cubans made up less than 3 percent of the total population. Cubans have migrated to the suburbs more rapidly than have Hispanics as a whole. By 1980, 35.2 percent of Cubans in the metropolitan area lived in the suburbs, compared with 27.3 percent of all Hispanics. West suburban Melrose Park and Stone Park and north suburban Skokie had the most Cubans, with more than 400 each. The 1990 census showed the same pattern, with about forty percent of the Cubans in suburbia.

"Guilt Wave"

Between 1959, when Castro's revolution toppled the United States-backed Cuban government, and 1973, when Castro halted emigration from Cuba, an estimated 20,000 refugees arrived in the Chicago area, according to Catholic Charities of Chicago, which helped to relocate most of them.

Fleeing a communist country, they were welcomed openly by the United States government, which provided generous public aid. "Cubans came on a guilt wave; they were viewed as victims. They fit in well with the prevailing anti-communist sentiment," declares Armando Triana, a business management professor at DePaul University who fled Cuba with his parents in 1960. The Trianas were among the first wave of refugees — predominantly white-skinned and middle-class — who came between the 1959 coup and the early 1960s. Many were men at the peak of their earning powers who became entrepreneurs here, taking advantage of the large established Hispanic market. Not surprisingly, many pulled themselves back up in dramatic fashion. "This country was already discovering the Hispanic when the Cubans came. Qualified Hispanics were needed and Cubans fit the bill. The other groups resented that Cubans came last and jumped ahead," says Isidro Lucas,

Pictured here is Cuban immigrant Roberto Perez, who fled Castro's communism and like many of his fellow refugees achieved business or professional success in Chicago. In the 1980s Perez was a regional manager of a large food distribution firm.
Courtesy of Chicago Reporter.

Spanish-born Midwest deputy director of the United States Commission on Civil Rights.

Cubans controlled some of the city's major Hispanic resources. In addition to Miyares' WBBS-TV and Casa Central, run by Alvarez, there was the Federation of Hispanic Chambers of Commerce, whose president was Roberto Perez in 1985. When Perez came to the United States from Cuba in 1961, he left behind everything he had built: a family, a home, a career. He came, he says, because he hoped to get his family out so that he could raise his children outside of communism. In Cuba, Perez had been general manager of an American firm. When he arrived in New York, he got work lifting boxes in a warehouse. "I needed the money to bring my family up from Cuba. I slept in a closet. I lost twenty-seven pounds," Perez recalls. After a stint fixing record players — something he knew nothing about — he brought his wife and two sons to Chicago, where he landed a job as a salesman for New York-based Goya Products, a Hispanic food manufacturer. With a trailer full of canned goods, he made the rounds. "In Chicago, I was the company," he said. While the thought of returning kept many Cubans uprooted, Perez quickly settled down. "I told my family that we can live limiting ourselves in order to go back to Cuba, or we can live here normally without thinking we'll go back in a year. I said, 'Let's try to live like we lived in Cuba,'" he said. Today, Perez is regional manager for Goya Products, which now operates here out of a large warehouse and employs thirty full-time workers.

Perez is also president of the local Cuban-American Chamber of Commerce. Many of the 182 retail stores, restaurants, and other businesses listed with that organization are located in Logan Square. Other firms dot Hispanic business strips throughout the city, making the small Cuban population highly visible. More Cubans are self-employed than are whites: 10 percent of Cuban households in Cook County in the 1980s claimed income from self-employment, compared with 3.8 percent of all Hispanic and 9.1 percent of white households.

But the stereotype of the Cuban as a self-made business success neglects a large portion of the population. Almost one-third of the Cuban workforce in 1980 held jobs as operators, fabricators, and laborers; and one in ten Cuban families lived below the poverty line in 1979. Thirty percent of Cuban adults reported that they had never attended high school. When Armando and Luz Delia Reyes came from Cuba in 1971, they left behind no thriving business in the capital but a farm in the interior of the island. With little education, they found work in Chicago's factories. Armando landed a night job as a welder; Luz Delia got work on an assembly line. The Reyeses were part of a second wave of refugees, less prosperous and more rural than the first, which streamed in between 1965 and 1973, many to reunite with their families. In Cuba, they had been factory workers, farmers, tradesmen, and clerks, or small businessmen who had lost their shops. Almost one-quarter were black, mulatto, or of Asian descent — minorities traditionally discriminated against in Cuba. Many were women, children, or the elderly, all considered nonproductive by the Cuban government, which prohibited males aged fourteen to twenty-four from leaving the island.

"The second wave was more of an economic migration. They were people who had not had the success in Cuba to want to leave immediately. They left with less of a motivation to return," maintains Triana. Reyes left, he says, because "there was too much misery. There was money but no food." The Reyeses brought three of their children, but left behind a fifteen-year-old son who was not allowed to leave until 1980. "When we came we didn't know anyone. That's hard. We were very depressed. The church was a blessing from God," Luz Delia recalled. The Reyeses were among some 1,350 families relocated to Chicago by Casa Central and Church World Service, an organization of fourteen Protestant denominations.

For the first month, the First Spanish United Church of Christ provided living quarters, food, job referrals, and emotional support for the Reyeses and other refugees, who also received some federal aid. "The miracle was to see them come and a few months later have an apartment and a job," says Alvarez. "They didn't need much help. They didn't care where they worked or what they did. You pushed them and they kept going."

Communist Wound

For years, the Cuban community remained on the fringes of political movements spearheaded by other Hispanics. Outside of the Cuban-American Chamber of Commerce, anti-Castro groups remain the largest organizations in the Cuban community, although the violent right-wing extremist groups active on the east coast are not visible here. "For Cubans there is nothing more important in life than freeing Cuba. We suffered under communism; communism shattered our lives. Every time you touch that wound we bleed," comments Guillermo Bauta, a member of La Junta Patriotica, a national right-wing, anti-Castro group. "The Cuban right-wing stance alienates other Hispanics. There was a backlash in the late '70s and early '80s when Cubans were excluded and attacked. We were seen as spies," says Llanes.

The stereotype of Cubans as right-wing extremists persists, although there has emerged a new generation less concerned than its parents with fighting communism. Raised in the United States, some younger Cubans identify more closely with the issues affecting Hispanics here.

The motivation, skills, and opportunities of the first and second waves of Cuban refugees often meshed to result in success. In contrast, the third wave of Cubans, those who came on the boatlift from Mariel in 1980, face a harsher reality and have been plagued by a negative stereotype. Unlike earlier Cuban immigrants, most were young, low-skilled single men, many black, who stepped into a shrinking job market. Some were prisoners and social misfits pressured by Castro to leave Cuba. They were held in detention centers upon their arrival and until late 1984 were not eligible for immigrant status. Reared in a communist country, many had problems adjusting to a capitalist system.

"More important than the language barrier has been the lack of cultural orientation. In Cuba, you lived day to day, and not for the future. Everything was planned for you. You had fewer responsibilities," asserts Juan Coll, a job counselor for the Catholic Charities Cuban Refugee Program, who came on the 1980 boatlift. Program supervisor Isabel Erviti says: "Most of the Cubans have found work and are adjusting to life here, but with difficulty. There is also a core group that has not adjusted — they receive public assistance and are doing little to improve their plight," she says. "What characterizes the 1980 Cubans is their mobility. Some of them have seen the entire country. They move at the drop of a hat, always looking for something better."

A quarter century ago, the more prosperous members of the Cuban population fled a revolution in their homeland. Over the years they were joined here by Cubans from the lower echelons of the island's society. Twenty-five years after the revolution, Chicago's Cuban community includes wealthy professionals, shopkeepers, factory workers, and the unemployed — a microcosm of the society the first immigrants left behind.

References

1. Bureau of the Census, "Condition of Hispanics in America Today." A report of hearings of the Subcommittee on Census and Population of the House Committee on Post Office and Civil Service. The hearings were held September 13, 1983. This pamphlet describes the demographic conditions and trends of the Hispanic population in the U.S., taking into account the differences among the national groups.
2. Bureau of the Census, "General Population Characteristics" (report number PC80-1-B15 Illinois, August 1982). Detailed data on Hispanics in Illinois by major group. Includes breakdown and detailed characteristics of Hispanic residents in Chicago and suburban communities.
3. Bureau of the Census, "1980 Census Summary File Tape 4." Data for Table 1 were obtained from census tables PB2, PB3, PB6, PB7, PB9, PB10, PB17, PB46, PB57, PB72, PB76, PB82, PB83, PB101, PB106, HB3.
4. Bureau of the Census, "Supplementary Report, Ancestry of the Population by State: 1980." Report number PC80-S1-10. Table 3 provides a breakdown of the ancestry reported by persons of Hispanic origin who did not identify themselves as Mexicans, Puerto Ricans, or Cubans.
5. Chicago Area Geographic Information Study, "Public Service Report Number One: Population Change, 1970 to 1980" (Chicago: Northeastern Illinois Planning Commission, June 1981). Population changes are provided by black, white, Hispanic, and others for basic geographic units, including metropolitan area, counties, city, and city census tracts.
6. City of Chicago Department of Planning, "Chicago Statistical Abstract 1980: Community Area Profiles" (Chicago: City of Chicago, December 1983). Detailed census profiles include population, age, income, and education figures for Hispanics in each of the city's community areas.
7. City of Chicago Department of Planning, "Forecast of Population for Chicago" (Chicago: City of Chicago, January 1984). Brief report on projections for growth of the Hispanic, non-Hispanic white, and non-Hispanic black populations in the city of Chicago. Projects that 30.2 percent of the city's residents will be Hispanic by the 2010.

8. City of Chicago Department of Planning, "1980 Census Reports: Population, Part 1" (Chicago: City of Chicago, June 1982). Table 8 provides a breakdown of the major Hispanic groups by community area.

9. City of Chicago Department of Planning, "Selected Characteristics: Chicago's Spanish-Speaking Population" (Chicago: City of Chicago, 1973). Based on the 1970 U.S. Census, provides a demographic profile of local Hispanics in community areas.

10. Chicago Panel on Public School Finances, "Dropouts from the Chicago Public Schools: An Analysis of the Classes of 1982, 1983, 1984" (Chicago: A Report of the Chicago Panel on Public School Finances, April 1985). Provides dropout figures for Hispanics in each of Chicago's public high schools. Based on Board of Education student files.

11. Wilfredo Cruz, "Population Growth Fuels Latino Drive for Political Power," *Chicago Reporter*, July 1981 (Vol. 10, No. 7). Chronicles several efforts by Hispanics to obtain representation at the ward level after the election of Mayor Jane M. Byrne.

12. Elrick and Lavidge, Inc., "Media Habits of Hispanic Consumers in the Chicago Metropolitan Area" (Chicago: A report for Asencio and Associates, March 1985). A statistical report of the findings of a survey of Hispanic heads of households on their media habits by national groups.

13. Ford Foundation, "Hispanics: Challenges and Opportunities" (New York: The Ford Foundation, June 1984). A look at the demographic, economic, social, and political situation of Hispanics nationally, taking into account some of the significant differences among the major groups. Provides a brief history of each of the groups in the U.S.

14. Floreal H. Forni, *The Situation of the Puerto Rican Population and its Viewpoints About Racial Relations* (Chicago: Community and Family Study Center, University of Chicago, 1971). A report on a survey of attitudes of Puerto Ricans in Chicago's West Town community area conducted soon after the 1966 riots.

15. Hispanic Policy Development Project, "The Hispanic Almanac" (New York: The Hispanic Policy Development Project, Inc., 1984). A demographic profile based on the 1980 U.S. Census of Hispanics in the top twenty Hispanic centers in the country. This comprehensive, easy-to-use study provides extensive statistical and historical profiles of the major Hispanic groups.

16. Immigrants' Protective League of Chicago and the School of Social Service Administration of the University of Chicago, "Mexican Colonies in Chicago," *The Social Service Review* (December 1928, Vol. 2, No. 4). Based on an M.A. thesis cited below by Anita Edgar Jones. A brief but meticulously detailed description of the Mexican community in Chicago in the 1920s.

17. Anita Edgar Jones, "Conditions Surrounding Mexicans in Chicago" (M.A.

thesis, University of Chicago, 1928). A description of the lifestyle of early Mexican immigrants. Includes historical photographs.

18. Ben Joravsky. "Blacks Vote Latino; Latinos Vote White," *The Chicago Reporter,* May 1984 (Vol. 13, No. 5). A precinct-by-precinct analysis of Hispanic voting patterns in Chicago in the March 1984 Democratic primary.

19. Ben Joravsky and Jorge Casuso, "Hispanic Vote Emerges as New Battlefront in Council Wars," *The Chicago Reporter,* Sept. 1984 (Vol. 13, No. 9). An analysis of the political role of Hispanics in Chicago after the election of Mayor Harold Washington.

20. Louise Ano Nuevo Kerr, "Mexican Chicago: Chicano Assimilation Aborted, 1939-1954," *Ethnic Chicago* (Grand Rapids, MI: Eerdmans, 1984). A description of the historical development of Chicago's Mexican Community. Provides education and income data for Mexicans in 1950. Includes several historical photographs.

21. Evelyn M. Kitagawa and Karl E. Taeuber, eds., *Local Community Fact Book, Chicago Metropolitan Area: 1960* (Chicago: Chicago Community Inventory, University of Chicago, 1963). Provides the earliest published census material on Puerto Ricans and Mexicans in Chicago. Contains a detailed profile of the housing conditions of Puerto Ricans in the city.

22. Jose Llanes, *Cuban Americans: Masters of Survival* (Cambridge, MA: Abt Books, 1982). First-person accounts by Cuban refugees of their experiences in the U.S., presented within a helpful historical framework. Includes demographic profile of the different waves of immigration.

23. Emily G. McKay, "Recent Hispanic Polls: A Summary of Results" (New York: Hispanic Policy Development Project, Feb. 1984). A summary of the findings of four national surveys of Hispanics in business, politics and the media on various issues, including education, employment, and immigration.

24. Gary Orfield and Ricardo M. Tostado, eds., "Latinos in Metropolitan Chicago: A Study of Housing and Employment" (Chicago: Latino Institute, 1983). Quantifies the Chicago area's Hispanic community, with a focus on where they live, employment, and housing.

25. Elena Padilla, "Puerto Rican Immigrants in New York and Chicago: A Study in Comparative Assimilation" (M.A. thesis: University of Chicago, 1947). A participant/observer account of the acculturation patterns in the mainland's two largest Puerto Rican communities.

26. Magalay Queralt, "Understanding Cuban Immigrants: A Cultural Perspective," *Journal of the National Association of Social Workers* (March-April 1984, Vol. 29, No. 2). Brief demographic and cultural profile of Cuban immigrants with implications for social workers.

27. Gerald William Ropka, *The Evolving Residential Pattern of the Mexican, Puerto Rican and Cuban Populations in the City of Chicago* (New York:

Arno Press, 1980). Based on a thesis for Michigan State University completed in 1973. Traces population trends of major Hispanic groups by community area. Provides bibliography.

28. Clarence Senior, "Puerto Rican Emigration" (Rio Piedras, P.R.: University of Puerto Rico Social Science Research Center, 1947). Policy development paper prepared for the Puerto Rican government. Provides a detailed explanation of the factors behind the large and sudden exodus of Puerto Ricans to the mainland.

29. Irving Spergel, "Violent Gangs in Chicago: Segmentation and Integration" (Chicago: University of Chicago School of Social Service Administration, April 1983). Based on police records, this extensive study provides detailed data on gang violence in Chicago's neighborhoods. Presented from a social work perspective.

30. The Public Agenda Foundation, "Moving into the Political Mainstream" and "Moving Up to Better Education and Better Jobs" (New York: The Hispanic Policy Development Project, February 1984). Summaries of the findings of a national survey of 448 Hispanic elected and appointed officials on how they view the obstacles facing Hispanics, their opportunities, and the outlook for the 1980s.

31. United States Commission on Civil Rights, "Puerto Ricans in the Continental United States" (United States Commission on Civil Rights, 1975). A detailed discussion of the problems facing Puerto Ricans on the mainland. Includes recommended solutions and some historical information.

32. U.S. Census, 1990.

33. V. Lance Tarrance and Associates and Peter D. Hart Research Associates, "Hispanic and Black Attitudes Toward Immigration Policy" (Washington D.C.: Federation for American Immigration Reform, June-July 1983). The findings of a national survey. Includes Hispanic's view on immigrants.

34. John Walton and Luis M. Salces, "The Political Organization of Chicago's Latino Communities" (Chicago: Northwestern University Center for Urban Affairs, 1977). Provides a history of Hispanic neighborhoods and categorizes the types of Hispanic community organizations that existed in the city.

35. Yankelovich, Skelly, and White, "Spanish USA, 1984" (New York: A report on the findings of a study commissioned by the SIN Television Network, 1984). A national market research study about attitudes, lifestyles, and media habits of Hispanics in the U.S.

CHAPTER 13

The Chinese in Chicago:
The First One Hundred Years

SUSAN LEE MOY

I. Chinese Immigrants and Chinatown

The Chinese began migrating to the United States in the early 1850s. Poor living conditions and political unrest during the Ching Dynasty (1644-1911) caused them to look for a better life. The Chinese had migrated to other parts of Asia and Southeast Asia for decades before they came to America. The poorer peasants, farmers, and lower classes were the hardest hit by the economic, social and political turmoil in China caused by the Taiping Rebellions, the Reform Movement, and the western encroachment of China. The Chinese government was deteriorating under poor dynastic rulers.

Early immigrants to America were basically from six districts of Kwang-tung Province in southern China. Since Canton was one of only five ports opened to the Westerners at that time, Cantonese people were the first to make contact with Americans. They migrated to America shortly after hearing about the California gold rush of 1848, and they found ample employment in the newly open eastern frontier of California. They filled the great labor need on the farms and small industries rapidly rising in California.

The United States welcomed these Asians with open arms; they were hard-working and worked for very low wages. In fact, employers encouraged more laborers and farmers to come to the United States. Chinese were employed by Union Pacific Railroads to complete the transcontinental railroad in 1869. At times Chinese were used as strike-breakers during the many labor disputes of the era because the Chinese could not and did not belong to any unions. The Chinese worked to reclaim much of the waste land of California into productive farms. They worked in the shrimp and fishing industries. Chinese made up almost thirty percent of California's population in the 1860s. Ninety-five percent of early Chinese immigrants were male.

The economic situation was good for these immigrants, so they wrote to tell fellow clansmen to come to America. The Chinese population increased rapidly: it doubled itself in one decade — 1860 to 1870 — dispersing Chinese throughout California. No Chinatowns, per se, were established during this time, but the Chinese did work and live together in their mining fields and work camps. There was generally an interpreter at the work camp who served as liaison between the Chinese workers and the employers.

But good economic conditions and open immigration for the Chinese came to a harsh end during the late 1870s. A combination of factors brought this into being: recession, high unemployment, and the rising "white America" sentiments, all of which had a profound affect on Chinese immigrations to the United States. It was the beginning of growing anti-Chinese legislation and exclusion laws aimed specifically at the Chinese. Americans who pushed for these laws claimed that the Chinese were undesirable because they were heathens who would not assimilate and acculturate into American society. They claimed that the Chinese, because of their willingness to accept low-paying jobs, were even taking work away from American women and children. The Chinese were not, in fact, generally in direct competition with white workers; they often took work others did not want in laundries, sweatshops, and as railroad laborers. But because they continued to wear traditional clothing and long queues and had their obvious distinct racial features, they became the scapegoat for faltering economic conditions in California.

The major exclusion law went into effect by 1882: the Exclusion Act, by which Chinese laborers were denied entry into the United States, and Chinese already in America were denied American citizenship. The 1924 Immigration Act excluded aliens who were ineligible for United States citizenship. (There were a host of measures, specifically aimed at the Chinese on the lawbooks in the United States and in California, between 1853 and 1924; reference to them is made later on in the chapter.) Without doubt, the Chinese population in America slowly declined after these laws were enforced, reaching its lowest point in 1920.

Even though economic and social conditions for the Chinese population in America were poor, conditions back in China were even worse. Chinese began to cluster_together in ghettos of American cities and towns for survival. They shared living and eating quarters and provided protection from their host country because they were often targets of mob attacks. These clusters were the forerunners of today's Chinatowns.

The Chinese began to look eastward in the United States, where anti-Chinese sentiments were not as strong, and better employment was to be gained. Major cities like Chicago, New York, and Boston began attracting Chinese immigrants from the west coast. By 1880 the Chinese population had made a substantial growth as a direct result of their continual eastward migration from California. The Chinese population in Chicago in 1890 was a mere 567; it doubled itself by 1900 to 1,209. The Columbian Exposition of 1893 attracted

The headquarters of the Chinese-American Society of "Highbinders," located on the
second floor of the middle building, which in 1907 was located in Chicago's first
Chinatown at Clark and Van Buren.   Courtesy of Susan Lee Moy.

many more people to Chicago and therefore created many more service jobs
for everyone, including the Chinese, who were engaged by that time mainly in
the laundry business and a few in the growing popularity of chop suey houses.

The first Chinese community in Chicago was established in the 1880s,
located south of the downtown area on Clark and Van Buren streets. This area
became known as the first "Chinatown" in Chicago. It included a few grocery
stores, two Tong organizations (Hip Sing Tong, and On Leong Tong), several
family associations, the Pao Huang Hui Restore Emperor Society and a Chinese
Baptist Mission. The majority of Chinese did not live in this small area; they
had learned from previous experience not to congregate and thus to be conspicuous. They lived behind their storefront laundries scattered around the city.

The majority of these Chicago Chinese came from the Toi Shan district
of Canton China. Like the Greek immigrants, they wrote home to tell fellow
clansmen and relatives to join them. The result was that a complete village in
China was thus transported to Chicago. In the early development of "China-

Shown here is a World War I–era photo of what is known today as Chicago's "Chinatown." The location is Cermak Road.   Courtesy of Susan Lee Moy.

towns," one sees the predominance of one family name in a community. In Chicago, the Moy family holds the majority: it is recognized that Moy Dong Jue and his brothers were the earliest residents of Chicago. They were local merchants who were able to bring along their wives and thus establish the first Chinese families in Chicago.

The majority of the Chinese men who immigrated to America were sojourners. They did not intend to make America their permanent home; they planned only to stay and work for a number of years to earn enough money to support their family and to retire well in China. It was the firm belief of older Chinese that they should die and be buried in their ancestral family homes. Therefore, if and when a Chinese person in America died before returning to China, his bones — after seven years of interment — were eventually sent back to his native village for proper burial.

There are two distinct Chinese sections in Rosehill Cemetery. The first section was the first burial place of the Chicago Chinese during the late 1880s to 1940s. In about 1945 the Chinese were no longer allowed burial at Rosehill site because there

The coming of age of the American-born generation of Chinese who are shown here in 1936 forming a social organization.   Courtesy of Susan Lee Moy.

was lack of land, and the Chinese created unkempt grounds by burning incense, paper money, and candles. The Chinese had to go southwest out of Chicago to find another resting place. Mt. Auburn Cemetery in Stickney, Illinois, is the second Chinese cemetery in the Chicagoland area. Rosehill has since opened up its plots to the Chinese; they are concentrated in the second section of the cemetery away from the original Chinese section, much of which has been leveled off.

The Chinatown that most Chicago people are familiar with is located on Wentworth Avenue and Cermak Road. Due to high rents, the growing Chinese community, and internal political tension over territorial rights between the two Tong organizations, the Chinese began looking for a different location away from Clark and Van Buren and moved to Wentworth Avenue in about 1910. They found Cermak Road (22nd Street), with its low rent and ample storefronts and apartments, suitable to their needs, and they established themselves within a square block of Cermak and Wentworth Avenue. At that time this area was just outside of the red-light district and was an old Italian and Croatian neighborhood. The original Chinatown on Clark Street remained until 1975, when it was razed to build the Metropolitan Correctional Center.

The Chicago Chinese population continued to grow steadily during the 1920s and 1930s, the majority of whom were employed in either the laundry or restaurant-related businesses. This was the time of the emergence of the first generation of Chinese Americans: being born and raised in America, they considered America home and had no desire to return to China, even though many were sent to China at a young age to receive a formal Chinese education. Many tried to find employment outside the Chinese community. During the Depression years the language barrier was no longer an obstacle, but jobs were not readily available due to the economic conditions, and there was still some discrimination.

As other local ethnic groups moved out of the Wentworth area, the Chinese began moving farther south along the Wentworth area, establishing more restaurants, gift shops, and grocery stores to attract the wider community. Chinese food was beginning to be very popular because it was not only inexpensive but delicious. Housing in the area was poor: many of the homes were over fifty years old by the time the Chinese moved in. But the majority did not want to purchase homes because their intent was to still return to China with their American-born families. Another problem was that many people would not sell to the Chinese: subtle housing discrimination was evident at that time.

The physical area of Chinatown reached its full capacity by the early 1960s; Chinatown was now a seven-square-block area. The Chinese were now making major improvements in the area, building new townhouses and condominiums. They had begun to purchase homes and make renovations. After the communist takeover in China in 1949, the Chinese could no longer return to China, so they began earnestly to invest their time and money in a permanent home here. Also, the emergence of a second generation of Chinese Americans was firmly established in Chicago. They found educational and job opportunities opened up to them, and this was their home — the only one they knew. The Chinese today are moving and purchasing property in the Bridgeport area, just south of Chinatown. The community was able to purchase the abandoned Santa Fe Railway yards north of Archer Avenue, and there are plans for more townhouses and stores for local Chinese residents.

The Chinese community has more than doubled itself twice since the 1950s; and since then, many Chinese have moved outside of Chinatown and into the suburbs.[1] During the first major influx of *new* immigrants, caused by the communist takeover of China in the 1950s, the population went from 3,000 to 6,000. The final repeal of the Exclusion Laws in 1943, as well as new refugee acts, brought many more Chinese to America, including Chicago. The family reunification program brought great stability to the Chinese community. Not only were Chinese continually entering Chicago, but many more

---

1. Interviews with early immigrants and Tin Chiu Fan, "Chinese Residents of Chicago" (unpublished M.A. Thesis, University of Chicago, 1926).

Pictured here are Chinese students in the 1920s, some in western dress and some in traditional dress, who are studying at the University of Chicago.   Courtesy of Susan Lee Moy.

native-born Chinese were now part of the total Chinese population. By 1960 there was also an appropriate ratio of Chinese females to Chinese males; for almost fifty years the number of males had been disproportionately high due to American immigration laws and China's own refusal to allow Chinese women to leave.

The second influx came when China and America opened up relations in the mid 1970s, and a number of Chinese from mainland China began to once again apply for visas to the United States. Prior to this, the majority of Chinese immigrating were from Hong Kong, Taiwan, or were ethnic Chinese from Southeast Asia after the fall of Saigon. The Chinese population of Chicago doubled itself for the second time from 6,000 to 12,000 by 1970; and the 1980 Census showed a continued growth to 28,000 Chinese in the Chicagoland area.

The influx of new immigrants to the Chinatown area during the 1980s was mainly from mainland China. They were relatives of the Chinese already settled in America, and they came under family sponsorship. Chinatown experienced a tremendous growth of both population and a demand for services to accommodate the needs of these new immigrants. Like the needs of the first Chinese immigrants, housing, education, and social services were of foremost importance. The major difference was that these services were now being provided by American social service agencies operating within the Chinese community. The influence and power of traditional Chinatown organizations have

Here a Cantonese-American opera group performs in Chinatown.   Courtesy of Susan Lee Moy.

diminished, and the number of residents needing services could not be handled by Chinese family associations alone. The resources provided by family associations were limited. Still, many of the services catering to the new Chinese immigrant community, such as insurance, tax preparation, real estate investment, newspaper, radio, and travel agencies, are provided by immigrants themselves, who understand the language and the needs of more recent immigrants.

About the same time that the Cantonese-speaking Chinese were immigrating to America in the nineteenth century, another group of Chinese were arriving on the East Coast. They were mainly Mandarin-speaking Chinese from Northern China, and they were from a higher social and educated class. They came not as laborers but as foreign students to study in American universities. The first Chinese person to graduate from Yale University was Yung Wing in 1854. He returned to China and was instrumental in bringing many more young Chinese men to America.

This group of Chinese students had little contact with the local Chinese from Southern China. First, because they spoke different dialects and did not necessarily understand each other, even though the Chinese written language is the same in both regions. Many of the early laborers were also semi-literates. Second, the foreign students' knowledge of the English language made them less dependent on traditional community mutual aid and family associations for help. Third, the social class difference was evident. The students might go into Chinatown to purchase Chinese supplies and occasionally eat at the local restaurants, but their contact was minimal.

These foreign students created their own organizations for social and political reasons. The communist take-over of mainland China also brought more Mandarin-speaking Chinese to Chicago from northern China and Taiwan. They sought out fellow North Chinese for help and support and ignored the local Cantonese-speaking Chinese community.

The fall of Saigon in 1975 brought additional Chinese immigrants. Many ethnic Chinese were being expelled from Vietnam by that communist government because they were businessmen and capitalists, and thus considered enemies of the state. The local Chinese in Chicago began to sponsor and provide aid to these new emigrés. Many of these Southeast Asian Chinese spoke both Cantonese and Mandarin dialects, which had helped them in their businesses in Vietnam. The majority of Chinese who migrated from Southeast Asia were originally from the Fukien province and spoke their own dialects as well.

Regardless of native dialect, the Chinese continued to help fellow countrymen. After a while these Southeast Asians naturally formed their own community groups. They understood their own heritage and problems better than anyone else. They settled mainly in the Uptown area of Chicago, where they received the most social services through Travellers Aid and Catholic Charities. When they arrived in the 1970s, there was a sizable Chinese community in the Uptown area on Broadway and Argyle Avenue because they had purchased homes there to be near their laundries or restaurants. Some moved to the suburbs to find better homes and education for their children.[2]

Because the original Chinatown on Clark and Van Buren was razed to build the Metropolitan Correctional Center, the local Chinese needed another location to continue their business, which they found on Argyle Street with its

2. Ibid.

Chinatown gateway erected by the Chinese community of Chicago with deep appreciation for the generosity and cooperation from City of Chicago.
Courtesy of Masako Osako.

ample storefronts and low-rent facilities. Argyle Street was a rundown and undesirable thoroughfare at the time, with many flophouses and taverns and a sizable transient population. The Hip Sing Tong established its new headquarters on Argyle Street and tried to encourage more Chinese to invest and establish businesses in the area. Many were skeptical of this new northside Chinatown and were reluctant to invest. But the surge of Southeast Asians and its ethnic Chinese provided the impetus to make Argyle Street a viable Asian business community.

Many of the new residents had been businessmen in Southeast Asia. After they had settled and learned the language after one or two years, they owned their own businesses that catered to their own as well as the wider community. Now after almost fifteen years in Chicago, the Southeast Asian Chinese have established themselves firmly in the city, having founded their own social and political organizations. The two different groups of Chinese share a commonality in that they are Chinese; for political and social purposes they support each other. Otherwise, they are very much independent of each other because their history and needs are different.

Chinatown will continue to be a viable part of the Chinese community for many years to come for several reasons: first, the constant influx of new immigrants with the need to be near family and social services; second, the hub of Chinatown still represents a common heritage for all Chinese Americans —

something to return to for cultural information and restaurants and grocery stores; third, the wider community continues to share an interest in visiting a Chicago-version of China and can do so without really having to leave home. Unlike Jewish communities, where the social mobility of its inhabitants quickly moved them out of an area, many middle-class Chinese do choose to live in or near Chinatown. Therefore, they continue to help the Chinese community and Chinatown itself to grow and prosper.

Chinatown is looked upon as a place to live or visit by choice, no longer a place of refuge from the hostile community that forced them to cluster together for protection. Other Asian groups have developed in Chicago over the years, but there is no recognized Japan town or Indian town. When other Asian groups migrated to America, they came better prepared socially and educationally. The social atmosphere and period in which they came were more open and acceptable to Asian immigrants in America.

II. Chinese-American Demography

The 1924 immigration law caused the break-up of many families, because the law excluded alien wives of both Chinese and Japanese citizens by birth but did not exclude their children born after the father had established residence in the United States. In many cases, when the mother and child arrived in the United States, the child was permitted to enter and the mother was deported to her home country. It was, therefore, very difficult for Chinese men to have a healthy family life in the United States. The only exception was that these men were permitted to be joined by their sons. Chinese devised their own means of by-passing these unfair rules and regulations, a method known as "paper sons." I will present an in-depth look into this method below.

The absence of Chinese women in America had an adverse effect on Chinese-American history. American immigration laws, including the 1882 Exclusion Act, contributed to a sex ratio imbalance (see the graph on p. 389). According to Stanford Lyman (1974), there were five distinguishable effects of the shortage of women among the Chinese in America.

1. Establishment and maintenance of a homeless men's community, even though these men were married and their wives were in China. They were labeled "married, bachelor."
2. Introduction of prostitution and other vices such as gambling.
3. Growth of illegal practices designed to bring Chinese, both male and female, into America.
4. Delay in the creation of a second generation of Chinese Americans.
5. An even greater consolidation of the traditional power elite in Chinatown.

POPULATION AND SEX RATIO OF CHINESE-AMERICANS, COTERMINOUS UNITED STATES, 1860–1970

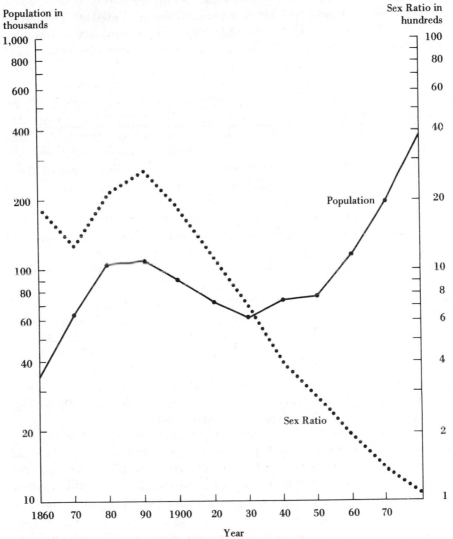

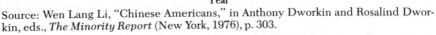

Source: Wen Lang Li, "Chinese Americans," in Anthony Dworkin and Rosalind Dworkin, eds., *The Minority Report* (New York, 1976), p. 303.

The consequence of these five conditions prolonged the existence of an isolated and closed Chinese community in America. It also reinforced the negative stereotype of the Chinese. Men without a family life led lonely lives and depended on one another for socialization and recreation, needs that had to be met by family associations. The majority of male immigrants to Chicago were married and had had at least one child in China prior to their departure. This was to ensure their return and also their monetary support of the family left behind.

Many women in early Chinese-American history led lonely lives too. Their husbands left them to migrate to America in the early part of their marriage, and they were left to obey and take care of the older generation with whom they lived. If their husbands were fortunate enough to save enough money to return to China after many years of absence, the couples were reunited. Many more times they never saw their husbands again and only received an occasional letter and money to cover necessary household expenses and support for the child and the older generation. Because one wage earner in the family was not sufficient, the son was looked upon to add to the family income. As soon as he was old enough to earn a living, he was sent to America to join his father. A mother was then without a son to keep her company; thus the son had to marry so that his wife could be filial and watch his mother for him. Families were and are still an important part of Chinese culture. Many of the men who immigrated to America returned to China as old men ready for retirement. Couples had to get reacquainted with each other again after so many years of separation.

The introduction of prostitution into the Chicago Chinese community was partly a response to an unbalanced sex ratio. But prostitution among Chinese women was limited due to the smaller community and the lack of Chinese females for such employment. Many Chinese girls, ages thirteen to sixteen, were brought over to the United States to become "slave girls"; they entered the United States as the wives of Chinese merchants and officials, the only way they could legally enter the United States. Tong organizations were involved in illegal sale of these slave girls, and many were shipped from one Chinese community to the other throughout the United States. Some of these women were "brought out" to become respectable wives of local residents. A California woman named Donalina Cameron rescued and saved many Chinese slave girls from their unfortunate lives, taught them to read and write, and instructed them in household skills so that they could be productive citizens.[3]

The Chinese also practiced concubinage. The wealthier a man became, the more wives he had. Many Chinese men in America continued this tradition and also took second wives: they were either brought over from China when immigration law allowed it, or the Chinese men married native-born Chinese

3. Standford Lyman, *Chinese Americans* (New York, 1974).

Pictured here are two Chinese-American families about 1890 posing in their
traditional best garments for a photo to be sent back to relatives in the homeland.
Courtesy of Susan Lee Moy.

women. This number, of course, was not large, and it was even smaller in
Chicago because of its limited size.

The largest influx of Chinese women into America came after the repeal
of Chinese exclusion laws in 1943 and the enactment of the War Brides Act and
Family Reunification and Refugee Acts. A small number of Chinese men in
Chicago served in the armed forces during World War II. After their service,
they were allowed to bring over their wives under the War Brides Act. Complete
Chinese families were firmly established during this time. Wives and children
worked and lived in the husband's business, usually a laundry venture. The
majority of the women began to take charge of the family business so that their
husbands could find other jobs to help augment the family income. The woman
could then still raise her family and work at the same time. She learned to read
and write English, along with her children, as they went off to school.

The divorce rate remained low among Chinese, partly due to the close
Chinese family ties. There remained a "shame-culture" element that prevented
Chinese from divorcing: marital split-ups dishonored not only the immediate
family but the entire clan. The actual number of divorces are not available, but

the number is presumed small.[4] Chinese intermarriage with the Caucasian community was once banned; anti-miscegeneration laws were in effect in many states of the Union. Today the percentage of Chinese marrying outside their race is growing, though the rate is much smaller than that of the Japanese, as outlined by Masako Osako in the next chapter.[5] Ms. Osako believes that Japanese Americans may become the first non-whites to merge biologically into the dominant American society through their continual intermarriage. This will not hold true for the Chinese for many years to come.

Many Chinese entered the United States illegally and by ingenious ways. When the quota for Chinese migration was only 105 per year in the early part of this century, the entrants often came under false names or as "paper sons" of immigrants who were resident aliens (and were thus allowed to bring their sons to America beyond the 105 quota). Large numbers of these resident aliens made trips back to China, and upon returning to America, they would report the birth of a male child so that some day he would be allowed to enter the United States. Even if the child was female, it was often reported as a male. Those legal papers were then bought and sold among the Chinese. Children who were dead were not reported, so that their names and status could be purchased, thus enlarging the number of entrants much beyond the meager annual quota.

Some Chinese were smuggled into the United States from Mexico and Canada. Some entered with false papers, and many Chinese males came under bogus names, though they were called by their correct family names within their Chinese community. This was common knowledge and practiced by many Chinese in America, and it generally went unnoticed by Americans, who had difficulty with Chinese names. In 1953 the so-called Confession Program permitted many Chinese families to change to their correct family names. It brought a great relief to some who had been disguising their existence for years.

Chinese Crimes

Since Chinese males did not have the time to participate in traditional American pastimes such as the movies, dance-halls, and dining out, they participated in Chinese gambling games because it was a familiar form of recreation. Their work schedule permitted them to gamble in Chinatown on their half day off. But the Chinese kept gambling to the confines of the Chinese community. Opium smoking, a practice encouraged for the Chinese in the early nineteenth century by the British colonial power, was practiced by a small number of Chinese in America. Their opium dens were for the Chinese only, though a few Americans were found practicing opium smoking.

4. Carol Wilson Green, *Chinatown Quest* (Sacramento, 1974).
5. See pages 409-37 below.

As a whole, the Chinese engaged in Chinese vices that did not affect the wider non-Chinese community. Crime and its prevention was controlled by the Chinese themselves. They did this partly to keep others from knowing their problems, but also because they did not understand or trust the American legal system, which, in part, caused their predicament.

The Second Generation of Chinese Americans

Stanford Lyman's argument concerning the absence of Chinese women in America is that it hampered the growth and social mobility of Chinese in America, compared to that of other ethnic groups who came at or about the same time. The lack of women delayed the creation of the second generation of Chinese Americans; while children of other ethnic groups were being born and raised in America and became assimilated and acculturated into American society, children of Chinese immigrants were not. First, the number of children was small because the number of women bearing Chinese children in Chicago was minimal. Second, the opportunities opened to other ethnic groups were not necessarily opened to the Chinese because of their distinct differences in culture and language. Third, the male children of Chinese immigrants were immigrants themselves. They continued the cycle begun by their immigrant fathers before them: they came to America when they were of age and left behind their wives and children.

The Japanese moved up the social ladder more rapidly than did the Chinese because they brought over their wives and families sooner. And though the Chinese came at the same time as did many other European immigrants, they took at least three generations to become as assimilated and acculturated as the Europeans had become in one.

Chinese Men Consolidated Their Leadership

The fifth point of Lyman's argument is that the consolidation of the traditional power elite in Chinatown was so strong because the men depended on local organizations to provide them with services one would normally receive through the family.

Today the ratio of men to women has reached a healthy balance. The presence of women has eliminated the five adverse effects of American immigration and exclusion laws adduced by Lyman. Chinese women today can be seen in all professions; they have struggled along, with the help of the women's movement.[6]

6. Lyman, *Chinese Americans.*

III. Occupations of the Chinese Americans

When the Chinese first came as laborers to the United States in the 1840s, they reclaimed much of the wasteland of California into productive farms, and they later worked in mining and railroad camps. Some were houseboys in wealthy California households, and others worked in small industries in the growing California economy. The Chinese were welcomed laborers to the west coast because employment was abundant and they were willing to work long hours and accept low wages.

The recession of 1870 and an on-going anti-Chinese movement on the west coast caused a high rate of unemployment and harassment for those Chinese already in California. They began earnestly to look for employment outside California, in places where they would not be in direct competition with the wider non-Chinese community.[7] The predominance of the Chinese laundry establishment during the early part of the twentieth century came about by necessity and not by choice. The need for clean clothes by the miners was met by the Chinese. Since many could not mine the gold fields because of a variety of discriminating laws, they chose to do "women's work" for the early prospectors and settlers of the frontier. When the Chinese began migrating eastward across the United States, they found that those same domestic skills were of value to them in the larger cities of Chicago, New York, and Boston. Entering the laundry business was a form of employment that met Chinese criteria: they were self-employed; they were not in direct competition with white workers; the start-up capital was nominal; and the skills needed were minimal.

The first Chinese laundry in Chicago was opened one year before the Great Chicago Fire of 1871. This laundry was located at the rear of 167 W. Madison Street, and it had no business name. The next year the number of laundries in Chicago increased to eighteen — fifteen of them in the downtown area. During the years 1874 to 1879 the growth of the number of laundries was slow, with a concentration along Madison, Clark, State, and Randolph streets. On the average, half of these laundries failed each year, due to lack of business; but this did not stifle the opening of more laundries throughout the Chicago area.[8]

A major expansion of the Chinese laundry business began in the 1880s. In one year alone, the number of laundries jumped from 18 to 97; by 1883, the number of Chinese laundries was at nearly 200. This resulted from a large influx of Chinese immigrants from the west coast. As Chicago became more and more industrialized and the metropolis expanded, the Chinese continued to service the ever-growing urban population. The 1893 Columbian Exposition in Chi-

7. Alexander Saxon, *The Indispensable Enemy* (Berkeley, California, 1971).
8. Margaret Gibbons Wilson, "Concentration and Dispersion of the Chinese population in Chicago" (Ph.D. diss., University of Chicago, 1969).

Man Sun Wing Co., a Chinatown grocery store, sells fresh shrimp, ducks, beef, aged chickens, and baby pigs (all advertised in Chinese characters); but also note the federal food stamp sign.   Courtesy of Susan Lee Moy.

cago created a big demand for washing the clothes of thousands of visitors who came into Chicago for the exhibition. The number of Chinese laundries during the Exposition went up to 313.

A change in the distribution of Chinese laundries occurred at the turn of the century: those formerly located in the downtown area were greatly reduced, while outlying ones increased, probably because of the rent increase in the downtown area. By 1903 only sixteen Chinese laundries remained in the Loop area, and the overall number of laundries decreased by nearly 100. The Exposition of 1893 was over, the demand was not as great as it had been the previous decade, and economic depression hit most Chicago industries.

Laundries began to disperse to the South Side because of the construction of Lake Shore Drive and its surrounding new neighborhood. A tendency toward dispersal still was noticeable in the 1900s: Chinese laundries were found in thirty-seven of the seventy-six community areas of Chicago, and by the next decade the Chinese had expanded themselves to forty-three of the seventy-six communities. The number of Chinese laundries reached its highest peak in

1928, when there were 794 laundries in the city alone. Those living in Chicago during the '40s and '50s were very familiar with the neighborhood Chinese Hand Laundry, with its distinguishable red-painted sign and small and simple storefront.[9] By 1980 there were fewer than a dozen Chinese Hand Laundries in the Chicago area. The advent of automatic washing machines and laundromats reduced the need for this once well-known occupation.

As many Chinese laundries as there were in Chicago, there never developed a Laundry Alliance like that in New York. Because the Chinese laundryman was tied to his place of business, the Chinese traveling *grocery* store was developed. (Ting C. Fan noted that 14 percent of the Chinese population was engaged in trade and transportation occupations.) Local Chinese grocery stores in Chinatown placed some basic groceries on a truck and set out on a route each day to visit the isolated laundryman. Not only did these trucks provide needed groceries, they also were an opportunity for the laundryman to catch up on local news and gossip. If the laundryman had time to purchase groceries himself in Chinatown, how would he bring them back home? Generally, the laundryman did not drive an automobile; he relied solely on public transportation. To increase business, many grocery trucks included laundry supplies in their inventory. Even Jewish tailors visited numerous Chinese laundries to offer their services; they realized that these men needed at least one suit for rare special occasions.

A laundry business was required to obtain a city license, which cost $15 in 1929. Laundrymen learned business skills from fellow family members or Chinese clansmen. Since the early laundry business was completely done by hand, and the pressing done with small, heavy, hot irons, the process was long and tedious. The laundryman usually worked fourteen to sixteen hours a day, six and a half days a week. The monetary returns were small because he had to pay rent, pay himself and other workers in the laundry, provide sleeping quarters on the premises, and provide the daily meals for everyone in the shop.

The Chinese Consolidated Benevolent Association required that any two laundries should be no less than 600 feet from each other. This was in hope of reducing direct competition. The Chinese laundryman was limited to a half day of work on Sunday so that he could get some rest, purchase necessary supplies, and socialize. He only had a few hours to go to Chinatown to meet with fellow clansmen and to play a few games of majoong and fan tan, perhaps to gamble.

The percentage of Chinese engaged in the laundry business dramatically declined over the years due to many factors. In the early development of the Chinese community in Chicago, approximately 90 percent of the men were engaged in the laundry business. By 1926, when Ting C. Fan wrote his dissertation on the Chinese residents in Chicago, the number had dropped to 35 percent. By the 1930s, occupations in Chinese restaurants had emerged as the

9. Ibid.

Chinese-American businessmen in 1927 in Chicago. Seated in the center is Bow
Nom Lee, a restauranteur.   Courtesy of Susan Lee Moy.

second most important business. After nearly fifty years in Chicago, the Chinese
food business remains an economic mainstay for the community.[10]

As in the laundry business, the Chinese sought self-employment through
restaurant ownership, and they hired their own family and clansmen first, or
were in partnership with them. The Chinese restaurant catering business was
dispersed to the wider community of Chicago much as the Chinese laundry
business had once been. Many failed launderers went directly into the Chinese
restaurant business. The 1960s and 1970s saw the greatest increase in neighborhood Chinese restaurants.

The popularity of the Chinese restaurant business began with the preparation of chop-suey, which was invented in New York in 1896. Legend has it
that it was concocted by the chef of the Chinese diplomat Li Hung Chang while
he was visiting the United States. The chef had to make a dish that appealed to
the American palate and used Chinese ingredients that were found in America.
He gave the dish the name *chop-suey,* which literally means "hash." Surprisingly,
the American public loved it and soon demanded more chop-suey houses. But
another type of Chinese restaurant was also established that catered to the
Chinese themselves; it provided the foods like those of home, and it was usually
found in Chinatowns.

10. Fan, "Chinese Residents in Chicago."

The Chinese restaurant business was an enterprise in which the Chinese were not in direct competition with non-Chinese workers. They sought to avoid such competition because it had brought about anti-Chinese riots on the West coast. Three major Chinese restaurants that catered to the American public, fully equipped with an orchestra and a dance floor, which was popular in the 1920s, were King Yen Lo at 227 S. Clark, King Joy Lo on State and Van Buren, and Joy Yet Lo at Clark and Van Buren Streets. The majority of the waiters in these restaurants were native-born Chinese who used their bilingualism to provide gainful employment. This second generation of Chinese Americans incorporated their western education into the Chinese business.

The Mon Sang Association, formed on September 1, 1918, was the first Chinese labor union. Thirty-six head waiters from various Chinese restaurants met to set wage and working conditions for themselves and other workers. By 1925 they had demanded a six-day workweek and had set minimum wage as follows:

Cooks . . . . $ 7.00 per day
Waiters . . . . $25.00 per week
Store Clerks . . . . $50.00 per month

When some of the Chinese population relocated around 1910 to Cermak and Wentworth Avenue, many Chinese followed and established other new restaurants. The oldest restaurant was Guey Sam on 22nd Street, which was established in 1901. In the mid 1920s, it relocated to a larger and newly built building at 2205 S. Wentworth Avenue. The building was owned by non-Chinese but was built to accommodate a new restaurant.

A rough estimate of Chinese restaurants today in the Chicagoland area is 800-900. There are many small restaurants that fail every year, but the number of Chinese restaurants continues to flourish and grow in Chicago and its suburbs along with population expansion. Cantonese cooking was the cuisine served in the early Chinese restaurants. Egg rolls and won ton soup were introduced in the 1920s. As more people became acquainted with Chinese food, more traditional dishes were introduced on the menus. The predominance of Cantonese food is due to the fact that the majority of Chinese engaged in the restaurant business were Cantonese; their cuisine has always been popular, even in China. The influx of Mandarin-speaking Chinese and American travelers brought Mandarin, Szechuan, and Hunan cuisine into the general public consumption. Many Cantonese restaurants included other cuisines in their menus, as did a new crop of Mandarin restaurants that appeared in the Chicagoland area. The popularity of Chinese restaurants also naturally developed a need for manufacturing, import, and supply-related businesses to accommodate the restaurants.

Today a majority of second- and third-generation Chinese Americans have completed a college education. They have left the traditional Chinese occupations and can be found in both white-collar and blue-collar professions. The majority of Chinese are employed in the technical fields of engineering, computer sciences, and medicine. They have experienced little discrimination in their choice of occupations. They are prized and welcomed employees because they show a strong Chinese work ethic, as their Chinese predecessors did; but they no longer have to work for lower wages and longer hours. And they continue to show entrepreneurial talents for owning and developing their own business.

IV. Political Life of the Chicago Chinese

As with any other ethnic group, the politics of the home country were foremost on the minds of the Chinese. It was the conflicting political situation at home that brought the immigrants to American shores. The Chinese were very interested in the political situation at home because their intention was to return to China someday. They wanted to ensure that they would return to a more stable government and a more stable economy so they would not have to leave home again — nor would their sons and grandsons.

One of the earliest Chinese political groups formed in the United States was an offshoot of the San Dan Hui, the Triad Society. This organization, calling itself the I Hing of Patriotic Rising, was founded in San Francisco between 1850 and 1860. This was during the Taiping Rebellion (1850-1864), from which many of the immigrants were refugees. In Chicago, St. Louis, and Philadelphia, this organization referred to itself as the Hung Shun Tong. Its main objective was to overthrow the Manchu dynasty (which came from Manchuria and ruled China from 1644 to 1912) and replace it with a Chinese dynasty. In America its functions encompassed mutual aid and brotherhood among immigrants as well.[11]

When the Taiping Rebellion failed in ideology, it was replaced by another group that believed in a reform movement to stabilize the political turmoil in China. The Chung Kuo Hsien Cheng, Hui, or as it was better known, the Pao Huang Hui, Save the Emperor Association, was established in the United States as well as in Southeast Asia. They were able to receive monetary support from immigrants. This reform movement was guided by the famous Chinese reformer K'ang Yu-wei (1858-1927), who travelled extensively around the world seeking support not only from overseas Chinese but from other heads of government.[12]

K'ang and his followers wanted to return power to the emperor and

11. Stewart Calin, *The I Hing of Patriotic Rising-Chinese Secret Societies* (San Francisco, 1970).

12. Jung-Pang Lo, K'ang Yu-Wei, *A Biography and Symposium* (Tempe, Arizona, 1967).

Chinese diplomats visit Chicago in the early 20th century. Note the upper-class dress and mandarin hats typical to their class.   Courtesy of Susan Lee Moy.

modernize China through reforms. K'ang believed that China would be better off under a constitutional monarchy than as a republic. But there was a growing nationalist group that opposed K'ang and wanted a republic and democratic government. K'ang's ideas rendered him an exile: he would be arrested if he stayed in China. It is important to note that the Save the Emperor Associations throughout the United States and Canada established activities designed to make life more bearable for the immigrants. The organization provided the community with educated members to provide newspapers and information about fellow Chinese communities, as well as the activities of their home country. K'ang Yu-wei visited Chicago on September 12, 1905. The local chapter of the Save the Emperor Association was established at 315 S. Clark Street.

The success of the revolution in China in 1911 was a blow to the Reform Association both in its ideology and its commercial enterprises overseas. The establishment of the Republic of China under the Kuomintang Party, led by Dr. Sun Yat-sen (1866-1925), gave the overseas Chinese a great sense of pride and accomplishment. They felt that their support and contributions helped to make China once again a strong and powerful nation. The Chicago chapter of the T'ung Meng Huie, predecessor of the Nationalist Party, had been established in 1909, and Dr. Sun Yat-sen had visited Chicago on December 8 of that year. The Chicago chapter raised $3,000 for the new revolutionary army.

The success of the new republic was short-lived, however, as the threat from the Japanese imperial government was growing on the northern battle front, and the expanding communist movement from the central front strangled a government that was not unified. Once again, overseas Chinese were called upon to support the mother country. By the 1920s a growing number of Chinese were native-born and their political affiliations were more American than Chinese; however, they did support their parents' political views. Some of them even went to China for the first time to educate and train the Chinese in Western military instruction.

The first large-scale community show of unity by Chinese in Chicago occurred during their anti-Japanese campaigns, which came after the Japanese had invaded Manchuria (bordering China) on September 18, 1931. The Chinese community, though small, remained relatively close-knit because they all hailed from the same area in Canton, China. Their campaigns, which lasted until the end of the war in 1945, brought the Chicago Chinese community even closer together and brought to the attention of the wider non-Chinese community the plight of the Chinese prior to America's involvement after Pearl Harbor in 1941. Every community member was to support these campaigns in one form or another: the money raised provided relief funds for war-torn China; children were taught songs to sing at fund-raising functions; businessmen, laundrymen, and workers were required to make nominal contributions according to their income, a collection conducted by the Chinese Consolidated Benevolent Association. If one did not contribute, he would be ostracized by the community and made to wear a placard stating his crime. The Chinese in America also purchased war bonds issued by the Republican government of China, but the takeover by Japan made those bonds totally worthless. Many older Chinese invested a good portion of their savings in those bonds.[13]

With the success of the Communist party in China and the Nationalist party fleeing to Taiwan, the Chinese became less involved in Chinese politics. By this time a little over half of the Chinese population in Chicago were

---

13. Interviews with immigrants by author.

Chicago's Chinese parade to protest the Japanese invasion of Manchuria in 1931.
Courtesy of Susan Lee Moy.

native-born Americans, and they began to look to American politics for their rights. At the same time, the older generation's hope of returning to China was finally destroyed. The Communist government prevented further immigration — as well as emigration. Their own lives in America were now better: the exclusion laws had been repealed; Chinese families were united; and the opportunities for the Chinese to become naturalized citizens was realized. Up until 1943, the Chinese were the only ethnic group denied the right to become naturalized citizens, which in turn denied them the right to vote and have a voice in American politics. The Confession Program of 1952 lessened the fear of American government and the fear of exclusion.

In American politics the Chinese Americans have generally supported the Democratic party. Traditionally, the Democrats have given Chinese Americans opportunities. In Chicago there are no Chinese holding any political office; however, they are employed in city government offices. The major appointments to city government came when Bernarda Wong, the executive director of the

The sale in Chinatown of relief war bonds to help victims of the Japanese invasion of China.   Courtesy of Susan Lee Moy.

Chinese American Service League, was appointed to the Library Board in the 1980s. She was instrumental in bringing an expanded branch of the Chicago Public Library to the Chinese community. The new facility opened in 1990.

In 1989, William Lui, professor of sociology at the University of Illinois at Chicago, was the first Chinese appointed to the Chicago Board of Education. He was replaced by Raymond B. Lee in 1990. Raymond Lee and other business community leaders were instrumental in demanding a new and larger public school facility for the Chinese community. The local public school, "John C. Haines," had been built in 1874 and was in need of a major renovation to house the growing Chinese community. It had educated three generations of Chinese Americans. Raymond Lee was also appointed to the Chicago Park District in 1988, and George Eng became deputy commissioner of Public Works of Chicago.

V. Chinese American Community Organization

Unlike European immigrants, who gravitated to the Christian churches for guidance, the Chinese first looked to their family organizations for guidance and support. For this reason family associations became dominant power structures in the early Chinese communities. The predominantly male society perpetuated these associations, and they were formed along family surnames or

A traditional family altar in Chinatown belonging to the Lee Family Association.
Courtesy of Susan Lee Moy.

district or clan allegiance; they provided mutual aid, employment, housing, and socialization. The power and influence of these family associations diminished with the reunification of families and the social services that came to be provided by agencies outside of the traditional community organizations. Today the family associations are symbolic organizations with little usefulness within the community. There is no denying the need for and usefulness that these family organizations once provided, but membership in local family associations, churches, and political organizations is not of utmost importance now to the Chinese community. The influence of these organizations have lessened as the community has changed from a single dominant group to a very heterogenous

A girl dressed for
the lunar New Year
celebration about 1915
in Chicago. Courtesy of
Susan Lee Moy.

Chinese population. The assimilation and acculturation of succeeding generations weakened participation or association with Chinese-language organizations.

Though religion was a very important part of European immigrant history
to Chicago, this was not true of the early Chinese and Japanese immigrants.
But religion has become an integral part of Chinese culture: they have adapted
Buddhism, Taoism, and animalism into their culture; Confucianism, which is
more of a philosophy than a religion, has been so integrated into Chinese culture
that it is hard to set it apart. Chinese belief in spirits and the use of the almanac
and astrology have guided and provided for their spiritual needs. The main

A Chinese-American dragon brightens up a festival in Chinatown.
Courtesy of Susan Lee Moy.

tenets of Confucianism emphasize the importance of filial relationships, piety, and self-conduct for harmonious relationships, both personally and profession-ally; they have dominated the behavior of Chinese no matter where they have migrated throughout the world.

Early Chinese immigrants, therefore, did not set up separate or elaborate places of worship. Nor did they need to have the time or the money to devote to their spiritual needs. The needs of survival, such as housing and employment, were of constant concern. They sometimes set up small altars and shrines to various deities and family ancestors in the *privacy* of their homes. Today, as more fresh immigrants arrive in Chicago, they have brought their religious practices with them and practice them more actively. There are still no separate religious temples for the Chinese, as one might find in Hong Kong or Taiwan. There are Buddhist temples in the Chicagoland area for the Japanese and Southeast Asian communities. Many Chinese homes have small shrines to honor dead ancestors, still emphasizing the importance of the family; but this practice is rapidly disappearing with the passing of each generation in America as the Chinese become more assimilated and acculturated into American middle-class society.

Many more Chinese in Chicago have adopted Christianity than in their homeland. Christians had a large Chinese mission since the mid-nineteenth century, though the Catholics began sending Jesuits to China much earlier, during the fifteenth century. Their mission was to convert the "heathen" Chinese from their pagan practices to a European Christian religion. This practice was continued when the Chinese migrated to America. The Protestant churches were foremost in establishing missions within the Chinese-American communities; the Midwest was the Bible belt, and Chicago had the most Chinese Sunday Schools of any city in the early part of the twentieth century.

The earliest record of a Chinese Baptist mission was in 1878, located in the heart of the Chinese community on Clark Street. Other smaller Chinese Sunday Schools were established near Chinese laundries on the West and South sides of Chicago. Services and English classes were held on Sunday afternoons to accommodate the working schedules of the Chinese laundryman. Today these Chinese Sunday Schools conducted by the Baptist mission no longer exist. The Chinese Christians have taken over their churches and provide the religious training for themselves. The Chinese Christian Union Church on Wentworth Avenue, an interdenominational church, is a direct result of the Baptist influence on the Chinese community and has affiliates in the northern suburbs and in Bridgeport. The language used in the church services reflects the congregation: English, Cantonese, and Mandarin. The Catholic church influence came much later to the Chinese-American community. The first Catholic mission was under the direction of Franciscan priests and nuns. Chinese Catholics of Chinatown now share the Italian Catholic church St. Marie Incoronata on Alexander Street; many of the Catholics in the community are converts from Hong Kong who had practiced Catholicism there. The Catholic church under the Maryknoll Sisters established the St. Therese School for the Chinese community.

Beyond family associations and religion, Chinese newspapers play a vital role: the Chinese keep informed of local and national news through the Chinese-language newspapers. These newspapers are circulated among the various Chinese communities throughout the United States. There are four dailies in the Chicago area today. A Mandarin-speaking television program on Channel 26 was established in 1983; and a local radio station, Global Communication, was established in 1989. Presently, there is no Chinese-American newspaper published in English that focuses on Chinese-American needs and concerns. Most Chinese Americans read American newspapers if they do not read or write the Chinese language, but also even if they are bilingual.

VI. Conclusion

Chinese Americans make up 23 percent of the total Asian population of the United States; they have remained the largest Asian group for the past century. The 1990 United States Census indicates that there are 1,645,472 Chinese in America. The Chinese population in Illinois is 49,936, ranking it sixth nationally, behind Massachusetts, New Jersey, Hawaii, New York, and California. The largest concentration of Chinese remains on the two coasts, and Illinois is the largest Midwest concentration of Chinese (as well as for many other Asian groups).

In Chicago there are nearly 35,000 Chinese; 10,000 live in the Chinatown area. With the continual increase of their population through natural progression and the influx of new immigrants, the Chinese have become a viable ethnic group in Chicago. Today's Chinese population is no longer a homogeneous grouping of Cantonese laborers: it is a heterogeneous population consisting of Cantonese, Indo-Chinese, Taiwanese, mainland immigrants, native-born Chinese, and racially mixed Chinese. The early immigrants were from the lower and lower-middle classes. Some of today's newcomers are better-educated professionals as well as being from the blue-collar and agricultural/laboring classes. The uniqueness that each of these groups brings into the Chinese Chicago community has blended with Chicago's ethnic history.

The continuing awareness of Chinese Americans of their unique heritage varies in degree. Chinese Americans after the first generation have tried very hard to blend into the mainstream of American society. Many have gone to the point of dissociating themselves from the community, language, and culture. But this is not the case with the majority of Chinese Americans, whether they are second or fifth generation. Part of this sense of pride in being Chinese Americans (even though they may no longer speak the language) is their sense of strong family ties. The success of the Chinese Americans is partly attributable to their sense of family responsibility, along with their strong work ethic and a sense of the struggling of their past generations.

The achievements of the Chinese community can be attributed to the struggles, sacrifices, and hard work of the early immigrants. The strong cohesiveness of the Chinese family (whether they are physically together or miles and worlds apart) in their struggle for survival contributed to their success of today. The importance of education, the ultimate measure of success in Chinese culture, was and is still instilled in the younger generation. The early immigrants, even though they themselves were semi-literate, worked long hours and endured great hardships so that their sons could enjoy better educations and lifestyles. These college-educated Chinese Americans have brought honor and respect to their families and the Chinese community as a whole. The success of Chinese Americans and their acceptance by the wider community have paved the way for widespread acculturation and assimilation for many of the third and fourth generations.

CHAPTER 14

Japanese Americans:
Melting into the All-American Melting Pot

MASAKO OSAKO

I do not know of any group in the history of our country who has suffered so much without justification and who has come out of it to make such a great contribution with never a scar of resentment or faltering in their love of and loyalty to country.

— Illinois Congressman Barrat O'Hara

There is a good chance that in a few generations the . . . members of the Chicago Japanese-American population will have dwindled, and this ethnic group will biologically melt into the dominant white society.

— Masako Osako, 1992

"Japanese-Americans are the 'model minority': they are law-abiding, polite, clean, hard-working, and assimilate readily to dominant American values." For years this has been the accepted wisdom regarding the Japanese as an ethnic group, and perhaps such traits remain characteristic of many Japanese Americans, whether living in Hawaii, on the West Coast, or in the Midwest. Yet today the community is more restive; some Japanese Americans are uncomfortable with the "quiet American" image and are reluctant to be typified too easily as "the model minority which has successfully integrated." Like other American ethnics, Japanese Americans are increasingly concerned with problems of group survival in a mass society, and they seek to preserve ethnic traditions, to identify social problems, and to rectify the injustices of discrimination. But the young are abandoning endogamy — they are marrying outside the Japanese community — at a rapid rate.

How did Japanese-Americans earn their image? How did they achieve success despite the severities of past discrimination? The answer lies partly in

409

the strength of their traditions, particularly family and community structures, as well as in the harsh reality of racial oppression. In the dynamic interaction between the ethnic group and the host society, certain consequences of assimilation follow. The Japanese-American family and community changed significantly in the crucible of assimilation.

Chicago's Japanese Americans underwent strikingly different experiences from those of their sister communities in Hawaii and on the West Coast: they were forced to relocate three times in alien milieus — to the West Coast, to the internment camps during World War II, and finally to the Midwestern metropolis — in a matter of only one generation. Moreover, the community in Chicago has been little affected by the expanding community of Japanese nationals in recent years.

Large-scale Japanese-American migration to Chicago began after World War II, as the relocation centers in the West closed. As late as 1940, there were only 390 persons of Japanese origin in the city of Chicago; but the figure boomed to 10,829 by the 1950 census. Today there are 16,000 in the greater Chicago area. Until the mid-1950s, the South Side (the Hyde Park-Kenwood area) and the near North Side along Clark Street were the major centers for Japanese. Today their residences are spread out all over the city, with more than one-third, especially the younger generation, living in suburbs such as Skokie, Evanston, and Des Plaines. The group's migration to predominantly white, middle-class suburbs suggests their social mobility and successful assimilation into American society.

Social Origin and Immigration

Japanese Americans began to immigrate to the United States around 1880, and eventually slightly more than 190,000 — excluding migrants from Hawaii after its annexation — arrived on American shores.[1] It was during the years 1900 to 1924 that a large majority arrived in America: an estimated 89 percent of the total of Japanese immigrants entered in this twenty-four-year period.[2] At first, most of the immigrants were young, unmarried male sojourners who intended to return home after making their fortunes. In contrast, after the ratification of the final form of the Gentlemen's Agreement in 1908, by which the Japanese government voluntarily limited its immigrants to America, young brides dominated the ranks of new arrivals from Japan. Following the traditional Japanese custom of arranged marriage, a young man residing in the United States could marry a girl in Japan by exchanging photos and being assisted by a go-between.

1. The immigration statistics of Japanese Americans suffer from various inconsistencies and inaccuracies. For details, see William Petersen, *Japanese Americans* (New York, 1971), pp. 14-219.
2. Roger Daniels, "The Issei Generation," in Akemi Tachiki et al., *Roots: An Asian American Reader* (Los Angeles, 1971), pp. 138-149.

The influx of women ended in 1924 with the ratification of the Omnibus Act, which denied admission to aliens ineligible for citizenship, including most people from Asia and Africa. Fortunately, by this time a large majority of Japanese immigrants were married. By 1924 the basic unit of the Japanese-American community had been transformed from a single male to a family.

A great majority of Japanese immigrants to America were from the farming class, which comprised 90 percent of Japan's population in the nineteenth century.[3] Like many traditional peasants, Japanese farmers generally lived close to subsistence level, though there were class distinctions even among them based on wealth, especially land ownership.[4] Typically, a Japanese village was composed of a handful of landlords, a sizable number of land-owning independent farmers, and a majority of full- or part-tenants. The part-tenant owned his own plot, but since it was too small to provide for his family, he leased an additional piece of land from his wealthier neighbors. The full-tenant, with no or little land of his own, was sometimes called a "water-drinking peasant" (Mizunomi byakushō) because he filled his stomach with water when food was scarce. Many immigrants were from middle or lower socioeconomic groups, but they were respectable people whose parents enjoyed enough trust from fellow villagers and relatives that they could borrow money to finance the son's travel expenses to the United States. Unlike the early Japanese immigrants to Hawaii, who were plantation workers, few of those who landed on the West Coast were so poor as to be indentured laborers.[5]

Life in the Japanese village was taxing and precarious. With limited arable land and dense population, farming was both labor-intensive and capital-intensive. Farm labor was also strictly regulated by a seasonal schedule, such as rice transplantation in June, weeding during the summer months, harvesting in mid-October, and planting of winter wheat in late October. The list of work to be performed was endless: gathering grasses to make compost, bargaining with fertilizer merchants, cleaning ditches, tending cows, feeding silk worms, and so forth. In addition, each task required skill, experience, and perseverance. A common saying, "The peasant is anxious to use the helping hand of even a cat," illustrates this demanding work. Furthermore, floods, drought, pestilence, and rising taxes and fertilizer prices were familiar perils.

Understandably, all the farm family members were required to work, and their contribution to household productivity was an important determinant

---

3. See Harry Kitano, *Japanese Americans* (Englewood Cliffs, N.J., 1969), p. 15; Leonard Bloom and Ruth Reimer, *Removal and Return: The Socio-economic Effects of the War on the Japanese Americans* (Los Angeles, 1949), Ch. 1.

4. See John Embree, *A Japanese Village: Suyemura* (Chicago, 1939); Edward Norbeck, *Changing Japan* (New York, 1962); Tadashi Fukutake, *Japanese Rural Society* (London, 1972).

5. See Petersen, *Japanese Americans*, pp. 9-37; Ichikawa Tomonori, "Hi-Kosatsu" [A Social Geographical Study of Japanese Indentured Emigrants to Hawaii from Kuchida Village in Southern Hiroshima Prefecture], *Shigaku Kenkyu (Historical Journal*, 99), 33-52.

of their status and power. For example, despite the widespread myth of subjugated Japanese women, many centers of the silk industry, where women were
the principal weavers, were known for petticoat government.[6] Similarly, even
though Confucianism, Japan's official doctrine during the Tokugawa period
(1600-1868), preached the importance of respect for aged parents, the old
farmer's status declined as he became feeble and unproductive. Beardsley
states:

> A grandfather merits respect, but in addition his ties with other household
> members become warmer as his exercise of authority diminishes. Skilled
> handicrafts, menial tasks, and some babytending become his main economic
> functions.[7]

In Japan the younger sons were almost invariably less fortunate than their
eldest brother, for to prevent the subdivision of already small plots, the Japanese
practiced primogeniture.[8] The sons other than the heir were encouraged to
leave home to find opportunities to earn a livelihood elsewhere, such as industrial employment or as a son-in-law in a family without a male heir. Thus
it was no coincidence that many of the male immigrants were younger sons.
This was probably a favorable factor in Japanese immigration to the United
States, for they were accustomed to hard work and determined to establish
themselves in nonfamilial employment.

Rural Japan in the late nineteenth century, where the *Issei** were raised,
was undergoing social change from being a largely self-sufficient economy
under a feudal system to becoming an expanding commercial economy with
growing industrialization.[9] During nearly 300 years of the Tokugawa regime,
the village was basically an economically and socially self-contained unit, with
peasants bound to the land, caught up by intricate networks of obligatory social
relations. But the restoration of imperial rule in 1868 abolished the hereditary
caste system of four rigid classes, and with it peasants gained the right of
occupational and geographical mobility. In addition, during the second half of
the nineteenth century, various modernizing measures were introduced, such
as compulsory elementary education, a nationwide postal system, a banking
system, and universal military conscription. These changes inevitably touched
the lives of the emigrating Issei. Therefore, despite their rural and relatively
low-class origin, the majority of the Issei had the equivalent of an eighth-grade

6. William Goode, *World Revolution and Family Patterns* (Englewood Cliffs, N.J., 1966),
p. 346.

7. Richard Beardsley et al., *Village in Japan* (Chicago, 1959), p. 220.

8. See Marion J. Levy, Jr., "Contrasting Factors in the Modernization of China and Japan,"
Economic Development and Cultural Changes 2 (Oct. 1953), 161-197.

9. Edwin Reischauer, *Japan: The Story of a Nation* (New York, 1974), pp. 99-145.

*The first generation Japanese immigrants are called *Issei* (literally, number one generation).
Their children are *Nisei* (second generation), and their grandchildren *Samsei* (third generation).

education[10] and were familiar with the demands and disciplines of a commercialized economy. They were also sensitive to national pride, since they had experienced military victories over China (1895) and Russia (1905).

Adjustment

Most Japanese immigrants to the West Coast of the United States found jobs in farming and in service industries: prior to World War II, approximately two-thirds of the Japanese urban dwellers were in service industries;[11] the farming Issei started out as hired laborers on farms producing vegetables and fruits.[12] Gradually the latter began to work on their own land, either as tenants or owners. Despite the anti-Japanese sentiment, some Caucasian landowners were willing to lease plots to Japanese farmers once they realized that the leasing was safe and profitable. At times a Japanese immigrant, eager to cultivate his own land, proposed to lease even previously barren land.[13] By 1930, twenty years after the peak immigration period, few of California's Japanese farm work force were still hired laborers.

Past experience of intensive work habits and farming techniques in Japan and the solidarity of the ethnic group contributed much to their advancement. Japanese farmers, living in clusters in such places as Fresno, San Joaquin, and Sacramento, not only exchanged information about land availability, lease opportunity, and market conditions, but also pooled money to purchase land and farm equipment. Eventually, Issei farmers developed a business structure that could handle all aspects of agricultural operations, such as seed and fertilizer purchase, farming, harvesting, retailing, and wholesaling. This cooperative network, coupled with the Issei's specialization in certain products like strawberries and cantaloupes, contributed to the farmers' survival in the face of persistent anti-Japanese measures, for example, anti-alien land acts and the boycotts of Japanese farm products. The number of Japanese farmers decreased from 5,152 in 1920 to 3,956 in 1930, and Japanese-owned acreage decreased in that decade from 361,276 to about half that figure. And yet, by 1941, Japanese farmers raised 42 percent of California's truck crops.[14]

10. See Petersen, *Japanese Americans,* 9-14.

11. Kitano, *Japanese Americans,* pp. 15-22; Ichibashi, *Japanese in the United States,* Chs. 8-10.

12. See Masakua Iwata, "The Japanese Immigrants in California Agriculture," *Agricultural History* 36 (1962), 33-52.

13. For the decline of Japanese agriculture in California, see Thomas Bailey, "California, Japan and the Alien Land Legislation of 1913," *Pacific Historical Review* 1 (1932), 36-59; Iwata, *op. cit.*; John Modell, "The Japanese of Los Angeles: A Study in Growth and Accommodation, 1900-1946" (Ph.D. diss., Columbia University, 1969).

14. There is a controversy concerning the extent to which the Alien Land acts impeded Japanese agriculture in California. On one hand, Nisei scholars like Masakuzu Iwata and Harry Kitano emphasize their dire emotional and economic impact on the Japanese farmers. On the

The Issei farmer's survival was achieved by the extremely hard and long labor of every family member, including the wives and children. The Japanese were charged with possessing an unfair superior advantage in economic competition because of their "thrift, industry, low standards of living, willingness to work long hours and the women working as men. . . ."[15] And for their effort they had to pay a penalty. When consumers complained about the rising prices of farm products and white farmers became alarmed about their declining share in the market, the success and visibility of Japanese farmers made them an easy target of racial discrimination.

Japanese immigrants, however, were not exclusively farmers. In the pre–World War II days nearly one-third of the Issei lived in urban centers, such as Los Angeles, Seattle, Tacoma, and Portland. Anti-Japanese sentiment and the Issei's lack of English-language skills narrowly limited the kinds of jobs they could obtain. Generally, factory jobs were unavailable to them except for low-paying, menial, and nonunionized ones like canning and slaughtering, which few whites would want. A large majority of urban Japanese opted for small business operations, such as fruit-stands, restaurants, laundries, and barber-shops. Domestic service positions for young people and gardening for former peasants were also common occupations. Little skill and capital needed to enter the business are the common characteristics of these trades. Miyamoto reports:

> . . . the restaurant cooking of that day was relatively simple; all one had to know was how to fry an egg, toast bread, and fry a steak. It was known as a "fry cook."[16]

As in the case of Japanese farmers, the Issei in cities progressed from hired hands and apprentices to business owners in urban occupations. For instance, among the Japanese-Americans in Seattle in 1935, 46 percent of income earners operated small businesses. Moreover, another 25 percent were in white-collar occupations, such as clerks, teachers, and stenographers. Fewer than 19 percent were service or manual workers.[17]

What contributed to the Issei's social mobility? Seattle and other western cities were still expanding in pre–World War II days, and this aided the Issei's

---

other hand, non-Japanese scholars like Roger Daniels, Carey McWilliams, and John Modell interpret the land acts as less potent. For instance, Daniels termed the 1920 law "an empty gesture, an ineffective irritant; it caused much litigation, but in no way significantly affected land tenure in the state." *Politics of Prejudice* (Berkeley, 1962), p. 88. See Petersen, *Japanese Americans,* for further discussion.

15. This charge was made in 1920 by V. S. McClatchy, vocal advocate of the Japanese Exclusion Act of California, quoted in Iwata, "The Japanese Immigrants in California Agriculture," p. 30.

16. Shotora Frank Miyamoto, *Social Solidarity among the Japanese in Seattle* (Seattle, 1939), p. 74.

17. *Ibid.,* p. 70.

business expansion. But more important, historians and sociologists argue, community solidarity and cooperation contributed much to the success.[18] For commercial establishments, the ethnic community was the major source of both customers and suppliers. For example, Japanese restaurants used Japanese laundries, food suppliers, cooks, and waitresses, and catered to Japanese customers. *Kenjinkai,* prefectural associations, were particularly helpful in starting a business. For instance, Miyamoto reports:

> People from the same prefecture often cooperated in particular trades. For example, the first Japanese barber in Seattle was from Yamaguchi-ken. After he became established he helped his friends from the same ken with training and money, so that eventually most of the Japanese barbers in Seattle were from Yamaguchi-ken. Other businesses followed similar patterns.[19]

The traditional financial practice of Japan, *tanomoshiko,* helped to finance many of the new business ventures in the absence of bank loans and government assistance. *Tanomoshiko* is a combination of an investment fund and credit service. Each member contributes a certain amount of money at designated intervals and receives a lump sum when his turn comes up. Its purpose and scale varied from several women forming a group to purchase wrist watches to a large *tanomoshiko* capable of financing the purchase of a sizable real estate holding. The system was clearly built on absolute trust, for nothing bound a person to pay his or her share except honor. The prevalence of *tanomoshiko* in the pre–World War II Japanese community in America is clearly indicative of ethnic solidarity.

For several decades Japanese descendants continued to live in a largely self-sufficient and self-contained "Japanese ghetto," relatively isolated from the dominant society. They built language schools, movie houses, churches, and temples. Although — unlike Japanese farmers — city Issei were not in competition with other Americans, their isolation did not help dispel the dominant society's suspicion and apprehension about Japanese. This was so even though crime and juvenile delinquency rates were extremely low among Japanese descendants.

Discrimination

For some time racial discrimination against Orientals had been an established practice in California. At first, it was the anti-Chinese movement. During the 1860s and 1870s thousands of Chinese laborers were brought in to build rail-

18. For community solidarity, see Ichibashi, *Japanese in the United States;* Kitano, *Japanese Americans,* pp. 14-18; Kenji Ima, "Japanese Americans: Making of Good People," in Gary and Rosalind Sworkin, eds., *The Minority Report* (New York, 1976), pp. 254-296. See also Edna Bonacich and John Modell, *The Economic Basis of Ethnic Solidarity: Small Business in the Japanese American Community* (Berkeley, 1980).

19. Miyamoto, pp. 74-75.

roads and work in mines; but with the completion of the railroads and the economic recessions in the 1880s, Californians began to regard the Chinese as unwanted competitors for jobs. The exclusion act of 1882 — suspended for ten years, renewed in 1892, and made indefinite in 1902 — officially banned the entry of Chinese immigrants into this country. In the late nineteenth century, Japanese laborers were brought in to fill the room vacated by the declining Chinese population. But as early as the turn of the century, Japanese farmers succeeded in their enterprises and, with the help of recessions, eased the labor shortage. This time public opinion turned against the Japanese, who inherited the anti-Oriental fears previously directed at the now-excluded Chinese.

Californians' anti-Japanese feelings were expressed in numerous incidents.[20] On February 5, 1905, the *San Francisco Chronicle*, an influential paper on the Pacific Coast, carried a front-page article charging the threat of "Yellow Peril." For months similar stories appeared almost daily. The Japanese victory over a major European power in the Russo-Japanese war of 1905 also stimulated fears of a war between the United States and Japan. During the same year, the Japanese and Korean Exclusion League was formed in San Francisco, the first of many West Coast anti-Japanese groups. The league was financed mostly by the Building Trade Council, and of the 231 organizations affiliated with it in 1908, 195 were labor unions. In the following year the "School Crisis" in San Francisco attracted international attention. The city board of education ordered that Chinese, Japanese, and Korean children be sent to a segregated Oriental public school in the Chinese quarter. The alleged reason was overcrowding in white schools, because many schools were destroyed in the great earthquake and fire of April 1906. The city's attempt at racial segregation was prevented, however, when the U.S. Attorney General threatened suit against the school board on constitutional grounds. But a considerable sector of California public opinion denounced the whole affair as an unwarranted intrusion of the federal government into state and municipal matters. In truth, San Francisco politicians had deliberately exploited the race issue to divert public attention from an investigation of municipal graft. The issue was settled at a White House meeting in February 1907. President Theodore Roosevelt persuaded the San Francisco authorities to abandon school segregation, and in return he promised to negotiate with Japan for further limitations on Japanese immigration to the United States. The outcome was the so-called Gentlemen's Agreement of 1907–1908, under which Japan refused exit visas to its nationals going directly to the United States seeking work.

In California, the Gentlemen's Agreement did not slake the thirst of anti-Japanese extremists. Violence against Japanese was common, and in 1913

20. Numerous scholarly works have been published on the subject of discrimination against Japanese. For example, Roger Daniels, *The Politics of Prejudice* (Berkeley, 1962); Sidney L. Gulick, *The Japanese American Problem: A Study of the Racial Relations of the East and the West* (New York, 1914); Dorothy S. Thomas and Richard Nishimoto, *The Spoilage* (Berkeley, 1946).

California passed an Alien Land Bill, which prohibited "aliens ineligible for citizenship" from purchasing land. Aliens could lease agricultural land for a maximum of three years only; lands already owned by or leased to aliens could not be bequeathed. Even though the Japanese effectively undermined this bill by purchasing land under the names of their American-born children or friends, they were acutely aware of possible law suits as well as the confiscation of their land.

The persecution was intensified further. In 1920, California tried to plug the loopholes that had made the 1913 land law more or less ineffective. This time the Japanese lost the right even to lease agricultural land, and they were forbidden to act as guardians of native-born minors with respect to property that they themselves could not legally own. Historian Iwata reports that the Japanese share of California's farm product dropped from 12.3 percent in 1921 to 9.3 percent in 1925.[21] To survive, Japanese farmers, despite their reputation for being law-abiding, had no choice but subtly to circumvent the tightening laws.

Throughout the 1920s and 1930s the insecurity resulting from clandestine use and ownership of land, as well as the boycotts of Japanese farm products, deeply troubled Issei farmers. Many living Issei can still recall confrontations with agitated white farmers and their supporters when they drove to the market with a truckload of fresh vegetables. The Issei would return home with a truckload of spoiled produce, having lost several hundred dollars, and fearful for their safety.

The persecution of Japanese descendants on the West Coast entered a new stage when on December 7, 1941, the Japanese Empire executed a surprise attack on Pearl Harbor. The Issei were now regarded as enemy aliens. Anti-Japanese sentiment became nationally acceptable. A Hearst columnist wrote on January 29, 1942:

> I am for the immediate removal of every Japanese on the West Coast to a point deep in the interior . . . let 'em be pinched, hurt, hungry. Personally, I hate Japanese. And that goes for all of them.[22]

The range of those attacking the Japanese descendants was remarkably wide, including trade unions, civic organizations, and religious groups. Only some Quaker groups and the American Civil Liberties Union provided visible support to protect Japanese civil rights.

21. Iwata, p. 7.
22. Quoted in Kitano, p. 32.

On March 2, 1942, the United States Commander in charge of the Western Defense Area ordered an evacuation of all persons of Japanese ancestry from the Pacific coastal states for relocation into the interior of the nation.
Courtesy of the War Relocation Authority.

Internment

On January 29, 1942, the first of a series of orders by U.S. Attorney General Francis Biddle established security areas along the Pacific Coast that required the removal of all enemy aliens from these areas. On February 19, 1942, President Roosevelt signed the infamous Executive Order 9066, which (1) designated military areas where military commanders could exclude persons, and (2) authorized the building of "relocation" camps to house excluded persons. On March 2, 1942, General John DeWitt, then commander in charge of the Western Defense Area, issued an order to evacuate all persons of Japanese ancestry from the western half of the three Pacific Coast states and the southern third of Arizona. "Persons of Japanese ancestry" were defined as all those with as little as one-eighth Japanese blood. More than 111,000 of the 126,000 Japanese in the United States were affected by the order. Of this group, Kitano reports that two-thirds were United States citizens.[23]

At the internment camps, located in remote and barren areas of Arizona, California, Arkansas, Utah, Wyoming, and Idaho, the evacuees began a life in a state of physical and emotional shock. They were kept behind barbed wire and guarded by armed soldiers. The fruit of their thirty years of hard labor was gone. Many had completely lost faith in America, once a promised land, and had to survive the confinement with no knowledge about when and if they would ever return to their home and community. After a period of initial adjustment and shock, the camp life settled down into a dismaying but on the surface orderly routine.[24] Both men and women worked at the camp workshops doing menial tasks for a few dollars a week. There was plenty of time to kill. Men and women took up hobbies, classes, and community work. But the sense of powerlessness, boredom, and constriction was pervasive.

In addition to the inconvenience, hardship, and frustration, the internment experience involved varied elements that undermined the traditional fabric of the Japanese community and family. For instance, in the camp, age suddenly lost much of its significance as a sign of status and privilege, essentially because the War Relocation Authority regarded individuals as equals in employment and in the supply of provisions. In addition, Japan and its culture were summarily dismissed as the enemy and undemocratic. The tradition of community autonomy ceased to exist; and its cultural emphasis on hard work and achievement had little meaning in the federal relocation center.

The impact of these changes was most severe on Issei men. Since the camp authority made all the major political and economic decisions for the residents, the household head's status declined sharply: he was no longer a principal wage earner; he could not set a respectable model for his children; he himself was visibly powerless with respect to the external authority; and above all, he lost confidence in his old cultural heritage and in himself. On the other hand, the younger Nisei could cope with the situation better than his father could. He had American citizenship, a command of English, and less attachment to Japanese culture. Added to this changing status of the two generations, the WRA's policy of appointing only American citizens to administrative positions resulted in the Nisei's ascendance and eventual assumption of leadership in the community and, to a limited extent, at home. This fast and drastic shift in power and status induced considerable frustration and stress among the Issei:

23. Kitano, p. 33; see also Allan R. Bosworth, *America's Concentration Camps* (New York, 1967); Leonard Broom and John Kitsuse, *The Managed Casualty* (Berkeley, 1956).

24. Several Nisei scholars have written revealing personal accounts of life in the relocation camp. For example, Raisuke Kitagawa, *Issei and Nisei: The Internment Years* (New York, 1967); Bill Hosokawa, *Nisei: The Quiet Americans* (New York, 1969). See also Masako Osako, "Aging and Family among Japanese Americans: The Role of Ethnic Tradition in the Adjustment to Old Age," *The Gerontologist* 19 (No. 5, 1979), 448-455.

The men looked as if they had suddenly aged ten years. They lost their capacity
to plan for their own futures, let alone those of their sons and daughters. . . .
In one sense, it was more a matter of morale than morals.[25]

Significantly, however, as Kitagawa points out, the Issei father did not lose
affection and concern for his loved ones, and "no immorality to speak of, say, in
terms of irregular sex relations, existed."[26] Furthermore, after leaving the relocation center, even though the Issei were more dependent on their own children than
before, most of them resumed life as responsible citizens and family men.[27]

Why did not the abrupt and drastic status change of the Issei lead to apathy
or antisocial behavior, as it often did in the case of other ethnic minorities, such as
blacks and Indians? We have already seen that in the traditional Japanese village
older people were expected to render their authority to the younger generation at
a culturally prescribed time. What happened to the Issei in the camp, then, is in
principle consistent with the course of events in traditional rural Japan, even
though the transfer in the camp was carried out more brutally. Thus the basic
cultural continuity between traditional practice and camp experience eased the
possibly harmful impact of the new environment upon family solidarity.

Of course, cultural continuity by itself was not a sufficient condition to
maintain family cohesion. The strong Japanese emphasis on the importance of
kinship solidarity must have prevented some households from breaking up.[28]
Similarly, the cultural definition of the woman's role helped to ease the adverse
impact of the internment on the family. Since the Japanese mother traditionally
played a major role in managing domestic tension when there was strife between
husband and son, she mediated between them and comforted the one who was
defeated. She managed to play this role effectively because the internment
affected her life and status more benignly than that of her spouse. Moreover,
for the first time in her life she had time for taking hobby classes and socializing
with friends in the camp.[29]

Even though a large majority of families kept themselves together, the level
of family solidarity varied from one household to another. In their study of family
life in and after the relocation camp, Bloom and Kitsuse do recognize such
variations and observe that families controlled by authoritarian fathers were more
vulnerable than those whose members were tied together primarily by affection.[30]
The presence of families and individuals who could not successfully cope with the
pressures of the internment does not contradict our interpretation, for families
incorporated the cultural traits discussed above with variations.

25. Kitagawa, *Issei and Nisei*, p. 91.
26. *Ibid.*, p. 92.
27. Petersen, pp. 131-143; Kitano, pp. 44-46.
28. See Beardsley et al., *Village in Japan*; Robert Bellah, *Tokugawa Religion* (New York, 1957);
Ezra Vogel, *Japan's New Middle Class* (Berkeley, 1964).
29. Kitagawa, pp. 91-92.
30. Bloom and Kitsuse, *The Managed Casualty*, p. 40.

At the internment camps, located in remote and barren areas of the interior, the evacuees began life again in a state of physical and emotional shock. Most severely affected were Issei men, whose status as heads of households declined sharply because the War Relocation Authority made the major economic and political decisions for residents. Courtesy of the War Relocation Authority.

In many ways, the relocation camp had the characteristics of a prison; but in other important ways it did not. For example, the relocation authority kept the family as the basic unity and eventually took an initiative in relocating its residents. As early as 1942, when it became clear that there were no real grounds for the fear of Japanese-Americans as a threat to national security, the WRA authority began to plan moving its residents to regions other than the Pacific Coast. The first group of camp inmates who left the center were students: they went to attend colleges in the Midwest and East. Other Nisei followed, aided by YMCA and Quaker groups in finding employment and housing. Finally, the Issei parents followed their children. One by one, they moved to cities like Pittsburgh, Milwaukee, New York, and Chicago.

Two weary but proud Issei mothers hold flags signifying that each has four sons serving in the United States armed forces.   Courtesy of the War Relocation Authority.

Settling in Chicago

There was a small Japanese population in Chicago prior to World War II. The first-known Japanese national was Kamenosuke Nishi, who moved to this city from San Francisco in 1893 to open a gift shop at the time of the Columbian Exposition.[31] He is said to have amassed $700,000 from the successful management of a store at the corner of Cottage Grove and 27th Street. Handfuls of other Japanese managed small shops or worked at restaurants. The size of the ethnic group increased slowly. As late as 1927, there were only 300 Japanese

31. Ryoichi Fujii, *Shikago Nikkeijinshi* [History of Japanese Americans in Chicago] (Chicago, 1968), p. 85. This section draws heavily from Mr. Fujii's work.

Japanese-Americans, despite the pain of being put into relocation centers, volunteered to serve in the U.S. forces in World War II.   Courtesy of Mosako Osako.

nationals in the city. They worked mostly in small shops and restaurants, with the exception of Japanese firms such as Mikimoto Pearls and Nippon Shipping Company. Partly because the group was small, unlike their counterparts on the West Coast, they continued to conduct their daily lives in Chicago without public persecution, even during World War II.

The first arrival of internment camp residents in Chicago is recorded on June 12, 1942. The substantial migration occurred from March of the following year through 1950; of 110,000 nationally interned, nearly 30,000 Japanese Americans moved to Chicago. Many stayed in this city permanently, but almost half returned to the West Coast when the region was freed from the classification of a military sensitive zone. The westward exodus ended by 1960, stabilizing the ethnic population in Chicago at around 15,000.

Pictured here on the right is Ross Harano of the Japanese-American
Citizens League, now chairman of the Illinois Consultation on
Ethnicity, thanking former Illinois Attorney General Neil Hartigan for his
support of a federal "redress" law that won reparation payments for
surviving Japanese-American internees.   Courtesy of Ross Harano.

There were important reasons why Chicago seemed inviting. Most important, there were jobs in this city. Unlike Detroit or Pittsburgh, Chicago was
never dominated by a single industry; it had various light manufacturing and
service industries. Clothing, printing, and furniture and cabinet factories existed
in large numbers here.[32] Even though the Issei were largely farmers or small
storekeepers with little industrial skill or English-language proficiency, they had

32. U.S. Government Census Bureau, *Japanese, Chinese, and Filipinos in America* (Washington, D.C., 1973). During World War II, labor shortages were a problem in the city. Elmer E.
Shirrell, Midwest Regional Director of the WRA, tried to recruit Japanese Americans from the
relocation camps. "Employers in Chicago are clamouring for American Japanese workers because
3,500 job offers are going begging. . . . Chicago must find 375,000 new workers by December 1
[1943], if the city is to carry its allotted load of the war contract" (*Chicago Tribune*, Oct. 1, 1943).

the proverbial manual dexterity. They were valuable to craft factories such as clothing and furniture makers. Since all Japanese women took sewing lessons as young girls, they were highly skilled seamstresses. Furthermore, hotels and restaurants were abundant in Chicago, and their jobs required neither prior training nor English-language ability.

Compared to the West Coast, Chicago appeared to be more open to Asian immigrants. Even during World War II, the Japanese experienced little overt discrimination, such as physical attacks. Moreover, a number of employers, among them Stevens Hotel, Edgewater Beach Hotel, McGraw-Hill Publishing Company, and Curtiss Candy, were willing to hire Japanese. The relative lack of anti-Japanese feeling was clearly seen in local newspapers. In contrast to the Hearst papers, which spearheaded anti-Japanese sentiments in California, four of the five major Chicago dailies supported the Japanese settlement.[33] From 1943 to 1945, several favorable articles appeared in local papers. For example, on August 12, 1943, Elmer E. Shirrell, Midwest regional director of the War Relocation Authority, was quoted as saying, "Employers are pleased with the quickness and adaptability of their Japanese help."[34] And on September 5, 1945, a headline in the *Chicago Tribune* read: "Jap-Americans sent to Chicago making good: 10,000 prove they are good citizens."

The appearance of ample opportunity and the relative absence of discrimination encouraged many Japanese to migrate to Chicago. But there were problems. The problem of adjustment was serious for many Issei. In the West they had spent most of their lives as farmers and shopkeepers in segregated Japanese communities. Now, in their old age, they were forced to begin a new life in the city; now they had to work with non-Japanese workers and live next door to non-Japanese neighbors. Misunderstandings resulting from language deficiency were common. Many Issei were obliged to work in unskilled jobs that failed to use their occupational skills. To ease the frustration, some took to drinking and gambling. Not surprisingly, however, a large majority held steady jobs and kept the family intact.

Another problem was the hesitation of many Chicagoans to offer jobs and apartments to Japanese applicants.[35] The mass media were generally favorable to the Japanese Americans' arrival, but because of the negative, propaganda stereotypes fostered during the war, many managers were reluctant to hire Japanese. Similar attitudes existed among landlords and apartment owners. Community leaders visited prospective employers to explain that their apprehension was groundless. And, pressured by the relative labor shortage during the war, they hired a few Japanese — reluctantly at first. As the workers proved to be reliable and hardworking, they gradually opened up more positions to other Japanese Americans. A similar pattern can be observed in apartment

33. Fujii, *Shikago Nikkeijinshi*, p. 95.
34. *Ibid.*, p. 98.
35. *Ibid.*, pp. 104-111.

leasing. It was no accident that the resettlers first congregated in the Hyde Park-Kenwood and North Side areas: the former was a racially transitional area (today almost exclusively black, except for the University of Chicago area) and the latter was a mixture of commercial and industrial areas with low residential values. There was initial resistance on the part of apartment owners, but when they realized that Japanese families were clean, quiet, and punctual in paying the rent, their reluctance disappeared. A Caucasian neighbor is said to have mentioned, "Simply by looking at the sidewalk you can tell where the Japanese live, because they keep not only the front yard, but also the sidewalk, clean."

The inability of the Japanese to purchase burial sites was still another crucial problem.[36] In 1942, for example, a Japanese nurse was killed in an automobile accident. Since no cemetery would accept her body, it was kept in a funeral home for an entire week. Finally she was buried in Montrose Cemetery, in a small communal plot that had been purchased by the Japanese Mutual Aid Society. In a separate incident, another cemetery discovered the Japanese background of an individual already buried there, and threatened his family with exhumation of the body. The Montrose communal burial plot was small, since it was purchased when the Japanese population in the city was a few thousand, and the problem of burial sites became acute as the Japanese population mushroomed to over 20,000 and many of the Issei became old.

In 1947 the Japanese Mutual Aid Society queried twenty-six cemeteries in the city about their policy on accepting the burial of Japanese.[37] Only three of them replied, and only one positively. Realizing the seriousness of the matter, the society appealed to the City Human Rights Commission, which subsequently organized a meeting between the representatives of cemeteries and the leaders of the Japanese community. But the managers, using constitutionally guaranteed freedom of enterprise as their sacred right, would not change their discriminatory stand. An unexpected break came when "Washington Merry-Go-Round" journalist Drew Pearson did a broadcast about the plight of Japanese Chicagoans who had no funeral plots in which to bury their deceased. Soon the *Chicago Daily News* took up this issue. To avoid the reputation of racial bias, the municipal offices pressured the cemetery owners to cooperate. Finally, a few cemeteries agreed to sell plots to Japanese. Today Japanese tombs are concentrated in three of the ten graveyards in the city of Chicago, with only a few in the suburbs.

To overcome the discrimination and adjustment problems of such bizarre experiences, Japanese-Americans initially found the support of community groups critically important. But the eventual success was gained basically through the hard work and determination of each individual Japanese person.

---

36. *Ibid.*, pp. 146-149; see also Japanese American Mutual Aid Society of Chicago, "History of Japanese American Mutual Aid Society" (undated brochure).

37. Fujii, p. 148.

In the very beginning of the postinternment period, a few Japanese groups were organized by former community leaders on the West Coast and in the camps, as well as old residents in Chicago. In cooperation with Christian organizations, notably Quakers and the YWCA, they aided newcomers in settling. Finding jobs and living quarters was their main function. In addition, community leaders contacted government offices, cemetery managements, apartment owners, and employers to counteract anti-Japanese sentiment. They were successful in breaking trends, but their effort bore fruit because Japanese quickly gained their colleagues' and neighbors' acceptance through hard work and honesty.

That these social service functions to fellow Japanese Americans were soon lessened indicates the success of these community groups. As early as 1946, the Japanese Mutual Aid Society organized a campaign to send relief materials to wartorn Japan, diverting their attention from service to fellow Japanese Americans. Ryōichi Fujii, local historian of Chicago Japanese Americans, reports that in November 1947 the Japanese community in Chicago donated 5,500 pounds of clothing and $7,000 in cash to be shipped to Japan.[38] Similar efforts were repeated several times during the following years when the Asian homeland was devastated by floods, earthquakes, and other natural calamities. Reflecting the successful adjustment of the Japanese Americans in Chicago, only two organizations today continue to render social services to the community members: the Japanese American Service Committee offers a wide range of services to the Japanese-American community, including counseling, educational and cultural programs, social events, hot meals for the aged, and Issei sheltered-workshops; the Chicago Mutual Aid Society offers a limited number of small loans to its members.

The reduced activities of social service organizations is understandable given the income profile of Japanese Americans provided by the Census Bureau. Gradually, the proportion of households under the poverty level had declined to 6 percent by 1970. At the same time, the censuses of 1950, 1960, and 1970 suggest an expanding middle-class segment among Japanese Americans.

Current Social Attainment

Most of the Issei are now retired or deceased, and a large portion of the Sansei are still in school. Therefore, the Nisei still constitute the bulk of the Japanese-American labor force. There are several indications that many Japanese-American males in Chicago have attained comfortable middle-class status. According to the 1970 Census, 20.0 percent were professionals, 23.1 percent occupy managerial positions, and 22.8 percent were in white-collar occupations. Similarly, 37.4 percent were college graduates and 85 percent had high school diplomas. The figures for Japanese-American males in the state of Illinois, which

38. *Ibid.*, pp. 141-146.

closely approximate the Chicago SMSA statistics, reveal a stabilizing trend from 1970 to 1980. The total proportion for the high-prestige occupations "Managerial, Officials, etc." and "Professional, Technical and Kindred Workers" remained virtually constant from 43.9 percent in 1970 to 43.1 percent in 1980. Similarly, the proportion of Japanese-American males in the medium-prestige occupations, "Craftsmen, Foremen, etc." and "Clerical, Sales, and Kindred Workers" changed little from 35.3 percent in 1970 to 36.7 percent in 1980.

These occupational and educational accomplishments, when contrasted with the past data, indicate a remarkable intergenerational mobility. According to the 1950 Census, of Japanese male descendants aged forty-five years and over, who were mostly Issei, only 3.4 percent were professionals and 17.9 percent white collar. Similarly, the group's schooling was limited: in 1950, 4.8 percent were college graduates and 31.7 percent had high school diplomas.

This achievement, however, does not mean that Japanese Americans are today completely free from the influence of racial discrimination and prejudice. Patricia Roos has found that the Japanese Americans' average earnings and status are less than those of Caucasians. She argues that "wage discrimination, structural unemployment, and minimal upward mobility within work organizations" plague Japanese and other Asian-Americans. She attributes these signs of underachievement in part to the lack of verbal skill and the nonassertiveness of Japanese Americans.[39]

For the leaders of the Japanese American Citizens' League (JACL), this is not a surprise, for they have counseled many cases of job discrimination through its affirmative action subcommittee. The subcommittee has taken up several cases for investigation, but lack of funding is preventing the processing of more cases. The typical complaint is concerned with promotion. For instance, an engineer is on the verge of quitting his job after ten years of service in a Chicago camera company, because, despite his fine technical performance, the management has promoted all the others in the department except him. The JACL complains that the employers are pressured by both white and black groups, but since Asians are generally neither assertive nor organized, they are the last ones to be promoted. A JACL member observed:

> A typical Nisei professional is a graduate of a local state university with a B.A. degree in engineering or science. He works for an organization of varying size as a technical staff member, but his career history does not indicate an orderly promotion pattern. He is likely to remain as a technical staff member with little managerial or supervisory responsibility. In short, the Nisei's occupational attainments often fail to be commensurate with academic credentials.[40]

39. See Masako Osako, "Aging and Family among Japanese Americans."
40. Although quantitative evidence is not yet available for Japanese-Americans, several articles argue similar points regarding Chinese Americans. For example, Wen Lan Li, "Chinese

Having properly qualified the so-called success story of Japanese Americans, we are now ready to ask: Why did Japanese Americans, despite race and past persecution, attain substantial upward mobility in the United States? The significance of this accomplishment is particularly evident in view of their agrarian and relatively lower-class origins and the severity of racial discrimination, which culminated in their wartime internment. Historians and sociologists find a common explanation in two strains in the Japanese tradition: its normative stress on discipline, hard work, achievement, and education on the one hand, and the solidarity of family and community on the other. For example, Harry Kitano observes: ". . . appeals to obligation, duty, and responsibility . . . and ethnic identification" account for the Japanese-American's achievement.[41] The Issei exerted pressure on the Nisei to conform to the cultural norms through cultivating the feeling of shame and guilt, a traditional socializing technique. Underachievers were made to feel guilty and ashamed by remarks like, "With these poor grades on your report cards, I wouldn't dare to face your teacher at the next school conference." Another equally effective means of reinforcing desired behavior was an appeal to ethnic identity. Many Nisei recall the Issei's admonition, "Japanese boys don't cry like that" or "Good Japanese don't think about things like that."

The emphasis on hard work and ethnic pride are effective in inducing desired behavior when the parents themselves live by these norms and provide secure, loving homes. Most Issei presented a reasonably close model, working hard and keeping the family intact, despite adverse circumstances. Of course, there were some Issei fathers who drank, gambled, and even beat their wives. Some Nisei still have harsh words about their fathers, but virtually all of them recall their mothers as hardworking, loving, and strong — protecting the children from society's harassment as well as from the father's anger and despair. A Nisei woman reminisces about her mother:

> My mother helped father in their produce shop. In the morning while he went to the market, she cooked breakfast, cleaned the house and prepared the store. After father returned, she unloaded with him, arranged and sold vegetables and fruits. While doing all these, somehow she found time to do our laundry, sew our clothes, and supervise our homework. I remember my exhausted mother, ironing our dresses late at night so that we would look neat at school.

Clearly, the stable and close family was instrumental in raising Nisei into responsible adults.

Americans: Exclusion from the Melting Pot," in Gary and Rosalind Dworkin, eds., *The Minority Report;* John T. Ma, "The Professional Chinese Americans," in Yuan-Li Wu, ed., *Economic Conditions of Chinese Americans* (Chicago, 1980).

41. Kitano, p. 68.

Spanning the generations: Issei, Nisei, Sansei. A grandfather (Issei) and granddaughter (Sansei) enjoy each other's company at a Kenjinkai picnic in Montrose Park, June 1979.   Courtesy of Masako Osako.

The Japanese-American family could maintain its effective role because the ethnic community supported its efforts. The support was rendered in two ways. First, by maintaining the ethnic culture intact, the community legitimated the traditional emphasis on discipline and education. Second, the community aided the Issei in counteracting racial discrimination and economic pressure. It is plausible that without such support many Japanese-American families could have succumbed to the stress, failing to raise children into respectable, well-adjusted adults.

Suburbanization and Interracial Marriage

Family and community played a vital role in the assimilation and ascendancy of Japanese Americans. But today there are signs of changes in these institutions. During the last fifteen years Japanese Americans have begun moving to the Chicago suburbs. Most upper-middle-class suburbs, except Kenilworth and Lake Forest, are now completely open to Asian residents. The loosening of racial barriers in the suburbs and the Japanese Americans' attainment of middle-class status occurred at about the same time. Presently, one out of four Chicago Japanese-American households is in the suburbs. The suburbanites are younger, better educated, and have higher incomes. They are predominantly white-collar or professional workers, and their decision to move is like that of other Americans — largely influenced by the desire for better schools for their children.

What happens to their ties with family and ethnic community after the move? Generally, their participation in the organized activities of the ethnic community in the city becomes less frequent, even though some maintain contact as members of church and temple. When the children are in school, the suburban Nisei parents are involved in local groups such as PTA and Boy Scouts.[42] As the children reach their teens, the wives generally obtain jobs and thus lose considerable time for and interest in community activities, either those of Japanese Americans or white Americans. The contact with Japanese American friends in the city also becomes less frequent and more formal, as the Nisei leave the city for the suburbs. City-dwelling and suburban Nisei share fewer common issues and have greater traveling distances for visits.

A sizable minority of suburban Nisei are now arriving at a state in the life cycle where their children have left them for college, jobs, or their own families. Now many of them have both time and money. Are those people returning to the Japanese-American community? Their personal friendships with fellow Japanese Americans sometimes revive in late middle age. They may join group tours organized by ethnic travel agents. But because they are employed by non-Japanese enterprises, they are largely independent of the ethnic community in the city. Furthermore, even though some suburbs have a sizable Japanese-American population, there have been few instances of Japanese clubs or groups in these places.

Admittedly, the move to the suburbs generally diminishes the frequency of contact with fellow Japanese Americans, but kinship ties remain strong. This author's study indicates that suburban and city-dwelling Japanese Americans feel equally committed to a child's filial responsibility to parents. As expected, however, intergenerational contact is less frequent between suburban-living children and their parents in the city. The children now visit their parents perhaps once a week to share a meal and some chore.

---

42. The information about the effect of suburbanization is primarily drawn from the present author's recent study of 250 Japanese-American families in Chicago.

Whether or not the Japanese Americans continue to maintain close ties with relatives in the future depends in part on a new development in Japanese-American mating patterns. While only 15 percent of the Nisei have married non-Japanese, as many as one-half of the *Sansei* (the third generation) are choosing spouses from other ethnic groups.[43] The 1980 Census figures are highly consistent with this finding. Of Japanese-American males born in the Chicago area, as few as 37 percent in the 25 to 34-year-old category are married to women of the same race, compared to 86 percent for the 45 to 64-year-old group. While the figures for the 15-24-year-old category are too small to make a generalization, none of the twenty-one counted in the census married women of the same race. Most Sansei children in the Chicago area grow up among non-Japanese people. Given the dispersion of Japanese in the schools and the increasing acceptance of marriage with non-Japanese among the Nisei parents, the trend is likely to continue. Eventually, Japanese Americans may become the first nonwhites to merge biologically into the dominant American society.

What happens to kinship interaction when Japanese Americans marry outside their ethnic group? Beyond the point that the total preservation of cultural patterns would be slim, it is impossible to generalize; there is a wide variation from one case to another. In one instance, an only daughter married a Caucasian boyfriend against the family's wishes; her family severed ties with her. Adding to her plight, the marriage soon failed. Rumor has it that this young woman, a semifinalist in the National Merit Scholar competition, has dropped out of college and become a bar waitress. In another case, a Sansei boy married an Irish-American girl, the third child among nine, whom he met while both had part-time jobs at a grocery store. Now he is in business school and she is a teacher trainee. The couple lives next door to his parents, and his grandparents, who live on the same block, delight in the smaller siblings of their new Irish granddaughter-in-law.

A Current Trend:
Expanding Business Community of Japanese Nationals

The expanding activities of corporations from Japan have brought about another major change in the Chicago Japanese-American community. During the 1960s, fewer than a hundred Japanese companies had offices in Chicago. These were primarily engaged in cross-national border business such as transportation, travel, or import/export. Importers were often specialized in quaint gift items from the East such as fans, pearls, and china. However, following

---

43. See Darrel Montero and Gene Levine, "Socioeconomic Mobility Among Three Generations of Japanese Americans," *Journal of Social Issues* 29 (No. 2), 33-48. See also Sylvia J. Yanagisako, *Transforming the Past: Tradition and Kinship Among Japanese Americans* (Stanford, 1989).

vigorous industrial development in Japan through the 1960s and 1970s, the number of Japanese corporations with an office in the Chicago area grew to nearly 200 by 1980. By this time, the nature of these businesses had also increased in variety. As the import of Japanese industrial goods such as electronics and automobiles increased, manufacturing companies set up service and sale offices across the Midwest. These were followed by parts suppliers and then machinery makers. In the early '80s, a cluster of some 100 firms formed an industrial park in the Elk Grove area, north of O'Hare Airport. Then banks began to move into downtown Chicago to serve American offices or subsidiaries of their customers in Japan. While The Bank of Tokyo and Dai Ichi Kangyo Bank (the largest bank in Japan) started their operations in the 1950s, it was only in the '80s that other major banks opened branch offices in Chicago. By 1990 all of Japan's top fifteen banks had operations in the city. Attracted by the reputation of Chicago as the second largest financial center in the United States, especially in the field of futures and options, major securities firms such as Nomura Securities and Daiwa Securities opened representative offices in the 1980s, joined by insurance and real estate companies that sought a variety of investment opportunities in the Midwest.

Today approximately 300 Japanese corporations have offices in the greater Chicago area, employing some 1,700 Japanese expatriates and a few thousand local employees. It is estimated that these Japanese nationals and their dependents amount to more than 3,500, or approximately 25 percent of the total Chicago-area population of Japanese ancestry. Following New York and Los Angeles, Chicago has the third largest concentration of Japanese businesses in the United States.[44]

Clearly, the visibility of Japanese businesses in Chicago, as elsewhere in the United States, is increasing. Toyota, Nissan, and Mazda cars are ubiquitous; so are Sony, Panasonic, and Toshiba electronics products. The Japanese influence is also visible in corporate financing. Today, nearly all major real estate financing in the city of Chicago involves the participation of a Japanese bank or insurance company. Japanese ownership of real estate (either full or partial) also includes such well-known structures as the AT&T Building and Morton International Building. Additionally, a large portion of the bonds issued by the city of Chicago and the state of Illinois are guaranteed by Japanese banks, such as Mitsubishi Bank and Industrial Bank of Japan.[45]

The Japanese businesses' presence is indeed significant in Chicago. How has it affected the experience of Japanese Americans in Chicago? One possible effect might be that the expanding Japanese business sector would absorb indigenous Japanese-American talents and delay their integration into the

44. Japanese American Chamber of Commerce and Industry, *JCCC Directory 1990* (Chicago, 1990).

45. *Ibid.*, pp. 160-170.

mainstream of U.S. society. However, such a development is not occurring, due mainly to a common Japanese personnel policy. The Chicago branch office of a Japanese corporation is typically staffed with three classes of employees: managers from the Japanese head office; professional or technical staff hired in Chicago; and clerical staff who are generally locally hired women. Japanese management does not have any reason to actively seek Japanese-American talent, for most office positions involve dealing with American customers and thus can be handled equally well by any qualified Americans or Japanese. A small number of staff who deal with Japanese clients must, of course, have a Japanese-language skill comparable to that of a Japanese national; but only a limited number of Nisei and virtually no Sansei possess such a command of the Japanese language. At the same time, from the perspective of talented Nisei and Sansei, Japanese firms do not offer attractive opportunities, since their chances for promotion are limited. As a result, in Japanese-managed offices, it is more common to find Japanese Americans in clerical and manual positions than in professional positions. Thus, unlike in New York, where some Japanese offices have opened up top positions to Americans, in Chicago ambitious Japanese Americans, particularly well-educated Sansei, tend to seek employment in non-Japanese firms, furthering their integration into the dominant American society.

The presence of a prosperous national group could potentially bring political benefits to the ethnic community through visibility, interpersonal contact, and economic strengths. However, in the case of Chicago Japanese Americans, such a benefit has failed to materialize. With a few exceptions, Japanese Americans do not occupy high-ranking positions, either elected or appointed, in city and state government. Such exceptions are the result of talented Japanese-American individuals' own efforts or the support of Asian-American groups, but not the aid of the Japanese business community. A major reason for this situation is that the indigenous Japanese-American community and the Japanese business community have by and large maintained separate existences with little interpersonal contact except for certain ceremonial occasions, such as a party to welcome a visiting Japanese dignitary.[46] As mentioned above, the activities of the former center around those ethnic group organizations such as Japanese American Service Committee (social service agency), Japanese American Citizens League (advocacy group), Buddhist temples, Christian churches, Kenjinkai (prefectural association), and various organizations of Asian Americans. On the other hand, Japanese nationals' organizational memberships are largely limited to Japanese American Society, Japanese American Chamber of

46. The case of Ross M. Harano, Chief of the Crime Victims Division at the office of Illinois Attorney General Neil Hartigan, may serve as an illustration. Harano has been active with the Japanese American Service Committee, Japanese American Citizens' League, American Indian Business Association, and numerous other Asian-American organizations, but he has no affiliations with groups whose memberships are primarily Japanese nationals.

Commerce, and various alumni associations of Japanese universities. Only a small number of Japanese Americans, mostly those who work on jobs that cater to the Japanese business community (e.g., bilingual law firms and travel agencies) are members of these groups.

More importantly, the Japanese nationals and Japanese Americans do not share common concerns. For the former, the main concerns include United States-Japan trade agreements that may restrict their business operations and the education of their children, who must re-enter the competitive Japanese educational system after three to five years in the United States. On the other hand, the major concerns of Japanese Americans in Chicago include the redress of damages associated with the internment during World War II and the establishment of a nursing home for Issei elderly.[47] The ethnic community began planning for the 180-bed JASC-supported nursing home in the early 1980s, and continued into the 1990s. Donations were widely solicited among Japanese Americans and Japanese corporations as well. However, response from the Japanese business community was disappointingly small. Reportedly, major Japanese corporations (many of which are among the world's one hundred largest) have donated only a modest sum, to the chagrin of the fund-raising committee. This is a manifestation of different priorities of Japanese Americans and Japanese nationals. Thus, the presence of Japanese nationals has had little or no effect upon the increasing assimilation of Japanese Americans.

Conclusion

Many Japanese-Americans today do not wish to be characterized as "the model minority," because the label implies the assumption that to be like "idealized" whites (i.e., hardworking, law-abiding, and middle class) should be the goal of minorities. And yet it cannot be denied that the Nisei and Sansei in Chicago have pursued largely middle-class occupations and lifestyles. The assets that Japanese Americans brought to this land — respect for hard work and education, familiarity with modern commercial and employment systems, and cohesive family and community — all contributed to their remarkable social mobility. An irony is that their very success in social mobility and assimilation appears to be inducing rapid changes in, if not the reduced importance of, their ethnic institutions.[48] Nearly one out of four Japanese Americans has moved to Chicago suburbs, and a large majority of them work for non-Japanese enter-

47. In 1988, forty-three years after the end of World War II, Congress authorized $1 billion in payment for Japanese Americans who were interned during the war. For the history of Japanese Americans' struggle to obtain the redress, see William M. Hohri, *Repairing America: An Account of the Movement for Japanese-American Redress* (Pullman, WA, 1988) and Roger Daniels et al., eds., *Japanese Americans, From Relocation to Redress* (Salt Lake City, 1986).

48. *The Chicago Shimpo: Japanese American News*, May 9, 1990, p. 1.

prises. The Nisei family tie is still very strong, measured in terms of interaction, exchange of services and goods, and sense of filial obligation; but the Sansei, many of whom are now reaching young adulthood, are different. They are politically more aware, they take their middle-class status for granted, and above all, they are marrying non-Japanese in large numbers. Whether or not the Japanese-American family will continue to retain distinctively Japanese elements, such as a sharp division of labor between the sexes, a strong sense of family loyalty, and an emphasis on discipline and success, is not at all certain. The census finding that the proportion of Japanese-American males in high-prestige occupations (i.e., managerial, professional, and technical jobs) remained virtually stable from 1970 to 1980 may indicate a declining commitment to upward mobility among ethnic group members.

Such an emerging trend appears to be more pronounced in Chicago than it does in regions like Hawaii and the West Coast, which have larger Japanese populations. The ethnic community in these centers is more persistent in part because of the large size. In contrast to 16,042 Japanese descendants in metropolitan Chicago, there are 117,190 in the Los Angeles area, and 190,218 in Honolulu. The residents of larger ethnic concentrations have more opportunity to work with, live with, and marry fellow Japanese Americans. Moreover, ethnicity is a politically recognizable force in Hawaii and on the West Coast, but in Chicago the Japanese-American population is too small to gain sizable political influence or clout. The Chicago political situation does not encourage Japanese ethnic group members to maintain a keen interest in the community as a whole.

Another major difference between Chicago and the cities with larger Japanese-American populations can be found in the ethnic group's relationship with Japanese *nationals*. Students from Japan and employees of Japanese firms and their families predominate among Japanese nationals in Chicago, and there is little interaction between these Japanese nationals and the descendants of immigrants from Japan. The former keep to themselves, and the latter say that they are "aloof" or "condescending." The West Coast and Honolulu situations differ from Chicago. For instance, the Japanese-American population is so large in these regions that even prestigious Japanese banks and businesses, for instance, find it profitable to establish branches to serve the American ethnic community. There the descendants of immigrants are not to be ignored but to be regarded as coveted clients.

It should also be pointed out that, in contrast to the Midwest, the Japanese-American communities in Hawaii and California rapidly absorb new arrivals from Japan who intend to become American citizens. Although the exact figure of new arrivals is not known, nursing homes for Issei aged are primarily staffed by Japanese nationals, and *Kenjinkai* (prefectural association) parties commonly employ Japan-born music groups. This new blood serves to perpetuate and update Japanese-American culture. Such an infusion is absent in Chicago. On the contrary, some Japanese Americans, feeling resentful of the Japanese nationals' alleged condescension, make it a policy to dissociate them from ethnic Japanese organizations. For example, several years ago the Midwest chapter of the Japanese American Citizens' League (JACL) did not participate in the protest against a radio station that broadcast anti-Japanese campaign messages claiming that Japan's aggressive business practices in the auto and steel industries were depriving Illinois residents of jobs. The civic group did not wish to be identified with Japanese national affairs.

Among various developments in the Japanese-American community, potentially the most significant is the rapidly increasing rate of Sansei interracial marriage. If the present high rate continues, assuming little geographical mobility and zero population growth for the ethnic group, in two generations three-quarters of the new Japanese-American children will be of mixed blood. Since interracial marriage is expected to increase, and younger Japanese-American generations are known for having small families, there is a good chance that in a few generations the full members of the Chicago Japanese-American population will have dwindled, and this ethnic group will biologically melt into the dominant white society.[49]

Our next research task seems to be to identify the social, demographic, and political contexts in which a racial minority biologically melts into a majority white population. Is such melting due to the small size of the ethnic population, its middle-class status, or the prestige of its mother nation as a superpower? Speculations are interesting, but this is certainly a profound issue that deserves a more systematic inquiry by future scholars of American ethnicity.

49. See Milton M. Gordon, *Assimilation in American Life* (New York, 1964); Thomas Sewell, "Ethnicity in a Changing America," *Daedalus* 107 (Winter 1978), 213-237.

CHAPTER 15

Asian Indians in Chicago:
Growth and Change in a Model Minority

PADMA RANGASWAMY

Chicago's Asian Indian population has enjoyed nearly thirty years of steady, continuous growth. They are busy living up to the myth of the model minority and at the same time trying to face up to the challenges that threaten it.

— Padma Rangaswamy, 1994

The myth of the model minority is at once true and false of the vibrant and fast-growing Asian Indian community of Chicago. On the one hand, the community is dominated by a highly educated, professional elite of doctors, engineers, scientists, and college professors who earn handsome salaries, live in comfortable suburban homes, drive luxury cars, and send their children to Ivy League schools. This group has broken almost every rule governing old immigration theories. Indeed, they are called "new" immigrants not only because they arrived recently but because they differed from the old immigration in significant ways. They were neither poor nor wretched, like the immigrants of yore; nor did they flee from a miserable existence in India. Instead of clustering in city ghettoes as previous immigrants have done, they moved rapidly into affluent suburban neighborhoods, climbed the economic ladder, and captured the American dream with remarkable ease. At the other end of the spectrum are the newly arrived, still-struggling Indian immigrants who lack language and professional skills, need basic job training, and are trapped in the clutches of a depressed economy. They find the adjustment to America slow and painful, and are yet to attain the self-sufficiency and confidence needed to move away from their own countrymen. Both groups, however, share the same rich cultural heritage of India and are unified in their attempts to recreate it and experience it anew in America. Supported by an intricate infrastructure of religious and cultural institutions, strengthened by professional and social special-interest ethnic groups, and catered to by an enterprising merchant community that can import practically anything they want from India, Chicago's Asian Indian population has enjoyed nearly thirty years of steady and continuous growth. They are busy living up to the myth of the model minority and at the same time trying to face up to the challenges that threaten it.

If it were not for the enumeration of Asian Indians as a separate ethnic group for the first time in the 1980 U.S. census, the dramatic growth of the Asian Indian community in Chicago — as elsewhere in the United States — might have remained an easily recognizable but difficult-to-assess phenomenon. We might not have known, for instance, that Indians had a growth rate of 125 percent between 1980 and 1990, representing one of the fastest-growing subgroups under the Asian-American umbrella, or that they numbered 815,000 nationwide in the 1990 census, equivalent to 11 percent of the Asian American population. The figures for the Chicago metropolitan area are equally impressive. There are 57,992 Asian Indians in Chicago and its six surrounding counties according to the 1990 census (an 82 percent growth over 1980), and they account for fully 25 percent of all Asian Americans in the area.[1]

Both the atypical characteristics and the rapid growth of the Indian immigrant population, in the United States in general as well as Chicago in particular, need to be understood in a larger context. If the Indians are so well educated and belong to the upper class in their own country, what are they doing in the United States? Why Chicago? Why not New Delhi, Bombay, Calcutta, or Madras? There are many complex answers to these question, and thereby hangs a fascinating and intriguing tale of Indian immigrants and what draws them abroad to distant lands.[2]

The American Context

Indians have a long and checkered history of immigration to the United States. The first lone Asian Indian set foot in America in 1820, and he was followed by a trickle of merchants, seamen, travelers, and missionaries amounting to no more than 700 up to the turn of the century.[3] The first significant wave of immigration to the United States took place between 1900 and 1910, when more than 3,000 agricultural workers, mostly Sikhs from Punjab, came to the Pacific Coast. They entered

---

1. Source: 1990 U.S. Census Bureau.

2. Asian Indians will henceforth be referred to as "Indians" in the text. Only in the American context do Indians need qualifiers like "East Indians" or "Asian Indians," so as not to be confused with the native American Indians. Since it is established that we are speaking of Indians from Asia, the term "Indians," which is the only term Indians themselves are comfortable with, should suffice. Arthur W. and Usha M. Helweg, *An Immigrant Success Story. East Indians in America* (Philadelphia: University of Pennsylvania Press, 1991), p. 142.

3. Joan M. Jensen, "East Indians," in *Harvard Encyclopedia of American Ethnic Groups*, S. Thernstrom, ed. (Cambridge: Harvard University Press, 1980), pp. 296-301.

America at a time when anti-Asian sentiment was rampant, and though they tried to live peacefully, working on the Western Pacific Railroad and the lumber mills of Washington, they aroused the hostility and suspicion of white Americans, especially the Asiatic Exclusion League and the American Federation of Labor, who campaigned vigorously against the "ragheads" and the "Hindoo menace." Driven down the Pacific Coast, the Sikhs were forced to seek refuge in the rural areas of California's Central Valley. Here they reverted to their agricultural traditions, and in spite of being discriminated against, they became successful farmers and some rose to distinction as prominent citizens.[4] There is a Sikh community in California that traces its religious and cultural heritage to these first immigrants.[5]

Immigration from India to the United States virtually stopped when Congress passed exclusion laws in 1917 and 1924. It picked up again shortly after 1946, when the Asian quota was relaxed to allow limited immigration, naturalization of Indian residents, and non-quota immigration of family members: about 6,000 Indians entered the United States between 1947 and 1965.[6]

After 1965, the number of Indians who entered the United States increased dramatically. According to Immigration and Naturalization Service (INS) figures, a total of 469,000 Indians were admitted as immigrants between 1961 and 1990. The increased inflow from India was a direct result of changes in the immigration law in 1965 that abolished the national origins quota, provided for family unification, and granted visas to those having skills, professions, or talents needed in the United States. This time around, the Indian immigrants were radically different from the earlier group. Not only were they well-educated, they came from all over India (not just from Punjab), they settled all over the United States (not just in California), and the women came in equally large numbers as the men (there were no women in the first group). The unprecedented transformation of the American economy from an industrialized to a post-industrialized era demanded the kinds of skills that Indians had in abundance, and the Midwest, as the traditional heartland of industrial America that was endowed with a broad economic base, attracted Indians in large numbers.[7]

4. Dalip Singh Saund, one of these farmers who became the first (and so far only) Indian U.S. Congressman. He was elected from California and served two terms — from 1957 to 1963 — and was on the House Foreign Relations Committee.

5. Joan M. Jensen, *Passage from India: Asian Indian Immigrants in North America* (New Haven: Yale University Press, 1988); Brett Melendy, *Asians in America: Filipinos, Koreans & East Indians* (Boston: Twayne Publishers, 1977); Ronald Takaki, *Strangers from a Different Shore: A History of Asian Americans* (Boston: Little, Brown & Co., 1989).

6. S. Chandrasekhar, ed., *From India to America: A Brief History of Immigration: Problems of Discrimination, Admission & Assimilation* (La Jolla: Population Review, 1982).

7. Those who came from India to fill this need were part of a broader trend in immigration where non-European immigrants far outnumbered their European counterparts. See Surinder M. Bhardwaj and N. Madhusudana Rao, "Asian Indians in the United States" in *South Asians Overseas,* Colin Clarke, Ceri Peach, and Steven Vertovec, eds. (Cambridge: Cambridge University Press, 1990), pp. 197-217.

The Indian Context

But the paradigm of America as the land of golden opportunity is a partial and inadequate model for explaining the presence of Indians in Chicago and other metropolitan areas of the United States. The question Why leave India? still remains unanswered. For a deeper understanding of the mindset of the Indian immigrant, we need to briefly visit newly independent India and the milieu in which the Indian immigrants came of age.

Unlike many other Asian Americans, such as the Koreans or the Vietnamese, Indians learned English in grade school and spoke the language fluently long before entering America. Many Indian immigrants attended convent schools or public schools modelled on the British education system. This legacy of colonialism has given them an enormous advantage and helped them gain a firm foothold in America, both professionally and in the society at large. Having graduated from American-style engineering colleges and medical institutions in India, they are very comfortable with the American professional culture and the work ethic here.

Besides this, the West has always held a certain glamor and mystique for the middle class Indian. In the 1950s and 1960's, many Indians went abroad for higher education and on their return landed lucrative jobs with prestigious public and private companies. Going *phoren* ("foreign" in playful Indian parlance) became a craze. After 1965 the steady stream of Indians going abroad became a virtual tidal wave. The reasons given for the "brain drain" (the phenomenon of educated Indians leaving for the West) are numerous, and the most commonly cited are: the prestige of higher education abroad (a carry-over of the colonial mentality); the exasperating bureaucracy and the corruption of the "license" raj in India (so-called because of the bribe-ridden system of issuing licenses or permits for every civic amenity, home utility, or industrial undertaking); and the lack of employment opportunities for highly educated professionals. The high unemployment rates for doctors and engineers in India during these years, and the enormous disparity in professional incomes between India and the United States, are also important factors. But the personal and individual circumstances of migration for the Indian immigrant are as varied and sometimes as unfathomable as those for any other immigrant from any other part of the world. Generally speaking, the decision to immigrate involved the entire family and was not taken individually or in isolation.[8]

For the Indian, the lure of higher education as well as the professional and business opportunities in America was also balanced with the knowledge that in this high-technology, information-oriented era, India was only a long-distance phone call or a sixteen-to-twenty-hour plane ride away. "Leaving" India was not a one-way journey, and it was definitely worth the experiment. Many

8. Helweg & Helweg, pp. 27-44.

TABLE 15.1
Asian Indians in the United States

	Asian Indians	Distribution of Asian Indians in the U.S.	Asian Americans	Asian Indians as % of Asian Americans
U.S.	815,000	100%	7,274,000	11.2%
Northeast	285,000	35%	1,335,000	21.3%
Midwest	146,000	17.9%	768,000	19%
South	196,000	24%	1,122,000	17.5%
West	189,000	23.1%	4,048,000	5%

Source: Statistical Abstract of the United States 1992 U.S. Dept. of Commerce, Economic and Statistical Administration Bureau of the Census.

Indians who had been reared on the ideals of Gandhi and Nehru and the urgent need to build a strong and independent India, were convinced that their stay in America would only be temporary and that they would return to their homeland where they belonged as soon as they had made some money. But as more and more Indians came across to America and became financially success-ful, they found it more and more difficult to return. Instead, they used the "preference" system to bring their immediate relatives over. Many of these family members were nonprofessional, and so the community gradually changed in character from an exclusive, professionally trained elite to a more motley group, increasingly diverse in economic and occupational status, but still knit together by kinship ties. The family bond remains strong and resilient and is perhaps the single most important force keeping the community together. A close look at Chicago's Indian immigrants and their special lifestyles will show how, despite the occupational and income differences, Indians are united by their strong belief in family ties, as well as their religious and cultural traditions.

The Chicago Asian Indians

The Indians in Chicago are in many ways representative of Indians in the large metropolitan centers of New York, Los Angeles, or Houston. An extensive survey of first-generation Indian immigrants in the Chicago area was conducted by the author in 1992 to study the community firsthand. Results of the survey (based on 573 respondents) are used throughout this essay to describe the main characteristics of the Chicago community. Statistics show that, at least with respect to basic demographics, Indians in Chicago are no different from Indians in other parts of the United States.[9] Indians flock to those areas that offer

9. Very often, other South Asians, namely the Pakistanis, Sri Lankans, and Bangladeshis are lumped together with Indians. The U.S. census, however, enumerates Asian Indians separately from

TABLE 15.2
Growth of Asian-Indian population in Chicago and suburbs
(with 1990 population of over 500)

	1980	1990	Growth
Chicago	11,209	16,386	+46%
Suburbs	20,649	41,606	+102%
County			
Cook	23,062	39,225	+70%
DuPage	6,381	14,172	+122%
Kane	510	754	+48%
Lake	1,012	2,257	+123%
McHenry	130	305	+135%
Will	763	1,279	+68%
Suburb			
Addison	445	1,087	+144%
Bensenville	212	619	+192%
Bolingbrook	406	566	+39%
Carol Stream	243	646	+166%
Des Plaines	482	1,051	+118%
Downers Grove	448	698	+56%
Elk Grove Village	508	637	+25%
Elmhurst	277	504	+82%
Evanston	314	632	+101%
Forest Park	443	540	+22%
Glendale Heights	593	1,177	+99%
Hanover Park	453	964	+113%
Hoffman Estates	497	1,347	+171%
Lombard	317	642	+103%
Morton Grove	223	622	+179%
Mount Prospect	458	1,291	+182%
Naperville	327	1,468	+349%
Niles	266	557	+109%
Oakbrook	151	736	+387%
Schaumburg	541	1,218	+125%
Skokie	880	2,292	+160%
Westmont	299	570	+91%
Wheaton	261	531	+103%
Wheeling	150	545	+263%
Woodridge	290	637	+120%

Source: 1990 Census of Population, General Population Characteristics, Illinois, Table 6 1980 Census, Table 15.

TABLE 15.3
Occupational distribution of Asian Indians

Occupation	Census 1980	Chicago survey 1992
Managerial and Professional	48.5%	53%
Technical, sales, administrative support	24%	28%
Service	7.8%	—
Operators, fabricators, and laborers	9.6%	3%
Self-employed	8%	5.7%

Source: 1980 Bureau of the Census
We, the Asian and Pacific Islander Americans
U.S. Department of Commerce, Table 7
The Chicago survey, 1992

opportunities in science, medicine, engineering, commerce, and real estate, no matter where these places may be on the map of the United States.

Indians are remarkably evenly distributed not only all over the country but all over the suburban map of Chicago. The most striking characteristic of the population distribution of Indians in metropolitan Chicago is that there is hardly a suburb that does not have at least a small number of Indian residents. Not only do Indians have the skills and money to strike out on their own; it seems that they enjoy their privacy, and having other Indians for neighbors is not particularly important to them. Yet they maintain their togetherness in other ways: by thronging at temples for religious festivals, meeting regularly at social functions, or forming associations to preserve their professional and economic interests.

During the 1970s and early 1980s, a large concentration of Indians could be found on Chicago's North Side, around Broadway and Kenmore and Sheridan, but as soon as they could afford it, these Indians moved out into the suburbs. Today, only the newer immigrants, many of whom do not own cars and cannot drive long distances, prefer to live on the North Side, close to the ethnic shopping on Devon Avenue. Most other Indians live in the suburbs, particularly the north, northwest, and west suburbs. While the city of Chicago experienced a 46 percent growth in its Indian population between 1980 and 1990, the suburbs saw a far more dramatic rise of 102 percent. Table 15.2 shows the growth of the Indian population between 1980 and 1990 in Chicago and those suburbs where Indians are most populous.

---

the other South Asians. In Chicago, there are frequent references to the "Indo-Pak" community, and this calls for clarification regarding the numerical strength of each community. There are 64,200 Indians in Illinois, compared to 9,085 Pakistanis, 311 Sri Lankans and 263 Bangladeshis. David M. Reimers, *Still the Golden Door: The Third World Comes to America* (New York: Columbia University Press, 1985), pp. 61-91, 114-117; Raymond B. Williams, "Asian Indians" in *Dictionary of American Immigration History* (Metuchen, N.J.: The Scarecrow Press, 1990), pp. 45-51.

TABLE 15.4
Select demographic data on Asian Indians

	India Abroad survey 1985	Chicago survey 1992
College graduates	90%	94%
Postgraduate degrees	70%	69%
Income over $50,000	65%	69%
Own their own home	69%	81%
Own investment property in India	23%	29%

Source: Arthur W. and Usha M. Helweg, *An Immigrant Success Story* (Philadelphia: University of Pennsylvania Press, 1991), p. 262. The Chicago survey, 1992.

Occupationally, too, the Indians of Chicago reflect the same characteristics as Indians in the entire United States. The Chicago survey showed an occupational distribution for Indians very close to that of the 1980 census (Table 15.3).[10]

Comparison of the Chicago survey with another 1985 survey of readers conducted by the New York-based but nationally distributed newspaper *India Abroad* confirms the theory that Chicago Indians are fully representative of Indians in the United States, even with respect to education, income levels, and home ownership (Table 15.4).

Without discounting the differences that no doubt exist among Indian immigrants in the United States, it is still valid to look at the Chicago group and see how its characteristics might reflect those of the entire Indian immigrant population in the United States. Other demographic data on the Chicago-area population (as revealed by the 1992 survey) shows that most (91%) are married, between thirty-five and fifty-four years of age (67%), and have two or three children (69%).[11]

The Language Issue

While the proficiency of most Indians in English can be explained by their educational background in India, it must also be attributed to the fact that Indians do not have any other common language in which to communicate among themselves. Though Hindi is the national language of India, most Indi-

10. Figures from the 1990 census were not available specifically for the Asian Indian group at the time of publication.

11. The first major study of the post-1965 Indian immigration was conducted by Paramatma Saran in New York. His works on Indian immigration include: Paramatma Saran and Edwin Eames, eds., *The New Ethnics: Asian Indians in the United States* (New York: Praeger, 1980); and Paramatma Saran, *The Asian Indian Experience in the United States* (Cambridge: Schenkman, 1985).

TABLE 15.5
Major languages of Asian Indians

	Chicago	Kalamazoo
Gujarati	30%	26%
Hindi	18%	9%
Punjabi	9%	16%
Telugu	8%	7%
Malayalam	8%	5%
Tamil	6%	4%
Kannada	5%	7%
Bengali	4%	—
Marathi	3%	5%
Urdu	3%	2%
Sindhi	2%	5%
Konkani	2%	0.4%

Source: Arthur W. and Usha M. Helweg, *An Immigrant Success Story* (Philadelphia: University of Pennsylvania Press, 1991), p. 263. The Chicago survey, 1992.

ans prefer to speak in their native tongue, which could be any one of at least fourteen regional languages recognized by the Indian government and taught in schools in India. (These are not dialects but full-fledged languages, with their own scripts and advanced literature.) Most of the major Indian languages are well represented in the Indian community of Chicago.

A comparison of the native languages of Chicago Indians (as revealed by the 1992 survey) and those of Indians surveyed in Kalamazoo, Michigan, in 1984 shows significant parallels. Gujaratis, the traditional merchant community from the western coast of India, dominate the scene, followed closely by the Hindi- and Punjabi-speaking people of North India. Indians from four of the major South Indian states, which speak Telugu, Malayalam, Tamil, and Kannada, make up more than one quarter (27 percent) of the Indians in Chicago (Table 15.5). Other languages not listed above but which are native languages of Chicago Indians include Oriya, Marwari, and Kashmiri.

There is thus a bewildering variety of languages spoken among Indians, but what makes the issue even more intriguing is the fact that language is not merely a medium of communication. It is an entire culture, a way of life, with its own tradition of music, dance, theater, literature, and even cuisine. And so it is that scores of regional associations exist in Chicago, each one with an active and healthy membership list, devoted to propagating its own culture. A list of Indian associations obtained at the Consulate General's office in Chicago shows that there is at least one association for each one of these linguistic groups, with some groups, like the Gujaratis, having four or five different associations.

TABLE 15.6
Religions of Asian Indians

	Atlanta		Chicago	
Hindus	83%	(182)	80%	(442)
Christians	5%	(10)	7%	(41)
Muslims	4%	(9)	5%	(25)
Sikhs	6%	(13)	4%	(21)
Jains	2%	(4)	3%	(15)
Zoroastrian	2%	(4)	1%	(3)

Source: John Y. Fenton, *Transplanting Religious Traditions: Asian Indians in America* (New York: Praeger, 1988), 106. The Chicago survey, 1992.

It is important to understand the complex relationship between language, regional identity, and ethnic origin among Indians. Supposedly, Tamilians speak Tamil and are from the state of Tamil Nadu; yet Indians who have never lived in Tamil Nadu and who do not speak a word of Tamil might still call themselves Tamilians, because their ancestry is Tamil and this is the only way they can distinguish themselves from people who belong to other parts of India.[12] One would have expected that in the United States these linguistic/regional identities would be somewhat blurred and a pan-Indian identity would take over. But the sheer number of Indians from each one of the major regions of India has enabled the Chicago Indians to preserve their regional identities. Indeed, many community leaders worry about the divisiveness of these groups and the jealousies and intergroup rivalries that sometimes prevent them from maintaining a united front, even on important national occasions like the annual celebration of Indian Independence Day on Michigan Avenue. Second-generation Indians who have grown up in Chicago area schools identifying strongly with other Indian children, no matter what their regional identities, strongly resent this groupism on the part of their parents. They are determined that their own Indianness will be nonregional and nonsectarian in nature. While groupism definitely exists within the Indian community (some Gujarati families, for instance, have never associated with or spoken to Indians from other regions, and so it is with Punjabis or Bengalis or any other group), it is difficult to determine the extent of its deleterious effects. Without an urgent cause for which they should come together, Indians are happy to pursue their narrower identities. Only time and circumstances can tell if they are capable of transcending this groupism and embracing a national Asian-Indian identity on larger issues.

12. See Maxine Fisher, *The Indians of New York City: A Study of Immigrants from India* (Columbia: South Asia Books, 1980) for an anthropologist's view of the multilayered ethnicity of Indians and the organizational lines along which they form their group identities.

By not acting as a single large group, they are certainly undermining the power of their numbers and the influence they could wield in America.[13]

The Importance of Religion

The religions of the Indians of Chicago are no less diverse than their native languages, nor is the relationship of religious affiliations to regional identities any less complex. For instance, Gujaratis can be Hindus, Jains, Muslims, Christians, or Zoroastrians.[14] No official figures are available for the breakdown of the Indian population in the United States by religion, but primary research done in Atlanta in 1985, as well as the 1992 Chicago survey, show the distribution given in Table 15.6 (see p. 447 above).

The dominant religion for Indians in Chicago, as in India, is Hinduism; but all the other religious groups are present here in large enough numbers to have built their own elaborate houses of worship in the greater Chicago area. The following is only a partial list of the major temples and religious institutions in Chicago's Indian community:

- Chicago Mar Thoma Church, Des Plaines
- Chinmaya Mission, Hinsdale
- Consultative Committee of Indian Muslims in U.S. & Canada, Chicago
- Gita Mandal, Chicago
- Hindu Temple of Greater Chicago, Lemont
- India Catholic Association of America, Buffalo Grove
- International Society for Krishna Consciousness, Chicago
- Islamic Foundation, Villa Park
- Jain Temple, Bartlett
- Nirankari Universal Brotherhood Mission, Chicago
- Sikh Gurudwara, Palatine
- Sri Venkateswara (Balaji) Temple, Aurora
- SwamiNarayan Temple, Wheeling
- Zoroastrian Association of Metropolitan Chicago, Hinsdale

The proliferation of temples, mosques, and gurudwaras is testimony to the importance of religion in the lives of Indians, but to say merely that Indians are highly religious does not quite capture the complexity of their attitudes

13. It would be interesting to compare this trend with trends in other metros such as New York and Los Angeles. Many Indians feel that groupism is far more pronounced in Chicago but are at a loss to explain why this is so.

14. See Raymond Brady Williams, *Religions of Immigrants from India and Pakistan: New Threads in the American Tapestry* (Cambridge: Cambridge University Press, 1988), pp. 11-14, for a full discussion of how religious affiliations are related to ethnicity.

toward religion. Most of the Indians who live in Chicago have not been part of organized religion in India; rather, religion is "in the air" in India, a living, breathing tradition that Indians do not have to make a conscious effort to imbibe. The lighting of a lamp at an altar in the home, sometimes as simple a setting as a kitchen counter, infuses an Indian home with a religious aura. Religion is everywhere — on TV, in the movies, in street processions, and in family gatherings. Temple visits in India are usually reserved for very special occasions, unless one happens to be located down the street from home, in which case a person just makes casual visits to the temple now and then. Here in the United States, the Indians feel impelled to enforce their religious identity in structured ways, for example, by visiting the temple every Sunday to pray. Perhaps this is because, without a peg on which to hang their religious identity, many Indians fear that it may be lost irretrievably, especially for the second generation.

According to the Chicago survey, 79 percent of Indians consider religion important or very important in their lives; 50 percent visit a temple often or regularly (another 37 percent visit sometimes), while 69 percent celebrate religious functions often or regularly. Given this importance of religion in their lives, a surprising number (55 percent) said they would be agreeable to their children marrying outside their religion. It is difficult to tell exactly what this means. It could be that Indians are simply relaxed about their religion; or it could mean a genuine tolerance on the part of a highly educated and liberal-minded group of Indians; or it could be just a pragmatic acceptance of the possibility that the second-generation Indians might indeed marry outside their religion whether their parents like it or not. Many second-generation Indians have found American marriage partners in school or college, following the American tradition, and despite strong misgivings, even the most conservative of Indian parents are accepting this trend. They have little choice. Most also hold that the children of earlier immigrants did not have a large pool of other Indians their age from which to pick a spouse. With the rapid increase in the Indian immigrant population, many Indian parents hope that miscegenation will not be on the rise.[15]

Those parents who hope their children will marry within the community are making a concerted effort toward that end. So the temples of Chicago have become the focal point of culture propagation among second-generation Indians, something that the first generation sees as a very critical issue, if not *the* single most important issue, at this stage in their development as an ethnic group. Temples are more than just a place to conduct religious services. Lan-

---

15. The Chicago survey asked immigrants questions about dating and marriage outside the community: 17 percent of those surveyed said they themselves or an immediate relative were married to Americans; 39 percent disapproved (16 percent strongly disapproved) of their children marrying Americans, but an equal number, 39 percent, were neutral to the idea.

guage and culture classes, targeted especially toward the children, are held here
regularly. Temples also serve as a venue for things as diverse as meditation
sessions, weddings, christenings, and many social events, including youth camps
and summer fests.

The history of temple building in Chicago is also the story of bitter
infighting among rival groups. Leaders from the South Indian immigrant community, especially doctors from Andhra Pradesh, dominate the boards of Hindu
temples, and differences of opinion among board members have often stymied
progress and diluted the resources available for development. The difficulties
involved in fund raising (budgets run into millions of dollars) and satisfying
the demand of various linguistic-regional communities under one religious
umbrella have also strained board relations to the breaking point. But the fact
that the two major Hindu temples, one in Lemont and the other in Aurora, are
both well patronized and serve the needs of about 100,000 Midwesterners
testifies to the creative energies of Indians in Chicago. Both temples have gran-
diose plans for expansion.[16]

Most temples in Chicago have followed similar growth patterns: they
have started out in the 1970s and 1980s as small organizations and slowly
developed into full-fledged institutions where thousands of devotees gather
for important religious events. Tracing the growth of one of the oldest and
fastest-growing of these institutions — the Hindu Temple of Greater Chicago
in Lemont — will serve as a typical example. The magnificent eighty-foot-tall
Rajagopuram, or front tower, of the Sri Rama Temple rises high atop the
heavily wooded northern bluffs of the Des Plaines River Valley in suburban
Lemont. This imposing, tapering structure is embellished with intricately
carved figures of the gods and goddesses of Indian mythology. Gazing upon
it, one can almost forget one's surroundings and be transported to the heart
of South India, at the center of its glorious temple traditions. Indeed, this
authentic re-creation was made possible only by the generous support of the
Tirumala Tirupati Devasthanam, the management of one of South India's
holiest shrines, who supplied the professional services of craftsmen and the
images of deities from India.

The temple began in 1977 as a small group of volunteers meeting in a
basement. They developed plans to raise funds and to purchase a site for a
temple that would serve the needs of all Hindus in Chicago. It took several years
to raise the money, which came from fund-raising dance recitals and banquets
(a favorite method amongst Indians), financing from Indian-owned banks in
the Chicago area, and interest-free loans from India. A twenty-acre site was
purchased in Lemont for $300,000 in 1981, and on June 17, 1984, the then chief
minister of Andhra Pradesh, N. T. Rama Rao, laid the foundation stone for the
temple. The *Kumbhabhishekham,* or dedication ceremony, was held on July 4,

16. *India Tribune,* October 17, 1992, p. 21.

1986, and resident priests from India began offering the full gamut of temple services. The temple contains the three main *Vaishnava* deities of Rama, Venkateswara, and Radha-Krishna. A grand Ganesha-Shiva-Durga temple is also being built in the same complex to accommodate the needs of the *Shaivites,* who form the other major Hindu sect. A large hall and several smaller rooms on either side of it provide ample space for Sunday language classes, prayer groups, youth seminars, and social and cultural events.

So many houses of worship have been founded in Chicago in recent years in a similar manner, the latest being the Jain Temple in Bartlett, that some of the early immigrants worry about whether these institutions will be supported in later years by the second generation, when fresh immigration from India might slacken or be cut off completely. For now, however, the need for religious services in each group is higher than ever before, and the majority of immigrants themselves seem to be caught up in the excitement of building a strong foundation for future generations.

Politics as Usual

Indians are still too few in number to have a significant impact on Chicago politics, but they are quite active and involved, especially at election time. They acquire naturalization rights at a fairly rapid rate (57 percent, or 326, of the Chicago survey respondents were United States citizens), and an overwhelming majority (91 percent) of those who are eligible to vote say they do exercise that right. This would indicate that they acquire American citizenship for more than just the convenience of an American passport for international travel.

Chicago politicians have a healthy respect for the fund-raising capabilities of Indians, the wealthiest of whom are happy to spend hundreds of dollars a dinner plate for the privilege of having their picture taken with a prominent politician. Many of the associations are quite successful in getting politicians to make personal appearances at their annual event. Illinois Democratic Senator Carol Moseley Braun was guest of honor at the annual dinner dance of the Club of Indian Women held in May 1993. Minor city and state politicians show up regularly at Indian functions, eager to become more visible in the Asian-American community. Indians in the city of Chicago traditionally vote Democratic, while suburban Indians sometimes vote Republican, as many did for Governor Edgar of Illinois. But Democratic Senator Paul Simon has a strong following in Chicago and the suburbs among Indians who consider him a friend of India.

There are some attempts to build a strong coalition with other Asian-American groups like the Chinese and the Koreans. For instance, Indians are members of the Chicago Asian American Political Action Council, which has very specific political aims, such as electing an Asian American for mayor in

Lincolnwood before the turn of the century.[17] The Indo-American Democratic organization also routinely declares its support for Asian-American candidates at the local and national level.

As for Indians themselves gaining political office, the figures are pretty dismal as of now. There are only five elected Asian-Indian officials in the United States, the youngest of whom is a twenty-six-year-old dentist who was elected alderman of Darien's Ward 3 in suburban Chicago on May 3, 1993.[18] It is difficult to predict if and when the Indian community, whose members are wealthy and talented, will ever wield much influence in politics. So far there has been no urgent cause that would serve as a rallying point, except for the issue of enumeration of Asian Indians as a separate category in the 1980 census. Many Indians thought it would hurt them to be identified as a minority, but that has not been the case. The Association of Indians in America, an organization that fought hard for separate enumeration, is justifiably proud of its political achievement. In recent times the AIA has been very active fighting racial attacks, hate crimes, and employment discrimination against Indians. It certainly seems that when Indians wish to be heard they will raise their voices, even if it is only in concert with the voices of the other Asian-American groups.

The involvement of Indians with politics in India is a far more volatile issue. In the Chicago survey, 86 percent said they kept in touch with developments in India (46 percent said they kept in touch often or regularly). Not only are they well aware of what goes on in India, they take a stand on political issues. The Hindu-Muslim rioting in India provoked by the tearing down of the Babri Masjid mosque on December 6, 1992, resulted in demonstrations and rallies in Chicago. Hindus and Muslims marched on Devon Avenue to express their solidarity with each other and condemn the rioting. Those concerned about the democratic and secular fabric of India feel a duty to take a stand whenever there is trouble in the home country.[19]

On another level, there is a strong divide in the Indian community along Hindu-Muslim lines. Because religious institutions have become the focus of so much cultural and social activity, Hindus and Muslims of India tend to socialize separately, and their relationship is affected by the conflicts in India. The Vishwa Hindu Parishad, a religious organization with a huge base in the United States and a strong following in Chicago, occasionally invites speakers from the Bharatiya Janata Party to speak to the Indians in the United States.[20] The Bharatiya Janata Party is the leading opposition party in India and is poised to fight future elections on a fundamentalist level with the strident cry of "India is for Hindus." As with the earlier problem of Sikh separatism in India, there

17. *India Tribune*, March 27, p. 24.
18. *India Tribune*, May 22, p. 22.
19. *India Tribune*, December 12, 1992, p. 21.
20. The VHP was recently banned by the Indian government for unlawful action in inciting rioting mobs. *India Tribune*, June 12, 1993.

are charges that Hindu fundamentalism is being fueled and encouraged by money from immigrants in the United States. This kind of politico-religious activity probably exists, but not on a scale that affects the everyday life of the Indian immigrant community.

Occupational Diversity

What is of most urgent concern to Asian Indians in Chicago is their professional and economic well-being. A majority of Indian engineers and scientists work quietly and successfully in the corporate environment, in places like Fermi Labs, Argonne National Laboratories, ATT, Bells Labs, and Amoco. Many of them, like Nobel laureate Chandrasekhar of the University of Chicago, have gained top honors in their fields. But a large number of the immigrants who came in the 1980s encountered unemployment and were forced to take up menial jobs or jobs way below their qualifications. This situation was aggravated with the influx of nonprofessional immigrants, who came as siblings under the family unification immigration laws. These immigrants took jobs as insurance sales-men, clerk typists, cab drivers, janitors, or dishwashers. The more enterprising among them opened restaurants or grocery stores or travel agencies, occupa-tions that did not demand professional qualifications. Several Dunkin' Donuts franchises all over Chicagoland are owned and operated by Indians and some-times staffed entirely by family members, a practice that keeps the money in the family and makes the venture more profitable.

Not all of these business ventures are started by nonprofessionals or those who were unsuccessful in their job search. Many a qualified engineer has been known to give up his job and set up shop, opening a restaurant or a jewelry business because it has meant more independence, a far higher income, and no fear of being passed over for promotion merely because he is Indian. Some rich housewives have recently joined the trend, opening boutiques and jewelry stores that cater to an elite clientele. Indian doctors in Chicago form an exclusive group whose inordinately high income levels and professional interests set them some-what apart from the engineers and scientists. They have learned the art of organizing and lobbying to protect their interests. Almost all the doctors in the Chicago survey belonged to the American Medical Association, the India Medi-cal Association, or the Chicago Medical Association. Their organizational affil-iations help them to be on the lookout for legislation adversely affecting them, and they are quick to rally against it. They have also been the financial bulwark of the Indian community, contributing generously to religious, cultural, and social service institutions, especially in the formative years.

The nonprofessionals look more to their families for support and security during hard times. There is no indication that unemployment among Indians is swelling the ranks of welfare recipients, or that it has become a major problem.

While not all is smooth sailing in immigrant paradise, Indians are still looking to their own families and communities to help them solve their problems.

Most of the Indian merchants are concentrated on a small stretch of Devon Avenue, also known as Gandhi Marg. This is the mecca for Indian shoppers who come from a radius of almost three hundred miles to experience the sights, the sounds, the smells, and the taste of India. The transformation of a street on Chicago's North side into "India town" took place in the 1970s, when Jewish businesses moved out of the area and Indian merchants moved in.[21] Several sari shops and electronics goods stores sprang up almost overnight, catering to the needs of immigrants, who carried gifts from these stores for their friends and family when they went back to India on frequent visits.[22] In the last few years, especially since the Gulf War, merchants say their traditional business has dropped drastically. Indians now buy more for themselves — to satisfy their own needs in the United States. Instead of goods from Devon Avenue finding their way to India, goods from India are being imported for consumption in the United States. Stores are stocked with pure silk sarees, exquisitely embroidered ethnic outfits, and ornate gold jewelry (much in demand because of the increase in second-generation Indian weddings) — all imported from India. Restaurants that import their chefs and serve authentic Indian cuisine do a brisk business. A kiosk at a street corner sells regional language publications from the Indian subcontinent (in each one of the major regional languages), as well as major English-language publications such as *India Today, Femina,* and a host of popular film magazines. Indian merchants, especially those in the restaurant and jewelry businesses, are anxious to make further inroads into the American market, where they feel they have the greatest potential. Given its ability to adapt to changing market conditions, it is difficult to predict how and when Devon Avenue will be further transformed as it reaches out to a wider clientele.

Another development worthy of note is the sprouting of new Indian businesses — grocery and video stores, boutiques, restaurants, and jewelry stores — out in the suburbs. Naperville, Westmont, and Elk Grove Village are some of the suburbs with clusters of Indian-owned stores. But even these stores, though they rely heavily on the Indian community for their business (some are patronized by the Caribbean community also), are looking more and more toward the larger American market to maximize their sales.

Community Organizations

It is difficult to sift through the plethora of Indian associations and organizations to assess which of them are the most valuable to the community. Two

21. "Asians add to suburban melting pot," *Chicago Tribune,* September 23, 1991.
22. Helweg & Helweg, p. 128.

outstanding social service organizations have provided much-needed help, especially for the newer immigrants. One is the Indo-American Center, founded by M. G. K. Pillai and run by a staff of dedicated volunteers, and located in the heart of the Indian shopping center on Devon Avenue. It serves as an outreach center of the Immigration office in Chicago and helps conduct citizenship interviews. The center also holds classes to teach elementary English to elders and to provide information to tourists, research students, and faculty members seeking information on India. Its senior citizens' club is a popular place for the parents of Indian immigrants to come to play bridge, volunteer their services, or merely get together with other fellow Indians. What makes the center unique is that it is secular in nature, and it targets for help those immigrants who need it most and can least afford it. It also tries to build in them a political awareness of their rights and interests. As part of the Asian American Coalition network, the center participates in interethnic programs and generally keeps the community in the forefront of happenings in Chicago. (Other umbrella organizations like the Federation of India Associations, Alliance of Midwest Indian Associations, and Association of Indians in America are also secular and have their branches in Chicago, but their concern is more with issues affecting all Indians in the United States. The Indo-American Center is more closely aligned with goings-on in Chicago than these other pan-Indian organizations.)

The other organization worthy of note in Chicago is *Apna Ghar* (a Hindi-Urdu phrase meaning "Our Home"), which provides Asian families in crisis with multilingual, multicultural support services. Founded in 1989 by five Asian-American women in the Chicago area who were responding to reports of increasing domestic violence in Asian-American homes (mostly from India, Pakistan, Korea, and Iran), the shelter has grown into a professionally run, partly state-funded facility that takes in women and children victimized by domestic violence and abuse. To date, *Apna Ghar* has provided shelter to 146 women and approximately 80 children. Ironically, many of them are from the homes of the highly educated and prosperous elite, where the tensions of living in a foreign culture coupled with the lack of an extended family support structure sometimes cause interpersonal relationships to collapse completely. *Apna Ghar* is another instance of self-help in which the Indian community is trying hard to solve its own problems before they get out of hand. One of its founders, Kanta Khipple, was the only Asian Indian to be honored by Chicago's "Culture in Action." Her name and a brief description of her work are inscribed on a rock near Daley Plaza in downtown Chicago.[23]

One other Chicago-based service organization, India Development Service, merits mention since it is an example of a widening trend on the part of Indians in Chicago to try to bring about social and economic change in India. IDS was founded in 1974 as a nonpolitical and nonsectarian organization with

---

23. "Kanta Khipple Makes Community Proud," *Spotlight*, May 28, 1993.

Asian Indian dancers in Chicago performing traditional dances to
appreciative audiences.   Courtesy of Padma Rangaswamy.

the objective of participating actively in India's development process. Since then,
it has sponsored integrated rural development projects, helped in the transfer
of appropriate technology, and supported social action, research, and education
for the disadvantaged and needy in India. This same spirit of "giving back to
the motherland" has also been manifested by individuals acting in an independent
capacity. Doctors, scientists, and engineers donate their expertise, medical
equipment, and research services to Indian institutions either on their visits to
India or through their own foundations.[24]

Arts and Fun

Nothing draws Indians together like an evening of song and dance. The entertainment
industry in Chicago is a flourishing business, capitalizing fully on the
Indian's penchant for nostalgia for the homeland. Both classical and popular
Indian culture have found their own niche, and there is no dearth of an audience
for both kinds of events, featuring top celebrities from India who regularly tour

24. *India Tribune,* March 27, 1993 and May 15, 1993.

A young Indian dancer strikes a pose in *Bharata Natyam,* the classical dance form of South India, now taught in several dance schools run by Indians in the Chicago area.   Courtesy of Padma Rangaswamy.

major capitals that have large Indian populations. Chicago is an important stop on that international circuit.[25]

The classical appeal had its roots in the desire of immigrant parents to inculcate a sense of Indian heritage in their children. While it was difficult to get five- and six-year-olds enthusiastic about Sanskrit lessons at the Hindu temple, they could always be counted on to attend *Bharata Natyam* or *Kathak* dance lessons with greater zeal.[26] Natyakalalayam is a dance school headed by Hema Rajagopalan, who began in the early 1970s by giving Bharata Natyam lessons to a few children in the basement of her home in Lombard. Today the school has studios in two locations and regularly conducts dance dramas with traditional costumes, elaborate sets, and a live orchestra from India. The Dilshad Khan school in Chicago provides training in Kathak to students as young as three years of age. The raison d'etre for these dance schools is, of course, the second generation, and the success of these schools points to a continuum of Indian culture for the future. Music lovers have the India Classical Music Society, which sponsors concerts by India's most famous luminaries, including Bhimsen Joshi, Ali Akbar Khan, L. Subramaniam, to name a few. Another favorite pastime

25. Helweg & Helweg, p. 115.
26. The classical dance styles of South and North India respectively.

for music lovers is the soiree, or private music party, where an outstanding singer may be the main feature of the evening but the party winds up in the wee hours of the morning with old-time sing-along favorites that bring back poignant memories of the immigrants' youth in India.

The most impressive crowds, however, are reserved for the stars of Bombay's movie industry, otherwise known as Bollywood. Every year there are at least one or two major events sponsored by the Patel merchants of Devon Avenue featuring top draws such as Amitabh Bachan, Sri Devi, and teenage heartthrob Amir Khan. These stars play to packed halls in Rosemont Horizon (ticket prices are from $40 to $100 and more), and members of the audience, some of whom drive hundreds of miles for the event, range from grandmothers to babes in arms. As Amir Khan bumps and grinds on the stage to hit songs from his latest movies, Indian teenagers scream and swoon as they would at a Michael Jackson concert. The popularity of Hindi movies is seen in the proliferation of video stores in Chicago.[27] There is also a movie theater, The Gateway on Lawrence Avenue, that screens Indian movies regularly. It is because of Hindi videos that many second-generation Indians have any familiarity at all with the Hindi language. Many Indian parents who would scorn Hindi movies as frivolous and trashy if they were in India encourage their children here to watch them. As the lowest common denominator of Indian culture, the movies bring "Indianness" closer to Indian children who, parents are afraid, are bombarded by American influences outside the home.

Song and dance routines from Indian movies are the main features of ethnic Indian television programming in Chicago. *Chitrahar,* a TV program started by an enterprising housewife named Vichitra Nayyar, has been broadcasting Indian programs on Channel 26 for eleven years now. Over the years it has expanded to include weekday programming and to cover other cities such as Atlanta and Detroit. *Vision of Asia* and *Everest Television* of New York also broadcast to Chicago. *The Super Broadcasting Company,* with a program called *Bharat Darshan,* regularly brings Indian movies into Chicago area homes via cable television.

Programming on ethnic television is slowly gaining in the breadth of its coverage and its polish. Whereas in the early years it consisted of amateur clips from Indian movies, it now includes interviews with Indian personalities, current news from the Indian subcontinent, replete with authentic footage, and a more professionalized presentation. Though it has a long way to go before reaching true sophistication, it promises to be an important area of growth. Ethnic Indian radio programs are also popular and holding their own (there are more than a half dozen listed in the Midwest India/Pakistan/Bangladesh Yellow Pages), but their contribution is limited so far to providing pleasant music for their listeners.

The print media that serves the Indian community in Chicago is another

---

27. There is also an astonishing selection of videos in the different regional languages of India.

growing enterprise. Two major English-language newspapers, the *India Tribune* in Chicago and *Spotlight* in Carol Stream, are published weekly. The Chicago survey indicated that 75 percent of Indians read these newspapers for news about India; almost a third (32 percent) read newspapers and magazines published in India and distributed locally.

Family Ties

Family life for Indians in the United States owes its success to the fact that women immigrants came in as large numbers as did the men. (The earlier immigration had no women to speak of — they were barred by law — and many Sikhs either returned to their families in India or wound up marrying Mexican women.) The 1990 census shows that the gender distribution for Indian immigrants in Illinois is 53 percent male to 47 percent female. For most years since 1965, women have been immigrating at the same rates as men; in 1973 the ratio was 53 percent female immigrants to 47 percent male, as large numbers of wives joined their husbands who already lived in the United States. Indians also have one of the highest percentages among ethnic groups of married couple families (91 percent), and one of the lowest figures for female householder families with no husband present (3.8 percent).[28]

In a typical sequential migration process, the husband came to the United States first, secured a job, and after building an economic base, sent for his wife from India. If he came as an unmarried student, chances are that he went back to India to get married and then brought his wife over to join him. The wife, who had probably attended college in India but was not necessarily equipped for a career, nevertheless quickly entered the job market, acquiring some marketable skills like accounting or computer analysis along the way. The women who had received professional training in India, in science or medicine or engineering, actively pursued their careers here. But when children were born, they made adjustments to accommodate the demands of the home and family. Indian women, even the professionals who are loath to give up their careers for full-time motherhood, try to ensure that the welfare of the family as a unit is never compromised for the sake of personal or individual satisfaction. Very often parents or parents-in-law are invited over from India to care for the children so that both parents may continue to be employed. The result is that even though Indians have been here really only since about 1965, many families have three generations in a household, with all the hierarchal nuances that exist in a traditional extended Indian family.

The presence of immigrants' siblings, who came under the family reuni-

---

28. Source: 1990 Census of the Population, General Population Characteristics, Illinois, Table 51.

fication quota, also adds to the kinship network.[29] Very often the parents are in this country only to sponsor the entry of a second or third child into the United States, the preference categories being such that an immigrant can bring in a brother or sister faster by first sponsoring a parent, who, in turn, can sponsor his or her remaining children. Once this function is fulfilled, the parents either return to India for good (many of them cannot make the social adjustment to a life here), while others stay on and help take care of the grandchildren. In any case, there is much shuttling back and forth between India and the United States for this older generation, who are inevitably caught up in the spiral of their children's decision to immigrate.

In the patriarchal Indian culture, the eldest son takes over the reins as head of the family when his parents grow old, and he becomes responsible for the welfare of his parents. This is a source of tension for the Indian family: sons whose parents are in India are guilt-ridden because of their inability to fulfill their traditional duty; sons whose parents have agreed to immigrate are subject to increased pressures and anxieties, because in addition to the usual generation gap there is the added strain of the clash of two diverse cultures, with the immigrants themselves in the middle playing mediator between grandparents and grandchildren.

The grandparents provide the link to the old country by speaking at home in the mother tongue, teaching the grandchildren Indian ways and customs, and generally filling in for parents who are busy with their own careers. But they also have to put up with brash, "disrespectful," and what they call "Americanized" behavior from the grandchildren; and they suffer the loneliness of being away from their homeland in their twilight years. The immigrant, especially the son, while he is happy that he can have his parents living with him and can provide for them as is his duty, also has to face the fact that they sometimes find their circumstances distressing.

The Indian woman's role in the family is probably the most pivotal in holding it together. Her upbringing in India is such that no matter how highly educated or Westernized or career-minded she may be, she still considers herself the primary homemaker. Often, she is almost as well educated as her husband (though, as mentioned before, among the newer immigrants, some women may not even have gone past high school), is eager and able to contribute to the family income, and because she is still the primary homemaker, she finds herself trying hard to live up to the same "superwoman" image as is her American counterpart. Earlier surveys[30] showed that Indian women were only too glad to be in America, away from the demands of an extended family, and thrilled to be running their own household without interference from the elders. But interviews conducted in Chicago in 1992 show that attitudes and circumstances

29. Helweg & Helweg, pp. 134-145.
30. Saran & Eames, 1980. See also Sathi Das Gupta, *On the Trail of an Uncertain Dream* (New York: AMS Press, 1989).

have changed over the years. Women miss the support normally provided by the extended family — for example, victims seeking shelter in *Apna Ghar* bemoan the lack of restraining influences on an abusive man — and have felt the debilitating effects of isolation. (Over the years, many Indian families in Chicago have partially solved this problem by bringing over their relatives.) Another aspect of life in India that Indian women miss is the availability of servants to take care of household chores. Only the affluent Indian families in Chicago, especially those where the women are pursuing lucrative careers, regularly employ maids, whereas in India even a middle-class housewife can afford to hire household help.

There is no doubt that women who have immigrated to America have gone beyond the areas traditionally defined for them in India. But the same is true of women in India as well, so it is difficult to determine how these women, as *immigrants,* have developed over the years. They certainly feel that they have had greater opportunity and freedom to pursue their own interests. Many women have achieved personal and professional satisfaction as they might never have done in India; but others have fallen through the cracks because they were ill-equipped and bereft of support.

Most Indian parents measure their success in life by their children, and the second generation growing up in America has been the focus of all their concerns. Though most Indian children are still in their teenage years or younger, the Chicago area colleges are already receiving second generation Indians in increasing numbers. The University of Chicago's South Asia department reports that while most of its students in the 1960s and '70s were Americans interested in Indian languages and cultures, today the majority of its students come from the homes of Indian immigrants. These children are anxious to rediscover their roots and gain an intellectual understanding of a culture that they have already experienced on the inside but which they realize is different from Indian culture in India.

The second generation has concerns that are quite different from those of their parents, though they arise from the same set of conditions. While their parents have felt discriminated against in their jobs and passed over for promotion in managerial positions, the children have had to confront racism head on. Growing up in Chicago-area schools, many of them have been harassed or beaten up in racial attacks. Suburban children report less of this, though they are fully aware of their differentness. Dating and sex are very thorny issues in Indian homes (which consider Western society corrupt and permissive), and many children choose not to discuss it with their parents, preferring to avoid confrontation altogether. Career choice is another area of dissension. It is taken for granted that Indian children will not stop at high school but go on to college, and young adults complain that they feel pressured to go into medicine, engineering, or law to satisfy their overachieving parents when they would rather pursue a career in social service or education. The question of marriage is the next big item looming on the immigrant agenda. Considerations of caste and social class, which many immigrants (and certainly all second-generation Indians) thought they had buried when they came to America, are resurrected and begin to plague family discussions like ghosts from a dim past. Indians know they are in the middle of flux and change. How much of that change they will be able to direct themselves and how much they will have to accept as they are carried with the tide is yet to be determined.

Indian culture and family life abroad has always had a vitality and ability to re-energize itself, mainly because it does not lose touch with the motherland. Indians who were ousted from Kenya and Uganda (and whose ancestors had been out of India for more than a century) were able to resettle in India because through all the in-between years they had kept in touch with relatives at home.[31] The Chicago immigration is fairly new, and perhaps it is to be expected that Indian immigrants here will remain in close touch with India at least for now, especially given the technological marvels of instant communication. Telephone companies and airlines, who advertise heavily in the Indian community, are aware of the volume of traffic between America and India.

The future of the Indian community in the United States depends on two main factors: how Indians fare in the United States and what options they have in India. The growth of the Chicago community provides evidence that Indians are here to stay and will continue to do well in an America that is tolerant of multiculturalism and rewards professional and technical skills.

31. Helweg & Helweg, p. 140.

CHAPTER 16

Koreans of Chicago:
The New Entrepreneurial Immigrants

JOSEPH AHNE

The Early Koreans in Chicago

The United States annexed Hawaii in 1898, and the islands became a territory in 1900. Three years later, 101 Korean laborers migrated to Hawaii to work in the sugar plantations. The day of their arrival, January 13, 1903, fixes the time of the beginning of Korean immigration to the United States. By 1905 the Korean presence in Hawaii had swelled: in different ships an additional 7,125 Korean laborers, including 637 women and 541 children, arrived in Honolulu. Within several years, about 2,000 of them relocated to the West Coast of mainland United States, while the Korean remainder either continued their laboring life in Hawaii or returned home to Korea, disappointed by the harshness of immigrant life.[1]

It is not known how many Koreans from the Hawaii plantations landed in Chicago, the capital of the Midwest. There is not much written material or historical record on the early Chicago Koreans. For oral history or secondary sources we have to rely on Korean community newspapers and other occasional reports. The evolution of Chicago's Korean community is related to the periods during which different groups of Koreans migrated to America. Chicago Korean history can be divided into three periods of time:

(1) the *Pioneer Period* (1915-1950), during which Koreans who settled down in the Windy City were made up of plantation laborers from Hawaii; emigrants from Korea proper escaping as political exiles from Japanese rule (1910-1945); and a small number of Korean students pursuing their scholarly work in Chicago.

---

1. Won-Yong Warren Kim, *Jaemi Hanin Osipnyonsa* [Fifty-Year History of Koreans in America] (Reedley, CA, 1959), p. 3.

Mr. Kyung Kim, the first
Korean settler in Chicago,
came to America at the
age of 15.
Courtesy of Joseph Ahne.

(2) the *Korean War and After* (1950-1967), during which many Korean refugees, war brides, and students came to the United States.

(3) and the bonafide *period of Major Immigration* (1968 to the present), when the Korean community finally emerged as a major ethnic group in Chicago and elsewhere, after the immigration law was changed in 1965.

The Pioneer Period (1915-1950)

There were no recorded Korean residents in Chicago prior to 1915, when a young Korean named Kyung Kim first came to the city. Thus concluded Kwang Dong Jo, a former reporter for *The Korea Times (Hankuk Ilbo)*, a Korean-language daily newspaper published in Chicago. Jo had interviewed Bestie Kim, Kyung Kim's wife, who was then living as an aging widow in New

York.[2] According to her story, there were a handful of Koreans living in Chicago by 1915: Kyung Kim, Mr. and Mrs. Phil Park, Mr. and Mrs. Il Sun Kim, Young Moon Kim, and Tae Eun Chung. In her interview with Jo, Mrs. Kim goes on to say:

> Kyung Kim, Chicago's pioneer Korean, first came to America in 1905 at the age of fifteen for better education. After having lived initially in Los Angeles for a few years, learning basic English language, he then in 1910 joined *So Nyun Byung Hak Kyo* (the Korean Boys Military League) in Hastings, Nebraska. The League was organized in June, 1910, by Yong-Man Park, a leading patriot, who attended the State University of Nebraska. Park provided patriotic/military training for young Korean volunteers to support the national independence movement in Korea. Kyung Kim was trained at the League for two years, enduring severe hunger and extreme hardship. And he then moved on to study architecture. Here in Chicago Kyung Kim himself engaged in a variety of businesses such as home construction and sales, owned a tailor shop and a restaurant at different times. By then Kim had become a very popular figure in the Korean community. (*The Korea Times*, August 2, 1979)

In a later feature story, reporter Jo described the wedding ceremony of Bestie Lim and Kyung Kim as a moving event for the small Korean society at that time:

> Once upon a time in 1928, an exotic wedding march came out from a Methodist church on Washington street in downtown Chicago. About 120, more than a majority of a little over 200 guests, were Koreans. It was rare to see so many Koreans gathered together at one place that almost the entire Korean population in Chicago seemed to have attended the wedding. Kyung Kim was then forty years old, as a successfully established businessman, widely known to all Korean communities throughout the States. His bride, Bestie Lim, was at her late 20's. She was studying at Ohio Wesleyan College after she came to the States at the age of 23 in 1924. The newly wedded couple settled down in the area of Kedzie and Wilson, which happened to be now Korea Town in the Albany Park area. Kyung Kim finally died in 1966 at 78 in New York, while Bestie remained living in a Brooklyn apartment.[3]

Jo's feature story also carried interviews and information about several other early Korean pioneers, including Phil Park, who is believed to have first come to Hawaii as a sugar plantation worker in 1903 and then moved to Chicago. He owned Diversey Cafeteria at Clark Street and Diversey on the North Side of

---

2. The interview was conducted in Spring 1979 as a part of a special series, "Chicago Korean Immigrant History," which was featured weekly from May 1979 to October 1980. I am much indebted to Mr. Jo's interview articles for the early Korean pioneers of Chicago in this paper.

3. *Hankuk Ilbo* [The Korea Times Chicago], January 9, 1980.

Chicago. Another was Tae-Eun Chung, who first supplied chop suey to an Anglo grocery store and later opened the Oriental Food Company in 1923. There was Il-Sun Kim, another migrant from the Hawaii sugar plantations who settled in Chicago via other cities in the mainland. He was known as a heavy drinker who caused a number of unpleasant episodes among Korean friends. Not much else can be gleaned from the records about this small worker migration.

The Student Generation

According to Jo's interview with Kwang-Sup Yum, he became the first Korean student to attend the University of Chicago, where he studied psychology in 1922. There were about ten Korean students by that time in the Chicago area. Around 1920, Se-Woon Chang had entered Northwestern University to study in the Mathematics Department. In early October 1921, Yeo-Taik (Thomas) Kim came to Chicago, and in July 1922, a handsome young man, Chang-Wha (Harry) Hwang, came to the University of Chicago Business School after studying a year in Paris and in Iowa respectively. At almost the same time, Jung-Yum (Andrew) Hyun came to Chicago as a student.

The Korean community then began to organize around those students. In fact, it is noteworthy that the first Korean Student Association was formed in Chicago on October 8, 1918, much earlier than that of Los Angeles, which was established on October 19, 1922. On April 30, 1921, the Korean Student Federation in North America was formed in New York. Four Chicago delegates (Young-Sung Kang, Myung-Jun Yang, Sung-Yum Hyun, and Jung-Yum Hyun) played such important roles in the birth of the Federation that in 1923 its headquarters was relocated to Chicago with the election of Kwang-Sup Yum as the president and Chang-Ha Hwang as the vice president.

In June 1924, the Korean Student Federation in North America held its annual meeting on the campus of the University of Chicago. The meeting was attended by about forty delegates from across the country, including Canada. The most exciting moment during the annual meeting was their enjoyment of *kimchi*, a kind of pickled cabbage served as a side dish, which is Korean "soul food." Thus these homesick student-expatriates got at least a taste of their distant and remote homeland.

The Birth of the Korean Church

No written documents date the beginning of the first Korean Church. According to an oral history, it was on August 30, 1919, when a small group of five or six Korean students informally gathered for fellowship and prayer. These informal meetings did not evolve into a regular Sunday service until July 27, 1924, when the Chicago Korean Methodist Church was officially organized by Young-So Kang, Kwang-Sup Yum, and Wong-Yong Kim.[4]

In his interview with the reporter Jo in the spring of 1979, Kwang-Sup Yum recalled that it was in March of 1924 when about ten students began to meet again for prayer and fellowship at the ground floor of a three-story apartment building owned by an American in the area of 39th street on the South Side. According to Yum's memory, there was no sermon but only prayers and fellowship time because of the unavailability of a licensed preacher. A year later, the meeting was moved to another place. Finally, the first ordained minister, Rev. Chang-Joon Kim, was provided for them through the financial assistance of the Home Missionary Society of the Methodist Church. Rev. Kim was well known in Korean history, for he was one of the "thirty-three Korean patriots" who signed Korea's Declaration of Independence from Japanese colonialism (Korea was under Japanese control from 1909 to 1945, when Japan surrendered to the United States ending World War II).

In the meantime, Won-Young Warren Kim, in his *Fifty-Year History of Koreans in America,* records a different date and meeting place of the initial Korean Church: the church began gathering in the basement of an American church on Lincoln Avenue on July 27, 1924. The charter members were Kyung-Kim, Young-So Kang, Jang-Soon Park, Won-Yong Kim, Eui-Suk Cha, Hui-Ryum Cho, and Kwang-Sup Yum. It seems most probable that the gathering first took place at the 39th Street location and then moved to Lincoln Avenue.

On May 8, 1927, the meeting place was moved to yet another building on Lake Park Avenue, and on February 5, 1928, it was relocated to Oakdale Avenue. The worship service was attended by about ten students in the beginning and gradually increased to some fifty. Considering that the total Korean population was smaller than one hundred people at that time, the church was obviously the center of the Korean society in Chicago. Several more guest preachers joined Rev. Chang-Joon Kim to lead the worship services on a rotation basis: Sung-Hak Cho was a student of theological studies at Garrett Biblical Seminary; other preachers were Min-Soo Bae, Rev. Sung-Kwon Han, Rev. Young-Soon Kim, and Hui-Ryum Cho (originally via Canada), who were all studying theology at Garrett Seminary. As a lay leader, Kyung Kim was the major financial supporter of the church, and Young-So Kang, Kwang-Sup Yum, and Nung-Ik Choi played active leadership in the church around 1930.

The Korean Methodist Church was not firmly established until April 12, 1936, when Rev. Eun-Taik Lee, who had come to study theology at Garrett Seminary, was officially appointed as the pastor. The church was by then a worship place as well as a student center. Yeo-Taik Kim, one of the early church members, recalled during his interview with reporter Cho that he was impressed by the indomitable dedication of Rev. and Mrs. Lee. So poor was the congre-

---

4. Bong-youn Choy, *Koreans in America* (Chicago: Nelson-Hall, 1979), p. 256.

gation that Lee had to peddle goods on streets at times to support the church and his own family. Mrs. Lee had odd jobs, sometimes doing embroidery work and sometimes housework at American missionaries' homes. Nevertheless, they never failed to display the joy of serving other fellow Koreans, despite the hardships. Rev. Lee pastored the Korean Methodist Church until he retired in 1964. He died at the age of ninety-one on September 10, 1990, in Chicago, where a few of his children still live.

In a nutshell, the history of the Korean community is the history of the Korean church that was organized by the early Korean students in the Chicago area. The Korean Methodist church gave the organized community its institutional shape. Thus, weekend services included more than preaching and praying; the church also functioned as a student center. In those days, the total Korean population was probably no more than one hundred, spread across the state of Illinois and neighboring states.

The Korean Church's Growing Role in the Community

Up to 1970, in addition to being a place of worship, the Methodist Church provided temporary shelter for Korean students or newly arrived Koreans, and functioned as a community information center. But with the increasing number of new immigrants after 1968, many new churches were formed in Chicago. The number increased dramatically from ninety-five Protestant churches and one Catholic church and four Buddhist temples in 1984 (see Map 16.1) to 150 Protestant churches, three Catholic churches and four Buddhist temples in 1990, according to the *1991 Korean Business Directory.* Of these 150 Protestant churches, sixty are in suburbs and ninety in the city, reflecting the upward mobility of the Korean population into the suburbs. In many cases, the church growth in numbers also resulted from church schisms caused by internal conflicts. A majority of the Korean churches are not free-standing congregations but share or rent from American congregations, who need the income to supplement their slumping collections as their memberships decline.

As Korean immigration increased, the clergy's role and functions were also stretched beyond the normal pastoral duties of preaching, visitation, and administration. During the new influx of the 1970s and early '80s, it became a major duty for Korean pastors to provide personal and social services for members and nonmembers alike. Such services included meeting new arrivals at O'Hare airport, giving them driving lessons, job hunting help, translations at hospitals, helping with utility companies and social security offices, and providing business consultations. Korean pastors had to be "jacks of all trades," providing a variety of material and spiritual services. Thus all Korean activities became centered around the churches. The first Korean church, now the First Korean United Methodist Church, has grown to a membership of 800 since it

MAP 16.1

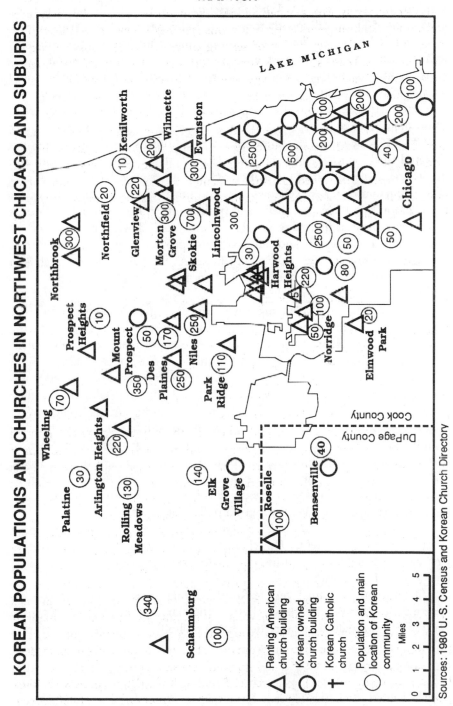

KOREAN POPULATIONS AND CHURCHES IN NORTHWEST CHICAGO AND SUBURBS

Sources: 1980 U. S. Census and Korean Church Directory

was relocated in 1980 to a former Jewish Temple in the hub of Korea Town. By 1991 there were at least ten Protestant churches with memberships ranging from 500 to 800; in addition, there were several congregations with an average of 150 to 300 members, and some small congregations in the 30-100 range. Presbyterian and Methodist are the main denominations among Korean Americans. In addition to the typical church programs, such as Sunday School and Women's Society, many Korean churches also offer classes in Korean language, history, music, and customs for the American-born generation in an effort to retain their heritage.

In a 1986 survey of 622 randomly selected Koreans in Chicago, Professors Kim and Hurh found that 477, or about 75 percent, had church affiliations and that more than one-half of them attend church once a week or more.[5] A part of this apparent piety is explained by the absence of other opportunities for socialization that the church helped to fulfill. Some business-minded Koreans such as insurance agents and real estate brokers also find that church attendance can be a good-will gesture and can sometimes provide business leads. Overall, Chicago's Koreans are very involved in Christian religious activities, which is in sharp comparison to the homeland behavior, where only 30 percent were counted as Christians as of 1985.

One of the most challenging issues confronting the Korean church is the language issue and the question of generations. Especially puzzling to the church and their parents is the *Iljomose* (the one-and-a-half generation). These Korean-born children came along with their parents at early ages, ten to sixteen, but have been socialized as preteens and teenagers in the United States and can easily fit into the major society, for they think, talk, and act like Americans. The same is true of the second generation, the *Ise.* The question that arises is, what will happen to those many Korean-language churches dominated by the *Ilse* (the first generation) after they are gone? Will Korean-speaking churches turn into English-speaking churches, as was the case in the early German church, the Japanese church, and even the Korean church in Hawaii? That seems to be happening: beginning in 1990, several Chicago Korean congregations have developed English language worship services for the younger generations, in addition to maintaining worship service in Korean for their immigrant parents. This change to two-language worship services is a reflection of the Korean community on the brink of transition from the first to the second generation.

Living with two languages, the Korean immigrant can be best understood from a socio-psychological perspective as "the marginal man," a person who is "in between two cultures or societies without wholly belonging to either one,"

---

5. Kwang Chung Kim, "Americanization of Korean Immigrants," in *Koreans in America,* Seong Hyong Lee and Tae-Hwan Kwak, eds. (Seoul, Korea: Kyungnam University Press, 1988), p. 90.

for "he is poised in psychological uncertainty between two social worlds. . . ."[6] Church life helps many Korean immigrants overcome the identity crisis. In the words of a theologian, "We Koreans are called by God to leave our homeland like Abraham and his children, who by faith went out, not knowing where they had to go." Chicago turned out to be one of the promised destinations.[7]

The Post–Korean War Period (1950-1967)

As in the case of the Early Pioneer Period, students continued to dominate the community leadership and the presidency of the Korean Association of Chicago during and before the Korean War period, when many political refugees and students came to this country for freedom and educational opportunities. There was also a small migration of Korean war brides at this time to Chicago. Yet because many of these women came from low-status groups, had compromised their Korean-ness, and had marginalized themselves even further by marrying foreigners and outsiders, they were never accepted as an integral part of the Chicago Korean community.

Korean-American Exemplar

If there is one single old-timer to be named as an exemplar, he is Dr. Paul (Bo-ra) Chung, who has witnessed the historical development of the Chicago Korean community for more than half a century. Dr. Chung is a most respected old-timer and leader among the student generations because he has set forth a role model in his successful career, which ranges from a student to an immigrant to a university professor to a diligent volunteer in the Korean community. To be more precise, Dr. Chung fits the role as a transitional leader between the student Pioneer Period and the Postwar Period. In 1937, he came to study at Northwestern University's Dental School, ambitious to introduce modern dentistry to Korea. After graduation, he taught and practiced dentistry in his homeland until 1948, when he returned permanently to Chicago.

He has been popular and revered in the diaspora and is often talked about within the Korean society, especially in the medium of Korean-language newspapers, because of his success and his voluntary services. In a personal interview, I was overwhelmed by his impressive story. He handed me copies of his *Nam-*

---

6. The concept of "marginal man" was originally developed by Robert E. Park, "Human Migration and the Marginal Man," *American Journal of Sociology* (33:1928), 881-893; Everett Stonequist, *The Marginal Man: A Study in Personality and Culture Conflict* (New York: Charles Scribner's Son, 1937), p. 55.

7. Sang Hyun Lee, "Called to Be Pilgrim: Toward a Theology of the Korean Immigrant" (unpublished paper, 1980).

kigosipun yiyaki (To Tell the Story), which appeared in the *Korea Central Daily* beginning on May 29, 1987, as an autobiographical feature column.

Dr. Chung recalled that it was on August 10, 1937, during a typical muggy Chicago summer, that he arrived on foreign soil. He spent his first night at the YMCA hotel on Chicago Avenue. It was a shameful and painful experience for him to have traveled overseas with a Japanese passport because Korea had been annexed by Japan (1909-1945). His first visit to the Korean Methodist Church was an emotionally unforgettable experience. He burst into tears when he saw the Korean national flag displayed inside the sanctuary (flying Korean flags was forbidden in his home country, which was under Japanese control).

At this church, pastored by Rev. Eun-Taik Lee, there were about fifteen Korean students and several other Koreans who were working as railroad construction laborers. Of the students, several of them later returned to their homeland to become prominent leaders in either the government or in social and economic endeavors. Dr. Chung particularly remembered his close friendship with the nationally renowned composer Ik Tae Ahn (1906-1965), who began to compose the Korean national anthem while studying cello in Chicago at the American Conservatory of Music in 1937. He later completed the song in Berlin, Germany. Such an act would have been severely punished in Japanese-occupied Korea. Of course, the anthem could not be played in Korea until after Japan had been defeated in 1945.

Dr. Chung had been born in North Korea in a Christian home; his father was raised by a grandmother who was an evangelist and who gave him the Christian name Paul. After graduating from the Seoul National University Dental School, he worked under Dr. John Boots, an American dentist-missionary, who later had a strong influence on his decision to come to Chicago for a further study in 1937. At that time it took about two weeks to travel by ship from Korea via Japan to the West Coast. He happened to arrive on a Saturday, when the immigration office was closed for the weekend. He spent his first night in the immigration detention center. Then he moved on to San Francisco, where about fifty Koreans were living, most of whom were laborers for a railroad construction company, and he continued his travel to Chicago by train, which took about three days. He was admitted to Northwestern University's Dental School with a one-year scholarship, owing to Dr. Boots's strong recommendation.

Dr. Chung recalled his early struggle to survive as a foreign student:

> Trying to save a five-cent subway ride, I often had to walk long miles between school and dormitory. My daily living expenses in those days included five cents for a one-way subway, eleven cents for lunch, and thirty cents for supper. In order to support myself, I often went along with the Reverend Lee to engage in peddling jobs with a carton box of sundry goods to factory workers in Gary, Indiana. Reverend Lee also had to support his family, for he was pastoring the church without any minimum compensation.

Dr. Chung described his peddling experience as such:

We used to go down to Gary by train on Friday afternoon. I'd hit bars and streets around the area where factory workers were concentrated, selling razor blades, wallets, perfumes, and other toiletries. On a lucky day, I could make about ten bucks in profit, which met about my weekly living expenses. Other fellow Korean students earned money as house boys for rich American families, cutting grass and working on yards. Once I was picked up by a police and spent a night at the police station for peddling without a permit.

Like most other expatriate students in the States at that time, Dr. Chung also volunteered much time and effort for the anti-Japanese movement. He appealed to American public officials about the oppressive Japanese colonization of Korea and engaged in fund raising for the Korean liberation movement. He was an activist until he graduated from Northwestern, where he earned a D.D.S. in 1938 and an M.S. in 1945. Later, in 1958, he was awarded an honorary Doctor of Law from Illinois Wesleyan University; and by 1973, Dr. Chung had professorships at several dental schools, such as Seoul National University, Northwestern University, and University of Illinois at Chicago.

Since there was no Korean consulate general office in Chicago until 1968, the Korean government appointed Dr. Chung as an honorary consul general to serve and look after the Korean residents in the area (1966-68). He has continued to be an honorary consul general since 1979. And he was also once active in many community groups such as the board chairman of the Korean Senior Citizens Association and as the president of the Korean-American Political League. Dr. Chung appeared in *Who's Who in America* (1974) and *Who's Who in the World* (1975). At the age of 80 now, he is still busy with many voluntary services attending community meetings.

In 1954 former founding President Syngman Rhee stopped in Chicago to meet members of the Anti-Japanese League after an official visit with President Harry Truman. Mayor Martin Kennelly of Chicago had a reception party for the Korean president at the Drake Hotel, to which Chicago Koreans were invited. During the presidential visit, the Chicago mayor asked President Rhee why there was no Korean diplomatic office. This prompted President Rhee to appoint Mr. Tae Eun Jung as a Korean consul to Chicago on the spot. Mr. Jung, then chairman of the Anti-Japanese League, was married to a Polish woman, had three children, and owned a chop suey wholesale business. Unfortunately, when Mr. Jung received the official credentials for Korean consul a month later, he was so overwhelmed by the honor that he died of a heart attack.

Among other one-time young students, some of whom are still active in the Korean community, is Ray Kim, who has owned the Ray Kim Ford dealership on the far North Side of Chicago since 1980. Joseph Lee, Rev. Lee's son, now a retired professional engineer for the state of Illinois Department of Transpor-

Syngman Rhee, the first president of Korea, (on left) with his Australian-born wife greets Dr. Paul Chung and the wife of the Reverend E. Lee (on right) during Rhee's visit to Chicago in 1954. Courtesy of Joseph Ahne.

tation and city of Evanston, has been actively serving the Korean community in many capacities. Another notable community leader from the student generation is attorney Kie-Young Shim, who graduated from Northwestern University Law School. He was elected to be the fourth, fifth, and thirteenth president of the Korean Association. With the increase of the Korean population the Association began to change its role and from mere fellowship and mutual support to that of interest-group politics. Active in city politics is Hae-Dal Paul Park, who once studied economics at the University of Chicago. He has owned a real estate office in Korea Town for many years, and now is serving as a commissioner of Chicago Economic Development, a patronage position he received for supporting Richard Daley during the mayoral election of 1989.

It was not until the late 1960s and the early 1970s that the numbers of the Korean immigrants began to increase rapidly as a result of the Immigration Act of 1965. By 1970 the census had classified Koreans as one of the major nationality groups in the country; it counted 3,673 in Illinois and 69,000 in the United States. This was a turning point: the Korean community began to change from the sojourner student generation to a permanent immigrant population when waves of Korean miners and nurses began to arrive in Chicago from Germany.

The Immigration Period (1968 to the Present)

The Influx of Korean Miners and Nurses

A unique group of Koreans, coal miners and nurses, came to Chicago from West Germany beginning in 1968. What is different about these Koreans is that they not only re-migrated from Germany but also came to look for *permanent* residence — in contrast to the earlier Korean student generation. In this sense, Korean miners and nurses from West Germany have played an important role in establishing a permanent Korean community in Chicago, and to some extent in other United States cities.

I have gleaned the historical background of the so-called *Dokil kwangby chulshin* ("Miners' Group from Germany") from my personal interviews and other information gathered about the pioneer Korean coal miners and nurses in West Germany. Korean migration to Germany was first initiated by the Korean government because of domestic and internal problems in Korea. This was the "push" factor; the "pull" factor came from West Germany's booming economy and its need for labor to keep its growing industries running. At the end of the devastating Korean War (1950–53), South Korea went through a socio-political transformation and an economically difficult period. In the late 1950s, Korean society was faced with a population explosion and high unemployment. This problem was largely caused by the post-Korean War baby boom, the flight of about one million North Korean refugees to South Korea, and the introduction of preventive Western medical technology, which reduced the mortality rate.[8]

Seeking a remedy, the South Korean military government (which took over power by a coup in 1961) embarked on an aggressive program for economic development. One of the innovative and unprecedented plans was its policy of emigration providing for the *export* of "surplus" Korean people. The new South Korean emigration law specifically stated that "this amendment, by encouraging people to emigrate to foreign countries, is designed to be geared to a population control policy and thus to contribute to the stability of the national economy."[9] Accordingly, the policy assumed that overseas workers and contract laborers would send money back home, thus helping their poor third-world homeland.

In 1963 the South Korean government negotiated with West Germany to send contracted workers for coal mining and the hospital industries, and in December of that year the first group of about 247 Korean "miners" left for West Germany for a three-year term. By 1974 about 7,000 miners were employed in such areas as Ruhr (Aachen, Essen), and about 10,000 nurses had been

8. Illsoo Kim, *New Urban Immigrants: The Korean Community in New York* (Princeton, 1981), pp. 48–51.

9. *Yimin Baeg-kwa* [*Emigration Encyclopedia*] (Seoul: Bak Moon Sa, 1964), p. 361, quoted in Kim, ibid., 52.

brought into the cities of West Germany from Korea. However, these Korean migrants were not considered to be official immigrants but merely temporary "guest workers" who would leave at the end of their contracts. It is interesting to note that these Korean miners were not real miners by training or experience in their homeland. To begin with, Korea has very few mines or miners. The majority of these "miners" were highly educated — in college or at least in high school — but unemployed young adults in their twenties, who took advantage of the opportunity to leave their economically troubled and socially unstable country. They were nicknamed *Haksa Kwangbu,* meaning "Miners with college degrees."[10] This migration was years before the Korean "economic miracle" of our time.

The Korean government recruited these overseas workers through written tests on German language and mining theory, background checks and personal interviews to exclude undesirables such as ex-convicts, military draft dodgers, political criminals, and physically unfit candidates. The process was highly selective, choosing only one of twenty applicants for these overseas jobs. One of the Korean miners in Germany, Mr. Sung Koh, who has lived in Chicago since 1968, shared the emotional experience of the day he left Korea for Germany:

> I can still remember or I don't want to remember again the heartbroken day of my departure for Germany. All I had in my mind was the fact that I blamed and despised my country, Korea, which had no room for me to make a living even from hand to mouth. After my parents died, I was raised by my grandmother, whom I was responsible to support . . . but I had to leave her behind. Oh, I felt so sad and shameful that I had to leave as a contracted worker as if I were a slave. (October 25, 1990)

By contrast, he seemed to have more positive feelings upon arrival in Germany. Mr. Koh noted:

> You mean my first impression in Germany? Uh . . . A lot of things new to me. Let's see, well . . . Yes, I was first impressed with the highway system. You know, I had never seen before such a fast-moving road in Korea. I was absolutely fascinated by the fact that German miners were driving their own cars to go to the mining sites. You know . . . it was beyond anybody's dream for even high-middle income people to afford a car in Korea. I just could not wait for a day I could drive my own car. Everybody was excited just to imagine a car, I mean a real car someday, forgetting all the sad memories in Korea. From day one, most of the Korean workers felt for sure that they came to a paradise in the world. (October 25, 1990)

---

10. *Dong-A Almanac* (Seoul: Dong-A Ilbo Co., 1975), p. 423.

But the realities of daily life and working conditions in coal mining were harsh and sometimes dangerous, especially for those without any experience as miners. As it turned out, Mr. Koh was never able to buy his dream car. The miners' daily wages were about 32 marks in German currency, much above what they would have earned in Korea; in addition, supplemental pay was given to married men and their dependent children.[11] Yet the miners did not have much cash left at the end of the month, after deducting their insurance premium and income taxes. Only their ruthless underconsumption and compulsive savings and ardent face-saving spirit enabled them to endure the difficulties.

But it did not take long for German supervisors to suspect the qualifications of the Korean miners. Whenever the German employers complained about the inefficient work performance, Koreans tried to excuse themselves, saying that Korea had far different working conditions, different kinds of tools, and of course there was the language barrier. By the time German employers discovered that their guest workers were inexperienced and bogus miners, they did not bother to deal with the falsification issue: there was no other labor available to replace the Koreans, and the three-year contract would soon expire anyway. A good number of these amateur Korean miners were injured and some were killed accidentally at work sites because of their inexperience. Mr. Koh recounted the psychological pressures and fears that he too might be killed in a deep mining tunnel some day. Often his only wish was to come home alive after each shift.

A group of Korean nurses also went to West Germany, and many of them married Korean miners. At the end of the contracts and facing an economic recession, West Germany began to expel Korean migrant workers. The United States, with its more generous immigration policies, was the most logical place for them to turn for remigration. America had a shortage of medical professionals at the same time that there was a change in the Immigration Act in 1965. That was a major pull factor. A majority of the Korean miners and nurses, many of them now as husband and wife, could easily obtain immigrant visas as workers or as visitors to enter the United States.

The number of Korean nurses who had migrated to West Germany was estimated at about 6,100 as of December 1973, according to the Nurses Association of Korea[12]; by contrast, a smaller number of 2,400 nurses had been admitted to the United States between 1965 and 1973. Although the number of Korean nurses in the United States had reached about 7,000 in 1976,[13] the

11. Jo-ja Kim, "A Study for the Enhancement of Korean Nurses in West Germany: Employment Status," *Daehan Ganho* (Nurses Association of Korea, March-April, 1975), p. 27, quoted in Kim, p. 148.

12. *Joong-Ang Ilbo* (The Korea Central Daily), April 17, 1978.

13. In April 1991, the bank negotiated to sell 51 percent of its stock to a John Hollen's investment group because of financial trouble due to alleged mismanagement. However, the bank board made a decision to sell it to a group of Korean investors in an effort to keep the pride of the first Korean-owned bank in Chicago.

statistics do not provide a specific breakdown on the number who came directly from Korea and those from Germany. Even so, it seems safe to assume that many, if not a majority, of those nurses had remigrated from Germany to the United States along with the Korean miners.

One nurse, who came to Chicago from Germany via Canada in 1968, related the background story of her migration:

> After graduating from a nursing school in Seoul, I could not find a job as a nurse due to the lack of hospitals and underdeveloped medical industries in those days in my country. To make the matter worse, you know, a nurse career was not a respected profession in Korean society anyway. I was so frustrated by the jobless situation, and a contracted nurse in Germany was not only a great job opportunity but also a once in a life chance to get out of the socially and culturally depressed Korean society. (Telephone interview, January, 1991)

She thought that the working conditions and pay at German hospitals were more than fair. In spite of some language difficulties, German head nurses were in general kindly and sympathetic and willing to help the Korean nurses. So she did not feel any racism as she sometimes experienced in American society. In contrast to the bogus miners, almost all nurses were graduates of legitimate nursing schools in Korea. Like many other nurses, this woman could have extended her contract with a German hospital. Nevertheless, she could not foresee for herself a better future in Germany than in North America. She first immigrated to Canada as a single, and later married a former miner who came to Chicago on a visitor's visa in 1967. Since then she has continued to work as a nurse, and her husband has now become an established owner-operator of a gas station. They have raised four children, sent one of them to college, and live comfortably in a north suburb of Chicago.

Unlike their counterpart miners, most Korean nurses who migrated from Germany found jobs in Chicago, though they were initially limited to nurse's aides at hospitals or nursing homes. Most states do not approve or recognize foreign-trained nurses until they have passed a state licensing exam for registered nurses, which became — along with the language barrier and the cultural adjustment to America — a major obstacle.

With the increasing number of Korean nurses, there was natural need to organize the Midwest Korean Nurses Association for mutual support and especially as an information exchange for employment opportunities as well as for passing the state exam. Since it was organized in 1969, the Association has played an important part in helping Korean nurses to advance their professional careers. There are now about 500 Korean nurses in the Chicago area, and the Association reports 200 dues-paid members. The Association has participated annually in community services such as free health checkups. It also sponsors educational and cultural seminars, with outside guest speakers such as Korean-born Professor Mi Ja Kim of the Nursing School, University of Illinois at Chicago. A large number of these nurses are employed at the Cook County Hospital, at Veterans Administration hospitals, and the Swedish Covenant Hospital on the North Side of the city, where Koreans have settled. Many of them still work as semiprofessionals and nurse's aides at nursing homes. The cutback in federal funding during the 1980s and the financial crunch at many hospitals forced layoffs of some Korean and other foreign nurses.

In many cases, Korean miners married nurses solely for the purpose of getting visas to come to America. Other Korean miners, without acceptable qualifications for entry, sought to a use a variety of means of entry. For example, Mr. Koh had remained unmarried for a number of years, awaiting his fiancée in Korea; yet he was determined to come to the United States to partake of its opportunities and make a success of himself. He was granted a temporary work visa as a Taekwondo (a Korean martial art) instructor at the United States embassy in West Germany by producing an invitation from a Korean friend in Chicago, and by showing that he had saved enough money to avoid welfare dependency in America.

When Mr. Koh finally arrived in Chicago in 1968, he found only a few other Korean miners from Germany. He estimated that there were then about 1,500 Koreans, most of whom were unmarried students plus a small number of Korean war brides married to American GIs. The number of Korean miners trickling in from Germany did reach about fifteen within a few months; then it soared to about 200, including their nurse-spouses by 1969. At that point the *Dongwoohoe* (Fellow Workers' Club) of German-Koreans was organized at Mr. Koh's martial art studio on Lawrence Avenue.

Unlike the Korean students, who were primarily confined to studying and who were transient "birds of passage" ready to return home, this new generation of Koreans from Germany was committed to settling down in Chicago, bringing their spouses and family members to America, moving into job markets and forming mutual interest groups. Chicago was to be their home. As a result, they would constitute the core of the Korean immigrant community and would exercise a major influence over its leadership and community activities.

The one-time migrant miners who are now old-timers and leaders in Chicago often remember the harsh conditions they faced in the early days. They were highly educated but without salable professional or vocational skills. Coupled with their lack of English-language fluency and a different occupational structure, it was almost impossible for them to land what they considered decent jobs. While many of their nurse-wives enjoyed professional jobs at hospitals, these miner-husbands had to work in factories or at other blue-collar jobs. Such a low occupational status was unbearable for many proud

Korean immigrants, who felt their higher education should land them higher on the job ladder. For instance, Mr. Koh felt humiliated by his first job as a low-ranked, part-time instructor at a Korean martial arts studio, working for small wages and having as part of his compensation being allowed to sleep on a cot at night. But he persevered and eventually opened his own martial arts studio, which prospered and is still in business at the same location after twenty-two years. His fiancée joined him in 1971.

Some miners opted to pursue further education at American universities to prepare themselves for better occupations, while others peddled wigs from pushcarts and backpacks, displaying samples on poles or carrying the products in their hands on the streets of South Side black neighborhoods. The 1970s was a time when Americans took to wearing wigs, and they were very much in vogue with black women and some men. As a result, some Korean immigrants succeeded and became millionaires in Chicago. A majority of them gradually moved into commercial businesses, since this seemed to be the fastest way to succeed in America. For example, Mr. Koh saved money from running several martial arts schools and from teaching martial arts at the Naval Training Center in Waukegan. The accumulated capital enabled his wife to open a Korean restaurant, which she ran for about ten years; now she owns a gift shop in a downtown hotel. Similarly, many of the former miners from Germany prospered as businessmen. For example, Kung-Ku Lee and Young-Shick Choi became board member-shareholders of Mayfair Bank, a Korean-owned bank, which was opened in 1987.[14] Two former miners, Hea-Bae Kim and Chang-Bum Kim, were elected as presidents of the Korean Association in Chicago, the leading fraternal organization of the Korean community.

Such success did not just come by accident but through a fierce pride in hard work and perseverance. The *Dongwoohoe* (Fellow Workers' Club) has continued to hold an annual banquet at Thanksgiving time for the last twenty years. Its members are no longer workers in the blue-collar sense. Most are now well-established small businessmen or sole owners of trading companies and other retail and wholesale businesses. Its annual attendance averages 200 to 300 family members, along with friends and community leaders as guests. Illinois Governor James Thompson proclaimed November 25th, 1989, to be the Day of "Dongwoohoe," thereby validating the miners' strong sense of being the bone and sinew, the ethnic heart and soul of the Korean community in Chicago. Korean-Americans mix their culture and their occupations. It is hard to tell where ethnicity leaves off and entrepreneurship begins.

14. For an in-depth analysis on socio-political and economic "push" factors of the Korean immigrants to the U.S., see Illsoo Kim, especially chapters two and three.

Chicago politician Neil Hartigan participates in a Korea Day parade in 1990.
Courtesy of Joseph Ahne.

Settlement Patterns and Characteristics

Korean Population Mobility

The Immigration Act of 1965 opened the way for the dramatic increase of Korean immigrants in the United States. As shown in Table 16.1, for example, in 1965 about 2,000 new Koreans were admitted to the United States. The number gradually grew to about 35,000 annually, beginning in 1985 and thereafter.

According to the 1990 census, 36,000 Koreans live in the Chicago metropolitan area. Of the total, about 22,000, or 62 percent, live in surrounding suburbs, particularly in the northern and northwestern suburban areas (see Map 16.1, p. 469 above). They are heavily concentrated in the white middle- and upper-middle class suburbs like Arlington Heights, Des Plaines, Glenview, Hoffman Estates, Lincolnwood, Morton Grove, Mt. Prospect, Niles, Northbrook, Schaumburg, and Skokie. Korean residents in the city are found in large sections of the Albany Park, North Park, Rogers Park, and Uptown areas. Lawrence Avenue, Montrose Avenue, Kedzie Avenue, and Lincoln Avenue are

TABLE 16.1
Number of Korean Immigrants Admitted to the U.S. (1950-1988)

Year	Number	Year	Number	Year	Number
1950-59	5,528	1971	14,297	1980	2,329
1960-64	9,647	1972	18,876	1981	32,663
1965	2,139	1973	22,930	1982	31,724
1966	2,492	1974	28,028	1983	33,339
1967	3,956	1975	28,362	1984	33,042
1968	3,811	1976	30,803	1985	35,232
1969	6,045	1977	30,917	1986	35,776
1970	9,316	1978	29,288	1987	35,849
		1979	29,248	1988	34,703

Source: Annual Reports by Immigration and Naturalization Service, 1950-1989.

major strips of Korean clusters. The 1990 census shows 62 percent in the suburbs, up from 52 percent in 1980 (see Table 16.2).

Why do these new immigrants keep coming to American cities? A long time ago Aristotle gave the most natural answer to such a basic question, which was that "men come to the city in order to live a better life." There are, of course, many complex factors that prod Koreans to leave their homeland, including the political instability caused by the military tensions between South and North Korea on the one hand, and by constant turmoil caused by student protests against the military regimes that took over after the coup in 1961, on the other. These problems were aggravated even more by an explosive population growth — from 25 million in 1960 to 40 million in 1984 — and the accompanying high employment, plus the ever-present scarcity of natural resources. All of these factors combined to "push" many educated middle- and upper-class Koreans to leave the home country.[15]

15. Kwang Chung Kim and Won Moo Hurh, "Koreans in Chicago" (unpublished manuscript, 1990). The same authors, in another survey in 1979, found that 61 percent of the males and 53 percent of the females among 615 Korean immigrants in Los Angeles have college degrees in Korea; 34 percent were counted for proprietors and managers at the time of the interview, whereas 25 percent of the respondents were in business in Korea. In *Korean Immigrants in America* (Cranbury, New Jersey, 1984), pp. 58, 105. A recent study also shows that 53 percent of Korean males and 45 percent of all Korean workers in Los Angeles are self-employed. In Pyung Kap Min, "Some Positive Functions of Ethnic Business for an Immigrant Community: Korean Immigrants in Los Angeles," final report submitted to the National Science Foundation, 1989. See also some of the essays, such as "Jewish Enterprise," in *Self-Help in Urban America*, Scott Cummings, ed. (Port Washington, NY, 1980), and the chapter on Greeks in this volume.

TABLE 16.2

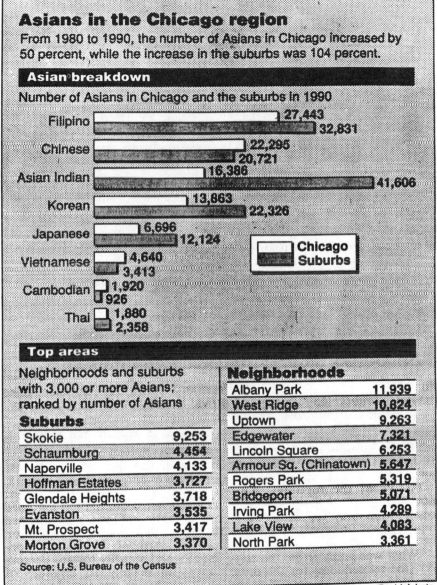

Asians in the Chicago region

From 1980 to 1990, the number of Asians in Chicago increased by 50 percent, while the increase in the suburbs was 104 percent.

Asian breakdown

Number of Asians in Chicago and the suburbs in 1990

	Chicago	Suburbs
Filipino	27,443	32,831
Chinese	22,295	20,721
Asian Indian	16,386	41,606
Korean	13,863	22,326
Japanese	6,696	12,124
Vietnamese	4,640	3,413
Cambodian	1,920	926
Thai	1,880	2,358

Top areas

Neighborhoods and suburbs with 3,000 or more Asians; ranked by number of Asians

Suburbs

Skokie	9,253
Schaumburg	4,454
Naperville	4,133
Hoffman Estates	3,727
Glendale Heights	3,718
Evanston	3,535
Mt. Prospect	3,417
Morton Grove	3,370

Neighborhoods

Albany Park	11,939
West Ridge	10,824
Uptown	9,263
Edgewater	7,321
Lincoln Square	6,253
Armour Sq. (Chinatown)	5,647
Rogers Park	5,319
Bridgeport	5,071
Irving Park	4,289
Lake View	4,083
North Park	3,361

Source: U.S. Bureau of the Census

Chicago Tribune/David Jahntz

The Entrepreneur Immigrants

Unlike the period of the early student pioneers, a large portion of the new Korean community is made up of educated middle- and upper-class Koreans "uprooted" from the major cities of Korea. According to a sample survey conducted by Professors Kwang Chung Kim and Won Moo Hurh in the Chicago area in 1986, three-quarters of 622 randomly selected Korean immigrants came from the city of Seoul. About 46 percent had college educations in their homeland; nearly 50 percent of the respondents were professional and technical workers in Korea; and about 28 percent were in sales and administrative jobs. Only 14 percent managed their own businesses, whereas about 30 percent of them claimed to engage in small business in Chicago.[16] The disparity in business proprietorships between the old country and the new poses a challenging question: what motivates the exceptionally high percentage of Korean immigrants to engage in small business in the big cities of the United States? This question must be put in the context of a tradition in Korea in which society has little respect for *Jangsa* (commercial business). In contrast, in Chicago it is not unusual to observe Koreans frequently talking about *Jangsa* at gatherings in churches, restaurants, and other community groups. The most popular topics include "Who made a fortune?" "What is the hottest business?" and "Where are good areas for business?"

Historically, self-employment has not been considered as an honored occupation in Korea.[17] Nonetheless, Asian Americans continue to lead in starting new businesses. In entrepreneurship, Koreans led all other minority groups in 1982 and 1987, according to a Census Bureau report (see Table 16.3). Many researchers have found that an intermeshing of complex factors helps to explain the rise of Korean entrepreneurship. Among the long list of causal factors most often cited are "ethnic class resources" such as money, education, a hard-work ethic, and some professional experience linked to high economic motivation; limited employment opportunities for an immigrant minority; strong family ties and mutually supportive ethnic group solidarity;[18] long hours of hard work and a willingness to take the risks of physical danger in crime-ridden inner-city neighborhoods; status inconsistency;[19] and the role of Korean entrepreneurs as "Middleman Minorities," who distribute products of the dom-

16. Ivan Light, "Disadvantaged Minorities in Self Employment," *International Journal of Comparative Society*, 20:31-45.

17. Illsoo Kim, *op. cit.*

18. Pyong Gap Min, *Ethnic Business Enterprise: Korean Small Business in Atlanta* (New York: Center for Migration Studies, 1988).

19. E. Bonacich, I. Light, and C. C. Wong, "Korean Immigrants: Small Business in Los Angeles," in *Sourcebook on the New Immigration*, R. S. Bryce-Laporte, ed. (New Brunswick, NJ: Transaction Books), pp. 167-184; see also I. Light and E. Bonacich, *Immigrant Entrepreneurs: Koreans in Los Angeles, 1965-1982* (Berkeley: University of California Press).

TABLE 16.3
Percentage of entrepreneurs among Asian-Americans

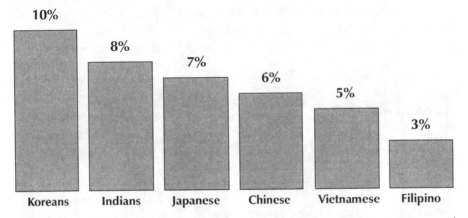

Source: Estimates by Professor William O'Hare, University of Louisville, from U.S. Bureau of the Census data for 1987.

inant group to minority customers.[20] Since human motivation is seldom singular and generally multicausal, it is likely that all of these variables have operated to greater and lesser degrees in propelling Koreans toward entrepreneurship and business start-ups.

Yet, in addition to these factors, there seems to be something else, which appears to be a "timely opportunity" created by the export-oriented economic policy of the South Korean government. That in itself may be a larger factor than is generally presumed in understanding the Korean concentration in small business in America. The same export-oriented urban economy that pulled rural labor into Korean cities to manufacture garments, wigs, toys, shoes, and electronic goods had to find large overseas markets for these goods. And this export-oriented economy created a "timely opportunity" for Korean immigrants to move easily into American business life.[21]

When President Park Chung-hee came to power by military coup in 1961, the South Korean government launched two five-year economic development plans aimed at building a major export economy. The result was almost miraculous: exports rose dramatically from a mere $41 million in 1961 to $10 billion in 1977. The United States and Japan became the major markets for these labor-intensive consumer goods. In an effort to meet national export goals,

20. Illsoo Kim, pp. 71-98.
21. Kim and Hurh, source in Note (15).

Oriental food store at N. Clark and Gregory. Run by a Korean manager, the store sells Japanese, Chinese, Philippine, and American goods, and advertises in all five languages. Courtesy of Masako Osako.

the government subsidized export manufacturers and trading companies with government loans, document payments, credit for the purchase of raw materials for export use, and other incentives. Largely owing to the expansion of the "export boom," well-educated, middle-class elites were recruited by the export-trading corporations to work their overseas markets. A majority of these representatives were first-time visitors to the United States. While getting some help from their Korean friends or relatives during their settling period, they often encouraged fellow Koreans already here to sell the Korean products with many promotional incentives. Many others chose to remain in this country eventually opening their own wholesale or retail businesses and selling Korean products with the knowledge they had gained in importing.

The impact of the Korean-government-sponsored export economy on Korean immigrant business in America was expressed by Johnny Koh, who once served as president of the Korean Trader's Association in Chicago:

In 1976 I came to Chicago initially as an overseas agent of a steel wire export company in Seoul. Upon arrival in America, I actually enjoyed American life styles more than doing my job. It was not easy for me as an inexperienced foreigner to compete in the American wholesale market anyway. In addition, I often felt insecure about my future in the company due to the company's merger. I finally decided to work for myself and changed my visa status from business visitor to permanent resident. In 1978 I started importing leather garments from Korea. Once I was overstocked with a large volume of unsold goods sitting in a warehouse. I was just desperate enough to invite some of my Korean friends to buy and resell them. And I also sold about $80,000 worth of merchandise to several Jewish merchants in Jew Town (Maxwell Street) on credit without any paper contract. I never collected that money. But the unfortunate experience with Jewish merchants rather helped me to become the first Korean to open a store in Jew Town. In 1978 I started selling leather garments and blue jeans for the lowest price in Jew Town. Absolutely no competition. I made a big money from the business. (June 12, 1991)

There were other Koreans who managed their own retail businesses successfully and became millionaires eventually. For instance, Eun Young Lee, a college graduate in Korea, began by selling wigs; Chang Keun Kim, now president of the Federation of Southside Korean Merchants, owned a clothing business; and Young Shik Choi was also in wigs. They all made such sizable fortunes from small businesses in "Jew Town" (as they call it) that they were able to open the Mayfair Bank. Mr. Koh estimates that there may be about one hundred Korean millionaires in Chicago who made their wealth from small retail businesses, of which at least thirty have derived their fortunes from the import-wholesale trade that was initially encouraged and subsidized by the Korean government.

The Korean American's penchant for business is confirmed by the survey of Professors Kwang Chung Kim and Won Moo Hurh, which showed that about 30 percent of working Koreans in Chicago are self-employed business owners. They are in three major types of businesses: 40 percent in the retail trade; 31 percent in personal services; and 7 percent in repair services. Most of the retail businesses are variety stores, food stores/restaurants, apparel stores, and real estate sales. Most of their businesses are family owned and operated by husband and wife. Most owners worked a long six- or seven-day week, with the men averaging sixty-one hours and the women putting in sixty hours in an effort to achieve their success ideal.[22]

The Chicago Korean business sample survey by Professors Kim and Hurh shows a high three-fourths of all married female respondents are working full time. This is in sharp contrast to the traditional customs in Korea, where most Korean wives are expected to stay home and take care of household work and childrearing. In fact, the employment rate among Korean immigrant wives in the Chicago area is higher than that of American

22. Kim and Hurh, "The Burden of Roles: Korean Wives in the U.S.," *Ethnic and Racial Studies* 11 (April: 151-167).

TABLE 16.4
Incomes of Metropolitan Chicago Ethnic Groups

Filipinos	$29,500
Asian Indians	$24,000
Japanese	$23,300
Whites	$22,500
Koreans	$21,700
Mexicans	$16,600
Vietnamese	$13,600
Blacks	$12,600

Source: U.S. Census 1980; Chicago Area Geographic Information Study prepared for Chicago REPORTER, March 1985. All dollar figures are rounded to the nearest one-hundred.

native-born wives.[23] This, of course, adds to the total household income: the 1986 survey showed that two-thirds of Korean Americans reported annual family incomes of $40,000 or more in 1985, apparently benefiting from two wage earners. The relatively high family income status of Korean immigrants is also supported by the earlier 1980 census data. With a median family income of $21,700, Koreans were almost equal to whites in the Chicago area, whose income was $22,500; their incomes were also far higher than those of Hispanics, Vietnamese, and blacks (see Table 16.4).

Classification of Korean Businesses

According to the 1991 *Korean Business Directory* (a Korean Yellow Pages that is published annually by *The Korea Times Chicago*), there are about 1,313 Korean businesses in eighty-one different lines of business in the Chicago area. But the Directory listed only about fifty businesses on the South Side of Chicago; and this is obviously an undercount, because many store owners whose customers are blacks and other non-Koreans did not bother to include themselves in the Korean Directory. Through direct contact with several Korean business leaders in major Korean business areas, I identified about 610 businesses in seventeen major Korean-clustered areas throughout the primarily black South and West sides of Chicago (see Map 16.2). However, the president of the Federation of the Southside Korean Merchants estimates the number to be even higher — between 850 and 1,000 — including those unidentified stores in scattered areas.

Korean businesses in the Chicago metropolitan area can be classified into

23. Joseph Ahne's field notes: *The Korea Times Chicago,* July 28, 1990; M. Mills, "Roseland is no bed of roses for Korean merchants," Chicago *Tribune,* July 10, 1990; K. C. Lee, "Korean Business," Chicago *Sun-Times,* March 16, 1990. Robert Gardner, B. Robey, Peter C. Smith, *Asian Americans: Growth, Change and Diversity* (Population Reference Bureau, October 1985, 32).

four major categories according to the origins of products and types of customers: (1) Korean products sold to Korean customers; (2) American products or technical services sold to Korean customers; (3) Korean labor-intensive service to the white majority; and (4) Korean products to ethnic minorities (see Table 16.5).

The businesses in the first category shown in Table 16.5 are mostly Korean goods and services for Korean consumers and are heavily concentrated in "Korea Town" in the Albany Park area (see Map 16.2). Densely clustered Korean businesses of the same kind are in severe price competition.

In Chicago, there are four *daily* Korean-language newspapers. They used to import the original newspapers daily via air transportation from home offices in Korea, reprint them here with additional news about Chicago Koreans as well as general American news, and distribute them by second-class mail. With the use of satellite technology, the local news can now be simultaneously printed in color in Chicago. In addition, three *weekly* newspapers are published in Chicago. There are also: one Korean television program, a cable program, and two radio shows that buy air time on American stations. The Korean-American media are probably the most sophisticated information clearinghouse and have the highest home subscription rates (approximately 10,000 daily subscribers) among all other ethnic media in Chicago.

Korean media go beyond mere news services; they are a very influential mechanism in Korean immigrant life. They provide publicity about Korean community issues, and they air opinions, educational information for American life adjustment and events, and news about South Korea. Videotape rentals are also a highly popular business, for many Koreans like to entertain themselves as well as see images of their homeland culture.

The businesses in the second category in Table 16.5 provide commercial American products or technical services to Koreans, who need a good deal of assistance in getting over the language problem and overcoming the lack of knowledge of American systems. The astonishingly high number of real estate agents reflects the high percentage of Korean home ownership in the suburbs. Both insurance and real estate sales can be defined by the "middleman minority theory," which provides American products and services to minority and immigrant customers.

The businesses in the third category are typical of Korean goods and services to Americans that are labor-intensive. A high proportion of their customers are the white majority. Korean penetration into the dry-cleaning business is perhaps the most visible to Chicagoans, particularly whites. *The Cleaners' Guide,* published in 1991 by the Korean-American Dry Cleaners' Association, lists some 2,300 dry-cleaning establishments in the Chicago area, of which about 2,000 are owned by Koreans. The Association estimates that there are 2,800 dry-cleaners in the state of Illinois, and about 80 percent of the total are accounted for by Korean owners. The Association is one of the strongest fraternal organizations among Koreans: it also provides such services as seminars

MAP 16.2

KOREAN BUSINESSES IN CHICAGO BY ZIP CODE

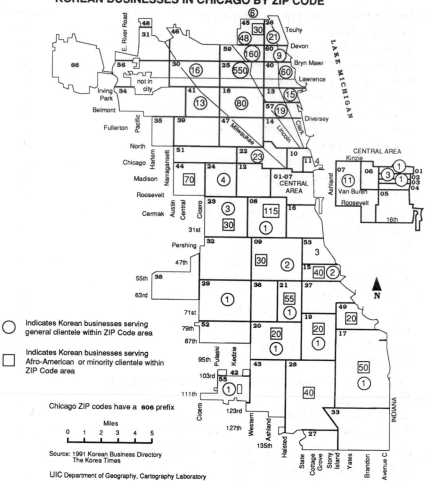

on "how to run a business," or even technical training, in addition to its occasional fellowship gatherings. Many Koreans have chosen the dry-cleaning business or flower shops as an alternative to doing business in high-crime areas and inner-city neighborhoods.

The businesses in the fourth category have been developed out of the growing trade activities between the United States and the developing nations in Asia, including Korea, Taiwan, Hong Kong, and recently China. Coupled with Korea's export-oriented economic development, Korean immigrants took advantage of the opportunity to import such low-priced consumer goods as wigs, jewelry, clothes, handbags, shoes, and other general merchandise from Korea and other Asian countries and sought to sell them in black and other

TABLE 16.5
Types and Numbers of Selective Korean Businesses

	Number
(1). Korean products to Korean customers	
Korean bakeries	6
Korean books	8
Korean imported cosmetics	6
Korean foods (wholesalers)	14
Korean grocery retailers	38
Korean restaurants	76
Korean-style night club/cafes	20
Korean imported gift shops	18
Oriental herbs and medicine stores	23
Korean video rental shops	34
Korean newspapers, radio & TV stations	13
(2). American products/technical services to Koreans	
Auto body shops, repairs and dealers	29
Construction, home repairs	57
Heating, plumbing repairs services	33
Travel agencies	22
Accounting, CPAs	40
Medical doctors and dentist offices	76
Insurance agents	52
Real estate brokers and agents	186
Beauty salons	51
(3). Labor-intensive service/products to the white majority	
Flower shops	32
Laundry and dry cleaners	2,000
Taekwondo (Korean martial arts) schools	36
(4). Korean imported products to ethnic minorities	
Fashion, clothing stores	41
General goods, clothes, shoes, wigs and beauty supplies in black neighborhoods	524
General goods, clothes in Hispanic areas	70
Wholesale import-traders	97

Source: '91 *Korean Business Directory,* The Korea Times

A shopping strip in Chicago's "Koreatown" on Lawrence Avenue.
Courtesy of Joseph Ahne.

minority neighborhoods. The wholesale importers numbered about ninety-seven in the *Korean Business Directory,* indicating a strong link between the products handled by Korean-American business and Korea's export economy.

Black and Korean Tensions

The wholesale traders are mostly located around Clark Street and Lawrence Avenue on the North Side of Chicago. Retail stores in the black and other minority neighborhoods are clustered in the following areas: (1) Madison-Pulaski (70 stores); (2) "Jew Town" at Halsted and Maxwell Street (115); (3) Englewood Shopping Mall at 63rd and Halsted (55); (4) Roseland area at 111th and Michigan Avenue (40); (5) 87th and Stoney Island Street (50); and (6) Milwaukee and Ashland (50). (See Map 16.2.) It is in these black and other minority communities where a large number of Koreans operate many businesses listed in the fourth category. They located there mainly because of the opportunities available after the exodus of the white, mostly Jewish, merchants. The children of these former Jewish merchants had moved into professional careers in the mainstream American society, forsaking the ghetto businesses of their forefathers.

Korean immigrants work hard at a business in which they have become a dominant force, dry cleaning. Courtesy of Joseph Ahne.

Sunny Koo, a devout Korean Christian businessman in the Englewood shopping mall, explained that fifty-five of the seventy-five businesses there were Korean-owned like his. They sold a variety of goods, including clothing, shoes, beauty supplies, and general merchandise. Koo related his interesting transformation from an overseas export-import agent to a retail store owner.

> After having some college education in Korea, I first came to New York in 1971 as an overseas representative of a Korean trading company, and after about one year I changed my mind to study political science at New York University. Before completing the school, I moved to Chicago looking for a job. Because of my loyal work in an American factory for several years, I was able to receive a permanent resident visa from the Immigration office. I then went back to Korea to find a bride, for there was not much choice of meeting Korean girls in Chicago. It was not until 1981 when I opened a store of women's hosiery, accessories, and general goods with a sum of my personal savings from employment.
>
> I have seen many Jewish merchants leaving the shopping mall to retire or to move to the suburbs. Stores in the mall used to be occupied by one hundred percent Jews up until around 1970, when Koreans began to buy out Jewish stores — now only one Jewish owner remaining. Depending on types and sizes of business, one could buy a small store for about $20,000 and a larger volume of business like apparel stores for about $50,000. Now the same

College-educated Korean immigrants became successful businessmen ranging from
wig merchants to bank owners. Here can be seen the Korean owners of Chicago's
Mayfair Bank, which was merged with another Korean bank in 1992.
Courtesy of Joseph Ahne.

businesses would cost an average of about $50,000 and $100,000 respectively.
I have not made a great fortune like some other fellow Koreans, but I made
a decent income in my business, being able to afford a home with children
in a northwest suburb. One thing I know for sure is, however, that I don't
want my children to take over the life-threatening business. I want them to
become successful professionals in America like Jewish descendants. In a
sense, I guess I am a Korean Jew in the ways of doing business and high
expectation of children. (July 29, 1991)

Korean businesses in the racial minority areas have been so successful that
their financial situations also affect the economic climate of Korean Town on

A group of blacks picket a Korean shopping mall.   Courtesy of Joseph Ahne.

the North Side, where many South Side Korean merchants shop and spend their earnings. However, the success and prosperity of Korean businesses is only one side of the story. The other side is that Korean entrepreneurs constantly face racial tensions with their black customers, in addition to daily threats of physical danger.

The picketing protest by blacks at Korean stores in the Roseland area at Michigan and 111st Street in 1991 is typical of the conflict seen around the country. Protesting blacks charged in several complaints that Korean merchants: (1) do not honor an exchange or refund policy; (2) do not hire black employees; (3) do not patronize black-owned banks; and (4) do not treat the black customers in a fair and respectful manner.

To these allegations the Korean merchants countered with their own grievances. They asserted that most Korean stores have honored refunds or exchanges according to the terms posted in all stores. However, many black customers demand refunds or exchanges for used or damaged goods. Concerning the black employment issue, Koreans responded with a survey done during the dispute showing that 73 blacks were being hired at 31 Korean stores, which compared to a total of 76 Koreans who were working at 41 Korean-owned stores in the same area. The survey also showed that five Korean stores were doing business at the neighborhood bank owned by African Americans. The remainder were banking on the North Side for the sake of safety and better services, including Korean-speaking tellers.[24] Most Korean stores are relatively small and are run by a husband and wife, with occasional help from their own family members. The small volume of business and thin profit margins make it hard to hire additional help. In addition, Korean storekeepers are constantly fearful of robbery and even of being killed for a few dollars.

Racial tensions in America are no longer mainly between whites and blacks, as was the case in the late 1960s and early '70s. Tension between blacks and the new immigrant minorities, largely from Asia and the Middle East, have reached a boiling point in major cities such as New York, Philadelphia, and Los Angeles. In fact, the Roseland dispute seemed to have evolved as a chain reaction to a highly publicized conflict between Korean greengrocers and a group of blacks in New York City, which drew national media coverage for almost a year. To deal with tensions, the Federation of the Southside Korean Merchants was formed with about 250 merchants in June 1990, and they consulted with Rev. Joseph Ahne on how to improve relations with the black community.

Observing such conflicts, the American media usually comment in sympathy with the Koreans as "successful new immigrants who advance through hard-working attitudes." Such praise makes Koreans feel proud and justified, and they don't realize that the same remarks add more fuel to the fire by making blacks angry. On May 21, 1990, for instance, Mike Royko in his regular Chicago *Tribune* column, entitled "Why not duplicate Koreans' success?" commented sarcastically on the black picketing at the Korean grocery in Brooklyn:

> . . . What's lacking is organization, and that's what blacks can learn from the success-driven Koreans. The Koreans don't wait for a bank to provide a loan. They have their own family and community financial support. They are private-enterprise-oriented. . . . Because of our history of welfare and social safety nets, many blacks look to government programs and social agencies. They're program-oriented. But the government isn't going to show anybody how to run a grocery store, a dry cleaning shop or teach anyone how to pool family or community money to get it started. . . . So instead of picketing Korean stores and being angry, envious and resentful, blacks might be wise to take another approach. Take a look at how the Koreans have done it, and give it a try yourself. If you can organize a boycott or a protest, take it one step further. Organize your own grocery store. It might not make the network news, but it could send your kids to college.

When the article was quoted in *The Korea Times*, the Koreans must have felt pleased that their hard work and modest successes had been recognized by a major big-city journalist. Yet blacks had just the opposite reaction. Blacks are often resentful of newcomers like Koreans, who open businesses in inner-city neighborhoods with what appears to be government or bank loans. Black leaders lament

24. Chicago *Tribune*, November 27, 1988, section 1, p. 25.

that they have little access to such financial resources. Such sentiments are typically shared even by sophisticated black national leaders like Joseph Lowrey, president of the Southern Christian Leadership Conference. Lowrey commented on Black-Korean tensions in Atlanta: "There is great resentment that these folks came in from overseas and find ready capital, whereas blacks have not been able to get the venture capital they need to start small businesses."[25]

However, most studies on how Koreans have raised money to go into business contradict this popular black misconception. In his survey on Korean businesses in Atlanta, Prof. Min found that about 26 percent of Koreans used money brought from Korea for one-half or more of their start-up capital. A high 63 percent of Korean merchants surveyed depended on personal savings for one-half or more of their initial capital. Overall, about three-fourths of the respondents started businesses mainly with their own personal sources. In sharp contrast, only about 10 percent of Koreans depended on commercial banks as the main source of start-up capital. And 2.5 percent of the respondents started businesses with funds from a *Kye*.[26] A *Kye* is a private Korean system of financial co-operatives whereby about ten to twenty members regularly contribute a small sum of monthly funds into a pot, which is given to a *Kye* member each month on a pre-assigned rotation basis. That continues until all members have received the pot for investing into a business. The system depends upon members trusting each other. Thus the black assumption that Koreans have easy access to bank credit and government loans is simply not true. Personal savings and loans from friends and relatives have been and are the most common source of capital for starting a Korean business.

In the meantime, black protesters say that they are not envious of Korean success in business. Instead, blacks are angry at being treated not as customers but as shoplifters by Korean store owners. Within the Korean community, many leaders acknowledge that Korean businessmen should change their attitudes toward black customers. Nevertheless, Korean entrepreneurs seem to find it difficult to do so in real business life when they are confronted by high rates of robbery and shoplifting every day. For instance, Mr. Kyung-Min Bank, a 34-year-old Korean shop owner in the Madison-Pulaski area, was killed during an armed robbery in January 1990; Mr. Ki-Bong Nam, a 53-year-old owner of a wig store at Ashland and 67th, was shot to death by a black teenage boy during an armed robbery on June 27 of that year; and at another Korean-owned electronic/jewelry store in the Madison-Pulaski area, a Korean employee was injured by a group of

---

25. Min, p. 79. For a view of how envy and resentment of outsider success fuels Korean-black tensions, see Thomas Sowell, "Middleman Minorities," *American Enterprise* (May-June 1993), 30-41.

26. *The Korea Times Chicago*, July 1, 1990.

A black-Korean joint choral concert during the 1991 Christmas season shows an effort to overcome Korean merchant–black shopper tensions.   Courtesy of Joseph Ahne.

about ten armed blacks on June 29, 1990.[27] Such a series of armed robberies attests the life-threatening reality of doing business in the inner city.

In addition to the garden-variety, day-in and day-out thefts and robberies, there was a large-scale West Side carnival of looting and rioting in June 1992 to celebrate the local basketball team, the Chicago Bulls, winning a national championship. West Side Korean businesses were among the major targets of looters and arsonists, who cut a trail of fire and pillaging through the heavily Korean business area.

One Korean leader lashed out in frustration, asking who else is willing to risk his life and supply of goods in such violent black neighborhoods. "What is intended by this violence?" he asked. "Do blacks want the stores vacant? Would they prefer to shop at expensive white stores outside the neighborhood when Korean merchants leave?" Despite such frustrations, many Koreans have agreed to work on improving customer relations and overcoming racial animosities. Some merchants have made donations of gifts, food, and scholarship awards to needy blacks during the holidays and Christmas.

Conclusion

Koreans are one of the fastest-growing immigrant groups in contemporary American society. They are well educated, accustomed to urban life, prepared to succeed, and have achieved remarkably high levels of upward mobility and economic progress as professionals, technicians, and especially as entrepreneurs. As businessmen they have brought some vitality back to dying and dead inner-city shopping districts. These areas saw an exodus of Euro-American immigrant merchants after the riots following the death of Martin Luther King, Jr., in 1968 and its swath of destruction through the small business community. Many of those fleeing proprietors were the aging sons and daughters of Jewish, Italian, and East European immigrants. Nothing filled those vacant storefronts and moribund business strips for more than a decade. And then slowly came a tide of newcomer entrepreneurs, including Middle Easterners, Indians, and above all Koreans. They breathed new life into those burned-out shells and are performing a genuine public service by making in-close shopping possible for inner-city residents.

Will the Korean newcomers repeat the history of the European immi-

27. Joseph Ahne's field notes; K. Alexander, "Koreans plan scholarships to heal rift with blacks," Chicago *Tribune*, June 12, 1991; and *The Korea Times Chicago*, January 12, 1991. A "structuralist" hypothesis as proposed by Ewa Morawska, which attempts to use a "co-ethnic enclave" to explain group success, does not work for Chicago's Koreans, the vast majority of whom make their living serving non-Koreans. "The Sociology and Historiography of Immigration," in V. Yans McLaughlin, ed., *Immigration, Reconsidered, Sociology and Politics* (New York: Oxford University Press, 1990), 207f.

grants who came before them? Some native-born observers and a few Korean-American intellectuals question whether Koreans can be assimilated into the majority society as were their European predecessors. The new immigrants, they point out, carry with them factors that are likely to slow assimilation, such as a strong homeland culture, ancient traditions, hardened customs, their own language, and tightly knit families. In addition, say the naysayers, they are different in appearance.[28] On the other hand, surveys and accumulating anecdotal evidence are picking up significant changes that are under way. Acculturation has already taken place in many areas of Korean life. We find that newcomers are diligently studying and learning the English language and adopting new cultural behaviors and customs. They are working hard to make a living and to get ahead in their new homeland, as did an earlier generation of immigrants. And eventually the American-born children of Korean descent, as is true of all other immigrant children of the past, are likely to be more American than Korean.[29]

28. *The Korea Times Chicago*, February 29, 1979.
29. Milton M. Gordon, *Assimilation in American Life: The Role of Race, Religion and National Origins* (New York, 1964), pp. 71f.

ETHNIC INSTITUTIONS

CHAPTER 17

The Ethnic Saloon:
A Public Melting Pot

PERRY R. DUIS

If the Saloon was a particularly public institution, it was also one that seemed ubiquitous, especially to its critics. It was not only public space, but it also seemed to be universal space. But when many anti-liquor publicists railed against the barroom menace, they incorrectly tended to assume that all drinking places were either "low dives" or "gilded dens." What they failed to recognize was that the saloon, being both a small business and essentially an extension of the sidewalk, reflected the diversity of Chicago, perhaps more than any other social institution. With a license to population ratio that reached as low as one for each 150 men, women, and children, almost any narrow community of tastes could be sufficient to support a license. It might be a particular ethnic group or those seeking a special atmosphere or physical location. Just as the variety of licensing systems created variations in barrooms from city to city, so too did different tastes create an enormous diversity of drinking places within a city.

Accessibility meant that the neighborhood, its residents, and the users of the public space outside the swinging doors were the major factors in creating the variety of barrooms. Proprietors who could not cope with that fact failed; those who could adjust turned a profit.

Ethnic Space

The saloon in the tenement districts had to adjust to many changes in the neighborhood. It had to weather the shocks of unemployment and strikes. It had to adjust to the changing land-use patterns in some areas when commercial and industrial districts expanded into residential areas. The character of the housing stock changed, usually undergoing a decline in quality. But most important of all, the ethnic character of neighborhoods was constantly changing.

503

The saloonkeeper, whose business was practically an extension of the sidewalk, soon realized an important fact: the city's tenement residents did not all use public and semipublic places in the same way. Rather, their ethnic backgrounds and traditions, although modified in the urban matrix, produced certain distinct differences in the street life of each group. This variety, in turn, had its parallel in the several ethnic forms of saloons.

Ethnic specializations had developed in many of the street trades and survived when those activities moved indoors. Italians and Greeks operated pushcarts or green groceries and were most numerous among those who eventually opened fruit and produce stands. Jews were predominant among the rag pickers and owned the more permanent versions of those same activities, the junk and pawn shops. Most of the portable craftsmen, such as scissors grinders and itinerant handymen, were Germans; when they accumulated enough capital, they opened construction firms or engaged in other artisan activities. Even the army of newsboys on Chicago's street corners was unevenly distributed among different nationalities. One study, conducted by the Chicago Federation of Settlements, revealed that more than a fifth of the news vendors were Italian children, a number far larger than their proportion of the population in 1903.[1]

National origins shaped other forms of public behavior as well. Whereas the Jewish Sabbath was often celebrated in the privacy of the home, the most important Italian religious days involved the whole community. In Chicago's South Side (Wentworth Avenue) Sicilian colony, the Festa della Maria Virgina included a large procession and sidewalk booths containing religious shrines. One description of the annual mid-August event pointed out that "in such public celebrations and in the persistence of tradition and customs we find the village of the old world often transplanted and flourishing with little change in the heart of our great cities."[2] Native costumes, dances, street games, and music added further to the distinctions between the various ethnic enclaves.

National origins contributed to ethnocentrism and interethnic hostility. Contemporaries made frequent reference to it. Irish disliked Italians and Jews, and mixed with them only for political purposes; Canadians and English-born immigrants disdained all other groups.[3] In Chicago, ill feelings imported from the homeland set Poles against Prussians and Irishmen against Englishmen. According to one source, when Italians moved into a building, everyone else moved out.[4]

Juvenile gangs in cities often organized along ethnic lines and contributed

1. Woods, *City Wilderness*, pp. 85-86; Woods, *Americans in Process*, pp. 106, 118, 125; "Analysis . . . Pawnbrokers," pp. 10-11; Krausz, *Street Types, passim*; B.G., Sept. 27, 1891.

2. Woods, *Americans in Process*, pp. 224-39; Evelyn Boylan Epsey, "Old World Customs Continued in Chicago," *By Archer Road* 3 (Sept., 1909), 3-5; "Celebrating a Feast Day," *By Archer Road* 3 (Sept., 1909), 3-5; B.G., Oct. 4, 5, 1891, on the North End.

3. Woods, *Americans in Process*, pp. 61-70; C.T., Nov. 19, 1883.

4. *Ibid.*

to the most violent and noticeable conflict.[5] Chicago settlement worker George Nesmith believed that such discord was itself a reason to develop small parks in tenement districts. These breathing spaces would improve the standard of local health, but the more that open spaces were decentralized, the easier it would be to adapt each of them to the uses of the specific nationality surrounding it.[6]

There were many complex reasons for these ethnic differences in public behavior. Some traditions had been part of the cultural heritage brought from the old country. Others were acquired after the settlement in the city. But what is significant is the role that ethnic traditions played in the development of saloons as public places, for their ubiquity and adaptability made them important institutions in almost every neighborhood. This could happen because each group modified the saloon to meet its own unique demands. As a result, there was really no such thing as "the saloon"; rather, there were as many different kinds of saloons as there were neighborhoods.

The variety of ethnic saloons seems confusing. Every group had its favorite beverage, spoke its own language freely, told its own jokes over the bar, and enjoyed its own delicacies at the free lunch sideboard. Most saloon groups, however, fit easily into four basic categories. The first may be called "universals": consisting primarily of the Irish and the Germans, they were widely dispersed across the city and entertained a clientele of mixed ethnic background. They were predominant in Chicago's Loop and enjoyed the patronage of busy thoroughfares. Their counterpart might be labeled "ethnocentric": these were bars that catered to a single ethnic group and were located within that group's neighborhoods. While outsiders were not necessarily unwelcome, the proprietors made no special effort to attract the trade of other language groups. A third group consisted of nonsaloon ethnics who utilized other social institutions in place of the saloon. Finally, there were the black residents' saloons: while their activities roughly resembled those of the ethnocentric groups, the growing level of discrimination and segregation they faced created a unique situation.

Our Own Saloons: The Ethnocentric Bar

The ethnocentric saloon was a sign that a neighborhood had turned inward. The ties of language or customs were much stronger than the centrifugal forces of ethnic intermixing and dispersal. This characteristic was not confined to immigrants from any particular region of the world. Members of the so-called

---

5. Jacob N. Burnes, *The Story of West End House* (Boston: Stratford Publishing Co., 1934), n.p.; William Foote Whyte, "Race Conflicts in the North End," *New England Quarterly* 12 (Dec., 1939), 623-42; William Foote Whyte, *Street Corner Society* (Chicago: University of Chicago Press, 1943). The article contains material omitted in the book.

6. Nesmith, "The Housing of Wage-Earners," p. 173.

"old immigration," as well as the new, found the saloon to be a comfortable complement to their ethnicity. Scandinavian saloons, especially those run by Swedes, were located almost entirely within their tightly concentrated neighborhoods. During the mid-nineteenth century, the Swedes had settled in the poverty-stricken Near North region of Chicago, and as late as the 1890s they were still welcoming drinkers along Chicago Avenue on the North Side to accommodate a small settlement. During the 1870s, many lodging house keepers also operated bars in their basements; these places were usually filled with the newest arrivals.[7]

A few Danes and Norwegians owned places on the fringe of the neighborhood, but they, like the Swedes, designed their places to appeal to a narrow ethnic audience. In biographical sketches, such as those in the *History and Souvenir of the Liquor Interests,* the most prominently mentioned feature was their interest in serving neighborhood families. Nearly all featured Swedish punch, and a few even posted it on their signboards. Axel Nilsson operated a "Texas" buffet adjoining his bar, while Scandia Hall hosted ethnic labor meetings, and Swedish singing societies met at Andrew Johnson's. Even within the liquor business itself, the Scandinavians were among the first to create their own ethnic liquor dealers' association.[8]

Among the more notable of the ethnocentric saloons were those operated by Italians. These displayed several distinctive characteristics. They were probably the only barrooms where the drink sold was of relatively minor importance in attracting customers. Most Italian households made and stored an ample supply of the community's staple beverage, a native red wine; any surplus was easily sold to neighbors by the jug or by the drink. This meant that in Italian communities the favorite drink was as easily obtainable outside the barroom as it was within. Bartenders sold wine but never consciously tried to cut into this trade. Instead, they catered to the interests of the brewing companies that had set them up in business and tried to convert their customers to "American" drinks like beer and whiskey.[9]

The Italian saloon attracted a narrow clientele that did not depend on the street traffic that passed its door. The casual non-Italian drinker who stopped in because it was convenient was a rare customer. Contemporary observers

7. Ulf Beijbom, *Swedes in Chicago: A Demographic and Social Study of the 1846-1880 Immigration* (Upsala: Laromedelsforlagen, and Chicago: Chicago Historical Society, 1971), pp. 258-59.

8. *Ibid.; H.C.S.,* pp. 210-11.

9. *M.C.* 26 (Apr. 16, 1910): 45; Rocco Brindisi, "The Italian and Public Health," *Charities* 12 (May 7, 1904), 486; Woods, *Americans in Process,* p. 204; "Chicago Commons Study of Prohibition," p. 7; Frederick Bushee, "Italian Immigrants in Boston," *Arena* 17 (Apr., 1897), 733; *The Italians in Chicago,* U.S. Commissioner of Labor, Ninth Special Report, 1897, p. 725; Rudolph Vecoli, "Chicago's Italians Prior to World War I: A Study of Their Social and Economic Adjustment" (Ph.D. diss., University of Wisconsin, 1963); Humbert Nelli, *Italians in Chicago, 1880-1930* (New York: Oxford University Press, 1970).

frequently commented that in the Hull House neighborhood, only Italians patronized Italian saloons.[10] The negative publicity of the press undoubtedly drove away many non-Italians. The appellation "dago bar" was a common synonym for criminal saloons in exposé stories about the city's low life, and this usage probably attached a certain stigma to the Italian drinking places in at least one segment of the public mind.[11]

The Italian saloon survived primarily because it provided certain services to the neighborhood. Customers seemed to flock to the places simply to pass the time and visit. Many men held unskilled jobs and were idle during whole seasons of the year. During summer they sat on benches in public places, but in the colder months and at night year round, they filled the barrooms. Many customers came in just to read the newspapers. On Chicago's polyglot West Side, the bars all carried copies of *L'Italia.*[12]

Many other customers sought information about jobs. They could not have found a better place in Italian neighborhoods than the saloon: the proprietor was also a labor boss. A number of barrooms served as employment agencies for railroads, hiring labor for track maintenance gangs. And when these seasonal workers departed, the saloons of the neighborhood seemed almost deserted. As *L'Italia* commented: "The saloons of South Clark Street, of Fourth Avenue, of Ewing, Taylor, Desplaines, and the small decent cottages are empty. No longer are there deafening shouts, the pounding of fists on the tables, the playing of cards or the drinking of beer. Goodbye to the days passed idly, seated near the hearth, around the benches of the saloon, along the streets. All are at work!"[13]

Other saloons became involved in the padrone business. They operated in the midst of large numbers of poor and uneducated bachelors who were the victims of the labor exploitation business. The saloonkeeper became the intermediary between the individual workers and the larger society. The helpless immigrants already admired him as an authority on politics, law, and even the rules of card games. He could also get them jobs, and in return the barroom proprietor could enlarge the meager profits of the liquor business in an impoverished neighborhood. As a result, an unknown number of lower-class Italian saloons — probably twenty or thirty in Chicago alone — were also headquarters for padrone operations.[14]

10. Woods, *Americans in Process,* pp. 201-2; Woods, *City Wilderness,* pp. 45-46; Alessandro Mastro-Valerio, "Remarks upon the Italian Colony in Chicago," *Hull House Maps and Papers,* pp. 135-36; Jane Addams, *The Second Twenty Years at Hull House* (New York: Macmillan, 1930), pp. 221-22.

11. *C.F.P.* 42 (Oct. 24, 1914): 8; *C.D.N.,* Feb. 2, Mar. 19, 1884.

12. Bushee, "Italian Immigrants," pp. 726-28; Woods, *Americans in Process,* pp. 128, 202-6; Vecoli, "Chicago's Italians," pp. 298-301.

13. *L'Italia,* July 20, 1889; Vecoli, "Chicago's Italians," pp. 302-37.

14. *Ibid.,* pp. 245, 253-54, 260, 266-70.

A Bohemian-style beer hall near Bohemian National Cemetery, ca. 1918.
Courtesy of Perry Duis.

The social structure of its neighborhood largely determined the character of the Italian saloon. Unmarried males made up a substantial portion of the populace. Most had migrated by themselves and saved or spent their money at their own discretion. Many moved in with families or rented small rooms.[15] Even in places that were comparatively uncrowded and not a slum, the physical environment encouraged alternatives to home leisure activities. As one commentator put it, "The decreased size of the tenements and rooms everywhere makes it evident that the life not only of the laborers, but of middle class as well, must find an increasing part of its expression outside of the home."[16] The saloon filled that need.

Another group that tended to frequent its own barrooms was the Bohemian population: Chicago's colony became one of the largest in the United States. Beginning with a few emigré intellectuals in the 1850s, it had grown to several thousand by 1900. But the majority of the people, unlike the earliest arrivals, were poor. Those with tailoring skills opened sweatshops, while many others became involved with the monotonous job of cigar making. Their poverty placed them in some of Chicago's most dilapidated neighborhoods,

15. *Ibid.*, pp. 91-92; Bushee, "Italian Immigrants," p. 728; Natalie Walker, "Chicago Housing Conditions, X: Greeks and Italians in the Neighborhood of Hull House," *American Journal of Sociology* 21 (Nov., 1915), 285-316.

16. Robert A. Woods and Albert I. Kennedy, *The Zone of Emergence* (Cambridge: M.I.T. Press, 2nd ed., 1969), p. 303.

first in Prague, a slum located just southwest of the downtown, and by the 1870s in Pilsen. The latter was a settlement of run-down frame buildings that escaped the conflagration of 1871. Poor sanitation and rear alley tenements, in which over a quarter of the population still lived in 1914, made the district one of the shabbiest in the city.[17]

Many families supplemented their incomes by renting to lodgers, and the overcrowding that resulted helped orient the social life of the community away from the home. But a lively street life was difficult amidst the unpaved byways strewn with garbage, and the intensive use of land precluded the establishment of beer gardens as they had existed in the old country. Sunday strolls, another tradition, were difficult because Chicago's large parks were so far away. Instead, much of the socializing remained indoors. In the 1860s they opened the Slovanska Lipa, a community building, and by the end of the next decade they had also established a pair of *sokols*, or gymnastic societies. These institutions, along with church parishes, became the principal centers of Bohemian leisure and benevolent activities.[18]

The saloons provided a valuable supplement to this active community organization. They provided the usual attractions of tables for playing cards and subscribed to *Svornost* and *Denni Hlasatel*, the local newspapers. But the meeting hall upstairs or next door was in many ways the most important part of the Czech or Slovak saloon. Substantial evidence indicates that no other ethnic group in the city made as frequent use of that type of saloon facility. Certain barrooms became the centers of the local Free Thought movement, which actively protested the dominant role of the Catholic church in the community and sought to establish their own informal educational system. "Free thinkers" had become social outcasts and in some parts of the community encountered difficulty in gaining access to many meeting facilities. And so certain saloons became their unofficial headquarters.[19]

Dozens of other community groups rented the saloon halls. They held large weekend dances to raise funds for various benevolent purposes and made them the focus of neighborhood social life. Institutions such as the Utulna A. Sirotcinec, or Old People's Home, depended almost entirely on these gatherings for funds. An inexpensive bar permit license from the city and a twenty-five-

17. Josepha Zeman, "The Bohemian People in Chicago," *Hull House Maps and Papers*, pp. 115-30; Helen Wilson and Eunice Smith, "Chicago Housing Conditions, VIII: Among the Slovaks of the 20th Ward," *American Journal of Sociology* 20 (Sept., 1914), 145-69; *C.T.*, Mar. 7, 1886; Emily G. Balch, *Our Slavic Fellow Citizens* (New York: Charities Publication Committee, 1910), p. 277.

18. Zeman, "The Bohemian People," pp. 120-21; *C.T.*, Mar. 7, 1886; Pierce, *A History of Chicago*, 3:33-34; Jakub Horak, "The Assimilation of Czechs in Chicago" (Ph.D. diss., University of Chicago, 1920), pp. 1-50; *Denni Hlasatel*, Apr. 23, 1911, Apr. 23, 1913.

19. *Ibid.*, Mar. 13, 1896, Nov. 25, 1907, Dec. 2, 1911; L. O. Cleminson to Victo von Borosini, Apr. 8, 1913, Civic Committee Minutes, VIII, City Club of Chicago Papers, C.H.S.; Hayner, "Effect of Prohibition," p. 16.

dollar federal tax stamp allowed the revelry to continue until 4:00 a.m., long past the normal saloon closing hour. The most serious problem was in finding a hall to rent; some were booked up months, even years, in advance. One group solved that problem by purchasing an entire saloon, just so they would have their own hall to use each weekend.[20]

A fourth group that frequented the barrooms of their fellow countrymen were the Poles: Chicago and the other industrial cities of the Great Lakes region became the home of thousands.[21] In 1890 there were only 24,086 Poles in Chicago; two decades later there were 126,059. Not only did they grow rapidly in numbers, but they also distinguished themselves by remaining in compact communities longer than other groups. That fact, along with their poverty, directly shaped their community life.[22]

There were four major Polish communities in Chicago. The oldest was on the near Northwest Side, around Milwaukee Avenue and Division Street. Later settlements developed just west of Bohemian Pilsen, out near the stockyards of Packingtown, and finally, near the steel mills of South Chicago. These communities suffered from the common problems of tenement neighborhoods: garbage in the streets, filthy food, unwholesome milk, and overcrowded housing. But in the case of the Poles, the misery was compounded because the neighborhoods they inherited were third or fourth hand. What had been decayed tenements when the Germans left had deteriorated even more with the arrival and departure of the Irish, Scandinavians, and the North-Side Italians. But the Poles held tenaciously to housing that was within walking distance of work.[23] And when they erected magnificent churches like St. Stanislaus Kostka, built in 1892, they also created community anchors that later resisted decades of residential mobility.[24]

The Polish saloon was devoid of distinguishing characteristics. It had a few tables and a bar; it sold both whiskey and beer, but little wine. It was strictly an indoors institution, and it sold enough beer to keep the Polish-dominated White Eagle Brewing Company busy. But what was most curious about the Polish saloonkeeper was the way he came under attack within his own community. Other ethnic groups had their temperance societies, but probably no other nationality of dealers was subjected to such a constant stream of verbal abuse as were the Poles.[25]

20. *Denni Hlasatel,* June 7, 1901, Jan. 4, 1904, Nov. 23, 1910, Feb. 12, 1912; *C.T.,* Jan. 26, 1880.

21. Justin Galford, "The Foreign-born and Urban Growth in the Great Lakes, 1850-1950: A Study of Chicago, Cleveland, Detroit and Milwaukee" (Ph.D. diss., New York University 1957), *passim; Woods*

22. U.S. Census, 1890, *Population,* I, pp. 670-75; *Ibid.,* 1910, *Population,* II, pp. 989, 1007-15.

23. Hunter, *Tenement Conditions,* pp. 26, 41, 54, 59, 64; Edith Abbott, *The Tenements of Chicago, 1908-1935* (Chicago: University of Chicago Press, 1936), pp. 133-34.

24. Joseph J. Parot, "The American Faith and the Persistence of Polonia, 1870-1920" (Ph.D. diss., Northern Illinois University, 1971).

25. *The Public Good* 2 (Oct. 28, 1886), 6; George, "The Saloon Problem," p. 90; Hayner, "the Effect of Prohibition," p. 76.

Several factors contributed to such overt antisaloon feelings. First, there was the problem of image: Poles, as was true among the later immigrant groups, seemed especially sensitive about the way they appeared to outsiders. Saloonkeepers, by filling their countrymen with whiskey, degraded the respectability of Polonia. *Dziennik Zwiazkowy*, a local newspaper, editorialized, "We implore you to behave yourself respectably, as cultured people. How can we ever hope to gain any respect among other nationalities when disorderly drunken conduct is permitted among Poles."[26] Leaders implied what sociologists like William I. Thomas and Florian Znaniecki later concluded, that the unsettling conditions of immigration had created an extraordinary amount of social disorientation among the Poles.[27]

According to the newspapers, drink did its most serious damage to the traditional family structure. Parents no longer provided a positive example for their offspring to follow. "Men are drunkards, women are drunkards, and the innocent looking at this get used to bad habits," complained the *Narod Polski*.[28] But it was the dance hall issue that aroused the greatest amount of anxiety in the community. This problem, like that of housing, became more difficult to solve because of the relatively late arrival of the Poles. Near the turn of the century a dancing craze swept the imagination of Chicago's young people. Saloons in many parts of the city, including Polish neighborhoods, opened halls. And when the children of the most recent immigrants began to attend, the saloon was drawn into the common intergenerational conflict. "The fondness of dancing," complained one observer, "makes young girls subject to excessive spending. Their clothes wear out quickly and soil easily, so more often the thoughtless girl buys dresses, ribbons, and other adornments, instead of saving her hard earned cash."[29] Moreover, young girls gambled and drank in front of everyone, "so openly and publicly that it looks as if all gentlemen Saloonkeepers belong to the same protection as our glorious police."[30]

Some of these antisaloon attacks may have been rooted in a traditional ethnic bias imported from the homeland. As *Abstynet*, a community temperance tract, complained:

> In Poland, most of [the] saloons are operated by Jews, because a real Pole and Catholic thinks himself too respected and too honorable to operate such a vile business. And this is the reason that saloonkeepers and saloons in Poland are insulted and become mean to the Polish people. And for that reason Poles are filled with antipathy and anti-Semitic aversions. In America it is the

26. *Dziennik Zwazkowy*, Dec. 10, 1910; *Narod Polski*, Jan. 17, 1900, Jan. 8, 1913.
27. William I. Thomas and Florian Znaniecki, *The Polish Peasant in Europe and America*, 6 vols. (Boston: Richard H. Badger, 1920), 5:209.
28. *Narod Polski*, Jan. 8, 1913.
29. *Ibid.*, July 6, 1904.
30. *Ibid.*, July 5, 1911; *Dziennik Zwazkowy*, Nov. 30, 1914.

opposite. Polish Catholics are operating saloons because it is simpler and more profitable than any other business.

To be a saloonkeeper every ordinary man with the ambition of a good drunkard or plenty of "gab" will do. Even the brewery helps them financially when it comes to the rent, fixtures, merchandise, and furniture; they give them these for credit.

Poles willingly give their support to their countrymen, go to the saloon and support them in the name of patriotism, and saloonkeepers good-heartedly serve them drinks of any kind, domestic or imported.

Business is going good. Support your fellow countrymen with the aim of solidarity.[31]

But despite the complaints of temperance interests, the number of Polish saloons continued to grow.

Ethnic Universals

The other kind of ethnic saloonkeepers, the "universals," included the Germans and Irish, as well as the "Americans" who were either of native stock or the descendants of earlier foreign-born arrivals. Their bars were widely dispersed around the city. Few wards in Chicago lacked an Irish saloon; and because Germans were much more numerous than the Irish, a "Kraut" saloonkeeper could be found even in such unlikely places as the South Chicago steel mill district or the teeming near West-Side neighborhood of Hull House. In 1893 the latter area was predominantly Italian, Austro-Hungarian, Russian (Jewish), and Polish; Germans and Irish were a very small percentage of the population. Nonetheless, of the 118 saloons, no fewer than fifteen had German proprietors, and eight were operated by Irish.[32]

Chicago's Irish community dispersed rapidly: the city experienced a large German migration that submerged the Irish — culturally if not politically. People talked of Chicago as a German city rather than an Irish one. The ranks of the Irish declined proportionately as well as absolutely as the decades passed: in 1870 they constituted 13.4 percent of the total population; in 1880, 8.8 percent. By 1890 there were 70,028 Irish in the city, or 6.4 percent of the total population; this also represented only about 15 percent of the foreign-born. During the next two decades the number of immigrant arrivals and births failed to offset the deaths and dispersals to suburban and other out-of-city locations, and the absolute number fell by nearly 4,000. The influx of

---

31. *Abstynet*, Nov., 1911.
32. *List of Names of Parties Who Sell or Keep Intoxicating Liquors, 1868*, Boston, City Doc. 140, 1868.

This Irish-style saloon, which advertised its whiskies and catered mostly to men, was
owned by celebrated Chicago politician, Michael "Hinky Dink" Kenna.
Courtesy of Perry Duis.

other groups, in the meantime, reduced the Irish percentage figures to about
half of their previous level.[33]

Despite this statistical decline, Chicago's Irish continued to enter the
saloon business in large numbers. In part, this reflected a national trend: Census
figures indicate that from the turn of the century until 1920, the Irish actually
demonstrated a rather stable or slightly increasing tendency to remain in the
retail liquor business across the generations. Nearly every other ethnic group
saw the first arrivals enter the saloon trade in larger numbers than their proportion of the population, but the next generation did so in decreasing numbers.
In Chicago the Irish actually became increasingly entrenched in the business.
In 1880, 410 — or 14.7 percent — of the city's 2,782 saloonkeepers recorded in

33. Ruth M. Piper, "The Irish in Chicago, 1848 to 1871" (M.A. thesis, University of Chicago,
1936), pp. 47-62; *C.T.*, Apr. 13, 1874.

A German-style saloon on Chicago's Westside in the 1880s.   Courtesy of Perry Duis.

the federal census were Irish; in 1900, the 1,286 Irish bar proprietors made up 21 percent of the 6,130 saloonkeepers.[34]

Most Irish barrooms were more distinguished for the facilities they lacked than for those they contained. The interiors often were unspectacular: marble wainscoting seldom adorned the walls, and the spittoons bore evidence of thousands of kicks. The lunch was plain, more of a standard fare than something designed to attract crowds. The favorite drink was whiskey; only gradually did the Irish accept the German's brew, which was probably due in part to the fact that Irishmen who purchased breweries in the 1870s and 1880s could appeal to the ethnic pride of their fellow countrymen. Perhaps the most unusual characteristic of Irish bars was their aversion to tables; they were stand-up places. There was an old myth that an Irishman could down a greater volume

    34. E. P. Hutchinson, *Immigrants and Their Children, 1850-1950* (New York: John Wiley & Sons, 1956), pp. 172-175.

of whiskey if he remained in an upright position. But then, the Germans, who enjoyed drinking at tables, had their own legendary abilities to consume heroic quantities of alcohol. "If a Slav ever tried to imitate a German in his drinking habits, he will drink himself to death," complained a Polish newspaper.[35]

The typical German saloon is also difficult to describe. The downtown places were fancy and primarily serviced the noon-hour trade; they were not designed to appeal to family or neighborhood social life. The German bars in the outlying neighborhoods, however, tended to be quite different. Where the Irish bar tended to be dimly illuminated, the lighting in a German place was as bright as daylight. This may have reflected a more substantial investment or a superior building, but it also probably reflected the family orientation of the place. The German saloon was as much a family institution as the Irish bar was a man's world. Unescorted women were not welcome because they might be prostitutes, but the entire family was, including the children. Thus, the common complaint that the saloon destroyed the family had far less relevance in German communities.

There were also few comments about crime in German saloons, leading some observers to believe that the barroom was a stabilizing rather than a disruptive influence in the immigrants' adjustment to Chicago life.[36] The peaceful barroom of Otto, Fritz, or August was usually depicted in the press as an honest operation. Disreputable women seldom entered, and drunkenness was uncommon.[37] As one German saloonkeeper who operated in the North Center area of Chicago commented: "The story goes that when a German comes to America, he looks for just three things — a saloon, a church, and a singing society. . . . When Germans drink they do not get mad, but just happy and want to sing and be friendly."[38]

Some German theaters and Turner halls (gymnasium headquarters of athletic societies) served beer, but the unique form of German drinking place was the beer garden. This institution traced its origins back to the continental custom of enjoying an outdoor Sunday afternoon with the family. Transplanted to urban America, the Turners frequently enjoyed outings at picnic grounds like Colehour's in South Chicago. Entrepreneurs like Peter Rinderer also realized the potential profits in locating a beer garden on the outskirts of a crowded city like Chicago; in 1865 he opened Ogden Grove, named for the land company from whom he purchased the ground. Others followed and combined their beer gardens with inns that were designed to accommodate traveling farmers. Thus, a person who sold the family livestock or grain in the city could enjoy an

35. *Narod Polski,* Mar. 28, 1900; George, "The Saloon Problem," p. 90; Addams, *Twenty Years,* p. 222.

36. Webster, "The Saloon and Juvenile Delinquency," pp. 3-4; George, "The Saloon Problem," p. 91.

37. *C.F.P.* 30 (May 18, 1907):4; George, "The Saloon Problem," p. 91.

38. "Northcenter, Document 5," p. 4 in Vivien Palmer Scrapbooks, II, C.H.S.

The German-American beer garden often served food in addition to beer and sought
family patronage, unlike the stand-up Irish male-centered watering holes.
Courtesy of Perry Duis.

overnight stopover at Chicago's Bismarck Gardens, as well as a beer in an
outdoor setting.[39]

The beer gardens were as varied as other public drinking spots. No two
of them were exactly alike, but most were as ornate and attractive as the competition demanded. All had tables and chairs rather than a bar, and the food
they served was often as important as beer in attracting trade. Music was
essential, and what started as small brass bands eventually evolved into orchestras, famous soloists, and vaudeville-type performances. Fischers, on the
shores of Lake Michigan on the northern edge of Chicago, advertised its cool
breezes and bathing beach. As the years passed, mechanical contrivances rivaled
natural features. In 1901, when the Keeley Brewing Company built the commodious Heidelberg Gardens (which seated 444 at 121 tables), it installed a
rock fountain on which a gardener had induced moss to grow. Thirteen years
later, Frank Lloyd Wright's Edelweiss Garden (more commonly known as Midway Gardens) featured an electric fountain that played colored lights on the
water sprays.[40]

Most of these places were more impersonal than the corner saloon. Nearly
all collected admission fees as a cover charge: this was usually a quarter — a
fairly large amount for the late 1880s — which made up for the freeloaders who
wanted to do a lot of listening but only a little drinking. Public transit also

39. Unidentified clipping, May 20, 1888, Harpel Scrapbooks, S4-12, C.H.S.
40. *Ibid.*

became an increasingly important factor in the trade. Resorts in both cities clustered near streetcar lines; a location at an intersection was considered especially choice.[41]

The beer gardens were especially attractive to families, who found them pleasant places to spend a summer afternoon. Some reform-oriented commentators thought that the mixed company was a favorable influence on drinking practices.[42] But temperance advocates argued that children and young men and women were exposed to the evils of the drink trade at a tender age; the presence of attractive young girls and drink at the same location aroused irresistible temptations among men.[43] Finally, the influx of large numbers of strangers on Sundays worried many residents.[44]

On the surface, the Germans and Irish seemed to have a community of interests in the liquor business: members of both groups had invested a great amount of money in the business; both had been in it a long period of time; and both claimed a common enemy in the "temperance cranks." But, in fact, there was a great deal of hostility between the two ethnic groups. The problem of language divided the Chicago liquor dealers' associations before they had a chance to become influential. The Irish became irritated when the Germans insisted on using their native tongue during meetings, which the latter said they did because many of their members knew no English. The resulting split never completely healed. The Irish, despite their numbers, always held little more than a secondary role in the hierarchy of the liquor dealers' protective associations. In fact, only one Irishman, Thomas Nolan, ever headed the county-wide federation known as the Cook County District.[45]

The dissension went far beyond matters of language. Germans and Irish operated barrooms all over the city, not merely in their own neighborhoods, and they were competitors in a very real sense of the word. Had their clientele been drawn wholly from the small ethnic islands and enclaves, as it was with most other foreign-born groups, the conflict may not have been so sharp. But even this factor was overshadowed by others. Differences in drinking habits added further political overtones. The Irish claimed that the idea of a differential license rate, with beer assessed at a lower rate than whiskey, was a plot hatched by German saloonkeepers and legislators: the "Krauts" could have their beer at a lower annual fee than the whiskey-drinking Irish could have their whiskey. When the matter of Sunday closing came up, the German claimed that the Irish, who lacked the traditions of the continental Sunday, cared little whether the saloons were officially open or closed. The Irish, they argued, had no particular

41. *Ibid.*

42. *Public Good* 1 (Nov. 26, 1885), 1.

43. *M.C.* 8 (Mar. 1, 1902), 1.

44. *N.E.T.* 2 (May 30, 1885), 6.

45. *C.T.,* Aug. 15, 1880, March 17, 19, 1881; C.F.P. 27 (Jan. 9, 1904), 5, 31 (Mar. 14, 1908), 6.

attachment to Sunday opening, and if an Irish barkeeper chose to stay in operation that day, he could always pay off the Irish cop. The German, on the other hand, suffered while the Irish laughed.[46]

The Saloon and the Blacks

Black residents faced institutional as well as residential segregation. Social customs had excluded them from certain places for many years, but those exclusions grew in scope and rigidity with the increasing numbers of new arrivals from the South. Although there had been a civil rights law — which gave blacks full access to public and semipublic places — on the books since 1885, there was no guarantee of enforcement. The legal machinery of the state, county, and city usually took the side of the minority group, but the punishment given offenders was minimal.[47] In 1893, for instance, Chapin and Gore refused to serve a black customer in one of their downtown locations; the fine was twenty-five dollars.[48]

The defendants in early public accommodations suits claimed that the state law did not specifically mention saloons. In 1896 the Illinois Supreme Court remedied that shortcoming by identifying a long list of businesses, including saloons, that were to be covered by the act; and in 1903 the General Assembly finally amended the statute to recognize its broader coverage.[49] Even then, there was no guarantee of service for blacks. Because it was not classified as a criminal law, the police made no arrests for its violation; someone had to go to court and institute a civil action. In one notable case, J. S. Thurman, a black attorney, was refused service at Riley and Early's saloon on Randolph Street downtown. He collected $200 in damages when the defendants refused to show up in court. The black press gave the case considerable publicity, prompting *Mida's Criterion* to warn its liquor-dealer readers that "the civil rights business is a two-edged sword, and it does not pay to monkey with it, especially in Chicago."[50]

The liquor dealers themselves frequently ignored the official city position on the matter. Confrontation led to occasional physical violence. For instance, during the long 1905 teamsters' strike, blacks attacked Ludwig Lewi's saloon at

46. *Ibid.*

47. Spear, *Black Chicago*, pp. 6-7, 41-43; Chicago Commission on Race Relations, *The Negro in Chicago* (Chicago: University of Chicago Press, 1922), pp. 232-234.

48. *M.C.* 9 (Feb. 16, 1893), 19; Paul L. Dunbar, "The Color Line in Chicago," *The Pilgrim* 7 (July, 1903): 9-10; *C.T.*, Feb. 7, 1883, is racist in tone.

49. *Cecil v. Green* 161 Ill. 265 (1896); Spear, *Black Chicago*, pp. 41-43; Chicago Commission on Race Relations, *The Negro in Chicago*, pp. 232-233.

50. *M.C.* 20 (Apr. 16, 1904), 63; *C.F.P.* 27 (Apr. 9, 1904), 4; C.R.-H., July 14, 1905; "Douglas, Document 8," p. 4, Palmer Scrapbooks, IV, C.H.S.

29th and Armour. The neighborhood was undergoing a racial transition, and Lewi had been known to exclude blacks. The use of 600 blacks as "scab" labor by the team-owning interests added to the tensions. One day in late May, Lewi's bartender shot and killed a black man who was involved in a fight just outside the door. In retaliation, blacks beat the owner and a friend severely and vandalized and looted the inside of the barroom.[51]

The racial issue placed the liquor dealers' association in an awkward position. On the one hand, it had to maintain peaceful relations with city hall: there were literally dozens of ways that city officials could use to seek revenge if they did not. The association had also featured Abraham Lincoln's experience at barkeeping in New Salem in its anti-temperance propaganda. On the other hand, saloon men wanted the right to serve whomever they wished to, and in the long run the association ended up supporting the idea of racial exclusion. Although it was never a publicly stated policy, its own lawyers defended members in discrimination suits. And when Chicago blacks founded their own liquor dealers' group, the Chicago association refused their offer of affiliation. It also remained silent when Oscar DePriest, the city's first black alderman, introduced an antidiscrimination bill in the City Council. This legislation would have required the mayor to revoke the license of any business, including saloons, that refused service to Negroes. Dealers breathed more easily when the bill died in committee.[52]

Even though blacks were excluded from many saloons, other barrooms provided them with substantial employment opportunities. Census data for Chicago revealed that they held 116 bartending jobs in 1900 and 137 a decade later; another estimate claimed that in 1914 about 12 percent of the black men in that city worked in saloons and poolrooms.[53] The number of black proprietors, however, declined after the turn of the century, from forty-eight in 1900 to thirty-three in 1910 to twenty-three in 1916. The exact cause of that trend is impossible to establish, although racial prejudice undoubtedly influenced it.[54]

In Chicago the saloonkeeper was an important part of the black business community. Whereas white barrooms seldom advertised in the daily press, the *Broad-Axe* carried numerous news stories that told of new openings, remodeled storefronts, and expanded facilities. These not only served to generate revenue for the weekly Negro press, but ads for places like the Elite Care and the Railroad

---

51. *Broad-Axe*, May 27, 1905.

52. *C.F.P.* 32 (Jan. 30, 1909), 4; *Proceedings of the Chicago City Council*, June 12, 1916, p. 648; *Chicago Defender*, June 17, 1916; *C.T.*, June 14, 1916.

53. Epple, *Liquor Laws of Massachusetts*, p. 135; Louis Epple, *Supplement to the Liquor Laws of Massachusetts* (Boston: City of Boston Printing Department, 1917), p. 74; *Bryant v. Rich's Grill* 216 Mass. 344 (1912).

54. U.S. Census, 1890, *Occupations*, p. 516; U.S. Census, 1910, *Occupations*, p. 544; brewery ads, *Broad-Axe*, Dec. 3, 1904, Sept. 18, 1909; Junius B. Wood, *The Negro in Chicago* (Chicago: Chicago Daily News, 1916), pp. 11-12; Louise DeKoven Bowen, *The Colored People of Chicago* (Chicago: Juvenile Protective Association, 1913), pp. 10-11.

Inn also informed readers of where they would be welcome. Business directories aimed at black consumers featured long lists of barrooms, interspersed with laudatory self-help biographical sketches.[55] For example, I. C. Harris's *Colored Men's Professional and Business Directory* for 1885-86 proclaimed: "As an enterprising businessman, J. H. Howard [who owned two saloons] can, beyond a doubt, be classed among the most energetic and exemplary colored businessmen in our city. Through tact, energy and perseverance, at the same time dealing consistently with his fellow men, he has been able to make a front rank with other leading men of business and demonstrates by genius and merit what the Negro may accomplish if he is accorded half a chance in his eventful race of life."[56]

Direct appeals to customers on the basis of race were also common where the establishment was a pioneer or a "first." Barrooms that opened in changing neighborhoods were anxious to inform the black community of their establishment. Since most of these areas contained housing that was less densely packed together and in better condition than in the slums, the open-air quality of a few places was a prominent part of the advertising. The Chateau de Plaisance, 5318-26 South State, featured "band concerts, vocal solos, roller skating," as well as food and drink. Noting that "State Street cars pass the door," it called itself a "summer resort" and boasted that "Ladies and Gentlemen . . . will find the desired spot at the only amusement park and pavilion owned and controlled by negroes in the world."[57]

Other saloon advertisements conveyed a defensive tone. Readers of the *Broad-Axe,* for instance, were told that Charles Gaskin "does not permit any kind of gambling . . . and [that] it makes no difference how many times the police raid places where gambling is conducted, it does not interfere with his business." Other places were careful to emphasize that they did not admit women.[58] The reasons for these pronouncements may lie in a growing sensitivity to race pride expressed in some quarters. Not unlike the temperance attitude in many white ethnic neighborhoods, the *Broad-Axe* considered the debauchery usually connected with saloons to be a significant impediment to progress. Although it continued to accept liquor advertising, it frequently criticized parents who sent children to buy their beer or abandoned their families during the evening hours in order to hang around saloons.[59] "Afro-American

55. *Rhea's New Citizen's Directory of Chicago* (Chicago: Press of W. S. McCleland, 1908), n.p.; Ford S. Black, *Black's Blue Book* (Chicago: Ford S. Black, 1916), p. 32; see e.g., *Broad-Axe,* Sept. 9, 1905, Aug. 4, 1906.

56. I. C. Harris, comp., *Colored Men's Professional and Business Directory* (Chicago: I. C. Harris, 1885), n.p.

57. *Rhea's New Citizen's Directory,* n.p.; *Broad-Axe,* June 3, 1905, Aug. 14, 1909.

58. *Ibid.,* Oct. 12, 1907, Oct. 2, 1909.

59. *Ibid.,* Dec. 16, 1905, Mar. 10, 1906, Mar. 5, 1910, Jan. 1, 1911.

women in the Town of Lake," it complained, "frequent saloons, fill up with beer and whiskey. Then they enter churches where they holler and shout for Jesus!"[60]

Defensive advertising was also employed to counteract the white stereotype of black saloons as dives and criminal establishments. Undoubtedly, some of them were lower class, generally reflecting the economic status of their users, and some actually were involved in crime.

The Non-Participants: Greeks, Jews

Poverty, overcrowded housing conditions, and the resulting use of public space did not automatically result in greater patronage of saloons. A variety of social and cultural factors considerably modified the pattern of leisure and economic mobility that developed among some ethnic groups in both cities. Some neighborhoods had little dependence on the barrooms and the attractions they offered. These residents did not necessarily support antiliquor movements, but they remained indifferent. They chose alternative centers of social activity and routes of economic advancement.

The Greeks of Chicago were no strangers to the street. They engaged in peddling and operated open-air fruit stands in their own neighborhoods and elsewhere, hoping to talk middle-class matrons into purchasing fruit to take home to their children. One estimate in 1886 contended that over half of the 200 or so Greeks in the city were sidewalk fruit salesmen.[61] They lived in what became known as the Greek Delta, a triangular block bounded by Halsted, Blue Island, and Taylor streets. This was in the heart of congested near West Side, the polyglot neighborhood that surrounded Hull House. There were a few saloonkeepers of Greek descent. Grace Abbott and the Immigrant Protective League found fifteen in 1909, a slight increase over those counted in the 1900 census, and their location in the heart of the community would seem to indicate local usage. But it was the coffeehouse, or *kaffeneion*, that functioned as the primary social gathering place. Most of these had the simplest of facilities — a few tables and plain chairs — and the fare consisted of coffee, tea, cider, soft drinks, ice cream, and native confections like baklava.[62]

---

60. *Ibid.*, Dec. 16, 1905.

61. Grace Abbott, "A Study of the Greeks of Chicago," *American Journal of Sociology* 15 (Nov., 1909), 379-393; George Kourvetaris, *First and Second Generation Greeks in Chicago* (Athens: National Centre for Social Research 1971), pp. 43-53, 71-77; Walker, "Chicago Housing Conditions: Greeks and Italians," pp. 285-316; Woods, *City Wilderness*, p. 46; Woods, *Americans in Process*, pp. 122-23; William I. Cole, *Immigrant Races in Massachusetts: The Greeks* (Boston: Massachusetts Bureau of Immigration, [1914]).

62. Jeremiah Jenks and W. Jett Lauck, *The Immigration Problem*, 3rd rev. ed. (New York: Funk & Wagnalls, 1913), p. 126; Abbott, "A Study of the Greeks," p. 386; Massachusetts, *Report of the Commission on Immigration*, House Report 2300, 1914, pp. 202-204; Theodore Saloutos, *Greeks in the United States* (Cambridge: Harvard University Press, 1964), pp. 78-83.

The social role of the *kaffenia* was not unlike that of the saloons. Fraternal societies, mutual aid, and charity groups used them for meetings. Most Greek immigrants were unmarried males who lived in crowded rooms, so they escaped the privatizing effect of family life. The *kaffenia* were simply places where men met and conversed, and this activity alone probably sustained most of the 138 places in the Delta.[63] As one commentator described it:

> There are hundreds of these restaurants standing side by side and all occupying ancient one and two story brick and wooden houses. In many cases, these buildings are very dilapidated and deteriorated. Sanitation on the whole, is not very good. The coffee shops do not have clean appearances and in reality are not very clean. . . .
>
> On the side of social life of the "Delta" are the coffee shops. Each one stands for a district of the "old country," and men go to the coffee house which bears the name of their district. They sit around the tables and talk about conditions — political, social, and economic — of Greece and their respective districts, drinking Turkish coffee or inhaling the heavy smoke of a Turkish pipe. Or they play cards — pinochle or "Thirty-One" — smoking cigarettes and arguing very vociferously at times. To observe this district at its most picturesque moments, walk down the various streets on Saturday or Sunday night. For the most part the arc lights along the curb supply little illumination, so that the neighborhood has a dingy and shadowy appearance. But the apparently endless row of coffee houses are all brightly lighted and may be seen at their gayest on Halsted Street. One also finds seemingly endless numbers of tables inside these places, most of which are occupied by the dark and mustached sons of Hellas.[64]

Like their Greek neighbors, Jewish immigrants also made intensive use of public areas, but not saloons. Peddlers and outdoor stands of every variety were very common. The street, even if muddy and littered, was a welcome refuge from the tenement and the sweatshop, and a lively social life evolved on door sills and steps of buildings. Like other foreign-born residents, many Jewish families took in lodgers to supplement their incomes, and the overcrowding that resulted placed even more of a burden on the limited housing facilities.[65]

63. *C.T.*, Mar. 11, 1886; *Salonika*, Nov. 1, 1913, Dec. 19, 1914, Oct. 2, 1915.

64. Quoted in Paul F. Cressey, "The Succession of Cultural Groups in the City of Chicago" (Ph.D. diss., University of Chicago, 1930), pp. 148-49.

65. Immigrant Protective League, *Annual Report, 1909-10*, p. 23; Theodore Sachs, *A Study of Tuberculosis in Chicago, with Special Reference to the Statistics Collected in the Jewish District* (Chicago: Municipal Tuberculosis Sanatarium, 1905), pp. 195-240; Hunter, *Tenement Conditions*, pp. 12, 32, 36, 59, 92, 94, 119, 149, 158, 185; Edith Abbott and Sophonisba Breckenridge, "Chicago Housing Conditions, IV: The West Side Revisited," *American Journal of Sociology* 17 (July, 1911), 1-34; Abbott, *Tenements of Chicago*, pp. 85-92; Woods, *Americans in Process*, p. 240; Ben Rosen, "The Trend of Jewish Population in Boston," *Federated Jewish Charities of Boston* 1 (Jan., 1921), 12-14; *B.G.*, Apr. 23, 1900; July 14, 1901.

But even these conditions did not produce much saloon patronage. That institution meant little to Jewish social life. Barrooms were scarce in Chicago's ghetto, even along the few blocks of busy Halsted Street that ran through the Maxwell Street market area of the near West Side.[66]

Instead, most drinking among Jews was confined to religious ceremonies or done in the privacy of the family or the worship service. There was also a wide variety of alternative institutions that provided places for sociability. Cigar stores, soft-drink parlors, and candy shops furnished newspapers and a few tables and chairs for spontaneous and unstructured socializing. A system of private charities removed the need for the philanthropic activities associated with saloons, while lodges and synagogues kept members busy with community welfare projects. Finally, the Yiddish theater, one of the most creative and best patronized of ethnic entertainments, drew potential customers away from saloons.[67]

Changes in this pattern, however, were clearly underway by the turn of the century. Jews exhibited a stronger tendency to move into the retail liquor business in the second generation than in the first. Although statistical precision is difficult because the census made no distinction between Jews and their Russian and Polish gentile conationalists, there is strong indication that only the Italians displayed a stronger intergenerational increase in the number of saloonkeepers. The reasons for this are not entirely clear. Both Jews and Italians saw a permanent store building with one's name over its door as a desired economic goal: indoor businesses were usually considered to be of higher status than the street trades. Also, the fact that Jews had occasionally been the public-house keepers in European countries may have contributed; some, perhaps, were only returning to a traditional family business.[68]

The Yiddish press viewed the growing prominence of the saloon as another sad example of assimilation. American-born children acquired the tastes, habits, ideas, and social institution of the larger city. Editors blamed the decline of the Yiddish theater on youths who went outside the neighborhood for entertainment. Some patronized saloons elsewhere in the city, but when they found other Jews operating bars near the ghetto, public drinking seemed

66. Charles Zeublin, "The Chicago Ghetto," in *Hull House Maps and Papers*, pp. 94-95; Late Levy, "Health and Sanitation," in Charles S. Bernheimer, ed., *The Russian Jew in the United States* (Philadelphia: John C. Winston, 1905), p. 320; Melendy, "The Saloon," p. 435; Woods, *City Wilderness*, pp. 40-41; Woods, *Americans in Process*, p. 241; Cole and Durland, "Report on Substitutes," pp. 331-32.

67. Minnie F. Low, "Philanthropy, Chicago," in Bernheimer, *The Russian Jew*, pp. 87-99; *B.G.*, Jan. 28, 1900; I. K. Friedman, "Amusements and Social Life, Chicago," in Bernheimer, *The Russian Jew*; Zeublin, "The Chicago Ghetto," p. 104; Addams, *Twenty Years*, p. 222; Seymour Pomrenze, "Aspects of Chicago Russian Jewish Life, 1893-1915," in Simon Rawidowicz, *Chicago Pinkas* (Chicago: College of Jewish Studies, 1952), pp. 126-129.

68. Hutchinson, *Immigrants and Their Children*, pp. 172-175; Balch, *Our Slavic Fellow Citizens*, pp. 140-141; on Jewish mobility, see Thernstrom, *Other Bostonians*, pp. 111-144.

more acceptable than it had to their parents. It was this tension between assimilation and the need to preserve the community and its customs that led
the *Daily Jewish Courier* to support the temperance movement.[69] This was an
unprecedented action, but the newspaper's rationale speaks for itself:

> We should not only sympathize with our neighbor, the Gentiles, in their
> fight against inebriety, but we must also apply all our energies to help them
> root out this plague, which is so dreadfully contagious. Gradually our young
> Jewish people are being dragged into this marsh. . . .
>
> Until now we are still sharing the reputation of being a sober people but
> this holds good in so far as the immigrant is concerned and it hardly applies
> to their offspring, the first generation of Americans. The more Americanized
> we get, the more impregnated we become with the general faults of our
> neighbors. It is no uncommon occurrence nowadays to see a young Jew
> indulging in liquor, and not exactly in Jewish districts on Purim or Simchas
> Torah. . . .
>
> The Jewish neighborhoods have their saloons and wine-joints where young
> Jewish people spend their time at the bar or in provisional rooms where one
> can drink and do everything that should not be done. There is nothing new
> in seeing Jewish girls standing on street corners, waiting for a friend to go to
> a Jewish saloon to spend an evening at a table covered with liquors. . . . There
> is no excuse for us to stand aloof and witness unconcernedly how the serpent
> of inebriety inoculates its poison into the best elements of our youth.[70]

Bootstraps

The structure of the retail liquor business helped to promote the ethnic diversity
among saloons. Would-be proprietors needed little capital to open, and so even
the poorest among the recent immigrants could realize the dream of rapid social
mobility. The proof was in the front door key he carried in his pocket. The
competition among barrooms also meant that the brewers who bankrolled their
retail outlets were especially interested in tapping new consumer markets. The
recently arrived immigrant communities, trapped in the tenement districts,
provided rich opportunities. Brewers had previously concentrated their efforts
in those same inner-city districts where they had already secured the necessary
buildings. All they needed were personnel who could speak the language, tell
the proper stories, and prepare the right food for the lunch. The task was made
easier by the high rate of failure, since the constant turnover of proprietors
made room for incoming ethnic groups.

Those changes are reflected in what the census statistics tell us about

---

69. Friedman, "Amusements and Social Life," pp. 249-252.
70. *Daily Jewish Courier,* Mar. 6, 1914.

saloonkeepers and bartenders and how their ethnic backgrounds changed during the last two decades of the nineteenth century. First, the figures for 1880 reveal that native-born people still operated a surprising number of saloons in Chicago. The data do not distinguish between immigrants and the offspring of immigrants; indeed, some of them might be the thirty-year-old sons of those who fled the potato famine. By 1900 the native-born were of far less importance, though, accounting for 23.1 percent of the saloonkeepers and 44.2 percent of the total city work force. Furthermore, Chicago workers born in America apparently found greater opportunities in other kinds of economic activity. Only .01 percent of Chicago's U.S.-born workers joined the retail liquor business.[71]

The 1880 census figures also lend credibility to some ethnic stereotypes, while revealing significant flaws in others. First, there is the image of the Irish saloonkeeper: while tradition held that every other Celt wore a bar apron, the Irish actually demonstrated no particular affinity for the liquor business in 1880. Chicago's Irish, only 12.5 percent of the work force, claimed 14.7 percent of the liquor jobs; even then, only 1.7 percent of all Irish workers in Chicago became saloonkeepers or bartenders.

The Germans demonstrated the most consistent interest in the liquor business. Furthermore, nationally no ethnic group in 1880 had a greater proportion of its workers in the liquor business: 2.9 percent of all German workers could be found behind the counter, over four times the proportion found among the Irish. The German-born constituted 21.3 percent of Chicago's working population, but they made up 42.8 percent of the bartenders and saloonkeepers. Within the German community the same percentage (2.9 percent) of workers went into the trade.

Chicago also contained a scattering of less-numerous ethnic groups. The share of the saloon market claimed by the English-born, English-Canadians, and Scandinavians in the city was smaller than their population should have warranted. Of greater interest are those groups whose numbers are lumped together in the mysterious category labeled "other." Although their individual identities remain unknown, they probably included those people commonly classified as "new immigrants": French-Canadians, Poles, Russians, Russian Jews, Austro-Hungarians, and Italians. This category operated more than its share of saloons, although the figures do not reveal individual ethnic associations. Chicago's newer immigrants were a much more significant factor in the liquor business, making up 7 percent of the city's working population and 11.3 percent of its saloonkeepers. Furthermore, their attraction to the saloon trade was even more significant, since 2.3 percent of the population classified as "other" went into the liquor trade. That meant that only among the Germans did a larger portion of the group (2.9 percent) choose the liquor trade as their

71. The 1880 census did not separate men and women or saloonkeepers and bartenders in each job category.

occupation. That figure would prove to be the beginning of an important trend in Chicago.

Unfortunately, the next census did not specify the ethnicity of occupational groups, but the 1900 census did, and the twenty-year interval provides enough time to document some trends. First, there was an apparent decline in the percentage of native-born dealers and bartenders. Their proportion of all bartending and saloonkeeping positions fell from 23.1 percent to 18.1 percent. However, that decline was only relative: the total number of native-born in both job categories actually increased from 642 to 1,931.

The native-born were not the only group to undergo a relative decline in the retail liquor business. The Germans, for instance, lost considerable ground in Chicago. Where they had accounted for 42.8 percent of all bartender and saloonkeeper jobs in 1880, that figure stood at 36.3 percent in 1900. The actual number of Germans in the liquor trades did increase — in fact, more than tripled, from 1,192 to 3,879 — in the same period; but that expansion failed to keep pace with the growth of other nationalities in the business. Thus, while the proportion of Germans among the total work force climbed from 21.3 percent in 1880 to 24.7 percent in 1900, their share of liquor dealerships declined. Likewise, statistics indicate that a smaller proportion of Germans entered the liquor business: whereas 2.9 percent of all Germans in Chicago had gone into the business in 1880, only 2.2 percent found it attractive in 1900. The imbalance between proprietors and bartenders in 1900 means that there were 2,298 German saloonkeepers and 1,524 bartenders in Chicago. This meant that Germans either operated one-man businesses or employed other ethnic groups behind the bar.

If the native-born and Germans were finding the liquor business less attractive in the last two decades of the century, who was replacing them? Some of the smaller groups among the older nationalities assumed a slightly larger proportion of the trade, but there was no consistent pattern. The British-born and English-Canadians in Chicago held a declining share of liquor jobs, but the share claimed by Scandinavians increased sharply from 0.1 percent in 1880 to 4.8 percent in 1900, a change that was much greater than their population increase would have warranted. Thus, the larger share of the people who were displacing Germans and native-born were representatives of other groups.

The ethnic pattern of the Irish in Chicago's liquor trade evolved in a distinct direction: the proportion of Irish in the combined liquor trades declined slightly, from 14.7 percent to 14.4 percent. Chicago's total Irish working population also remained roughly the same, increasing modestly from 12.5 percent of the total 14.3 percent. The Irish behind bars tended to be the proprietors; 21 percent of Chicago's proprietors were Irish, but only 5 percent of the bartenders were sons of Erin.

Significant was the role assumed by the later immigrant groups: they were 26 percent of the total of all saloon employees in 1900. That statistic proved to be of great importance, for saloon licenses were widely distributed among Chicago's newcomers. French-Canadians, only a tiny portion (2 percent) of the city's work force, claimed 1.3 percent of the barroom jobs, while Russians held 2.5 percent of these jobs and were 2.1 percent of the populace. Those were only the smallest among the groups. Poles got 4.7 percent of the jobs, while Austro-Hungarians got 6.2 percent, and Italians, 5.1 percent; another 5.6 percent of the jobs were distributed among a variety of newly arrived people. Moreover, the newcomer was more likely to be a proprietor than a mere bartender. The Windy City really was a place of great opportunities. The greater the ethnic diversity of people, the greater the need for saloons to service the needs of each group.

In Chicago, until 1906, the liquor license fee remained at $500 — quite moderate. Before that date, there also was no limit on the number of licenses issued in Chicago and thus no premium to drive up the value of the annual permit. Brewers could establish as many outlets as they could afford, and the resulting overcompetition brought their agents into the newest and poorest neighborhoods in search of entrepreneurial talent. That fact was reflected in the way that young men in ethnic neighborhoods turned to the liquor business to seek their fortunes. The Italian communities provide the most dramatic contrast Chicago's 213 Italian saloonkeepers (including one woman) and 313 bartenders served 8,830 Italian men and 810 women. Thus, 6.2 percent of all Italian men entered the liquor trade, making it the largest proportion of any ethnic group to concentrate in the retail liquor business at any time in the history of the city. Not even the Irish or the Germans could equal that record.[72]

Conclusion: A Mirror of City Life

The story of the saloon as an ethnic institution in Chicago was shaped by three basic factors. First, and perhaps most obvious, was the fact that the saloons of some ethnic groups were more open and more accessible to the general population than were those of other nationalities. Irish and German places, dispersed and assimilated, were often in locations to be convenient to an anonymous stream of traffic, although some bars representing both ethnic groups drew their customers from a narrow neighborhood base. Other ethnic groups, including Scandinavians, Bohemians, Italians, and Poles, were divided from fellow drinkers by language, food, and internal customs. Greeks and Jews, meanwhile, generated their own substitutes for saloons. Black Chicagoans became saloonkeepers in much greater numbers, operating both Levee district dives

72. In Chicago the proportion of native-born workers in all fields fell from 44.2 percent in 1880 to 21.7 percent in 1900. The 1910 census did not break down the foreign-born by nationality, but it did show that native-born whites increased their share of the total saloon-related jobs from 18.1 percent in 1900 to 36.8 percent; the total percentage of the Chicago labor force that was native-born white stood at 47.2 percent (U.S. Census, 1910, *Occupations,* pp. 539-540, 544-547).

that drew "sports" of all races and nationalities and ethnocentric bars to serve the emerging Black Belt.

Second, the heterogeneity and social class of the street life surrounding the saloon had an obvious impact on the activities inside. Bars in the "portal of entry" neighborhoods, where the most recently arrived immigrants lived, serviced customers who were most often poor, clung most tightly to ethnic customs, and seldom spoke English. The migration of ethnic groups outward led to more homogeneous areas, where fewer of the customers depended on the barroom for the necessities of life or emergency relief. Ultimately, the free lunch on the sideboard became more Americanized. Thus, the status of the Irish and German saloons as ethnic universals came, in part, from the economic mobility and assimilation of those two nationalities.

Cheap beer, comparatively cheap licenses, the lack of a premium, the domination by aggressive breweries, easy entry into the business, and the tendency to allow over-competition among too many outlets all allowed great flexibility in responding to the heterogeneous immigrant tide. Native-born, German, and Irish barkeepers gave way to an increasing number of the so-called new immigrants. None of the latter nationalities made up more than a small percentage of the trade by themselves, but as a group they claimed an important share of the business. Thus, the saloon in Chicago became an important avenue of social mobility for the newcomer.

CHAPTER 18

Ethnic Sports

STEVEN S. RIESS

Urban sport was strongly influenced by ethnic history, demography, and culture, as these interacted with such elements of urbanization as spatial patterns, racism, and prejudice. The sporting experiences of non-WASP urbanites differed significantly from those of members of the core culture — on the basis of their immigrant heritage (norms, customs, values), income levels, degree of assimilation, and their concentration in large, crowded cities. The disproportionate presence of newcomers in major cities posed a serious threat to old-stock Americans and their culture. At the turn of the century, over three-fourths of New Yorkers and Chicagoans were of foreign origin, a ratio that was even exceeded in some eastern industrial towns. In 1920, when just half of the national population lived in cities, over 80 percent of the new immigrants — 84 percent of the Irish and 67 percent of German newcomers — resided in cities, mainly in major cities. Blacks comprised the smallest urban ethnic group in 1900, but when they migrated north, 70 percent settled in cities, crowding into ghetto communities.[1]

The athletic participation of white ethnics and black urbanites was influenced by the cultural baggage they brought from their points of origin, the timing of their arrival, their social class, degree of acculturation, and the spatial relationship in their slums or zones of emergence, which influenced access to sports facilities. Many voluntary institutions were developed to sustain tradi-

---

1. Raymond A. Mohl, *The New City: Urban America in the Industrial Age, 1860-1920* (Arlington Heights, Ill., 1985), p. 24. In 1900, half of the foreign born (49.5 percent) lived in cities with over 25,000 inhabitants, including three-fourths of Russians, two-thirds of Irish, Italians and Poles, and half of Germans. U.S. Census Office, *Twelfth Census of the United States Taken in the Year 1900: Population*, vol. 1 part 1 (Washington, D.C., 1901). Second-generation immigrants were usually about as urban as their parents were. Niles Carpenter, *Immigrants and Their Children* (1927; rep. New York, 1969), p. 21. For a survey of ethnic sports in Chicago, see Gerald R. Gems, "Not Only a Game," *Chicago History* 18 (Summer 1989), 4-21. See also Gems, "Sport and Culture Formation in Chicago, 1890-1940" (Ph.D. diss., University of Maryland, 1989).

tional pleasures or to introduce newcomers to American games. The sporting interests of second-generation immigrants were often opposed to those of their parents, who had little interest in or experience with sports. But the American-born frequently became ardent sports fans as they sought Americanization.

The Old Immigrants

The Irish-American Community

The Irish prominence in urban sport, established in the antebellum era, continued after the Civil War. In Irish neighborhoods the traditional male bachelor subculture continued to provide a focal point for their association life. But besides promoting manliness and solidarity, as in the past, sport also provided both a means to encourage and express Irish nationalism and a vehicle for social mobility.

In the 1870s and 1880s, independence leaders in Ireland had revived long-forgotten Irish sports like hurling and Gaelic football as means to promote Irish nationalism. To show solidarity with the revolutionaries and to encourage ethnic pride, Irishmen living in the United States quickly adopted these sports, forming an ethnic subcommunity that gave members dignity and a heightened sense of nationalism. Among the first organized groups to play these sports was the Irish Athletic Club of Boston in 1879. The club's inaugural meet featured such traditional sports as goaling, trapball, and stone throwing. Five years later, the Gaelic Athletic Association (GAA) was formed in Ireland to promote traditional Hibernian sports, and through them greater self-esteem and national pride. Branches of the GAA were soon established in American cities, where it became best known for its Sunday track and field meets at sites like Gaelic Park in the heart of Chicago's South Side Irish community. Political clout in that neighborhood protected the games in the face of Sabbatarian opposition. Irish sports were also promoted by overtly political organizations, most notably the Clan-Na-Gael (United Brotherhood), a secret revolutionary society that arranged athletic meets to gain favorable publicity, attract adherents, and promote Irish nationalism.[2]

While traditional Irish pastimes continue to be played in Irish neighborhoods to the present day, they became far less important in the community than American sports. Sports like baseball, boxing, and basketball provided a

---

2. Stephen Hardy, *How Boston Played: Sport, Recreation and Community, 1865-1915* (Boston, 1982), pp. 137-38; New York *Clipper* 24 (26 Aug. 1876), 173; Brooklyn *Eagle*, 5 July 1891; *Spirit* 116 (29 Sept. 1888), 376; 116 (6 Oct. 1888), 416-17; 116 (20 Oct. 1888), 492; 116 (27 Oct. 1888), 518; 116 (3 Nov. 1888), 561; Chicago *Tribune*, Sept. 28, 1892. On the history of the GAA, see W. F. Mandle, "The IRB and the Origins of the Gaelic Athletic Association," *Irish Historical Studies* 20 (Sept. 1977), 418-38; *idem, Sport in History: The Making of Modern Sporting History,* Richard Cashman and Michael McKernan, eds. (St. Lucia, Queensland, 1979), pp. 180-204.

major focal point around which Irishmen living in the slums or the zones of emergence organized their social life and secured self-esteem. Most young Irish-American athletes played in their own neighborhoods on teams they organized, often by block, to compete against boys from across the street or from different neighborhoods. These aggregates were commonly based on a youth gang, which formalized as the members got older into a "social and athletic club" (SAC) and gave members — generally at least sixteen to eighteen years old — a greater sense of belonging and status than just "hanging out" on the corner with their peers. SACs first gained popularity around the turn of the century in predominantly Irish sections of cities like Chicago, and they were later copied by other ethnic groups. The initiative in organizing a club was usually taken by an outside agent, such as a politician, a saloonkeeper, or a youth worker. A typical SAC had a spartanly furnished clubhouse, usually in a streetfront or the back room of a store, where members spent their free time shooting pool, tossing dice, or playing cards. They generally had about one hundred members who enjoyed the camaraderie of the clubs, along with SAC-sponsored stags, dances, and athletics. SACs sponsored baseball, football, and other team sports; obtained uniforms; and scheduled matches with other SACs. SACs had the potential to be destructive, asocial agencies or positive integrative forces that replaced the uncontrolled, pugnacious behavior of street punks with the cooperative values taught through team sports.[3]

One of the most prominent aspects of the SACs was their political character. They depended heavily on political assistance to get organized, secure a charter, become well-known, and succeed. As sociologist Frederick Thrasher, the leading student of the SACs, pointed out in 1926:

> The tendency of the gangs to become athletic clubs has been greatly stimulated by the politicians of the city. It has become a tradition among gangs throughout Chicago that the first source of possible financial aid is the local alderman or other politician. . . . The ward "heeler" often corrals a gang like a beeman does his swarm in the hive he has prepared for it. The boss pays the rent and is generous in his donations for all gang enterprises. He is the "patron saint" of the gang and often leads the grand march or makes a speech at gang dances and in return his proteges work for him in innumerable ways and every gang boy in the hive is expected to gather honey on election day. It is doubtful if this sort of athletic club could long survive if it had to depend solely upon the financial backing of its own members. Former SAC members commonly ended up as Democratic machine aldermen, police captains, or gamblers.[4]

3. Frederick M. Thrasher, *The Gang: A Study of 1,313 Gangs in Chicago*, abr. ed. (Chicago, 1963), pp. 13, 48, 52, 60, 124, 315-18.

4. *Ibid.*, 175, 316 (quote); see also Mike Royko, *Boss: Richard J. Daley of Chicago* (New York, 1971), pp. 37, 38.

The preeminent Chicago SAC was the Ragen Colts, whose territory was the impoverished Back of the Yards district on the South Side, though in time it also terrorized neighborhoods west of that area. Founded in 1908 by politico Frank Ragen, a future county commissioner who rented them a clubhouse and bought uniforms and sporting equipment, the Colts rapidly gained fame for their athletic prowess and notoriety for their slugging and political intimidation. In the words of one member, "when we dropped into a polling place, everyone else dropped out." The gang became infamous as a lawless group that terrorized the Southwest Side, the better Irish neighborhoods, and the nearby black community on the east side of Washington Park. During the Chicago Race Riot in July 1919, the Colts played a prominent role in attacking black Chicagoans. One historian of the riots blamed their violence on the Colts' antipathy to the growing number of black workers at the stockyards, Republican Mayor William H. Thompson's support of black civil rights, and the increased presence of black ballplayers and picnickers in Washington Park. By this time the Colts were accurately described as "athletic only with their fists and brass knuckles and guns." SACs were becoming less social and athletic and more a hangout for rough young men who had graduated from youth gangs.[5]

The German-American Turnverein

Ethnic athletics in German-American neighborhoods revolved around the *turnverein*, an important community center as integral a part of German culture as the beer garden, German-language theaters, and German choral societies. Membership nationally reached 13,387 in 1880, up from about 5,000 in 1859; it then nearly tripled a decade later, to 35,912 in 1890. The members were mainly lower-middle and middle-class first- and second-generation Germans. A majority of senior members in the 1880s were blue-collar workers (55.5 percent), and virtually all the rest (44.2 percent) were white-collar workers, predominantly petty bourgeois. Virtually all of the manual working members were craftsmen, mainly printers, brewers, and cigarmakers — all typically German occupations (see Table 3). In all, the membership constituted a hard-working, respectable element who resided in heavily German urban villages.[6]

    5. Thrasher, *Gang*, 318; William M. Tuttle, Jr., *Race Riot: Chicago in the Red Summer of 1919* (New York, 1974), pp. 32-33, 54-55, 156, 199-200 (quote), 236-38; Allan H. Spear, *Black Chicago: The Making of a Negro Ghetto, 1890-1920* (Chicago, 1967), pp. 201, 206, 213, 216; *Chicago Commission on Race Relations: The Negro in Chicago* (Chicago, 1922), p. 237 (quote). On Italian-American SACs in Chicago in the early 1960s, see Gerald D. Suttles, *The Social Order of the Slum* (Chicago, 1968).

    6. Henry Metzner, *A Brief History of the American Turnerbund* (Pittsburgh, 1924), pp. 17-24, 29-30; Benjamin G. Rader, "Quest for Subcommunities and the Rise of American Sport," *American Quarterly* 29 (Fall 1977), 360. For a history of the turners in Chicago, see Theodor Jannsen, *Geschichte der Chicago Turn-Gemeinde* (Chicago, 1897).

The social backgrounds of members in the oldest, and what were presumably the most prestigious, societies varied substantially from city to city.
The Boston and Williamsburg (Brooklyn) turnvereins were nearly 90 percent
blue collar, as were more than two-thirds of the membership in Cincinnati and
Philadelphia. Yet in Milwaukee and Chicago, newer Midwestern cities with large
and prosperous German communities, the proportions were markedly different.
Four-fifths of the Milwaukee turnverein were white collar; one-third of its senior
members (34.6 percent) had high-level white-collar jobs. The Chicago *turngemeinde*, the city's oldest and most prestigious society, was 70.6 percent white
collar, and that increased to 82 percent by the turn of the century. Chicago's
large and vital German community could support several separate turner units
with its combined membership of about 5,000 in 1890, the most of any city. At
least two of the other units were primarily working class. Still, the turners were
probably less class based than any other major sport organization. Certain units
in New York and St. Louis were evenly divided between white-collar and blue-
collar workers at a time when most German Americans were blue-collar workers. Respectable, hardworking German immigrants from different social classes
could exercise and socialize together in a gemütlich atmosphere because they
shared the same culture and values. Unlike the antebellum cricket clubs, the
turnvereins did not, as a matter of course, evolve into purely status communities.[7] The *turnhalles*, located in the heart of German neighborhoods, were social
centers that provided far more than places for physical exercise. A major turn-
halle like that of the Chicago turngemeinde, located in the center of the city's
North Side German community, had a well-equipped gymnasium, of course,
but also a billiard room, library, club room, dining room, and one of the largest
dance halls in the city. German-language theatrical productions were staged
there, and it was also a forum for public debates.[8]

7. One hundred twenty-two men in the *Chicago City Directory*. None were unskilled, and
just nine were semiskilled. On left-wing turners, see Ralph Wagner, "Turner Societies and the
Socialist Tradition," in *Workers Culture in the United States, 1850 to 1920*, Hartmut Keil, ed.
(Washington, 1988), pp. 221-239. The Aurora Turner Hall, opened in 1868, was the uncontested
center of the German labor movement, and German culture and social life on the Northwest Side
into the 1890s. See Klaus Ensslen, "German-American Working-Class Saloons in Chicago: Their
Social Functions in an Ethnic and Class-Specific Cultural Context," in *ibid.*, p. 176. While Aurora
is considered a working-class turner society, one history of the society described members after
1877 as "mostly workers or small businessmen who sought to further the labor movement." Fees
that year were dropped from $5 to $2. Membership in 1884 reached 240, with 360 children
attending turner school. Membership peaked at 527 in 1890, then declined because of the hard
times that came with the depression of 1893. See "The Aurora Turnverein," from *Der Western:
Frauen-Zeitung* 15 (22 Nov. 1896), in *German Workers in Chicago: A Documentary History of
Working-Class Culture from 1850 to World War I*, Hartmut Jeil and John B. Jentz, eds. (Urbana,
1988), pp. 160-69 (quote, 164).

8. *Illinois Staats-Zeitung*, 26 Aug. 1861, 3 Oct. 1881; Chicago *Times*, 20 Jan. 1873, in Works
Progress Administration, Illinois, *Chicago Foreign Language Press Survey*, University of Chicago
Library, Special Collections, Chicago, Ill. (hereafter cited as CFLPS).

The goals of the turners were to maintain the German character of their communities, encourage physical fitness, and improve conditions of working-class folk. They were politically active as a pressure group on ethnocultural issues such as the preservation of the Continental Sabbath and the use of German as the primary language of instruction in neighborhood public schools. They tried to improve the quality of urban life by advocating better health through the construction of gymnasiums in all schools, physical education and gymnastics for public school students under the supervision of trained instructors, and the development of municipal parks. The turners were strong advocates of trade unionism and socialism. During the 1870s their national organizations supported such traditional socialist demands as worker control over the means of production, as well as general social reforms such as compulsory school attendance, regulation of monopolies, government inspection of factories, restrictions on child labor, and the eight-hour day. Turner halls were frequently utilized by unions for meetings and public debates. By the 1880s an influential minority in the overtly socialist turnvereins, people like August Spies in Chicago, began to openly avow anarchism.[9]

By 1890, Chicago, with thirty-four societies and 5,000 members, was the stronghold of the turner movement. Following Haymarket, many socialists joined the turners to avoid antisocialist police campaigns. Relations between middle-class and socialist turners exploded after Haymarket, resulting in a realignment: conservatives and progressives split apart and formed their own societies. The precipitating event was the Chicago turngemeinde's expulsion of social democrat Julius Valteich in 1891 for his radical views, an action that was overturned by the North American Turner Association (NATA), which had been momentarily taken over by political radicals. In response, the 800-member Turngemeinde and three other middle-class Chicago units, the Central Turnvereine, the Sudseite Turngemeinde, and the Germania Turnvereine dropped out of the NATA for one year.[10]

The Chicago district became more socialist in the 1890s, and in 1901 many turners participated in the founding of the Socialist Party of America. Once the socialists created their own institutions, their ties with the turners weakened; in addition, the turner movement became increasingly bourgeois, reflecting the general economic well-being of the city's German-American community. By the early 1900s the turners were largely a middle-class ethnic social organization whose members preferred to divorce politics from athletics. The movement soon went into a decline. It was becoming more German-American than German, reflected by the use of English at its meetings and in its publication, and

9. *Ibid.*

10. *Chicago Tribune,* 20 February, 22 May 1891; Chicago *Abendpost,* 17 Sept. 1891; Jannsen, *Geschichte der Chicago-Turngemeinde,* pp. 75-76.

it did not appeal to highly assimilated folk, who were more interested in baseball and nickelodeons than gymnastics and German culture.[11]

The turners languished during World War I because of anti-German sentiments, renaming themselves after American heroes such as Lincoln to set themselves apart from the enemy. The movement survived in Chicago — with sixteen units — as late as 1926, bolstered by recent immigrants, who comprised 30 percent of its membership.[12]

The New Immigrants

While ethnic sports facilitated the adjustment of old immigrants in their urban villages, they were far less important among the new immigrants from eastern and southern Europe, who had little if any sporting tradition and would not become ardent sportsmen in America. In general, they regarded sports as a childish pursuit and ridiculed their peers who were interested in sports. Those who ventured into athletic institutions like the YMCA were quickly put off by Americans, who made fun of them. Instead, hardworking male newcomers, exhausted by backbreaking jobs, preferred relaxation to physical exertion pleasures, and they enjoyed themselves at ethnic saloons, clubs, and coffeehouses, or at family gatherings and religious festivals.[13]

The Bohemians

One of the few new immigrant groups who came to America with any sporting heritage at all, the Bohemians established themselves in heavily Czech neighborhoods such as Pilsen on the near Southwest Side of Chicago and in other industrial areas in the Midwest. In 1862, as part of a Romantic resistance movement against the ruling Austrians, Bohemian nationalists had organized the *sokol* movement. Its philosophy, modeled after the turnverein, sought to develop nationalism and strong bodies and minds for the future revolution. The sokol tradition in America goes back almost as far as it does in Bohemia: a unit was established in St. Louis in 1865. The primary goals of American sokol units were to promote physical culture and to encourage newcomers to identify with their fellow Bohemians and their language and culture. By 1900 there were 184 units in the United States, whose members were mainly working-class

11. Chicago *Tribune,* 20 Feb. 1891; *Illinois Staats-Zeitung,* 7 May 1900, CFLPS; Wagner, "Turner Societies," pp. 235-36; Ensslen, "German-American Working Class Saloons," p. 176. On the use of non-German languages at turner meetings, see *Chicago Arbeiter Zeitung,* 30 June 1908, CFLPS.

12. Metzner, *American Turner Bund,* pp. 17-30.

13. W. C. Smith, *Americans in the Making* (New York, 1939), p. 312.

people or small merchants who were freethinkers. Hostility between freethinkers and devout Catholics eventually caused the latter to organize their own sokols. The example of the sokol encouraged other Slavic peoples to organize their own athletic associations for similar purposes. The Polish Falcons, for example, were organized in 1867 and were first imported to America twenty years later, when the first nest was established in Chicago.[14]

The sokol hall was normally one of the largest buildings in a Bohemian neighborhood — and the center of its cultural and social life. It often housed the community's major recreational institutions, such as the Czech theater and choral societies. Sokols sponsored annual gymnastic exhibitions and family holiday outings that would include sokol drills and folk dancing. The physical culture programs emphasized calisthenics, which did not appeal to the second generation. In Chicago's Pilsen community, the sokol leaders met the challenge of attracting the interest of the American-born by organizing Sunday Bohemian baseball leagues for them. This got the youth involved in the sokol and encouraged them to sustain their ethnic identity. The quality of play was quite high: by 1910 several Chicago Bohemians had made the major leagues. Their achievement was a source of great pride in the community, even among those who were not baseball fans.[15]

The Jews

The brief tradition of the Bohemians completely surpassed that of the two million eastern European Jews who migrated to the United States between 1880 and 1914 to escape pogroms and anti-Semitism. They were stereotyped as weak, unhealthy, physically unfit, and unaccustomed to respectable, "manly" labor. The noted sociologist E. A. Ross described them as "the polar opposite of our pioneer breed. Not only are they undersized and weak-muscled, but they shun bodily activity and are extremely sensitive to pain." The presence of these strangely garbed, bearded, Yiddish-speaking Orthodox Jews embarrassed German-American Jews and unleashed a wave of anti-Semitism that resulted in restricted admission to colleges,

14. Vaclad Vesta, ed., *Panorama: A Historical Review of Czechs and Slovaks in the U.S.A.* (Cicero, Ill., 1970), pp. 22-26, 133-136, 145-146; *Svornost*, 12 Aug., 6 Sept., 25 Nov. 1878; 8 Apr. 1890, CFLPS; Jakub Horak, "The Assimilation of Czechs in Chicago" (Ph.D. diss., University of Chicago, 1920), p. 92. On the Polish experience, see Arthur L. Waldo, "The Origins and Goals of the Falcons," in *Polish Falcons in America: Sixty Years of District IV, 1904-1964* (Pittsburgh, 1965), pp. 5-7. On the paramilitarism of the sokols, falcons, and the Ukrainian Sich (an anti-Communist organization complete with air corps established to fight the U.S.S.R. in the early 1930s), see *Denni Hlasatel*, 30 Apr., 21 May, 17 June 1917; *Dziennik Zwiazkowy*, 15 Sept. 1915, in CFLPS; Myron Kuropas, "Ukrainian Chicago: The Making of a Nationality Group in America," in Peter d'A. Jones and Melvin G. Holli, *Ethnic Chicago* (Grand Rapids, 1984), pp. 165-73.

15. Chicago *Times*, 1 June 1887; *Svornost*, 8 Apr. 1890; *Denni Hlasatel*, 2 Apr. 1910; 16 Sept. 1911, in CFLPS; Steven A. Riess, *Touching Base: Professional Baseball and American Culture in the Progressive Era* (Westport, CT, 1980), pp. 37, 191.

prestigious men's clubs, and well-known athletic clubs. Until then, the prosperous German Jews had been hardly distinguishable from other German Americans in their social and athletic activities, having served as leaders of turnvereins and gained prominence in mainstream sports ranging from thoroughbred racing to professional baseball as participants and entrepreneurs.[16]

Philanthropic German Jews accepted the responsibility of assisting the new Jewish immigrants to adjust to life in the New World by establishing settlement houses and other social agencies that helped the newcomers find jobs, secure housing, and acculturate. Settlement houses established in inner-city slums, such as the Educational Alliance (1893) in New York's Lower East Side and the Jewish People's Institute (1908) in Chicago's West Side ghetto, sought to sustain a Jewish identity among their clients while helping them to become good citizens. Youth workers emphasized athletics to attract Jewish youth and to encourage good health habits, improve morality, and build character, while disproving negative stereotypes about Jewish manliness.[17]

The Catholics

The most important Catholic group to utilize athletics to uplift inner-city youth was the Catholic Youth Organization (CYO), established in Chicago in 1930 by Auxiliary Bishop Bernard J. Sheil. Sheil recognized that young Catholics such as Studs Lonigan and his like were being drawn away from the church by the competition of such exhilarating pleasures as drinking, fighting, and womanizing. The church — along with the family and schools — apparently had lost its historic function as agent of socialization and had little relevance to the needs of young Catholic males in the 1920s and 1930s. Sheil wanted to find a way to bring the young men back into the fold.[18]

16. Edward A. Ross, *The Old World in the New: The Significance of Past and Present Immigration to the American People* (New York, 1914), pp. 289-90. On German-American attitudes, see Cary Goodman, *Choosing Sides: Playground and Street Life on the Lower East Side* (New York, 1979), pp. 37-40; Chicago *Messenger*, 1 Nov. 1909; Chicago Hebrew Institute, *Observer*, Nov. 1912; Dec. 1913; Jan. 1918, in CFLPS. On German-Jewish sports participation, see *The Jewish Encyclopedia*, s.v. "Sports"; Bernard Postel, Jesse Silver, and Roy Silver, eds., *Encyclopedia of Jews in Sports* (New York, 1965); Riess, *Touching Base*, p. 87. In his classic *The Ghetto* (Chicago, 1956), p. 170, sociologist Louis Wirth argues that the gap between German and Russian Jews was better demonstrated by their social clubs than by different religious institutions.

17. Goodman, *Choosing Sides*, pp. 37-40; Morris J. Frank, "Activity of the Jews in Athletics," *The American Hebrew* 83 (18 Sept. 1908), 477; "The Jewish Athlete," *ibid.*, 83 (12 Oct. 1908), 544; "The Jewish Athlete," *ibid.*, 84 (11 Dec. 1908), 171; Gerald R. Gems, "Chicago's Jewish People Institute," *American-Jewish History* (in press).

18. John R. Betts, *America's Sporting Heritage, 1850-1950* (Reading, MA, 1974), pp. 281-282; Ellen Brewer, "Bishop Bernard Sheil and the Formation of the Catholic Youth Organization" (seminar paper, University of Chicago, 1979); Roger L. Treat, *Bishop Sheil and CYO* (New York, 1951).

The Catholic church's concern about the protection of its youth in America dated back to the early nineteenth century, when it created parochial schools to counter Protestant influence in the public schools. In the early 1900s, when most Catholics were unassimilated urbanites of new immigrant stock, bishops worried that adult-directed boys' organizations like the YMCA and the Boy Scouts would undermine the faith of good Catholics by promoting the values of the Protestant core culture to the detriment of their own religious heritage. Two decades later, the church was still on the defensive, despite the efforts of Chicago's Cardinal Mundelein and others in the hierarchy to Americanize their communicants.[19]

The emphasis on education and socialization continued into the 1930s. Pope Pius XI's 1929 encyclical, "Christian Education of Youth," urged that full attention be given to the complete supervision of all aspects of Catholic education. The problem of coping with a perceived hostile environment was exacerbated by the onset of the Depression, which created high levels of unemployment and left many young men with free time and nothing constructive to do. These concerns struck home in Chicago, which had the largest parochial school system in the country, and they prompted Bishop Sheil to devise a program of supervised recreation for older boys as a partial solution to some of the church's problems. He believed that athletics would help Americanize the second generation, promote citizenship, and enable young men to direct their antisocial energies in a positive direction. Sports would fill up idle time and promote sexual and moral continence. Sheil publicized the CYO to the non-Catholic community as an organization that would prevent juvenile delinquency and premarital sex and sold the program to the church by emphasizing that it would bring boys closer to their religious heritage and save those who had fallen away.[20]

The CYO began operations in 1931 with a huge boxing tournament and a ten-team basketball league. Sheil originally relied on local parishes to train and instruct members, but since their facilities were inadequate, he set up a training center in the Loop. By 1938, three-fifths of the city's parishes had CYO units serving more than 10,000 boys in recreational, educational, religious, and social programs. The CYO became best known for teaching boxing, which generated a lot of favorable publicity. Sheil emphasized boxing because it appealed to poor and working-class youth, the people he wanted to bring into the

19. Brewer, "Bishop Sheil," pp. 2-6; see also James W. Sanders, *The Education of an Urban Minority: Catholics in Chicago, 1833-1965* (New York, 1972), which focuses on the efforts of the archdiocese to acculturate its youth.

20. Brewer, "Bishop Sheil," pp. 6-9. On the success of the CYO and other adult-organized recreational programs in fighting juvenile delinquency in this era, see Betts, *America's Sporting Heritage*, p. 331; Chicago Recreation Commission, *Recreation and Delinquency: A Study of Five Selected Chicago Communities* (Chicago, 1942), pp. 236-44.

CYO. Boxing did just that, and the CYO became an important training ground for talented boxers, three of whom made the 1936 Olympic team.[21]

CYO branches were soon established all over the country, and by 1940 they were reaching 150,000 Catholic youth. Besides boxing, the CYO sponsored a baseball league and the largest basketball association in the United States. Its philosophy, which differed significantly from the Protestant-inspired athletic associations founded in the late nineteenth century, reflected a Catholic perspective: it did not fear the influence of women as teachers for older boys, as the late Victorians had. The CYO used sports, not to build manly, healthy, and physically muscular Christians, but rather to save souls. In addition, the CYO always served a heterogeneous lower-class Catholic clientele, while Protestant boys' workers started out with a homogeneous middle-class population.[22]

Urban Space and Ethnic Sports

The choice of sports among athletically inclined ethnic youth was heavily influenced not only by their social class and ethnic heritage but also by the spatial and social patterns of the neighborhoods in which they lived. Second- and third-generation youth living in the more well-to-do communities in the suburban fringe, or even the moderate income zone of emergence, had many different opportunities available to them than did slum dwellers. Residents of the inner city, who had high drop-out rates and less free time if they were employed, had less exposure to sports in school. In addition, they had virtually no access to distant suburban parks that had the space for outdoor sports like baseball. In fact, until the turn of the century, they did not even have small parks within walking distance.

Baseball

The best baseball players were mainly recruited from upper-lower- and lower-middle-class urban families, the kinds of people who lived in the zones of emergence or even the suburban fringe. Major league rosters before 1920 were dominated by American, Irish, and German players who lived in localities that had sufficient space for baseball. The Irish lived in urban sections of the country where the sport had been popular from an early date, so they had a head start on other ethnic groups. In Irish neighborhoods everyone followed the sport, and many communities, such as the Southwest Side of Chicago, the locale of James T. Farrell's novels, had plenty of space to play ball in the nearby parks.

21. Brewer, "Bishop Sheil," p. 9; Chicago Recreation, 3:71.
22. Brewer, "Bishop Sheil," pp. 11, 12-18; Sanders, *Urban Minority,* pp. 195-196.

An all-Italian cast, 1936-1937: (from left) Tony Lazzeri, Joe DiMaggio, Zeke Bonura, and Frankie Crosetti.   Courtesy of D. Bukowski.

Furthermore, neighborhood teams were often sponsored by SACs, local politicians, or saloonkeepers.[23]

White Sox Park drew many of the South Side Irish in Chicago — not just because the owner of the White Sox, Charles Comiskey, was Irish but also because the park was just a few blocks from Bridgeport, a heavily Irish community. Irish attendance was also facilitated by the work schedule of many Irish in construction or in city employment, which permitted afternoon recreation, as well as Sunday ball and cheap tickets — since Comiskey operated the largest 25-cent section in the major leagues. A dramatic sport whose frequent lapses

23. Riess, *Touching Base*, pp. 35-36, 85-186; James T. Farrell, *My Baseball Diary* (New York, 1957), pp. 29-30.

in action gave spectators a chance to talk over the game and drink beer, baseball fit in well with the norms of the Irish bachelor subculture. It was a manly sport, rarely attended by Irish womenfolk, and it provided Irishmen with a topic of conversation with their sons, whom they would take along to the games.[24]

The Irish familiarity with the sport, their opportunities to play the game, and their proficiency enabled them to achieve great success in baseball. By the 1880s and 1890s they had many role models to emulate, such as "King" Kelly, John J. McGraw, and Ed Delahanty, and parents encouraged talented young men to practice so they could become professional ballplayers and earn high wages. By the early 1890s, one-third of all major leaguers were believed to be Irish, and they soon comprised a large proportion of managers as well; in 1915, for instance, eleven of sixteen major league managers were sons of Erin.[25]

By comparison, the new immigrant groups had very little success in breaking into the major leagues during this period. There was not a single rookie of new immigrant stock in 1910, and just two Italians and one Bohemian out of 133 first-year men in 1920. Baseball was enormously popular with the second-generation newcomers, who ardently followed the exploits of their heroes and favorite teams in the local press but seldom attended games because of the expense. Boys liked to play baseball, which was fun and demonstrated that they were not greenhorns but "real Yankees." However, the lack of playing space in the crowded inner city was the key factor that made it difficult for second-generation youths to secure the skills and experience necessary to become professionals. Because of spatial limitations that consigned slum youths to the streets, their ballplaying was often constricted to cognate games like stickball, and they had to develop special rules to conform to the idiosyncrasies of their playing area ("anything hit to right field is out"). Other factors also constrained them: limited discretionary time for working youth, afternoon attendance at Hebrew School, low rates of attendance at secondary school (where they could play on interscholastic teams with other talented players under the supervision of trained coaches), parental opposition, and limited community support. Before the 1920s, Yiddish-, Italian-, and Polish-language newspapers almost never covered baseball, although it did become a staple of the Czech and French-Canadian press. Immigrant parents, especially eastern European Jews, saw baseball as a silly sport played by men in short pants, a waste of time that introduced their sons to some of the worst features of the host society. In 1903 a Jewish father wrote to the Yiddish *Forward* (New York): "What is the point of this crazy game? It makes sense to teach a child to play dominoes or chess . . . but not baseball. . . . I want my boy to grow up to be a *mensch*, not a wild American runner." Jewish

24. Riess, *Touching Base*, pp. 33, 36.
25. *Ibid.*, pp. 185-86.

parents felt that baseball was a dangerous game that required too much physical exertion![26]

A similar story of intergenerational conflict concerned an Italian youth named Nick and his immigrant mother. When the son was brought before the Chicago Juvenile Court on charges of misconduct, his mother told the judge: "Nick no wanna work. He big man, 14, and wanna to play ball all day. Father say, 'You go-to-day and work in restaurant with your uncle. . . .' He makes faces, cusses, laughs, and runs out to play ball. . . . He very bad boy. . . . He no wanna work. . . . He get up at noon and go out to play. That not right. I go out to the ball game and say, 'Nick, come home with me from these bad boys and work.' He laugh at me, make a face, tell me to go home and to mind own business. He like nothing but ball. . . . The father work hard. Have heart trouble. Nick ought to help."[27]

In the 1920s, if not before, several major-league teams made a concerted effort to recruit ethnic ballplayers to build up fan interest. The Giants, for example, signed Moses Solomon, the "Rabbi of Swat," to a brief trial in 1923; three years later brought up Andy Cohen, who was widely publicized as a ghetto boy making good. Born in Baltimore, Cohen had actually grown up in Waco, Texas, and was educated at the University of Alabama — hardly the typical Jewish inner-city youth. Even though New York contained half of the American Jewish population in 1920, the city produced less than its proportionate share of major leaguers. Baseball players did not come from the poorest, most crowded neighborhoods. Jewish superstar Hank Greenberg, for instance, was not a product of the inner city but grew up in the 1920s in a middle-class household in the relatively prosperous and spacious Bronx.[28]

The other new immigrant groups achieved greater success in baseball; though, until 1935, Slavs and Italians together comprised just 7 percent of all major leaguers. In the next few years, second-generation new immigrants began flocking into the major leagues, attracted by the pay and the prestige. In 1941, 8 percent of big leaguers were Italians and 9.3 percent Slavic — more than double their share of the national white population. These groups were more geographically dispersed, were less urban or concentrated in ethnic neighborhoods, and had greater parental support than Jewish boys, whose elders stressed education rather than obtaining a well-paid "manly" job. The first Italians and Slavs were less likely

26. *Ibid.*, pp. 36-37, 184-91; Allon Schoener, ed., *Portal to America: The Lower East Side* (New York, 1967), pp. 67-68; Irving Howe, *World of Our Fathers* (New York, 1976), p. 259 (quote).

27. National Commission on Law Observance and Enforcement, *Report on the Causes of Crime*, vol. 2, no. 13 (Washington, D.C., 1931), pp. 4-5, quoted in William Carlson Smith, *Americans in the Making: The Natural History of the Assimilation of Immigrants* (New York, 1939), p. 312.

28. Riess, *Touching Base*, pp. 186, 189-190; Tilden G. Edelstein, "Cohen at Bat," *Commentary* 76 (Nov. 1983), 53-56; William M. Simons, "The Athlete as Jewish Standard Bearer: Media Images of Hank Greenberg," *Jewish Social Studies* 44 (Spring 1982), 95-112. Data on Jewish players' birthplaces based on biographical sketches in Postal, *Jews in Sports*.

to come from cities like New York or Boston, which had limited open space and inadequate baseball facilities, than from smaller cities or metropolises like Chicago, where there was more space to play baseball and where the sport was strongly emphasized and supported by active amateur programs.[29]

Basketball

One of the most popular indoor sports was basketball, a team game invented by Dr. James Naismith to provide football players with wintertime exercise. Because it did not require much space or costly equipment — a rag ball and a peach basket could suffice — it fit well with the inner-city environment. The spatial factor was a clear advantage for basketball over baseball: as Basketball Hall of Famer Barney Sedran remembered, "It was difficult for an East Side youngster like myself to play baseball because there were no diamonds nearby." However, basketball was played in school yards, settlement houses, and churches, and that was why, he felt, his neighbors became so proficient in basketball. The sport spread like wildfire through Eastern and Midwestern cities.[30]

During the 1920s and 1930s urban basketball maintained a very strong ethnic character. Ethnic fraternal groups organized athletic clubs for basketball and other sports to facilitate sporting competition and social events among the second generation, who were unwelcome in prestigious WASP voluntary athletic organizations. In the 1930s there were Serbian, Lithuanian, and Polish national basketball championships. Ethnic championship games in Chicago could draw in excess of 10,000 spectators. Interethnic competition also purportedly provided a broadening experience, though one might argue that it encouraged as much ethnic hostility as friendship and understanding. In Chicago one of the most popular events was an annual exhibition game between the CYO and B'nai Brith All-Stars.[31]

The ethnic dimension was also very strong, if not stronger, at the professional level. Before World War II, professional basketball in major urban areas was very much an ethnic community entertainment. The best-known teams, like the New York Celtics, often started out as ethnic clubs and maintained that identity when they recruited new talent. These teams were important community institutions that instilled ethnic pride in their fans and gained respect from

29. Riess, *Touching Base*, pp. 191-192.

30. Quoted in Postal, *Jews in Sports*, p. 92; see also Frank, "Jews in Athletics," p. 477. On the early history of basketball, see Larry Fox, *Illustrated History of Basketball* (New York, 1974), pp. 9-57; and Albert Applin, "From Muscular Christianity to the Marketplace: The History of Men's and Boy's Basketball in the United States, 1891-1957" (Ph.D. diss., University of Massachusetts, 1982). Ted Vincent, *Mudville's Revenge: The Rise and Fall of American Sport* (New York, 1981), pp. 247-253.

31. John H. Mariano, *The Italian Contribution to American Democracy* (Boston, 1921), pp. 144-148.

other ethnic groups. Games were often played at dance halls, where they preceded an evening of dancing — all for fifty cents a couple.[32]

Professional basketball players active before 1940 were nearly 90 percent urban, and almost one-third of them came from New York City. Three-fourths of a selected sample of prominent players were either German, Jewish, or Irish. While they were presumably from lower-class backgrounds, an exceptionally large proportion (74.6 percent) had attended college, even though entrance into the professional sport before the 1930s did not require college experience. Salaries were generally modest, and players active in weekend leagues during the Depression, such as the midwestern National Basketball League, all held full-time jobs outside of basketball.[33]

The Prize Ring

The sport that probably best fit in with the urban slum environment was pugilism. Because boys and young men from different ethnic backgrounds were constantly getting into fights to protect their honor or their turf, self-defense was a very useful skill to learn. Jewish boys coming home from school or walking to a swimming pool often had to cross neighborhood lines where Irish lads were waiting to beat them up to guard their territory, to extort money, or just to have fun at their expense. They learned to fight back, either to break the vicious cycle or to protect those weaker than themselves. Neighborhood settlement houses and local boxing gymnasiums provided excellent coaching, which helped boys learn to defend themselves and build up their self-confidence. The ability to fight well in the streets and in the gym was a means for these youths to prove their manhood, to win respect from their peers, and, for some, to gain training for a possible future occupation.[34]

Inner-city youths who learned to discipline their street fighting in the ring might take advantage of their training to become professional pugilists. For boys who lacked more traditional means of advancement, boxing had long been an escape from the slums. However, only young men from the poorest neighborhoods chose to become prizefighters, because it required intensive training and certain physical punishment. Novices who became sufficiently proficient might be recruited to fight at a Knights of Columbus smoker, for example, and thus develop a reputation leading to a paying bout at a local bar/boxing club. Between 1870 and 1920 the sport was totally dominated by Irish pugilists. In the 1890s, for instance, nine of the American world champions in various weight

32. Vincent, *Mudville's Revenge,* pp. 247-55.

33. Computed from biographical data in Ronald L. Mendell, *Who's Who in Basketball* (New Rochelle, 1973). Mendell's focus on the more notable players may have skewed the study sample.

34. Riess, *Touching Base,* pp. 188-189; Daniel Bell, *The End of Ideology* (Glencoe, IL, 1960), pp. 127-150; and esp. Steven A. Riess, "The Jewish-American Boxing Experience, 1890-1940," *American Jewish History* 74 (March 1985), 223-54.

divisions were of Irish descent, including John L. Sullivan, heavyweight champion from 1882 to 1892 and the most prominent sportsman of the nineteenth century. Sullivan, whose picture was displayed in virtually every saloon, was regarded with awe as the toughest man in the world. While lace-curtain Irish Americans were embarrassed by Sullivan's profession and bawdy lifestyle, most Irishmen regarded him as the champion of their race. Between 1900 and 1920 there were more Irish champions (thirteen out of forty-seven) and more contenders (40 percent in the late 1910s) than from any other ethnic group. However, their predominance was beginning to decline, partly because of improving opportunities for other kinds of success for Irish youth, but mainly because of the growing competition from impoverished second-generation newcomers.[35]

The sons of eastern and southern European immigrants enjoyed considerable success in prize fighting, the sport with which they were most identified by the general public. Boxers were often desperate, driven youths at the bottom of the social ladder who lived in neighborhoods like New York's Lower East Side, Chicago's Near West Side, and San Francisco's Mission District. They were tough kids, usually ex-street fighters whose idols were either local boxers or hoodlums, who engaged in the only well-paying occupations these poor youths saw open to them as an escape from poverty. Jewish, Italian, and Polish youths highly esteemed the ability to fight: it was a sign of manliness and was a useful skill because of the frequency of interethnic gang fights at public parks and playgrounds and other border areas separating rival groups. In Chicago, for example, there was a good deal of hostility in the early 1920s between the Jewish and Polish communities located along Roosevelt Road, the West Side's major commercial district, where Jewish businessmen and pedestrians were regularly attacked by Polish thugs, and also at Douglas Park, a "no-man's land" that divided the two ethnic communities. Hoodlums and other tough Jews organized gangs euphemistically called "social and basement clubs" to retaliate against Poles and other enemies. One day in 1921, the equilibrium at Douglas Park was upset when Jewish boys playing baseball were attacked by a gang of Polish lads. The news spread rapidly to the nearby poolrooms, and Jewish reinforcements quickly arrived, eager to "wallop the Polock." Such defenders of the community, like the Miller brothers' gang (one-fourth of whom were boxers) and gangsters like "Nails" Morton, became local heroes in such confrontations. Street fighters who acquitted themselves well in such confrontations might be encouraged by friends or interested observers to learn the formal art of boxing at neighborhood gyms or settlement houses.[36]

---

35. Computed from the names of champions in Bert R. Sugar, ed., *Ring Record Book and Boxing Encyclopedia* (New York, 1981). For Sullivan's life, see Michael T. Isenberg, *John L. Sullivan and His America* (Urbana, IL, 1988); on the elite Irish and Sullivan, see Hardy, *How Boston Played*, pp. 174-175.

36. Thrasher, *Gang*, pp. 133-34, 138; Riess, "Jewish-American Boxing," pp. 225-47; Mark Haller, "Organized Crime in Urban Society: Chicago in the Twentieth Century," *Journal of Social History* 5 (Winter 1971-72), 221-27.

Second-generation newcomers achieved a good deal of quick success in the prize ring. The first Jewish-American world champion was bantamweight Harry Harris, a Chicagoan of English extraction who won his crown in 1901, shortly followed by Abe Attell of San Francisco, a Russian Jew who was featherweight champion from 1901 to 1912. In the 1910s the number of Jewish champions was exceeded only by the Irish. The first Polish champion was middleweight Stanley Ketchell (1908-11), and the first Italian titlist was bantamweight Pete Herman (1917-20), a generation before either group would have a major-league batting champion. Furthermore, Italian fighters in the mid-1910s were third in the number of contenders after the Irish and Germans. Most of the prize fighters of Italian and eastern European stock were small and slightly built, as were most of their fellow countrymen, and they found their niche in the lower weight classifications. During the 1920s and 1930s there were twenty-four Italian-American and fifteen Jewish-American champions. More contenders in the late 1920s were Jewish than any other group; they were superseded by the Italians in the mid-1930s. However, neither group approached the prominence in the sport that the Irish had earlier achieved.[37]

Ethnic boxers became popular heroes among the second generation, and even the immigrants who normally frowned on boxing were proud when their youths won championships and proved the courage and manliness of their people. In the 1930s, Jews on the West Side of Chicago and all across the country felt such a pride for Barney Ross, just as Italians did for Tony Canzoneri. Ross, like many second-generation fighters, strongly identified himself with his ethnic heritage and wore a Star of David on his trunks. When Ross was a rising amateur, his neighbors followed him all over Chicago to cheer him on, and they glowed with pride when he turned professional and went on to win world championships in the lightweight (1932) and welterweight (1934) divisions. Ross and other Jewish pugilists usually drew opponents who were Irish or Italian whenever possible, because promoters knew that such ethnic rivalries generated enormous excitement and helped attract large crowds.[38]

---

37. Champions and their ethnicity drawn from Sugar, *Ring Record Book*. On ethnic succession in prize fighting, see Thomas H. Jenkins, "Changes in Ethnic and Racial Representation among Professional Boxers: A Study in Ethnic Succession" (M.A. thesis, University of Chicago, 1951), esp. pp. 85-89. On Jewish-American prize fighters, see Riess, "Jewish American Boxing," pp. 223-47; William M. Kramer and Norton B. Stern, "San Francisco's Fighting Jew," *California History* 53 (Winter 1974), 333-345; Postal, *Jews in Sports*, pp. 144-180. The Eastern European Jews were building on a boxing tradition that dated back to London's West End ghetto in the late eighteenth century. See John Ford, *Prizefighting: The Age of Regency Boximania* (New York, 1972); Todd Endelman, *The Jews of Georgian England, 1714-1830: Tradition and Change in a Liberal Society* (Philadelphia, 1979). On Italian pugilists, see Frederick G. Lieb, "The Italian in Sport," *Ring* 2 (March 1924), 16-17.

38. See, e.g., Jewish *Daily Forward*, 25 Feb. 1925, quoted in Wirth, *The Ghetto*, pp. 252-253; Barney Ross and Martin Abrahamson, *No Man Stands Alone: The True Story of Barney Ross* (Philadelphia, 1957).

Still a Champ

An ethnic representative of Chicago's Westside Jewish-American district, Barney Ross with a Star of David emblem on his trunks slugged his way to a world championship. Courtesy of Steve A. Riess.

Boxing was an enormously popular sport during the Depression. Neighborhood gyms and small boxing clubs were kept busy as thousands of young men tried to become professional boxers. They were drawn by the glamor and the large purses won by champions like Barney Ross, who earned $500,000 in the ring. But even the modest winnings of amateurs, who sold the medals they won for five or ten dollars, or professionals who fought preliminaries for fifty dollars were attractive. There were about 8,000 professional boxers in the 1930s, although only a fraction of them ever became contenders. Boxing was the most democratic American sport, open to talented athletes regardless of size or ethnicity; and presuming one had capable and well-connected management, success was based solely on merit.[39]

Former fighters fared worse than any other professional athletes after retirement, even though champions earned more money more quickly than any other athlete. Titlists like Barney Ross and Joe Louis made huge amounts of money but ended up broke because of fast living, gambling debts, and crooked management. Boxers came from poor backgrounds, did not understand the need to save for the future, and thus indulged in some of the worst cases of conspicuous consumption when the money was rolling in. Most boxers, of course, did not make the big money. Between 1938 and 1951, just 7.1 percent of a sample of 127 fighters achieved national recognition, and 8.7 percent became local headliners. The rest (84.2 percent) never advanced beyond semi-windup or preliminary matches. Boxers rarely left the ring prepared for retirement, having saved little of their earnings, having few marketable skills and little if any education, and being, more than likely, at least mildly punch-drunk (60 percent).[40]

African-American Sports

The sporting options of black urban residents were influenced not only by such factors as class, culture, and space, of course, but also by their race. At the turn of the century, most urban blacks lived in southern cities. They comprised the majority in Charleston and Savannah, nearly half of Memphis, and two-fifths of Atlanta, Birmingham, Charlotte, Nashville, and Richmond. Unlike the European immigrants, blacks were completely familiar with and actively involved in the American sporting culture. However, in the post-Reconstruction South, their athletic experiences were totally segregated, either by law or custom. Black athletes could not compete with whites, and seating at commercial spec-

39. Ross and Abrahamson, *No Man Stands Alone*, pp. 141, 159.

40. S. Kirson Weinberg and Henry Arond, "Occupational Culture of the Boxer," *American Journal of Sociology* 57 (Mar. 1952), 460-61, 465, 469; see also Nathan Hare, "A Study of the Black Fighter," *Black Scholar* 3 (Nov. 1971), 2-8.

tator sports like horse racing and baseball was segregated. The black sporting life was, by necessity, centered within black neighborhoods. Black communities in larger cities supported at least two black baseball clubs, while fraternal organizations, churches, and politicians organized picnic games at black-owned fairgrounds or in black sections of municipal parks.[41]

At the turn of the century, black populations in northern cities were rather small — 15,000 in Chicago, for example — but beginning in 1916 large numbers of blacks migrated north to escape racial violence, get better jobs, secure civil rights, and enjoy a more sophisticated lifestyle. Black populations in industrial cities in the North doubled in a decade; by 1920, Chicago had more than 100,000 black residents. Consequently, black ghettoes fostered an enormous development and expansion of black social and cultural institutions in segregated settings.

Although black amateurs were usually able to compete against whites, black athletes in northern cities encountered considerable discrimination. Like the Irish and the new immigrants, black athletes had to form many of their own sports clubs, which ranged from track and field and baseball to cycling, because white status and ethnic clubs would not admit them. Black athletic associations themselves sorted out individuals by class or origin, just as white clubs did.[42] Black access to semipublic and public sports facilities was limited by expense, discretionary time, accessibility, and discrimination. In the late nineteenth century, separate black YMCA's were established in several cities; as early as 1889, black community leaders in Chicago considered establishing a separate black branch, but integrationist sentiment at the time defeated the proposal. After the turn of the century, white hostility to blacks in the Y movement became so sharp that they were virtually shut out. As a result, prominent black Chicagoans in 1910 initiated a campaign for a Y in their own neighborhood. The building was completed three years later at a cost of $190,000, with generous contributions from philanthropist Julius Rosenwald and various local meatpackers and industrialists, who further demonstrated their concern by purchasing memberships for their black employees.[43]

Black or integrated teams that traveled outside the growing black neighborhoods to play white teams in white neighborhoods often encountered rough

41. David Goldfield and Blaine Brownell, *Urban America: From Downtown to No Town* (Boston, 1979), p. 260; Howard Rabinowitz, *Race Relations in the Urban South, 1865-1890* (Urbana, Ill., 1980), pp. 185, 187, 189-190, 389n, 30, 228-230.

42. Hardy, *How Boston Played*, pp. 138, 153; Brooklyn *Eagle*, 5 May 1894; New York *Times*, 18 Oct. 1914, 14 Aug. 1917. For a detailed study of sports in one black community, see Rob Ruck, *Sandlot Seasons: Sport in Black Pittsburgh* (Urbana, Ill., 1987).

43. C. Howard Hopkins, *The History of the Y.M.C.A. in North America* (New York, 1951), pp. 213, 472; David M. Katzman, *Before the Ghetto: Black Detroit in the Nineteenth Century* (Urbana, Ill., 1973), pp. 79, 161; W. E. Du Bois, *The Philadelphia Negro: A Social Study* (1899; rep. New York, 1967), p. 232; Kenneth L. Kusmer, *A Ghetto Takes Shape: Black Cleveland, 1870-1930* (Urbana, Ill., 1976), pp. 50-58; Spear, *Black Chicago*, pp. 46-47, 52, 100-101, 162, 174, 227.

treatment on the playing field and even tougher situations off the field. In the 1910s, when an integrated Chicago basketball team went to play in a white section, trouble often followed: "On the way over here fellows on the outside bailed them out, but our fellows sure got them on the way home. There were three black fellows on the team and those three got just about laid out. Our team wouldn't play them, so there was a great old row. Then, when they went home some of our boys were waiting for them to come out of the building to give them a chase. The coons were afraid to come out, so policemen had to be called to take them to the car line. The white fellows weren't hurt any, but the coons got some bricks."[44]

Boxing

The most popular spectator sports in the black community were prize fighting and baseball. Although black fighters encountered less discrimination than other black athletes — which reflected the low status of the sport — they were subject to terribly abusive language from white fans. At a time when black professional athletes were being forced out of thoroughbred racing, cycling, and organized baseball, blacks were achieving considerable renown in the prize ring. Between 1890 and 1908 there were five black world champions, though many prominent contenders never even got title matches because champions like John L. Sullivan drew the color line.[45]

Top black fighters usually lived in Northern black communities, where they would be treated with respect, could get more fights, found opportunities for investment in businesses, such as Jack Johnson's Café de Champion (a cabaret in Chicago's black belt), and enjoyed the pleasures of the demi-monde. In working-class black communities, black pugilists were heroes and had such a wide following that a historian discovered that "black attendance at boxing matches outdrew the Sunday sermon." Black fans preferred to see mixed bouts in which their idols could win symbolic racial victories, but local customs or city and state laws often restricted interracial contests for fear of fomenting racial antagonisms. Immediately after Jack Johnson successfully defended his heavyweight crown on July 4, 1910, against former champion Jim Jeffries, "the Great White Hope," there were racial conflicts in cities across the country. Many

---

44. Chicago Commission on Race Relations, *Negro in Chicago*, p. 253.

45. See, e.g., Riess, *Touching Base*, pp. 194-196, 217n, 124; Robert Peterson, *Only the Ball Was White* (Englewood Cliffs, N.J., 1970), chaps. 1, 2; Marshall W. Taylor, *The Fastest Bicycle Rider in the World* (Worcestor, Mass., 1928); David K. Wiggins, "Issac Murphy: Black Hero in Nineteenth-Century American Sport, 1861-1896," *Canadian Journal of History of Sport and Physical Education* 10 (May 1979), 15-32; *idem*, "Peter Jackson and the Elusive Heavyweight Championship: A Black Athlete's Struggle against the Late-Nineteenth Century Color Line," *Journal of Sport History* 12 (Summer 1985), 143-168; Randy Roberts, *Papa Jack: Jack Johnson and the Era of White Hope* (New York, 1983); Al-Tony Gilmore, *Bad Nigger! The National Impact of Jack Johnson* (Port Washington, NY, 1975).

communities subsequently barred exhibitors from showing films of the fight for fear of generating more incidents.[46]

Over the next several decades, boxing continued to attract black interest because it was the only democratic professional sport. One expert estimated that there were as many as 1,800 black pros during the 1930s. Like their white peers, they were attracted by the opportunity to make a name for themselves, earn a living, escape the ghetto, and perhaps get rich. At a time when no other major professional sport was open to blacks, African-American pugilists were achieving great success. The 1930s produced five black champions, including Henry Armstrong, who won three different titles, and Joe Louis, the first black to fight for the heavyweight championship since Jack Johnson. Champion from 1937 to 1949, Louis represented to white America what the ideal Negro should be; but to his own community, Louis symbolized black power, racial pride, and an insistence that blacks be accepted in American society. He was a role model for ghetto youths like Malcolm Little (Malcolm X), who became an amateur fighter. His victories were received with great glee in Northern black communities, where thousands took to the streets to celebrate, deriving, as Lena Horne remembered, "all the joy possible from this collective victory of the race."[47]

Blacks quickly achieved dominance in the ring. By 1948, nearly half of all contenders were black — a reflection of both widespread black poverty and the success of role models like Joe Louis. Italians were second in the number of contenders, and Mexican-Americans, a new group to achieve prominence in boxing, third.[48] The ethnic succession in the ring reflected the changing racial and ethnic complexion of the inner city as older ethnic groups who were doing better economically moved out and were replaced by the new urban poor. This dynamic was epitomized by the absence of Jewish fighters from the lists of contenders: Jews had formerly dominated the sport, but as they became better educated or succeeded as entrepreneurs, they moved to the urban periphery or the suburbs. They no longer needed to get their brains knocked out to make a living.

46. Elizabeth Pleck, "Black Migration to Boston in the Late Nineteenth Century" (Ph.D. diss., Brandeis University, 1974), p. 188 (quote). (My thanks to Stephen Hardy for bringing this to my attention.) Roberts, *Papa Jack*, chaps. 5, 7-9; Gilmore, *Bad Nigger!* chaps. 5-6; New York *Times*, 6, 9, 10-12, 14, 17 July 1910; "The Prize Fight Moving Pictures," *Outlook* 95 (16 July 1910), 541-542. Mixed bouts were barred in New York from 1912 to 1916. See, e.g., New York *Times*, 29 Dec. 1911, 7 Jan. 1912, 6 June 1915, 17 Jan., 18 Feb. 1916; *National Police Gazette* 103 (6 Sept. 1913), 10; 107 (12 Feb. 1916), 10; 108 (1 Apr. 1916), 10; "Smith-Langford Cancelled," *Boxing and Sporting World* 1 (4 Oct. 1913), 4; New York *World*, 17 Jan., 29 June, 7, 8, 11, 12 July, 8 Aug. 1916.

47. On white attitudes toward Louis, see Anthony Edmonds, *Joe Louis* (Grand Rapids, 1972), chaps. 4-6; Frederick C. Jaher, "White America Views Jack Johnson, Joe Louis and Muhammed Ali," in *Sport in America: New Historical Perspectives*, Donald Spivey, ed. (Westport, CT, 1985), pp. 158-73, 177-82. For black attitudes, see Lawrence W. Levine, *Black Culture and Black Consciousness: Afro-American Folk Thought from Slavery to Freedom* (New York, 1977), 433-38. Quote is from Lena Horne and Richard Schickel, *Lena* (Garden City, NY, 1965), p. 75.

48. In the late 1940s, boxers were typically ex-street fighters, often from broken homes, with unemployed fathers. Weinberg and Arond, "Occupational Culture," p. 460.

Basketball: The Ghetto Game

Class and environment — the main reasons that blacks achieved ethnic success in boxing — are also the primary factors behind current black dominance in professional basketball (75 percent of the National Basketball Association in 1980). Professional ballplayers had always been disproportionately urban, particularly from major cities, and that pattern still holds. In the 1960s and 1970s nearly all NBA players (91.3 percent) were urban; and nearly half were from *large* cities (49.5 percent), usually from the inner city, where boys did not have much money or many constructive alternatives for their free time other than sports.[49] Over the past thirty years, basketball has been the major athletic passion of black ghetto youth, as it had once been for Jewish, German, and Irish youth. As Pete Axthelm pointed out a few years ago, "Other young athletes may learn basketball, but (inner) city kids live it." The playground is their heaven, wrote journalist Rick Telander, where city youths study the moves of their heroes, develop their own, and try to make a reputation for themselves. They practice diligently for hours a day, all year long, motivated by the immediate gratification of prestige at neighborhood courts and the longer-term goals of starring in high school, getting a college scholarship, and ending up in the NBA. This, of course, is a pipe dream, since only 4 percent of high school players are good enough to play in college, much less the NBA. Unlike earlier cohorts of inner-city basketball players, the latest generation devoted *all* their attention to their game and little to their brain, with the result that even if they excelled in college basketball and achieved a degree of fame, there was a strong chance they would end up right back in the ghetto where they had started.[50]

Baseball in the Urban Black Community

Baseball was originally the most important sport in the black communities. Unlike the immigrants from overseas, rural black migrants were very familiar with the national pastime. Until 1898, when blacks were barred from organized baseball by a common understanding among racist owners, there had been about fifty professional black ballplayers, including two in the majors in 1884.

49. Computed from Ronald L. Mendell, *Who's Who in Basketball* (New Rochelle, NY, 1973); see also John F. Rooney, Jr., *A Geography of American Sports: From Cabin Creek to Anaheim* (Reading, MA, 1974), pp. 154-174. Between 1946 and 1983, two-thirds of all college All-Americans (Division I) came from metropolitan areas with over 500,000 residents at a time when those cities comprised just half (49.5 percent) of the national population. New York produced the most (13.5 percent), followed by Chicago (6.3 percent), Philadelphia, and Los Angeles (3.8 percent each). In 1970 they were the leading procurer of Division I players, with ratios approximately equal to their share of the national population (Chicago *Sun-Times*, 13 Dec. 1983).

50. Pete Axthelm, *The City Game* (New York, 1970), pp. ix-x, book iii; Rick Telander, *Heaven Is a Playground* (New York, 1976).

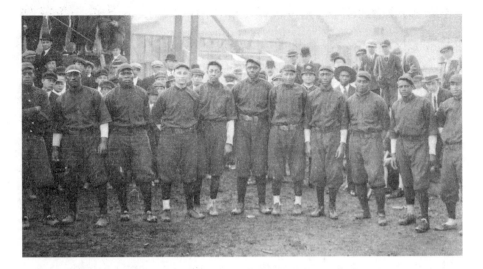

Chicago's Negro Union Giants baseball team lining up to play Milwaukee's Polish Kosiusko Reds about 1911. Courtesy of Golda Meir Library Special Collections, Milwaukee.

Blacks responded to being shunned by forming their own professional teams. By 1900 there were five salaried black teams, including two in Chicago despite the small size of its black community. The Unions, first organized in 1886, became professionals in 1896, playing in Chicago on Sundays when their fans were off work, and touring local towns during the week. Manager Frank Leland left in 1902 to form the Union Giants (renamed the Leland Giants in 1904), which were owned by Robert R. Jackson and Beauregard F. Moseley, local black politicians. The club played at Auburn Park (79th and Wentworth), where general admission was 25 cents; boys got in for 15 cents.[51]

In 1906, former Union and Leland Giant pitcher Rube Foster was recruited by the Philadelphia Giants to be player-manager, and he brought along with him most of his teammates. They won the city semipro championship, and in 1907 they joined the all-white City League, the finest semiprofessional association in the United States, amassing an overall record of 110-10. The Leland Giants won the league championship in 1908 and were, in a description in the *Spalding Baseball Guide,* "as good as the Major Leagues." The team drew crowds

51. The standard history of black baseball is Peterson, *Only the Ball Was White,* esp. chaps. 2-3; see also Bruce Chadwick, *When the Game Was Black and White: The Illustrated History of the Negro Leagues* (New York, 1992). On black baseball in Chicago, see Peterson, *Only the Ball Was White,* pp. 62-66; Spear, *Black Chicago,* pp. 79, 117-18. The Leland Giants Baseball and Amusement Association also owned the well-known Chateau de la Plaisance, a combination dance hall and skating rink. In 1910 Moseley tried to organize a National Negro Baseball League, but had no success. See *ibid.,* 118.

of up to 15,000, and in 1909 played a three-game post-season series with the Cubs, one of the first between blacks and major leaguers. The Cubs swept the series, but the Giants acquitted themselves well, losing two of the games by just one run. In 1910 there were three black nines, a touring Union Giants, the Leland Giants (now controlled by Rube Foster), and the Giants, established by Frank Leland after he had been deposed from his old team. Foster's club played at its owners' Normal Park (69th and Halsted) one season. In 1911, Foster renamed the team the American Giants, and with partner tavernkeeper John M. Schorling, son-in-law of Charles Comiskey, relocated to the recently abandoned White Sox field at 39th and Shields, across the street from the growing Black Belt. The club had a record of 123-6, and was so popular that one Sunday in 1911 it drew 11,000 fans, surpassing both the Sox and Cubs, who were both in town that day. The Giants won consecutive city championships in 1911 and 1912, with Foster serving as the league's booking agent. His Giants became a symbol of pride in the community, and Robert Abbott of the *Defender* urged "all race loving and race building men and women" to support it.[52]

The success of black baseball was strongly influenced by the Great Migration north during the mid-1910s because it created greater opportunities for African-American businessmen. Most black teams up to that time were owned by white entrepreneurs who scheduled games and rented ballparks. Black journalists deplored these conditions, urging that profits "should be received by the Race to whom the patrons of the game belong." After World War I, Rube Foster, sole owner of the Chicago American Giants since 1916, initiated a movement to wrest control of black baseball from white promoters and put it into the hands of black entrepreneurs. Foster believed that the growing black urban communities provided a potential market for a top-flight Negro league, and he also argued that since all players and two-thirds of the spectators were black, the profits should remain with the race.[53]

In 1920, Foster organized the Negro National League (NNL), with eight mainly Midwestern franchises, all but one of which were owned and operated by black businessmen. NNL teams played from forty to eighty league contests and a total of about 200 games a year, including exhibitions. Tickets cost 25 cents. Negro League historian Robert Peterson estimates that weekend crowds exceeded 5,000, but the average attendance was only about one-third of that.

52. Spear, *Black Chicago*, pp. 117-118; John B. Holway, *Blackball Stars: Negro League Pioneers* (Westport, CT, 1988), pp. 13-17; *Spalding's Official Baseball Guide of Chicago 1906 . . . 1910* (New York, 1906-1910); (Chicago) *Broad Ax*, 30 Apr., 14 May, 6, 27, 1910; *Chicago Defender*, 12 Dec. 1908; 4 Mar., 23 Apr., 11, 25 June, 23 July 1910; 20 Feb. 1915; *Chicago Daily News*, 10 Jan. 1910; *New York Age*, 14 Apr., 5 May, 21 July 1910; 5 Jan. 1911; Chadwick, *When the Game Was Black and White*, pp. 31-33; Peterson, *Only the Ball Was White*, p. 66 (quote). On Rube Foster, see Charles E. Whitehead, *A Man and His Diamonds* (New York, 1980); and John Holway, "Rube Foster: The Father of Black Baseball," in his *Blackball Stars.*

53. Riess, *Touching Base*, pp. 38, 196-97; Peterson, *Only the Ball Was White*, p. 257.

Although the league was highly regarded by the black press and urban fans, it struggled financially and lasted through twelve shaky seasons. Of the original eight teams, only the American Giants lasted from start to finish in 1931. Two years later, a second Negro National League was established by numbers bankers, one of the few lucrative, albeit illegal occupations in African-American neighborhoods during the Depression.[54]

Negro League teams in the era between the wars were prominent community institutions, and cities without NNL franchises were regarded as second rate. Opening-day games became important public rituals, embellished with such ceremonies as pregame parades or the throwing out of the first ball by celebrities like Lena Horne or politicians like Congressman William Dawson of Chicago. Fans dressed up for opening day, and according to historian W. Donn Rogosin, "society pages of the black newspaper gushed with baseball stories that suggested opening day's importance for a culture with limited opportunities to partake in American tradition." Games during the season were part of community activities ranging from beauty contests to "Stop Lynching" campaigns.[55]

The biggest event in black baseball — and the single most important sporting event in the black community outside of Joe Louis's fights — was the annual East-West All Star Game. In 1893, Gus Greenlee initiated this black all-star game in Chicago. The event never drew fewer than 20,000 spectators, with a top of over 51,000 for the 1943 game at Comiskey Park, where most of the games were played. The ballpark was located across the street from one of the most important black communities in the United States. Fans from all social backgrounds, including out-of-town tourists, flocked to the field. The game became a highlight in the social calendar of the black elite, who sat in expensive $1.50 seats, where everybody could see them.[56]

Ironically, at the same time that the Negro leagues reached their height of popularity, a major movement had developed to integrate organized baseball, which eventually meant the end of the Negro leagues. Black sportswriters, civil-rights organizations, and left-wing political groups made the integration of baseball a political issue. The first to play major-league baseball was Jackie Robinson, and his courage, perseverance, outstanding play, and "class" made him a great hero in black communities, his exploits front-page news in the black press. As Branch Rickey had hoped, Robinson's presence in the Brooklyn Dodgers lineup had a positive impact on black attendance, which had previously been limited. During his rookie season in 1947, black Kansas Citians took a five-hour train ride to St. Louis, traveling under Jim Crow conditions, to see

54. Foster's team averaged $85,000 in gate receipts in each of its first six NNL seasons, but the other clubs took in as little as $10,000. Peterson, *Only the Ball Was White*, pp. 86, 89, 90, 114-115; W. Donn Rogosin, *Invisible Men: Life in Baseball's Negro Leagues* (Boston, 1983), pp. 14-17, 103-108, 213.

55. *Ibid.*, pp. 14-17, 22-23, 93-94.

56. *Ibid.*, pp. 25-26.

Jackie play in segregated Sportsman's Park. When Robinson made his first appearance at Wrigley Field, he drew a record crowd of 46,000. Thousands of blacks attended, wearing their best Sunday clothes. At the time blacks were almost never seen on the North Side, and as Chicago journalist Mike Royko remembered, "It was probably the first time . . . (blacks and whites) had been so close to each other in such large numbers."[57]

The integration of baseball, a slow and torturous process, was not completed on the major-league level until the late 1950s. The worst abuses of black athletes and spectators did not end until the civil-rights demonstrations and economic boycotts of the 1960s and the implementation of federal civil-rights legislation. Professional baseball was one of the first American institutions to accept blacks on virtually equal terms, an important symbolic achievement because baseball is the national pastime. The process of integration had a significant impact on black urban life, promoting racial pride, securing grudging respect from white fans, and demonstrating a potential for future gains in race relations.[58]

Conclusion: Sport, Race, and Ethnicity in the American City

The sporting culture of urban ethnic groups was a product of their cultural heritage, social class, and of discrimination. Yet while these variables affected all groups, some were more important for different categories of ethnic cohorts than others: the Old World heritage for the European immigrant, economics for second-generation white ethnics, and racism for blacks. The old immigrants brought over a sporting tradition that remained a vital part of their cultural life in America. However, the new immigrants had little if any athletic heritage, and sports did not have much of an appeal to these newcomers. Sports played a prominent role among all second-generation immigrant groups, serving as a major step toward assimilation. Success in sports was a means of disproving negative ethnic stereotypes and gaining respect from the outside community. Athletic accomplishments were a source of ethnic pride, they cemented social relationships among street-corner youths, and they provided a potential vehicle for social mobility.

Black urbanites, completely familiar with the American sporting culture, still faced severe limitations because of classism and racism. Nonetheless, sports were of crucial significance in black communities for recreation and other social purposes. Urban blacks, less successful at building their local institutions than were the European immigrants, used sports, along with the church, press, and politics, to develop a sense of community in their neighborhoods.

57. Jules Tygiel, *Baseball's Great Experiment: Jackie Robinson and His Legacy* (New York, 1983), pp. 40-41; Rogosin, *Invisible Men*, p. 218. Quote is from *Chicago Daily News*, 26 Oct. 1972, cited in Tygiel, *Baseball's Great Experiment*, p. 196.
58. Tygiel, *Baseball's Great Experiment*, pp. 265-284, 305, 311-319, 343-344.

CHAPTER 19

Ethnic Crime: The Organized Underworld of Early 20th Century Chicago

MARK H. HALLER

For 26 years I lived in West Side 'Little Italy,' the community that has produced more underworld limelights than any other in Chicago. . . . Since then I have seen many of my playmates shoot their way to the top of gangdom and seen others taken for a ride.

— anonymous University of Chicago student, 1934

In America's major cities, like Chicago, an organized underworld had emerged by the late nineteenth century. Central to the organized underworld were those who provided illegal goods and services to customers. They included the backers of policy gambling syndicates, the organizers of sports bookmaking, the madams and vice entrepreneurs within the city's lively red-light entertainment districts, along with the rising bootleggers of the 1920s. Often the city's labor racketeers and career thieves had multiple links to the criminal entrepreneurs.[1] One way to understand the organized underworld is to explore the various ways that the underworld was rooted in the experiences and structure of the city's neighborhoods and ethnic groups.[2] There were at least three interrelated aspects that might be examined: first, the importance of the underworld in providing

---

1. This is a considerably revised version of an article that first appeared as "Organized Crime in Urban Society: Chicago in the Twentieth Century," *Journal of Social History* 5 (Winter 1971-72), 210-234.

2. The following are useful historical studies analyzing the relationship of crime to the social structure of the city: John Landesco, *Organized Crime in Chicago*, 2nd ed. (Chicago, 1968); St. Clair Drake and Horace R. Cayton, *Black Metropolis: A Study of Negro Life in a Northern City* (New York, 1945), II, esp. chaps. 17 and 19; William F. Whyte, *Street Corner Society: The Social Structure of an Italian Slum*, 2nd ed. (Chicago, 1955), chaps. 4 and 5; Daniel Bell, "Crime as an American Way of Life: A Queer Ladder of Mobility," *The End of Ideology*, rev. ed. (New York, 1961), chap. 7; and Humbert S. Nelli, *The Italians in Chicago, 1880-1930: A Study in Ethnic Mobility* (New York, 1970), chap. 5 and pp. 210-222.

social mobility for immigrants and their children; second, the diverse patterns by which different ethnic groups became involved in criminal activities; and third, the broad and pervasive economic and social impact of the organized underworld on many of the city's working-class and ethnic neighborhoods.

Crime and Mobility

During the period of heavy immigrant movement into the cities of the Northeast and Midwest, criminal enterprises and racketeering provided paths of upward mobility for many young men raised in ethnic slums. The gambling entrepreneurs, vice promoters, bootleggers, and racketeers often began their careers in the ghetto neighborhoods; and frequently these neighborhoods continued to be the centers for their entrepreneurial activities. One study of the leaders of Chicago's underworld in the late 1920s found that 31 percent were of Italian background, 29 percent of Irish background, 20 percent Jewish, and 12 percent black. None were native whites of native white parents.[3] A recognition of the ethnic roots of criminal activities, however, is only a starting point for understanding their relationship to ethnic mobility.

At the risk of oversimplification, it can be said that three paths lay open to young persons from ethnic neighborhoods. The vast majority became, to use the Chicago argot, "poor working stiffs." They toiled in the factories, filled menial service and clerical jobs, or opened mom-and-pop stores. Their mobility to better jobs was, at best, incremental. A second, considerably smaller, group followed respectable paths to relative success. Some of this group went to college and entered the professions; others rose to management positions in the business or governmental hierarchies of the cities. There existed, however, a third group of interrelated occupations which, although often not regarded as respectable, were open to uneducated and ambitious ethnic youths. Crime was one such occupational world, but there were others.

One was local machine politics. Many scholars have, of course, recognized the function of politics in providing mobility for some members of ethnic groups.[4] In local politics, a person's ethnic background was often an advantage

---

3. William F. Ogburn and Clark Tibbitts, "A Memorandum on the Nativity of Certain Criminal Classes Engaged in Organized Crime and of Certain Related Criminal and Non-Criminal Groups in Chicago" (Unpubl. ms., July 30, 1930), pp. 9-11, in Charles E. Merriam papers, Univ. of Chicago Library, Chicago, IL.

4. For general discussion of urban politics and ethnic mobility, see Harold Zink, *City Bosses in the United States: A Study of Twenty Municipal Bosses* (Durham, NC, 1930); Robert K. Merton, *Social Theory and Social Structure* (Glencoe, IL, 1957), esp. pp. 71-72; and Eric L. McKitrick, "The Study of Corruption," *Political Science Quarterly* 72 (Dec. 1957), 505-506. For specific reference to Chicago, see Joel A. Tarr, "The Urban Politician as Entrepreneur," *Mid-America* 49 (Jan. 1967), 55-67; and Harold F. Gosnell, *Machine Politics, Chicago Model*, 2nd ed. (Chicago, 1968), esp. chap. 3.

rather than a liability. Neighborhood roots could be the basis for a career that might lead from poverty to great local power, considerable wealth, or both.

A second area consisted of those businesses that prospered through political friendships and contacts. Obviously, construction companies that built the city streets and buildings relied on government contracts. But so did banks in which government funds were deposited, insurance companies that insured government facilities, as well as garbage contractors, traction companies, and utilities that sought city franchises. Because political contacts were important, local ethnic politicians and their friends were often the major backers of such enterprises.[5]

A third avenue of success was through leadership in the city's labor unions. The Irish in Chicago dominated the building trade unions and most of the other craft unions during the first twenty-five years of this century. But persons of other ethnic origins could also rise to leadership positions, especially in those unions in which their own ethnic group predominated.[6]

Another path of mobility was sports. Boxing, a peculiarly urban sport rooted in the neighborhood gymnasiums, was the most obvious example of a sport in which Irish champions were succeeded by Jewish, Polish, and black champions. Many a fighter, even if he did not slug his way to national prominence, could achieve considerable local fame within his neighborhood or ethnic group. He might then translate that local fame into success by becoming a fight manager, saloon keeper, politician, or racketeer.[7]

A fifth area often dominated by immigrants was the entertainment and night life industry of the city. In Chicago, immigrants — primarily Irish and Germans — ran the city's saloons by the turn of the century. During the 1920s, Greek businessmen operated most of the taxi-dance halls. Restaurants, cabarets, and other nightspots were similarly operated by persons from various ethnic groups. Night life also provided careers for entertainers, including bar girls, singers, comedians, vaudeville performers, and jazz musicians. Jewish comedians of the 1930s and black comedians of our own day are only examples of a larger phenomenon in which entertainment could lead to local and even national recognition.[8]

---

5. For example, Joel A. Tarr, "J. R. Walsh of Chicago: A Case Study in Banking and Politics, 1881-1905," *The Business History Review* 40 (Winter 1966), 451-466.

6. Royal E. Montgomery, *Industrial Relations in the Chicago Building Trades* (Chicago, 1927); Italian involvement in labor leadership discussed in Nelli, *Italians in Chicago.*

7. For a general depiction of sports in the city, see Steven A. Reiss, *City Games: The Evolution of American Urban Society and the Rise of Sports* (Urbana & Chicago, 1989).

8. Backgrounds of saloonkeepers from *History of Chicago and Souvenir of the Liquor Interest* (Chicago [1892]), pp. 136-254; concerning Greek ownership of taxi-dance halls, see Paul G. Cressey, "Report on Summer's Work with the Juvenile Protective Association of Chicago" (typewritten paper, Oct. 1925), in Ernest W. Burgess papers, Univ. of Chicago Library. Jewish comedians of the 1930s included Bert Lahr, Fannie Brice (who married Nicky Arnstein, a gambler and con man), Eddie Cantor, George Jessel, Groucho Marx, Willie Howard, and Jack Pearl; see review in *New York Times Book Review* (Nov. 23, 1969), p. 1. For an interesting general discussion of the intersection

The organized underworld of the city, then, was not the only area of urban life that provided opportunities for ambitious young men from the ghettos.

Ethnic Specialization

Some have suggested that each ethnic group, in its turn, took to crime as part of the early adjustment to American urban life.[9] While there is some truth to such a generalization, the generalization obscures more than it illuminates ethnic experiences and the structure of crime. In important respects, each ethnic group was characterized by different patterns of adjustment; and the patterns of involvement in the organized underworld often reflected the broader patterns by which each ethnic group struggled to find a niche within the larger society. Some ethnic groups — Germans and Scandinavians, for instance — appear not to have made significant contributions to the development of the underworld. Among the ethnic groups that did contribute, there was specialization within crime that reflected the group's assimilation to American urban life.

In Chicago, by the turn of the century, for example, the Irish predominated in two areas of crime. One was labor racketeering, which derived from the importance of the Irish as leaders of organized labor in general.[10] The second area was the operation of bookmaking and policy gambling syndicates. Irish importance in gambling reflected both their background in Ireland and the opportunities that they found in the New World. For the Irish peasants in Ireland, one of the few pleasures was to watch the British lords race their horses and to place bets on the outcome. Being selected as a jockey or a trainer was an opportunity for a poor Irish boy to escape from grinding poverty. Many of the Irish, then, arrived in America as lovers of the turf, and participation in horse racing seemed like the mark of gentlemanly achievement.[11]

Following the Civil War, thoroughbred racing in America rapidly became a national and urban sport and entered upon its golden years as the nation's most popular sporting activity. At the track and off-track, fans sought opportunities to bet on their favorites. The rise of horse racing came as the Irish and their children were seeking opportunity in their new homeland; in Chicago, as

of crime and entertainment, see Stephen Fox, *Blood and Power: Organized Crime in Twentieth-Century America* (New York, 1969), chap. 3.

9. Bell's "Crime as an American Way of Life" is often associated with this idea.

10. For discussions of Chicago labor racketeering, see Montgomery, *Industrial Relations, passim;* John Hutchinson, *The Imperfect Union: A History of Corruption in American Trade Unions* (New York, 1970), esp. chaps. 4 and 9; and the extensive correspondence in the Victor A. Olander papers, folders 115 and 266-268, in Library of the University of Illinois—Chicago.

11. Discussion of the Irish politics-gambling complex based primarily on Herman F. Schuettler, Scrapbook of Newspaper Clippings . . . 1904-1908, 2 vols, in Chicago Historical Society; see also Citizens' Association of Chicago, *Bulletin* No. 11 (July 31, 1903).

in many other cities, they were poised to seize the expanding opportunities to make betting possible. The first step was often the ownership of a saloon, from which the owner might move into both politics and gambling. Many Irish saloonkeepers ran horse betting or encouraged other forms of gambling in rooms located behind or over the saloon. Successful operators could become coordinators of bookmaking syndicates and back the betting in numerous neighborhood barbershops, pool halls, cigar stores, and newspaper kiosks.[12]

The Irish predominated in other areas of gambling as well. At the turn of the century, they were the major group in the syndicates that operated the policy games, each with hundreds of policy writers scattered in the slum neighborhoods to collect the nickels and dimes of the poor who dreamed of a lucky hit. They also outfitted many of the gambling houses in the Loop, which offered roulette, faro, poker, blackjack, craps, and other games of chance. Furthermore, many top police officers were Irish and rose through the ranks by attaching themselves to the various political factions of the city. Thus a complex system of Irish politicians, gamblers, and police shared in the profits of gambling, protected gambling interests, and built careers in the police department or city politics. Historians have long recognized the importance of the Irish in urban politics. In Chicago, at any rate, politics was only part of a larger Irish politics-gambling complex.

The Irish politics-gambling complex remained intact until about World War I. By the 1920s, however, the developing black ghetto allowed black politicians and policy operators to build independent gambling and political organizations linked to the Republicans in the 1920s and to the Democratic city machine in the 1930s. By the 1920s, in addition, Jewish gamblers became increasingly important, both in controlling gambling in Jewish neighborhoods and in operations elsewhere. Finally, by the mid-1920s, bootleggers under Capone took over gambling in suburban Cicero and invested in Chicago gambling operations. Gambling had become a complex mixture of Irish, black, Jewish, and Italian entrepreneurship.[13]

By the twentieth century, the Irish played little direct role in managing prostitution. Italians had moved into important positions in the vice districts by World War I, especially in the notorious Levee district on the South Side. (Political protection, of course, often had to be arranged through Irish political leaders.)[14] But just as the Irish blocked Italians in politics, they also blocked Italians in gambling, which was both more respectable and more profitable than prostitution. Hence, the importance of Prohibition in the 1920s lay not in

12. This and the next paragraph based on Haller, "Rise of Gambling Syndicates."

13. Development of gambling in the 1920s can best be followed in the extensive files of the Chicago Crime Commission, esp. file No. 65.

14. For descriptions of Italian involvement in South Side vice, see McPhaul, *Johnny Torrio*, pp. 69-155; Kobler, *Capone*, chaps. 3 and 4; and investigators' reports, Merriam papers, Boxes 87, 88.

initiating an organized underworld (gambling continued both before and after Prohibition to be the major enterprise within the underworld); rather, Prohibition provided Italians with an opportunity to break into a major field of criminal enterprise that was not already monopolized by the Irish.

This generalization, to some extent, oversimplifies what was in fact a complex process. At first, Prohibition opened up business opportunities for large numbers of individuals and groups, and the situation was chaotic; as a result, the ethnic backgrounds of the bootleggers were remarkably diverse. Some bootleggers were Irish, including one set of O'Donnell brothers on the far West Side and another set on the South Side. Southwest of the stockyards there was an important organization, both Polish and Irish, coordinated by "Pollack" Joe Saltis. And on the near North Side a major group — founded by burglars and hold-up men — was led by Irishmen like Dion O'Banion, Poles like Earl (Hymie) Weiss and George (Bugs) Moran, and Jews like Jack Zuta and the Gusenberg brothers. There were, finally, the various Italian gangs, including the Gennas and the Aiellos.[15]

The major bootlegging gang, the one associated with the name of Al Capone, was itself a diverse coalition. By 1925, there were four leading figures: Al Capone; his older brother, Ralph Capone; his cousin, Frank Nitti; and Jack Guzik, who was Jewish. They rapidly recruited partners to establish bootlegging activities in the Loop and in the suburbs south and west of the city. Very early, they worked closely with Irishmen like Frankie Lake and Terry Druggan in the brewing of beer; Jack Guzik offered his brother-in-law, Louis Lipschultz, a partnership in beer distribution in the western suburbs. The success of the partners brought worldwide fame to Capone, a media favorite, and earned wealth and notoriety for many ambitious men who worked with Capone and his partners. They commanded such resources that, in the late 1920s and 1930s, they moved into gambling, racketeering, and entertainment. As a result, they captured a central position in organized crime and provided a basis for the growing influence of Italians within the Chicago underworld.[16]

Jewish immigrants fleeing the rising discrimination and pogroms of Eastern

15. Many accounts of Chicago bootlegging concentrate on the Capone group; development of the other groups can be followed in the extensive files of the Chicago Crime Commission.

16. Of the many accounts of the rise of Capone and his partners, the best are Kobler, *Capone*, and McPhaul, *Johnny Torrio*; see also Fred D. Pasley, *Al Capone: The Biography of a Self-Made Man* (New York, 1930). For an analysis of the structure through which Capone and his partners operated, see Haller, "Illegal Enterprise: A Theoretical and Historical Interpretation," *Criminology* 28 (May 1990), 217-23. The movement of Capone associates into racketeering can be followed in the Olander papers, folders 266-268; a series of stories in the Chicago *Tribune*, March 19-27, 1943; Virgil W. Peterson, *Barbarians in Our Midst: A History of Chicago Crime and Criminal Justice* (Boston, 1952), chaps. 9-14; and Demaris, *Captive City*, pp. 22-29. Despite their success in crime, Italians did not displace the Irish from politics. In 1929, out of 99 ward committeemen in Chicago, 42 were Irish and only one was Italian; see Ogburn and Tibbitts, "Memorandum on Nativity," p. 45.

MAP 19.1

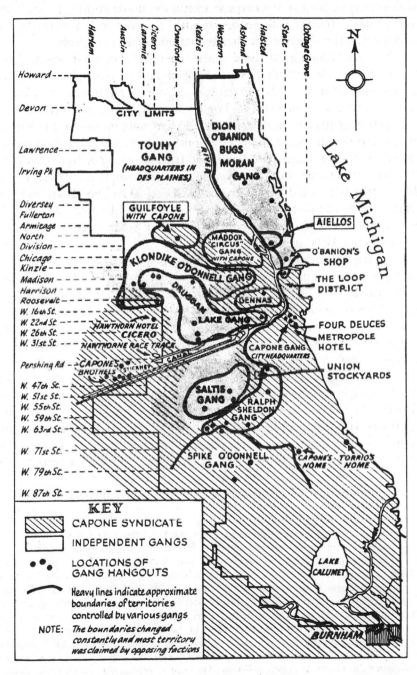

One of the divisions of Chicago into gangland "fiefs" during Prohibition times.
Courtesy of the Chicago Tribune.

Europe and Russia flocked to the United States at the turn of the century. Accustomed to seeking a living in peripheral activities in the cities and towns of their country of origin, some Jewish immigrants and their children found opportunities in the red-light districts of American cities. Indeed, in New York the appearance of Jewish madams and pimps triggered a flurry of anti-Semitic charges. By World War I, Chicago Jews had made important inroads into vice, especially in vice districts on the West Side. In the 1920s, with the dispersal of prostitution, several Jewish vice syndicates operated on the South and West Sides.[17]

In the 1920s, with the rise of bootlegging throughout the United States, persons of Jewish background became significant entrepreneurs. Nationally, they probably constituted half the leading bootleggers during the brief thirteen years of Prohibition. In cities like Philadelphia and Cleveland, for instance, they were the dominant ethnic group. In Chicago, despite the importance of Jack Guzik, who was Capone's partner, Jews played a less prominent role.[18]

Although Jews took part in Chicago's vice, gambling, and bootlegging, they made a special contribution to the underworld by providing professional or expert services. Even before World War I, Jews were becoming a majority of the bail bondsmen in the city. And by the 1920s, if not before, Jews constituted over half the fences who disposed of stolen goods. (This was, of course, closely related to Jewish predominance as junk dealers and their importance in retail selling.) Jews were also heavily overrepresented among defense attorneys in the criminal courts. The entrepreneurial and professional services of Jews clearly reflected broader patterns of Jewish adaptation to American urban life.[19]

Black achievements as criminal entrepreneurs were linked to the relationship that some blacks had to the sporting world and the night life entertainment of the city. By 1900, Chicago's famous red-light district, the "Levee," was located in the area around 22nd and State Streets (south of the Loop) and offered an array

17. On Jewish vice in New York and elsewhere, see Edward J. Bristow, *Prostitution and Prejudice: The Jewish Fight against White Slavery, 1870-1939* (New York, 1982); and Arthur Goren, *New York Jews and the Quest for Community* (New York, 1970). On the role of Mike de Pike Heitler and other Jews in West Side vice before World War I, see Murray, *Madhouse on Madison Street,* chap. 30; and investigators' reports in Merriam papers, esp. Box 88, folders 1 and 6. On Jewish syndicates in the 1920s, see the following investigative reports in the Juvenile Protective Association papers: "Law Enforcement and Police," Nov. 29, 1922, and Dec. 3, 1922, folder 94; and "Commercialized Prostitution," Dec. 10, 1922, folder 92. For Jewish gamblers, see Chicago Crime Commission file No. 65.

18. For an overview of bootlegging, see Haller, "Bootleggers as Businessmen: From City Slums to City Builders," in David E. Kyvig, ed., *Law, Alcohol, and Order: Perspectives on National Prohibition* (Greenwood Press, 1985), chap. 9.

19. Bradstreet reports on 30 major bail bondsmen are attached to a letter of Assistant Corporation Counsel to Harry J. Olson, April 9 and 29, 1913, in Chicago Municipal Court papers, folder 24, Chicago Historical Society. Ethnicity could be established for 18, of whom 9 were Jewish. Half of the 30 bail bondsmen were saloonkeepers. By the late 1920s, Jews constituted 51 percent of bail bondsmen (out of 150 studied); see Ogburn and Tibbitts, "Memorandum on Nativity," p. 48. Figures on Jewish fences and defense attorneys in Ogburn and Tibbitts, pp. 15 and 47-48.

of houses of prostitution, cabarets, gambling parlors, vaudeville theaters, Chinese opium smoking dens, and other exciting or forbidden forms of entertainment. In the rooming houses and cheap hotels of the Levee, many of the city's pimps and professional thieves made their homes. Nearby, a growing Chinese population built the city's Chinatown. Camouflaged within the district were those few bars where Chicago's gay residents could participate openly in a social life. In the Levee, where outcasts and respectable people mingled and where customers flocked to sample forbidden pleasures, there was a relaxation of the rules that normally separated the city's dwellers by race and by class. Talented blacks, faced with sharp discrimination and growing segregation in the city, could often make opportunities for themselves in the world of entertainment.[20]

By the time of the World's Columbian Exposition in 1893, blacks were finding opportunities within the district. For visitors to the Exposition, Vina Fields offered the city's finest parlor house, with some forty "sporting women" to entertain her customers. The Exposition also made ragtime tunes popular and thus initiated a process by which black musicians were sought after to perform in cabarets and other outlets. By that time, too, black gamblers like John "Mushmouth" Johnson ran gambling houses and sometimes even became partners with whites in operating the city's popular policy gambling syndicates. By the turn of the century, then, the district was — ironically enough — already the most integrated area of Chicago.

By the 1920s, with the decline of the Levee, two new entertainment districts emerged in the city. One, located on the near North Side, featured night clubs and speakeasies controlled by whites and aimed at white customers. The other was "The Stroll," the famous black entertainment district located along South State Street from 31st to 39th streets in the heart of the rapidly emerging black ghetto. In the 1920s, musicians from New Orleans, Kansas City, and other cities mingled there, and Chicago rapidly emerged as the center for the development of jazz in the United States. Louis Armstrong, Joe "King" Oliver, Earl "Fatha" Hines, Cab Calloway, and Alberta Hunter were among those whose talents were honed along The Stroll. In the fancy cafes, the elegant theaters and ballrooms, the "black and tan" cabarets, and the numerous speakeasies, black and white customers heard the best jazz of the era, watched comedians and dancers in exciting floor shows, and tried out the latest dances on the crowded dance floors.[21]

20. This and the next four paragraphs are based on Haller, "Policy Gambling, Entertainment, and the Emergence of Black Politics: Chicago from 1900 to 1940," *Journal of Social History* 24 (Summer 1991), 719-739.

21. Haller, "Policy Gambling"; see also Dempsey J. Travis, *An Autobiography of Black Jazz* (Chicago, 1983); Thomas J. Hennessey, "From Jazz to Swing: Black Musicians and their Music, 1917-1935" (Ph.D. diss., Northwestern Univ., 1973), pp. 7-12, 54-108, and chap. 7; Leroy Ostranski, *Jazz City: The Impact of our Cities on the Development of Jazz* (Englewood Cliffs, NJ, 1978), chaps. 4-6; John Steiner, "Chicago" in Nat Henthoff and Albert J. McCarthy, eds., *Jazz: New Perspectives on the History of Jazz* (New York, 1959); and George D. Bushnell, Jr., "When Jazz Came to Chicago," *Chicago History* 1 (Spring 1971), 132-41.

The emergence of the Stroll was tied to the emergence of the South Side black ghetto. With the Great Migration of blacks from the rural south to the urban north, blacks became increasingly segregated within a black belt that, in 1930, extended for nearly five miles along South State Street from the end of the Loop to 63rd Street. By the early 1920s black politicians had fashioned local Republican organizations that were tied to the wing of the Republican party dominated by Mayor William Hale (Big Bill) Thompson. As early as 1921, for instance, Dan Jackson was head of the so-called "Second Ward Syndicate," which provided police and political protection for gambling and entertainment along The Stroll. A leader in the Republican ward organization, Jackson was himself a leading policy backer, owner of gambling houses, and promoter of cabarets. In the 1930s, when the Democratic Party emerged as the dominant force in city politics, the Jones brothers — Edward, George, and McKissack — allied themselves with the Democrats and seized the opportunity to emerge as the city's leading policy gambling operators.[22]

At the same time that some whites created a violent underworld in the city centered in bootlegging, black gambling entrepreneurs, allied with the entertainment and political leaders of the Black Belt, were part of a relatively independent black underworld. Because of the much greater discrimination against blacks than against European immigrants, the leaders of black gambling syndicates emerged from higher-status backgrounds than did the bootleggers. Their parents were often middle class, they sometimes had college educations, and they created an underworld culture less violent and more tied to the community than that of the white underworld.

Until there has been more study of comparative ethnic patterns, only tentative hypotheses are possible to explain why various ethnic groups followed differing patterns. Because many persons involved in gambling or bootlegging initiated their careers with customers from their own neighborhoods or ethnic groups, the degree to which a particular ethnic group sought a particular illegal service would influence opportunities for criminal activities. If members of an ethnic group did not gamble, for instance, then ambitious members of that ethnic group could not build gambling syndicates based upon local roots.

An ethnic group's attitude toward the legitimacy of law and law enforcement also affected career opportunities in illegal ventures. Those groups that became most heavily involved in underworld activities had immigrated and migrated from regions in which they had understandably developed deep suspicions of government authority: the Irish fleeing British rule in Ireland, Jews escaping the discrimination and pogroms of Eastern Europe and Russia, Italians emigrating from southern Italy or Sicily, or blacks leaving the miseries of the American South. Within a community suspicious of courts and government officials, a person in trouble with the law could retain roots and even respect

22. Haller, "Policy Gambling."

in the community. Within a community more oriented toward upholding legal authority, on the other hand, those engaged in illegal activities risked ostracism and loss of community roots.

In other ways, too, ethnic lifestyles evolved differently. Among both Germans and Irish, for instance, friendly drinking was part of the pattern of relaxation. Although the Irish and Germans were the major managers of Chicago's saloons by 1900, the meaning of the saloon was quite different for the two groups. German saloons and beer gardens were often part of family entertainment and generally excluded gambling or prostitution; Irish saloons, part of an exclusively male social life, often featured gambling and fit more easily into the world of entertainment associated with criminal enterprise. In terms of violence, it appears that southern Italians had the highest homicide rate in Europe. There was, in all probability, a relationship between the cultural factors that sanctioned violence and private revenge in Europe and the violence with which some Italian bootleggers fought their way into a central position in Chicago's underworld.[23]

There were, at any rate, many ways that the immigrant background and the urban environment interacted to influence the ethnic experience with the underworld. For some ethnic groups, involvement in organized crime was not an important part of the adjustment to American urban life. For other groups, involvement in the organized underworld both reflected and influenced their relatively unique patterns of acculturation.

Economic Impact

The economic role of underworld activities was an additional factor underlying their impact on ethnic communities and urban society. The underworld was important because of the relatively great wealth of the most successful criminals, because of the large numbers of persons directly employed by organized crime, and because of the still larger numbers who supplemented their income through various part-time activities. And all of that does not even count the multitude of customers who bought the goods and services offered by the bootleggers, gambling operators, and vice promoters in the city.

During the first thirty or forty years after an immigrant group's arrival, successful criminal entrepreneurs might constitute a disproportionate percentage of the most wealthy members of the community. (In the 1930s, perhaps one-half of the blacks in Chicago worth more than $100,000 were policy kings;

---

23. Italian homicide rate mentioned in Rudolph J. Vecoli, "Contadini in Chicago: A Critique of the *Uprooted*," *Journal of American History* 51 (Dec. 1964), 406. For a discussion of the ways that Italian criminals reflected aspects of south Italian values, see Francis A. J. Ianni, "The Mafia and the Web of Kinship," *The Public Interest* 22 (Winter 1971), 78-100.

Italian bootleggers in the 1920s may have represented an even larger proportion of the very wealthy among immigrants from southern Italy.)[24] The wealth of the successful criminals was accompanied by extensive political and other contacts that gave them considerable leverage both within and outside the ethnic community. They had financial resources to engage in extensive charitable activities, and often did so lavishly. Projects for improvement of ethnic communities often needed their support and contacts in order to succeed; and criminals often invested in or managed legitimate business enterprises in their communities. Hence, despite ambiguous or even antagonistic relations that they had with "respectable" members of their ethnic communities, successful criminal entrepreneurs were men who had to be reckoned with in the ethnic community and who often represented the community to the outside world.

In crime, as in other economic activities, the very successful were but a minority. To understand the economic impact of crime, it is necessary to study the many persons active at the middle and lower levels. In cities like Chicago the number of persons directly employed in criminal enterprises was considerable. A modest estimate of the number of full-time prostitutes in Chicago around 1910 would be 15,000 — not counting madams, pimps, procurers, and others in managerial positions. Or look at the policy racket: in the early 1930s an average policy wheel in the black ghetto serviced as many as 100 writers, and there were perhaps 5,000 policy writers in the ghetto. The policy wheels, during this period of heavy unemployment, may have been the major single source of employment in the black ghetto, a source that did not need to lay off workers or reduce wages merely because the rest of the economy faced a major depression.[25] Finally, during the 1920s, bootlegging in its various aspects was a major economic activity that employed thousands in manufacture, transportation, and retailing activities.

Yet persons directly employed constituted only a small proportion of those whose income derived from criminal enterprise. Many persons supplemented their income through occasional or part-time services. While some prostitutes walked the streets to advertise their wares, others relied on intermediaries who would direct customers in return for a finder's fee. During certain periods, such payments were sufficiently lucrative so that some taxi drivers would pick up only those passengers seeking a house of prostitution. Bellboys, especially in the second-class hotels, found the function of negotiating between guests and prostitutes a profitable part of their service. (Many of the worst hotels, of course, functioned partly or wholly

24. On blacks, this is my surmise from information in Drake and Cayton, *Black Metropolis,* II, pp. 514 and 546.

25. Estimate of number of prostitutes from City of Chicago Civil Service Commission, *Final Report, Police Investigation, 1911-1912* (Chicago, 1912), p. 12; for a lower estimate, see Vice Commission of Chicago, *The Social Evil in Chicago* (Chicago, 1911), p. 71. Figures on policy gambling from Gosnell, *Negro Politicians,* pp. 124-125, and Drake and Cayton, *Black Metropolis,* II, pp. 478-481.

as places of assignation.) Bartenders, newsboys, and waiters were among the many helpful persons who provided information concerning places and prices.[26]

Various phases of bootlegging during the 1920s were even more important as income supplements. In the production end, many slum families prepared wine or became "alky cookers" for the bootlegging gangs — so much so that after the mid-1920s, explosions of stills and the resulting fires were a significant hazard in Chicago's slum neighborhoods. As one observer reported:

> During prohibition times many respectable Sicilian men were employed as "alky cookers" for Capone's, the Aiello's or for personal use. Many of these people sold wine during prohibition and their children delivered it on foot or by streetcar without the least fear that they might be arrested. . . . During the years of 1927 to 1930 more wine was made than during any other years and even the "poorest people" were able to make ten or fifteen barrels each year — others making sixty, seventy, or more barrels.[27]

Other people, including policemen, moonlighted as truck drivers who delivered booze to the many retail outlets of the city. Finally, numerous persons, including bellboys, janitors in apartment buildings, and shoeshine boys, supplemented their income by retailing booze.

The many people who mediated between the underworld and the law formed another group that supplemented its income through underworld contacts. Large numbers of policemen, as well as bailiffs, judges, and political fixers, received bribes or political contributions in return for illegal cooperation with the underworld. Defense attorneys, bail bondsmen, and bankers in small banks provided expert services that were generally legal.[28]

For many of the small businessmen of the city, retailing the goods or services of the underworld could supplement business income significantly. Saloons, as already mentioned, often provided gambling as an additional service

26. Fred Cotnam, "Conversations with Bell-boys" (student term paper, winter 1929); Stanley Jenkins, "Prostitution and the Prostitute in a Study Centered around Hotel Life" (undated term paper); and Morris Carl Bergen, "The City as Seen by the Cab Driver" (term paper, July 1932); all in Burgess papers. Also investigators' reports, Nov. 1922, folder 94, and Report F-2 in "Commercialized Prostitution," folder 98, in Juvenile Protective Association papers.

27. Quotation from Raymond Sayler, "A Study of Behavior Problems of Boys in the Lower North Community" (research paper [1934]), p. 50, in Burgess papers. Explosions of stills in Chicago *Tribune,* Sept. 28, 1927. See also Cotnam, "Conversations with Bell-boys," and Cressey, "Report on Summer's Work," pp. 28ff.

28. On relations of criminals to politics, see references in footnote 8. For relations to police, see especially investigators' reports in Merriam papers, Boxes 87 and 88. Of many discussions of judges and criminals, see Judge M. L. McKinley, *Crime and the Civic Cancer — Graft,* Chicago Dailey News Reprints, No. 6 (1923), in Juvenile Protective Association papers, Suppplement 1, folder 58. An excellent general discussion of bail bondsmen is Arthur L. Beeley, *The Bail System in Chicago* (Chicago 1927), esp. pp. 39-46. A long description of defense attorneys for organized crime is in Sunday Chicago *Tribune,* April 8, 1934.

to customers. Large numbers of small businesses were outlets for handbooks, policy, baseball pools, slot machines, and other forms of gambling. A substantial proportion of the cigar stores, for example, were primarily fronts for gambling; barbershops, pool halls, newsstands, and small hotels frequently sold policy or would take bets on the horses. Drugstores often served as outlets for cocaine and, during the 1920s, sometimes sold liquor.[29]

The organized underworld also influenced business activity through racketeering. A substantial minority of the city's labor unions were racketeer-controlled; those that were not often used the assistance of racketeer unions or of their strongarm gangs during strikes. Underworld leaders, as a result, often exercised control or influence in the world of organized labor. Not as well known was the extensive racketeering that characterized small-business organizations. The small businesses of the city were generally marginal and intensely competitive. To avoid cutthroat competition, businessmen often formed associations to make and enforce regulations that would illegally limit competition. The Master Barbers Association, for example, set minimum prices, forbade a shop to be open after 7:30 p.m., and ruled that no shop could be established within two blocks of another shop. Many other kinds of small businesses formed similar associations: dairies, auto parts dealers, garage owners, candy jobbers, butcher shops, fish wholesalers and retailers, cleaners and dyers, and junk dealers. Many of the associations were controlled — or even organized — by racketeers who levied dues on association members and used a system of fines and violence to ensure that all businessmen in the trade joined the association and abided by the regulations. In return for control of the association's treasury, in short, racketeers performed illegal services for the association and thereby regulated certain kinds of small business activity in the city.[30]

Discussion of the economic influence of underworld activities would be incomplete without mentioning the largest group that was tied economically to the underworld, namely, the many customers for the illegal goods and services. Like other retailers in the city, some criminal entrepreneurs located their outlets near the center of the city or along major transportation lines and

29. On newsstands and gambling, see memo by C. O. Rison, private detective, to Chicago Federation of Labor, July 4, 1910, in John Fitzpatrick papers, folder 4, Chicago Historical Society. For other businesses acting as fronts for gambling, see Rison's many other reports for June and July 1910; also Nels Anderson, "Report of Visit to Ten Gambling Houses in Hobohemia," Jan. 1, 1923, Doc. 79; and Paul Oien, research notes describing many gambling places in Chicago, Summer 1935, in Burgess papers. On the sale of cocaine in drugstores, see esp. Informant No. 100, Lists of places for securing cocaine [1914], in Merriam papers, Box 88, folder 1.

30. Landesco, *Organized Crime*, chap. 7; Samuel Rubin, "Business Men's Associations" (term paper, winter 1926), and Philip Hauser and Saul Alinsky, "Some Aspects of the Cleaning and Dyeing Industry in Chicago — A Racket," research paper (1929), in Burgess papers. See also the various issues of Employers' Association of Chicago, *Employers' News*, during the 1920s, which reported business racketeering in detail; see also journalistic books such as Fred D. Pasley, *Muscling in* (Chicago, 1931), and Gordon Hostetter, *It's a Racket* (Chicago, 1929).

serviced customers from the entire region; others were essentially neighborhood businessmen with a local clientele. In either case, those providing illegal goods and services usually attempted to cultivate customer loyalty so that the same customers would return on an ongoing basis and advertise among their friends. Criminal entrepreneurs thrived because of wide customer demand, and a large proportion of the adult population of the city was linked to the entrepreneurs on a regular basis for purchase of goods and services.

Heroism and Ambiguity

Because of the diverse ways that successful criminal entrepreneurs influenced neighborhoods and ethnic communities, many of them became heroes — especially within their own communities. There is a variety of reasons for the admiration that they received. Their numerous philanthropies, both large and small, won them reputations as regular guys who would help a person in need. Moreover, they were often seen as folks who fought for their ethnic communities: they aided politicians from their communities to win elections in the rough, often violent politics of the slums, and thereby advanced their ethnic groups toward political recognition. Sometimes they were seen as fighters for labor unions and thus friends of labor. And, on occasion, they fought directly for members of their ethnic group. There was, for instance, the case of the three Miller brothers from Chicago's West Side Jewish ghetto. In typical ghetto pattern, one became a boxer, one a gangster, and one a policeman. The boxer and gangster were heroes among Jews on the West Side, where for many years Jewish peddlers and junk dealers had been subjected to racial slurs and violent attacks by young hoodlums from other ethnic groups. "What I have done from the time I was a boy," Davy Miller told a reporter,

> was to fight for my people here in the Ghetto against Irish, Poles or any other nationality. It was sidewalk fighting at first. I could lick any five boys or men in a sidewalk free-for-all.

When the Miller brothers and their gang protected the Jews of the West Side, the attacks against them abated.[31]

Particularly for youngsters growing up in ethnic neighborhoods, gangsters were often heroes whose exploits were admired and copied. Davy Miller modestly recognized this when he said:

> Maybe I am a hero to the young folks among my people, but it's not because I'm a gangster. It's because I've always been ready to help all or any of them in a pinch.

31. Quotation from William G. Shepherd, "How to Make a Gangster," *Colliers* (Sept. 2, 1933), 12.

Chicago's infamous gangster boss, Al Capone, is seen at the center on the ground
next to his kid sister. Also sitting left to right are Jack "Machine Gun" McGurn,
Frank Rio, Jimmy Amaratti. Standing left to right are unidentified, Louis Campagna,
Joe Guinta, James "Fur" Sammons, and "Polack Joe" Saltis.
Photo and identification courtesy of the John Binder collection.

An Italian student at the University of Chicago in the early 1930s remembered
his earlier life in the Italian ghetto:

> For 26 years I lived in West Side "Little Italy," the community that has pro-
> duced more underworld limelights than any other area in Chicago. . . . I
> remember these men in large cars, with boys and girls of the neighborhood
> standing on the running board. I saw them come into the neighborhood in
> splendor as heroes. Many times they showered handfuls of silver to youngsters
> who waited to get a glance at them — the new heroes — because they had
> just made headlines in the newspapers. Since then I have seen many of my
> playmates shoot their way to the top of gangdom and seen others taken for
> a ride.[32]

Nevertheless, despite the importance of gangsters and the world within which
they moved, their relations to ethnic groups and the city were always ambiguous.

32. First quotation from *ibid.*, p. 13; second from [anon], (research paper entitled "Introduction" [approx. 1934]), p. 10, in Burgess papers.

Because many of their activities were illegal, they often faced the threat of arrest and, contrary to common belief, frequently found themselves behind bars. Furthermore, for those members of the ethnic community who pursued respectable paths to success, gangsters gave the ethnic group a bad name and remained a continuing source of embarrassment. St. Clair Drake and Horace R. Cayton, in their book on the Chicago black ghetto, describe the highly ambiguous and often antagonistic relations of the respectable black middle class and the policy kings. In his book on Italians in Chicago, Humbert S. Nelli explains that in the 1920s the Italian-language press refused to print the name of Al Capone and covered the St. Valentine's Day massacre without suggesting its connection with bootlegging wars.[33]

The respectable middle classes, however, were not the only ones unhappy about the activities or notoriety of gangsters. Underworld activities sometimes contributed to the violence and fear of violence that pervaded many of the ethnic neighborhoods. Local residents often feared turning to the police and lived with a stoical acceptance that gangs of toughs controlled elections, extorted money from local businesses, and generally lived outside the reach of the law. Some immigrant parents, too, resented the numerous saloons, the open prostitution, and the many gambling dens — all of which created a morally dangerous environment in which to raise children. Especially immigrant women, who watched their husbands squander the meager family income on liquor or gambling, resented the laxity of enforcement. Within a number of neighborhoods, local churches and local leaders undertook sporadic campaigns for better law enforcement.[34]

The organized underworld, then, was an important and sometimes ambiguous part of the complex social structure of ethnic communities and urban society in the early twentieth century. For certain ethnic groups, criminal activities both influenced and reflected the special patterns by which the groups adjusted to life in urban America. Through crime, some members of those ethnic groups could achieve mobility out of the ethnic ghettos and into the social world that linked crime, politics, ethnic business, sports, and entertainment. Those who were successful possessed the wealth and contact to exercise broad influence within the ethnic communities and the city; the economic activities of the underworld provided jobs or supplemental income for thousands. Despite the importance of the underworld, however, individual gangsters often found success to be ambiguous. They were not always able to achieve secure positions or to translate their positions into respectability.

33. Drake and Cayton, *Black Metropolis*, II, pp. 490-94 and 546-50; Nelli, *Italians in Chicago*, p. 221.

34. On the attitude of immigrant mothers, see the many letters to Mayor Dever (1923-27) reporting speakeasies and begging the mayor to have them closed; William E. Dever papers, Chicago Historical Society, esp. folders 25-26. For a long article on the Chinese Christian Union's campaign to close Chinese gambling houses, see Chicago *News*, May 11, 1904. On activities of black and Polish churches, see Herbert L. Wiltsee, "Religious Developments in Chicago, 1893-1915" (M.A. thesis, University of Chicago, 1953), pp. 14 and 23.

CHAPTER 20

The Ethnic Church

EDWARD R. KANTOWICZ

Ethnicity is the skeleton of religion in America because it provides "the supporting framework," "the bare outlines or main features" of American religion.

— Martin E. Marty

The church, with its use of the old language, with its conservative continuance of Old World customs, with its strictly racial [ethnic] character, was the most important of the social organizations of the immigrant.

— H. Richard Niebuhr

America's religious pluralism owes much of its character to the ethnic diversity of the United States. One of the most distinctive features of religion in America, its division into a bewildering variety of denominations, is based on sociology as much as theology.[1] It's important not to exaggerate or overemphasize this main point, for religious divisions have many roots. Geography has exercised a powerful fracturing influence on the denominations. Most of the mainline English Protestant groups broke into Northern and Southern wings over the slavery issue before the Civil War, and some of these divisions persist today. Former president Jimmy Carter, for example, is a Southern Baptist. This does

1. H. Richard Niebuhr first made this point in his pioneering study, *The Social Sources of Denominationalism* (New York, 1929). See, particularly, chap. 8, "The Churches of the Immigrants," pp. 200-235. After the ethnic revival of the 1960s, church historians became more attentive to the ethnic factor. Martin E. Marty reviews the historiographic issues in "Ethnicity: The Skeleton of Religion in America," *Church History* 41 (March 1972), 5-21. The quotations at the head of this chapter are taken from these two sources.

not mean simply a Baptist who happens to come from the South. Rather, he is a member of the Southern Baptist Convention, one of the largest Protestant denominations in the United States.

Social class can also distinguish one religious grouping from another. In a land of social mobility, it is not unusual for a person to begin life as a Baptist or Methodist, then to change his affiliation to a more "high church" body such as the Presbyterians or the Episcopalians as his wealth and social status increase. Theological divisions also run strong and deep. Historians feel more comfortable searching out sociological explanations for events, but they should resist the temptation to reduce all theological disputes to matters of class or ethnicity. However arcane the points of theology may look to an outsider, committed believers argue passionately over them and frequently form wholly new denominations because of these disagreements.

So denominationalism has both social and theological sources. Yet the fact remains that ethnicity forms a sort of skeleton undergirding the limbs and torsos of religious bodies in America. When the census takers took a survey of American religion in 1916, they discovered that 132 of the 200 or so denominations conducted all or part of their services in a language other than English. Forty-two languages in all were reported.[2]

Ethnic Denominations

Nationalism has tended to fragment Christianity since the Protestant Reformation. The Treaty of Westphalia in 1648 ended more than a century of religious wars in Europe by imposing a settlement based on national territory. Under the principle of *Cujus regio, ejus religio,* the prince or king of each state in Europe decided the religion of the realm, and the people were expected to fall in line. Henry VIII had already imposed his state church in England. The Lutheran faith prevailed throughout Scandinavia and in many of the German states; Reformed Calvinism in Switzerland and the Netherlands; and Catholicism in France, Spain, Italy, and the Hapsburg Empire of Austria and Hungary.

When adherents of a state church in Europe immigrated to America, they naturally tried to transplant their religious institutions. The Lutherans are a good example of this impulse. American Lutheranism was a German creation from the very beginning, first brought to the colony of Pennsylvania by immigrants from the Rhineland in the mid-eighteenth century. By the middle of the next century, however, the Lutherans had become Americanized and their church was divided into three major synods, largely along regional lines. Then

2. Jay P. Dolan, "The Immigrants and Their Gods: A New Perspective in American Religious History," *Church History* 57 (March 1988), 66.

in the years between the Civil War and World War I, a new immigration transformed the Lutheran Church in America.

In the second half of the nineteenth century, approximately a million and a half German Lutherans arrived in the United States, along with a roughly equal number of Lutherans from Scandinavia. The majority of Germans affiliated with the doctrinally rigorous Missouri Synod, but many smaller German synods broke off from this group and became separate denominations. Originally, all the Scandinavian Lutherans organized the Augustana Synod in 1860, but within less than a decade the Danes and Norwegians broke away to form their own synods. By the end of the nineteenth century there were sixty-six separate Lutheran synods in the United States, distinguished largely by "linguistic differences, geographical separation, and varying degrees of Americanization."[3]

Chicago followed this national pattern quite closely. German immigrants founded First St. Paul's church on the North Side in 1843. Beginning in 1851, Rev. Henry Wunder served as pastor for the next sixty-two years; and largely through his influence other German congregations were founded and the majority of them affiliated with the Missouri Synod. The Scandinavians organized the First Norwegian Evangelical Lutheran Congregation in 1848 in the Sands district just north of the Chicago River. Swedes soon found the Norwegian dominance of this church distasteful, however, and organized the Swedish Lutheran Immanuel Congregation in 1853. By 1893 there were six different language groups of Lutherans — Germans, Norwegians, Swedes, Danes, Slovaks, and English — organized into about a dozen different synods.[4]

Similarly, the Methodist Episcopal church organized separate conferences for Germans and Swedes and a combined Dano-Norwegian conference. In these cases, an English denomination was not trying to preserve Old World traditions but rather was appealing to dissidents from state churches in their home countries on the Continent.[5] Adherents to the Reformed Calvinist tradition, with its emphasis on congregational autonomy, were not pulled apart quite so strongly by the divisive force of ethnicity as the Lutherans were. Since the individual congregation enjoyed almost complete authority, it mattered little if its members spoke a different language from those of the neighboring church. Still, the resulting mosaic could be quite diverse. In the 1920s, for

3. I have relied on the account in Sydney E. Ahlstrom, *A Religious History of the American People* (Garden City, NY, 1975), Vol. 2, pp. 215-223.

4. Robert C. Wiederaenders, "A History of Lutheranism in Chicago," Vol. 2 of the *Chicago Lutheran Planning Study* (National Lutheran Council, 1965), pp. 3-5; Ulf Beijbom, *Swedes in Chicago: A Demographic and Social Study of the 1846-1880 Immigration* (Uppsala, Sweden, 1971), pp. 231-265; Odd S. Lovoll, *A Century of Urban Life: The Norwegians in Chicago before 1930* (Northfield, MN, 1988), pp. 54-58.

5. Lovoll, *Century of Urban Life*, p. 109.

example, Chicago's Baptists embraced congregations speaking thirteen languages other than English.

In sum, the already strong tendency for Protestant churches to divide and subdivide was greatly accelerated by immigration from a variety of European nations in the late nineteenth and early twentieth centuries. In 1923, just as mass immigration from Europe was coming to an end, the Chicago City Directory listed 860 Protestant congregations gathered into 31 separate denominations. About half of these denominations were identifiably ethnic, including four German, four Swedish, two Norwegian, one Danish, one Slovak, and four African-American church groupings. Many of the predominantly English denominations, such as the Methodists, Baptists, and Congregationalists, listed numerous individual congregations that employed a foreign language. Only the two high-status Protestant denominations, the Episcopalians and the Presbyterians, appeared to be overwhelmingly English-speaking.[6]

The reason Protestant immigrants organized their own parishes and denominations is clear enough. Since Protestantism is a religion of the *Word*, as found in the Bible and preached from the pulpit, it is imperative that its church members be able to understand the words. The doctrines of Martin Luther or John Calvin, translated into English, were of no use to a Lutheran or Calvinist from Germany. An ethnic parish, moreover, served many social and economic functions for newly arrived immigrants. The historian of the Norwegians in Chicago has aptly described the wide-ranging activities of Erland Carlsson, the first pastor of the Swedish Lutheran Immanuel Congregation:

> Social work, as practiced by Carlsson, extended to include many services, from meeting immigrants at the railroad station to finding them a place to live and work, helping them overcome language barriers by being an interpreter, buying money orders, and assisting in many daily affairs. The religious impulse in this manner combined with a social program to form an indispensable immigrant institution.[7]

H. Richard Niebuhr, who first analyzed the "social sources of denominationalism" in 1929, added a cultural dimension to the practical functions of the ethnic parish:

> The preacher . . . was often the only educated man in the immigrant community. To him the old culture was not merely a mass of memories but a literature and an art expressive of a national genius. He expressed for his countrymen their inarticulate loyalties and fostered their sense for these cultural values.[8]

---

6. *Polk's Directory of Chicago, 1923* (Chicago, 1923), Vol. I, pp. 162-169.
7. Lovoll, *Century of Urban Life*, p. 61.
8. Niebuhr, *Social Sources of Denominationalism*, p. 223.

The ethnic parish, synod, or conference, therefore, served as a way station for immigrants, nourishing them spiritually and culturally after their long voyage and providing much practical assistance as well. A phrase that one historian has applied to Swedish Lutheranism in Chicago — "The pioneer church, a firm foundation for the uprooted" — applies equally well to many other Protestant churches.[9]

Jewish immigrants also followed national lines in their places of worship. Most of the Jews who immigrated in the early years of the American republic came from Germany. They quickly Americanized and tended to follow the Reform tradition in Judaism, which adapted the ancient rituals of the faith to the local national customs. In the late nineteenth century, however, nearly two million Jews arrived from eastern Europe. These newcomers spoke Yiddish, an amalgam of Hebrew, German, and Polish, and observed strictly Orthodox Jewish beliefs and rituals. So by 1900, two broad tendencies could be found in American Judaism. Those with German roots tended to be Reform or Conservative Jews, whereas the more recent immigrants from the Russian or Austro-Hungarian empires adhered to Orthodox Judaism. In Chicago the waves of immigrants from eastern Europe overwhelmed the older German Jewish population. By 1930, Chicago had 84 Orthodox congregations, and only 13 Reform and 8 Conservative congregations.[10]

Ethnic division proceeded even further among Jewish immigrants, however. The East European Jews came from almost totally Jewish small towns, or *shtetlach*, in the Russian Empire. Arriving in whole family groups, immigrants from the same *shtetl* settled together in American cities and formed *landsman-schaften*, or mutual aid societies, to help each other out. A *minyan*, or a quorum of ten adult males from one of these societies, might then organize a synagogue, which would also be composed entirely of Jews from the same locality in Europe.[11] So, for example, a group of Jews from the Crimean city of Mariampol formed a benevolent society in the Maxwell Street district of Chicago in 1870 and organized the first Orthodox synagogue in the city, Ohave Sholom Mariampol. An old legend concerning the founding of this synagogue reminds us that ethnic distinctions were not the only reasons for the division of congregations. Supposedly, a group of Jews from Mariampol who attended an older synagogue in Chicago were offended when a man recited *kaddish* while wearing a straw hat. Not only their place of birth but also their stage of assimilation impelled the Mariampolers to withdraw and form their own synagogue. As

9. Beijbom, *Swedes in Chicago*, p. 231.

10. Ahlstrom, *Religious History*, Vol. 2, pp. 467-480; Morris Gutstein, "The Roots and Branches: A Survey of the Chicago Jewish Community, 1845-1976," in *Faith and Form: Synagogue Architecture in Illinois* (Chicago, 1976), p. 21.

11. Much of the extensive literature on Jewish immigration focuses on New York City. For settlement background in Chicago, see Edward H. Mazur, *Minyans for a Prairie City* (New York, 1990), pp. 1-78.

greenhorns in America, they found the "swell" American dress of more assimilated Jews offensive.[12]

Overall, therefore, ethnicity has tended to fragment both Protestantism and Judaism in America. Both faith traditions place considerable emphasis on the autonomy of the individual congregation and are marked by frequent divisions into new groupings of congregations, but immigration has accentuated the centrifugal tendencies in both religions.

Ethnic Leagues in Catholicism

At first glance, the Catholic Church might seem largely immune to ethnic divisions. The Church of Rome considers itself universal in scope (the word *catholic* means "universal") and tries to impose uniformity of belief and ritual throughout the world. Indeed, before the Second Vatican Council of the 1960s, the Catholic mass and sacraments were conducted in Latin, a language equally unintelligible to immigrants and natives.

Furthermore, Catholicism is organized geographically, with each diocese carved into territorial parishes. Unlike many Protestants, who may travel a great distance to the congregation of their choice, most Catholics worship where they live. Early in this century, Archbishop James Quigley of Chicago set forth the ideal of one Catholic parish per square mile in the city. Quigley believed that "a parish should be of such a size that the pastor can know personally every man, woman, and child in it."[13]

This ideal of a neighborhood parish for all Catholics, however, proved unrealistic. As Catholic immigrants from Continental Europe flooded into American cities, they demanded separate parishes with priests of their own nationality to minister to them. The mass may have been celebrated in Latin, but the priest preached his sermon and listened to confessions in the vernacular. Furthermore, the parish was a community center for social organizations as much as a place of worship. Therefore, American bishops often allowed immigrant groups to organize national parishes, defined by language not territory, side by side with the territorial churches.

Germans organized the first national parishes in the United States. In 1846, just two years after Chicago received its first Catholic bishop, the diocese authorized two German-language parishes, St. Peter's and St. Joseph's. In the years that followed, many other German parishes were erected, as well as numerous Polish, Bohemian, Lithuanian, Italian, and Slovak churches. As a result,

12. Hyman Meites, *History of the Jews of Chicago* (Chicago: Jewish Historical Society of Illinois, 1924), pp. 116, 489-490.

13. Edward Kantowicz, "Church and Neighborhood," *Ethnicity* 7 (1980), 349-366; Ellen Skerrett, "The Catholic Dimension," in Lawrence McCaffrey et al., *The Irish in Chicago* (Urbana, IL, 1987), p. 49.

MAP 20.1

LOCATION OF CHICAGO PARISHES, 1916

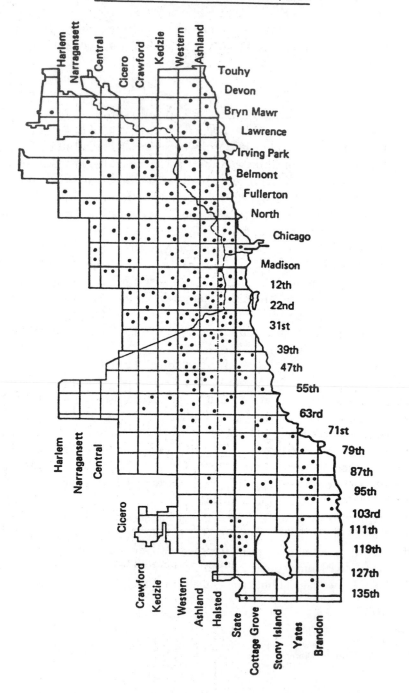

MAP 20.2

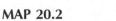

CHURCHES

A – All Saints
B – St. Bridget
C – St. David
D – Nativity of Our Lord
E – St. John Nepomucene
F – St. Anthony of Padua
G – Immaculate Conception
H – St. George
I – St. Barbara
J – St. Mary of Perpetual Help

Bridgeport, circa 1910.

many square-mile quadrants of Chicago had two, three, or as many as six or seven Catholic parishes.[14]

Map 20.1 shows the resulting geographical pattern in 1916, the year after Archbishop Quigley's death. The outer parts of the city — north of Fullerton Avenue, the whole Northwest Side, the West Side beyond Western Avenue — and most of the South Side east of State Street, where Catholics were in the minority amid black and white Protestants, fit the ideal of one parish per square mile reasonably well. The empty squares on the outskirts of the city were generally not settled yet in 1916. In the inner city, however, between State and Western, Fullerton and 55th, each quadrant is crowded with Catholic churches. This is due not merely to density of population and a high percentage of Catholics in these neighborhoods (though these were factors), but primarily to the presence of several different Catholic ethnic groups and thus a number of national parishes besides the territorial ones.

One of Chicago's most famous neighborhoods, Bridgeport on the South Side, home to five Chicago mayors, aptly illustrates the crowding of Catholic churches in a single district.[15] Roughly a mile and a half long by a mile wide, Bridgeport is clearly marked out by natural boundaries: the south branch of the Chicago River on the north, a short finger of the river (nicknamed Bubbly Creek) on the west, a wide swath of railroad tracks running along Stewart Avenue on the east, and the Union Stock Yards and a rail line just south of 39th Street on the south (see Map 20.2). For most of the twentieth century, Bridgeport counted ten Catholic parishes of five different nationalities. In 1910 the neighborhood was about 70 percent Catholic. The census listed 49,650 people in Chicago's 4th Ward, which included most of Bridgeport; the pastors of Bridgeport's Catholic parishes reported about 35,000 parishioners.[16]

The Irish had been the first to arrive in Bridgeport, imported to dig the Illinois and Michigan Canal in the 1830s and '40s; and it remained a largely Irish and German neighborhood until the end of the nineteenth century. Three territorial (though largely Irish) parishes and two German national parishes were organized in the nineteenth century, and a fourth territorial parish was added in 1905.[17] Just before the Chicago fire, a number of Bohemians moved down Halsted Street into the northeast sector of Bridgeport and founded the parish of St. John Nepomucene in 1870.

14. Though there is no overall narrative history of the Catholic Church in Chicago, Harry C. Koenig, ed., *A History of the Parishes of the Archdiocese of Chicago* (Catholic Bishop of Chicago, 1980), is a rich, encyclopedic source of information. Ellen Skerrett did most of the research for these volumes and should have been acknowledged on the title page.

15. Kantowicz, "Church and Neighborhood," pp. 351-361.

16. The parish population figures were drawn from the annual reports of the parishes, at the Archives of the Archdiocese of Chicago.

17. The territorial parishes and their founding dates are: St. Bridget, 1850; Nativity, 1868; All Saints, 1875; St. David, 1905; the German parishes are St. Anthony of Padua, 1873, and Immaculate Conception, 1883.

St. Bridget's, Bridgeport, 1905-6, James J. Egan and Charles H. Prindeville.
Following the example of Henry Hobson Richardson's Trinity Church in Boston,
many ethnic groups and denominations adopted Romanesque as a common style
in the late 19th century.   Courtesy of Edward R. Kantowicz.

At the end of the nineteenth century, a much larger Slavic group, the Poles,
began settling in Bridgeport, followed closely by a large Lithuanian immigration.
St. George's was founded in 1892, the first and largest Lithuanian church in the
city, the "mother church" of Lithuanian Chicago. A decade earlier, in 1883, the
Poles had organized St. Mary of Perpetual Help parish. St. Mary's of Bridgeport
did not contain the largest Polish settlement in Chicago, but the parish was large
enough to be divided in 1910, when the parish of St. Barbara was erected. Before
the changes in devotional practice brought about by the Second Vatican Council,
many Catholics observed a pious custom of visiting the Blessed Sacrament in nine
different churches on Holy Thursday. The residents of Bridgeport could make this
mini-pilgrimage easily on foot without leaving their own neighborhood.

Bridgeport was not unique, or even unusual, in Catholic Chicago.
Wherever immigrants clustered in multiethnic, working-class wards, each Cath-
olic nationality organized its own parish and thrust its church steeple skyward.
Lay people almost always took the initiative by forming a mutual aid society

under the patronage of some national saint and petitioning the bishop for a priest who spoke their language. Though the purpose of founding an ethnic parish was to preserve the language and culture of the homeland, the very process of parish building marked a departure from Old World ways. Instead of the state erecting and supporting the parish church, individual believers were adopting the American system of voluntary church support. The ethnic parish, therefore, was marked at birth as a transitional institution, simultaneously preserving immigrant customs and adapting itself to American law and practice.

Catholic parishes of each nationality were loosely federated into ethnic "leagues."[18] The individual parishes conducted elementary schools and organized a wide variety of social and charitable organizations; and they jointly financed high schools, hospitals, orphanages, and cemeteries. These leagues of the nations enjoyed no official status in Rome's canon law; they were not legally incorporated and were not recognized as separate denominations, as the Lutheran synods were. Yet an "ethnic league" was more than a figure of speech. The Polish pastors, for example, frequently met to set policy for the Polish cemeteries and orphanages and to assess the Polish parishes for joint building projects. Individual pastors commonly made loans to pastors of new parishes within their league. For example, when the St. Mary of Perpetual Help parish in Bridgeport was divided, Rev. Stanislaus Nawrocki loaned the pastor of the new St. Barbara parish — his brother, Rev. Anthony Nawrocki — $28,000 from parish funds. The entire operation remained, literally and figuratively, within the family.

The ethnic leagues were very exclusive in their staffing practices. In 1916, 99 percent of the Irish clergy engaged in parish work were assigned to territorial, English-speaking parishes. Similarly, 100 percent of the Polish and Slovak priests, 92 percent of the Lithuanian priests, 86 percent of the Italian priests, and 82 percent of the Bohemian priests labored within parishes of their own ethnic league. Even the Germans, who had been assimilating rapidly in some respects, retained 90 percent of their priests in German parishes. The Archbishop of Chicago generally relied on an informal "ethnic boss," either an auxiliary bishop or an influential pastor, from each nationality when making assignments to the ethnic leagues.

The priests of each league guarded their constituencies jealously, complaining frequently to the archbishop about "scavenger priests" in neighboring parishes who tried to lure Catholics of other nationalities into their churches in order to receive their mass stipends and Sunday donations. Charity not only began, but ended, at home. Each league functioned much like a Protestant synod or conference: it formed a virtual subdiocese or quasi-denomination.

18. Edward R. Kantowicz, *Corporation Sole: Cardinal Mundelein and Chicago Catholicism* (Notre Dame, 1983), pp. 71-72.

The Major Leagues

The statistics displayed in Table 20.1 reveal a clear division of the Chicago Catholic archdiocese into "major leagues" and "minor leagues" at the time when mass immigration from Europe had just ceased.[19] The territorial parishes (still largely Irish in 1926), along with the German and Polish national parishes, dwarfed the rest of the archdiocese, with 79 percent of the congregations and 81 percent of the church members. The three major leagues of parishes ranked at or above the archdiocesan average on most of the measures of institutional health recorded in the table.

The territorial parishes were fairly evenly distributed throughout the city, but the largest and most impressive churches stood along the main transportation lines west and south of the Loop, where Irish Catholics predominated. These territorial parishes were in some ways just as "ethnic" as the others, for they were heavily Irish. Many bore distinctive Irish names, such as St. Patrick, St. Jarlath, St. Bridget, and St. Columbkille. Their sanctuaries displayed numerous statues of Gaelic saints; and in at least one church, Holy Family, an altar carving portrayed Joseph, the foster father of Jesus, wearing a bowler hat, which must have been the height of fashion for Irish "swells" when the altar was donated. Just as the brave "Fr. Murphys" of Ireland had fought and died in the many rebellions against English rule, Chicago Irish pastors encouraged their parishioners to support the cause of freedom for their homeland. They permitted nationalist groups such as the Land League and the Ancient Order of Hibernians to hold meetings on an equal footing with purely religious organizations such as the St. Vincent de Paul Society or the Holy Name Society.[20]

Still, the territorial parishes were open to any Catholic who lived within their boundaries, and assimilated members of other ethnic groups, particularly descendants of early French settlers and an increasing number of German Americans, attended them. English was spoken at all the nonliturgical events of the territorial parishes, for the Irish immigrants had largely lost their native language before arriving in America. This fact alone set the Irish parishes off from all the other ethnic parishes. Also, by 1926 a huge proportion (79 percent) of the clergy ministering in the territorial parishes were American-born; indeed, two-thirds of these priests were born in Chicago.

The territorial parishes were comfortably average in size (about 2000 "souls," or 400 families each) and reasonably well supported financially. The $18.40 per capita that the parishioners donated in 1926 works out to nearly

19. I gathered these statistics at the Archives of the Archdiocese of Chicago while researching *Corporation Sole*. I analyzed them more thoroughly in a paper entitled "Men, Money, and Masonry: The Maturing of American Catholicism," delivered at the Perspectives on American Catholicism Conference at Notre Dame, November 19, 1982.

20. Skerrett, "The Catholic Dimension," pp. 41-42.

TABLE 20.1
Cross-section of Chicago archdiocese, by ethnic "leagues," 1926

League	Number of parishes	Number of church members	Americanization of clergy	Localization of diocesan clergy	Number of priests per parish	Solvency	Regularization	Per capita donations
Territorial (Irish)	183	367,300	79%	63%	2.1	1.5 to 1	1.95 to 1	$18.40
German	64	96,000	68%	54%	2.2	1.65 to 1	1.78 to 1	$17.28
Polish	54	258,800	53%	59%	2.4	1.88 to 1	1.85 to 1	$ 8.61
Bohemian	11	18,500	50%	27%	1.5	1.17 to 1	1.45 to 1	$12.25
Slovak	9	10,900	37%	0%	1.5	2.23 to 1	2.45 to 1	$13.53
Lithuanian	12	29,000	7%	12%	2.2	1.3 to 1	.95 to 1	$13.01
Italian	18	76,800	7%	17%	1.9	2.5 to 1	2.1 to 1	$ 3.25
Other (10 Nationalities)	29	39,000	42%	46%	1.8	2.6 to 1	1.5 to 1	$10.61
Archdiocesan totals	380	896,300	65%	57%	2.1	1.6 to 1	1.9 to 1	$13.58

Key to the Table

The number of parishes and church members and all financial data were calculated from the annual reports of the parishes filed at the archives of the Archdiocese of Chicago. The number of priests per parish was calculated from the Official Catholic Directory, and the Americanization and localization of the clergy was drawn from a collective biography assembled by the author from obituaries published in The New World.

• Number of church members was reported by the pastors. The criterion used by most pastors was probably more than just baptism but less than weekly church attendance. Probably anyone who made his Easter duty and contributed at least something to the support of the parish was enumerated.

• Americanization refers to birth in the United States, and localization to birth within the six-county archdiocese of Chicago.

• Solvency presents a ratio of parish debt to annual parish income.

• Regularization presents a ratio of ordinary parish income (pew rents, and regular Sunday and Holyday collections) to extraordinary income (raffles, bazaars, bingo, parish canvasses and appeals).

• Per capita donations presents the average contribution per person. It is probably more illustrative to convert this into an average family donation by multiplying it by five, the average size of a Catholic family at the time.

two dollars a week per family. The financial measure that I call "regularization" in the table (the ratio of ordinary revenue to extraordinary revenue) probably loomed more important to the Irish Americans of the early twentieth century than it would to us today, for it measured social respectability as much as it did financial stability. "Ordinary revenue," a term taken from the annual reports the pastor filed with the archbishop each year, denoted all pew rentals and the regular Sunday, holy day, Christmas, and Easter collections. All other sources of revenue — including bazaars, raffles, and bingo — were listed as extraordinary. The Irish ratio of ordinary to extraordinary revenue reached nearly 2 to 1 in 1926, illustrating that these parishes followed the normal financial procedures more closely than others. In the eyes of the archbishop, the Irish territorial parishes represented the norm and all the others were exceptions.

German parishes were also distributed throughout the city, but the German stronghold lay on the North Side. The ten North Side parishes accounted for nearly half of the church membership and financial support of the German League. St. Michael's, just west of Lincoln Park, and St. Alphonsus, on Lincoln Avenue, both conducted by the Redemptorist order of priests, were the largest German parishes in the city. Overall, the German parishes were a bit smaller than the Irish ones (about 1500 souls, or 300 families each), but on all the other measurements, such as Americanization of the clergy and financial support, they ranked very near the archdiocesan average. Nevertheless, the German League was declining numerically as more and more German Catholics became Americanized and attended territorial parishes; the German parishes had fewer members in 1926 than they had ten years earlier.

Perhaps the most distinctive feature of the German League was its orientation toward social action and charitable work. Following the tradition of German social Catholicism that developed in the nineteenth century, Chicago's German League fostered a rich variety of organizations to serve the poor and the unfortunate. The St. Vincent de Paul Society, for example, was founded in France in 1833 and swiftly spread to other countries. Male lay volunteers raised money at parish events, then distributed it personally to the needy of the parish. Fewer than half of the parishes in Chicago supported a St. Vincent de Paul Society early in this century, but nearly all the German parishes did. Msgr. Aloysius J. Thiele, the German boss of the archdiocese, also served as spiritual director for all the St. Vincent de Paul societies.

German Catholics were also preeminent in the field of institutional child care. In 1865 a group of priests and laymen had started the Angel Guardian German Catholic Orphan Society of Chicago. Quite independent of the archdiocese, this society held title to Angel Guardian Orphanage in the Rosehill district of the North Side, at Ridge and Devon Avenues, and three German Catholic cemeteries as well: St. Boniface, St. Mary, and St. Joseph. Profits from the cemeteries helped support

St. Michael's (Polish), South Chicago, 1907-9, William J. Brinkman. The soaring Gothic steeple dominated the steel mill district surrounding U.S. Steel's South Works. Courtesy of Edward R. Kantowicz.

the orphanage. The priests and nuns who cared for the children at Angel Guardian pioneered a new system of child care. In 1914 and 1915 the Orphan Society built small cottages at the orphanage and assigned a nun to act as "mother" for a small group of children. The cottage system was later adopted by the official orphanage of the archdiocese, St. Mary's in Des Plaines, Illinois.

A generation later, Msgr. Reynold Hillenbrand, a German Catholic who grew up in St. Michael's parish, was appointed rector of the newly opened St. Mary of the Lake Seminary in Mundelein, Illinois. Hillenbrand had read deeply in the social teachings of the popes and had worked out a synthesis of theology and social action built around the doctrine of the Mystical Body of Christ. At the seminary he trained a whole generation of Chicago priests in his Catholic action philosophy, thus earning for Chicago Catholicism a reputation for social liberalism. Hillenbrand and other German priests also experimented with a more participatory liturgy. One of his contemporaries, Fr. Bernard Laukemper,

St. Hyacinth (Polish), Logan Square, 1917-21, Henry Worthmann and J. G. Steinbach. Most of Chicago's Polish churches were built in a High Renaissance style that recalled the glory days of the Polish Commonwealth before the Partitions. Courtesy of Edward R. Kantowicz.

made St. Aloysius parish on the near Northwest Side a model of liturgical revival nearly thirty years before the Second Vatican Council.[21]

The Polish League formed the largest group of nonterritorial parishes, fifty-four congregations with over a quarter million members at its height in the 1920s. Polish parishes were found in all the city's districts of heavy industry, such as Bridgeport, Back of the Yards, and the South Chicago steel district; but the greatest number were concentrated on the Northwest Side, near St. Stanislaus Kostka, the mother church of Chicago's Polonia. The Northwest Side parishes, many of them administered by the Resurrectionist religious order, accounted for nearly 50 percent of all Polish church members. Polish parishes were much larger than those of other nationalities, averaging nearly 5,000 members (roughly 1,000 families). Several of the congregations approached 20,000 members, the largest in the archdiocese.[22]

21. Kantowicz, *Corporation Sole*, pp. 129-131, 197-202.
22. *Ibid.*, pp. 68-69.

Polish pastors ruled their parishes in an exceptionally authoritarian manner, like feudal lords. A great number of Polish priests had emigrated with their flocks, and thus the Polish league enjoyed the highest priest-to-parish ratio in the archdiocese. Only about half the Polish priests were American-born by the 1920s, lower than the archdiocesan average. Rather than the mixed lay-clerical orphan society that ran the German orphanages and cemeteries, a committee of Polish pastors exercised complete control over St. Hedwig's Orphanage and the three Polish cemeteries.

A Polish priest kept tabs on his constituents much as a ward boss or precinct captain did. Every year during Lent, the pastor and his assistants made a door-to-door canvass of the parish, collecting an annual subscription from each family. When a family paid the minimum subscription fee (somewhere between five and ten dollars in the 1920s), the priest gave each family member a registration card and reminded him or her to perform the Easter duty, that is, go to confession and receive communion at least once during the Easter season. Family members were required to hand in their cards when they made their confession. If a family failed in this obligation two years in a row, it was "stricken from the parish registry" and thus denied the right to baptize its children or solemnize its marriages in the church. This effectively cut them off from the Polish Catholic community.

Polish parishioners did not always meekly accept the priest's authoritarian direction. They rarely dared to neglect their Easter duty, because the consequences were so severe; but not every adult attended Sunday mass regularly. And even though the pastor preached the necessity for a Catholic education, many parents sent their children to the parish school for only the minimum two years required to prepare them for first communion. The spiritual life of the Polish parish, therefore, represented a delicate compromise between priestly commands and selective responses by the parishioners.[23]

The Minor Leagues

Two of the minor leagues of Eastern Europeans, the Slovaks and the Lithuanians, resembled the larger group of Poles. Their priests were largely foreign-born, and the people were staunchly nationalist and Catholic. The numerically small and poor Slovak congregations carried a much higher debt load than did the other ethnic leagues, and the Lithuanians relied on extraordinary fund-raising methods more than any other. Both groups were concentrated in the industrial districts of the South and West sides, with the Lithuanian mother church, St.

23. Mary Cygan, "Ethnic Parish as Compromise: The Spheres of Clerical and Lay Authority in a Polish American Parish, 1911-1930," Charles and Margaret Hall Cushwa Center for the Study of American Catholicism, Working Paper Series 13, No. 1, Spring, 1983.

George, in Bridgeport and the oldest and largest Slovak parish, St. Michael the Archangel, in Back of the Yards.

The Bohemians were more geographically concentrated than any other Catholic group in the city, with all but two of their parishes lying in a narrow belt of the West Side along 18th and 22nd streets, and extending out into Cicero and Berwyn. More importantly, the Bohemians stood out from other Eastern Europeans by the high proportion who proved indifferent to Catholicism or any other religion. All East European ethnic groups contained a nationalist faction that was at least mildly anticlerical or secularist in attitude; but Bohemian nationalism had developed into a virtual secular religion. The Catholic Austrian Empire had ruthlessly suppressed the Protestant followers of Jan Hus in the fifteenth century, and though Bohemia remained a nominally Catholic province, its leading intellectuals were generally self-styled atheists or "freethinkers." In the United States, the free-thought movement broadened its base and embraced a large number of Bohemian workers as well.

Bohemian freethinkers greatly outnumbered Bohemian Catholics in Chicago. Only about 17 percent of the Bohemians belonged to Bohemian Catholic parishes, whereas about 50 percent of the Slovaks and Lithuanians and a remarkable 78 percent of the Poles belonged to their own national churches. Only because of the evangelizing efforts of Benedictine priests from St. Procopius Abbey did a Bohemian League of parishes exist at all in Chicago.[24]

The remaining minor league, the Italian, also presented a missionary challenge to Catholic church authorities. The eighteen Italian parishes, distributed fairly widely around the city and inner suburbs — but with two important centers on the near West and near North sides — were quite large, averaging about 4,500 members each. But unlike the Polish parishes of similar size, Italian church membership was largely nominal, based on baptismal and marriage statistics, not church attendance or a yearly canvass. Italians gave little financial support to the church. In fact, most of the Italian parishes had been founded at the initiative of Archbishop Quigley and continued only with subsidies from the archdiocese. Italian indifference to the institutional aspects of Catholicism had deep roots in the Old Country. The Italian church had opposed the nationalist *risorgimento* in the nineteenth century, and the Papal States had long blocked Italian unification. In the case of both the Italians and the Bohemians, nationalism and Catholicism were antagonistic, conflicting forces. Thus the average Italian or Bohemian inherited a heavy weight of anticlericalism. In Poland and Ireland, however, the Catholic church supported the opposition to occupying powers, and thus the twin forces of nationalism and religion reinforced each other.

To sum up this survey of ethnic Catholicism early in the twentieth century, the leagues of ethnic parishes can be categorized as 1) assimilating groups: the

---

24. Kantowicz, *Corporation Sole*, pp. 69-71.

Irish (who comprised the "mainstream" in territorial parishes), the Germans, and the much smaller French group; 2) staunchly Catholic and nationalist groups: the Poles, Slovaks, Lithuanians, and a smaller number of Croatian and Slovenian parishes; 3) missionary groups: the Bohemians and the Italians. The differences between groups reflected their national histories in Europe and their stage of assimilation in America. To varying degrees, all the groups relied on ethnic parishes and pastors to preserve their national identities and help them adjust to the urban environment.

The Golden Age of Chicago Catholic Architecture

The twin spires of church steeple and factory smokestack dominated the ethnic neighborhoods of Chicago. The church buildings of each nationality nearly jostled one another as they proclaimed to God and man, "Here we are!" This is too cynical and simple an explanation, however, for the massive church edifices that scraped the soot-filled sky of Chicago. Status competition certainly impelled many pastors and parishioners to build a towering church, but there were other motives as well. The Catholic church building, adorned with statues, murals, stained glass, and golden altar vessels, was the only place of beauty in a raw immigrant neighborhood, an oasis of quiet and harmony amidst industrial cacophony. It was also a sacred space that elevated the minds and hearts of believers.[25]

Not every parish could afford to build a full-scale, free-standing church building. Of necessity, nearly every congregation began in a storefront or a makeshift wooden church. The Catholic bishops of Chicago encouraged pastors to build a school building first, wisely judging that the children would form the glue to hold the parish together. Worship services were conducted in the basement or the school hall. Only a little more than half the Chicago parishes ever raised enough money to build a full-scale church; the rest remained content with a combination church-school building.

Chicago experienced a tremendous building boom after the Chicago Fire of 1871, but Catholic immigrants were still too few in number and too poor to build many churches at that time. But in the 1890s, when Catholic numbers burgeoned, many parishes began building on a large scale, thus ushering in the golden age of Catholic church architecture in Chicago.[26] This golden age was marked by a rich variety of architectural styles. The nineteenth century was a period of tremendous eclecticism in architecture, as one historical revival followed another. Most early Chicago churches, just before and after the Fire, were

---

25. Ellen Skerrett has made this point very eloquently in "Whose Church Is It, Anyway?" *Commonweal* (November 18, 1988), 622-629.

26. Edward R. Kantowicz, "To Build the Catholic City," *Chicago History* 14 (Fall 1985), 4-27.

TABLE 20.2

Ethnic	Architectural Style					
League	Gothic	Romanesque	Renaissance	Other	Unknown	Total
Irish	31 (38%)	19 (23%)	18 (22%)	13 (16%)	0 (0%)	81 (100%)
German	17 (59%)	7 (24%)	1 (3%)	3 (10%)	1 (3%)	29 (100%)
Polish	3 (12%)	7 (27%)	13 (50%)	3 (12%)	0 (0%)	26 (100%)
Other	5 (17%)	14 (48%)	8 (28%)	1 (3%)	1 (3%)	29 (100%)
Total	56 (34%)	47 (28%)	40 (24%)	20 (12%)	2 (1%)	165 (100%)

Full-scale Catholic churches in Lake and Cook counties between 1891 and 1945.

built in the Gothic style, testifying to the power of the Victorian Gothic revival in England. But Henry Hobson Richardson's Trinity Episcopal Church in Boston (1877) stemmed the Gothic tide and inspired a host of Romanesque imitations in Chicago and across the country. The World's Columbian Exposition of 1893 then revived interest in Renaissance and classical designs of all kinds. Thus, by the end of the century, Catholic parishes had a large vocabulary of popular forms from which to draw.

A vanguard of local Catholic architects emerged in the 1890s to serve the ethnic leagues and manipulate the historical styles so popular at the time. In all, forty individuals or firms built 165 full-scale churches in Lake and Cook counties between 1891 and 1945. Only two Catholic churches were built by famous, mainstream architects. Solon S. Beman, the designer of George Pullman's model town, also built Holy Rosary Catholic Church in the Roseland neighborhood bordering on Pullman; and the firm of Burnham and Root erected St. Gabriel's Church near the Chicago stockyards. Chicagoans also called in outside architects from time to time.

Most of the forty architects, however, were local Chicagoans, born after the Civil War, had apprenticed with one of the important architectural partnerships, and were making their livings largely on Catholic church work. Seven architects (or partnerships) built a large share of Catholic churches (79 of 165) during this period. The most noteworthy were Henry J. Schlacks, who started his practice in the German League but eventually built for all the major groups, Joseph J. McCarthy, designer of Cardinal George Mundelein's St. Mary of the Lake Seminary, and a partnership of two German Protestants, Henry W. Worthmann and John J. Steinbach, who built the largest and most magnificent of the Polish churches.

If he knew how to read the architectural styles, a walker in the city could learn something of the history of the Catholic ethnic groups (see Table 20.2). Chicago's Irish churches, whose congregations represented mainstream Chicago Catholicism, employed the greatest variety of styles, reflecting the changing fashions in church architecture over the decades. Thus the earliest Irish churches built after the Fire, such as St. Anne and St. James on the South Side, St. Jarlath

Holy Name Cathedral,
Near North, 1874-75,
Patrick C. Keely.
Chicago's Catholic
Cathedral was built of
local Joliet limestone in
the prevailing Victorian
Gothic style right after
the Chicago Fire.
Courtesy of
Edward R. Kantowicz.

on the West Side, and Holy Name Cathedral, were all designed in a high Victorian Gothic style. James J. Egan's design for St. Bridget's of Bridgeport, however, built in the 1890s, reflected the Romanesque revival ushered in by Richardson; and the magnificent basilica of Our Lady of Sorrows showed the classical influence of the 1893 World's Fair.

The single most common style among the Irish churches, however, remained the Gothic. Though the Irish would rarely admit it, this style summed up their aspirations for respectability in the eyes of Victorian Protestants. The German Catholics favored Gothic even more heavily, building nearly two-thirds of their churches in that style. Two of Henry Schlacks's designs, St. Martin of Tours on the South Side and St. Paul's on the West Side, provide handsome examples of German Gothic workmanship. Though I do not have detailed information about German Protestant churches, an unsystematic look around the Chicago area suggests that German Protestants also favored Gothic. In this

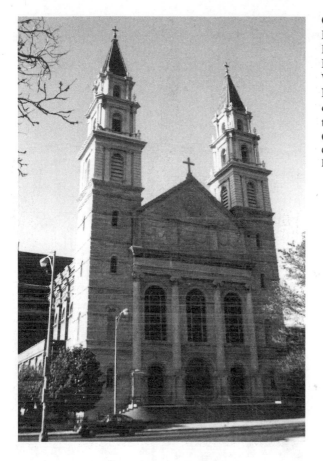

Our Lady of Sorrows
Basilica, East Garfield
Park, 1890-92, Henry
Englebert, John F. Pope,
William J. Brinkmann.
Neo-Classical facades
came into style at the
time of the World's
Columbian Exposition.
Courtesy of
Edward R. Kantowicz.

way both Catholics and Protestants harkened back to the days before Martin
Luther, when German Christianity was still united.

The social meaning of Gothic expressed in the previous paragraph is
admittedly very speculative, but the preference of the Polish League for Renaissance and baroque forms seems more clearcut. The glory days of the Polish
Commonwealth came in the sixteenth and seventeenth centuries, when it
formed the largest state in Europe, stretching nearly from the Baltic Sea to the
Black Sea, from the Oder River deep into White Russia and the Ukraine. The
Polish princes imported Italian architects and artisans to build their palaces and
churches in splendid Renaissance and baroque styles.

The Polish churches in Chicago, particularly the magnificent edifices that
Worthmann and Steinbach built along the Milwaukee Avenue corridor on the
Northwest Side, reflected the Renaissance glory of Polish Catholicism. Fully half
of the Polish churches employed classical Renaissance forms; only three Polish
churches in the archdiocese were built in the Gothic style. St. Mary of the Angels,

St. Martin of Tours (German), Englewood, 1894-95, Louis A. Becker and Henry J. Schlacks. Gothic was the most common style used by German Catholics, harkening back to the days before Martin Luther when German Christianity was still united. Courtesy of Edward R. Kantowicz.

with a soaring dome to rival St. Peter's in Rome, is the ultimate example of the Polish Renaissance style. Father Francis Gordon, a leading member of the Polish Resurrectionist order, commissioned this building as a Polish cathedral, or bishop's church, because he hoped to be named auxiliary bishop for the Poles of Chicago. The episcopal call never came, but the church testifies to his daring ambition and the generosity of his parishioners. Built over an eight-and-a-half year period around World War I and costing over $400,000, St. Mary's may not be the most beautiful church in Chicago but it is certainly the most audacious. Sadly, it deteriorated over the years and was closed for a time and threatened with demolition; but heroic fundraising efforts by its past and present parishioners allowed it to reopen in 1992.[27]

27. A word is in order about Romanesque, the simple, rounded style of the early middle ages which preceded the Gothic. No ethnic pattern is detectable in the use of Romanesque. Chicago

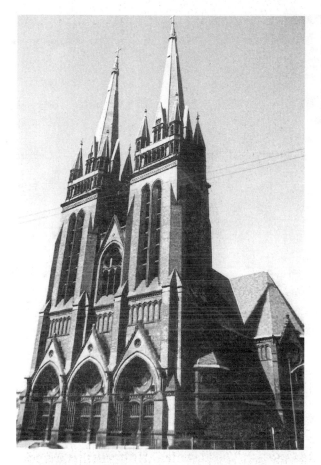

St. Paul (German),
Pilsen, 1897-99, Henry J.
Schlacks. A mature
example of German
Gothic by Chicago's
finest Catholic architect.
Courtesy of
Edward R. Kantowicz.

Other religious denominations also adopted distinctive architectural styles that reflected their national heritages (see sidebar, p. 599 below). English Protestants often imitated the church of St. Martin-in-the Fields, designed by Sir James Gibbs in London.[28] Greek, Russian, and Ukrainian Orthodox congregations usually built their churches in the Byzantine style of Constantinople. Interestingly, many Jewish synagogues also adopted Byzantine forms, in order to emphasize their Middle Eastern roots and to distinguish their houses of worship from the more common Catholic and Protestant styles. Few if any Jewish synagogues were built in Gothic.

Romanesque tended to be a modest, utilitarian style chosen most frequently by the less wealthy parishes in each ethnic league.

28. Cardinal George Mundelein, who was a vigorous Americanizer in the Catholic church, instructed his architect, Joseph McCarthy, to use this English model, as filtered through colonial New England, when he designed the seminary of St. Mary of the Lake.

St. Mary of the Angels (Polish), Bucktown, 1914-20, Henry Worthmann and J. G. Steinbach. One of the most audacious churches in Chicago, this was Worthmann and Steinbach's masterpiece for the "Polish League." Courtesy of Edward R. Kantowicz.

Ethnic Ecumenism

Ethnic parishes served the same basic functions that any religious institution did: worship, education, and charity. Different denominations performed these functions in varying ways. Catholics and Missouri Synod Lutherans built parochial schools alongside their churches to preserve both the religious and ethnic heritages of their people; other synods of Lutherans and most other Protestants adopted the American Sunday School as its primary means of cultural and religious education. Orthodox synagogues established *yeshivas* where young male Jews learned the intricacies of Hebraic Law.

All immigrants, however, wanted to praise God, learn more about the Word of God, and assist one another in a language they could understand. So ethnicity tended to fragment the Protestant, Catholic, and Jewish religions. Catholic bishops grudgingly conceded the right of non-English-speaking ethnic groups to organize their own parishes in order to keep them from falling away from the faith. German and Scandinavian Lutherans organized separate synods to preserve the beliefs and rituals of their state churches in Europe. Orthodox

Architectural Styles and Ethnic Groups

The nineteenth century was an era of architectural eclecticism, marked by successive waves of historical revivals. Different ethnic groups showed particular affinities for individual styles.

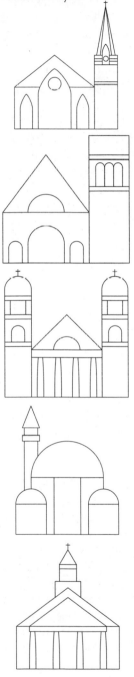

Gothic — This was the first style to be revived, in the 1830s and '40s. English Victorians adopted it as peculiarly their own. Both German Catholics and German Lutherans used the style widely, harking back to the Middle Ages when German emperors vied with the papacy for dominance in Christendom.

Romanesque — Henry Hobson Richardson revived this style with his Trinity Episcopal Church built in Boston in 1877. No ethnic pattern developed, as all denominations and ethnic groups adopted a modest, utilitarian version of Romanesque as a sort of lowest common denominator.

Classical, Renaissance, Baroque — The Chicago World's Fair of 1893 revived interest in classical forms. Italians showed a marked affinity for Renaissance styles, for obvious reasons, as did Poles, since Poland's days of greatness as a nation coincided with the Renaissance in Europe. The majority of Polish churches in Chicago are Renaissance or Baroque; only 3 are Gothic.

Byzantine — This was used primarily for Greek, Russian, and Ukrainian Orthodox churches; for Jewish synagogues; and for Moslem mosques. Jews adopted it in order to emphasize their Middle Eastern roots and to distinguish their houses of worship from common Christian styles. There were no Gothic synagogues.

Colonial — This traces its lineage directly to St. Martin-in-the-Fields, designed by Sir James Gibbs in London in 1726. Adopted by the New England Puritans in colonial times, it has been widely copied by Protestant denominations with English roots, particularly in small towns and suburbs. Interestingly, the Chicago Catholic cardinal of the 1920s, George Mundelin, used this style for the main chapel of his major seminary, in order to emphasize the Americanization of the Catholic Church.

Text by Edward R. Kantowicz; artwork by Greg Kantowicz.

Jews from a given *shtetl* in Eastern Europe gathered together in the same synagogue on Maxwell Street.

However, more than language was at stake. Even immigrants who spoke English, such as Irish Catholics or Scots Presbyterians, tended to worship together with people of their own nationality. An ethnic parish was a place where people felt comfortable together, where they could read between the lines when they talked to one another. It was a family, albeit a patriarchal one in most cases. As in any family, the children grew up and moved away from their parents; so the ethnic parish was a transitional institution. Even at the high point of ethnic fragmentation, early in the twentieth century, it is possible to overemphasize the divisive effects of ethnicity on religion. All the Catholic leagues remained faithful to the Pope of Rome; and though they didn't like it, the individual ethnic parishes all conceded legal title of their property to the archbishop of Chicago in his capacity as a *corporation sole*. Though it is easy to point out churches with distinctive ethnic names, such as St. Patrick, St. Stanislaus, and St. Boniface, many more Catholic church names reflected common dogmas and popular devotions. The city of Chicago was home to six Catholic churches named Immaculate Conception, representing four different ethnic groups; there were also six Sacred Heart churches, each one founded by a different nationality.

The Lutheran synods may have formed separate denominations, but they retained a lively sense of their communion as Lutherans, and the Confession of Augsburg remained a doctrinal touchstone for them all. The German Jews resented the greenhorn Russian Jews, but their common identity as the chosen people nevertheless impelled the former to much charitable work among the newcomers.

As the children of the immigrants adopted the English language and American ways, the ethnic parishes became less and less necessary. German Lutherans, for example, experienced an extended transitional process of many stages. First of all, the pastor found it necessary to perform occasional weddings or christenings in English; next he added an extra, English-language Sunday School class. Since the children learned English quickly in public schools and on the streets, the parish soon found itself with an all-English Sunday School and occasional English worship services. Eventually the English-language services became a regular Sunday feature, scheduled at a more convenient time than the German services, which were attended largely by older people. At long last, the parish would be entirely English. This process, however, took a long time. Most German Lutheran parishes were only reaching the final stages when World War I accelerated the change. Historians of Lutheranism in Chicago have concluded: "The World War, a change of pastorate, death of a prominent German member, and relocation of the church have been the most prominent in putting an end to German services. . . ."[29]

---

29. Wiederaenders, in "History of Lutheranism in Chicago," pp. 46-47, adopted this description of the transition process from Sharvy G. Umbeck, "The Social Adaptations of a Select Group of German-Background Protestant Churches in Chicago" (Ph.D. diss., University of Chicago, 1940), pp. 74-83.

German Catholic parishes followed a similar evolution, as did Catholic parishes of other nationalities at a slightly later date. However, a Catholic parish would not change location to follow its parishioners, as Protestant congregations often did, so it tended to remain ethnic for a longer time, a vestigial institution servicing the elderly in the inner city. The Catholic church also experienced considerable bureaucratic inertia in making clerical assignments to ethnic parishes. As late as 1948, only 14 percent of the German diocesan priests in parochial work in Chicago were assigned to non-German parishes. St. Nicholas in Evanston, one of the most suburban and least ethnic parishes of German origin, received its first non-German pastor in 1969.

Beginning in the 1920s, then accelerating greatly after World War II, the major trend in all denominations was toward merger and consolidation, a sort of ethnic ecumenism. The sixty-six Lutheran synods existing at the turn of the century, for example, gradually combined into fewer but larger denominations. Today the *Lutheran Annual* lists only ten Lutheran church bodies in the United States. The two largest of these, the Missouri Synod and the Evangelical Lutheran Church in America, encompass fully 90% of the Lutheran congregations, 93% of all ordained ministers, and 94% of baptized members.[30]

Three very large events of the twentieth century have eroded particularism in the American Jewish community. First of all, Americanization and material success erased the old *shtetl* consciousness of Jews; second, the Holocaust during World War II traumatized all Jews and tended to make distinctions among them pale into insignificance; third, the rise of Zionism and the establishment of the state of Israel have united all Jews in defense of their homeland.

In the Catholic church, the bishops have frowned upon ethnic parishes since World War I. The codification of canon law that Rome completed in 1918 required special permission for the erection of any new national parishes. In Chicago, Cardinal George William Mundelein tried to pursue a policy of Americanization. When he arrived in the city in 1916, he declared his dislike of hyphenism: "The people of the United States must be American or something else. They cannot serve two masters." Mundelein was a practical man, however, and he soon found he could not dismantle ethnic parishes without pushing their parishioners into schism, so he backed off and simply made it difficult to erect any new ones.[31]

Therefore, when Spanish-speaking newcomers arrived from Mexico and

---

30. Ahlstrom, *Religious History of the American People,* outlines the tortuous process of synodal consolidation in a long footnote, Vol. 2, pp. 222-223. The statistics are from *Lutheran Annual, 1989, of the Lutheran Church–Missouri Synod,* p. 657, and *1988 Yearbook: Evangelical Lutheran Church in America,* p. 496.

31. Kantowicz, *Corporation Sole,* pp. 72-83. A number of Polish priests in several cities had broken away from the Catholic church in the 1890s and organized a separate Polish National Catholic Church. This was the only major schism in American Catholicism, but it served as a warning to strong bishops like Mundelein.

Puerto Rico, the Catholic Church in Chicago did not welcome them as openly as it had previous immigrants from Europe. Cardinal Mundelein showed some flexibility toward the Mexicans: in 1925 he invited a Spanish religious order, the Claretians, to organize the Mexican parish of Our Lady of Guadalupe in South Chicago, which became known colloquially as the "Mexican cathedral." About the same time, Mundelein also handed over St. Francis Assisi, an old German church on Roosevelt Road, to the Claretians as a second Mexican national parish. The Claretians later extended their religious work to the Mexicans living in Back of the Yards; however, their storefont church in that neighborhood was not organized as a full-scale parish, only as a mission outpost. The Immaculate Heart of Mary vicariate was a decidedly second-class facility that looked like a garage with a church facade tacked on.[32] The archdiocese of Chicago officially recognized two and a half Mexican national parishes, but this fell far short of meeting the religious needs of the immigrant community. And in some ways the existence of so few national parishes made the religious status of Mexican Catholics ambiguous. When Mexican parents found their way to the nearest Catholic church to arrange a baptism for their child, the English-speaking pastor often told them to "go to the Mexican parish," which might be miles away and in a strange neighborhood.

Puerto Ricans, as American citizens by birth, were not granted any national parishes at all. By the time they arrived in Chicago after World War II, the Catholic church was expanding rapidly into the suburbs; so the last thing the Chicago bishops intended to do was build new national parishes in the city. In some ways Mexicans and Puerto Ricans resembled the Italian Catholic immigrants who arrived earlier in the century. Like the Italians, they did not bring many of their own priests with them and they remained largely indifferent toward the institutional church. They did not willingly support the church financially. Yet when the Italians came to Chicago, the archdiocese had actively promoted the formation of national parishes and subsidized them indefinitely. It did not leave them wandering around looking for a parish community that would welcome them, as it did with the Mexicans and Puerto Ricans. Preoccupied with suburban growth, Catholic authorities after World War II forgot that the ethnic parish was a tried and true institution of immigrant adjustment and neglected to promote it among the Spanish-speaking.

In addition, by the time Latinos became numerous in Chicago, parochial school education had been priced out of their reach. Before the Second Vatican Council, religious orders of sisters provided the teaching staff of parochial schools, and the local parish subsidized most of the costs. Tuition was free in many parishes, or a nominal dollar or two per month at most. From the 1960s

---

32. *Ibid.*, pp. 72-74; Charles Shanabruch, *Chicago's Catholics: The Evolution of an American Identity* (Notre Dame, 1981), pp. 181-185, 210-211; Koenig, *History of the Parishes,* Vol. 1, pp. 285-286, 444-447, 691-695.

on, however, lay teachers replaced the teaching sisters, and yearly school tuition soared to $500, then $1,000 and even more per child. Latino parents, with large families and yearly incomes near or below the poverty level, could not afford Catholic schools, as their immigrant predecessors had.

For all their coolness toward the ethnic parishes, however, Chicago Catholic bishops did not close or consolidate many of the older ones until very recently. They preferred to let the ethnic leagues evolve and dissolve slowly on their own. However, in January 1990, Cardinal Joseph Bernardin, impelled by financial stringency, announced the wholesale closing of thirty-seven parishes and schools over the following eighteen months. Most of these were former national parishes in the older industrial neighborhoods of the city.[33]

In the archetypal neighborhood of Bridgeport (see Map 20.2, p. 581 above), two of the parishes, All Saints and St. Anthony, had already been consolidated a number of years before 1990. The mass closings of 1990 cut the number of parishes in half, when St. Bridget, St. John Nepomucene, Immaculate Conception, and St. George were shuttered. As a final gesture to its ethnic heritage, St. George, the oldest Lithuanian church in the city, donated all its statues and other furnishings to a parish in Lithuania. The Irish territorial parish of Nativity, home parish of Mayors Richard J. Daley and Richard M. Daley, was not touched. Ethnicity may not have counted for much in the archdiocese anymore, but clout did.[34]

European immigrants believed that they were building their churches for the ages; but, in fact, they were not. The edifices may have looked magnificent from a distance, but most were relatively humble constructions, fashioned from common Chicago brick, not stone or marble. In less than a hundred years, many have begun to crumble; all of them require expensive maintenance, which was often deferred indefinitely by frugal pastors. Ethnic communities have proven even less lasting than the churches, as children and grandchildren of immigrants attained some economic success and moved to the suburbs.

Yet it would be incorrect to conclude that the ethnic church is a vanishing institution. Chicago is still a magnet for immigrants. Some Polish Catholic churches have burgeoning congregations of recent arrivals from the *Solidarnosc* generation in Poland. Though bishops have been reluctant to create national parishes for Latinos, many formerly European ethnic churches have become thriving Mexican, Puerto Rican, or Filipino parishes simply by the strength of numbers. Another common pattern in older Catholic parishes finds one mass on Sunday celebrated in English, another in Polish (or Lithuanian, or Bohemian), and a third in Spanish.

So long as immigrants find the city attractive, there will be a need for way stations on the journey between one country and another, and between this world and the next.

---

33. Chicago *Tribune*, January 22, 1990, pp. 1, 4; January 23, 1990, sect. 2, p. 1; *The New World*, January 26, 1990, pp. 9-16.

34. Chicago *Tribune*, June 29, 1990, section 2, p. 8; *The New World*, July 6, 1990, pp. 2-6.

CHAPTER 21

Chicago's Ethnic Neighborhoods: The Myth of Stability and the Reality of Change

DOMINIC A. PACYGA

Chicago's neighborhood history centers on the reality of change, rather than on the myth of stability. . . . It was attitudes concerning race, ethnicity, and class that influenced the choices Chicagoans have historically made. To a large extent, technological advances did not so much alter as reinforce trends in place since the Yankees drove the French and Indians out of the old settlement in the 1830s.

— Dominic A. Pacyga

Chicago's neighborhoods and ethnic groups have often been the objects of investigation and speculation. Sociologists, urban anthropologists, and historians have all looked at the city's varied residential areas. Novelists have described urban life by focusing on Chicago's neighborhoods. Politicians constantly try to reach voters by singing the praises of neighborhood and community. Class, race, and ethnicity have been constant factors in the description of these districts.

Chicagoans themselves have cataloged parts of the city by typologies of economic activity and residential dwellers. Some of these identifications persist even after realities have changed. Chicago is a large city, and cognitive maps are not quickly updated by those who know only parts of it well. For example, the district centering on the intersection of Division Street, Milwaukee, and Ashland Avenues on the city's near Northwest Side in the West Town Community Area was long identified as Polish in ethnicity. This was held to be true even though Jews, Italians, Scandinavians, Germans, and Ukrainians all lived close by and mingled with the Poles at various times in the history of Chicago. Even after

I would like to thank Kathleen Alaimo and Ellen Skerrett for their help with this article.

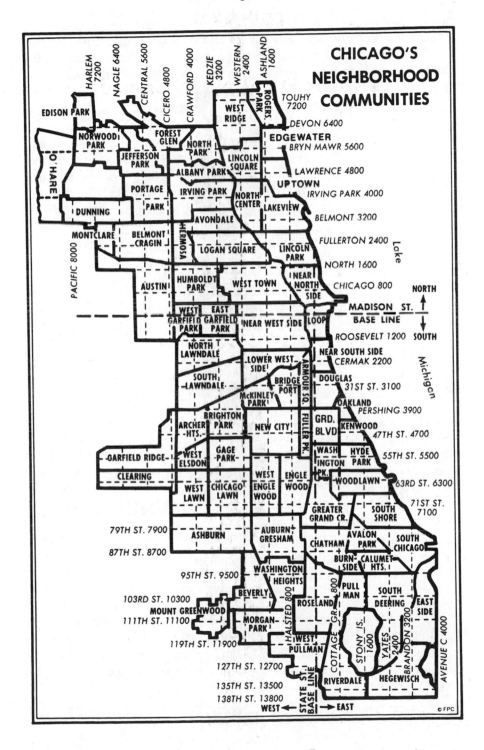

CHICAGO'S NEIGHBORHOOD COMMUNITIES

many Polish Americans had left West Town and Hispanic residents came to dominate the area, the city named a small park at the intersection Polonia Triangle. Bridgeport, in turn, is still referred to as Irish, perhaps because of the Daley family and other Irish-American politicians who called the area home, though this neighborhood has historically had a varied ethnic base. Pilsen, just to the north of Bridgeport, still carries a Bohemian name, though the neighborhood in 1991 contained the largest Mexican community in the city. Lithuanian Marquette Park includes among its residents many Irish, Polish, and other European Americans as well as the second largest Arab-American community in the United States. By the late 1980s, Marquette Park also included growing Hispanic and African-American populations adding to the district's diversity. Change has been and remains a constant factor on the streets of Chicago's neighborhoods.

Most Chicago neighborhoods were shared by more than one ethnic group. This was generally true despite the identification of any particular district with one particular group. Irish, German, Mexican, Greek, Jewish, Polish, and Czech families, among others, lived on the city's near West Side even though most outsiders considered this area to be Italian. In Back of the Yards, a neighborhood long identified with Polish Chicagoans, twelve different Catholic churches had been erected by the 1930s, testifying to the ethnic diversity of the district and to the fact that ethnic Chicagoans constantly moved in and out of these industrial neighborhoods. Only African-American neighborhoods remained physically segregated in Chicago. Even Chinatown contained large non-Asian populations long after its identification as a Chinese residential community. Indeed, most working-class Chicago neighborhoods were spatially integrated, that is, various communities of people lived together. They remained, however, socially segregated: members of various ethnic groups created their own cultural and social institutions and remained generally apart from each other, at least in the first generation.[1]

The *neighborhood,* for the pioneering Chicago School of Sociology, was a mosaic of social worlds segregated like plants in a garden and in competition with one another. The capitalist market economy ensured a kind of Darwinian struggle for survival for both groups and functions. A proprietary sense of place, as well as human prejudices, segregated groups of individuals from others. Later

---

1. On the Italians of Chinatown, see *Santa Maria Incoronata Church Golden Anniversary Book, 1904-1954* (Chicago, 1954); *Santa Lucia Silver Jubilee Book* (Chicago, 1968). On the demographic development of Back of the Yards, see Robert Slayton, *Back of the Yards: The Making of a Local Democracy* (Chicago, 1986); James R. Barrett, *Work and Community in the Jungle: Chicago's Packinghouse Workers, 1894-1922* (Urbana and Chicago, 1987); Louise C. Wade, *Chicago's Pride: The Stockyards, Packingtown, and Environs in the Nineteenth Century* (Urbana and Chicago, 1987) For a discussion of the development of the West Side, see Dominic A. Pacyga and Ellen Skerrett, *Chicago: City of Neighborhoods* (Chicago, 1986), chap. 6. For a look at the ethnic and racial history of Chicago, see *Historic City: The Settlement of Chicago* (Chicago, 1976).

investigators such as Gerald Suttles continued to see segregation and competition. A more recent look at urban neighborhoods by Ira Katznelson even describes the creation and use of what he calls "city trenches." What emerges from the sociological and historical literature is an image of the American city as battleground between groups competing for the finite rewards and limited services of the urban industrial economy.[2]

The whole problem, then, of neighborhood succession emerges as a major factor in the history of Chicago and of the American city as a whole. Yet the myth of neighborhood stability still remains as a potent force. The question of stability in the face of constant change presents itself to Chicagoans of every ethnic, racial, or class group.

Neighborhood change occurred early on in the history of Chicago. Yankee settlers from the Eastern United States quickly displaced the French and Indian residents of the Chicago area after the rebuilding of Fort Dearborn in 1816. As Jacqueline Peterson has shown in the first essay in this collection, along with the arrival of the Easterners came cultural change. The old French-Indian Creole culture that had dominated the Upper Midwest quickly disappeared. When the Potawatomi bands, painted in the colors of death, made their way through the streets of Chicago and danced out of sight they began a tradition of leaving the city behind to newcomers and moving on to another settlement. In a very real sense, Chicago went through neighborhood change with its very founding in the 1830s. A new ethnic group, the Yankees, began to dominate Chicago.[3]

The Yankees quickly made the city their own. Being the dominant cultural group in the city and the nation, the Yankees are not often treated as an ethnic group, but they certainly acted like one. New Englanders and others from the East Coast established organizations, including churches and schools such as the Latin School. They also came to dominate neighborhoods, and they were among the first to leave the core of the city and move to suburbs — *before* the Civil War. The expansion of Anglo-Saxon Protestant neighborhoods and communities across the city and the early ring of suburbs, many of which later became part of the city in the annexation frenzy of the late nineteenth century, is marked in the institutional legacy this group left behind.

The Anglo-Saxons tended to move south and north along the lakefront and directly west of the city center. The very rich settled first in the southern part of the downtown area and then farther south, in the Prairie Avenue District. Many members of the white Protestant middle class began to move even farther out as transportation systems allowed them to spread across the prairie. Three early suburbs, Evanston, Hyde Park, and Oak Park, soon became dominated by

2. Robert E. L. Ferris, *Chicago Sociology, 1920-1932* (Chicago, 1970), p. 25; Gerald D. Suttles, *The Social Order of the Slum: Ethnicity and Territory in the Inner City* (Chicago, 1968); Ira Katznelson, *City Trenches: Urban Politics and the Patterning of Class in the United States* (Chicago, 1981).

3. Jacqueline Peterson, "Chicago's Founding Fathers," in this volume.

these native white Protestants as they left the core of the city behind to Irish, German, and Scandinavian immigrants, who were flooding into the city by the 1850s. The new rail system that developed in Chicago after 1848 allowed the development of a new kind of Chicagoan, the commuter. The pattern of the well-off leaving the central city behind was set early in Chicago's history. After the Civil War, the South Side of the city expanded greatly as Anglo-Saxon settlement pressed farther and farther south.

Green spaces laid out by Frederick Law Olmsted surrounded the town core of Hyde Park, which attracted middle-class residents. The combination of the Illinois Central Railroad commuter line and the new system of parks seemed to ensure a bright future for Hyde Park and much of the emerging South Side. Large and fine homes appeared on the tree-lined Douglas, Grand Boulevard, Washington Park, Hyde Park, and Kenwood streets. Protestant churches appeared on these same streets as more and more families made their way south along the fine boulevard system that was developed to complement the new parks. These middle-class Protestant families left behind them the hustle and bustle, the dirt, and the noise of the industrial city from which they had profited. Their escape from the city seemed complete: the Illinois Central Railroad provided convenient and dependable transportation for these suburban pioneers; the South Parks and accompanying boulevard system, as well as nearby Lake Michigan provided a "civilized" setting for the upwardly mobile urban dweller. Stability and civility seemed to be the standards of the day.[4]

In reality, however, the city was not far behind. Other ethnic groups soon followed the Yankees into Chicago's middle class and out of the center city. The very economic and technological success of the Yankee elite brought a quick end to their "ethnic" neighborhoods; rapid change continued to be a reality in a city built on the ideas of progress, growth, and technology. Transportation technology, especially, began to transform the South Side. In the 1880s, cable cars appeared on South Side streets, pushing as far south as 39th Street. Between 1887 and 1889, a new east-west horsecar line made its way across the city on 26th Street. Finally, between 1890 and 1892, the South Side "Alley El" was constructed, connecting Jackson Park and much of the South Side with the downtown area. This change in transportation configurations meant changes in residential patterns. Soon other groups moved down the boulevards of the South Side, and the Anglo-Saxon Protestants moved on.

Irish, German, and Jewish families began to move down the boulevards and close to the cable car lines and the new elevated railroad stops. Irish working-class families had begun to move into the South Side before the Civil War, founding St. James parish at 26th and Wabash in 1855. After the war, many

---

4. For the development of these South Side neighborhoods, see Glen E. Holt and Dominic A. Pacyga, *Chicago: A Historical Guide to the Neighborhoods, The Loop and South Side* (Chicago, 1979); see also Pacyga and Skerrett, *City of Neighborhoods*, chaps. 9, 10, and 11. For Olmsted and the South Parks, see Victoria Post Ranney, *Olmsted in Chicago* (Chicago, 1972).

newly upwardly-mobile Irish families made their way farther south. By the early 1890s, prominent Catholic Irish families, including those of John and Michael Cudahy, settled in the Douglas community near 35th Street and Wabash Avenue. De La Salle Institute stood prominent among the important institutions founded by the Irish in this stretch of the South Side. The boys' high school opened in 1892 on the northeast corner of 35th and Wabash. The school quickly made its mark in the educational history of Chicago.[5]

Along with the arrival of upper-middle-class Irish families in the Douglas community, leading Jewish families also made their way to the South Side neighborhood. In 1881, Michael Reese Hospital opened its doors at 29th Street and Cottage Grove. In 1889 the Standard Club, an elite men's organization created in 1869 by Chicago's German-Jewish community, moved to 24th Street and Michigan Avenue, just to the north of the district. Kehilath Anshe Ma'ariv (K.A.M.) Synagogue opened in 1890 at 33rd and Indiana Avenue. The area assumed the sobriquet Jewish Gold Coast.

Meanwhile, the African-American middle class also began to look to the South Side to locate its new institutions. The first meeting of Olivet Baptist Church took place downtown in 1853. Forty years later, however, as its membership grew, the congregation built a new place of worship at 27th and Dearborn streets. In 1917 this large black church purchased the building of the First Baptist Church at 31st and South Park Boulevard, which the white assembly had constructed in 1876. The Anglo-Saxon congregation simply moved farther south. The history of these various institutions speaks to the history of change in these middle-class communities and neighborhoods, especially during the World War I period and immediately after, when African-American migration to Chicago from the South began to increase. Chicago's black population doubled during the war, and it doubled again in the 1920s.[6]

The German-Jewish Standard Club eventually relocated in the Loop. K.A.M. sold its building on 33rd and Indiana to the Pilgrim Baptist Church, an African-American congregation, in 1922, just thirty-two years after it had opened. By that time, the great majority of the members of that Hebrew congregation had moved to neighborhoods farther south; K.A.M.'s members built

5. Holt and Pacyga, *Historical Guide*, p. 50; *De La Salle Institute Centennial History, 1889-1989* (Chicago, 1989); Rev. Msgr. Harry C. Koenig, S.T.D., ed., *A History of the Parishes of the Archdiocese of Chicago*, 2 vols. (Chicago, 1980) I, 454-460; The Chicago Fact Book Consortium, *Local Community Fact Book Chicago Metropolitan Area Based on the 1970 and 1980 Censuses* (Chicago, 1984), pp. 96-99.

6. Allan H. Spear, *Black Chicago: The Making of a Negro Ghetto, 1890-1920* (Chicago, 1967), 177-178; William M. Tuttle, Jr., *Race Riot: Chicago in the Red Summer of 1919* (New York, 1982), p. 98. For a discussion of the impact of the Great Migration on Chicago, see James R. Grossman, *Land of Hope: Chicago, Black Southerners, and the Great Migration* (Chicago, 1989). The classic sociological study of the Great Migration and the development of Black Chicago is St. Clair Drake and Horace R. Cayton, *Black Metropolis: A Study of Negro Life in a Northern City*, 2 vols. (New York, 1970).

a new temple at 50th and Drexel in Hyde Park. Other Hebrew congregations witnessed the same basic history. In 1899, Temple Isaiah was dedicated at 4501 S. Vincennes Avenue; twenty-one years later, the temple moved to Hyde Park farther south. In 1912, Sinai Temple opened at the southwest corner of 46th and Grand Boulevard; in 1944 that temple also moved to Hyde Park. The Lakeside Club, one of the South Side's most important Jewish institutions, located at 42nd Street and Grand Boulevard, opened in 1893 just as South Side Jews were coming into their own in the middle-class areas of the city. It was sold to an African-American congregation in 1924 and was burned down by arsonists that same year.[7]

The Catholic population of the South Side also witnessed change. Irish Catholics founded Corpus Christi Parish in 1901, and they constructed a magnificent church in 1915 at 49th and Grand Boulevard. Seventeen years later, Corpus Christi became a black Catholic parish. The black middle class moved south along the boulevards, just as the Anglo-Saxons, the Irish, and the Jews had before them, and opened churches and social centers as they did.[8] The short-lived Douglas Center operated at 3032 S. Wabash Avenue in 1903; and in May 1910 the Negro Fellowship League Reading Room and Social Center for men and boys was opened at 2830 S. State Street. Ida B. Wells played a crucial role in both of these organizations. Robert T. Motts opened the Pekin Theater at 27th and State Street in the early 1900s. Everywhere across the South Side, change took place rapidly as the city expanded across the prairie.

The fact that many of the white ethnic institutions in these South Side areas lasted for a generation or less is a sign of the quick pace of change. Some of the larger organizations such as Michael Reese Hospital and De La Salle Institute, which had a citywide following, remained beyond the ethnic turnover of these communities; but transformations took place in all of these institutions. Chicagoans kept moving across the cityscape. However, this is not to say that change occurred peacefully or without resistance. Especially in the case of racial change, resistance could be quite stiff. In 1919 a race riot shook the city, leaving thirty-eight dead and several hundred injured. Much of the fighting took place on the South Side between African Americans and recently upwardly-mobile ethnic groups of a West European heritage, particularly the Irish. These latter groups had just succeeded in taking hold of many areas that were now undergoing racial succession. The building of Corpus Christi church in 1915 on Grand Boulevard, near the center of the conflict, gives testament to this. The white ethnic middle class felt most threatened by the spread of African-American neighborhoods. Later racial conflicts often involved Eastern and Southern

---

7. Pacyga and Skerrett, *City of Neighborhoods,* pp. 301-357.
8. Koenig, *Parish Histories,* I: 216-219; Alfreda M. Duster, ed., *Crusade for Justice: The Autobiography of Ida B. Wells* (Chicago, 1970), pp. 279-307.

European ethnics in large numbers as these newer groups entered the middle class.[9]

These middle-class ethnic areas, whether Anglo-Saxon, Irish, or German Jewish, saw rapid racial succession in the period before World War II. The argument could be made that the reality of change was a middle-class phenomenon, and that working-class ethnic communities and neighborhoods witnessed more and longer periods of stability. Yet it was the constant influx of new immigrants to replenish neighborhoods being left by the more acculturated that gave the illusion of stability to these neighborhoods. In reality, Chicago's ethnic working-class neighborhoods witnessed demographic shifts too.

While the middle and upper classes created their neighborhoods first along the lakefront and on the West Side of the city, working-class Chicagoans settled near the branches of the Chicago River. Here the industrial might of the city could be seen. Massive industrial plants, grain elevators, lumber yards, and packinghouses were located near the sluggish stream making its way across the prairie. These huge capitalist ventures contrasted with the commuter rail lines, parks, and universities of the wealthier residential parts of Chicago. Soon vast working-class neighborhoods rose to provide homes for industrial laborers and their families. The near Southwest and Northwest Sides emerged as industrial residential districts even before the Civil War. Two diagonal streets, Archer Avenue on the Southwest Side and Milwaukee Avenue on the Northwest Side, were intimately connected with the formation of these districts. To the southwest of the city, the digging of the Illinois-Michigan Canal provided much of the impetus for development: Archer Avenue first served as a service road for this huge construction project, which was built between 1836 and 1848. Industry also located along the North Branch of the river, creating the Milwaukee Avenue corridor.[10] These two arteries acted as funnels for the ethnic populations that came to work in Chicago's industries and inhabit the districts connected to them. Here, too, transportation changes proved crucial for the movement of ethnic groups across the cityscape.

In 1847 the Irish canal workers who had been settling along Archer Avenue, southwest of the city in the old Hardscrabble district, increasingly known as Bridgeport, founded the mission of St. Bridget parish. By 1850, St. Bridget's parish became the mother church of the Irish working-class parishes of the Southwest Side. Soon other Catholic and Protestant ethnic groups

9. The best general discussions of the riot are Tuttle, *Race Riot,* and Chicago Commission on Race Relations, *The Negro in Chicago: A Study of Race Relations and a Race Riot* (Chicago, 1922). For a discussion of the role of Irish and Polish South Siders in the riot, see Dominic A. Pacyga, "Race, Ethnicity, and Acculturation: Chicago's Poles and Irish and the 1919 Race Riot," in Michael Ebner, Kathleen Conzen, and Russell Lewis, eds., *American City History: Modes of Inquiry* (Chicago: The University of Chicago Press, forthcoming).

10. William Cronon, *Nature's Metropolis: Chicago and the Great West* (New York, 1991), gives a detailed description of the industrial development of the city in the nineteenth century.

founded churches in the neighborhoods adjacent to Archer Avenue. Germans, Poles, Lithuanians, and French Canadians established overlapping settlements in the Bridgeport and McKinley Park neighborhoods.[11] The working-class Irish meanwhile moved west down Archer Avenue to Brighton Park and formed St. Agnes parish in 1878, just more than three miles from St. Bridget's. In 1889 the French Catholics, in turn, created another parish, St. Joseph and St. Ann, on 38th and California, replacing the old St. Jean de Baptiste church farther east in McKinley Park. Eventually four more ethnic Catholic parishes were carved out of the territory once covered by the parish of St. Agnes. The creation of these various parishes gives testimony to the movement of these ethnic groups across the prairie as the city expanded.[12]

The number and ethnic diversity of these churches was hardly unusual. Most of Chicago's neighborhoods, particularly working-class neighborhoods, saw these kinds of developments during the one hundred years of intense European immigration that flowed into the city. In Back of the Yards, just to the east of Brighton Park, twelve Roman Catholic parishes stood challenging the packinghouse smokestacks for dominance of the sky. Each of these represented further migration into the district. In the 1890s, when Mary McDowell arrived in the Back of the Yards to open the University of Chicago Settlement House, the area was already changing from a district dominated by the Irish and Germans to one that was primarily Slavic in character. By World War I, more than thirty Roman Catholic churches surrounded the Chicago Stockyards in the Bridgeport, Canaryville, McKinley Park, and Back of the Yards neighborhoods, testifying to the strength of the stockyards as an economic-industrial base on the Southwest Side. Add to these the parishes of Englewood, Brighton Park, Gage Park, and other neighborhoods that developed just beyond the Stock Yard District, and you get the image of an ever-widening pool of Catholic and Protestant ethnic groups across the Southwest Side of Chicago.[13]

While succession had always been a factor in the history of Chicago's neighborhoods, the twenty-year period after 1945 saw the pace of change accelerate. Race seemed to be more of an actor in neighborhood change than it had been in the 1919 Race Riot, which set racial boundaries in Chicago for

11. *Auksinis Jubiliejus Sv. Jugio Parapija, 1892-1942* [Golden Jubilee Book of St. George Parish, 1892-1942] (Chicago, 1942); Vivien Palmer, ed., "Documents History of Bridgeport Community, Chicago," Document No. 3 informant an Irishman born in Bridgeport and christened in 1856, dated August 1925, typed manuscript, Chicago Historical Society. See also Koenig, *Parish Histories*, I: 97-99, 145-151, 519, 604-608.

12. Koenig, *Parish Histories*, I: 28-30; Holt and Pacyga, *Historical Guide* pp. 150-153. For a discussion of Irish Catholic parishes, see Ellen Skerrett, "The Catholic Dimension" in Lawrence J. McCaffrey, Michael F. Funchion, Ellen Skerrett, and Charles Fanning, *The Irish in Chicago* (Urbana and Chicago, 1987).

13. Mary E. McDowell, The Foreign Born (Immigrants in the Packing Industry), p. 1 in Mary Eliza McDowell Papers, Chicago Historical Society, box 2, folder 12; *Catholic Map Directory of the City of Chicago* (Chicago, 1954), pp. 32-33, 38-39, 45, 49.

twenty years. World War II, however, with its massive mobilization of Chicago's industry, greatly influenced the city's demographics. Indeed a second great migration of Southern blacks occurred during the Second World War, once again putting pressure on the racial boundaries that had been more or less in place since the early 1920s. A wartime housing shortage kept racial lines drawn during the war, but soon after the armistice and the subsequent economic boom, the effect of the new migration was quickly felt on both the South and West sides of the city.

The South Side Black Belt pushed farther south along the boulevards of the city. African Americans found housing opportunities in neighborhoods adjacent to their traditional settlements, which had long shunned them. White Chicagoans meanwhile took part in a national trend and began leaving the inner city in large numbers and heading to the suburbs. This round of suburbanization during the post–World War II boom seemed to be something new; but in reality it was simply the continuation of a trend that had started earlier but had been partially disrupted by twenty years of depression, war, and readjustment. Arnold Hirsch has vividly portrayed the tensions of this period in his study of racial conflict in the city after 1940. Eastern and Southern European ethnics, who had begun to move into better neighborhoods after World War II, found themselves in conflict with African Americans, who also hoped to improve their residential and economic conditions. The roots of those conflicts lay in the American urban tradition of expansion and change.[14]

The 1920s is a crucial decade for understanding the changes of the twentieth century. In that ten-year period the automobile came to have its first large-scale effect on the American city. The growth of new residential neighborhoods on the fringes of the older industrial neighborhoods came about, in large part, because of the automobile, even though public transportation still served these newly settled districts. Most of these neighborhoods benefited from rapid transit, street-car, or new bus lines in the post–World War I era. Yet the spread of the Chicago bungalow throughout the outlying districts owes much to the emergence of the automobile. Neighborhoods such as Gage Park, Chicago Lawn (Marquette Park), and Garfield Ridge on the Southwest Side, and Portage Park, Belmont-Cragin, and Jefferson Park emerged as growing residential areas during this period.

Portage Park reached residential maturity in 1924: the majority of its homes were one- and two-family buildings. In 1930, 80 percent of all houses were single-family homes, and Portage Park had become part of the bungalow belt. This far Northwest Side community area had 24,439 residents in 1920; the population had shot up to 64,203 ten years later. Portage Park's largest immigrant groups in 1930 were the Germans, Poles, and Scandinavians; Poles predominated in the southern section of the district.

14. Arnold R. Hirsch, *Making the Second Ghetto: Race and Housing in Chicago, 1940-1960* (Cambridge, 1983), pp. 1-39.

Belmont-Cragin underwent a tremendous growth in the 1920s: in 1920, census takers counted 13,492 inhabitants in this Northwest Side area; ten years later there were 60,221 residents, one-third of whom were foreign-born. Residential construction reached its peak in the 1920s: in that decade's first eighteen months alone, residential construction exceeded the previous ten years. Jefferson Park also experienced a dramatic increase in population during that decade, from 5,825 to 20,532.

On the Southwest Side the movement out of the stockyards district also increased in volume in the 1920s. Czechs and Poles followed the Germans and Irish southwest from Bridgeport, McKinley Park, and the Back of the Yards. In 1920 the population of Gage Park stood at 13,692; ten years later, it had more than doubled to 31,500. Neighboring Chicago Lawn saw its greatest growth during the same decade: the population grew from 14,000 to over 47,000 in 1930. Garfield Ridge contained a population of 2,472 in 1920; by 1930 the population had risen to 6,050. These figures, when compared to those for the Northwest Side, indicated that much of the Southwest Side remained undeveloped even after the 1920s.

With the onset of the Great Depression and the war, those neighborhoods remained undeveloped. Yet the demographic and economic trends that would remake the city after 1945 were already in place in the 1920s. White ethnics continued to flow out of the core of the city, leaving older settlements behind to either African Americans, other ethnic groups, or, in the case of the Eastern and Southern Europeans, more recent immigrants from their own groups. The automobile and the 1920s version of tract housing, the bungalow, encouraged this dispersion across the cityscape. However, the financial collapse of the 1930s slowed or stopped, and in some cases reversed, this trend. The outbreak of war in 1941 also kept residential expansion to a minimum. In many ways the trends, including the decentralization of American industry, seemed to be frozen by the emergencies of the 1930s and 1940s. After peace and readjustment, however, these trends re-emerged in much stronger forms and transformed Chicago.

The outlying parts of the Southwest Side saw unprecedented growth in the 1950s. Garfield Ridge blossomed from a small, almost rural community of just over 6,000 inhabitants in 1940 to 12,900 inhabitants in 1950, and 40,449 in 1960. But older communities closer to the Loop along Archer Avenue saw their populations decrease: Brighton Park's population fell from more than 45,000 in 1940 to just over 38,000 in 1960 and to 30,770 in 1980. Bridgeport, McKinley Park, and Back of the Yards also witnessed population losses during that period. Meanwhile, outlying districts like Mount Greenwood and West Lawn continued to see increases until the 1970s, when the continued outward movement of Chicagoans had a negative impact on these community areas.[15]

Racial succession marked the postwar period as the most important and visible kind of population turnover in the city's history. As Arnold Hirsch and

15. *Fact Book,* pp. 29-30, 38-40, 48-50, 144-146, 149-158, 161-162, 165-169, 187-188.

others have pointed out, new residential construction boomed after World War II. From 1945 to 1959, more than 680,000 new homes were constructed in the Chicago metropolitan area, more than 77 percent of them in the suburbs. Seventy-six percent of the new buildings were single-family dwellings, and the great majority of the construction took place on the southwest, northwest, and southeast fringes of the city.[16] These areas quickly became known as bastions of white ethnic groups who had for the most part left the inner ring of neighborhoods by the 1970s. The outward flow of middle-class Chicagoans of every economic and ethnic background, which had been initiated by the Anglo-Saxons one hundred years earlier, continued. The process of ethnic and racial succession also continued, as the city became transformed by the economic, technological, and demographic shifts of the postwar era.

West Englewood on the Southwest Side is a good example of the succession process as it manifested itself in the period after 1960. A small African-American population had existed in the neighborhood from the late nineteenth century onward; in 1930, blacks made up 3.1 percent of the neighborhoods' population. During World War II the black population of West Englewood began to rise. The district was located just south of the stockyards district, and black packinghouse workers found the area desirable. Various attempts were made to stabilize the area, but in the 1950s, during the postwar residential building boom, 14,000 whites left the area. High white fertility rates disguised the trend, but by the 1960s, racial succession seemed unavoidable, especially in the eastern sections of the community area.

In 1970, African Americans made up 48.3 percent of West Englewood's population, and ten years later they comprised 98.1 percent of the population. It was during this period that Rev. Francis Lawler, an Augustinian priest and teacher at St. Rita High School, emerged as a local leader of the white population and led the failed attempt to keep the area to the west of Ashland Avenue predominantly white. He eventually represented the district in the city council. Racial antipathy reached great heights as West Englewood went through racial change. White middle-class and working-class residents left the area in great numbers after 1968. While whites and blacks still shared the neighborhood in 1970, this proved to be a very temporary arrangement. The pattern of racial change also brought the usual process of local economic disinvestment. Businesses left the Ashland Avenue and 63rd Street shopping strip. In turn, the housing stock, rather old and poorly maintained, fell into decline. The traditional pattern of segregation, integration, and resegregation reasserted itself quickly in West Englewood.[17]

Meanwhile, the neighborhoods to the west of Western Avenue, especially Marquette Park and Gage Park, acted in a defensive mode as the African-American population increased in and then overwhelmed West Englewood. When Dr. Martin

16. Hirsch, *Second Ghetto* pp. 27-28.
17. *Fact Book,* pp. 169-172.

Luther King, Jr., led an open-housing march into these areas in 1966, whites threw stones at him and rioted. West Englewood became a symbol of racial succession and economic disinvestment while Gage Park and Marquette Park became symbols of the urban racism of the North.

Marquette Park and Gage Park were part of that expanding bungalow belt of the 1920s. These areas also saw some residential expansion in the post–World War II period. From 1960 to 1980, Gage Park maintained a population that was well over 90 percent white. African Americans made no inroads during this twenty-year period, while neighborhoods to the east went through racial succession. In 1980 Hispanics made up only 6.3 percent of Gage Park's population; ten years later, however, that would change. By 1990, whites made up only 54.9 percent of the community area's population; and even though African Americans still accounted for only 5.1 percent, the Hispanic percentage rose to 39.2 percent. Hispanics, primarily Mexicans, provided the numbers that actually reversed a fifty-year long decline in population.

Chicago Lawn, known locally as Marquette Park and situated south of Gage Park, also saw changes in the years after the 1966 riots. As late as 1970, Chicago Lawn was 99.6 percent white. By 1980, however, the white percentage had dropped to 83 percent, with a small black and Hispanic population, and the 1990 census found whites to be a 43 percent minority of residents, while blacks and Hispanics comprised 28.4 percent and 26.5 percent respectively. Both Chicago Lawn and Gage Park also contained large Arab populations. The white ethnic exodus from the city continued, though the rate of change was certainly slower than the racial turnover of West Englewood twenty years earlier. Gage Park and Chicago Lawn residents, along with those from other nearby neighborhoods, banded together to promote stability and diversity in 1989 under the guidance of the Southwest Catholic Cluster Project, which attempted to promote these districts as desirable places to live for all Chicagoans. This acceptance of diversity was a far cry from the opposition to the open housing marches in the 1960s.[18]

Technological change has had a tremendous impact on the post-1945 neighborhood. The automobile transformed the urban transportation system, and highways cut across the cityscape, increasing the speed of change. In the old Polish-dominated West Town district, adjacent to Milwaukee Avenue as it begins its run Northwest, the building of the Kennedy Expressway nearly destroyed the St. Stanislaus Kostka parish. The massive construction project tore at the very fabric of the Polish community and sped the ethnic change that was already beginning to take place as Hispanics moved into the community. The 1960 census showed that 25 percent of Chicago's Puerto Ricans lived in West Town. In 1990 Hispanics made up 62 percent of West Town's

18. *Fact Book,* pp. 161-162, 167-169; Chicago *Sun-Times,* February 24, 1991; Don Hayner, "Marquette Park — Quiet Change," Chicago *Sun-Times,* July 22, 1990; Michael J. Bela, "Southwest Side Coalition Seeks Ways to Create Racial Harmony," *New World,* April 14, 1989.

population[19] (indeed, a quarter of Chicago's Puerto Ricans lived in West Town already by 1960).

The automobile and the highway have not been the only forces at work in neighborhood change. Changes in communication and even in entertainment, such as the widespread use of the telephone and television, have all had their impact on community life. Even architecture, which has to an extent turned its back on the neighborhood street in order to create private family space, has had an impact on the social life of the city. Certainly there has been a good deal of privatization of life in the city since the 1940s.

The lure of what Robert Fishman calls the "new" city, which has been designed around these changes, is also evident. The expanding residential areas beyond the traditional industrial metropolis has attracted urban dwellers for a long time. It is not surprising, for example, that many of Chicago's Lithuanians are settling in Lemont, Illinois, far from their traditional South Side neighborhood in Marquette Park.[20] Chicagoans with the ability to segregate themselves from others continue to do so as they have from the beginning. Hispanics, African Americans, and Arabs now outnumber the Lithuanians and other Euro-ethnics of Marquette Park.

A recent study of Chicago and other American cities has pointed to the increased segmentation of urban residential districts since 1945. Ever since Jane Jacob's study of urban residential areas, sociologists, anthropologists, and urban planners have bemoaned the loss of urban diversity.[21] This trend however, has a long history: Chicagoans have always divided themselves by race and class. Historically, ethnicity too has played a role in the way Chicagoans organize themselves. Many times, different white ethnic groups shared the same neighborhood, but they segregated themselves socially by creating separate institutions, such as churches, schools, adult clubs, stores, taverns, and even street gangs.

There is a good deal of continuity in the history of Chicago's changing neighborhoods. That continuity, however, revolves around ethnic and racial segregation and succession. These trends have provided lasting influences on Chicago's ethnic neighborhoods. Chicago's neighborhood history centers on the reality of change rather than on the myth of stability. Technological shifts in industry and urban transportation have made such population turnover possible. Yet it has been attitudes concerning race, ethnicity, and class that influenced the choices Chicagoans have historically made. To a large extent, technological advances did not so much alter as reinforce trends in place since the Yankees drove the French and Indians out of the old settlement in the 1830s.

19. Ed Marciniak, *Reviving an Inner City Community* (Chicago, 1970), pp. 18-19; *Fact Book*, pp. 62-66; Chicago *Sun-Times*, February 24, 1991.

20. Robert Fishman, "America's New City: Megalopolis Unbound," *The Wilson Quarterly* (Winter 1990), 25-48; Tim Hadac, "Lithuanians Looking to Bolster Ethnic Character," *Southwest News-Herald*, July 29, 1989.

21. Larry Bennett, *Fragments of Cities: The New American Downtowns and Neighborhoods* (Columbus, OH 1990).

CHAPTER 22

Ethnic Cemeteries:
Underground Rites

HELEN A. SCLAIR

Chicago's population represents more than one hundred distinct ethnic groups. Most of these populations have been absorbed into the city at large, leaving very few external characteristics of their existence. Initially, churches and temples were identified with a single group; today these original congregations have moved elsewhere. Societies, vereins, and fraternals have been disbanded or transported in the migrations to the suburbs. The presumed permanence of the cemetery may be the sole viable sign remaining of what was once a vocal and visible community. In the discussion that follows we will examine representative ethnic cemeteries in the Chicagoland area.

Chicago's earliest burials were near Fort Dearborn and along the banks of the Chicago River.[1] The population was small and heterogeneous, drawn by activities at the fort and the trading posts. The town of Chicago attempted, by ordinance, to formalize burials by creating two cemeteries in August 1835. Both were located on the lakeshore, at the town's limits, one at Chicago and Rush, the other at Twelfth and Michigan.[2] When the Irish arrived to dig the Illinois and Michigan Canal, they preferred to be buried above the watertable and on higher ground at what is now called Saint James the Sag, north of Lemont.[3] Undoubtedly, the two town cemeteries were unsatisfactory from the outset, having been laid out directly on the shores of Lake Michigan, where they were buffeted by lake storms and the vagaries of shifting sands. Graves were shallow (only three to four feet deep), maintenance was difficult, and the result was

1. Alfred T. Andreas, *History of Chicago*, Vol. II (Chicago, 1885), pp. 448-454.
2. Bessie Louise Pierce, *A History of Chicago*, Vol. I (New York, 1937), p. 354. Map of Fractional Section No. Fifteen, Township 39 North, Range East of the 3D Principal Meridian, April 1836. Map of the Town of Chicago and Canal Lands, 1836, prepared by the commissioners of the Illinois and Michigan Canal, Chicago Historical Society.
3. *Caritas Christi Urqet Nos: A History of the Offices, Agencies and Institutions of the Archdiocese of Chicago*, Vol. I (Chicago, 1980), pp. 37-39.

unpleasant, unsightly, and unsavory. Sometimes decomposing remains were even exposed.[4]

Chicago was organized as a city in 1837. As the population and industry expanded, settlements began to extend toward the early town cemeteries. By 1842, four thousand people lived and worked in Chicago, and no longer were these burial grounds on the outskirts. In addition, the need for a well-managed larger cemetery, located on higher ground, had become apparent. The beach ridge on which the Green Bay Trail (Clark Street at North Avenue) was located, was available, and was selected. Although it was less than fifteen feet above the lake's water level, this land was seen as ideal for the "Chicago Cemetery." A sexton was hired to oversee the operation, and the removal of bodies from the two older cemeteries began. The city of Chicago now owned a new and improved burying ground.[5]

In that same year, the Roman Catholic Diocese of Chicago also purchased land for interring its departed souls, south of North Avenue between State and Dearborn streets.[6] Finally, there were places of burial that were deemed suitable for all the people of Chicago. Who were these people? They were Irish, German, English, Scotch, and Scandinavian — both Catholic and Protestant.[7] Grave markers were simple obelisks (some draped), urns, or slab headstones, which were the preferred form for Protestants in the Chicago Cemetery. Even in this early period the followers of Reformation religions objected to crosses and crucifixes, which were viewed as "papist." The old Catholic cemetery, on the other hand, had the crosses and crucifixes as its monuments, often made of wood or "marble" from Lemont.[8]

In outlying communities, in addition to Saint James the Sag (1837), other cemeteries were being laid out: Irish Saint Patrick in West Lake Forest (1840); Scotch Presbyterian in Millburn (1840); German Saint Joseph in Wilmette (1843); German Saint James in Sauk Village (1847); Irish Saint Patrick in Lemont (1849); Irish Saint Patrick in Wadsworth (1849). These cemeteries still exist today (all current cemeteries cited here are listed with their addresses at the end of this essay). Some of them now bury different ethnic groups and the newer arrivals.[9]

---

4. *City Council Proceedings Files, 1833-1871,* Illinois Regional Archives Depository, Northeastern Illinois University. A book pertaining to Chicago's earliest cemeteries and the populations buried therein is under preparation by the author. Much of the information for this article is derived from that source. William D. Pattison, "Land for the Dead of Chicago" (M.A. thesis, University of Chicago, 1952), pp. 20-24; Pattison, "The Cemeteries in Chicago: A Phase of Land Utilization," *Annals of the Association of American Geographers,* XLV, No. 3 (September 1955), 253, 254.

5. *City Council Proceedings.*

6. Pierce, p. 238.

7. *Historic City: The Settlement of Chicago* (Chicago, 1976), pp. 9-13.

8. Author's notes. An earlier name of Lemont was Athens, to promote the limestone industry.

9. Carl B. Pietras, "Catholic Cemeteries of the Archdiocese of Chicago" (M.A. thesis, Chicago State University, 1977), in the Archives of the Archdiocesan Cemeteries.

In south suburban Roseland, the True Holland Reformed Church, known as the "Dutch Church" or the "Holland Church," was built at 107th and Michigan in 1850. A small parish cemetery was located next to the church; names of ministers include Wust, Koopman, Ess, Kruikard, Flipse, Heemstra, and so forth. The living congregation moved to South Holland, and the dead were moved to Mount Greenwood. But apparently not all of the dead, for in 1928 and again in 1983, during construction at the old church-cemetery site, other coffins were discovered, which were also moved to Mount Greenwood.[10]

Chicago's one identifiable Native American Cemetery came into being through an Indian benefactor. Alexander Robinson and his family lived on the two sections of land that had been granted to him at the Treaty of Prairie du Chien in 1829. In addition, he was receiving two annuities for his aid in negotiating other treaties. Also known as Che-Che-Pin-Quay, Chief of the Pottawatomies, Ottawas, and Chippewas, Robinson and his wife, Catherine, and their Saint Xavier-educated children remained on their land near the Des Plaines River, opting not to move during the great Indian removal to the reservations west of the Mississippi River. Part of the Robinson tract became an Indian cemetery. Other Native-American burial sites exist, several of which have been built over and replaced by the more modern cemeteries of later users of the land.[11]

The first Jews that arrived in 1845 were German by birth. One of their initial acts was to purchase (for $45) nine-tenths of an acre for a burial ground in what is now Lincoln Park. In this case the burying ground was dedicated before the temple was; their temple, Kehilath Anshe Maariv, was not established until a year later.[12]

By the 1850s the deadly scourge of successive cholera epidemics had contributed to the need for expanded burial sites. In addition, the city's population was growing. The desperate conditions existing in the earlier cemeteries were being repeated in the burial grounds at North Avenue. Complaints against the continued burying of the dead so close to the city's water supply were often heard: the public feared that grave putrefaction might be contaminating their water. People also suspected that there might be a definite connection between the poorly buried dead and the potential for disease and death. The "Pest House," which was a warehouse for the plague-ridden and dying, and the nearby

10. Jan Helge and Paula Malak, *Churches of the Greater Roseland Area* (South Holland, 1988), pp. 28-29.

11. Alfred T. Andreas, *History of Cook County, Illinois* (Chicago, 1886), p. 108. Charles S. Winslow, ed., *Indians of the Chicago Region* (Chicago, 1946), pp. 159-162. A photograph in this book includes the tombstones of the Robinson family as they appeared in the 1880s. They were similar to those to be found in any cemetery of the era. The present boulder, erected in 1984, was deemed necessary after vandalism(s) had destroyed the original markers. At least four members of the family were buried there.

12. Morris A. Gutstein, *A Priceless Heritage* (New York, 1953), pp. 25, 433-435. *City Council Proceedings.* See note.

"Morgue" were located in the City Cemetery and only served to heighten public concern with the cemetery.[13]

Among the first to acknowledge the need to move their dead were the elders of the Jewish Cemetery. They purchased four acres of land at Belmont and Clark in 1856[14]; by 1889 that cemetery was full and not able to receive the deceased members of Kehilath Anshe Maariv. The congregation purchased new space at Addison and Narraganset. (This story of multiple removals of Jewish bodies is unique, for the moving of Jewish cemeteries is rarely undertaken; it represents a good example of the difficulty in locating suitable burial space in Chicago.) Earlier inscriptions on grave markers were frequently written in Hebrew, but later generations chose English. Most of these memorials are expansive yet plain, for the depiction of a human form in sculpture was not encouraged. Gray granite was most often the stone of choice.[15] An exception to the monochrome monotony at Mount Maariv is a rose-granite Corinthian column that marks the final resting place of the architect Dankmar Adler. It was designed by him and once stood as one of a pair at the entrance to a building at State and Randolph.[16] Winding roads and shade trees enhance this garden-like cemetery. The Jewish custom of leaving small stones or pebbles, rarely flowers, on the monuments as mementos of a visit can still be seen at Mount Maariv, as well as at all Jewish cemeteries.

Another German Jewish Cemetery was dedicated in 1854 by the Hebrew Benevolent Society on North Clark Street, and other temples purchased sections here as well. The area became known colloquially as Jewish Graceland.[17] (Graceland Cemetery was the only one of the three non-Catholic Victorian Cemeteries founded in the mid-nineteenth century that did not include a Jewish section; Rosehill and Oakwoods cemeteries had extensive Jewish holdings within their walls that have continued to the present time.) Markers were crammed in close together; and narrow carriage roads, which once divided the sections of the cemetery, are still visible. Remnants of the wrought-iron fence protrude near the sidewalk. Gnarled and dying catalpa trees loom overhead. The population once served by this cemetery has died or moved away, and burials are now infrequent. It is a saddening example of the cemetery that has buried the immigrant and ethnic generations but lost most of its connections to the living generation.[18]

Directly north of "Jewish Graceland," through the barbed wire, is

13. S. J. Bryan, compiled by *Report of the Commissioners and a History of Lincoln Park* (Chicago, 1899), pp. 13-42; *City Council Proceedings.*

14. Gutstein, pp. 27-30.

15. Author's observations.

16. Carl W. Condit, *The Chicago School of Architecture, A History of Commercial and Public Building in the Chicago Area, 1875-1925* (Chicago, 1952), p. 33.

17. *A Cemetery Guide to Jewish Cemeteries and Non-Sectarian Cemeteries with Jewish Sections in the Chicago area, Including a Map of Jewish Waldheim* (Chicago, 1984).

18. Author's notes.

Wunder's Cemetery, owned by First Saint Paul's Evangelical and Reformed Church. Many of the bodies interred here were moved from the congregation's original plot in the City Cemetery. This cemetery, dating from the 1850s, is the oldest German Protestant cemetery in Chicago. Many of the earliest monuments are inscribed in German.[19]

The Roman Catholics also recognized the need to move their cemetery. The diocese had owned land in Evanston since 1851, and Calvary Cemetery was consecrated in 1859 in this northern suburb.[20] Filled with crosses, crucifixes, and angels, many of the markers here also include fireman's helmets in their design because the fire department was a popular place of employment for Irish Catholics. Although in-ground burial was generally practiced by the Irish, there are many mausoleums in Calvary; this may be a recognition of the continued proximity to the lake, with its variations in level. The names on the monuments include Mulligan, Lynch, O'Neill, Cudahy, Murphy, Kelly — bespeaking its Hibernian origins.[21]

German Catholics in the Chicago diocese insisted on their own identity as a people with unique needs and rights: they wanted their own institutions for their children and their infirm and their own cemeteries for their dead. In 1863 representatives from the four German churches, Saint Peter, Saint Joseph, Saint Francis of Assisi, and Saint Michael, formed the German Roman Catholic Saint Boniface Cemetery Association — for the "burial of Catholics of German descent."[22] Although Calvary Cemetery in Evanston had been consecrated as a diocesan cemetery to serve the entire Catholic population, Germans did not look favorably on the Irish who wished to be buried there. Ethnic conflict was not only a fact of nineteenth-century life, but also of death.

Saint Boniface's board of directors was elected from the members of the German parishes. Memorials at Saint Boniface include the traditional wayside shrines of Germany as well as the ubiquitous crosses and crucifixes. Saint Boniface's board established that the surplus of the annual receipt would be expended for benevolent purposes, and the first recipient of this beneficence was the German Guardian Angel Orphanage on Devon at Ridge.[23] Calvary's profits, by contrast, were to be used for improvements in the cemetery itself. Its beautiful gateway on Chicago Avenue remains as one example of that policy: its columns are decorated with a tracery of lilies of the valley. Saint Boniface's original Gothic gate, which once included a bell that tolled as the

19. Gail Santroch, editor, *A Transcription of Wunder's Cemetery, Chicago, Illinois* (Chicago, Illinois), p. iii; *Proceedings of Common Council.*

20. Archdiocese of Chicago, *Centennial of Calvary Cemetery* (Chicago, 1959).

21. Andreas Simon, *Chicago, The Garden City* (Chicago, 1893), pp. 132-139.

22. *Ibid.*, pp. 140-143.

23. Roger J. Coughlin and Catherine A. Riplinger, *The Story of Charitable Care in the Archdiocese of Chicago* (Chicago, 1981), pp. 144-148.

funeral procession entered the cemetery, has been replaced by a more functional structure.[24]

The problems of ethnic separation in the Catholic cemeteries would not be eased until the mid-twentieth century. The attitudes exemplified by the dissension between Irish and Germans over their right to their own burial sites have mostly been resolved. But those attitudes are likely among the newer immigrant groups in Chicago.

Saint Henry's, a Luxemburg parish and cemetery, was consecrated in 1863 at Ridge and Devon.[25] The capacious church, dedicated to the patron saint of Luxemburg, commanded the view of the Luxemburg farming community in the surrounding countryside. This congregation chose to follow the German example of contributing extra moneys to nearby Angel Guardian Orphanage; the memorial styles in the cemetery were also typically German.[26] A constant factor in Chicago's institutional life has been ethnic succession, whereby newer ethnics replace older ones and take over their holy places and burying grounds. Today, Saint Henry's church has been renamed Angel Guardian to serve a Croatian congregation. The cemetery witnesses very few burials of Luxemburgers. More recently, newer portions of the cemetery are used for the interment of Hispanics. Angel Guardian Orphanage no longer exists; the extensive buildings have been renamed "Misericordia North."[27]

Polish and Bohemians were immigrating to Chicago in increasingly greater numbers in the late nineteenth century. At first, their communities were represented by the nationalistic parish churches. Their attitudes toward diocesan affairs were akin to those expressed by the Germans: they expected to have the right to have their own Polish- and Czech-speaking clergy, their own schools, and their own cemeteries. In 1872, Saint Adalbert's Cemetery was opened in Niles. Initially it was small, only a few acres. Each Polish or Bohemian parish would buy a section of land, then resell lots to the individual parishioners.[28] Memorials were similar to those in European cemeteries, and inscriptions were in Polish or Czech. The idea for creation of the Bohemian National Cemetery arose from an "unfortunate incident involving a Bohemian woman, Marie Silhanek, who died on July 25, 1876. Although a devout Catholic, she was denied burial at several Catholic cemeteries, by Father Joseph Molitor, priest of Saint James Church on DeKoven Street, then a predominately Bohemian enclave in Chicago, simply because she made no confessions prior to her death. This so aroused the Bohemian population of Chicago, then numbering about 30,000,

---

24. Pietras, p. 32.
25. Simon, pp. 136, 140.
26. *Caritas Christi*, pp. 841-847.
27. Author's notes.
28. Diane McClure, "The Bohemian Polish Catholic Cemetery Society of Chicago," *Chicago Genealogist 22*, 21-24.

St. Adalbert's Cemetery, Niles, Chicago.

The entry to St. Adalbert's Cemetery. Courtesy of Helen Sclair.

that a cry was raised for organizing a cemetery for Bohemian people, which would not be under ecclesiastical control."[29]

In March 1877, delegates of eight organizations met to organize and found the Bohemian National Cemetery. They decided that surplus funds earned by the cemetery would be used for Bohemian schools, a Bohemian library, and a Bohemian home for the aged.[30] In spite of strong objections by the township of Jefferson, the plan was to incorporate. One letter of complaint compared cemeteries to "glue-factories, brickyards, tanneries, rendering establishments, toll roads, sink holes for the depositing of offal, and the carcasses of the city's dead animals." In conclusion, wrote A. B. Munn, ". . . some of the most desirable residence property in the vicinity of Chicago, is located in the exact vicinity where the cemetery desires to go. Undulating enough for beautifully varied scenery, susceptible of perfect drainage, and ornamented with grand forest trees, it is even now, without the aid of art, a series of magnificent parks and natural gardens; and the time is not far distant when, in spite of our hitherto bad policy, these lands will be in great demand as residence property of a class of people whose wealth, intelligence and refinement will render them valuable acquisi-

29. Jaroslav E. S. Vojan, *The Semi-Centennial Jubilee of the Bohemian National Cemetery Association in Chicago, Illinois* (Chicago, 1927), p. 7. The "Saint James" should read "Saint Wenceslaus."

30. James W. Krakora, *Bohemian National Cemetery: The First 100 Years* (Cicero, 1977), pp. 461-463.

The Bohemian National Cemetery was originally founded to bury Czechs who were not Catholics in good standing. Courtesy of Helen Sclair.

tions to any community. . . . I most emphatically protest against granting the privilege of turning these beautiful parks into graveyards."[31] The "parks" Munn referred to were actually orchards and pastures.[32]

The Bohemian National Cemetery won lawsuits, defied all objections, and made the first burial on July 1, 1877. Since then it has been a cemetery for the population for which it was planned.[33] Record-keeping, reports to the delegates, and maintenance have all been very thorough. The cemetery grew as the community expanded, and the Board kept up with all the trends in cemetery management. At one time, Jens Jensen, the well-known landscape architect, was employed to plan the design for a new section of the cemetery.[34] Albin Polasek's bronze sculpture "The Grim Reaper" striding toward the portals of the Stejskal-Buchal mausoleum is an outstanding example of fine art in the cemetery. Section 16, filled with the bodies of those Western Electric employees who died in the Eastland Disaster, is a grim reminder of some of Chicago's history. The combination chapel-columbarium-crematorium is unique. The decorations on

31. Letter from A. B. Munn to Board of Town of Jefferson, June 27, 1877, *Proceedings of City Council Files, 1872-1944.* Author's note: The kind of attitude expressed in this letter prevailed at the founding of many cemeteries.

32. Author's observations.

33. Krakora, p. 49.

34. Vojan, pp. 75-76.

niches display each family's individuality, making this cemetery a museum of folk art. The gate's bell landmark is the only one remaining in Chicago to toll for the passing of the dead entering a cemetery.[35]

As Bohemians have moved to the western suburbs, some have elected to be buried in Mount Auburn, Stickney, Woodlawn, or Forest Park. But Bohemian National Cemetery continues today with the traditions it established 115 years ago.[36]

By the 1870s the small Jewish cemeteries located along Clark Street, as well as Oakwoods Cemetery, were becoming sold out. The Jewish community, long only Germanic in heritage, was being expanded by the arrival of Jews from Eastern Europe. These new populations, often more Orthodox in their religious practices, wanted their own cemeteries. As before, the temples purchased land to sell to members of the various congregations. They founded Jewish Waldheim,[37] which was not really one cemetery but more than 300 pieces of land representing the burial sites of various temples, shtetls, vereins, and landsmanschaften.[38] At one time, gates and fences were used to demarcate the various properties, but most of these have fallen into disrepair. Small, mausoleum-like buildings remain, though they are abandoned because of various legal interventions. These "houses," or Bet-Taharas, were originally used in the ritual washings, wrappings of the body, and overall preparations for immediate in-ground burial.[39] As cemeteries began to require grave-boxes or vaults to keep the disturbed land from caving in, the Jews discovered a way to continue their ancient burial practices by using boxes without bottoms. A memorial type, peculiar to some of the cemeteries at Jewish Waldheim, is the construction of mounded graves, usually with plantings of perennial flowers on top. Near Des Plaines Avenue is the uncommon Sephardic cemetery: memorials there are enormous horizontal slabs that cover the entire grave.[40]

The character of the Jewish cemetery began a rapid metamorphosis in the 1920s. A tendency toward cemeteries that resembled those used by "others" became the trend. They were still solely for the purpose of Jewish burial, but the rigorous regimental rows of stones were now more relaxed in their lawn types of memorialization. The earlier intense relationships with groups — religious or secular — began to fade. Newly developed Westlawn Cemetery in Norridge was laid out to resemble all others of the period. More space appeared between monuments, and the inscriptions tended to be chiefly in English. By

35. Author's notes.
36. *Ibid.*
37. Simon, p. 171.
38. *A Cemetery Guide*, p. 3.
39. "The name of the building is "Bet-Tahara." Letter to the author from David I. Jacobson, Piser Weinstein Menorah Chapels, November 27, 1989; Maurice Lamm, The Jewish Way in Death and Mourning (New York, 1969).
40. Author's notes.

1932, Rosemont Park was dedicated to continue this "modernistic" practice. Flower plantings on the graves were changed with the seasons; evergreens frame the monuments. Memorial Park in Evanston and the Jewish sections of Evergreen Cemetery continue these practices. The mausoleum at Rosehill Cemetery in Chicago became a very popular site for the new practice of "entombment" above ground.

The Jewish burial traditions remain the same, but memorialization is changing. The popularity of Palatine's, Shalom Memorial Park, with its ground level markers, has replaced the ancient steles of the past. No flowers appear on these graves, but the pebble remembrances do continue; and focal-point memorials are becoming popular in some of the sections. Very recently, a community mausoleum has been erected.[41]

Norwegians, Swedes, and Danes have lived in Chicago for most of the city's history.[42] Members of the Scandinavian community were first buried in the Chicago Cemetery in Lincoln Park. When that cemetery was abandoned in the 1860s and 1870s, bodies were disinterred during the day and carried on wagons through the city to the suburban cemeteries of Rosehill, Graceland, and Oakwoods at night. The living community continued to buy land in these newer cemeteries for burial of their dead.[43] By 1886 the Scandinavian churches recognized the need to establish their own burial sites and purchased land at Mount Olive for their own cemetery. Early monuments were rough-hewn obelisks and carved slabs, all of them massive and sturdy. Names in this cemetery included Stensland, Hjortdahl, Stangeland, Johnson, Benson, Anderson, Gunderson, and others.[44] A handsome Viking fountain, carved from granite, is near the gate.

South Side Scandinavians selected land for burial in Oak Hill Cemetery, Merrionette Park. Monuments and names were similar to those found at Mount Olive. These cemeteries were laid out on the "park plan," with rolling terrain, meandering roads and paths, and the comfort of shade trees. Both cemeteries had anticipated that the living populations would remain nearby, so that their dead would fill up the vast spaces that had been purchased. This did not happen. Early population dispersal scattered many Scandinavians to suburbs distant from the cemetery, while some assimilation served to further diminish the significance of a distinctive ethnic burying ground. Early in the twentieth century a large portion of Oak Hill was sold for an African-American cemetery; more recently, successive areas of Mount Olive have been sold to Armenians and Latvians. An additional section, never used for burial, has been converted to real estate development for town houses. The Scandinavians have moved to other communities and other cemeteries.[45]

41. *Ibid.*
42. *Historic City,* pp. 11, 19, 26, 37.
43. *Proceedings, 1833-1871.*
44. Simon, pp. 175-176.
45. Author's notes.

Two extensive German Protestant cemeteries were created by German Lutheran parishes, following the similar desires of the German Roman Catholic population. Concordia in Forest Park[46] and Bethania in Justice are analogous in their plans and development. Roads, trees, and chapels are well maintained, and monuments are imaginative but do not include any crucifixes. Some of the inscriptions are in German. Directly east of Concordia Cemetery is the property of Altenheim, the German Old People's Home. Its cemetery memorials are regimental in style; almost every marker is cast concrete.[47] Many other Protestant German cemeteries exist in the Chicago area. One example is Saint Lucas, a smaller version of Bethania and Concordia.[48]

Not all Polish cemeteries are Roman Catholic. For many years a group of Polish nationalists carried on continuing disputes with the authority in Rome, expressing their "desire for a more 'Polish' American church and an independence from the Irish-dominated American hierarchy."[49] In Chicago, Father Anthony Kozlowski set up the independent Church of All Saints to satisfy that desire. In September 1895, Archbishop Feehan excommunicated Kozlowski, who then proceeded to establish the Polish Old Catholic Church. (By 1897 the independent Polish National Catholic Church was being led from the see at Scranton, Pennsylvania.)[50] There are nine operating churches in Chicago and one cemetery, All Saints on Higgins Road. The older sections resemble older Polish Roman Catholic cemeteries of the same period — with crucifixes and angels used for memorialization; the newer sections are developed with ground level markers. This is the only cemetery in the city of Chicago with its own community hall and picnic grove.[51]

As the nineteenth century drew to a close, the ethnic populations continued to expand, by birth and by immigration. New cemeteries were platted. The earlier pattern prevailed: Mount Olivet was organized for South Side Irish in 1885; a short distance away, the South Side Germans organized Saint Mary's in Evergreen Park in 1888.[52] Increases in the Italian immigration saw the founding of more "national" cemeteries. Mount Carmel in Hillside and Sacred Heart in Winnetka were consecrated in 1900. These burial sites brought a new look to the Roman Catholic cemetery: above-ground burial was the preferred

46. Simon, p. 172.
47. Author's notes.
48. Coughlin and Riplinger, p. 158.
49. *Ibid.*
50. Edward R. Kantowicz, "Polish Chicago Survival Through Solidarity," Melvin G. Holli and Peter d'A Jones, eds., *Ethnic Chicago* (Grand Rapids, 1984), pp. 227, 228; *About the Polish National Catholic Church* (South Deerfield, MA, 1980).
51. Author's notes. Food is often associated with a funeral. Przybylo's House of the White Eagle (located immediately across the street from the entrance to Saint Adalbert's Cemetery) serves 3,500-4,000 meals on a typical Saturday. It is not unusual to find several hearses parked in the parking lot.
52. Simon, pp. 152, 156.

method of interment in Italy. Whenever financially feasible, expensive mausoleums replaced the less elaborate cross or simple marker; angels and crucifixes abounded; and photographs of the deceased became so commonplace that Mount Carmel began to look like a photo gallery. The Italians achieved their intention of transporting traditions from their homeland: their ancient, adored practices were highly visible in their cemeteries.[53]

Saint Casimir's Lithuanian Cemetery, consecrated in 1903, is the most startling of all cemeteries. Memorials in the oldest sections are similar to those found in any other Roman Catholic burial grounds of the time. But new immigrants began arriving after World War II,[54] and rather than continue the traditional memorialization of the old timers, the newcomers combined folk art with elegance in the new grave markers. There are several themes on these new gravestones. One is the concept of the wayside cross or chapel, often accompanied by a charming image of the "Worrier." There are representations of Our Lady of Vilnius, and tulips are carved on other monuments. Materials include traditional granite but extend to experimental uses of Cor-ten steel, stainless steel, and fiber glass. The new memorials are immense, defying comparison to any in any other cemetery. They rise from large, well-tended lots. Many of the distinctive sculptures have been created by Ramojus Mozaliauskas, a talented member of the Lithuanian community.[55] Two features of this lovingly tended cemetery are unique: it is the only Roman Catholic cemetery that includes the name of the community it serves, Lithuanian (the reader may recall that "Bohemian National" is not Catholic); and it is the only cemetery with its own stoplight at the entrance gate.

Protestant Lithuanians, often Lutheran, are buried in Willow Springs in the Lithuanian National Cemetery. Types of memorialization are similar to those to be found at Saint Casimir's. Lithuanian National is a smaller cemetery than Saint Casimir's, but graves in both cemeteries have the appearance of having received extremely good care from cemetery management as well as the families.[56]

African Americans have lived in Chicago since the days of the first Fort Dearborn. As the historical record indicates, two died among those massacred in the 1812 Indian attack.[57] For this early period, no evidence has been found to suggest that whites and African Americans were treated differently in death or in burial. The only determining factors appear to have to do with religion:

53. *Caritas Christi*, p. 42. Robert W. Habenstein and William M. Lamers, *Funeral Customs the World Over* (Milwaukee, 1960), pp. 515-526. Author's collection.

54. *Saint Casimir's Lithuanian Cemetery in Chicago, Illinois* (Chicago, 1976).

55. *Ibid.;* Jacqueline Hanks, "Saint Casimir's Cemetery," *Stone in America* (November 1988), 28-37.

56. *Lietuviu Tautiskos Kapines, Lithuanian National Cemetery* (Chicago, 1938); Kantowicz, p. 224.

57. Allan W. Eckert, *Gateway to Empire* (Everglades, 1983), pp. 633-656.

Protestant, Roman Catholic, or Jewish.[58] But by the 1880s the problems of Jim Crow had crept northward into Chicago. Where lots had been purchased in existing cemeteries, such as Oakwoods, Negro burials did continue; however, the purchase of new lots was being discouraged. Forest Home in Forest Park was available for burial, but that was a long way from the center of the black population.[59] By the turn of the century, burial plots for African Americans were becoming increasingly difficult to obtain. Thus they turned to the solution of many other ethnic groups: they bought their own cemetery. One Baptist church purchased land for a small cemetery, Mount Forest. In rapid succession, more cemeteries for African Americans were dedicated, such as Mount Glenwood, Lincoln, Burr Oak, and Restvale. These burial sites were all located in south suburban Cook County.[60] They were out of reach in this horse-and-buggy age for blacks living along the North Shore, particularly in Evanston. But North Side blacks gained access to beautiful Sunset Memorial Park, which was opened in Northbrook.[61] All of the above-mentioned cemeteries resembled the typical white non-sectarian cemeteries of the same period; monuments, roads, trees, and decorations are nearly identical.[62]

Anthropological studies of cemeteries in specific areas of the southern United States have discovered distinct ties to burial sites in Africa. African characteristics included the scraping (raking of the bare soil) of the grave and the mounding of the graves. Shells and broken crockery were often used as decorations; fences frequently enclosed each grave; common field stones or wooden slabs were used as markers. No Chicago-area African-American cemetery includes any remnant of these ancient traditions.[63]

An interview with Chicagoan Gladstone Trotter, Jr., whose family is buried in Citronelle, Alabama, revealed some evidence of the survival of African burial practices in the United States. A number of years ago, Trotter recalls, he participated in the sodding and "cleaning-up" of the family lots in Citronelle, and unknowingly replaced the African characteristics that had existed since the mid-nineteenth century. He and his family "wanted the graves to look like others." This is the only instance in which the present author was able to find a Chicago link to African burial practices.[64]

Another example of the "Americanization" of ethnic burial characteristics

58. Author's notes.

59. *Ibid.*

60. Roma Jones Stewart, "Cemetery Exploration," Afro-American Genealogical and Historical Society of Chicago, Inc., 2:4, December, 1987.

61. *Sunset Memorial Park,* brochure, n.d.

62. Author's notes.

63. Terry G. Jordan, *Texas Graveyards: A Cultural Legacy* (Austin, 1982), pp. 41-63. Gregory Jeane, "Rural Southern Gravestones: Sacred Artifacts in the Upland South Folk Cemetery." *Markers IV: The Journal of the Association for Gravestone Studies,* David Watters, ed. (University Press of America, Inc., 1987), pp. 55-84

64. Interview with Gladstone Trotter, Jr., May 10, 1991.

can be found in the large Chinese section of Mount Auburn Cemetery in Stickney. Generally, the Chinese have memorialized the dead with elaborate vertical monuments, festooned by columns of Chinese characters and adorned with pictures of the deceased. At Mount Auburn a dramatic change can be seen: the ground-level bronze markers prevail, which is the result of the regulations of the cemetery. The only concession to tradition is that in the middle of the "field" there stands a large, brilliant pagoda-style shrine used for incense offerings. In the spring and fall, family- and community-sponsored celebrations take place and are accompanied by the burning of incense at the graves and the offerings of special foods, such as golden oranges. Much human activity and participation is evident at these festivals for the dead, which is in contrast to the more somber and subdued style of European-American memorialization.[65]

One of the most colorful cemeteries in the Chicago area is on Higgins Road and is dedicated to the use of the Ukrainian Catholic parish of Saint Nicholas, a profusion of flowers — plastic, silk, and fresh-growing — decorate the graves. This is the only cemetery where polychromed granite monuments have been erected. Some markers are hand-wrought, in metal or wood; birch crosses are popular. One characteristic that is consistent throughout most of this folk-type cemetery is the symbol of the sun at the birth date and the bare unadorned cross next to the date of death.[66]

The Greek Orthodox community has long used its own burial space, located in two cemeteries: Evergreen in Evergreen Park on the South Side, and Elmwood in River Grove for the North Side community. The monuments there are large, with columns and statues included, creating temples reminiscent of their ancient Greek culture. Beautiful floral plantings and evergreens complement the memorials. An excursion near these burial sites at night is an experience to remember, for one sees flickering lights of the lamps on the graves, keeping perpetual watch, an eerie reminder of the presence of death.[67]

A much more elusive population in the area are the Gypsies. Yet there are sufficient numbers of them in death to create a large, highly visible community in the Forest Home Cemetery. Their monuments are expansive and elaborate and mix elements of religious devotion with those of their ancient customs. Photographs of the deceased are prominently displayed; offerings of food and drink are frequently found on the graves. Memorial decorations are changed for each season or holiday. Their funerals feature expensive floral pieces and the wail of Gypsy violins. The death of a Gypsy King or Queen will summon hundreds of the tribes from every corner of the country for the last rites.[68]

The final resting place of the Gypsies, Forest Home Cemetery, has long

65. Federal Writer's Project of the Works Project Administration for the State of Illinois, *The WPA Guide to Illinois* (New York, 1983), p. 587.
66. Author's notes.
67. *Ibid.*
68. Habenstein and Lamers, pp. 720-727.

The last resting place of Chicago's famous Haymarket anarchists is shown in this romantic depiction of Forest Home (Waldheim) Cemetery. Courtesy of Helen Sclair.

encouraged the policy of being available for the burial of those who might be refused interment elsewhere. The Haymarket Riot anarchists are buried there; the Communist party members are nearby. In addition, large portions of this cemetery are inhabited by Germans who might have had no particular affiliation with any of the church-related burial sites at nearby Concordia Cemetery.[69]

When Serbians came to the Chicago area, one of their first acts was to buy land in order to continue their monasteries, which included a church, a picnic grove, game fields, and, especially, a cemetery. Saint Sava's Serbian Orthodox Monastery, north of Libertyville, serves the population of a large area that extends from Milwaukee to Chicago to Gary.[70] In 1970, when Queen Victoria's great-grandson, King Peter of Yugoslavia, died in Los Angeles, he was transported there to be buried within the onion-domed church of Saint Sava's. The cemetery is built on a hillside that overlooks the Des Plaines River. Photographs of the deceased and inscriptions in the Cyrillic alphabet decorate most of the memorials. Flowers are planted on nearly every grave, many of which are outlined with low enclosures. Various foods, alcoholic beverages, and soft drinks are placed on the graves as offerings. (It is said that in Serbia, roving bands of Gypsies knew where they could always find sustenance — in a Serbian graveyard. In Libertyville these delicacies present problems because they attract rodents rather than humans.)[71] In the Serbian tradition, the living hold picnics for themselves at the site of the grave. Black granite was used for most of the earlier memorials; but more recently, brilliant rose, orange, and blue iridescent granites are preferred. Temporary simple wooden crosses mark new graves until permanent monuments can be obtained to replace them.[72]

A few miles west of Saint Sava's is the Monastery of the Most Holy Mother of God in the town of Third Lake. This land, purchased in 1977, is the home of the Free Serbian Orthodox Diocese of the United States and Canada. In addition to a monastery, church, and picnic grounds, a large dormitory is located there for use as a school or camp. The cemetery regulates the placement of stones so that all have an Eastern orientation.[73] Chicago's Montrose Cemetery has a large Serbian section, but there the head stones are simpler than those at the cemeteries in Lake County.[74]

The Japanese Mutual Aid Society of Chicago was formally launched in January 1935. Two of the goals of the society pertained to death: that the society would purchase centrally-located cemetery lots and that it would help pay for final

69. Author's notes.
70. Federal Writer's Project, p. 418. Also author's notes.
71. Interview with a monk, July 1986.
72. Author's observation.
73. *Monastery of the Most Holy Mother of God,* "Gracanica," n.d., brochure, author's collection.
74. Tom McGann, "Montrose Cemetery Nears 90th Birthday," *American Cemetery* (August 1991), Vol. 64, No. 8.

Japanese-American mausoleum used for Japanese Americans' burials in the 1930s.
Courtesy of Mosako Osako.

expenses of all who died without family or funds. Until this time, Japanese burials had been scattered throughout the various cemeteries of the city. A mausoleum in Montrose Cemetery was completed in 1937. When World War II heated up ethnic tensions, Japanese who died in Chicago were denied burial in many cemeteries. The timeliness of the Montrose Mausoleum became apparent.[75]

Before 1940, the Japanese population was fewer than 50. After the closing of the relocation campus there was an influx of about 20,000 Japanese Americans into Chicago. The mausoleum was added onto several times, lots around the mausoleum were purchased, and Memorial Day services are always observed. The historical fact that racial discrimination had been practiced until recent times was one of the principal incentives for the origin of the Society and its provision for burials.[76]

75. *Japanese Mutual Aid Society, 1934-1977* (Chicago, 1977). Masako Osako, "Japanese-Americans: Melting into the All-American Melting Pot?" Melvin G. Holli and Peter d'A. Jones, *Ethnic Chicago* (Grand Rapids, 1984), pp. 527-529.

76. *Japanese*, p. 4.

Indeed, most of these groups purchased land to guarantee their right of continuous community, especially in death. Some of this "permanent" land may disappear in its role as a cemetery if ongoing care can not be given by existing members of a given community.[77]

The most effective large-scale effort to assure permanence of cemeteries has been undertaken by the Chicago Roman Catholic Archdiocese. The Archdiocesan Cemeteries in the past sixty years have attempted to control landscaping and types of memorialization in order to improve maintenance. Before that time, a *laissez-faire* attitude prevailed that allowed families to erect monuments of their choosing without review by cemetery officials. They had selected materials such as limestone and marble, which lacked the characteristics of permanence, often becoming eroded and corroded by the weather and thus becoming potentially dangerous. Every kind of evergreen, deciduous shrub, and perennial was also permitted. In those cemeteries where families had once tended the graves of their loved ones, but now had died or moved away, such plantings became overgrown eyesores.[78]

The result today is that the Archdiocesan authorities have taken responsibility for more than 3,500 acres, with thousands of burials per year. Improved maintenance and interment procedures have reduced operating expenses. Although no one Protestant or Jewish cemetery even remotely equals the size and scope of the Archdiocesan system, many of their operating techniques have been adopted by the smaller cemeteries.[79]

Summary

We can see that many national and racial groups purchased cemetery land as an expression of their ethnicity in both life and death. Some were forced to do so because of discrimination, but even more did so by choice. But over time and with the passing of generations, we see an increasing homogenization of cemetery and burial styles. Some of the change was required by law (such as the regulation requiring Jews to use burial boxes), but even more of it came about by the adoption of styles more acceptable in America. An example of the latter is Gladstone Trotter, who "Americanized" an African-style family burial plot in the South. Accelerating such trends and working as a powerful standardizing force is the massive cemetery establishment of the Chicago Roman Catholic Archdiocese. Unrivaled in size, it not only accounts for a substantial number of all burials in

77. Author's observation.

78. National Catholic Cemetery Conference, *God's Acre* (Chicago, 1951); *Caritas Christi*, pp. 42-47.

79. Kenneth T. Jackson and Camilo José Vergera, *Silent Cities* (New York, 1989), pp. 48-59, 110-122. This represents one of the first books written to include material (some Chicago) on ethnic cemeteries; these authors include photographs and text that briefly examine the development of cemeteries in America.

Chicago, but acts as a forerunner and trendsetter that other groups are likely to emulate. Much of the change toward standardized burial practice is also the result of the fact that acculturation and assimilation march inexorably onward in America through both life and death. Convergence toward a broadly conceived "Americanized" burial style appears to be in the making. *E pluribus unum* would seem to be a fitting epitaph for the ethnic style in death.

AFRICAN AMERICAN

Burr Oak Cemetery
4400 W. 127th Street
Alsip, IL 60658

Lincoln Cemetery
12300 S. Kedzie Avenue
Blue Island, IL 60406

Mount Forest Cemetery
Marion Street
Thornton, IL 60476

Mt. Glenwood Cemetery
18301 Glenwood-Thorton Road
Glenwood, IL 60425

Restvale Cemetery
115th & Laramie
Worth, IL 60482

Sunset Memorial Lawns
3100 Shermer Road
Northbrook, IL 60062

BOHEMIAN (CZECH)

Roman Catholic

Saint Adalbert Cemetery
6800 N. Milwaukee Avenue
Niles, IL 60648

Protestant

Bohemian National Cemetery
5255 N. Pulaski
Chicago, IL 60630

Mount Auburn Cemetery
4101 Oak Park Avenue
Stickney, IL 60402

Woodlawn Cemetery
7600 W. Cermak Road
Forest Park, IL 60130

CHINESE

Mount Auburn Cemetery
4101 Oak Park Avenue
Stickney, IL 60402

DUTCH

Mount Greewwood Cemetery
111th Street and California
Blue Island, IL 60406

GERMAN

Protestant

Altenheim
7824 Madison
Forest Park, IL 60130

Bethania Cemetery
7701 Archer Avenue
Justice, IL 60458

Concordia Cemetery
7900 Madison
Forest Park, IL 60130

Forest Home (Waldheim)
863 Des Plaines Avenue
Forest Park, IL 60130

Saint Lucas Cemetery
5300 N. Pulaski
Chicago, IL 60630

Wunder's Cemetery
3963 N. Clark Street
Chicago, IL 60613

Roman Catholic

Saint Boniface Cemetery
4901 N. Clark Street
Chicago, IL 60640

Saint Joseph Cemetery
Cumberland and Belmont
River Grove, IL 60171

Saint Mary's Cemetery
87th & Hamlin
Evergreen Park, IL 60642

GREEK

Elmwood Cemetery
2905 Thatcher Road
River Grove, IL 60171

Evergreen Cemetery
87th & Kedzie
Evergreen Park, IL 60642

GYPSIES

Forest Home Cemetery
863 Des Plaines
Forest Park, IL 60130

IRISH

All Saints Cemetery
700 N. Des Plaines
Des Plaines, IL 60016

Calvary Cemetery
301 Chicago Avenue
Evanston, IL 60202

Holy Sepulchre Cemetery
6001 W. 111th Street
Worth, IL 60482

Mount Olivet Cemetery
2755 W. 111th Street
Chicago, IL 60655

Saint James the Sag Cemetery
Routes 53 & 171
Lemont, IL 60439

ITALIAN

Mount Carmel Cemetery
1400 S. Wolf Road (office)
Hillside, IL 60162

Sacred Heart Cemetery
905 Burr Street
Winnetka, IL 60093

JAPANESE

Montrose Cemetery
5400 N. Pulaski Road
Chicago, IL 60630

JEWISH

Jewish Graceland Cemetery
3919 N. Clark Street
Chicago, IL 60613

Rosehill Cemetery
5800 N. Ravenswood
Chicago, IL 60660

Jewish Waldheim Cemetery
1800 S. Harlem Avenue
Forest Park, IL 60130

Rosemont Park Cemetery
6758 W. Addison
Chicago, IL 60634

Mount Maariv Cemetery
3600 N. Narraganset
Chicago, IL 60634

Shalom Memorial Park
Rand Road & Route 53
Palatine, IL 60667

Oakwoods Cemetery
1035 E. 67th Street
Chicago, IL 60637

Westlawn Cemetery
7801 W. Montrose
(P.O. Chicago)
Harwood Heights, IL 60634

LITHUANIAN

Protestant

Lithuanian National Cemetery
Kean Avenue & 82nd Street
Willow Springs, IL 60480

Roman Catholic

Saint Casimir's
Lithuanian Cemetery
4401 W. 111th Street
Chicago, IL 60655

LUXEMBURG

Saint Henry's Cemetery
1929 W. Devon Avenue
Chicago, IL 60660

NATIVE AMERICAN

Robinson Burying Ground
N.W. Corner Lawrence &
E. River Rd. 30
Chicago, IL 60614

POLISH

Protestant

All Saints Polish National
Catholic Cemetery
9201 Higgins Road
Chicago, IL 60631

Roman Catholic

Holy Cross Cemetery
Michigan City & Burnham Ave.
Calumet City, IL 60409

Maryhill Cemetery
8600 N. Milwakee Avenue
Niles, IL 60648

Resurrection Cemetery
7200 S. Archer Avenue
Justice, IL 60648

Saint Adalbert's Cemetery
6800 N. Milwaukee Avenue
Niles, IL 60648

SCANDINAVIAN

Mount Olive Cemetery
3800 N. Narraganset
Chicago, IL 60634

Oak Hill Cemetery
11900 S. Kedzie
Merrionette Park, IL 60655
(P.O. Chicago)

SERBIAN

Most Holy Mother of
God Monastery
Route 45
Third Lake, IL 60046

Saint Sava's Serbian
Orthodox Monastery
Route 21, N
Libertyville, IL 60048

UKRAINIAN

Saint Nicholas Ukrainian
Catholic Cemetery
Higgins W. of East River Rd.
Chicago, IL 60631

NOTE: Members of these groups are occasionally in other cemeteries. The burial sites listed here are those most frequented by these ethnic groups.

Contributors

MELVIN G. HOLLI is professor of history at the University of Illinois at Chicago and co-author and co-editor of several books, including *Restoration: Chicago Elects a New Daley* with Paul M. Green, and *The Ethnic Frontier* (1977) and *The Biographical Dictionary of American Mayors, 1820-1980* with Peter d'A. Jones.

PETER d'A. JONES is professor of history at the University of Illinois at Chicago and the author of several books, including *Since Columbus, Pluralism and Poverty in the Americas, Henry George and British Socialism,* and *The Consumer Society.*

JOSEPH AHNE is a Korean-born clergyman, executive director of Chicago's Korean Community Council, and was recognized by the Chicago Commission on Human Relations for his work in improving relations between African Americans and the Asian business community. He is a doctoral student at the University of Illinois at Chicago, and this article represents some of the preliminary findings of his research.

WILLIAM BRADEN is a veteran reporter for the Chicago *Sun Times* and has written extensively about ethnic and political affairs.

DOMINIC CANDELORO received his Ph.D. at the University of Illinois, Champaign-Urbana. He was executive director of the Italians in Chicago NEH Project based at the University of Illinois at Chicago. He has published extensively on ethnic Italian Americans and is a staff member at Governors State University in Illinois.

JORGE CASUSO and EDUARDO CAMACHO are keen observers, researchers, and writers on Chicago's Latino communities. Mr. Casuso is a journalist, and Mr. Camacho is in private business in Chicago.

IRVING CUTLER, now retired, was professor and chairman of the department of geography at Chicago State University. He is the author of numerous articles and several books on urban affairs, including *Chicago: Metropolis of the Mid-Continent, The Chicago-Milwaukee Corridor,* and *Urban Geography.* He is a founding member of the Chicago Jewish Historical Society and serves on its board of directors.

PERRY R. DUIS is an associate professor of history at the University of Illinois at Chicago, an expert on Chicago and its cultures, and the author of *Creating New Traditions* and *The Saloon: Public Drinking in Chicago and Boston, 1880-1920.*

MICHAEL F. FUNCHION is professor of history at South Dakota State University and the author of *Chicago's Irish Nationalists, 1881-1890.* He completed his doctorate at Chicago's Loyola University.

JAMES R. GROSSMAN is director of the Center for Family and Community History at the Newberry Library and the author of *The Promised Land: Chicago, Black Southerners, and the Great Migration.*

MARK H. HALLER is professor of history at Temple University and the author of numerous studies on organized crime and criminality in American cities. He has most recently completed a study of a "crime family" in Philadelphia.

EDWARD R. KANTOWICZ was associate professor of history at Carleton University and is the author of *Polish-American Politics in Chicago* and *Corporation Sole: Cardinal Mundelein and Chicago Catholicism.*

ANDREW T. KOPAN is professor of education in the School of Education at DePaul University. He is an active facilitator in the field of education and ethnicity, and has written articles and books on the subject, including *Rethinking Urban Education, Rethinking Educational Equality,* and *Education and Greek Immigrants in Chicago, 1892-1973.*

MYRON B. KUROPAS is the author of *The Ukrainian Americans: Roots and Aspirations, 1884-1954* and was honored with the Kowaliv Award for excellence in Ukrainian studies. During the Ford administration he served as special assistant to the President for Ethnic Affairs.

SUSAN LEE MOY received her M.A. in Asian History from the University of Wisconsin–Madison. She is employed by the Chicago Board of Education as an elementary teacher and is an active member of various organizations in the Chinese community in Chicago.

ANITA R. OLSON was executive director of the Center for Scandinavian Studies at North Park College, and an expert and author of articles on Chicago's Swedes and Scandinavians.

MASAKO OSAKO was adjunct assistant professor of sociology at the University of Illinois at Chicago and has conducted extensive research on the subject of Japanese Americans and on the issue of gerontology. She is currently a vice president at the Industrial Bank of Japan, Chicago.

DOMINIC PACYGA is a doctoral graduate of the University of Illinois at Chicago, teaches at Columbia College, and is the author of numerous urban studies, including *Chicago: City of Neighborhoods* and *Polish Immigrants and Industrial Chicago.*

JACQUELINE PETERSON is an associate professor of history at Washington State University. She completed her Ph.D., a study of eighteenth- and nineteenth-century Indian and métis groups of the Great Lakes region, at the University of Illinois, Chicago, and has published extensively on that topic.

PADMA RANGASWAMY was educated in India and the United States and is currently researching the Chicago Asian-Indian community for her doctoral thesis at the University of Illinois at Chicago.

STEVEN S. RIESS is professor of history at Northeastern Illinois State University (Chicago), editor of the *Journal of Sport History,* and the author of numerous studies, including *City Games: The Evolution of American Urban Society and the Rise of Sports.*

HELEN A. SCLAIR is a learning disabilities teacher in the Chicago Public Schools. A native Chicagoan, she is a lecturer and the author of several articles on the area's cemeteries. Having discovered a trove of lost pre–1871 Chicago Fire documents, she is completing a volume on Chicago's nineteenth-century city cemetery.

Index